COMPANION ENCYCLOPEDIA OF PSYCHOLOGY

COMPANION
ENCYCLOPEDIA
OF
PSYCHOLOGY

Volume 2

EDITED BY

Andrew M. Colman

London and New York

First published in 1994
by Routledge
11 New Fetter Lane, London EC4P 4EE
29 West 35th Street, New York, NY 10001

© 1994 Routledge

Typeset in 10/12 pt Times Compugraphic by
Mathematical Composition Setters Ltd, Salisbury, Wiltshire
Printed in England by Clays Ltd, St Ives plc
Printed on acid free paper

British Library Cataloguing in Publication Data
A catalogue record for this book is available from the British Library.

Library of Congress Cataloging-in-Publication Data
A catalog record for this book is available on request.

ISBN 0–415–06446–5 (*set*)
ISBN 0–415–10704–0 (*Volume 1*)
ISBN 0–415–10705–9 (*Volume 2*)

CONTENTS

COMPANION ENCYCLOPEDIA
OF PSYCHOLOGY

VOLUME 2

8
DEVELOPMENTAL PSYCHOLOGY

INTRODUCTION

This section cuts across the others inasmuch as it is concerned with the development, across the lifespan from birth to old age, of all aspects of behaviour and mental experience dealt with in the other sections, including biological aspects of behaviour (section 2), sensation and perception (section 3), cognition (section 4), learning and skills (section 5), emotion and motivation (section 6), individual differences and personality (section 7), social behaviour (section 9), and psychopathology (section 10). The cross-references are too numerous to list exhaustively, because this section is conceptually parasitic on most of the others rather than being concerned with its own class of behavioural or mental phenomena.

Developmental psychology is strongly influenced by the work of the Swiss psychologist, philosopher, and biologist Jean Piaget (1896–1980). Piaget's main concern was the development of thinking, but his ideas, though highly controversial, pervade almost all areas of developmental psychology, and aspects of his work are discussed in every chapter in this section. There is no other major branch of psychological research that is so strongly influenced by the writings of a single individual.

Chapter 8.1 by George Butterworth is on infancy. Infancy (whose Latin roots mean "not speaking") is usually taken in developmental psychology to denote the period between birth and the acquisition of language, that is, approximately the first 18 months of life. This often causes confusion, because in everyday usage the word is often used loosely to include pre-school children up to 6 or 7 years of age. Butterworth discusses the development during infancy – the first 18 months – of perception, skilled behaviour, knowledge of physical objects and people, and language.

In chapter 8.2 Sara Meadows discusses cognitive development. She outlines and comments on three major theoretical approaches to cognitive development – Piagetian, Vygotskian, and information-processing approaches – before discussing in particular the development of memory, the acquisition of literacy, and sources of individual differences in cognitive development. Several of the topics dealt with in this chapter, including the acquisition of literacy, have links with chapter 5.3 (K. Anders Ericsson and William L. Oliver), which focuses on cognitive skills.

Peter K. Smith provides a wide-ranging survey of social development in chapter 8.3. Among the areas of social development that he covers are friendship and popularity, social skills, aggression and dominance, sex differences and sex roles, and ethnic awareness and prejudice. For a general discussion of social skills, see chapter 5.5 (Michael Argyle); for more information on general aspects of prejudice, see chapter 9.4 (James Vivian and Rupert Brown).

Chapter 8.4, by John C. Coleman, is devoted to adolescence. He outlines the major psychoanalytic and sociological theories of adolescence and discusses research into puberty, cognition during adolescence, and relationships of adolescents with adults. For detailed accounts of psychoanalytic theory see chapter 7.4 (Richard Stevens) and chapter 13.5 (Peter Fonagy).

Finally, chapter 8.5 is on ageing; John C. Cavanaugh surveys the research evidence relating to the effects of ageing on a wide range of psychological functions, including attention and reaction time, memory, intelligence, personality, and psychopathology. For detailed accounts of these psychological functions in general, see chapters 4.1 (memory: Alan Baddeley), 4.2 (attention: Michael W. Eysenck), 7.1 (intelligence: Robert J. Sternberg), 7.2 (personality: Sarah E. Hampson), 7.3 (personality: H. J. Eysenck), 10.1 (neuroses: J. Mark G. Williams and Isabel R. Hargreaves), and 10.2 (psychotic disorders: Chris Frith and Connie Cahill). The chapter closes with brief discussions of psychological aspects of grandparenting and widow-ʰood. See chapter 12.6 (Anthony Gale) for a discussion of ethical issues related to ageing.

Two technical concepts that are introduced in this section need clarification, namely *cohort effect* and *longitudinal study*. They are most easily explained by considering physical stature. In industrial societies, each generation of adults grows slightly taller than the last. A cross-sectional study of the heights of representative samples of adults of various ages would give the misleading impression that men and women shrink throughout adulthood. This would be due to a cohort effect – the tendency for the age-group samples or cohorts to differ in average height. The misleading impression would be dispelled if a longitudinal study, following the same sample of subjects over time, were carried out instead.

A.M.C.

682

INFANCY

George Butterworth
University of Sussex, England

Infancy is the period of development between birth and the onset of language, which covers approximately the first 18 months of life. There have been important discoveries about prenatal development and a great deal more has become known about the psychological origins of speech and language. The rather convenient markers, between birth and the appearance of first words, nowadays set only minimal boundaries with earlier and later stages of childhood.

HISTORY OF INFANCY RESEARCH

Systematic study of infants began in the nineteenth century. One of the earliest scientific studies was by Charles Darwin, who kept a diary of the development of his infant son William during the year 1844. He noted the baby's innate capacity for emotional expression, observations which were especially influential in Darwin's work on *The Expression of the Emotions in Man and Animals* (1872) and on Sigmund Freud in his theories of personality formation. Another particularly influential contribution was made by the German physiologist Wilhelm Preyer, who published a monograph *The Mind of the Child* (1895) based on observations of his own daughter from birth to $2\frac{1}{2}$ years.

The view of infancy that prevailed in the nineteenth century was most memorably captured by the philosopher and psychologist, William James, who described the world of the newborn baby as a "blooming, buzzing confusion, where the infant is seized by eyes, ears, nose and entrails all once" (James, 1890). This vivid phrase conveys an image of a passive infant, inundated by meaningless sensations, with little coherent awareness of self or of the outside world. The newborn was thought to have no more than reflex control of action and to be capable of seeing or hearing very little. One of the major scientific achievements since the mid-1960s has been radically to revise this nineteenth-century preconception in favour of an image of the infant as "competent" and well adapted to the demands of the physical and social environment.

By the early twentieth century, studies of babies had moved from single-case diary records to large-scale investigations. Two major schools of psychology soon emerged which generated rather dichotomous approaches to infant development. The behaviourist school, especially through John Watson, emphasized the importance of early experience in development. Watson and Raynor (1920) showed that irrational fears could be learned in infancy through the principles of association by classical conditioning, first demonstrated by Pavlov. An alternative emphasis was on intrinsic processes of biological growth. Arnold Gesell, who made extensive investigations of motor development in babies, is most closely associated with the "nature" side of the "nature–nurture" dichotomy, because of his stress on maturation. Gesell considered that the infant's motor development, from gaining of early head control to crawling and walking, unfolded on a rather inevitable biological timetable of "motor milestones".

The modern era of infancy research was inaugurated by Jean Piaget (1896–1980). Piaget rejected a dichotomy between nature and nurture in favour of an account of development that combines biology and experience. Piaget's main interest was in the intellectual development of babies. He studied his own three children in great detail to produce his "sensori-motor theory" of infant development (Table 1). He argued that development begins with a limited number of innate reflex actions which are triggered by specific sensory experiences. For example, babies are born with the sucking reflex which serves their nutritional needs. Soon, however, the baby applies the reflex to other objects, in repetitive exploration (circular reaction) and thus learns something of the variety of shape, texture, and consistency of objects.

Other biologically based reflexes, such as looking, listening, or grasping

Table 1 Piaget's hierarchical theory of intellectual development in infancy

Stage I   Reflexes
Age Birth to 6 weeks: e.g., sucking

Stage II   Primary circular reactions
Age 6 weeks to 3 months: first acquired habits, e.g., thumb sucking

Stage III   Secondary circular reactions
Age 3–9 months: goal-directed behaviour, e.g., visually guided reaching

Stage IV   Coordinated secondary circular reactions
Age 9–12 months: differentiation of means and ends in intentional acts, e.g., searching for a hidden object

Stage V   Tertiary circular reactions
Age 12–18 months: application of established means to new ends, e.g., baby climbs on stool to reach object hidden in cupboard

Stage VI   Representation
Age 18 months: mental combinations of means and ends
Insightful discovery of new means through active experiment, e.g., baby pulls in object through playpen bars using a stick

Toddler has concepts of object, space, time, and causes

are also applied to a variety of objects in exploration of the world; the senses become inter-coordinated and actions become hierarchically organized in goal-directed sequences. Through acting on the world the baby acquires basic knowledge of cause and effect and of the properties of physical and social objects.

Piaget therefore avoided the pitfalls of dichotomizing nature and nurture; he recognized both the intrinsic biological processes of growth and the role of the infant's actions in the construction of knowledge. However, research has shown that Piaget may have underestimated the abilities of infants and this needs to be taken into account to give a contemporary overview. This information comes from studies of the prenatal origins of behaviour and from the contribution of infant perception to the development of knowledge.

PRENATAL DEVELOPMENT

Human gestation takes 40 weeks between conception and birth. The germinal stage lasts 2 weeks after conception and is primarily a period in which the fertilized egg undergoes repeated division into identical copies. It ends when the fertilized ovum has become implanted in the uterus. The formation of the basic structures of the human occurs in the embryonic stage, which lasts to the eighth week. There is rapid differentiation of the fertilized egg, with formation of limbs, fingers, toes, and major sensory organs. By 8 weeks, the embryo is about 1 inch long, limb buds have appeared, eyes and eyelids have begun to form. The foetal stage from 8 weeks to birth coincides with major developments of the nervous system. The foetus rapidly takes on distinctively human characteristics so that by 12 weeks it is easily recognizable. By 16 weeks it is 6–7 inches long but it cannot survive outside the mother's body. By 23 weeks the foetus has a sleep–wake cycle synchronized with that of the mother. The foetus continues to develop for the normal gestational term of 40 weeks, although, like all biological phenomena, there is natural variation in the time of onset of birth.

The normal western baby at birth, around 40 weeks, weighs about 7 pounds and is about 21 inches long. The head, which has grown fastest in utero, is disproportionately larger than the body. Head and neck take up about 30 per cent of the total body volume by comparison to 15 per cent at 6 years and only 10 per cent in adults. It is worth remembering that the changing proportions of the body pose particular problems in gaining motor control in infancy.

Before the 1970s little was known about foetal behaviour before birth. Although pregnant women often note feeling foetal movements at about 16 weeks gestation, they are aware only of the most gross movements. In fact, depending on the measuring technique, up to 20,000 movements per day can be recorded in the foetus of less than 16 weeks gestational age. The advent of real-time ultra-sonic scanning in the 1970s has offered a safe means of imaging foetal movements in utero. Ultra high frequency sound (outside the audible range) is transmitted into the pregnant woman's abdomen. The echoes of the sound are picked up electronically and converted to a visual image which provides a view of the foetus as it moves.

De Vries, Visser, and Prechtl (1984) have described 15 distinctively different movement patterns in the 15-week foetus; these include foetal breathing movements, where the amniotic fluid is regularly inhaled and exhaled, stretching movements, turning movements, and slightly later thumb sucking. These well-coordinated movement patterns occur under the relatively weightless conditions of the foetal environment. Some, like the foetal breathing movements, seem related to similar action patterns in postnatal life, a phenomenon called *anticipation*, because the behaviours show organization that will be essential later in development.

After 24 weeks, finer degrees of movement control are observed, including expressive facial movements. Foetal activity resumes, in the increasingly cramped living quarters, and is now subject to sleep–wake cycles.

The first postural reflex, to be observed at 28 weeks, is the tonic neck reflex (TNR). This is a pattern of coordinated muscular activity in which the baby extends the arm and leg on the side to which the head is turned, while flexing the opposite arm and leg. This so-called "fencer posture" continues to the eighth postnatal month. The typical orientation of the head is thought to predict whether the baby will be right or left handed.

The general explanation of many of the foetus's spontaneous movement patterns is that they serve to exercise the developing system and aid the growing joints take their correct shape. Another possible function of prenatal activity is that it provides a high level of input to the developing ears, eyes and other sensory receptors. The cutaneous (skin), taste, and olfactory (smell) receptors and the vestibular and auditory systems are functional by 24 weeks gestation. The visual system is functional by the 26 weeks. Another possibility is that the continuous rotation and "crawling" movements of the young foetus may prevent adhesion to the uterine wall.

It is very likely that there is a continuous relationship between some foetal movement patterns and postnatal forms of behaviour. De Vries et al. (1984) describe a stretch and yawn pattern at 10 weeks foetal age which suggests continuity in the organization of yawning and stretching movements throughout life. Less obviously, there may also be continuity across loco-motor patterns. The crawling movements of the 6-month-old baby and the typical alternating walking movements of upright locomotion may be related to the so-called "stepping reflex", a cyclic stepping movement made by new-born babies when supported in an upright posture. The stepping movements may in turn be related to foetal movements which prevent adhesion to the uterine wall (Thelen, 1984).

Such observations on foetal behaviour have led to a re-evaluation of the status of the newborn. The radical shift in environment from prenatal to postnatal life, the extra weight of the body, especially the head, rapid growth and new possibilities for the control of action through vision may contribute to the general "helplessness" of the newborn. However, the period of intra-uterine life may have been rather effective in preparing the baby for independent existence, not only in terms of the repertoire of motor movements but also in some early perceptual abilities.

THE PERCEPTUAL WORLD OF THE NEWBORN: THE SENSES

The evidence suggests that all the basic sensory systems are functional from birth or before; even newborn babies will show preferences in vision, hearing, taste, and smell. They actively seek out to what they will attend and this implies that babies are not passively bombarded by sensory stimulation, as William James had assumed. We shall briefly review the sensory capacities of the newborn before turning to research on the information which the senses make accessible to the baby.

Vision

Relative to adult standards, vision in the newborn is very poor. The eyes have a fixed focal length because the lens does not accommodate properly until about 3 months. However, the fixed focal length of 21 centimetres coincides with the average distance of the mother's face from the baby when the infant is held at the breast. So, even though distant objects will be blurred, important social objects can be seen from birth. Newborns can discriminate between stationary black and white stripes one-eighth of an inch wide and a uniform grey surface. Moving the stripes to attract visual following movements actually yields much finer measures of visual discrimination. It is also known that newborns see in colour, probably trichromatically, as in normal (non-colour-blind) adults.

Stereoscopic binocular vision, which is particularly useful for depth perception, does not begin to develop until about 13 weeks. This seems partly to be a function of poor control over the convergence of the eyes (when we focus both eyes on the same object the eyes converge differentially according to the object's distance), partly a function of changes in the axes of alignment of the eyes in the early weeks of life, and partly a function of "tuning" the visual cortex of the brain so that the neural cells responsible for binocular vision receive the same information from both eyes. Extensive research indicates that binocular aspects of visual functioning depend on early visual experience during a "sensitive" period when the binocularly activated cells in the visual nervous system undergo fine tuning as a result of visual experience. There are important implications for the treatment of squint (strabismus). The effect of a squint is that binocular cells do not receive the same input from equivalent regions of the two eyes, so it is important to realign the squinting eye surgically if steroescopic vision is not to be adversely affected.

Newborn infant eye movements are very similar to those of adults. Successive shifts of visual fixation from object to object are known as saccades. Newborn infants follow moving objects by making a series of saccadic jumps whereas smooth tracking movements of the eyes develop at about two months. The scanning pattern is internally generated and not simply a reaction to incident visual stimulation. This is important because it again suggests that the newborn baby is well prepared to explore the visual environment. Newborns are particularly likely to pick out the external edges of visual objects, although they will shift their gaze to the interior of an object if it has internal movement. They do not simply search at random but scan for salient features of objects (for a review of infant vision see Atkinson & Braddick, 1989).

Hearing

The auditory system is functional from before birth (Rubel, 1985). The inner ear has reached its adult size by 20 weeks gestation. The middle ear, with its complex structure of bones and membranes which mediate hearing, is well formed by 37 weeks gestation, although it continues to change shape and size into adulthood. The external ear acquires its adult shape at 20 weeks gestation, but it continues to grow in size until the child is about 9 years of age.

It is becoming increasingly clear that infants are attentive to sounds from before birth. Since the middle ear of the foetus is filled with amniotic fluid, the conduction of sound is quite different in utero than postnatally. The most likely source of sound to be internally transmitted is the mother's speech, especially the patterning of sound onset and offset, at frequencies that are not masked by the internal noise of the mother's heart beat and blood circulation.

It has been shown that newborns can distinguish their mother's voice from the voice of another woman, which suggests that aspects of the mother's voice may become familiar to the child in utero (DeCasper & Fifer, 1980). Newborn babies generally prefer voices in the female range (average frequency 260 cycles per second) to the male range (on average one octave lower at 130 cycles per second). Adults and even children will adopt a higher pitched tone of voice when addressing babies, as if this is a particularly effective way of speech "getting through".

Smell and taste

Newborn babies show a similar aversion to a sour taste as do adults. They can also discriminate sweetness and show contented emotional expressions to sweet liquids (Steiner, 1979). Newborn babies show a similar range of expressions when presented with smells that are unpleasant (rotten eggs), or pleasant (a milky smell, honey, or chocolate). Neonates also recognize the smell of their own mother's breast milk within the first 6 days of life (Mac-Farlane, 1975).

Methods of studying perception in babies

The fact that babies show spontaneous visual preferences means that it is possible to study what the infant chooses to look at. The pioneer of this technique was Robert Fantz (1965), whose visual preference method has come to revolutionize our understanding of the perceptual world of the infant. The method is actually very simple. The infant is presented with a pair of visual targets, one to the left and the other to the right of the mid-line. The investigator notes the direction of the baby's first eye movement and the total amount of time that the infant fixates the target. It was soon established that babies prefer to look at patterns rather than plain surfaces; in one study it was found that newborns showed a preference for a face-like stimulus. Research has confirmed that newborns do indeed have a particular interest in faces and face-like stimuli (Johnson & Morton, 1992).

A variation of the Fantz technique involves presenting babies with the same stimulus repeatedly. This is called the habituation method, since it involves accustoming the baby to the visual object so that the object becomes progressively less interesting. Then, once the infant's attention has declined, a new object is presented. If the baby can perceive the difference between the old stimulus and the new one, she will show a marked interest in the new object. Thus, even where there is no initial preference between two stimuli, this method creates the potential for discriminating between a familiar stimulus and a new one, once again revealing what the baby perceives. Furthermore, the method also implies that the baby remembers something of the stimulus, since the procedure relies on the test material becoming increasingly familiar. Many contemporary studies of infant perception use variations of the visual preference and habituation methods to study not only vision but also aspects of audition, such as phonological perception (Kuhl & Meltzoff, 1986).

Perception of complex object properties in early infancy

Two very important features of visual perception are size and shape constancy. Changes in distance or orientation of an object from the observer result in differences in the projection of the retinal image. Size constancy refers to perceiving the real size of an object, despite the fact that the size of the retinal image varies greatly with the distance of the object. Shape constancy is the ability to perceive an object's real shape, despite any changes in orientation with respect to the observer which will result in changes in the projected shape of the retinal image.

Piaget believed that babies have to learn to coordinate touch with vision in order to perceive size and shape constancy. He suggested that having learned to grasp the object, the baby could twist and turn it, bring it further and nearer in the field of view, and gradually make the discovery of size constancy. The assumption is that "touch tutors vision" in early development. Piaget suggested that the visual world of the newborn baby is two-dimensional and lacking in depth, and that perception of shape and size constancy develops only slowly, during the first 6 months of life. A radical alternative to this traditional view of visual perception was developed by James Gibson (1966), who argued that perception should be considered an active process of seeking after information, with no privileged relation of any one sense over any other. While each of the senses has specialized functions, such as visual perception of colour or cutaneous perception of temperature, there is also information common to different senses. According to Gibson, perceptual systems have evolved to put the infant in direct contact with the real world from the outset. Competent perception could be a particular advantage, since the infant is typically much less able to make motor responses than to perceive: she will spend many months looking and listening before motor development allows physical exploration of distant objects.

The first demonstration of size and shape constancy in 3-month-old babies was made by Bower (1966). His finding has since been replicated in newborns by Slater (1990). Many new findings about the relations between sensory systems in early perception have come to light. These studies present a novel picture of the "competent" infant, well able to gain information about the world through perception.

Auditory-visual coordination

Wertheimer (1961) first showed that there is an innate coordination between seeing and hearing, such that when the newborn baby hears a sound, the eyes will be reoriented to the sound. These results have subsequently been extended by Castillo and Butterworth (1981), who showed that newborns look to a distinctive visual feature of the environment in order to locate the source of a sound. Vision and audition interact in sound localization from birth. This is not to say that these coordinations are fixed and unchanging. In fact, there is a complex development; the innate coordination lasts for the first 2 months and then eye movements to sound become increasingly difficult to elicit until 5 months, when the coordination reemerges. U-shaped functions are rather common in early development and imply developmental reorganization of perceptual systems to give rise to new abilities.

As mentioned earlier, infants recognize their mother's voice soon after birth and there is also evidence for an early olfactory preference for the mother. Bushnell, Sai, and Mullin (1989) found that 5-day-old babies preferred to look at their own mother rather than another woman. It is possible that an innate coordination between hearing and seeing helps babies rapidly discover what their mothers look like. Prenatal familiarity with the mother's voice, coupled with an innate tendency to look where a sound is heard, may be sufficient for the baby to learn rapidly the distinctive aspects of the mother's appearance. By 3 months there is definite evidence that babies know the characteristic faces and voices of both parents. In a study by Spelke and Owsley (1979) the baby heard a tape recording of the mother's voice over a loudspeaker placed exactly between the mother and father. Babies from 3 months looked towards the mother when the mother's voice was heard (and towards the father when the father's voice was played). This need not be a very precise auditory-visual memory but the infant is nevertheless familiar with the sound and sight of the parent and this has important implications for social and emotional development, as will be discussed below.

Other aspects of inter sensory perception in young babies have important implications for the acquisition of speech and language. Kuhn and Meltzoff (1982) showed that babies detect a correspondence between the auditory and visual information for vowel sounds. This ability to "lip read" might be very useful in acquiring language as it means that visual and auditory information for speech are to some extent overlapping. Meltzoff and Moore (1977) showed that newborn babies can imitate tongue protrusion, mouth opening, and lip-pursing movements. As in many other newborn behaviours, a U-shaped developmental function was found, with imitation of tongue and

691

mouth movements dropping out at about 3 months and reappearing at 12 months. The later form of imitation has a symbolic quality, as illustrated by Piaget, who observed his daughter use tongue protrusion in an attempt to understand how the sliding drawer of a matchbox might work. This observation shows that foundational abilities observed in the neonate should not be confused with more developed forms of the same behaviours seen later in development.

PERCEPTION AND THE DEVELOPMENT OF SKILLED ACTION

Perception has a particularly important part to play in the acquisition of skills in infancy. A motor skill is an organized sequence of goal-directed activity which is guided or corrected by feedback. Among the most important developmental precursors of skills are gaining control over the posture of the head by about 3 months, over sitting by about 6 months, and over standing towards the end of the first year. Vision serves an important role in gaining postural control since visual feedback from the stationary environment can be used to stabilize involuntary swaying movements when learning to sit or stand. Acquiring control over head and trunk enables new skills to be acquired, such as reaching and grasping, which depend on postural stability. The onset of independent locomotion also depends on good prior control of static postures. Each skill has a prolonged period of development and it is not surprising that infants with visual impairments are also delayed in postural control and the onset of locomotion.

The neonate is not entirely devoid of coordinated actions, indeed in some domains, such as sucking, the baby soon acquires very skilled control over the pressure and vacuum produced by the mouth in obtaining milk. In other domains, such as reaching to grasp something or in acquiring independent locomotion, only the most basic elements of the visual-motor coordination can be observed and skilled control takes many months to be acquired.

There is now quite extensive evidence for an innate eye hand coordination. Bower (1982) demonstrated that newborns will attempt to make gross, visually elicited, movements of the hand and arm in the vicinity of an attractive object. The visual object elicits a rather ineffectively aimed "swipe" with occasional contact. As the baby's aim gets better, contacts become more frequent; by about 4 months, the baby succeeds in grasping the object after contacting it. The actions of visually elicited reaching and tactually elicited grasping become coordinated and reaching begins to be visually guided in the course of the action (rather than "pre-programmed", as before). The infant begins to "anticipate" the object and the hand begins to open before contact so that, by 5 months, both reaching and grasping are coming under visual control. Once the right and left hand reach and grasp under visual guidance, they begin to collaborate and the baby will transfer objects from right to left,

Table 2 Integration of vision, action and memory in development of reaching and grasping

Age	Action pattern
9–12 months	Bimanual collaboration Differentiated grips between left and right hands
6–8 months	Integration of action and visual memory Search for hidden objects Transfer of objects between hands Development of finger grips
5–6 months	Reach is continuously guided to target by vision Mainly palm grips
Innate	Reached aimed at target by vision

in order to deal with more than one object at a time. This marks the beginning of a further integration of visually guided reaching with memory.

Table 2 illustrates the hierarchy of processes involved in the development of reaching and grasping and the approximate ages at which each level of skill is achieved.

Table 3 Locomotor development

Months	Motor behaviour
1	Lifts chin when prone; holds head erect for a few seconds
2	Lifts head up when prone
3	Rolls from side to back
4	Lifts head and chest when prone; holds head erect continually
5	Rolls from side to side
6	Sits with slight support
7	Can roll from back to stomach, stepping reactions
8	Tries vigorously to crawl; sits alone for short time
9	Can turn around when left on floor; makes some progress crawling
10	Stands when held up
11	Pulls self up by furniture
12	Crawls on hands and knees; side steps around inside cot
13	Stands alone
14	Walks alone
15	Climbs stairs
16	Trots about well
17	Climbs on a low chair; stoops
18	Can walk backwards
19	Climbs stairs up and down
20	Jumps; runs

Source: After Griffiths, 1954

Developments in the grips of babies can be observed well into the second year of life, as the infant first becomes able to grasp objects and then to gain finer and finer control over the fingers. Babies first grasp by pressing all the fingers against the object in the palm of the hand. These palm grips give way to more precise finger grips so that, by the end of the first year, the baby is able to pick up rather small objects in a "pincer grip" between the end of the index finger and the tip of the thumb. This precision grip is species-specific to humans. It involves full opposition of the fingers and thumb, so that they may be brought into contact for very skilled tool use, as for example in sewing or writing.

These observations once again show that the amount of pre-adaptive structure available in early development is greater than traditional theories would suppose, yet the baby only slowly gains the skills required to put the innate eye–hand coordination to use. Many other motor skills also come under visual control during infancy. Table 3 shows month by month the motor development to be expected in the average child (Griffiths, 1954).

ORIGINS OF KNOWLEDGE OF PHYSICAL OBJECTS IN HUMAN INFANCY

As adults we know that when one object is occluded by another, the hidden object continues to exist and to retain its physical and spatial properties. Furthermore, the movements of the object and its transformations are subject to regular physical laws and are therefore predictable. This is known as the "object concept", a shorthand way of expressing the fact that objects are permanent, substantial, and possessed of constant shape, size, and identity.

According to Piaget, the object concept stands at the foundations of thought. He was of the opinion that, until the child is about 18 months old, appearances and disappearances are not understood as the movements of single objects in space. His evidence came from infants' failure to search manually for hidden objects before 9 months. Indeed, he argued that for the young baby the object is a "mere image", lacking permanence, substantiality, and identity (Piaget, 1954). Piaget's theory rests heavily on the assumption that perception is insufficient to inform the developing child about the physical world. According to Piaget, infants fail to search for a hidden object because they do not perceive that it continues to exist once it disappears. If Piaget's interpretation of search failures is correct, then the physical universe of the infant must be very different to that of the adult.

However, Piaget's theory of the origins of foundational concepts has come under increasing criticism. One source of evidence against Piaget's theory came from infants born without arms or legs following the thalidomide tragedy. These babies often showed normal intellectual development, despite the fact that they lacked the opportunity for extensive physical interaction with objects (DeCarie, 1969). Other evidence against the Piagetian theory came from ingenious experiments based on the possibility that the infant may be capable of picking up information through the distal senses, especially through vision. Renée Baillargeon (1987a, 1987b) has systematically measured infants' perception of physical objects using the habituation method described earlier. Her technique involves habituating the baby, then changing the visual display in such a way that a basic physical law is broken. Changes in looking patterns reveal which changes in physical events babies perceive as possible or impossible.

For example, Baillargeon's experiments on perception of substance violate the principle that a solid object cannot move through the space occupied by another object (Baillargeon, 1987b). Babies of $3\frac{1}{2}$ months observe a screen, in the form of a drawbridge seen end-on by the infant, rotate repeatedly in a 180-degree arc. Once the infant has become habituated to this display, a large box is placed behind the screen and the infant is shown one of two test events. In one event, the physically possible case, the screen stops rotating when it is obstructed by the box. In a second, impossible event, the screen continues to rotate through a full 180 degrees, as if the box were no longer behind it. Babies looked longer at the impossible event than at the possible event. This suggests that infants perceive the continued existence of the hidden box and that they also perceive that the screen could not rotate through it. In subsequent experiments, Baillargeon went on to demonstrate that, by $6\frac{1}{2}$ months, babies understand not only that the screen should stop when there is a box behind it, but also that the screen will stop at different positions depending on the height of the box, or depending on whether the object behind the screen can be compressed or not. That is, the baby appropriately perceives occlusion and the possible physical interactions between rigid and elastic objects, and finds it unusual when the experimenter presents the baby with visual events that violate basic physical laws.

This evidence suggests that infants are able to perceive that solid objects cannot travel through the space occupied by other solids and that objects cannot appear at two separate points in space without travelling the distance between them. The important question is *why* does it take babies 8 or 9 months before they will search for hidden objects? Why is there this disjunction between *perceiving* the physical properties of objects and *using* the information to retrieve them? Baillargeon suggests that the limitation lies in planning sequences of action. The baby perceives the world appropriately, but until 8 or 9 months of age, lacks the ability to transfer information obtained through perception to memory, in order to regulate action.

ORIGINS OF KNOWLEDGE ABOUT PEOPLE IN HUMAN INFANCY

Whereas Piaget was mainly concerned to explain intellectual development in infancy, John Bowlby (1907–1990) was concerned to understand emotional development. He developed a unique synthesis of method and theory drawn from the traditions of Freudian psychoanalysis, recording of natural history, field studies of ethology (the study of animal behaviour in the natural environment), and cognitive developmental psychology, to explain the formation of the earliest attachment bonds between infant and mother (Bowlby, 1971).

A key idea in Bowlby's theory is that the mother provides a secure base from which the developing infant can explore the world and periodically return in safety. The evolutionary function of such attachment behaviour is thought to be to protect the child from predators; the further implication is that emotionally secure bonds between parent and child have basic survival value. Parental responsiveness to the exploratory instincts of the child is an important factor in establishing a secure attachment relationship; this in turn leads into a range of psychologically healthy developmental pathways. Securely attached infants feel free to explore a novel environment, so long as the mother is within sight. Bowlby argued that insecure patterns of attachment contribute to the formation of a neurotic personality, and that enforced, prolonged separations from loved parent figures, especially when a parent dies, may result in the long-term developmental links in psychopathology, such as depression in adulthood.

An early, practical application of his ideas arose in the changes that he effected in the hospitalization of young children in Britain. As a result of his work on prolonged and non-understandable separation, mothers were allowed to remain in hospital with their young children. Subsequent elaborations of the work have included large-scale epidemiological studies which have explored the role of family experiences as antecedents of depression and anxiety disorders (see Campos, Barrett, Lamb, Goldsmith, & Stenberg, 1983, for a review of socio-emotional development in infancy).

THE ACQUISITION OF LANGUAGE

A popular way to explain the fact that humans typically acquire language is by recourse to an innate "language acquisition device" (Chomsky, 1980). On this view, language is the near-inevitable consequence of the infant living in a particular linguistic community. An alternative theory, rather more consistent with the evidence reviewed above, is that language development brings together a variety of constituent processes, some of which can be observed very early in infancy, while others emerge with cognitive development. Some of the constituent perceptual abilities are not species-specific to humans, as in the case of phoneme perception (Kuhl & Meltzoff, 1986), while other abilities, such as pointing, are species-typical and closely linked to the comprehension and eventual production of speech. Early pre-speech abilities include sound perception and its counterpart in the production of babbling. Social interaction skills – such as "turn taking" between infant and mother, the emotional attunement of the infant to the mother, and attending jointly to objects and events with the mother – all lay the groundwork for communication through language (Butterworth & Grover, 1989; Harris, 1992). Motor development enables the infant to gain control over the articulatory and gestural systems, while cognitive development promotes their use in intentional communication, in gestures such as pointing and in speech. Babies comprehend single words at about 9 months, most babies produce single words at about the end of their first year. Subsequent development proceeds rapidly as babies build up a vocabulary with increasing speed and discover the names of objects. The first two-word combinations begin at around 18 months and thereafter the child acquires the rudiments of grammar. Infancy has come to an end: the walking, talking toddler is now relatively autonomous and ready for new knowledge.

FURTHER READING

Bower, T. G. R. (1982). *Development in infancy* (2nd edn). San Francisco, CA: Freeman.
Bremner, J. G. (1988). *Infancy*. Oxford: Basil Blackwell.
Butterworth, G. E. (Ed.) (1982). *Infancy and epistemology*. Brighton: Harvester.
Osofsky, J. D. (1987). *Handbook of infant development* (2nd edn). New York: Wiley.
Slater, A., & Bremner, G. (Eds) (1989). *Infant development*. Hove: Lawrence Erlbaum.

REFERENCES

Atkinson, J., & Braddick, O. L. (1989). Development of basic visual functions. In A. Slater & G. Bremner (Eds) *Infant development* (pp. 3–36). Hove: Lawrence Erlbaum.
Baillargeon, R. (1987a). Object permanence in $3\frac{1}{2}$ and $4\frac{1}{2}$ month old human infants. *Developmental Psychology*, 23, 655–664.
Baillargeon, R. (1987b). Young infants' reasoning about the physical and spatial properties of a hidden object. *Cognitive Development*, 2, 179–200.
Bower, T. G. R. (1966). The visual world of infants. *Scientific American*, 215(6), 80–92.
Bower, T. G. R. (1982). *Development in infancy* (2nd edn). San Francisco, CA: Freeman.
Bowlby, J. (1971). *Attachment*. Harmondsworth: Penguin.
Bushnell, I. W. R., Sai, F., & Mullin, J. T. (1989). Neonatal recognition of the mother's face. *British Journal of Developmental Psychology*, 7, 3–15.
Butterworth, G. E., & Grover, L. (1989). Joint visual attention, manual pointing and pre-verbal communication in human infancy. In M. Jeannerod (Ed.) *Attention and performance* (pp. 605–624). Hillsdale, NJ: Lawrence Erlbaum.
Campos, J. J., Barrett, K. C., Lamb, M. E., Goldsmith, H. H., & Stenberg, C. (1983). Socioemotional development. In M. M. Haith & J. J. Campos (Eds) *Handbook of child psychology* (vol. 2, pp. 783–916). New York: Wiley.
Castillo, M., & Butterworth, G. E. (1981). Neonatal localisation of a sound in visual space. *Perception*, 10, 331–338.
Chomsky, N. (1980). *Rules and representation*. New York: Columbia University Press.

Darwin, C. (1872). *The expression of the emotions in man and animals*. London: John Murray.

DeCarie, T. G. (1969). A study of the mental and emotional development of the thalidomide child. In B. M. Foss (Ed.) *Determinants of infant behaviour* (vol. IV, pp. 167–187). London: Methuen.

DeCasper, A. J., & Fifer, W. (1980). Of human bonding: newborns prefer their mothers' voices. *Science, 208*, 1174–1176.

DeVries, J. I. P., Visser, G. H. A., & Prechtl, H. F. R. (1984). Fetal motility in the first half of pregnancy. In H. F. R. Prechtl (Ed.) *Continuity of neural function from prenatal to postnatal life* (pp. 46–64). London: Spastics International Medical.

Fantz, R. L. (1965). Visual perception from birth as shown by pattern selectivity. *Annals of the New York Academy of Sciences, 118*, 793–814.

Gibson, J. J. (1966). *The senses considered as perceptual systems*. Boston, MA: Houghton Mifflin.

Griffith, R. (1954). *The abilities of babies*. London: London University Press.

Harris, M. (1992). *Language experience and early language development*. Hove: Lawrence Erlbaum.

James, W. (1890). *The principles of psychology*. New York: Holt.

Johnson, M., & Morton, J. (1992). *Biology and cognitive development*. Oxford: Basil Blackwell.

Kuhl, P., & Meltzoff, A. N. (1982). The bimodal perception of speech in infancy. *Science, 218*, 1138–1141.

Kuhl, P., & Meltzoff, A. N. (1986). The intermodal representation of speech in infants. *Infant Behaviour and Development, 7*, 361–381.

MacFarlane, A. (1975). Olfaction in the development of social preferences in the human neonate. In Ciba Foundation Symposium 33 (New Series), Parent–Infant Interaction (pp. 103–117) Amsterdam: Elsevier.

Meltzoff, A. N., & Moore, M. K. (1977). Imitation of facial and manual gestures by human neonates. *Science, 198*, 75–78.

Piaget, J. (1954). *The construction of reality in the child*. New York: Basic Books.

Preyer, W. (1895). *The mind of the child*. New York: Appleton.

Rubel, E. W. (1985). Auditory system development. In G. Gottlieb & N. A. Krasnegor (Eds) *Measurement of audition and vision in the first year of postnatal life* (pp. 53–90). Norwood, NJ: Ablex.

Slater, A. (1990). Visual memory and perception in early infancy. In A. Slater & G. Bremner (Eds) *Infant development* (pp. 43–71). Hove: Lawrence Erlbaum.

Spelke, E., & Owsley, C. J. (1979). Intermodal exploration and knowledge in infancy. *Infant Behaviour and Development, 2*, 13–24.

Steiner, J. (1979). Human facial expression in response to taste and smell stimulation. In H. Reese & L. P. Lipsitt (Eds) *Advances in child development and behaviour*, (vol. 13, pp. 257–295).

Thelen, E. (1984). Learning to walk: Ecological demands and phylogenetic constraints. In L. P. Lipsitt (Ed.) *Advances in infancy research* (vol. 3, pp. 213–257). Norwood, NJ: Ablex.

Watson, J. B. & Raynor, R. (1920). Conditioned emotional reactions. *Journal of Experimental Psychology, 3*, 1–130.

Wertheimer, M. (1961). Psychomotor coordination of auditory and visual space at birth. *Science, 134*, 1692.

8.2

COGNITIVE DEVELOPMENT

Sara Meadows
University of Bristol, England

<table>
<tr><td>

Some fundamental theoretical issues

Major theoretical approaches to cognitive development

Piagetian theory

Information-processing models

Vygotskian theory

Theories and issues in the development of cognitive skills

</td><td>

Memory development

Becoming literate

Domains of cognitive development

Sources of individual differences in cognitive development

Further reading

References

</td></tr>
</table>

Studying cognitive development, we are concerned with "the child as thinker", with someone who thinks, understands, learns, remembers, and so forth. These are activities that are not completely understood even in their adult forms; accounting for cognitive development requires not only an understanding of the adult form but also of how it is reached, that is, we need to note what changes there are in cognition between different ages and to explain how these changes come about. An enormous amount of research and theorizing has been produced in an attempt to describe and explain the course of cognitive development. The disciplines relevant to a full understanding range from developmental neuroscience through computer science to cultural anthropology: each of these addresses a slightly different range of questions and has its own methodologies and theories. Because of the volume and heterogeneity of relevant work, it is not possible to produce a comprehensive synthesis: this review focuses on some of the fundamental questions in the field and on some of the recent developments, addressing them through a brief account of three major theoretical paradigms and two important areas of cognitive activity. (For a more extensive account, see Meadows, 1993.)

SOME FUNDAMENTAL THEORETICAL ISSUES

A number of profoundly difficult theoretical questions underlie the study of cognitive development, and theorists' different assumptions about these questions surface in their answers (or in their unawareness that they need to be answered). One collection of questions has to do with the degree to which cognition is a coherent set of general skills, applicable to all sorts of problems and disciplines, available to all normally competent human beings as a permanent part of their repertory, independent of the knowledge they are applied to, and best described in abstract, formal terms, rather than an ad-hoc bundle of task-specific procedures, culturally constituted, heavily dependent on the knowledge base available, and re-created each time they have to be used. Beyond this are questions concerned with the nature of development: is it unidimensional, is it consistent over different areas, is it a gradual, steady, quantitative change, or a matter of more sudden, qualitative shifts? Is it a matter merely of change or one of progress and improvement? How far is development internally generated, and how far is it a matter of external shaping? More importantly still, how are externally given and internally generated cognitions combined? Is the developing cognitive person best described and best explained as an information-processing mechanism, as an adaptable organism, or as a participant in a social construction? How much does the child's cognition differ from the adult's? What are the causes of any cognitive differences (or indeed any similarities) – differences in brains? In the amount, the organization or the availability of information? In control and awareness? In processes? In practice and expertise? In social position and experience? Finally, there are a number of questions that are fundamental but outside the main body of work on cognitive development: what about individual differences in cognitive development? What internal and what external characteristics and events improve or worsen cognitive development? What are the developmental links between cognition and other psychological systems?

These are profound questions: the aim of this chapter is to begin to elucidate them.

MAJOR THEORETICAL APPROACHES TO COGNITIVE DEVELOPMENT

Much scientific work has grown from particular theoretical paradigms, as researchers sought to refine, extend, criticize, or refute some earlier piece of work. The major approaches to cognitive development stem from the work of Piaget, from the information-processing theorists of cognitive science, and from Vygotsky. Each deserves a brief review.

Piagetian theory

Piaget's theory of the development of cognition (Meadows, 1986, 1993; Piaget, 1983) has at its centre the child actively trying to make sense of the world, just as any organism must actively adapt to its environment. This cognitive activity is a special case of the adaptive processes that pervade all biological existence and evolution, "assimilation" and "accommodation". "Assimilation" is the relating of new information to pre-existing structures of understanding, and "accommodation" is the development of old structures into new ones at the behest of new external information or problems. These two together give rise to a series of structures of cognition, that is, to organized systems or "stages" of rules, categories, procedures, and so forth, which eventually amount to complex, comprehensive, coherent, flexible, and logically rigorous ways of understanding the world.

These stages are universal in that they can be applied to any cognitive problem, in that they operate at a consistent level across problems at any given moment, and in that all normal human beings develop them in the same order and at much the same rate, irrespective of cultural and educational differences, becoming increasingly logical, abstract, systematic, and flexible in their cognition as they move from infancy to adolescence. This cognitive improvement is caused by four interacting processes. These are organic growth, particularly the maturation of the central nervous system; the individual's experience of the actions performed on objects, both direct physical experience and indirect reflective experience of logico-mathematical rules and relations; social interaction, especially peer conflict rather than adult–child transmission of knowledge; and "equilibration", the most important and also the most problematic of the four.

Cognitive equilibration involves the idea that the organism needs to maintain a stable internal equilibrium within the changes and uncertainties of the outside world, and so automatically adjusts to the "perturbations" or "conflicts" which new or contradictory ideas or events produce in the cognitive system with just enough adjustment to get back to the original stable state or to get on to a new and better one where cognition finds a new more stable equilibrium. There are several conceptual roots of "equilibration majorante": in biologically programmed homeostatic mechanisms like those that stabilize the body temperature of warm-blooded animals; in the coherence, clarity, and consistency of logico-mathematical systems, in which no conflict or ambiguity is possible if the rules are properly applied; and in a belief that evolutionary adaptation involved a good and improving fit between the organism and the environment, and an unceasing progress towards better and better forms.

Piaget's is a rich and complex model that has made an immense contribution to developmental psychology, not least because it single-handedly put cognitive development at the top of the agenda, and also because Piaget sought to combine detailed observation of children's behaviour with the most profound questions about the nature of development, using ideas and evidence from biology, sociology, psychology, logic, and mathematics. It still has fervent adherents (Beilin, 1992). Nevertheless, it faces some significant difficulties Its abstract developmental processes – assimilation, accommodation, and (especially) equilibration – are hard to pin down conceptually or to observe or measure. Diagnosis of children's thinking has turned out to be problematic: their answers to questions seem to be somewhat unpredictably dependent on details of the questions and materials used (e.g., Donaldson, 1978; Light, 1986; Siegal, 1991); much post-Piagetian research has revealed surprising competence at considerably earlier ages than Piaget found. There is very little evidence for universal stages with consistent performance levels on all the tasks presumed to involve the same cognitive structure, and the more universal sequences found may be in a logically necessary order rather than a psychological one (Smedslund, 1980).

Piagetian theory emphasizes the individual child as the virtually independent constructor of his or her own development, an emphasis that undervalues the contribution of other people to cognitive development and excludes teaching and cultural influences. It seems possible that cognition is not so pure and abstract as Piagetian theory proposed, but may be rather more closely tied to particular tasks and routines, socially prescribed (Hinde, Perret-Clermont, & Stevenson-Hinde, 1985).

Information-processing models

Work in the "information-processing" tradition emphasizes precise analysis of how information is recognized, coded, stored, and retrieved in order to solve cognitive tasks, usually of a well-defined and tightly structured sort such as chess, balance-scale problems, or "Cannibals and Missionaries" (McShane, 1991) Researchers use the techniques of experimental cognitive psychology and computer science, and the central metaphor is that "people are in essence limited capacity manipulators of symbols" (Siegler, 1983, p. 129). Thus cognition involves the use of a fairly small number of basic cognitive processes in a structured way over a period of time, the same basic processes for all problems, though in different combinations and sequences. Cognitive development may involve development of basic processes, of the information base they are applied to, of the structure of the sequence in which basic processes are used, of the executive control of the whole system, or of combinations of these.

"Basic processes", such as recognition, categorization, association, coordinating different modalities and different information, appear in a rudimentary form even in the very youngest children (e.g., Butterworth, 1994; Harris, 1983; Kail, 1991), but undergo experience-related and age-related changes in speed, exhaustiveness, and flexibility. Learning and development use cognitive processes which are quite complex even from infancy; development here is a matter of refining cognitive tools rather than of creating them. It seems unlikely that cognitive development during childhood involves the appearance of completely new basic processes, though the processes inherited from infancy may well change. The information base that cognitive processes are applied to, on the other hand, clearly increases enormously during development. This is so obvious that many theorists have set it aside as uninteresting or even a contaminating variable, but later researchers suggested that the amount, organization, and availability of information may have important effects even on universal cognitive processes (Chi & Ceci, 1987; Keil, 1989).

The structured use of basic cognitive processes and executive control of processing are seen as major areas for developmental improvement, as discussion of memory and reading later in this chapter will describe: it seems clear that young children less often show deliberate strategic approaches to problems and have smaller and less flexible repertoires of strategies than older ones. This improvement, though age-related, may be connected with practice and the growth of expertise rather than with age per se.

There are various different information-processing accounts of how development comes about (Meadows, 1993; Sternberg, 1984) using similar ideas. Events that co-occur are associated; procedures that run many times become automatized; consistencies and inconsistencies are detected and sorted out. Earlier information-processing accounts, using serial processing as a model, emphasized executive control and monitoring: although there has only been a limited degree of success in producing a program that can act as a general problem solver, this approach has had some impressive results in modelling sequential logical problem solving in areas such as chess or the computation of whether a beam will balance. The development of Parallel Distributed Processing (PDP) or Connectionism promises progress with some of the cognitive areas that are less logical and sequential, such as the structure and acquisition of concepts (McClelland et al., 1986).

The basic hypothesis of PDP is that information processing involves a large number of units working contemporaneously in parallel, with units, like the neurons of the brain, exciting or inhibiting one another. Units that are active together have their excitatory connections strengthened and their inhibitory connections weakened; for units that are not active together inhibitory connections are strengthened and excitatory ones weakened. Thus over time a network that repeatedly receives the same input will develop high-strength connections so that units that have repeatedly been active together will come to excite one another more reliably and strongly than ever. Units act on small items of information ("subsymbols") and the whole network will come into play even if only some of the units are activated; no one sub-symbol is crucial and even the inclusion of a few incorrect or irrelevant ones will not throw the network if the general pattern of activation is correct. Networks can deal with possibilities and probabilities, rather than requiring complete and completely correct and non-redundant information as more traditional models do.

Connectionist models look closer to the biological structure of the brain, and their performance may be closer to the cognition of human beings on tasks such as pattern recognition in reading or the identification of what category a complex case belongs to (Clark, 1989). They look promising as models of the change that occurs during development or learning, and also of the effects of damage to a cognitive system. They will at least supplement traditional information-processing accounts of sequential problem solving with models of how problem solutions are learned and of how processing that is less linear is dealt with, and they may supersede them.

Vygotskian theory

Both Piagetian theory and the information-processing approach assume that there are psychological structures in people's minds that explain their behaviour, which are invariant across cultures, settings, and tasks, and which are essentially independent of the individual's relations to other individuals, to social practices, and to the cultural environment. Cognitive development is the individual construction of an internal mental model of external reality. Vygotskyian theory (Kozulin, 1990; Meadows, 1993; Tharp & Gallimore, 1988; Vygotsky, 1978, 1986) challenges this assumption; cognitive abilities are not internal and individualistic, but formed and built up in interaction with the social environment, interpsychological before they become internalized and intra-psychological. Children develop sophisticated cognitive competences despite starting with only rudimentary ones because adults are available as teachers or models to guide the child repeatedly through the relevant behaviour. The more expert person provides a context or "scaffolding" within which the child can act as though he or she was competent to solve the problem, and by so acting in such a context the child can indeed reach the solution successfully.

As the task becomes more familiar and more of it is within the child's competence, the adult can leave more and more for the child to do until at last he or she can undertake the whole task successfully. The child undergoes an apprenticeship in the skills of the culture, and by practising these skills and reflecting on them internalizes the cognitive tools that earlier members of the culture have developed. The developing thinker does not have to create cognition out of an unpeopled vacuum, but will first imitate and then internalize sole of the cognitive content and processes provided by others, and may in turn develop and pass on these skills. The internalized cognitive skills remain social, both in the sense that as mature learners we may "scaffold" ourselves through difficult tasks in an internal dialogue about our performance as our teachers once scaffolded our earlier attempts, and in the sense that for most individuals the only cognitive skills practised to a high level of competence are those that their culture offers; thus cognitive potential may be universal but cognitive expertise is culturally determined. Culturally given ways of thinking, remembering, categorizing, reading, and so forth build on and may supersede the biologically based ways we begin with.

As so much social interaction, and especially so much teaching, involves language, the Vygotskian model sees language development and cognitive development as becoming interrelated (Kozulin, 1990; Vygotsky, 1986). Children under about 2 years use vocal activity as a means of social contact and emotional expression, and are capable of systematic and goal-directed activity that does not require verbal operations. This first stage of "pre-intellectual speech" and "pre-verbal thought" is followed by a stage of "practical intelligence" in which there are parallels between the syntactic and logical forms of the child's language and the child's practical problem solving activity but no systematic or mutually useful links between them. Later, children start to use symbols external to themselves, such as language or other cultural tools, to help with their internal problem solving; at this stage they may use strategies such as talking themselves through problems or counting by using their fingers as aids. Finally such aids are internalized, and except in cases of great difficulty problem solving thought uses internal dialogue, while language can be used to reflect on and develop thought rather than as a prop to support problem solving. Language also changes immediate perception and action, which become more and more integrated into a cognitive system that is to a large extent represented through language and expressed in language.

There is still, incidentally, considerable controversy about the developmental relationship of cognition and language (Goodluck, 1991). A full discussion of this (or of language development itself) is beyond the scope of this chapter. However, cognition might play a role in the development of language. It has been argued that cognition is necessary for language, and therefore that children cannot use a linguistic form until they understand the cognitive point that it relates to; but there are quite frequent instances, both in normal development and in certain pathological conditions, of correct syntax or vocabulary use coupled with failure on tests of the concept involved (Cramer, 1991), and of bilingual children expressing a concept correctly in one language but not in the other (Slobin, 1985).

It has alternatively been argued that language is "modularized", that an innate Language Acquisition Device programs language development, and cognitive development is of only marginal importance (Chomsky, 1968; Fodor, 1983; Karmiloff-Smith, 1991). Researchers agree that there is genetic programming underlying some aspects of language development, for example in infants' early phonetic discrimination and also, perhaps, in children's syntactic and semantic development (Cromer, 1991; Gleitman & Wanner, 1982; Pinker, 1984); but Chomsky's argument rests on an underestimation of the variation in human language behaviour. Since the 1980s studies have emphasized the role of social interaction in language development, particularly the facilitating effects of the use of child-contingent language by adults talking with children (Dickinson & McCabe, 1991; Heath, 1983; Meadows, 1986; Okagaki & Sternberg, 1991; Wells, 1985).

This "fit" between adult and child language closely resembles Vygotskian scaffolding; it is worth noting, very briefly, that the differences of emphasis between a neo-Vygotskian approach, emphasizing how embedded cognitive functioning is in social experience, on the one hand, and the asocial information-processing approach and the individualism of Piaget's work on the other, parallel these differences of emphasis in work on language development. Both cognition and language include behaviour that is clearly influenced by social interaction (for example the skills of literacy) and other skills that are less socialized (for example memory). These areas are discussed below.

Vygotsky's emphasis on social interaction implies that more complex cognitive functioning may be possible in a dialogue between cooperating individuals than is possible for those individuals alone, thus that the level of an individual's functioning may depend on the social support currently available for cognition, and, very importantly, that instruction may be a facilitator of cognitive development rather than the irrelevance or the distortion that the Piagetian model suggests (Hinde et al., 1985; Meadows, 1993).

THEORIES AND ISSUES IN THE DEVELOPMENT OF COGNITIVE SKILLS

How do the three theoretical approaches described above appear in the light of data on children's cognitive behaviour at different points in development? They are not mutually exclusive; indeed there are some very interesting models of cognitive development that combine approaches, notably the work of Karmiloff-Smith (1986, 1991). I have already argued that each has strengths and weaknesses, and that different areas of "cognition" seem to bear different emphases. I shall now describe two major and contrasting areas of cognition, first memory, which is essential for all learning, is largely untaught and could be considered to be basically a biologically programmed capacity with a long evolutionary history and subject to only minor cultural modifications, and second, literacy, which although it comes to pervade much of the cognition of the literate and uses biologically based capacities, is clearly a major focus of educational effort and acculturation, and has not existed long or widely enough to be subject to much evolutionary selection. The skills of memory are more "natural", while those of literacy are a matter of "nurture"; comparing the two will illuminate the debate on the universality and generality of cognitive development and on what its causes are.

Memory development

The information-processing approach, which has dominated the study of memory, suggests four main candidates for the locus of development: the size of the memory, basic memory processes, strategies for remembering, and metamemory. It remains possible that the size of the memory stores increases as children grow older, though it has been impossible so far to separate change in capacity (argued for by the Piagetian information-processors Pascual-Leone and Case) from change in how much can be squeezed into an unchanging capacity as memory processes become quicker, more effective, and more automatic (Meadows, 1993). Certainly the amount of information known and rememberable increases enormously with development; certainly, too, neurons in the brain can form new interconnections throughout life, so that connectionist pathways continue to develop.

It appears that quite young infants are capable of feats of memory which suggest that basic processes are operating from the earliest months of life: they can habituate, recognize faces and voices, learn the contingencies between their own movements and those of a mobile, and so forth (Butterworth, 1993). Many memories persist for long periods of time in early childhood, though they may become less accessible as older children reinterpret and reorganize their knowledge. Changes in the knowledge base may occasionally lead to an improvement in memory, through a new understanding of what was known earlier (Piaget, 1983).

There certainly are changes in the use of memory strategies, with a major increase in the frequency and the efficiency of their use over the school years. Young children may remember things well, but they rarely use overt memory strategies (except in well-understood games such as hide-and-seek); deliberate memorization emerges in the early school years. What happens fits a Vygotskian pattern as culturally given strategies become superimposed on biologically programmed ones, with a resultant transformation in performance. Training in the laboratory, which highlights the better remembering that rehearsal, categorization, elaboration, or other memory strategies can bring about, may induce a persistent use of memory strategies; analogous experiences may occur during everyday domestic routines such as shopping, or in the early years of schooling. Finally there is improvement in metamemory, as children become more able to identify with certainty what they do and do not know, what their cognitive strengths and weaknesses are, what improves and what impedes their remembering, and how their current study is progressing at each moment. Here Vygotskian internalization, Piagetian reflection, and information-processing executive strategies would seem to be overlapping descriptions and explanations of the child's behaviour.

Becoming literate

Becoming literate is a central part of cognitive development for several reasons: literacy involves many linguistic, perceptual, attentional, memory, and cognitive skills; its development illustrates the variety of developmental processes; achieving an adequate degree of literacy is one of the prime aims of many educational systems; and literacy itself may determine what cognitive skills can be used even on tasks that do not directly involve being literate. A further reason why it is of particular interest is that a combination of careful experimental work and large sample assessment in schoolchildren has led us to a much more accurate understanding of what children do when they read and write, and hence to more understanding of how they may be taught (Goswami & Bryant, 1990; Meadows, 1993).

Children beginning to learn to read have behind them years of experience of spoken language, of visual and auditory discrimination, of remembering pieces of information until they build up into a meaningful whole, of obtaining information from a range of sources. Their task is now to apply these linguistic and cognitive skills to written text. Children who lack any of these skills to a significant degree have more difficulty in becoming literate than those who are more skilled. Expert readers do most of their reading by a combination of recognizing overlearned familiar words and the expectations as to probable content that their knowledge of the current topic and of text in general affords them (Ellis & Young, 1988). Beginning readers similarly learn to recognize familiar words and to guess from the context of topic and pictures. These strategies are not much use with unrecognizable words; but if these words are in the child's spoken vocabulary (and for a young child the spoken vocabulary will be considerably larger than the sight vocabulary) they will be identifiable if the child has a strategy that gives a sounded-out version of the written word.

It is at this point of linking written word with sound that many children have problems. The ability to discriminate between different speech sounds, in particular, has been shown to be a crucial component of progress in reading beyond the earliest stage when words are recognized as familiar patterns (Goswami & Bryant, 1990); children who cannot work out how an unrecognized written word would sound have only a very restricted access to its meaning (by guessing, which may be unreliable, or by asking a more expert reader, which may not be allowed) and are likely to make poor progress in learning to read. This lack of progress may in turn lead to such undesirable consequences as reading less, rarely using reading for either amusement or information, public and humiliating failure in school, falling behind in other areas of the curriculum where reading is necessary, loss of self-confidence and motivation to learn, and so forth. There are many useful strategies for reading, but the strategy of linking of seen and sounded words is a particularly important one between the earliest reading of a few familiar words and the expert stage when most words are familiar: at that stage it reduces memory load and eases recognition.

DOMAINS OF COGNITIVE DEVELOPMENT

The theoretical approaches of Piaget and information-processing researchers assumed that thinking and its development are essentially the same across all areas. Vygotsky, too, discussed very general forms of cognitive development, though his greater stress on acculturation admitted the possibility of much more variation in cognition. Later, there has been more research that looked at the different structures of understanding that build up in different "domains" of knowledge, and it has been claimed that cognition is to some extent "modularized", that is, that conceptual understanding of one domain may be quite different in its form, its origins, and its development from understanding of another domain. This focus admits that there may indeed be general abstract high-level cognitive processes (such as assimilation or internalization or categorization), which the domain-general approaches asserted were important, but that there are many examples of very localized cognitive expertise, where a high degree of skill is tied to particular content. Studies such as that of Chi (1978) on the memory of chess players and of Ceci (1990) on race-course handicappers illustrate this.

"Domain" refers to localized areas of cognition where processes and concepts form a fairly coherent whole, less closely related to other domains. There are some suggestions of innate or genetically programmed modules, which operate with minimal environmental support, for example a specialized faculty for language and language acquisition (Anderson, 1992; Chomsky, 1968; Fodor, 1983); others are areas of acquired expertise, such as the ability to write computer programs, which is the result of prolonged and intensive experience. Other sorts of domains that have been a focus of attention are the "naive" or "common sense" theories that divide our rich day-to-day experience into organized systems of knowledge, linking together particular sorts of event or concept as parts of the same domain. There seems to be, for example, a basic ontological distinction between people, other living things, and inanimate objects in most people's everyday understanding.

It seems that infants and children very rapidly develop basic understandings of the world which observe these ontological distinctions and which develop with time into the sorts of "folk" theories of psychology, biology and physics that adults use (Carey, 1991; Gelman, 1991; Perner, 1991). Research on the child's "theory of mind" suggests that by the age of 3 to 4 years they understand that people (but not inanimate objects) have desires and beliefs, and that the latter can be objectively false; these understandings arise from the social interactions of infancy, perhaps from a biologically programmed module (Anderson, 1992), but amount by the fourth year to a complex model of other people's mental lives. Similarly, notions of what objects are like in physical terms and of physical causality begin in infancy and develop in a coherent, if technically inadequate, theory of causation; and biology becomes increasingly clearly differentiated from both psychology and physics as ideas about growth, inheritance, and what it is to be alive become more and more refined.

The child's understanding of all these domains has early roots, followed by a long development, and is not necessarily correct, not even as correct as that of adults; the argument of theorists studying these sorts of domains is that theories that have a fair degree of internal coherence guide the classification of experience and the development of knowledge. The child has a notion of causality, for example, which can underpin performance on analogical reasoning tasks (Goswami & Brown, 1990) that are much more difficult if the basis for the analogy is non-causal, such as a semantic opposition. Children's basic understandings will allow them to give answers that are correct in principle even when their ignorance means that they are wrong about detail, as in their early appeal to a story character's beliefs as a reason for their actions, even when the only details they can give about the beliefs are vague or incorrect. Much work in this field is demonstrating earlier competence than the traditional approaches which deliberately used more abstract, formal content.

SOURCES OF INDIVIDUAL DIFFERENCES IN COGNITIVE DEVELOPMENT

All the work discussed so far looks for a single general path of cognitive development, attending only to differences that are age-related. It is perhaps assumed that a "normal" pattern of development has to be discovered before any exceptions to it can usefully be studied; or even that exceptions are non-existent or pathological, as in some Piagetian and information-processing work. If the possibility that cognition is domain-specific and culturally constituted is taken seriously, and it has to be if such cognitive tools as reading are to be studied, then there is far more obvious variation between individuals in cognitive development, and a consequent need to chart the causes of this variation. Elucidating the causes of individual differences will, I would argue, clarify the causes of "normal" development.

One possibility as a source of individual differences is that they are genetic, that is, that an innate variation in the individual's genetic programming leads, not necessarily directly or independently of other influences, to a particular form of cognitive development, just as genetic programming leads to differences in eye colour or number of toes. It is clear that certain major genetic anomalies cause abnormalities of brain development or functioning which lead to abnormal cognitive development; Down's Syndrome and Turner's Syndrome are examples where an abnormal amount of genetic material leads to the development of a child who has a number of physical and cognitive abnormalities. If a markedly wrong gene "messes up" (Scarr & Carter-Saltzman, 1982) the program for cognitive development, then it could be that smaller variations also have genetic roots, that subtler genetic peculiarities lead to subtler cognitive differences.

Exactly this argument appears in the study of "intelligence" (Anderson, 1992; Eysenck, 1982; Meadows, 1993); for example it is suggested that some brains are innately "faster" or "more efficient" in their basic processing because of their owners' comparatively favourable genes, and that therefore those individuals may think and learn better than individuals with "slower" brain speeds. Undoubtedly cognition depends on brain functioning, and this is to a considerable extent the result of a genetic program of development; but neuroscience is demonstrating that brain functioning, structure, and biochemistry are also the result of experience and learning continuing over the years of childhood and beyond (Greenough & Black, 1992; Meadows, 1993), and it may be more fruitful to look at differences in *experience* when searching for sources of individual differences in cognitive development.

To do this requires a much better conceptualization of what is relevant "experience" than any current theoretical perspective affords. The relevant experiences will be both physical and social. Several aspects of the physical environment are suspected of being damaging to cognitive development (Meadows, 1993), including various sorts of pollution and dietary deficiencies. The causal sequences are not yet perfectly clear, but nervous system damage and impairment of attention and motivation may be involved. Severe prenatal malnutrition, for example, may reduce the number of brain cells that develop, and this reduction may be handicapping in later cognitive development, though the evidence is not entirely clear; severe malnutrition in childhood certainly has adverse effects on health and energy which impede involvement in the exploration and education that normally lead to good cognitive development.

The brain is affected by environmental factors throughout life, as brain development continues throughout childhood, and new neural connections can be formed and lost throughout life. During the early years, there are periods of rapid proliferation of nerve cell connections followed by the selective dying-off of connections that have served no useful purpose; later development is a matter of the rearrangement of connections as new links supersede old ones, rather than of enormous increases in connectivity. Current work in developmental neuropsychology is transforming our understanding of the links between brain development and cognitive development in both normal and abnormal development, and a complex and exciting picture is emerging (for an introduction, see Meadows, 1993).

Studies of the effects of the social environment on cognitive development are not likely to provide a simpler set of influences than studies of the physical environment, and are complicated by the lack of an adequate grasp of how the social environment should be described and assessed (Meadows, 1993). Variables such as social class are associated with differences in cognitive development as assessed by school achievement, but do not indicate at all clearly what causes the association. The best candidate for social experience affecting cognitive development that a theory offers is Vygotsky's idea of "scaffolding" (Meadows, 1993; Tharp & Gallimore, 1988; Wood, 1988).

There have been several demonstrations that teaching problem solving in a Vygotskian manner facilitates children's performance on that problem and, perhaps, their ability to transfer what they have learned to another problem (Tharp & Gallimore, 1988; Wertsch, McNamee, McLane, & Budwid, 1980; Wood, 1988). Language development is similarly facilitated by Vygotskian child-contingent language (Wells, 1987). There is some evidence that parenting that is notably lacking in scaffolding and child-contingent discussion is associated with later difficulties in concentration and the development and elaboration of activities (Meadows, 1993). However, we know very little about how common scaffolding is in adults' dealings with children; whether more is better, or whether there is an "enough is as good as a feast" effect; whether the cultural differences that appear in language development apply also in cognition; whether there are alternative ways of getting the same good result (and it does seem clear that some cultures do not engage in what is recognized as scaffolding in Anglo-American settings); and whether there are stable differences between individuals in how much scaffolding they need for optimum development. Further, we do not know how scaffolding affects the child; it may provide models of cognitive skills, or of self-scaffolding, or encouragement, or lower failure rates, or a transformation of failure into a good opportunity to learn, or all of these: in other words, there may be a multitude of cognitive or motivational effects. One interesting prediction from the Vygotskian model is that the recipients of successful scaffolding not only may learn the tasks in question but also may learn to scaffold themselves through new learning, perhaps turning, effectively, into Piagetian learners. Further research is necessary to sort out these issues. So is further development of theory, beyond the assumption that cognition can be studied as independent of affect, motivation, and the social world.

FURTHER READING

Goodluck, H. (1991). *Language acquisition*. Oxford: Basil Blackwell.
Meadows, S. (1993). *The child as thinker: The acquisition and development of cognitive skills in childhood*. London: Routledge.

REFERENCES

Anderson, M. (1992). *Intelligence and cognitive development*. Oxford: Basil Blackwell.

Azmitia, M., & Perlmutter, M. (1989). Social influences on young children's cognition: State of the art and future directions. In H. W. Reese (Ed.) *Advances in child development and behavior* (vol. 22, pp. 90–145). New York: Wiley.

Beilin, H. (1992). Piaget's enduring contribution to developmental psychology. *Developmental Psychology*, *28*, 191–204.

Bronfenbrenner, U. (1979). *The ecology of human development*. Cambridge, MA: Harvard University Press.

Bryant, P. (1985). Parents, children and cognitive development. In R. Hinde, A.-N. Perret-Clermont, & J. Stevenson-Hinde (Eds) *Social relationships and cognitive development* (pp. 239–251). Cambridge: Cambridge University Press.

Butterworth, G. (1994). *Infancy*. In A. M. Colman (Ed.) *Companion encyclopedia of psychology* (pp. 683–698). London: Routledge.

Carey, S. (1991). Knowledge acquisition: Enrichment or conceptual change. In S. Carey & R. Gelman (Eds) *The epigenesis of mind* (pp. 257–291). Hove: Lawrence Erlbaum.

Case, R. (1985). *Intellectual development: Birth to adulthood*. New York: Academic Press.

Ceci, S. (1990). *On intelligence . . . more or less: A bio-ecological theory of intellectual development*. New York: Prentice-Hall.

Chi, M. (1978). Knowledge structures and memory development. In R. S. Siegler (Ed.) *Children's thinking: What develops?* (pp. 73–96). Hillsdale, NJ: Lawrence Erlbaum.

Chi, M., & Ceci, S. (1987). Content knowledge: Its role, representation and restructuring in memory development. In H. W. Reese (Ed.) *Advances in child development and behaviour* (vol. 20, pp. 91–142). New York: Academic Press.

Chomsky, N. (1968). *Language and mind*. New York: Harcourt Brace Jovanovich.

Clark, A. (1989). *Microcognition: Philosophy, cognitive science and parallel distributed processing*. Cambridge, MA: Massachusetts Institute of Technology Press.

Cromer, R. (1991). *Language and thought in normal and handicapped children*. Oxford: Basil Blackwell.

Dickinson, D., & McCabe, A. (1991). The acquisition and development of language. In J. F. Kavanagh (Ed.) *The language continuum: From infancy to literacy* (pp. 1–40). Parkton, MD: York Press.

Donaldson, M. (1978). *Children's minds*. London: Fontana.

Ellis, A. W., & Young, A. W. (1988). *Human cognitive neuropsychology*. London: Lawrence Erlbaum.

Eysenck, H. (Ed.) (1982). *A model for intelligence*. Berlin: Springer.

Fodor, J. (1983). *The modularity of mind*. Cambridge, MA: Massachusetts Institute of Technology Press.

Gelman, R. (1991). Epigenetic foundations of knowledge structures: Initial and transcendent constructions. In S. Carey & R. Gelman (Eds) *The epigenesis of mind* (pp. 293–322). Hove: Lawrence Erlbaum.

Gleitman, L. R., & Wanner, E. (1982). Language acquisition: The state of the art. In E. Wanner & L. R. Gleitman (Eds) *Language acquisition: The state of the art* (pp. 3–50). Cambridge, MA: Harvard University Press.

Goodluck, H. (1991). *Language acquisition*. Oxford: Basil Blackwell.

Goswami, U., & Brown, A. L. (1990). Melting chocolate and melting snowmen: Analogical reasoning and causal relations. *Cognition*, *35*, 69–96.

Goswami, U., & Bryant, P. (1990). *Phonological skills and learning to read.* Hove: Lawrence Erlbaum.

Greenough, W. T., & Black, J. E. (1992). Induction of brain structure by experience: Substrates for cognitive development. In M. Gunnar & C. A. Nelson (Eds) *Developmental behavioral neuroscience. Minnesota symposium on child development*, *24*, 155–200.

Harris, P. (1983). Infant cognition. In M. M. Haith & J. J. Campos (Eds) *Handbook of child psychology* (vol. 2, pp. 689–782). New York: Wiley.

Heath, S. B. (1983). *Ways with words.* Cambridge: Cambridge University Press.

Hinde, R., Perret-Clermont, A.-N., & Stevenson-Hinde, J. (Eds) (1985). *Social relationships and cognitive development.* Oxford: Oxford University Press.

Kail, R. (1991). Developmental change in speed of processing during childhood and adolescence. *Psychological Bulletin*, *109*, 490–501.

Karmiloff-Smith, A. (1986). From meta-processes to conscious access: Evidence from children's metalinguistics and repair data. *Cognition*, *23*, 95–147.

Karmiloff-Smith, A. (1991). Beyond modularity: Innate constraints and developmental change. In S. Carey & R. Gelman (Eds) *The epigenesis of mind* (pp. 171–197). Hillsdale, NJ: Lawrence Erlbaum.

Keil, F. (1989). *Concepts, kinds and cognitive development.* Boston, MA: Massachusetts Institute of Technology Press.

Kozulin, A. (1990). *Vygotsky's psychology.* Brighton: Harvester.

Light, P. (1986). Context, conservation and conversation. In M. Richards & P. Light (Eds) *Children of social worlds* (pp. 170–190). Cambridge: Polity.

McClelland, J. L., Rumelhart, D. E., & the PDP Research Group (1986). *Parallel distributed processing: Explorations in the micro-structure of cognition, vol. 2. Psychological and biological models.* Cambridge, MA: Massachusetts Institute of Technology Press.

McShane, J. (1991). *Cognitive development: An information-processing approach.* Oxford: Basil Blackwell.

Meadows, S. (1986). *Understanding child development.* London: Hutchinson.

Meadows, S. (1993). *The child as thinker: The acquisition and development of cognition in childhood.* London: Routledge.

Okagaki, L., & Sternberg, R. J. (Eds) (1991). *Directors of development: Influences on the development of children's thinking.* Hillsdale, NJ: Lawrence Erlbaum.

Perner, J. (1991). *Understanding the representational mind.* Cambridge, MA: Massachusetts Institute of Technology Press.

Piaget, J. (1983). Piaget's theory. In P. H. Mussen (Ed.) *Handbook of child psychology* (vol. 3, pp. 103–128). New York: Wiley.

Pinker, S. (1984). *Language learnability and language development.* Cambridge, MA: Harvard University Press.

Scarr, S., & Carter-Saltzman, L. (1982). Genetics and intelligence. In R. Sternberg (Ed.) *Handbook of human intelligence* (pp. 792–896). Cambridge, MA: Cambridge University Press.

Siegel, M. (1991). *Knowing children: Experiments in conversation and cognition.* Hove: Lawrence Erlbaum.

Siegler, R. (1983). Information-processing approaches to development. In W. Kessen (Ed.) *Handbook of child psychology* (vol. 1, pp. 129–212). New York: Wiley.

Siegler, R. (1986). *Children's thinking.* Englewood Cliffs, NJ: Prentice-Hall.

Slobin, D. I. (Ed.) (1985). *The cross linguistic study of language acquisition.* Hillsdale, NJ: Lawrence Erlbaum.

Smedslund, J. (1980). Analyzing the primary code: From empiricism to apriorism. In D. R. Olson (Ed.) *The social foundations of language and thought* (pp. 47–73). New York: Norton.

Sternberg, R. J. (Ed.) (1984). *Mechanisms of cognitive development*. New York: Freeman.

Tharp, R., & Gallimore, R. (1988). *Rousing minds to life: Teaching, learning and schooling in social context*. Cambridge: Cambridge University Press.

Vygotsky, L. S. (1978). *Mind in society: The development of higher psychological processes*. Cambridge, MA: Harvard University Press.

Vygotsky, L. S. (1986). *Thought and language*. Cambridge, MA: Harvard University Press.

Wells, G. (1987). *The meaning makers*. Sevenoaks: Hodder & Stoughton.

Wertsch, J. V., McNamee, G. D., McLane, J. B. & Budwid, N. A. (1980). The adult–child dyad as a problem-solving system. *Child Development, 51*, 1215–1221.

Wood, D. J. (1988). *How children think and learn*. Oxford: Basil Blackwell.

8.3

SOCIAL DEVELOPMENT

Peter K. Smith
University of Sheffield, England

During the years of infancy, social development takes place primarily with parents and adult caregivers. From birth and soon afterwards, babies possess reflexive abilities and learning capacities that assist the development of social interchanges with adults. They preferentially focus on the kinds of visual and auditory stimuli that adults typically provide when talking, and when putting their face close to an infant. Also, they enjoy the kinds of contingent responsiveness that are generally obtained from adults, for example, vocalizing when they coo or babble, cuddling them when they cry.

Some psychologists, such as Trevarthen (1977), strongly emphasize the early abilities of rhythm and intersubjectivity that the infant brings to these social interchanges. Others, such as Kaye (1984), rather emphasize the limited abilities of the infant in the first year of life, and the role of the adult caregiver in "scaffolding" the interactions by providing the right response to whatever the infant does, and timing responses appropriately to mesh in with the infant's timing. Certainly, the infant will be learning a great deal over the first 12 to 18 months, through observation and imitation.

Infants will also be learning to discriminate between different adults and caregivers, and typically are becoming attached to a small number of these towards the end of the first year. Despite evidence for some discrimination much earlier, the obvious signs of preferring a familiar caregiver to a stranger, and being reassured by the former but not by the latter, usually appear from 7 months on. This process of attachment has been described in detail by Bowlby (1969); he argues that the attachment system functions to provide a secure base for the infant to explore the physical and social environment. If alarmed or stressed, the infant will return to seek the proximity and reassurance of the attachment figure.

Some attachment theorists, such as Ainsworth, Blehar, Waters, and Wall (1978), and Main (1991), distinguish between secure and insecure attachment. A securely attached infant, when distressed, is reassured by the attachment figure. An insecurely attached infant, when distressed, will show some ambivalence to, or avoidance of, the attachment figure, or may show a disorganized response. These patterns of attachment (which measure a relationship between an infant and a particular caregiver) are measured by a procedure called the "strange situation", which re-enacts in miniature a situation involving an infant being mildly stressed by being left with a stranger, and assessing response to the caregiver on her or his return (Ainsworth et al., 1978). This procedure is applicable to infants aged 1 to 3 years. Beyond that age, attachment theorists prefer to talk about "internal working models" of relationships, which can be assessed by different means in middle childhood, and through to adulthood (Main, 1991).

Despite an earlier misplaced emphasis by Bowlby (1953) on the unique importance of mothers as attachment figures, it is now generally accepted that attachment figures can include fathers, grandparents, older siblings, and familiar non-family adults such as nannies or childminders; and that a child can be attached to several such persons. This recognition has to some extent defused the long-running controversy about whether infants can be left in non-family day-care situations without any adverse effects. It is generally felt that there are no necessary adverse effects consequent upon high-quality day-care (Clarke-Stewart, 1989), though some uncertainty still remains about the effects of intensive, early day-care on the quality of mother–infant attachment (Belsky, 1988).

EARLY PEER RELATIONSHIPS

By the age of 2 years, peers – other children of about the same age – become increasing sources of interest. In fact, peers seem to be especially interesting to children even in the second year of life. In one study of 12–18-month-old infants, two mother–infant pairs who had not previously met shared a play-room together. The infants touched their mothers a lot (remaining in proximity to them, as we would expect from attachment theory), but *looked* most at the peer, who clearly interested them (Lewis, Young, Brooks, & Michalson, 1975).

The interactions between under-2s often consist of just looking at another child and perhaps smiling, or showing a toy, or making a noise. In toddler groups an infant might make such overtures to another child once every minute or so, and any interactions are brief (Mueller & Brenner, 1977). This rather low level of peer interaction is probably because infants have not yet learned the skills of social interaction. Whereas adults can "scaffold" social interactions with infants, it takes young children some 2 or 3 years to become really competent at interacting socially with age-mates, knowing what are appropriate behaviours in certain situations, what behaviour to expect back, and waiting to take one's turn. There is some evidence that early peer experience (e.g., in toddler groups or day nurseries) can help this along. Some studies suggest that infants who are "securely attached" to their mothers are more confident and better able to explore both objects and peers, and to make new social relationships over the next few years (Bretherton & Waters, 1985; Turner, 1991).

SIBLINGS

The majority of us have siblings – brothers or sisters. Usually, siblings differ in age by only a few years. Although not exactly peers, they are generally close enough in age, and similar enough in interests and developmental stages, to be important social partners for each other in the family. Older siblings can show great tolerance for younger ones, and can act as important models for more competent behaviour. They can also show hostility and ambivalence; this has been observed in many different societies (Eibl-Eibesfeldt, 1989).

Dunn and Kendrick (1982) made observations in the homes of 40 firstborn children living with both parents in or near Cambridge, England. At first visit, a new sibling was due in a month or so, and the first child was usually nearing his or her second birthday. After the birth of the sibling they made further visits, when the second child was about 1 month old, and again at 8 months and at 14 months.

They found that many firstborns showed some signs of jealousy when the new sibling arrived. Although they had previously been the centre of attention from mother, father, or grandparents, the new brother or sister now got the most attention. Much of the jealousy and ambivalence of the firstborn was directed towards parents. Not many firstborns showed much overt hostility to the infant, but some showed ambivalence or hostility, as the following extract of conversation shows:

Child: Baby, baby (caressing her). Monster. Monster.
Mother: She's not a monster.
Child: Monster.

However, the great majority of the firstborns showed much interest and affection towards their new siblings seeking to please them, or being concerned if they cried. Overall, Dunn and Kendrick (1982) felt that the sibling relationship was one in which considerable emotions may be aroused – both of love and of envy.

This close and emotionally powerful relationship may also be an optimal situation in which to learn how to understand others. Siblings seem to be learning how to frustrate, tease, placate, comfort, or get their own way with their brother or sister. Dunn and Kendrick (1982) relate one incident in which 14-month-old Callum repeatedly reaches for and manipulates some magnetic letters which his 3-year-old sister Laura is playing with on a tray. Laura repeatedly says "no" gently. Callum continues trying to reach the letters. Finally, Laura picks up the tray with the letters and takes it to a high table that Callum cannot reach. Callum is furious and starts to cry. He turns and goes straight to the sofa where Laura's comfort objects, a rag doll and a pacifier, are lying. He takes the doll and holds it tight, looking at Laura. Laura now gets very upset, starts crying, and runs to take the doll.

Callum seems to have calculated how to annoy Laura so as to get his own back on her. These are interesting observations to compare with ideas about children's "theory of mind", as well as the critique of Piaget's ideas about egocentrism. But it is also worth bearing in mind that children can learn these social-cognitive skills with adults and peers, as well as with siblings. Research on only children appears to suggest that they do well on achievement and intelligence scores, and show no deficits in sociability or adjustment (Falbo & Polit, 1986).

THE SCHOOL YEARS

By 2 or 3 years of age a child is usually thought to be ready for nursery school. The period from 2 to 4 years does see a great increase in the skills children have with peers. Sociodramatic play (pretend role-play with others) and rough-and-tumble play (friendly play-fighting with a partner) become frequent in this age range. The child is also beginning to develop concrete operational thought and to be able to take the perspective of others in simple ways.

The increase in social behaviour in pre-school children was first documented by Parten (1932). She observed 2–4 year olds and described how they might be "unoccupied", an "onlooker" on others' activities, or, if engaged in an activity, they could be "solitary", in "parallel" activity with others, or in "associative" or "cooperative" activity with others. Parallel activity is when children play near each other with the same materials, but do not interact much – playing independently at the same sandpit for example. Associative activity is when children interact together at an activity, doing similar things, perhaps each adding building blocks to the same tower. Cooperative activity is when children interact together in complementary ways; for example, one child gets blocks out of a box and hands them to another child, who builds the tower. Parten found that the first four categories declined with age, whereas associative and cooperative activity, the only ones involving much interaction with peers, increased with age.

Most group activity involves just two or three children playing together, though the size of groups tends to increase in older pre-schoolers and in the early school years. A study of more than 400 Israeli children in outdoor free play found that group activity predominated, while parallel activity became very infrequent; the number of groups comprised of more than five children increased from 12 to 16 per cent between 5 and 6 years of age (Hertz-Lazarowitz, Feitelson, Zahavi, & Hartup, 1981). The size of children's groups continues to increase through the middle school years (about 9–12 years old), especially in boys, as team games such as football become more popular. The nature of children's groups changes again as adolescence is reached, when large same-sex cliques or gangs become common in early adolescence, changing as heterosexual relationships become more important in later adolescence.

CONCEPTIONS OF FRIENDSHIP

Usually we take friendship to mean some close association between two particular people, as indicated by their association together or their psychological attachment and trust. It is quite possible to interact a lot with others generally but not have any close friends.

How do children themselves conceive of friendship? Bigelow and La Gaipa (1980) asked Scottish and Canadian children, aged 6 to 14 years, to write an essay about their expectations of best friends. Based on a content analysis, Bigelow and La Gaipa suggested a three-stage model for friendship expectations. A "reward-cost" stage, based on common activities, living nearby, having similar expectations, was common up to 8 years. From 9 to 10 years, a "normative" stage emphasized shared values, rules, and sanctions. At 11–12 years, an "empathic" stage showed a more mature conception of friendship based on understanding, and self-disclosure, as well as shared interests. These and other studies suggest a shift towards more psychologically complex and mutually reciprocal ideas of friendship during the middle school years, with intimacy and commitment becoming especially important later in adolescence.

THE MEASUREMENT OF FRIENDSHIP: SOCIOMETRY

It is possible to build up a picture of the social structure in a group of children using a technique called sociometry. This can be done by observation. Clark, Wyon, and Richards (1969) observed nursery school children to record who was playing with whom, at intervals over a five-week period. They constructed *sociograms* (an example is shown in Figure 1). Each symbol represents a child; the thickness of lines joining two children represents the percentage of observations on which they were seen playing together. The concentric circles show the number of play partners a child has: if many, that child's symbol is towards the middle, if none, at the periphery. In this class there is one very popular girl who links two large subgroups; one boy and one girl have no clear partners.

Observation shows who associates with whom, but this may not be quite the same as friendship. An alternative is to ask each child "Who are your best friends?" The nomination data can also be plotted on a sociogram. If John chooses Richard as a best friend, but Richard does not choose John, this can

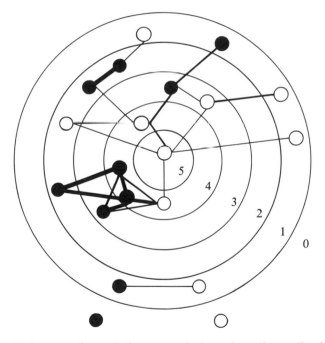

Figure 1   Sociogram of association networks in a class of pre-school children
Source: Adapted from Clark, Wyon, and Richards, 1969
Note: White circles represent girls, black circles represent boys

721

be indicated by an arrow from John to Richard; if the choice is reciprocated, the arrow would point both ways on the sociogram.

A common nomination method is to ask each child to name their three best friends. Some investigators have also asked children to say whom they do not like. There may be ethical objections to this (for example, such questions actually might bring about increased negative behaviour to unliked peers) but so far ill effects have not been found (Hayvren & Hymel, 1984). Researchers who have obtained both positive and negative nominations have not constructed sociograms (which would then look very complicated), but have instead categorized children as "popular", "controversial", "rejected", "neglected", or "average", according to whether they are high or low on positive and on negative nominations (see Table 1).

Coie and Dodge (1983) looked at the stability of these sociometric status categories between 8 and 11 years. They found that stability was highest for "rejected" children; 30 per cent of those rejected at 8 years were still rejected four years later, and another 30 per cent were "neglected". By contrast, those merely "neglected" at the start of the study tended to become "average".

Rejected children do seem to differ in their behaviour from most other children, in what seem to be maladaptive ways. Ladd (1983) observed 8 and 9 year olds in playground breaks. Rejected children, compared to average or popular children, spent less time in cooperative play and social conversation, and more time arguing and fighting, they tended to play in smaller groups, and with younger or with less popular companions. Dodge, Schlundt, Shocken, & Delugach (1983) looked at how 5 year olds attempted to get into ongoing play between two other peers. Popular children first waited and watched, then gradually got themselves incorporated by making group-oriented statements; by contrast, neglected children tended to stay at the waiting and watching stage, while rejected children tended to escalate to disruptive actions such as interrupting the play.

Children who are rejected in the middle school years (ages 9–12) may be

Table 1   Five types of sociometric status

POPULAR High on "liked most" Low on "liked least"	CONTROVERSIAL High on "liked most" High on "liked least"
AVERAGE	
NEGLECTED Low on "liked most" Low on "liked least"	REJECTED Low on "liked most" High on "liked least"

more in need of help even than those who simply keep a low profile and are ignored or neglected. The findings above suggest that rejected children are lacking in some social skills. This is a widely held view, and has been developed by Dodge, Pettit, McClaskey, & Brown (1986). They suggest that the social skills of peer interaction can be envisaged as an exchange model (see Figure 2). Suppose child A is interacting with child B. According to this model she has to (1) encode the incoming information – perceive what child B is doing, (2) interpret this information, (3) search for appropriate responses, (4) evaluate these responses and select the best, and (5) enact that response. Child B will be engaged in a similar process with respect to child A.

This model may be helpful in making the term "social skills" more explicit. If a child has a social skills deficit, where is this located? Does an over-aggressive child misinterpret others' behaviour (stage 2), or just too readily select aggressive responses (stage 4), for example?

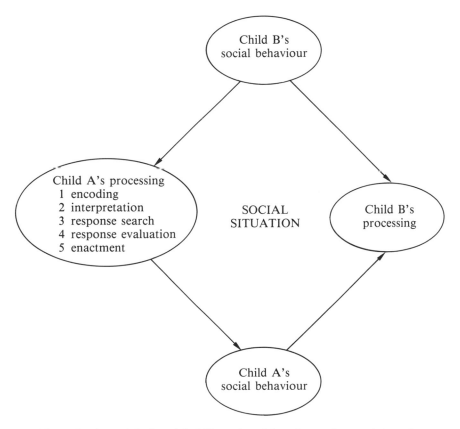

Figure 2 A model of social skills and social exchange in peer interaction
Source: Adapted from Dodge, Pettit, McClaskey, and Brown, 1986

However, not all behaviour labelled as maladjusted may be due to *lack* of social skills. Some aggressive children may be quite skilled at manipulating others. And some rejected children may be simply reacting to exclusion by the popular cliques and would not necessarily be rejected or lacking in social skills in other situations outside the classroom.

THE IMPORTANCE OF FRIENDSHIP

It seems likely that having friends is important for a child's development, but it is difficult to prove this. Parker and Asher (1987) reviewed many relevant studies, most carried out in the USA. They looked at three measures of peer relationships: peer acceptance/rejection (number and quality of friendships); aggressiveness to peers; and shyness or withdrawal from peers. They examined the relationship of these to three main kinds of later outcome: dropping out of school early; being involved in juvenile and adult crime; and adult psychopathology (mental health ratings, or needing psychiatric help of any kind).

They found a consistent link between low peer acceptance (or high peer rejection) and dropping out of school, and a suggestive link with juvenile/adult crime. There was also a consistent link between aggressiveness at school and juvenile/adult crime, with a suggestive link with dropping out of school. The data on effects of shyness/withdrawal, and on predictors of adult psychopathology, were less consistent, with any links or effects unproven at present.

Whatever the difficulties of proof, many psychologists believe that social skills training may be useful for those children who lack friends; this training is anyway usually directed to changing behaviours that are the correlates of peer rejection (such as high aggression, or high withdrawal).

SOCIAL SKILLS TRAINING

Attempts have been made by psychologists to help improve social skills in rejected or neglected children. Furman, Rahe, and Hartup (1979) observed 4 and 5 year olds who seldom played with other children. Some received special play sessions with a younger partner, to see if this might give them more confidence in social interaction. This did seem to help, more so than play sessions with a same-age peer or no intervention at all. Other researchers, working with middle-school-age children (about 9–12 years old), have used more direct means of encouraging social skills. A child might watch a film showing an initially withdrawn child engaged in a series of increasingly complex peer interactions. This has been shown to increase social interaction subsequently (O'Connor, 1972). Ogden and Asher (1977) used a more instructional approach, coaching 8- and 9-year-old children identified as socially isolated (neglected or rejected) on skills such as how to participate in groups, cooperate, and communicate with peers. They did this in special play sessions with the target child and one other peer. These children improved in sociometric status more than those who had special play sessions without the coaching.

FACTORS AFFECTING POPULARITY IN CHILDREN

Children differ in popularity and some less popular children may have less adequate social skills. But other factors are certainly at work. One such factor is physical attractiveness. Vaughn and Langlois (1983) obtained ratings of physical attractiveness for 59 pre-school children, and found a high correlation with sociometric preference. Other studies have found that ratings of physical attractiveness correlate with sociometric status.

Popularity may also be influenced by the composition of the peer group a child is in. Children tend to pick as friends peers similar to themselves. A child might tend to appear sociometrically neglected or rejected simply because he or she differs in social class, or ethnicity, from most others in the class.

AGGRESSION IN CHILDREN

It is not unusual for children to show aggression, and for young children this will often be shown in physical forms such us fighting, or in verbal taunts. Jersild and Markey (1935) observed conflicts in 54 children at three nursery schools, and described many kinds of conflict behaviour, such as taking or grabbing toys or objects held or used by another child and making unfavourable remarks about someone such as "You're no good at it" or "I don't like you". Some decline in conflicts occurred with age, and boys took part in more conflicts than girls. Nine months later, conflicts had become more verbal, but individual differences between children tended to be maintained. Cummings, Iannetti, and Zahn-Waxler (1989) similarly reported that aggressive boys tended to stay aggressive between 2 and 5 years of age, even though the overall level of physical aggression declined over this period.

Blurton Jones (1967) drew a clear distinction between physically aggressive behaviour, evidenced by beating or hitting at another with a frown or angry face, and rough-and-tumble play, where children chased and tackled each other, often smiling or laughing. These two kinds of behaviour can be confused because of their superficial similarity, but in fact most children are accomplished at telling them apart by at least 8 years of age (Costabile et al., 1991).

A number of researchers distinguish *verbal* and *non-verbal* aggression (based on the presence or absence of verbal threats or insults); *instrumental* and *hostile* aggression (based on whether the distress or harm is inferred to

725

be the primary intent of the act); and *individual* and *group* aggression (depending on whether more than one child attacks another).

CAUSES OF HIGH AGGRESSION

A certain amount of aggressive and assertive behaviour is normal. However, some children show high levels of aggression, often of a hostile or harassing nature, which can be quite stable over time and for which some adult intervention seems justified. If not dealt with at the time, children who show persistent high aggressiveness through the school years are at increased risk for later delinquency, antisocial, and violent behaviour (Farrington, 1991).

There is considerable evidence that home circumstances can be important influences leading to aggressive and later antisocial behaviour. Patterson, DeBaryshe, and Ramsey (1989) suggest that certain key aspects of parenting are involved. Children who experience irritable and ineffective discipline at home, and poor parental monitoring of their activities, together with a lack of parental warmth, are particularly likely to become aggressive in peer groups and at school. Antisocial behaviour at school is likely to be linked to academic failure and peer rejection, they argue; and in adolescence, especially if parental monitoring is lax, these young people are likely to be involved in deviant and delinquent peer groups. Their hypothesis is shown in Figure 3.

This approach suggests that the social skills of *parenting* are very important in preventing antisocial behaviour; interventions can focus on helping parents improve their child-management skills, for example via manuals and videotaped materials.

Bullying in schools is one kind of persistent aggressive behaviour that can cause great distress to victims (Smith & Thompson, 1991). It can be carried out by one child, or a group, and is usually repeated against a particular victim. The victim usually cannot retaliate effectively. While some bullying

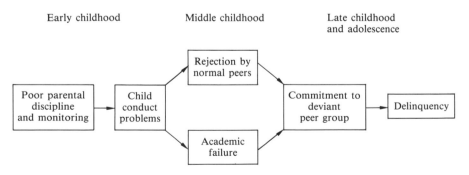

Figure 3   A developmental progression for antisocial behaviour
Source: Adapted from Patterson, DeBaryshe, and Ramsey, 1989

takes the form of hitting, pushing, taking money, it can also involve teasing, telling stories, and social exclusion. Research in western Europe suggests that bullying is quite pervasive in schools, probably to a greater extent than most teachers and parents realize, since many victims keep quiet about it. However, schools can take action to reduce the problem, by having definite "whole school" policies on the issue, improving playground supervision, raising awareness through curricular activities, and working intensively with individuals and small groups who are affected.

AGGRESSION, DOMINANCE, POPULARITY, AND LEADERSHIP

How does aggressive behaviour relate to popularity and leadership? One view is that aggressive children tend to be disliked and unpopular. Rejected children often show disruptive behaviour with peers, being disliked because of their unprovoked aggression. Some children, however, are quite aggressive but not clearly disliked. These are "controversial" children. Peers describe them as good leaders, but also as starting fights – a pattern of behaviour that appeals to some peers but not to others. Thus, some children may use aggressive behaviour in quite a socially skilled way, to acquire status in the peer group.

Sluckin (1981) made a detailed study of playground behaviour in an Oxford first school. He describes how a boy called Neill was known by his peers as the "boss" of the playground. Neill was seldom observed in actual fights (he was not physically strong), but he often tried to raise his prestige and manipulate social situations by verbal means. For example, in a race with Ginny, where they finished at the same time, Neill cried out "Yes, yes" (I'm the winner). Ginny called out "Draw", to which Neill replied "No, it wasn't, you're just trying to make trouble". Or, playing football, Neill said "I'm in goal, bagsee". Nick replied "No, I'm in goal". Neill retorted "No, John's in goal" and John went in the goal. Neill had kept the initiative, avoided a fight, but given the impression of being in charge (even though he did not get his own way entirely). Neill had a high-dominance status in the playground, and was clearly a leader of sorts, but was not especially popular. His leadership was often disruptive, since he always insisted on winning games.

Playground observations by Sluckin and others suggest that schoolchildren can rank others for dominance or fighting strength in a consistent way, and experiments confirm that this can be done reliably from about 4 or 5 years of age onwards (Sluckin & Smith, 1977). Winning fights is one criterion of dominance, but more generally it is taken as getting one's one way or influencing others. Thus, the concept is close to that of leadership.

In general, some children are popular, and often leaders, because they are socially skilled and assertive but not gratuitously aggressive. Another way of being a leader, or achieving high-dominance status, is to be a good fighter. This is a more controversial way, which may not bring true popularity with all one's peers. High aggression without the social skills to go with it, however, leads to unpopularity and rejection.

SEX DIFFERENCES AMONG CHILDREN

Up to 2 years there are not many consistent differences between girls and boys. The similarities certainly outweigh the dissimilarities; but girl infants may be more responsive to people, staying closer to adults, whereas boy infants may be more distressed by stressful situations that they cannot control. Girls also seem to talk earlier.

Observations of 2 year olds at home, and of 3 and 4 year olds in nursery classes, have found characteristic differences in choices of activity. Girls tend to prefer dolls, and dressing-up or domestic play; boys tend to prefer transportation toys, blocks, and activities involving gross motor activity such as throwing or kicking balls, or rough-and-tumbling. Many activities, however, do not show a sex preference at this age.

In nursery school children tend to select same-sex partners for play, and more so as they get older. By the time children are getting into team games from about 6 or 7 years onward, sex segregation in the playground is much greater. Girls prefer indoor, more sedentary activities, and often play in pairs; boys tend to prefer outdoor play and, later, team games. Girls tend to be more empathic, and remain more oriented towards adults (parents and teachers) longer into childhood; boys more frequently engage in both play-fighting and actual aggressive behaviour.

Lever (1978), in a study of 10–11-year-old children in American playgrounds, found that girls were more often in smaller groups of same-age pairs, while boys more often played in larger mixed-age groups. Girls put more emphasis on intimacy and exclusiveness in their friendships. Boys liked playing competitive team games that were more complex in their rules and role-structure, and that seemed to emphasize "political" skills of cooperation, competition,and leadership in their social relations.

STEREOTYPES OF SEX ROLES

Sex-role stereotypes are acquired early; these are beliefs about what is most appropriate for one sex, or the other. Kuhn, Nash, and Bruken (1978) showed pre-school children a female doll and a male doll, and asked which doll would do each of 72 activities, such as cooking, sewing, playing with trains, talking a lot, giving kisses, fighting, or climbing trees. Even $2\frac{1}{2}$ year olds had some knowledge of sex-role stereotypes (see Table 2). This sex-stereotyping increases with age and by the middle school years it is firmly established. In a study of 5- and 8-year-old children in England, Ireland, and the USA (Best et al, 1977), the majority of boys and girls agreed that females were soft-hearted whereas males were strong, aggressive, cruel, and coarse.

Table 2 Beliefs about boys and girls, held by both boys and girls aged $2\frac{1}{2}$ and $3\frac{1}{2}$ [a]

Beliefs about girls	play with dolls
	like to help mother
	like to cook dinner
	like to clean house
	talk a lot
	never hit
	say "I need some help"
Beliefs about boys	like to help father
	say "I can hit you"

Source: Kuhn, Nash, and Bruken, 1978
Note: [a] Only results at or approaching statistical significance are recorded

By 8 years of age children's stereotypes are very similar to those obtained with adults.

EXPLANATIONS OF SEX DIFFERENCES

The sex differences in behaviour and sex-role stereotypes so far discussed apply to western urban societies such as the UK and the USA. Barry, Bacon, and Child (1957) made a survey of the anthropological literature on child-rearing in 110, mostly non-literate, societies. In more than 80 per cent of societies, girls more than boys were encouraged to be nurturant, whereas boys more than girls were subject to training for self-reliance and achievement. In many societies responsibility and obedience were also encouraged in girls more than boys. Pressure for sex-typing is especially strong in societies where male strength is important for hunting or herding; it is less strong in societies with small family groups, where sharing of tasks is inevitable.

Sex hormones may have some effect on behaviour. In normal foetal development male sex hormones perhaps predispose boys to become more physically active and interested in rough-and-tumble play. This is consistent with evidence that such sex differences appear early in life, and in most human societies. However, biological factors do not in themselves explain the process of sex-role identification, and the variations in sex roles in different societies. Psychologists such as Bandura (1969) argue that children are moulded into sex-roles by the behaviour of adults, especially parents and teachers − the social learning theory approach. The idea of reinforcement is particularly important in this theory, which postulates that parents and others reward or "reinforce" sex-appropriate behaviour in children, for example encouraging nurturant behaviour in girls, and discouraging it in boys. Children may also observe the behaviour of same-sex models, and imitate them; for example, boys might observe and imitate the behaviour of male figures in TV films, in their playful and aggressive behaviour.

Kohlberg (1969) initiated a cognitive-developmental approach in this area, arguing that the child's growing sense of gender identity is crucial to sex-role identification. Children attend to and imitate same-sex models, and follow sex-appropriate activities, because they realize that this is what a child of their own sex usually does. This process has been termed "self-socialization" by Maccoby and Jacklin (1974), since it does not depend directly on external reinforcement. A number of studies have found development of gender identity and constancy to correlate with the degree of sex-typed behaviour.

While reinforcement does seem to have some effect, it looks as though its effects are being modulated by other factors. Any complete understanding of sex-role development will require an integration of biological factors, reinforcement, and social learning provided by others, with the cognitive-developmental view which provides an active role for the child himself or herself.

ETHNIC AWARENESS, IDENTITY, PREFERENCE, AND PREJUDICE

Besides differing by gender, people differ in terms of their racial or ethnic group; both are usually obvious from physical characteristics such as hair and skin colour, and facial appearance. There is not universal agreement on how people should be classified by ethnic group. Besides country of origin, other important dimensions are language (e.g., English Canadian and French Canadian) and religion (e.g., Muslim Indian and Hindu Indian).

As children grow up they will become aware that people differ by ethnic origin. By 4 or 5 years children seem able to make basic discriminations, for example between black and white; and during the next few years more difficult ones, such as Anglo and Hispanic. By around 8 or 9 years, children understand that ethnic identity remains constant despite changes in age, or superficial attributes such as clothing.

How do children react to, and evaluate, the ethnic differences which they become aware of from about 4 years? A number of studies of this kind have found that in a test situation where they can choose a doll, or photo, representing children of differing ethnicity, most white children choose or prefer the white doll (or photo) from 4 years, whereas black and other ethnic minority children are more divided, with (in some of the earlier studies) most of them choosing the white doll too. These preferences strengthen up to about 7 years. Beyond 7 years, black children tend to choose the black doll or photo more frequently. These studies were mostly carried out in North America or the UK, where whites form the dominant and more privileged social groups, and this probably influenced the results. The extent to which minority group children choose their own group has increased, at least among 7 to 11 years old (Milner, 1983), with the rise of ethnic minority group consciousness and pride in their own culture which has characterized North America and the UK since the 1970s.

Another way of looking at ethnic preference is more naturalistic, observing whom children actually choose as play partners, in playgroup or playground situations. Children often segregate by race, as well as by gender. Finkelstein and Haskins (1983) observed black and white kindergarten children in the USA. They found that these 5 year olds showed marked segregation by race, which increased during a year in kindergarten. However, neither black nor white children behaved differently towards other-colour peers from the way they behaved towards same-colour peers.

In older children too, segregation by race is noticeable. However, segregation by race seems to be less marked than segregation by sex, by the middle school period, and is not so evident among boys as girls, perhaps because boys play in larger groups than girls; when playing football, for example, ethnic group may be ignored in order to fill up a team with the requisite number of good players.

ETHNIC PREJUDICE

Preference is not identical with prejudice. Prejudice implies a negative evaluation of another person on the basis of some general attribute (which could be for example sex, race, or disability). Thus, racial prejudice means a negative evaluation of people as a consequence of their being in a certain racial or ethnic group. If a white child dislikes a black child because of some individual attribute, this is not prejudice. But if a white child dislikes a black child (and black children) because of colour, this is racial prejudice. The experience of prejudice can be very damaging and at times tragic. This is vividly brought to life in a case study at one school, *Murder in the Playground* (MacDonald, 1989).

Prejudice can be measured by asking children to put photos of other children from different ethnic groups along a scale of liking (Aboud, 1988), or to assign positive adjectives such as "work hard" and "truthful", or negative adjectives such as "stupid" or "dirty", to all, some, one or none of photos representing different ethnic groups (Davey, 1983). The results are rather similar to those of ethnic identity; prejudice seems to increase from 4 to 7 years, mainly at the expense of minority ethnic groups. During middle childhood, white children tend to remain prejudiced against black or minority group children, while the latter show a more mixed pattern but often become more positive to their own group.

Aboud (1988) has argued that before about 3 or 4 years of age, ethnic awareness is largely absent and prejudice is not an issue; but that from 4 to 7 years, children perceive other ethnic groups as dissimilar to themselves, and because of this tend to have negative evaluations of them. From 8 years onward, children become able to think more flexibly about ethnic differences, and in terms of individuals rather than groups, so that their earlier prejudice can be modified.

Schools have been a focus for work to reduce racial prejudice in children. A multiracial curriculum approach which emphasizes the diversity of racial and cultural beliefs and practices and gives them equal evaluation, may help in this process. Procedures such as Cooperative Group Work (Cowie & Rudduck, 1991) bring children of different race (and sex) together in common activities, and may thus reduce ethnic preference and prejudice in the classroom.

INFLUENCES ON SOCIAL DEVELOPMENT: SUMMARY

The early important influences on the social development of the child are clearly parents or caregivers. Through caregiver—infant interactions the infant acquires basic social skills and develops social attachments.

As the child enters school and progresses to middle childhood, the influence of peers becomes more important. Social participation and friend-ships with peers, and sociometric status in the peer group, appear to relate in significant ways to later development. To some extent, the peer group is an autonomous world with different systems, customs, and culture from the adult world (Sluckin, 1981). Nevertheless, the family continues to exert an influence, through patterns of attachment, management practices of parents (including a direct influence on the out-of-school peer network), and the effects of siblings. The older child, too, is increasingly aware of, and influenced by, the expectations of society for someone of their age, gender, ethnicity, and social background, as mediated by peers and by socializing influences such as schools, and the mass media. By adolescence, the sep-aration from parents is becoming more complete, and the young person is moving toward a mature sense of identity and social being.

FURTHER READING

Aboud, F. (1988). *Children and prejudice*. Oxford: Basil Blackwell.
Bowlby, J. (1988). *A secure base: Clinical applications of attachment theory*. London: Tavistock.
Dunn, J. (1988). *The beginnings of social understanding*. Oxford: Basil Blackwell.
Hargreaves, D., & Colley, A. (Eds) (1986). *The psychology of sex roles*. London: Harper & Row.
McGurk, H. (Ed.) (1992). *Childhood social development: Contemporary perspect-ives*. Hove: Lawrence Erlbaum.

REFERENCES

Aboud, F. (1988). *Children and prejudice*. Oxford: Basil Blackwell.

Ainsworth, M. D. S., Blehar, M. C., Waters, E., & Wall, S. (1978). *Patterns of attachment: A psychological study of the strange situation.* Hillsdale, NJ: Lawrence Erlbaum.

Bandura, A. (1969). Social learning theory of identificatory processes. In D. A. Goslin (Ed.) *Handbook of socialization theory and research* (pp. 213–262). Chicago, IL: Rand McNally.

Barry, H., III, Bacon, M. K., & Child, I. L. (1957). A cross-cultural survey of some sex differences in socialization. *Journal of Abnormal and Social Psychology, 55,* 327–332.

Belsky, J. (1988). Infant day care and socioemotional development: The United States. *Journal of Child Psychology and Psychiatry, 29,* 397–406.

Best, D. L., Williams, J. E., Cloud, L. M., Davis, S. W., Robertson, L. S., Edwards, J. R. Giles, H., & Fowles, J. (1977). Development of sex-trait stereotypes among young children in the United States, England and Ireland. *Child Development, 48,* 1375–1384.

Bigelow, B. J., & La Gaipa, J. J. (1980). The development of friendship values and choice. In H. C. Foot, A. J. Chapman, & J. R. Smith (Eds) *Friendship and social relations in children* (pp. 15–44). Chichester: Wiley.

Blurton Jones, N. (1967). An ethological study of some aspects of social behaviour of children in nursery school. In D. Morris (Ed.) *Primate ethology* (pp. 347–368). London: Weidenfeld & Nicolson.

Bowlby, J. (1953). *Child care and the growth of love.* Harmondsworth: Penguin.

Bowlby, J. (1969). *Attachment and loss: I. Attachment.* London: Hogarth.

Bretherton, I., & Waters, E. (Eds) (1985). Growing points of attachment theory and research. *Monographs of the Society for Research in Child Development, 50* (1–2).

Clark, A. H., Wyon, S. M., & Richards, M. P. M. (1969). Free-play in nursery school children. *Journal of Child Psychology and Psychiatry, 10,* 205–216.

Clarke-Stewart, A. (1989). Infant day care: Maligned or malignant? *American Psychologist, 44,* 266–273.

Cole, J. D., & Dodge, K. A. (1983). Continuities and changes in children's social status: A five-year longitudinal study. *Merrill-Palmer Quarterly, 29,* 261–282.

Costabile, A., Smith, P. K., Matheson, L., Aston, J., Hunter, T., & Boulton, M. (1991). Cross-national comparison of how children distinguish serious and playful fighting. *Developmental Psychology, 27,* 881–887.

Cowie, H., & Rudduck, J. (1991). *Cooperative group work in the multi-ethnic classroom.* London: BP.

Cummings, E. M., Iannotti, R. J., & Zahn-Waxler, C. (1989). Aggression between peers in early childhood: Individual continuity and developmental change. *Child Development, 60,* 887–895.

Davey, A. (1983). *Learning to be prejudiced: Growing up in multi-ethnic Britain.* London: Edward Arnold.

Dodge, K. A., Schlundt, D. C., Shocken, I., & Delugach, J. D. (1983). Social competence and children's sociometric status: The role of peer group entry strategies. *Merrill-Palmer Quarterly, 29,* 309–336.

Dodge, K. A., Pettit, G. S., McCluskey, C. L., & Brown, M. M. (1986). Social competence in children. *Monographs of the Society for Research in Child Development, 51,* 2.

Dunn, J., & Kendrick, C. (1982). *Siblings: Love, envy and understanding.* Oxford: Basil Blackwell.

Eibl-Eibesfeldt, I. (1989). *Human ethology.* New York: Aldine de Gruyter.

Falbo, T., & Polit, D. F. (1986). Quantitative review of the only child literature: Research evidence and theory development. *Psychological Bulletin, 100*, 176–189.

Farrington, D. P. (1991). Childhood aggression and adult violence: Early precursors and later-life outcomes. In D. J. Pepler & K. H. Rubin (Eds) *The development and treatment of childhood aggression* (pp. 5–29). Hillsdale, NJ: Lawrence Erlbaum.

Finkelstein, N. W., & Haskins, R. (1983). Kindergarten children prefer same-color peers. *Child Development, 54*, 502–508.

Furman, W., Rahe, D. F., & Hartup, W. W. (1979). Rehabilitation of socially withdrawn preschool children through mixed-age and same-age socialization. *Child Development, 50*, 915–922.

Hayvren, M., & Hymel, S. (1984). Ethical issues in sociometric testing: impact of sociometric measures on interaction behavior. *Developmental Psychology, 20*, 844–849.

Hertz-Lazarowitz, R., Feitelson, D., Zahavi, S., & Hartup, W. W. (1981). Social interaction and social organisation of Israeli five- to-seven-year olds. *International Journal of Behavioral Development, 4*, 143–155.

Jersild, A. T., & Markey, F. V. (1935). Conflicts between preschool children. *Child Development Monographs, 21*. Teachers College, Columbia University, New York.

Kaye, K. (1984). *The mental and social life of babies*. London: Methuen.

Kohlberg, L. (1969). Stages and sequence: The cognitive-developmental approach to socialization. In D. A. Goslin (Ed.) *Handbook of socialization theory and research* (pp. 347–480). Chicago, IL: Rand McNally.

Kuhn, D., Nash, S. C., & Bruken, L. (1978). Sex role concepts of two- and-three-year-olds. *Child Development, 49*, 445–451.

Ladd, G. W. (1983). Social networks of popular, averge and rejected children in school settings. *Merrill-Palmer Quarterly, 29*, 283–307.

Lever, J. (1978). Sex differences in the complexity of children's play and games. *American Sociological Review, 43*, 471–483.

Lewis, M., Young, G., Brooks, J., & Michalson, L. (1975). The beginning of friendship. In M. Lewis & L. Rosenblum (Eds) *Friendship and peer relations* (pp. 27–65). New York: Wiley.

Maccoby, E. E., & Jacklin, C. N. (1974). *The psychology of sex differences*. Stanford, CA: Stanford University Press.

MacDonald, I. (1989). *Murder in the playground*. London: Longsight.

Main, M. (1991). Metacognitive knowledge, metacognitive monitoring, and singular (coherent) vs. multiple (incoherent) model of attachment: Findings and directions for future research. In C. Murray Parkes, J. Stevenson-Hinde, & P. Marris (Eds) *Attachment across the life cycle* (pp. 127–159). London: Routledge.

Milner, D. (1983). *Children and race: Ten years on*. London: Ward Lock Educational.

Mueller, E., & Brenner, J. (1977). The origins of social skills and interaction among playgroup toddlers. *Child Development, 48*, 854–861.

O'Connor, R. D. (1972). Relative efficacy of modeling, shaping and the combined procedures for modification of social withdrawal. *Journal of Abnormal Psychology, 79*, 327–334.

Oden, S., & Asher, S. R. (1977). Coaching children in social skills for friendship making. *Child Development, 48*, 495–506.

Parker, J. G., & Asher, S. R. (1987). Peer relations and later personal adjustment: Are low-accepted children at risk? *Psychological Bulletin, 102*, 357–389.

Parten, M. B. (1932). Social participation among preschool children. *Journal of Abnormal and Social Psychology, 27*, 243–269.

Patterson, G. R., DeBaryshe, B. D., & Ramsey, E. (1989). A developmental perspective on antisocial behaviour. *American Psychologist*, *44*, 329–335.

Sluckin, A. M. (1981). *Growing up in the playground: The social development of children*, London: Routledge & Kegan Paul.

Sluckin, A. M. & Smith, P. K. (1977). Two approaches to the concept of dominance in preschool children. *Child Development*, *48*, 917–923.

Smith, P. K., & Thompson, D. A. (Eds) (1991). *Practical approaches to bullying*. London: David Fulton.

Trevarthen, C. (1977). Descriptive analyses of infant communicative behaviour. In H. R. Schaffer (Ed.) *Studies in mother–infant interaction* (pp. 227–270). London: Academic Press.

Turner, P. (1991). Relations between attachment, gender, and behavior with peers in preschool. *Child Development*, *62*, 1475–1488.

Vaughn, B. E., & Langlois, J. H. (1983). Physical attractiveness as a correlate of peer status and social competence in preschool children. *Developmental Psychology*, *19*, 561–567.

8.4

ADOLESCENCE

John C. Coleman
Trust for the Study of Adolescence, Brighton, England

In seeking to understand adolescence we are brought face to face with a variety of puzzling issues. In the first place no one is entirely sure when adolescence begins, and when it ends. It may be convenient to use the teenage years – from 13 to 19 – as one definition, but it hardly fits the facts. At one end puberty may commence at 10 or 11, and parents or teachers may describe the behaviour of girls or boys as "adolescent" well before they reach the age of 13. At the other end, those remaining in higher education, or still living at home in their early 20s, may be manifesting confrontational or dependent behaviour which is strikingly similar to that of a typical 14 year old.

We have only to consider current legislation to do with young people to see that age is a deeply confounding factor. Is adulthood reached at 16, 17, or at 18? Is a 10 year old a child or a young person? When do parental responsibilities cease? Asking such questions simply brings us face to face with the anomalies of the legal systems in many countries, anomalies that have a profound effect on young people themselves. The fact is that chronological age, although giving us a broad indication of the adolescent stage, cannot be a precise definition. Around the edges, and particularly at either end, the definition of adolescence remains uncertain, and this itself reflects an important feature of the phenomenon.

The second problem associated with adolescence has to do with the possibility that it is a stage that is to some extent artificially created. Many were influenced by Margaret Mead's classic book *Coming of Age in Samoa* (1928). In this book she describes a society in which individuals pass from childhood to adulthood with no trauma or stress. The existence of rites of passage enable boys and girls to be clear about when and how they should assume adult roles and responsibilities, and this clarity ensures that the long transition and the ambiguity of status are not experienced. Although it is generally agreed now that Mead viewed Samoan society through rose-coloured spectacles, none the less the sense continues to linger that western society, through its emphasis on continued education and the prolonged economic dependence of young people on their parents, encourages adolescence to be a difficult period.

Indeed, the teenage consumer has an important place in an industrial economy. The spending power of those who have as yet no adult responsibilities is formidable, and advertising and the media have devoted much of their energies to ensuring that this market not only remains in place, but also is expanded as far as possible. Such pressures undoubtedly play a part in creating younger and younger adolescents whose needs – for music, fashion, and so on – can be met only by new products.

However, this argument can be taken only so far. While it is certainly true that teenage consumers are an important element in western economies, that does not necessarily mean that our economic system – capitalism – has created adolescence. Adolescence has existed in one form or another since the Greeks, as we know from the writings of Plato. Two thousand years ago youth was seen as the political force most likely to challenge the status quo, and even in Elizabethan times, according to Shakespeare, the young were more likely to be "wronging the ancientry" and "getting wenches with child" than doing anything useful. A study by Montemayor (1983) analysed relationships between parents and adolescents in two historical periods – the 1920s and 1980s. He was able to show not only that issues of disagreement remained remarkably similar over the two periods, but, even more important, that levels of conflict within families were almost exactly the same. Clearly, therefore, in spite of enormous social and economic changes in the twentieth century, the phenomenon of adolescence has changed little. It is often said that the concept "the teenage years" came about after the end of the Second World War, and came to public notice in the 1950s with films such as James Dean's *Rebel without a Cause*. Montemayor's research shows this not to be true: it may be that the term "teenager" came into our vocabulary at that time, but adolescence itself has been around for very much longer. In fact the first substantial study of the psychology of adolescence was written by G. Stanley Hall; the date – 1904.

While adolescence is quite clearly affected by social and economic factors, and may manifest itself differently depending on the cultural and historical context, some form of transitional stage is common to most societies. The period of the transition will obviously vary both between and within societies. Thus, for example, in the United States and Britain work opportunities, housing, entry into further education, and family circumstances all affect the way adolescence shades into adulthood, and the length of time the transitional stage is allowed to continue.

Irrespective of when the stage ends, however, in most western countries there are particular characteristics of adolescence that are of general relevance. There seems little doubt, for example, that almost all young people experience ambiguity of status. Between the ages of 15 and 17 uncertainties about their rights, and lack of clarity about where they stand in relation to the authority of the parents, are issues familiar to many teenagers. "When do I become an adult?" is a tricky question to answer, and is likely to lead to confusion, not least because a different answer would be given by a police officer, a doctor, a teacher, a parent, and a social worker.

What is adolescence? It is a complex stage of human development, having some common features, but also involving enormously wide individual variations. In this chapter I shall be outlining some well-known theories of adolescence, as well as reviewing the results of some of the major research studies. I shall be concentrating on the common features of adolescence, but we should not lose sight of the fact that a stage which lasts for a minimum of six years cannot possibly be encapsulated in a few pages, and generalizations need to be treated with some care.

TRADITIONAL THEORIES

There is general agreement by all who have written about adolescence that it makes sense to describe the stage as being one of transition. The transition, it is believed, results from the operation of a number of pressures. Some of these, in particular the physiological and emotional pressures, are internal; while other pressures, which originate from peers, parents, teachers, and society at large, are external to the young person. Sometimes these external pressures carry the individual towards maturity at a faster rate than he or she would prefer, while on other occasions they act as a brake, holding the adolescent back from the freedom and independence which he or she believes to be a legitimate right. It is the interplay of these forces which, in the final analysis, contributes more than anything to the success or failure of the transition from childhood to maturity.

So far two classical types of explanation concerning the transitional process have been advanced. The psychoanalytic approach concentrates on the psychosexual development of the individual, and looks particularly at the psychological factors which underlie the young person's movement away from childhood behaviour and emotional involvement. The second type of explanation, the sociological, represents a very different perspective. While it has never been as coherently expressed as the psychoanalytic view, it is none the less of equal importance. In brief, this explanation sees the causes of adolescent transition as lying primarily in the social setting of the individual and concentrates on the nature of roles and role conflict, the pressures of social expectations, and on the relative influence of different agents of socialization. Let us now look more closely at each of these explanations.

Psychoanalytic theory

The psychoanalytic view of adolescence takes as its starting-point the upsurge of instincts which is said to occur as a result of puberty. This increase in instinctual life, it is suggested, upsets the psychic balance that has been achieved by the end of childhood causing internal emotional upheaval and leading to a greatly increased vulnerability of the personality. This state of affairs is associated with two further factors. In the first place, the individual's awakening sexuality leads him or her to look outside the family setting for appropriate "love objects" thus severing the emotional ties with the parents which have existed since infancy. This process is known as disengagement. Second, the vulnerability of the personality results in the employment of psychological defences to cope with the instincts and anxiety which are, to a greater or lesser extent, maladaptive. An excellent review of psychoanalytic thinking as it applies to adolescence may be found in Lerner (1987).

Regression, a manifestation of behaviour more appropriate to earlier stages of development, and ambivalence are both seen as further key elements of the adolescent process. According to the psychoanalytic view, ambivalence accounts for many of the phenomena often considered incomprehensible in adolescent behaviour. For example, the emotional instability of relationships, the contradictions in thought and feeling, and the apparently illogical shift from one reaction to another reflect the fluctuations between loving and hating, acceptance and rejection, involvement and noninvolvement which underlie relationships in the early years, and which are reactivated once more in adolescence.

Such fluctuations in mood and behaviour are indicative also of the young person's attitudes to growing up. Thus, while freedom may at times appear the most exciting of goals, there are also moments when, in the harsh light of reality, independence and the necessity to fight one's own battles become a daunting prospect. At these times childlike dependence exercises a powerful attraction, manifested in periods of uncertainty and self-doubt, and in behaviour that is more likely to bring to mind a wilful child than a young adult.

A consideration of ambivalence leads us on to the more general theme of non-conformity and rebellion, believed by psychoanalysts to be an almost universal feature of adolescence. Behaviour of this sort has many causes. Some of it is a direct result of ambivalent modes of relating, the overt reflection of the conflict between loving and hating. In other circumstances, however, it may be interpreted as an aid to the disengagement process. In this context if the parents can be seen as old-fashioned and irrelevant then the task of breaking the emotional ties becomes easier. If everything that originates from home can safely be rejected then there is nothing to be lost by giving it all up.

Non-conformity thus facilitates the process of disengagement although, as many writers point out, there are a number of intermediate stages along the way. Baittle and Offer (1971) illustrate particularly well the importance of non-conformity and its close links with ambivalence:

> When the adolescent rebels, he often expresses his intentions in a manner resembling negation. He defines what he does in terms of what his parents do not want him to do. If his parents want him to turn off the radio and study this is the precise time he keeps the radio on and claims he cannot study. If they want him to buy new clothes, "the old ones are good enough". In periods like this it becomes obvious that the adolescent's decisions are in reality based on the negative of the parents' wishes, rather than on their own positive desires. What they do and the judgements they make are in fact dependent on the parents' opinions and suggestions but in a negative way. This may be termed the stage of "negative dependence". Thus, while the oppositional behaviour and protest against the parents are indeed a manifestation of rebellion and in the service of emancipation from the parents, at the same time they reveal that the passive dependent longings are still in force. The adolescent is in conflict over desires to emancipate, and the rebellious behaviour is a compromise formation which supports his efforts to give up the parental object and, at the same time, gratifies his dependence on them. (p. 35)

To summarize, three particular ideas characterize the psychoanalytic position. In the first place adolescence is seen as being a period during which there is a marked vulnerability of personality, resulting primarily from the upsurge of instincts at puberty. Second, emphasis is laid on the likelihood of maladaptive behaviour, stemming from the inadequacy of the psychological defences to cope with inner conflicts and tensions. Examples of such behaviour include extreme fluctuations of mood, inconsistency in relationships, depression, and non-conformity. Third, the process of disengagement is given special prominence. This is perceived as a necessity if mature emotional and sexual relationships are to be established outside the home.

Sociological theory

As has been indicated, the sociological view of adolescence encompasses a very different perspective from that of psychoanalytic theory. While there is no disagreement between the two approaches concerning the importance of the transitional process, it is on the subject of the causes of this process that the viewpoints diverge. Thus, while the one concentrates on internal factors, the other looks at society and to events outside the individual for a satisfactory explanation. As will become apparent, it is implicit in the sociological viewpoint that both socialization and role assumption are more problematic during adolescence than at any other time.

Why should this be so? First, features of adolescence such as growing independence from authority figures, involvement with peer groups, and an unusual sensitivity to the evaluations of others all provoke role transitions and discontinuity, of varying intensities, as functions of both social and cultural context. Second, any inner change or uncertainty has the effect of increasing the individual's dependence on others, and this applies particularly to the need for reassurance and support for one's view of oneself. Third, the effects of major environmental changes are also relevant in this context. Different schools, the move from school to university or college, leaving home, taking a job, all demand involvement in a new set of relationships which in turn leads to different and often greater expectations, a substantial reassessment of the self, and an acceleration of the process of socialization. Role change, it will be apparent, is thus seen as an integral feature of adolescent development.

Socialization is seen as problematic for the following reasons. In the first place, the adolescent is exposed to a wide variety of competing socialization agencies, including the family, the school, the peer group, adult-directed youth organizations, the mass media, political organizations, and so on, and is thus presented with a wide range of potential conflicts, values, and ideals. Furthermore, it is commonly assumed by sociologists today that the socialization of young people is more dependent upon the generation than upon the family or other social institutions. Marsland (1987) goes so far as to call it "auto-socialization" in his description of the process:

> The crucial social meaning of youth is withdrawal from adult control and influence compared with childhood. Peer groups are the milieu into which young people withdraw. In at least most societies, this withdrawal to the peer group is, within limits, legitimated by the adult world. Time and space is handed over to young people to work out for themselves in auto-socialisation the developmental problems of self and identity which cannot be handled by the simple direct socialisation appropriate to childhood. There is a moratorium on compliance and commitment and leeway allowed for a relatively unguided journey with peers towards autonomy and maturity. (p. 12)

Both the conflict between socialization agencies and the freedom from clearly defined guidelines are seen as making socialisation more uncertain, and causing major difficulties for the young person in establishing a bridge towards the assumption of adult roles. Brake (1985), in his discussion of youth subcultures, makes similar points, and it is a common assumption among those writing from the sociological point of view that the social changes since the early 1970s have created ever-increasing stresses for young people.

To summarize, the sociological or social-psychological approach to adolescence is marked by a concern with roles and role change, and with the processes of socialization. There can be little doubt that adolescence, from this point of view, is seen as being dominated by stresses and tensions, not so much because of inner emotional instability, but as a result of conflicting pressures from outside. Thus, by considering both this and the psychoanalytic approach, two mutually complementary but essentially different views of the adolescent transitional process have been reviewed. In spite of their differences, however, the two approaches share one common belief, and that is in the concept of adolescent "storm and stress". Both these traditional theories view the teenage years as a "problem stage" in human development, and it is important therefore to see whether this view is borne out by the research evidence.

THE RESEARCH EVIDENCE

Broadly speaking, research provides little support for these traditional theories, and fails to substantiate much of what both psychoanalysts and sociologists appear to believe. To take some examples, while there is certainly some change in self-concept, there is no evidence to show that any but a small minority experience a serious identity crisis. In most cases, relationships with parents are positive and constructive, and young people do not in large part reject adult values in favour of those espoused by the peer group. In fact, in most situations peer-group values appear to be consistent with those of important adults rather than in conflict with them (Coleman & Hendry, 1990). Expectations of promiscuity among the young are not borne out by the research findings, nor do studies support the belief that the peer group encourages antisocial behaviour, unless other factors are also present. Lastly, there is no evidence to suggest that during the adolescent years there is a higher level of psychopathology than at other times. While a lot still needs to be learned about the mental health of young people, almost all the results that have become available so far indicate that, although a small minority may show disturbance, the great majority of teenagers seem to cope well and to show no undue signs of turmoil or stress.

Support for this belief may be found in every major study of adolescence that has appeared in recent years (Feldman & Elliott, 1990). Most would agree with the views of Siddique and D'Arcy (1984) who, in summarizing their own results on stress and well-being in adolescence, write as follows:

> In this study some 33.5 per cent of the adolescents surveyed reported no symptoms of psychological distress, and another 39 per cent reported five or fewer symptoms (a mild level of distress). On the other hand a significant 27.5 per cent reported higher levels of psychological distress. For the majority the adolescent transition may be relatively smooth. However, for a minority it does indeed appear to be a period of stress and turmoil. The large majority of adolescents appear to get on well with adults and are able to cope effectively with demands of school and peer groups. They use their resources to make adjustments with environmental stressors with hardly visible signs of psychological distress. (p. 471)

There would appear to be a sharp divergence of opinion, therefore, between theory and research. Beliefs about adolescence that stem from traditional theory do not in general accord with the results of research. We need now to consider some of the reasons for this state of affairs. First, as many writers have pointed out, psychoanalysts and psychiatrists see a selected population. Their experience of adolescence is based primarily upon the individuals they meet in clinics or hospitals. Such experience is bound to encourage a some-what one-sided perspective in which turmoil or disturbance is over-represented. For sociologists, on the other hand, the problem is often to dis-entangle concepts of "youth" or "the youth movement" from notions about young people themselves. As a number of commentators have observed, youth is frequently seen by sociologists as being in the forefront of social change. Youth is, as it were, the advance party where innovation or alteration in the values of society are concerned. From this position it is but a short step to use youth as a metaphor for social change, and thus to confuse radical forces in society with the beliefs of ordinary people (Brake, 1985).

Another possible reason for the divergence of viewpoint is that certain adolescent behaviours, such as vandalism, drug-taking, and hooliganism, are extremely threatening to adults. The few who are involved in such activities therefore attain undue prominence in the public eye. The mass media play an important part in this process by publicizing sensational behaviour, thus making it appear very much more common than it is in reality. One only has to consider critically the image of the teenager portrayed week after week on the television to understand how, for many adults, the minority comes to be representative of all young people. All three tendencies mentioned so far lead to an exaggerated view of the amount of turmoil that may be expected during adolescence, and thus serve to widen the gap between research and theory.

Obviously the two traditional theories have some value, and it would be wrong to leave the impression that neither is any longer relevant. Perhaps the most important contribution made by these theories is that they have provided the foundation for an understanding of young people with serious problems and a greater knowledge of those who belong to minority groups. In this respect the two major theories have much to offer. However, it must be recognized that they are now inadequate as the basis for an understanding of the development of the great majority of young people. The fact is that adolescence needs a theory, not of abnormality, but of normality. Any viable theoretical viewpoint put forward today must not only incorporate the results of empirical studies, but also acknowledge the fact that, although for some young people adolescence may be a difficult time, for the majority it is not a period of serious instability.

PUBERTY

Having considered theoretical approaches to adolescence, the rest of this chapter will be devoted to outlining three key areas of development –

puberty, cognition, and relationships with adults. Many other topics could have been included, but limitations of space have meant that selectivity has been inevitable. Puberty, and the physical growth that accompanies it, is important for a number of reasons. In the first place puberty has a range of physiological effects which are not always outwardly apparent to observers, but which can none the less have a considerable impact on the individual. Second, rates of maturation vary enormously leading inevitably to questions of normality and comparability between young people. Furthermore, especially early or unusually late developers have particular difficulties to face, which again have marked implications for classroom performance and behaviour. Third, physical development cannot fail to have psychological consequences, often affecting self-concept and self-esteem, factors which themselves play a major part in motivation and learning. Thus it can be seen that an understanding of puberty is essential in making sense of adolescent development as a whole.

Adults often fail to appreciate that puberty is accompanied by changes not only in the reproductive system and in the secondary sexual characteristics of the individual, but also in the functioning of the heart and thus of the cardiovascular system, in the lungs, which in turn affect the respiratory system, in the size and the strength of many of the muscles of the body, and so on. One of the many physical changes associated with puberty is the "growth spurt". This term is usually taken to refer to the accelerated rate of increase in height and weight that occurs during early adolescence. It is essential to bear in mind, however, that there are very considerable individual differences in the age of onset and duration of the growth spurt, even among perfectly normal children. This is a fact that parents and adolescents themselves frequently fail to appreciate, thus causing a great deal of unnecessary anxiety. In boys the growth spurt may begin as early as 10 years of age, or as late as 16, while in girls the same process can begin at 7 or 8, or not until 12, 13, or even 14. For the average boy, though, rapid growth begins at about 13, and reaches a peak somewhere between 14 and 15. Comparable ages for girls are 11 for the onset of the growth spurt and 12 for the peak age of increase in height and weight. Other phenomena associated with the growth spurt are a rapid increase in the size and weight of the heart (the weight of the heart nearly doubles at puberty), accelerated growth of the lungs, and a decline in basal metabolism. Noticeable to children themselves, especially boys, is a marked increase in physical strength and endurance (see Tanner, 1978, for a full description).

Sexual maturation is closely linked with the physical changes described above. Again, the sequence of events is approximately 18 to 24 months later for boys than it is for girls. Since individuals mature at very different rates, one girl at the age of 14 may be small, have no bust, and look very much as she did during childhood, while another of the same age may look like a fully developed adult woman, who could easily be taken for someone four or five years in advance of her actual chronological age.

The changes discussed above inevitably exercise a profound effect upon the individual. The body alters radically in size and shape, and it is not surprising that many adolescents experience a period of clumsiness in an attempt to adapt to these changes. The body also alters in function, and new and sometimes worrying physical experiences, such as the girl's first menstrual period, have to be understood. Perhaps most important of all, however, is the effect that such physical changes have upon identity. As many writers have pointed out, the development of the individual's identity requires not only the notion of being separate and different from others, but also a sense of self-consistency, and a firm knowledge of how one appears to the rest of the world. Needless to say, dramatic bodily changes seriously affect these aspects of identity, and represent a considerable challenge in adaptation for even the most well-adjusted young person. It is unfortunate that many adults, having successfully forgotten much of their own adolescent anxiety, retain only a vague awareness of the psychological impact of the physical changes associated with puberty.

COGNITION

In a short review such as this it is possible only to draw attention to the major themes, and to highlight one or two of the most significant areas of work in this field. For those wishing to read further, good general discussions of cognition in adolescence are to be found in Coleman and Hendry (1990), Serafica (1982), and Conger and Petersen (1984). Changes in intellectual functioning during the teenage years have implications for a wide range of behaviours and attitudes. Such changes render possible the move towards independence of both thought and action; they enable the young person to develop a time perspective that includes the future; they facilitate progress towards maturity in relationships; and finally they underline the individual's ability to participate in society as worker, voter, responsible group member, and so on. We cannot consider these changes without looking first at the work of Piaget, for it is he who has laid the foundation for almost all subsequent work on cognitive development. It will be worthwhile also to discuss briefly some work on adolescent reasoning and to review ideas on both moral and political thought in adolescence.

The work of Jean Piaget, the Swiss psychologist, is the most obvious starting-point for a consideration of cognitive development during the adolescent years. It was he who first pointed out that a qualitative change in the nature of mental ability, rather than any simple increase in cognitive skills, is to be expected at or around puberty, and he has argued that it is at this point in development that formal operational thought becomes possible (Inhelder & Piaget, 1958). A full description of Piaget's stages of cognitive growth is not possible here. According to Piaget, in early adolescence the individual moves from a stage of concrete operations to one of formal operational thought. With the appearance of this stage a number of capabilities become available to the young person. Perhaps the most significant of these is the ability to construct "contrary to fact" propositions. This change has been described as the shift of emphasis in adolescent thought from the "real" to the "possible", and it facilitates hypothetico-deductive logic. It also enables the individual to think about mental constructs as objects that can be manipulated, and to come to terms with notions of probability and belief.

This fundamental difference in approach between the young child and the adolescent has been neatly demonstrated in a study by Elkind (1966). He showed dramatic differences between 8 and 9 year olds and 13 and 14 year olds in their capacity to solve a concept-formation problem by setting up hypotheses and then testing them out in logical succession. However, it is clear that formal operational thought cannot be tested using a single problem task. Any investigator must use a range of tests in an attempt to construct some overall measure of the individual's ability to tackle problems of logical thought in a number of areas. In relation to this it is important to bear in mind that the development of formal thinking is certainly not an all-or-nothing affair, with the individual moving overnight from one stage to another. The change occurs slowly, and there may even be some shifting back and forth before the new mode of thought is firmly established. Furthermore, it is almost certain that the adolescent will adopt formal modes of thinking in one area before another. Thus, for example, someone interested in arts subjects may use formal operational thinking in the area of verbal reasoning well before he or she is able to utilize such skills in scientific problem solving.

In addition to these points, research has indicated that in all probability Piaget was a little too optimistic when he expressed the view that the majority of adolescents could be expected to develop formal operational thought by 12 or 13 years of age. While studies do not entirely agree on the exact proportions reaching various stages at different age levels, there is general consensus that up to the age of 16 only a minority reach the most advanced level of formal thought (Coleman & Hendry, 1990).

One area of particular interest to researchers in the field of cognitive development is that of moral and political thought. How is this changed by formal operations? Do young people pass through different stages of thinking where morals and politics are concerned, and if so, what is the nature of such stages? As far as moral thinking is concerned it is once again Piaget's notions which have formed the springboard for later thinking on this subject, enabling Kohlberg to develop his "cognitive-developmental" approach.

Kohlberg (1969) elaborated Piaget's early ideas into a scheme that has six different stages. His method was to present hypothetical situations concerning moral dilemmas to young people of different ages, and to classify their responses according to a stage theory of moral development. Some of Kohlberg's most interesting work involved the study of moral development in different cultures. He showed that an almost identical sequence appears to occur in widely different cultures, the variation between cultures being found in the rate of development, and the fact that in more primitive societies later stages of thinking are rarely used.

As in the case of moral judgement, the young person's political ideas are likely to be significantly influenced by his or her level of cognitive development. Since the 1960s a number of writers have become interested in the shift that takes place during the adolescent years, from a lack of political thought to – in many cases – an intense involvement in this area of life. How does this occur and what are the processes involved? At what age do adolescents begin to show an increasing grasp of political concepts, and what stages do they go through before they achieve maturity of political judgement? One of the most important early studies was that undertaken by Adelson and O'Neill (1966). They approached the problem of the growth of political ideas in an imaginative way by posing for young people of different ages the following problem: "Imagine that a thousand men and women, dissatisfied with the way things are going in their own country, decide to purchase and move to an island in the Pacific; once there they must devise laws and codes of government". They then explored the adolescents' approach to a variety of relevant issues. They asked questions about how a government would be formed, what would its purpose be, would there be a need for laws and political parties, how would you protect minorities, and so on. The investigators proposed different laws, and explored typical problems of public policy.

The major results may be discussed under two headings – the changes in modes of thinking, and the decline of authoritarianism with age. As far as the first is concerned, there was a marked shift in thinking from the concrete to the abstract, a finding which ties in well with the work discussed above. The second major shift observed was the decline in authoritarian solutions to political questions. The typical young adolescent appeared unable to appreciate that problems can have more than one solution, and that individual behaviour or political acts are not necessarily absolutely right or wrong, good or bad. The concept of moral relativism was not yet available for the making of political judgements. In contrast, the 14 or 15 year old is much more aware of the different sides of any argument, and is usually able to take a relativistic point of view. Thinking begins to be more tentative, more critical and more pragmatic.

Work in this area has been well reviewed by Furnham and Stacey (1991). As they indicate, we now know a lot more about the ways in which thinking in the political arena develops. It is a topic of particular interest, not only because of its obvious implications for education and government, but also because of the manner in which intellectual change can be seen to interact with social behaviour. This is not to say that other areas of cognitive development are not of equal value and importance, and it is to be hoped that this chapter may act as a signpost, if nothing more, towards issues of general interest.

RELATIONSHIPS WITH ADULTS

One of the central themes of adolescent development is the attainment of independence, often represented symbolically in art and literature by the moment of departure from home. However, for most young people independence is not gained at one specific moment by the grand gesture of saying goodbye to one's parents and setting off to seek one's fortune in the wide world. Independence is much more likely to mean the freedom to make new relationships, and personal freedom to take responsibility for oneself in such things as education, work, political beliefs, and future career choice.

Many forces interact in propelling an individual towards a state of maturity. Naturally both physical and intellectual maturation encourage the adolescent towards greater autonomy. In addition to these factors there are, undoubtedly, psychological forces within the individual as well as social forces within the environment that have the same goal. In the psychoanalytic view, mentioned earlier, the process of seeking independence represents the need to break off the infantile ties with the parents, thus making new mature sexual relationships possible. From the perspective of the sociologist, more emphasis is placed on the changes in role and status which lead to a redefinition of the individual's place in the social structure. Whatever the explanation, it is certainly true that the achievement of independence is an integral feature of adolescent development, and that the role of the adults involved is an especially important one.

In understanding this process it is necessary to appreciate that the young person's movement towards adulthood is far from straightforward. While independence at times appears to be a rewarding goal, there are moments when it is a worrying, even frightening, prospect. Childlike dependence can be safe and comforting at no matter what age, if, for example, one is facing problems or difficulties alone, and it is essential to realize that no individual achieves adult independence without a number of backward glances. It is this ambivalence that underlies the typically contradictory behaviour of adolescence, behaviour that is so often the despair of adults. Thus there is nothing more frustrating than having to deal with a teenager who is at one moment complaining about adults who are always interfering, and the next bitterly protesting that no one takes any interest. However, it is equally important to acknowledge that adults themselves usually hold conflicting attitudes towards young people. On the one hand they may wish them to be independent, to make their own decisions, and to cease making childish demands, while on the other they may be anxious about the consequences of independence, and sometimes jealous of the opportunities and idealism of youth. In addition it should not be forgotten that the adolescent years often coincide with the difficulties of middle age for parents in particular. Adjusting to unfulfilled hopes, the possibility of retirement, declining physical health, marital difficulties, and so on may all increase family stress, and add further to the problems faced by young people in finding a satisfactory route to independence.

Research evidence has not provided much support for the notion that wide-ranging conflict between adults and young people is the order of the day. Noller and Callan (1991), in reviewing the data available, come to the conclusion that the general picture that emerges from experimental studies is one of relatively harmonious relationships with adults for the majority of young people. Of course adolescents do seek independence, of that there is no dispute, and so the question arises as to how common sense and research evidence can be fitted together. In the first place it is clear that some adolescents do, temporarily at least, come into conflict with or become critical of adults. In addition there is no doubt that some adults do become restrictive, attempting to slow down the pace of change. Research has shown that there are a number of factors that affect the extent of the conflict occurring between the generations. Cultural background, adult behaviour, age, and social class all need to be taken into account.

Other aspects of the situation need also to be borne in mind. For example, there is undoubtedly a difference between attitudes towards close family members, and attitudes to more general social groupings, such as "the younger generation". Thus, for example, teenagers may very well approve of and look up to their own parents while expressing criticism of adults in general. Similarly, parents may deride "drop-outs", "skinheads", or "soccer hooligans" while holding a favourable view of their own adolescent sons and daughters. Another fact that needs to be stressed is that there is a difference between feeling and behaviour. Adolescents may be irritated or angry with their parents as a result of day-to-day conflicts, but issues can be worked out in the home, and do not necessarily lead to outright rejection or rebellion. Furthermore, too little credit is given to the possibility that adults and young people, although disagreeing with each other about certain things, may still respect each other's views, and live or work together in relative harmony. Thus there seems to be little doubt that the extreme view of a generation gap, involving the notion of a war between the generations, or the ideas of a separate adolescent subculture, is dependent on a myth. It is the result of a stereotype which is useful to the mass media, and given currency by a small minority of disaffected young people and resentful adults. However, to deny any sort of conflict between teenagers and older members of society is equally false. Adolescents could not grow into adults unless they were able to test out the boundaries of authority, nor could they discover what they believed unless given the opportunity to push hard against the beliefs of others. The adolescent transition from dependence to independence is almost certain to involve some conflict, but its extent should not be exaggerated.

CONCLUSION

Adolescence is, to many, a confusing concept. Its definition is uncertain, its characteristics contradictory, and much behaviour associated with this stage in development is difficult to understand. Classical theories of adolescence – those originating from psychoanalysis and sociology – have been helpful in unravelling some of the more extreme types of behaviour and, in the case of psychoanalysis, contributing to developments in the treatment of disturbance. None the less, empirical evidence shows wide individual variation in the abilities of young people to adjust to the transition from childhood to adulthood.

Many factors, such as family context, maturational timing, educational ability, and so on, will contribute to the adolescent's capacity to cope with the social and emotional changes inevitable during the teenage years. However, based on the research that has appeared in many different countries since the 1960s, it appears to be the case that the majority of young people, in western countries at least, do not suffer a major identity crisis, nor do they experience a serious breakdown in relationships within the family. While all will have conflicts and pressures to deal with, most appear to do so without excessive trauma.

As I have indicated, there is wide individual variation in adjustment, and in considering adolescence, and the factors that contribute to young people's experience of growing up, two important dimensions need to be kept in mind. First, the social circumstances of childhood and adolescence cannot be ignored. As one example of this, since the early 1980s we have become more aware of the impact of poverty, and its devastating consequences on the occupational and family careers of young people. Second, culture too plays a major role in facilitating or hindering individuals' opportunities to make the full use of their potential. Questions of ethnic identity, widely differing attitudes to the roles of boys and girls in the family, living through racial prejudice or harassment – such things may loom very large indeed in the lives of individual adolescents.

Adolescence is an important transitional stage in human development. If we wish to understand it, however, we need to remember that no generalizations, even in relation to one culture, one country, one location even, will do justice to the complexity of the adolescent experience. Theory and research have taken us a long way forward since Hall's publication of 1904, but we still have much to learn before we can fully grasp the complexity of the second decade of life.

FURTHER READING

Coleman, J. C., & Hendry, L. (1990). *The nature of adolescence* (2nd edn). London and New York: Routledge.

Feldman, S. S., & Elliott, G. (1990). *At the threshold: The developing adolescent*. London: Harvard University Press.

Kroger, J. (1989). *Identity in adolescence: The balance between self and other*. London: Routledge.

Noller, P., & Callan, V. (1991). *The adolescent in the family*. London: Routledge.

REFERENCES

Adelson, J., & O'Neill, R. (1966). The development of political thought in adolescence. *Journal of Personality and Social Psychology*, *4*, 295–308.

Baittle, B., & Offer, D. (1971). On the nature of adolescent rebellion. In F. C. Feinstein, P. Giovacchini, & A. Miller (Eds) *Annals of adolescent psychiatry* (pp. 22–57). New York: Basic Books.

Brake, M. (1985). *Comparative youth subcultures*. London: Routledge & Kegan Paul.

Coleman, J. C., & Hendry, L. (1990). *The nature of adolescence* (2nd edn). London and New York: Routledge.

Conger, J., & Petersen, A. (1984). *Adolescence and youth* (3rd edn). New York: Harper & Row.

Elkind, D. (1966). Conceptual orientation shifts in children and adolescents. *Child Development*, *37*, 493–498.

Elkind, D. (1967). Egocentrism in adolescence. *Child Development*, *38*, 1025–1034.

Feldman, S. S., & Elliott, G. (1990). *At the threshold: The developing adolescent*. London: Harvard University Press.

Furnham, A., & Stacey, B. (1991). *Young people's understanding of society*. London: Routledge.

Hall, G. C. (1904). *Adolescence*. New York: Appleton.

Inhelder, B., & Piaget, J. (1958). *The growth of logical thinking*. London: Routledge & Kegan Paul.

Kohlberg, L. (1969). *Stages in development of moral thought and action*. New York: Holt, Rinehart & Winston.

Lerner, R. M. (1987). Psychodynamic models. In V. B. Van Hasselt & M. Hersen (Eds) *Handbook of adolescent psychology* (pp. 53–76). Oxford: Pergamon.

Marsland, D. (1987). *Education and youth*. London: Falmer.

Mead, M. (1928). *Coming of age in samoa*. New York: Morrow.

Montemayor, R. (1983). Parents and adolescents in conflict: All families some of the time and some families most of the time. *Journal of Early Adolescence*, *3*, 83–103.

Noller, P., & Callan, V. (1991). *The adolescent in the family*. London: Routledge.

Serafica, F. C. (Ed.) (1982). *Social-cognitive development in context*. London: Methuen.

Siddique, C. M., & D'Arcy, C. (1984). Adolescence, stress and psychological well-being. *Journal of Youth and Adolescence*, *13*, 459–474.

Tanner, J. M. (1978). *Foetus into man*. London: Open Books.

AGEING

John C. Cavanaugh
University of Delaware, USA

Roughly a century ago, Oliver Wendell Holmes, a member of the United States Supreme Court and a poet, wrote that "to be 70 years young is sometimes far more cheerful and hopeful than to be 40 years old". Holmes's use of "young" to describe a 70 year old and "old" to describe a 40 year old is far more than a literary device. It is possible that he was trying to make the same point as late twentieth-century psychologists: growing old is as much, if not more, a state of mind that a state of inevitable playing out of some genetic programme.

The inclusion of a chapter on ageing in this volume is recognition of a profound revolution: the restructuring of the world's population from one that is dominated by youth to one that now includes many older people as well. This revolution has changed the way people experience daily life (e.g., death is now viewed as the province of the old in industrialized nations) and each other (e.g., knowing one's great-grandparents is now common), as well as how governments interact with citizens (e.g., the need to develop programmes for long-term care). All of this has happened without fanfare and in spite of world wars and numerous natural disasters.

This chapter is about understanding the revolutionaries, elderly people in modern society. Clearly, our overview must be selective. Thus, we shall consider a few areas of cognitive development (attention, reaction time, memory, and intelligence), personality, depression and dementia, retirement, grandparenting, and widowhood. Readers desiring more complete coverage have many options at both the introductory level and the professional level, as noted below under "Further Reading".

THE CONTEXTS OF AGEING

In order to understand the ageing process, it is necessary to use a multidisciplinary framework that includes various influences on development. The biopsychosocial model provides a context for considering influences in three major arenas: biological, psychological, and social. This model highlights the fact that ageing is not the result of any one of these influences alone; rather, all three must be considered together. The biopsychosocial model consists of four main components, each of which focuses on a different set of issues: interpersonal factors, intrapersonal factors, biological and physical factors, and life cycle factors. We shall consider each of these factors briefly.

Interpersonal factors include all of the various aspects of social support an individual has in his or her present situation. For example, the degree to which someone has a collaborative relationship with family and friends and the interpersonal skills one has for dealing with interpersonal relationships are aspects of interpersonal factors. In general, these factors describe the social milieu in which an individual exists.

Intrapersonal factors reflect personal characteristics such as age, gender, genetic inheritance, and physiological systems such as the central nervous system. In addition, intrapersonal factors include psychological characteristics such as personality, intelligence, sensory-perceptual functioning, and motor functioning. In short, intrapersonal factors involve all of the aspects of a normal functioning individual.

Biological and physical factors represent degenerative influences of chronic illness, functional incapacities, and physical diseases (such as cardiovascular diseases, cancer, and the like). These factors reflect processes that ultimately lead to death. These disease factors play a very important role in understanding ageing, as many of them are associated with negative images of ageing. For example, many people erroneously believe that most older people get Alzheimer's disease. (In fact, the incidence is roughly 10 per cent of people over age 65.) Because biological and physical factors represent decline, they play a major role in setting the overall context of ageing.

Life cycle factors include four distinct things: past social experiences (e.g., accomplishments, adversities, stressful events, economic changes); past physical experiences (e.g., acute diseases, psychobiological predispositions to disease, psychological disorders); current functioning (e.g., current hopes, motivation, attitudes towards ageing); and future perspectives (e.g., anxieties, hopes, and dreams about what life will be like). Life cycle factors help place people in a specific historical time in relation to their own lifespan and sociocultural history.

Most of the research reviewed in this chapter pertains to intrapersonal factors. That is, the emphasis is on normal individual development across adulthood. However, we shall consider a few topics represented by the remaining factors (e.g., Alzheimer's disease).

ATTENTION AND REACTION TIME

The information-processing model has been adopted by researchers in cognitive ageing as a general framework in which to study how people deal with incoming stimuli and how these processes change over time. Some age differences have been noted in some of the early aspects of information-processing, such as decreases in encoding speed and increased susceptibility to backward masking (Kline & Schieber, 1985). Unfortunately, little research has been conducted on these early steps in information-processing; consequently, we do not know how these age differences affect later phases. Much clearer, though, are age differences in attention and reaction time.

Attention

Although everyone has some intuitive understanding of what attention is, it turns out to be rather difficult to define precisely. About the best researchers can do is describe three interdependent aspects of it: selectivity (referring to the limited ability to process information), capacity (referring to how much information can be processed), and vigilance (referring to how long we are able to maintain focused attention).

Selectivity

Several different aspects of age differences in attentional selectivity have been studied. The evidence indicates that older adults have more difficulty than younger adults visually searching a display for specific target stimuli (Plude & Hoyer, 1985). In particular, while older and younger adults are equally able to extract information about the target (such as colour) automatically, older adults have more difficulty putting all the pieces of information about the target together. When the task involves identifying the location of a target, older adults have more difficulty than younger adults unless a cue appears that provides unambiguous information about where the next target will be (Plude & Doussard-Roosevelt, 1990). Other research indicates that older adults are sometimes as able to switch their attention as well as younger adults on visual tasks (Hartley & McKenzie, 1991). Specifically, older adults are able to switch from a narrow focus (such as on the centre letter of a five-letter word) to a broad focus (such as all five letters).

The most prominent age differences in attention appear as a function of the task. For example, McDowd, Filion, and Oseas-Kreger (1991) showed that when relevant and irrelevant information are both presented in the same modality (such as visually), older adults distribute their attention more equally between the two types of information than do younger adults. However, when relevant information was presented in one modality (say, visually) and irrelevant information in another (say, auditorially), older and younger adults show similar patterns of attention allocation.

Capacity

How much information adults can process at the same time is typically examined in divided attention tasks, in which people are asked to perform two tasks at once. Age differences emerge as a function of task complexity. When divided attention tasks are relatively easy, age differences are typically absent. However, when the tasks become more complicated, age differences favouring younger adults are found (McDowd & Craik, 1988).

Vigilance

Little research has been done examining age differences in how long people can maintain attention. What little there is suggests that older adults are not as accurate as younger adults at identifying targets correctly, but no age differences appear in the rate at which performance declines over time. Specifically, it appears that older adults are not as alert as younger adults while performing vigilance tasks. Moreover, older adults' performance does not improve to the level of younger adults' performance even after considerably longer training periods (Fisk & Rogers, 1987).

Reaction time

Results from hundreds of studies point to a clear conclusion: people slow down as they age (Salthouse, 1985). Indeed, the slowing-with-age phenomenon is so well documented that many gerontologists accept it as the only universal behavioural change yet discovered. Evidence to back up this claim comes from several sources, including simple, choice, and complex reaction time tasks (Salthouse, 1985). Two aspects of the actual response made in reaction time tasks appear to change with age. First, older adults do not prepare to respond as well as younger adults. Second, the complexity of the response differentially affects older adults; the more complex the response, the more older adults are slowed relative to younger adults.

Three interventions help older adults perform better on reaction time tasks. First, practice with making rapid responses improves older adults' performance, but usually does not close the age gap completely. Second, using real-world tasks can help as well. Salthouse (1984) reported age differences on standard reaction time tasks but no age differences on a typing task, due to the fact that typists had learned to compensate for slower reaction times by being able to anticipate upcoming letters. Finally, people who engage in sustained aerobic exercise have better reaction time performance relative to sedentary people (Baylor & Spirduso, 1988).

MEMORY

More research has been conducted on memory than on any other topic in cognitive ageing. Our survey of this large literature will focus on several topics of current interest: working memory, secondary memory, storage and retrieval processes, prose, everyday memory, self-evaluation, clinical issues, and remediation.

Working memory

Working memory is a small-capacity store that deals with items currently being processed. There is growing evidence that the capacity of working memory declines somewhat with age (Salthouse, 1991), with the result being poorer quality information being passed along the system. The difficulty appears to involve how efficiently working memory operates. For example, older adults show a loss of efficiency in working memory with age even with substantial practice on a mental arithmetic task. Because changes in efficiency may potentially affect many other aspects of information-processing, some researchers (Salthouse, 1991) argue that age-related changes in working memory may underlie cognitive changes in general.

Secondary memory

Secondary memory involves the ability to remember rather extensive amounts of information over relatively long periods. Typically, secondary memory is studied through recall and recognition paradigms involving the retention of many different types of material. The results from hundreds of studies point to several conclusions. Older adults tend to perform worse than younger adults on recall tests, but these differences are less apparent or may be eliminated on recognition tests (Poon, 1985). Older adults tend to be less efficient at spontaneously using strategies, such as putting items into categories, during study. When instructed to do so, however, older adults not only do so, but show improved performance as well. Overall, these data show that older adults are not as good as younger adults at devising ways to learn and remember information on their own, but are able to benefit to some degree from cues during learning and retrieval. Age differences can be reduced in several ways, such as slowing down the rate of presentation of information, allowing older adults to practise the task, and by using familiar information.

Storage and retrieval processes

The age differences in performance on secondary memory tasks imply age differences in the underlying processes of storage and retrieval. The available evidence suggests that: first, changes in memory with ageing are a result of decrements in both storage and retrieval; second, these decrements are more substantial for retrieval; and third, these decrements occur in specific sub-components of storage and retrieval and do not generalize to all of them (Howe, 1988). For example, older adults are less likely to use connections between incoming words and words they already know to help remember the stimuli, but, once the connections are made, older adults remember them as well as younger adults (Howe, 1988). Moreover, older and younger adults are equally good at using generic retrieval strategies, but younger adults are better at using specialized retrieval strategies (Howe, 1988).

Prose memory

How well adults remember the material they read is a rapidly-growing area in memory research. Whether one finds age differences in prose memory depends on several things. In general, age differences in remembering prose are minimised when tasks are made more naturalistic by providing unlimited study time, using long text passages, and requiring only a general summary rather than details. Several other factors are also important. Adults with little education and who have low verbal ability tend to do much worse on prose memory tasks than other groups (Meyer, 1987). How much people know about the topic they are reading also matters; high prior knowledge is usually an asset. Rapid presentation of reading material tends to differentially penalize older adults. Finally, when text material is clearly organized, with emphasis on structure and the main ideas, older and younger adults perform equivalently in distinguishing between the main ideas and the details.

Everyday memory

Despite the large number of studies investigating age differences in memory, little is known about how memory performance changes in everyday life. This is largely because the tasks used in most research on memory ageing involve list learning. In everyday life, many other tasks are faced, such as remembering where something is located or what actions were performed earlier. Due to the concern about the potential lack of generalizability of list learning to everyday life, several researchers began investigating memory in other tasks.

Results from several studies of memory for location indicate that older adults perform better in familiar settings and use different search strategies than younger adults. Actually performing actions (rather than merely watching them) helps older adults remember activities (Cohen & Faulkner, 1989). However, older adults are more likely to claim that they remember performing actions that they in fact only observed (Cohen & Faulkner, 1989). Several researchers (e.g., Poon & Schaffer, 1982) have shown that older adults are consistently superior to younger adults in remembering to remember (e.g., remembering to mail a postcard on a certain day).

Self-evaluation

Because memory is used by many older adults as a means of judging their overall cognitive competence, it is important to establish whether the evaluations they make are a reflection of accurate information. Research on the processes underlying memory self-evaluations examines this issue. Older adults tend to rate their memory as poorer than younger adults rate theirs. It appears that older adults know less about the internal workings of memory and its capacity, view memory as less stable, expect that memory will deteriorate with age, and perceive that they have less control over memory (Dixon & Hultsch, 1983). Older adults report that remembering names is especially troublesome, but report no more problems remembering appointments and errands than do younger adults (Cavanaugh, Grady, & Perlmutter, 1983).

If asked to predict how well they will do on a task they have not seen, older adults tend to overestimate their performance while younger adults tend to be more accurate. However, if they are allowed to see or practise the task first, older adults are just as accurate as younger adults in predicting their performance.

Clinical issues

The large research literature on age differences in memory have helped establish guidelines for distinguishing between normal and abnormal ageing. In general, normative age-related decrements in memory do not significantly interfere with daily life. If such interference is observed, then the changes may not be normative and should be investigated further. Whether such changes indicate a serious pathology such as dementia depends, however. Many physical and mental disorders may affect memory performance, including depression, certain nutritional deficiencies, and several types of medications. If abnormal memory changes are suspected, a full diagnostic work-up should include a complete physical examination, blood tests, neurological screening, and neuropsychological tests.

Remediation

If a memory impairment has been identified, or if an older person simply desires to compensate for normative changes, several types of remediation approaches are available. First, memory strategies may be trained. Yesavage (1983) has developed a successful programme to train older adults to use imagery strategies to help themselves remember names. Similar training programmes have been developed for retrieval strategies. For example, Camp and McKitrick (1991) report the successful application of a spaced retrieval strategy to persons with Alzheimer's disease to help them learn the names of staff members. Second, memory exercises such as rehearsing a grocery list over and over appear to.work as well. Third, the most popular approach has been the use of external strategies, such as making lists and keeping appointment calendars (Cavanaugh et al., 1983).

INTELLIGENCE

Research on the development of general intellectual skills has followed two main research traditions: the psychometric tradition and the cognitive-process tradition. The psychometric tradition includes all the standardized intelligence tests, and emphasizes how many items are answered correctly in each of several domains. In contrast, the cognitive-process approach stresses the qualitative nature of intelligence by emphasising the thought processes underlying the response rather than its accuracy. Each approach paints a different picture of intellectual development across adulthood.

Psychometric approach

The psychometric approach is based on the notion that related intellectual skills are hierarchically organized into an overall structure of intelligence. To date, researchers have identified numerous intellectual abilities at two different levels in the hierarchy. First, the primary mental abilities are those that are tapped by various intelligence tests. Second, the primary mental abilities are themselves organized into secondary mental abilities.

In a complex longitudinal study begun in 1956, Schaie tests seven cohorts of people every seven years. Based on two separate sets of fourteen-year longitudinal data, Schaie and Hertzog (1983) demonstrated age changes on five primary mental abilities: number, work fluency, verbal meaning, inductive reasoning, and spatial ability. The magnitude of the decline in individuals between age 50 and 60 was minimal. However, the changes in people over age 60 was large enough for individuals to notice the difference in everyday life.

Relationships among the various mental abilities tapped directly by intelligence tests have been studied as well. Two of these higher-order abilities that have received the most attention are fluid and crystallized intelligence. Fluid intelligence refers to innate abilities that are not the product of experience or education, but are thought to provide the basis for learning. Typically, research findings show that fluid intelligence declines across adulthood (Horn, 1982). In contrast, crystallized intelligence is the result of experience and education, and typically shows stability or improvement across adulthood (Horn, 1982).

In an attempt to explain the different developmental patterns of fluid and crystallized intelligence, researchers have identified several important variables. One of the most important is cohort effects, which relate to differences in key experiences as a function of when people were born (Labouvie-Vief, 1985). For example, individuals born in the 1930s did not have computers as part of their educational experience like those born in the 1970s did. Such differences become reflected in how and what people learn, which in turn affects their scores on intelligence tests. Additionally, educational level, occupation, personality, health, and the relevance of test materials have also been shown to explain part of the age changes (Labouvie-Vief, 1985). Nevertheless, even when moderators are taken into account, age differences between younger and older adults are never completely eliminated (Schaie & Hertzog, 1983).

The normative declines in fluid intelligence have led some authors to speculate whether such changes are simply inevitable or are due to lack of practice. That is, it is possible that declines in fluid abilities reflect changes in cognitive demands placed on adults, and not an inevitable part of the ageing process. Baltes and Willis (1982) initiated a series of studies called Project ADEPT examining this issue by training adults on primary mental abilities that show decline over time. Baltes and Willis demonstrated that people's performance on these abilities improved significantly after training, supporting the view that the observed declines may not be inevitable and irreversible.

Subsequently, other researchers have confirmed Baltes and Willis's (1982) results. Some have shown that direct training may not be essential for improved performance; for example, there is some evidence that an anxiety reduction programme may work about as well as direct training in improving performance. In addition, researchers have established that improvements following training persist. Willis and Nesselroade (1990) reported results from a seven-year follow-up to the original Project ADEPT study. After initial training in 1979, participants received booster sessions in 1981 and 1986. Significant improvement was still evident at the long-term follow-up, even in people in their late 70s and early 80s. These results demonstrate that training effects are powerful, even in the oldest participants in Willis's research.

Piagetian research

A second major approach to the study of intelligence emphasizes the cognitive processes underlying thought rather than the product of thought. This second approach is exemplified by Piaget's theory, which focuses on the growth of knowledge and how the structure of knowledge changes over time. Because Piaget's theory is described in detail elsewhere, we shall concentrate here on its implications for adult development and ageing.

Piaget believed that formal operations marked the end of cognitive development, although there are hints that he may not have been entirely convinced of this (e.g., Piaget, 1972). In any case, researchers in this tradition have generally believed that formal operations was the culmination of cognitive development, and looked for evidence of stability in formal operational reasoning across adulthood. They found little evidence of it. Some studies report that relatively few adults demonstrate formal operational reasoning, and others show that older adults do not perform as well as younger adults on formal operational tasks.

There are several problems with this line of research, however. First, the studies were cross-sectional, opening them to criticisms based on cohort differences. Second, the age differences demonstrated may be due more to personal preference than to a lack of ability. That is, older adults may simply have a lack of interest in solving problems that demand formal logical reasoning. Third, researchers may have been looking for the wrong thing. Specifically, it is also possible that the reason for the failure to find substantial evidence for formal operational reasoning is that adults have moved on to a different type of thinking.

Postformal thought

Since the early 1970s, evidence has been mounting that adults approach certain types of problems in fundamentally different ways than adolescents. In particular, problems involving social situations, that are ill structured, or that

761

require life experience are solved differently by middle-aged and older adults (Cavanaugh, Kramer, Sinnott, Camp, & Markley, 1985; Commons, Sinnott, Richards, & Armon, 1989). Postformal thinking involves acceptance of more than one correct solution, tolerance for ambiguity, acknowledgement of practical or real-world constraints, and acceptance of contradiction. Labouvie-Vief (1985) also argues that adult postformal thinking involves the integration of emotion with logic, and sees the main goal of adult thought as effectiveness in handling everyday life.

Wisdom

One of the relatively few positive stereotypes about ageing is that older adults become wise. Despite this belief, wisdom is seldom the focus of research on older adults' cognition. What little has been done has emphasized a connection between wisdom and expert knowledge. Smith and Baltes (1990) describe a wise person as one who has "exceptional insight into human development and life matters, exceptionally good judgement, advice, and commentary about difficult life problems" (p. 495). Wisdom is apparently not the same thing as creativity; wisdom is more related to the growth of expertise and insight whereas creativity is associated with generating a new solution to a problem. For a person to be wise, he or she needs to have accumulated relevant life-experience. In this sense, wisdom is associated with age. However, simply being old does not guarantee that one will be wise (Smith & Baltes, 1990).

PERSONALITY

Perhaps no other area in ageing research has engendered as much controversy as personality. At issue is a fundamental question: does personality change across adulthood? Answers to this question generally localize around two discrepant views. On the one hand, trait theorists believe that stability in personality is normative. In contrast, ego and cognitive theorists believe that change is the rule.

Personality traits

Many investigators have examined the relative stability of personality traits, but Costa and McCrae (e.g., 1980) are among the few who have developed a theory of personality in adulthood based on this research. In their view, personality consists of five dimensions: Factor I, Extraversion (or Surgency, including warmth, gregariousness, assertiveness, activity, excitement seeking, and positive emotions); Factor II, Agreeableness-Antagonism; Factor III, Conscientiousness-Undirectedness; Factor IV, Neuroticism (or Emotional

Stability, including anxiety, hostility, self-consciousness, depression, impulsiveness, and vulnerability), and Factor V, Openness to Experience (or Culture, or Intellect, including fantasy, aesthetics, openness to action, values, feelings, and ideas) (see also Goldberg, 1983).

Costa and McCrae's data on stability are impressive. For example, they reported correlations ranging between .68 and .85 for various traits measured 12 years apart. Other researchers report high stability over an 8-year span, while one study reported high stability over 30 years. Clearly, such evidence on very long-term stability in personality traits in individuals between 20 and 90 years of age provides strong support for the position that personality remains constant across adulthood.

Nevertheless, some researchers have found change on a few specific traits. For example, Haan, Millsap, and Hartka (1986) reported significant shifts in self-confidence, cognitive commitment, outgoingness, and warmth. However, the shifts were not orderly or universal, and did not represent a "mid-life crisis". Rather, the changes appeared to reflect life cycle experiences that forced people to change. Overall, the weight of the evidence suggests that personality traits are unlikely to change except in very specific situations.

Thomae (1980) argues that adults' personalities change only to the extent that people believe they need to change and have the motivation to carry out the process. This view fits well with notions such as personal control that also highlight the importance of people's perceptions of reality as an important determinant of behaviour. Thomae's view is also highly consistent with theories of psychotherapy that emphasize the importance of the client's desire to change as basic to the success of the therapeutic process.

Life satisfaction

As typically operationalized, life satisfaction means the degree to which people are happy with their current life situation and have positive well-being. Hundreds of studies on this issue have shown conclusively that life satisfaction is not related to age (Larson, 1978). However, life satisfaction is related to neuroticism and extraversion, as well as a host of other variables such as health, social class, gender, and immediate life situation.

Gender role identity

The shared cultural beliefs of what constitutes appropriate characteristics for women and men vary across groups. Most important for our present discussion, gender role stereotypes also vary with age. In western societies, old men are stereotypically viewed as less masculine and more peaceable, whereas old women are viewed as matriarchs overseeing extended families. Evidence from several studies indicates that changes occur in the statements

763

adults of different ages endorse about femininity and masculinity. In general, the findings reveal a tendency for older women and men to endorse similar self-descriptions: women and men appear most different in late adolescence and young adulthood and become increasingly similar in late-middle and old age (Huyck, 1990).

Mid-life crisis

A concept central to most ego development theories of adult personality is the notion that middle-aged adults experience a mid-life crisis in which there is a general upheaval in all aspects of their lives. Despite considerable effort, researchers have largely been unable to document a crisis unique to mid-life (Haan et al., 1986). Instead, researchers report that individuals may periodically undertake a re-evaluation of their lives, but tend to do so on their own timetable rather than being driven by calendar time.

PSYCHOPATHOLOGY AND TREATMENT

There is a growing realization on the part of clinicians that assessing older adults requires a far more careful consideration of the interplay among biological, psychological, and social influences. This realization has resulted in a major emphasis on multidisciplinary assessment as a requirement for diagnosing physical and psychosocial problems. Indeed, the biopsychosocial model can be applied to all aspects of older adults' lives (Cavanaugh, 1993).

Although older adults may experience the entire spectrum of mental disorders, two dominate the literature: depression and dementia. Both represent significant problems for elderly people and in many cases present diagnostic difficulties to clinicians.

Depression

Contrary to the image that older people are prone to depression, the incidence of severe depression among elderly people is lower than that in younger adults (Nolen-Hoeksema, 1988). Older adults differ somewhat from younger adults in their symptoms of depression. Specifically, older adults may not label their sad feelings as depression, and are more likely than younger adults to show signs of apathy, subdued self-depreciation, expressionlessness, changes in arousal, withdrawal, and inadequate self-care. In addition, the physical symptoms accompanying depression (e.g., loss of appetite and sleep disturbances) must be evaluated carefully to rule out an underlying physiological problem.

Treatment of depression in elderly people is accomplished through the same types of interventions used with younger adults. Antidepressant medication (e.g., heterocyclics) are effective, but dosage levels need to be carefully monitored. Behavioural and cognitive behavioural psychotherapy are both highly effective with most older adults with depression (Gallagher & Thompson, 1983).

Dementia

The term dementia does not refer to a specific disease, but, rather, to a family of diseases that have similar symptoms. Roughly a dozen types of dementia have been identified, all of which are characterised by cognitive and behavioural deficits involving some form of permanent damage to the brain. The most common form of dementia is Alzheimer's disease.

Alzheimer's disease

Alzheimer's disease is a form of progressive, degenerative, and fatal dementia, accounting for as many as 70 per cent of all cases of dementia. Alzheimer's disease is characterized by large numbers of specific microscopic changes involving neurons: neurofibrillary tangles (abnormal, twisted fibres that are produced inside neurons), neuritic plaques (amyloid protein deposits that form in conjunction with dead neurons), and granulovacuolar bodies (deposits of granular material in the neuron). At present, definitive diagnosis of Alzheimer's disease can only be accomplished by conducting a brain autopsy. Most researchers believe that Alzheimer's disease has a genetic component, although the nature of this link remains unclear (Breitner, 1988), but mutations involving the genes responsible for the production of amyloid protein may provide an important lead (Goate et al., 1991). At present, there is no effective treatment or cure.

Alzheimer's disease is tentatively diagnosed on the basis of cognitive and behavioural changes: declines in memory, learning, attention, and judgement; disorientation in time and space; difficulties in word finding and communication; declines in personal hygiene and self-care skills; inappropriate social behaviour; and changes in personality. These symptoms tend to be vague initially and worsen steadily over time. However, the rate of deterioration is highly variable across individuals.

Caregiving

The vast majority of people with Alzheimer's disease and other forms of dementia (e.g., Huntington's chorea, multi-infarct dementia) are cared for at home by family members. Caregivers generally report feeling stressed and burdened (Kinney & Stephens, 1989). They report a host of negative effects: chronic fatigue, anger, depression, loss of friends, loss of time to themselves, dissatisfaction with other family members, physical and mental strain, lower life satisfaction, and lower well-being. Nevertheless, caregivers also show considerable ingenuity in devising strategies to help their loved ones deal with the cognitive impairments due to their disease (Cavanaugh et al., 1989).

RETIREMENT

A person's occupation has an important influence on his or her sense of identity. Withdrawing from an occupation, then, is not a trivial thing. Although it is tempting to view retirement as an all-or-none state (either one is employed or not), the actual state of affairs is far more complex. For this reason, retirement is best viewed as a complex process by which people withdraw from full-time participation in an occupation.

Deciding when to retire reflects considerations of many factors, including health, financial status, and personal attitudes toward retirement. Typically, poor health and excellent finances are the major factors in a decision to retire early. The relationship between attitudes toward retirement and the decision to retire are more complicated. In general, people who have professional occupations or who are self-employed do not look forward to retirement as much as blue-collar workers do. Middle-level managers with high incomes and good pension plans, though, are the most favourable about retiring.

Adjustment to retirement

Retirement is a stressful life transition that affects relationships with family, friends, and the community at large. Understanding how people cope with retirement is best accomplished by placing retirement in the broader context of life transitions. Thus, past behaviours and attitudes during people's employment years influence people's adjustment to retirement. For example, people who were strongly work-motivated are likely to experience more adjustment problems than people who were not. Atchley (1989) argues that successful adjustment to retirement depends on the degree to which people are able to build on their past in order to maintain a sense of continuity in their lives.

Overall, the research literature suggests that most people are satisfied with their retirement situation. One interesting trend is that retirees are increasingly concerned with financial security, and many express a desire to work at least part-time. However, the expressed desire to work appears to be based on concerns about financial security rather than a fundamental dislike for retirement. Adjustment to retirement appears to be helped by advance planning. Specifically, Kamouri and Cavanaugh (1986) reported that individuals who completed a pre-retirement education programme had more realistic views of retirement than individuals who did not participate. Holding realistic views assists individuals in understanding the lifestyle changes that occur following retirement, which in turn is an important influence on overall satisfaction.

GRANDPARENTING

Being a grandparent is an important source of identity for many older adults. How individuals act as grandparents varies considerably across individuals and cultures, ranging from playing very structured and formal roles to being remote and distant. Researchers have shown that people derive several positive meanings from grandparenthood, such as being able to indulge or spoil their grandchildren, the importance of seeing their family line continue and being perceived as a wise elder (Miller & Cavanaugh, 1990). Thomas (1986) reports that satisfaction with grandparenthood is higher in grandmothers and that the opportunity to nurture and support grandchildren is an important source of satisfaction.

Relationships between grandparents and grandchildren vary with the ages of the people involved as well as with culture. Typically, children under age 10 are closer to their grandparents than are older children and adults, and grandparents tend to enjoy younger children more. Some authors have suggested that grandmothers and granddaughters have better relationships than grandfathers and grandsons due to the importance of matrilineal kin-keeping issues in most societies.

Because of increased divorce rates in many industrialized countries, a growing issue among grandparents is contact with grandchildren after the divorce of the parents. Few places have clearly articulated policies covering grandparental visitation rights. Most grandparents desire continued contact, and see themselves as innocent victims in the parents' divorce.

WIDOWHOOD

Experiencing the death of a spouse is certainly a traumatic event for most people. Widowhood is more common for women; in western societies roughly half of women over age 65 are widows, but only about 15 per cent of the same-aged men are widowers. This difference reflects gender differences in average longevity as well as a tendency for women to marry men older than themselves.

Considerable research supports the notion that widowhood has different meanings for women and men. In general, a woman's reaction depends on the kind of relationship she had with her husband. To the extent that she defined herself in terms of her husband, widowhood causes her serious adjustment problems (Lopata, 1975). In contrast, women who define themselves in more diverse ways experience much less loss of identity following the death of their spouse.

Many people believe that the loss of a one's wife presents a more serious challenge to adjustment than the loss of one's husband. Perhaps this is because a wife is often a man's only close friend or because men may be less equipped to live out their lives alone. However, as men share more of the housekeeping tasks these gender differences begin to decrease. It is the case, however, that men are generally older when they are widowed than are women. Thus, to some extent the greater overall difficulties reported by widowers may be due to this age difference. Indeed, at least one study showed that if age is held constant, widows report higher anxiety than widowers.

Regardless of age, men have a clear advantage over women in the opportunity to form new heterosexual relationships. Interestingly, though, older widowers are actually less likely to form new, close friendships than are widows. This difference may simply be a continuation of men's lifelong tendency to have few close friendships.

ACKNOWLEDGEMENTS

The writing of this chapter was supported by NIA research grant AG09265-02 and by a research grant from the AARP Andrus Foundation.

FURTHER READING

Binstock, R. H., & George, L. K. (Eds) (1990). *Handbook of aging and the social sciences* (3rd edn). San Diego, CA: Academic Press.
Birren, J. E., & Schaie, K. W. (Eds) (1990). *Handbook of the psychology of aging* (3rd edn). New York: Van Nostrand Reinhold.
Poon, L. W., Rubin, D. C., & Wilson, B. A. (Eds) (1989). *Everyday cognition in adulthood and late life*. Cambridge: Cambridge University Press.
Sinnott, J. D., & Cavanaugh, J. C. (Eds) (1991). *Bridging paradigms: Positive development in adulthood and cognitive aging*. New York: Praeger.

REFERENCES

Atchley, R. C. (1989). A continuity theory of normal aging. *The Gerontologist, 29*, 183–190.
Baltes, P. B., & Willis, S. L. (1982). Enhancement (plasticity) of intellectual functioning: Penn State's Adult Development and Enrichment Project (ADEPT). In F. I. M. Craik & S. Trehub (Eds) *Aging and cognitive processes* (pp. 353–389). New York: Plenum.
Baylor, A. M., & Spirduso, W. W. (1988). Systemic aerobic exercise and components of reaction time in older women. *Journal of Gerontology, 43*, 121–126.
Breitner, J. C. S. (1988). Alzheimer's disease: Possible evidence for genetic causes. In M. K. Aronson (Ed.) *Understanding Alzheimer's disease* (pp. 34–49). New York: Scribner's.
Camp, C. J., & McKitrick, L. A. (1991). Memory interventions in Alzheimer's-type dementia populations: Methodological and theoretical issues. In R. L. West & J. D. Sinnott (Eds) *Everyday memory and aging: Current research and methodology* (pp. 155–172). New York: Springer-Verlag.
Cavanaugh, J. C. (1993). *Adult development and aging* (2nd edn). Pacific Grove, CA: Brooks/Cole.

Cavanaugh, J. C., Grady, J. G., & Perlmutter, M. (1983). Forgetting and use of memory aids in 20 to 70 year olds' everyday life. *International Journal of Aging and Human Development*, *17*, 113–122.

Cavanaugh, J. C., Kramer, D. A., Sinnott, J. D., Camp, C. J., & Markley, R. J. (1985). On missing links and such: Interfaces between cognitive research and everyday problem solving. *Human Development*, *28*, 146–168.

Cavanaugh, J. C., Dunn, N. J., Mowery, D., Feller, C., Niederehe, G., Frugé, E., & Volpendesta, D. (1989). Problem-solving strategies in dementia patient–caregiver dyads. *The Gerontologist*, *29*, 156–158.

Cohen, G., & Faulkner, D. (1989). The effects of aging on perceived and generated memories. In L. W. Poon, D. C. Rubin, & B. Wilson (Eds) *Everyday cognition in adulthood and late life* (pp. 222–243). New York: Cambridge University Press.

Commons, M. L., Sinnott, J. D., Richards, F. A., & Armon, C. (Eds) (1989). *Adult development: vol. 1. Comparisons and applications of adolescent and adult developmental models*. New York: Praeger.

Costa, P. T., Jr, & McCrae, R. R. (1980). Still stable after all these years: Personality as a key to some issues in adulthood and old age. In P. B. Baltes & O. G. Brim, Jr (Eds) *Life-span development and behavior* (vol. 3, pp. 65–102). New York: Academic Press.

Dixon, R. A., & Hultsch, D. F. (1983). Structure and development of metamemory in adulthood. *Journal of Gerontology*, *38*, 682–688.

Fisk, A. D., & Rogers, W. (1987) *Associative and priority learning in memory and visual search: A theoretical view of age-dependent practice effects*. Paper presented at the National Institute on Aging Conference on Aging and Attention, Washington, DC, November.

Gallagher, D., & Thompson, L. W. (1983). Depression. In P. M. Lewinsohn & L. Teri (Eds) *Clinical geropsychology* (pp. 7–37). New York: Pergamon.

Goate, A., Chartier-Harlin, M.-C., Mullan, M., Brown, J., Crawford, F., Fidani, L., Guiffra, L., Haynes, A., Irving, N., James, L., Mant, R., Newton, P., Rooke, K., Roques, P., Talbot, C., Williamson, R., Rossor, M., Owen, M., & Hardy, J. (1991). Segregation of a missense mutation in the amyloid precursor protein gene with familial Alzheimer's disease. *Nature*, *349*, 704–706.

Goldberg, L. R. (1993). The structure of phenotypic personality traits. *American Psychologist*, *48*, 26–34.

Haan, N., Millsap, R., & Hartka, E. (1986). As time goes by: Change and stability in personality over fifty years. *Psychology and Aging*, *1*, 220–232.

Hartley, A. A., & McKenzie, C. R. M. (1991). Attentional and perceptual contributions to the identification of extrafoveal stimuli: Adult age comparisons. *Journal of Gerontology: Psychological Sciences*, *46*, 202–206.

Horn, J. L. (1982). The aging of human abilities. In B. B. Wolman (Ed.) *Handbook of developmental psychology* (pp. 847–879). Englewood Cliffs, NJ: Prentice-Hall.

Howe, M. L. (1988). Measuring memory development in adulthood: A model-based approach to disentangling storage-retrieval contributions. In M. L. Howe & C. J. Brainerd (Eds) *Cognitive development in adulthood* (pp. 39–64). New York: Springer-Verlag.

Huyck, M. H. (1990). Gender differences in aging. In J. E. Birren & K. W. Schaie (Eds) *Handbook of the psychology of aging* (3rd edn, pp. 124–132). San Diego, CA: Academic Press.

Kamouri, A., & Cavanaugh, J. C. (1986). The impact of pre-retirement education programs on workers' pre-retirement socialization. *Journal of Occupational Behavior*, *7*, 245–256.

Kinney, J. M., & Stephens, M. A. P. (1989). Caregiver Hassles Scale: Assessing the daily hassles of caring for a family member with dementia. *The Gerontologist, 29,* 328–332.

Kline, D. W., & Schieber, F. (1985). Vision and aging. In J. E. Birren & K. W. Schaie (Eds) *Handbook of the psychology of aging* (2nd edn, pp. 296–331). New York: Van Nostrand Reinhold.

Labouvie-Vief, G. (1985). Intelligence and cognition. In J. E. Birren & K. W. Schaie (Eds) *Handbook of the psychology of aging* (2nd edn, pp. 500–530). New York: Van Nostrand Reinhold.

Larson, R. (1978). Thirty years of research on the subjective well-being of older Americans. *Journal of Gerontology, 33,* 109–125.

Lopata, H. Z. (1975). Widowhood: Societal factors in life-span disruptions and alternatives. In N. Datan & L. H. Ginsberg (Eds) *Life-span developmental psychology: Normative life crises* (pp. 217–234). New York: Academic Press.

McDowd, J. M., & Craik, F. I. M. (1988). Effects of aging and task difficulty on divided attention performance. *Journal of Experimental Psychology: Human Perception and Performance, 14,* 267–280.

McDowd, J. M, Filion, D. L., & Oseas-Kreger, D. M. (1991). *Inhibitory deficits in selective attention and aging.* Paper presented at the meeting of the American Psychological Society, Washington, DC, June.

Meyer, B. J. F. (1987). Reading comprehension and aging. In K. W. Schaie (Ed.) *Annual review of gerontology and geriatrics* (vol. 7, pp. 93–115). New York: Springer.

Miller, S. S., & Cavanaugh, J. C. (1990). The meaning of grandparenthood and its relationship to demographic, relationship, and social participation variables. *Journal of Gerontology: Psychological Sciences, 45,* 244–246.

Nolen-Hoeksema, S. (1988). Life-span views on depression. In P. B. Baltes & R. M. Lerner (Eds) *Life-span development and behavior* (vol. 9, pp. 203-241). Hillsdale, NJ: Lawrence Erlbaum.

Piaget, J. (1972). Intellectual evolution from adolescence to adulthood. *Human Development, 15,* 1–12.

Plude, D. J., & Doussard-Roosevelt, J. A. (1990). Aging and attention: Selectivity, capacity, and arousal. In E. A. Lovelace (Ed.) *Aging and cognition: Mental processes, self-awareness, and interventions* (pp. 97–133). Amsterdam: North-Holland.

Plude, D. J., & Hoyer, W. J. (1985). Attention and performance: Identifying and localizing age deficits. In N. Charness (Ed.) *Aging and human performance* (pp. 47–99). Chichester: Wiley.

Poon, L. W. (1985). Differences in human memory with aging: Nature, causes, and clinical implications. In J. E. Birren & K. W. Schaie (Eds) *Handbook of the psychology of aging* (2nd edn, pp. 427–462). New York: Van Nostrand Reinhold.

Poon, L. W., & Schaffer, G. (1982). *Prospective memory in young and elderly adults.* Paper presented at the annual conference of the American Psychological Association, Washington, DC, August.

Salthouse, T. A. (1984). Effects of age and skill in typing. *Journal of Experimental Psychology: General, 113,* 345–371.

Salthouse, T. A. (1985). Speed of behavior and its implications for cognition. In J. E. Birren & K. W. Schaie (Eds) *Handbook of the psychology of aging* (2nd edn, pp. 400–426). New York: Van Nostrand Reinhold.

Salthouse, T. A. (1991). *Status of working memory as a mediator of adult age differences in cognition.* Invited address presented at the American Psychological Association, San Francisco, CA, August.

Schaie, K. W., & Hertzog, C. (1983). Fourteen-year cohort-sequential studies of adult intelligence. *Developmental Psychology*, *19*, 531–543.

Smith, J., & Baltes, P. B. (1990). Wisdom-related knowledge: Age/cohort differences in responses to life-planning problems. *Developmental Psychology*, *26*, 494–505.

Thomae, H. (1980). Personality and adjustment to aging. In J. E. Birren & R. B. Sloane (Eds) *Handbook of mental health and aging* (pp. 285–301). Englewood Cliffs, NJ: Prentice-Hall.

Thomas, J. L. (1986). Gender differences in satisfaction with grandparenting. *Psychology anal Aging*, *1*, 215–219.

Willis, S. L., & Nesselroade, J. R. (1990). Long-term effects of fluid ability training in old-old age. *Developmental Psychology*, *26*, 905–910.

Yesavage, J. A. (1983). Imagery retraining and memory training in the elderly. *Gerontology*, *29*, 271–275.

9
SOCIAL PSYCHOLOGY

INTRODUCTION

Social psychology is the study of social behaviour and the mental experience of individuals in social contexts. It includes the study of social effects on aspects of behaviour and mental experience that are studied more generally in other branches of the discipline. But at the heart of social psychology lie a number of psychological phenomena that are quintessentially social – that do not arise, or in some cases cannot even be conceived of, in individuals divorced from their social contexts.

Chapter 9.1, by Klaus Jonas, Alice H. Eagly, and Wolfgang Stroebe, introduces and provides a general overview of the social psychology of attitudes and persuasion. The authors explain the relationships between attitudes, beliefs, and behaviour before discussing research into the main strategies of persuasion and their implications for the design of persuasion campaigns via the mass media. Among the persuasion strategies that they discuss are those based on incentives and rewards, including classical and operant (or instrumental) conditioning; for a detailed general discussion of conditioning, see chapter 5.1 (Nicholas J. Mackintosh), and for examples of practical applications of conditioning methods in other areas, see chapter 5.2 (Donald M. Baer).

In chapter 9.2 Peter B. Smith summarizes what has been discovered about social influence processes, apart from persuasion and attitude change. Among the forms of social influence that he covers are the effects of the mere presence of other people on an individual's behaviour (social facilitation), social loafing, group polarization, conformity and minority influence, leadership, and obedience to authority. Smith's account of social facilitation and social loafing is closely related to parts of chapter 6.3 (Russell G. Geen), which discusses them from the point of view of social motivation.

In chapter 9.3 David J. Schneider introduces attribution and social cognition. Attribution theory is concerned with how people infer traits, motives, and abilities from the behaviour of others, and social cognition concerns the ways in which people perceive and understand all aspects of their social environments. This chapter provides a comprehensive survey of leading theoretical contributions and research findings related to these processes. There are numerous links with section 4, which is devoted to cognition in general.

Chapter 9.4, by James Vivian and Rupert Brown, focuses on prejudice and intergroup conflict. This chapter deals with the major research findings and theories of prejudice, including theories of the authoritarian personality, belief similarity, frustration-aggression, stereotyping, relative deprivation, realistic conflict, and social identity. This chapter concludes with a section on strategies for prejudice reduction and conflict resolution.

Finally, chapter 9.5, by Peter Bull and Lesley Frederikson, is on non-verbal communication. The authors discuss the role of non-verbal cues in the expression of emotion, gestures accompanying speech, individual differences in encoding and decoding non-verbal signs, and non-verbal communication in interpersonal relationships. The chapter concludes with the practical applications of research into non-verbal communication. For more information on the expression of emotion, see chapter 6.1 (Brian Parkinson); for more on the application of non-verbal communication research to social skills training, see chapter 5.5 (Michael Argyle).

A.M.C.

9.1

ATTITUDES AND PERSUASION

Klaus Jonas

Universität Tübingen, Germany

Alice H. Eagly

Purdue University, Indiana, USA

Wolfgang Stroebe

Rijksuniversiteit te Utrecht, The Netherlands

The campaign against smoking, an exceptionally effective persuasion campaign, began in 1964 with the publication of the report of the United States Surgeon-General's Advisory Committee on Smoking and Health (1964). Persuasive materials carried by the media emphasized the unhealthy consequences of smoking, and compulsory health warnings were introduced on tobacco advertisements and cigarette packages. Increases in excise taxes on tobacco made smoking considerably more expensive. Largely as a result of this anti-smoking campaign, smoking is no longer perceived as glamorous, but as a health risk and an addiction. Moreover, especially in the USA, smoking has declined substantially.

This chapter examines some of the psychological processes involved in effective persuasion campaigns. The first part of the chapter introduces the concepts of attitude, belief, and behaviour, and analyses the relations between them. The second part focuses on two general strategies of persuasion – namely, the use of rewards or incentives to change attitudes and the use of persuasive argumentation.

ATTITUDES, BELIEFS, AND BEHAVIOURS

The concept of attitude

Attitude may be defined as a psychological tendency to evaluate a particular entity with some degree of favour or disfavour (see Eagly & Chaiken, 1993; Zanna & Rempel, 1988). For example, one might have an attitude towards reducing agricultural subsidies in the European Community. The entity towards which people hold an attitude (e.g., reducing agricultural subsidies) is called an *attitude object*. Anything that is discriminable or is an object of thought can be evaluated and therefore can function as an attitude object. Examples of attitude objects thus include people, one's own behaviour (e.g., smoking), concrete objects like one's car, and more abstract entities like social policies and ideologies. Attitudes may be positive or negative and differ in their extremity as well.

People can express their attitudes in various ways, through their cognitions, affects, and behaviours. *Cognitions* refer to the thoughts, or beliefs, that a person has about the attitude object; a belief is any perceived link between an attitude object and an attribute. *Affects* refer to the feelings, moods, emotions, or sympathetic nervous system activity that a person experiences in relation to an attitude object. *Behaviours* refer to a person's overt actions with respect to the attitude object and include intentions to behave that are not necessarily expressed in action. In general, a person's cognitions, affects, and behaviours are positive (i.e., have favourable implications for the attitude object) to the extent that the person holds a positive attitude and are negative (i.e., have unfavourable implications for the object) to the extent that the person holds a negative attitude.

Relations between attitudes and beliefs

Several algebraic models attempt to describe precisely the relation between attitudes and beliefs. Among these approaches is Fishbein and Ajzen's (1975) expectancy-value model, which assumes that one's attitude is a function of one's beliefs when these beliefs are represented as the sum of the expected values of the attributes one ascribes to the attitude object. According to this approach, each attribute has an expectancy and a value attached to it. The *expectancy* is the individual's subjective probability that the attitude is characterized by the attribute, and the *value* is the individual's evaluation of the attribute. For example, a person may have a definite expectancy (high subjective probability) that *European integration* (attitude object) will contribute to *political stability in Europe* (positively evaluated attribute). To predict an attitude from such beliefs, the expectancy and value terms associated with each attribute are multiplied together, and these products are added (see Equation 1). By this approach, people should hold positive attitudes towards things that they think have good attributes and negative attitudes towards things that they think have bad attributes.

$$\text{Attitude} = \Sigma \text{ Expectancy} \times \text{Value} \tag{1}$$

Despite the success of this model, its implicit assumption that people form attitudes by summing a number of attributes of the attitude object has been questioned. Sometimes people may proceed more efficiently by taking into account only one or a very few attributes of the attitude object (e.g., McGuire, 1985), or they may form attitudes based on their affective responding or their behaviours rather than their beliefs.

Relation between attitudes and behaviours

If attitudes influence overt behaviour, people with positive attitudes towards a given attitude object should engage in behaviours that approach, support, or enhance it, and those with negative attitudes should engage in behaviours that avoid, oppose, or hinder the object. However reasonable it may seem that attitudes should be related to behaviours in this way, considerable controversy surrounds the ability of attitudes to predict behaviour. Central in this debate was Wicker's (1969) review of 42 studies of the attitude-behaviour relation, which found an average correlation of only about .15 and led him to conclude that attitudes are typically unrelated or only slightly related to overt behaviours. Although Wicker's and other critics' conclusions were initially accepted by many social scientists, important principles by which attitude-behaviour correlations can be increased were subsequently set forth.

From a psychometric perspective, much of the variation in attitude-behaviour correlations can be understood in terms of the *reliability* and *validity* of an investigator's measures of behaviour. A single instance of behaviour is an unreliable indicator of an attitude because the performance of the behaviour depends upon many factors in addition to the attitude. For example, whether an environmentalist places used bottles into a recycling bin during a particular week may depend not only on his or her attitude towards environmental preservation but also on factors like opportunity, time, or resources. Yet when a number of somewhat unreliable behavioural indicators of an attitude are aggregated into a composite behavioural index, the non-attitudinal factors that influence the single behaviours should tend to cancel one another. Because such a composite behavioural measure should more reliably reflect the underlying attitude, it should show a higher correlation with attitude. This *aggregation principle*, initially proposed by Fishbein and Ajzen (1974), has been effectively demonstrated in a number of studies.

A single behavioural observation may be not only an unreliable measure of attitude, but also a relatively invalid measure because it embodies specific features that are not incorporated into the attitude that the social scientist has chosen to study. As Ajzen and Fishbein (1977) pointed out, each single behaviour incorporates (1) a specific *action*, (2) directed at a *target*, (3) in a *context*, (4) at a *time* or occasion. In contrast, many of the most commonly studied attitudes indicate only the target of an attitude (e.g., one's attitude towards a healthy lifestyle is an "attitude towards a target"). Such general attitudes can be expressed by a variety of specific actions performed in a variety of contexts and times. For example, an individual's positive attitude towards a healthy lifestyle can be manifested in a wide range of actions such as jogging, eating a balanced diet, giving up smoking, and reducing consumption of alcoholic beverages; these actions can be performed in a variety of contexts and times. To be a maximally valid indicator of attitude towards a healthy lifestyle, a composite index of behaviours should consist of a representative sample of all the behaviours that are relevant to this attitude. Yet the range of relevant behaviours would be much narrower for a more narrowly formulated attitude such as attitude towards jogging before breakfast each morning. In general, correlations between attitudes and behaviours increase to the extent that the two measures are defined at the same level of generality in terms of their action, target, context, and time elements (see Ajzen & Fishbein, 1977). Ajzen (1988) has labelled this generalization the *principle of compatibility*.

Attitudinal models of behaviour

Expectancy-value models

Fishbein and Ajzen (1975) proposed a theory for predicting behaviour from attitude and other variables. The type of attitude considered by this theory is attitude towards one's own behaviour (e.g., one's attitude towards voting in favour of a particular political party or candidate). This *theory of reasoned action*, which is restricted to the prediction of volitional or voluntary behaviours, assumes that the proximal cause of a behaviour is one's intention to engage in it. Intention represents motivation to perform a behaviour in the sense of the individual's conscious plan to exert effort to carry out the behaviour. Intention to engage in a behaviour is itself a function of the person's attitude towards engaging in the behaviour, and her or his perception of the extent to which significant others think that she or he should engage in the behaviour. This latter component is called *subjective norm*. This model can be stated algebraically as follows:

$$B(f)BI = w_1 A_B + w_2 SN. \tag{2}$$

In this equation B refers to behaviour, BI to behavioural intention, A_B to attitude towards the behaviour, and SN to subjective norm; w_1 and w_2 are empirical weights indicating the relative importance of the attitudinal and normative components. Attitude towards the behaviour (A_B) is itself a function of one's beliefs about the perceived consequences of the act multiplied by the evaluation of each consequence (i.e., a form of Equation 1). Subjective norm is a function of one's perceptions of other people's preferences about whether one should engage in the particular behaviour (weighted by one's motivation to comply with these perceived preferences).

The theory of reasoned action has been tested in numerous studies of quite diverse behaviours, including voting, weight loss, consumer behaviour, and family planning behaviour (Ajzen & Fishbein, 1980). According to a meta-analysis of this research (Sheppard, Hartwick, & Warshaw, 1988), the theory has been well supported. Specifically, the mean correlation in the studies reviewed in the meta-analysis was .66 for the prediction of intention from attitude and subjective norm. For the relation between intention and behaviour, the mean correlation was .53.

Among the criticisms of the theory of reasoned action is the view that limiting the model to volitional behaviours excludes actions that one cannot engage in merely by deciding to do them. Behaviours such as having a party, for example, require resources, cooperation, and specialized skills (Liska, 1984). Also challenged was the reasoned-action assumption that attitude and subjective norm are sufficient proximal causes of intentions. To circumvent these criticisms, many revisions of the theory have been proposed, all of which retain as their central feature the ideas that people form attitudes towards behavioural acts by scrutinizing the consequences of acts and that these attitudes then impact indirectly or directly on behaviour. Best known among these variant models is Ajzen's (e.g., 1988, 1991) *theory of planned behaviour*. This model, which is designed to predict non-volitional as well as volitional behaviours, adds to the reasoned action model a new predictor of intention (and behaviour) labelled *perceived behavioural control*, which is defined as one's perception of how easy or difficult it is to perform the behaviour. Perceived control is in turn a function of the individual's beliefs about how likely it is that he or she possesses the resources and opportunities required to execute the behaviour. Research has shown that the addition of this variable can often improve the prediction of intention and behaviour; yet models adding a variety of other variables have also improved prediction under certain circumstances (see Eagly & Chaiken, 1993).

Spontaneous processing model

The models of behaviour discussed so far conceive of people as rational decision-makers who form behavioural intentions by thinking about the consequences of future actions. Although these models do not imply that individuals have to weigh all the possible consequences of behavioural alternatives before they act, their assumption that actions are controlled by intentions suggests that behaviour presupposes some deliberative cognitive processing. However, as Fazio (1990) argued, such deliberative thinking occurs only when individuals are able and willing to think about their future actions. People are more likely to expend cognitive effort on such thinking if important outcomes are involved and if they have the time and peace of mind to deliberate. When outcomes are unimportant or when there is little opportunity to deliberate, attitudes might affect behaviour through a more spontaneous process.

Fazio (1986, 1990) reasoned that such spontaneous behaviour is influenced, not by the attitudes towards behaviours considered in the expectancy-value tradition, but by more general attitudes – that is, attitudes towards the entities or targets towards which behaviours are directed. For example, one's attitude towards a particular brand of breakfast cereal, rather than one's attitude towards *purchasing* this cereal on a particular trip to the store, might determine whether one purchases it.

From Fazio's perspective, attitudes are associations between the attitude object and an evaluation. The sequence that links an attitude to behaviour is initiated when the attitude is accessed from memory. The likelihood that the attitude is spontaneously activated when a person observes an attitude object (or a cue associated with it) is a function of the *accessibility*, or ease of recall, of the attitude. Accessibility depends, in turn, on the strength of the individual's mental association between the attitude object and her or his evaluation of the object. Repeated activation of the link between the attitude object and its evaluation strengthens the association. To the extent that this association is strong, the evaluation is accessed easily and quickly in response to cues conveyed by the attitude object. According to Fazio, only attitudes with high associative strength have a high probability of spontaneous (and automatic) activation. Once such an attitude is activated, it instigates attitude-congruent perceptions of the attitude object (i.e., positive perceptions if the attitude is positive and negative perceptions if it is negative), and these perceptions in turn evoke attitude-congruent behaviour.

Consistent with Fazio's (1986) theory, higher accessibility (operationalized by the speed with which an attitude-relevant cue elicits an evaluative response) is related to higher attitude-behaviour consistency. Moreover, accessibility may account for the influence of several variables on the magnitude of attitude-behaviour correlations. For example, the reason why attitudes based on direct experience are better predictors of behaviour than attitudes based on indirect experience may be that they are more accessible from memory (see Fazio, 1986).

In conclusion, contemporary psychologists have provided two approaches to understanding the psychological processes by which attitudes affect behaviour. The first approach consists of a family of expectancy-value models that treat attitudes towards behaviours as causes of behaviours and regard the perceived consequences of behaviour as determinants of these attitudes. The second approach predicts behaviour from more general attitudes and emphasizes that attitudes that are more accessible from memory are more likely to direct behaviour.

STRATEGIES OF PERSUASION

Webster's (1986) unabridged dictionary defines "to persuade" as "to induce by argument, entreaty, or expostulation into some mental position" or "to win over by an appeal to one's reason and feelings" (p. 1687). Although the term *persuasion* thus focuses on argumentation, as the Latin root of the word would suggest, a broader interpretation of the term would encompass other forms of social influence such as the use of incentives and rewards. Reflecting such breadth, our discussion focuses on persuasion through the use of rewards or incentives as well as argument-based persuasion.

Reward- and incentive-based persuasion

The study of incentive-based persuasion concerns the extent to which attitudes and behaviour can be influenced by rewards and punishments. Early theorists generally believed that attitudinal responses are automatically strengthened by their immediate consequences through processes of *classical* and *instrumental* conditioning (e.g., Lott & Lott, 1968; Staats & Staats, 1958; Verplanck, 1955). However, with the emergence of cognitive theories of social learning (e.g., Bandura, 1986), psychologists began to emphasize the *informative* and *incentive* functions of reinforcements.

Classical conditioning of attitudes

Through classical conditioning a stimulus that is initially incapable of

781

eliciting a particular response (the conditioned stimulus) acquires the ability to do so through repeated association with a stimulus that already evoked this response (the unconditioned stimulus). In Pavlov's (1927) classic experiment on dogs, a tone that was presented repeatedly just prior to food eventually elicited salivation, a response previously evoked only by the food.

Instead of using food as an unconditioned stimulus, Staats and Staats (1958) used words that elicited positive affect (e.g., *vacation*, *gift*) or negative affect (e.g., *bitter*, *failure*). These words were presented auditorially to subjects immediately after the visual presentation of the name of a nationality in what was apparently a learning experiment. For half of the subjects, Dutch was consistently paired with positive adjectives and Swedish with negative adjectives; for the other half, the pairing was reversed. The presentation of other nationalities consistently paired with neutral words was intended to disguise the purpose of the experiment. When the target nationalities were later rated on an evaluative scale, the nationality that had been associated with positive words was rated more positively than the nationality paired with negative words. Interpreting their findings in terms of automatic conditioning processes, Staats and Staats reasoned that the positive or negative reaction initially evoked by the adjectives had been passed on to the nationality name by mere association.

The conditioning processes modelled by experiments of this type may have important implications for understanding the development of prejudice, because social groups (e.g., national or racial groups) are often systematically associated with negative information in the media. Classical conditioning may also offer an explanation for the effectiveness of advertising practices that pair brand names with positive but seemingly irrelevant stimuli (e.g., a photograph of a handsome man or beautiful scenery).

Instrumental or operant conditioning of attitudes

Consistent with Skinner's (1957) assertion that human verbal behaviour is subject to the same operant conditioning principles that govern much animal learning, numerous studies during the late 1950s and 1960s investigated the instrumental, or operant, conditioning of people's attitudinal statements and other verbal behaviour. Whereas in classical conditioning the organism has no control over the reaction that is originally elicited by the unconditioned stimulus and later by the conditioned stimulus, in operant conditioning the organism must produce a response first, before it can be strengthened or weakened by differential reinforcement.

Studies of instrumental conditioning of attitudes typically used a question-and-answer format in which the experimenter queried subjects about their attitudes towards some issue and then reinforced responses in a particular attitudinal direction. For example, in one early study, subjects were interviewed by telephone about the educational policy of their university

(Hildum & Brown, 1956). The telephone caller verbally reinforced some subjects by responding with "good" whenever their responses implied a favourable attitude towards university policy, and other subjects were reinforced for answers implying a negative attitude. Consistent with predictions, subjects reinforced for positive attitudes increasingly agreed with favourable statements, whereas the trend was reversed for subjects reinforced for negative attitudes.

Role of cognition in conditioning processes

Interpretations of classical and instrumental conditioning of attitudes in terms of behaviourist theories which assume that conditioning is an automatic, affective process were challenged by cognitively oriented psychologists who argued that conditioning processes are based on learning the contingencies, or relationships between events, that characterize the conditioning experiment. According to cognitive reinterpretations of classical conditioning of attitudes, subjects in these studies typically recognize the systematic relationship between the adjectives and the nationality names. They may then merely respond to the demands of the experimental situation by telling the experimenter what they think she or he wants to hear (e.g., Page, 1969), or they may form beliefs about these nationalities on the basis of the information conveyed by the adjectives (e.g., Fishbein & Ajzen, 1975).

Similarly, cognitive reinterpretations of instrumental conditioning of attitudes assume that subjects typically become aware of the contingency between their responses and the receipt of reinforcement. For example, Insko and Cialdini (1969) suggested that the interviewer's "good" response has two consequences: first, it informs subjects of the attitudinal position held by the interviewer, and second, it establishes positive rapport between subjects and interviewers. Subjects' friendly feelings towards the interviewer then motivate them to conform to the interviewer's attitude.

Although behaviourist and cognitive interpretations of conditioning were hotly debated during the 1970s, this controversy has never been resolved. Existing empirical evidence does not rule out the possibility that attitudinal conditioning may sometimes influence attitudes without mediation by higher-order cognitive processes (see Eagly & Chaiken, 1993).

Incentive-induced attitude change

Consistent with the expectancy-value models of behaviour presented earlier in the chapter are the attempts of powerful institutions such as governments to change the "costs" of a given behaviour through monetary incentives, taxation, or legal sanctions. For example, by increasing taxes on tobacco and alcoholic beverages, governments have had some success in inhibiting unhealthy behaviours such as smoking and drinking excessive alcohol (see

Moore & Gerstein, 1981; Novotny, Romano, Davis, & Mills, 1992). Like the demand for most commodities, the demand for alcoholic beverages and cigarettes responds to changes in price, and increases in price result in decreased sales of alcoholic beverages (e.g., Johnson & Oksanen, 1977) and cigarettes (e.g., Walsh & Gordon, 1986). Moreover, evidence for the successful use of legal sanctions to discourage risky behaviours comes from studies demonstrating the considerable impact of laws mandating the use of seat-belts (e.g., Fhanér & Hane, 1979).

Limiting this approach is the tendency for changes in the "price" of a given behaviour to influence mainly the attitude towards purchasing the product or service that enables one to engage in the behaviour. Consistent with the assumption that attitude towards a behaviour reflects the perceived consequences of the behaviour, one's attitude towards *buying* alcoholic beverages might become more negative, given the price constraints, whereas one's attitude towards the critical behaviour itself (i.e., *drinking* alcoholic beverages) might remain positive. Consequently, although a marked increase in the price of alcoholic beverages is likely to induce people to buy fewer alcoholic beverages, they might drink at their old level of consumption when the price constraints are not in effect (e.g., when drinks are freely available at a party).

Despite the narrow impact of such incentive-based programmes, under certain conditions incentive-induced behaviour change could produce more general attitude change. Consider, for example, the use of positive incentives to induce individuals to engage in behaviours for which they have negative expectations. Should these expectations be *unrealistically* negative, their experience with the behaviour would allow them to view it more positively. Also, communicators can imply that rewards would follow, not from behaviour change, but from broader changes in attitudes and beliefs (see Hovland, Janis, & Kelley, 1953).

Attitude change is also likely when individuals are induced to engage in a behaviour that is *discrepant* from their attitudes. There is evidence from research conducted in the cognitive dissonance tradition (Festinger, 1957) that under certain conditions engaging in attitude-discrepant behaviour to gain some reward or avoid some penalty produces a negative state of arousal known as *cognitive dissonance*. In order to reduce this aversive state, people may change their attitude in the direction of greater consistency with their behaviour. According to cognitive dissonance theory, dissonance should be greater when the reward for the attitude-discrepant behaviour is *small* rather than large, because the lack of external justification for engaging in the behaviour increases the dissonance that follows from the behaviour's inconsistency with the attitude.

This negative relation between the size of a reward and the amount of attitude change induced by attitude-discrepant behaviour was demonstrated in a classic study by Festinger and Carlsmith (1959) and has been frequently replicated in subsequent research (see Eagly & Chaiken, 1993). However, subsequent research also uncovered a number of limiting conditions. Specifically, the negative relation between the magnitude of reward and the amount of attitude change occurs only when subjects feel free to refuse to engage in the attitude-discrepant behaviour and when this behaviour has negative consequences either for themselves or for other people.

Finally, offering incentives for the performance of a particular behaviour can result in a more negative attitude towards this behaviour. This so-called *overjustification effect* is likely to occur when people are rewarded for engaging in a behaviour that they already find intrinsically interesting and pleasurable (e.g., Lepper, Greene, & Nisbett, 1973). The positive attitude towards the behaviour is undermined by the positive incentives, perhaps in part because people attribute their behaviour to the incentives rather than to their intrinsic interest in the behaviour (see Bem, 1972).

In conclusion, both attitudes and behaviours may be changed through incentives and rewards. Yet the psychological processes by which these effects may occur are diverse and include classical and operant conditioning, the learning of contingencies, the reduction of cognitive dissonance, and the attribution of one's behaviour to external rewards and costs.

Argument-based persuasion

The study of argument-based persuasion concerns the extent to which people's attitudes, beliefs, and behaviour are changed by relatively complex information consisting of a verbal communication or message. Research in this area has traditionally been oriented to understanding the categories of variables highlighted by Lasswell's (1948, p. 37) classic question, "Who says what in which channel to whom with what effect?" *Who* thus refers to the characteristics of the communicator or message source, *what* refers to the content of the message, *in which channel* refers to the medium through which the message is communicated, *to whom* refers to the characteristics of the recipients of the message, and *with what effect* refers to the nature of the changes that the message produces. Research in this area has not produced "laws of persuasion" in the form of general relationships between particular independent variables and amount of persuasion. Instead, relations involving a particular independent variable typically interact with other variables. For example, communicator credibility or communicator likability, two of Lasswell's "who-variables", generally have a positive impact on the persuasiveness of a message, but this effect is much stronger under some circumstances than others and is sometimes absent or even reversed from its usual direction.

To make sense out of such phenomena, psychologists have produced theories of persuasion that illuminate the psychological processes that are relevant to persuasion and take into account the circumstances under which each process is likely to be important. This process-theory approach to understanding persuasion began with the work carried out at Yale University under the direction of Carl Hovland (Hovland et al., 1953).

Subsequent decades have witnessed increasingly complex theories of persuasion that have illuminated more and more of the relations observed in the thousands of persuasion experiments that have appeared in the empirical literature (see Eagly & Chaiken, 1993; Petty & Cacioppo, 1986a). In these experiments, subjects usually receive a relatively complex verbal message containing a number of arguments that support an overall position on an issue. Subjects give their responses, ordinarily on questionnaires designed to assess, in addition to change in attitudes and beliefs, a number of the mediating processes that may underlie their tendencies to change or resist changing.

Theories of systematic processing

Some persuasion theories have emphasized what might be termed systematic processing by highlighting the importance of message recipients' detailed processing of message content. This approach began with Hovland et al.'s (1953) suggestion that the impact of persuasive communications can be understood in terms of a sequence of processes − attention to the message, comprehension of its content, and acceptance of its conclusions. By this approach, independent variables that influence persuasion act not only directly on people's tendencies to accept the messages' conclusions, but also indirectly through their impact on two causally prior processes, attention and comprehension. Persuasion could fail to occur because of omissions in any of these three information-processing phases: recipients could fail to attend to the message, fail to comprehend its content, or fail to accept what they have comprehended. Persuasion variables such as the inclusion of vivid or pallid imagery in persuasive argumentation might have their impact through any of these processes. For example, vivid imagery might attract attention, yet distract recipients from comprehending message content, or directly facilitate acceptance of the information.

Information-processing model

McGuire (e.g., 1972) proposed a longer chain of processes that are relevant to persuasion: presentation, attention, comprehension, yielding (or acceptance), retention, and behaviour. This perspective assumes that after exposure to the message, recipients must pay attention to it in order for attitude change to be produced. Subsequently, the overall position it advocates and the arguments provided to support this position must be comprehended. Also, recipients must yield to, or agree with, the message content they have comprehended if any attitude change is to be detected. If this change is to persist over a period of time, recipients must retain their changed attitudes.

Finally, if impact is to be observed, recipients must behave on the basis of their changed attitudes. McGuire argued that the failure of any of these steps to occur causes the sequence of processes to be broken, with the consequence that the subsequent steps do not occur.

Empirical work relevant to McGuire's model has emphasized in particular the mediating role of the two steps involving reception of message content: attention to the message and comprehension of its content. Reception of message content should in general facilitate persuasion, at least under the ordinary circumstances in which the message contains cogent persuasive arguments. Moreover, many independent variables may act simultaneously on reception of message content and yielding to it. For example, message recipients' intelligence may facilitate their ability to comprehend messages but reduce the likelihood that they would yield to them. Because the relative importance of these two processes would depend on the nature of the situation, the model makes a number of predictions. Concerning recipients' intelligence, for example, the model predicts that more intelligent recipients will be more persuaded than less intelligent recipients by complex, well-argued messages for which the positive relation between intelligence and message reception should be the primary determinant of persuasion. In contrast, less intelligent recipients will be more persuaded than more intelligent recipients by simple, poorly argued messages for which the negative relation between intelligence and yielding to the message should be the primary determinant of persuasion. Such predictions have received moderately good support (see Eagly & Chaiken, 1993; Rhodes & Wood, 1992).

Cognitive-response model

Also illustrating the systematic approach to understanding persuasion is the cognitive-response model initially proposed by Greenwald (1968) and developed by several social psychologists (see Petty, Ostrom, & Brock, 1981). This perspective reflects the general proposition that people's attitudes are a function of the cognitions that they generate about the objects of their attitudes. This approach thus emphasizes the mediating role of the idiosyncratic thoughts or "cognitive responses" that message recipients generate as they receive and reflect on persuasive communications. Messages should be persuasive to the extent that they evoke favourable thoughts and unpersuasive to the extent that they evoke unfavourable thoughts. Moreover, these effects of the favourability of recipients' thoughts should be magnified to the extent that they engage in extensive message-relevant thinking.

This cognitive-response perspective produced numerous persuasion experiments, each of which manipulated a variable that impacted on extent of message processing (e.g., distraction, message repetition, issue involvement) and crossed this variable with a single other variable – namely, the quality of the arguments given by the message, a factor that reliably affects the favourability of recipients' message-relevant thoughts. The general pattern of findings in these cognitive-response experiments is well known: the favourability of recipients' thoughts (as controlled by argument quality) determines persuasion only to the extent that recipients process the message relatively thoroughly and therefore react to the quality of the arguments. For example, distraction, a variable that can disrupt recipients' abilities to think about message content, has differing impact, depending on the quality of the arguments contained in the message. With high-quality messages that elicit predominantly favourable thoughts, distraction should inhibit these favourable thoughts and therefore inhibit persuasion; with low-quality messages that elicit predominantly unfavourable thoughts, distraction should inhibit these unfavourable thoughts and therefore facilitate persuasion. Petty, Wells, and Brock (1976) confirmed these hypotheses in an early cognitive-response experiment. Although quite a few additional persuasion variables have been investigated within this tradition, the theory none the less is relevant mainly to those variables that are clearly related to message recipients' abilities or motivation to engage in message-relevant thinking.

Dual-process theories

Subsequent persuasion theories took on a broader mission than the systematic processing theories did. Whereas the systematic theories had emphasized message reception and cognitive elaboration of persuasive argumentation, the newer theories consider in addition the idea that people adopt attitudes on bases other than their understanding and evaluation of the semantic content of persuasive argumentation. This general dual-process approach has gained considerably in popularity in recent years. Among dual-process theories are the elaboration likelihood model (Petty & Cacioppo, 1986a, 1986b), which incorporates a peripheral route to persuasion, and the heuristic-systematic model (Chaiken, 1980; Chaiken, Liberman, & Eagly, 1989), which considers simple decision rules or heuristics that mediate persuasion. These theories emphasize contrasting modes of processing and trade at least in part on the idea borrowed from cognitive psychology that cognitive processing can be carried out at a superficial or deeper level. Following the general notion that people process information superficially and minimally unless they are motivated to do otherwise, these attitude theories thus stress that message recipients must have sufficient motivation to turn to more effortful, systematic forms of processing persuasive communications. They must also have the capacity to engage in this more deliberative form of processing.

In the elaboration likelihood model, Petty and Cacioppo (1986a, 1986b) postulated a *central route to persuasion*, which they identified primarily with the message-relevant thinking that served as the mediating process in the cognitive response approach. They postulated in addition *a peripheral route to persuasion*, which they conceptualized quite broadly as the product of any of a variety of mechanisms that cause persuasion in the absence of scrutiny of persuasive arguments. The peripheral route would thus encompass cognitive mechanisms such as heuristic decision rules and attributional reasoning, affective mechanisms such as classical and operant conditioning, and social relational mechanisms such as maintaining role relationships and favourable self-identities. The principal idea of the elaboration likelihood model is that message recipients follow the central route when situational and individual difference variables ensure high motivation and ability for issue-relevant thinking (i.e., when elaboration likelihood is high); they follow the peripheral route when motivation or ability (or both) are low (i.e., when elaboration likelihood is low).

This perspective has led to a range of interesting predictions. Prototypical predictions are that when elaboration likelihood is high, persuasion is influenced by the quality of persuasive arguments, but when elaboration likelihood is low, persuasion is influenced by peripheral cues, which are variables capable of affecting persuasion without influencing recipients' scrutiny of the arguments contained in messages. Illustrating this approach is Petty, Cacioppo, and Goldman's (1981) study in which source expertise functioned as a peripheral cue. Subjects listened to a message advocating senior comprehensive exams, a policy the university was ostensibly considering for the following year (establishing "high personal relevance", which should induce high motivation to think about the message) or the following decade (establishing "low personal relevance", which should induce little motivation to think about the message). Subjects were exposed to either high-quality or very low-quality arguments favouring this recommendation, and the message was said to be based on a report prepared by either a local high school class (low source expertise) or the "Carnegie Commission on Higher Education" (high source expertise). As predicted, the results showed that in the low relevance conditions, source expertise influenced subjects' attitudes and argument quality did not, whereas in the high relevance conditions source expertise had no impact on attitude whereas argument quality did.

The heuristic-systematic model also postulates two mediational paths to persuasion (Chaiken, 1980; Chaiken, Liberman, & Eagly, 1989). This theory's concept of systematic processing resembles central processing in the elaboration likelihood model. In contrast, heuristic processing is more narrowly formulated than peripheral processing because it focuses on simple decision rules that message recipients use to judge the validity of messages. For example, as a consequence of invoking the simple rule that "experts' statements can be trusted", message recipients may agree more with expert than inexpert communicators without having fully absorbed or evaluated the semantic content of the argumentation contained in a message. Because heuristic processing is associated with a particular type of psychological mechanism, this conceptualization has produced several unique hypotheses regarding the persuasive impact of communication variables that serve as heuristic cues. In particular, the model's assumption that heuristics are learned knowledge structures has suggested several cognitive principles that govern their operation and therefore their impact on persuasion. Specifically, these heuristics must be available (i.e., stored in memory for potential use) and accessible (i.e., activated or accessed from memory) in order to influence persuasion. In addition, cognitive heuristics vary in their strength or perceived reliability; more reliable heuristics have more judgmental impact than less reliable heuristics. These principles have suggested novel mechanisms by which certain variables may influence persuasion.

In conclusion, social psychologists have provided several theories of argument-based persuasion and have conducted extensive research to test these models. The earlier theories emphasized the systematic processing of message content, whereas later theories added the assumption that people are often not sufficiently motivated to engage in message-relevant thinking and therefore base their decision to accept or reject a persuasive message on heuristic cues or other peripheral processes. These newer theories have allowed investigators to cast a much wider net among independent variables and to make effective predictions about the conditions under which these variables influence persuasion.

IMPLICATIONS FOR THE DESIGN OF PERSUASION CAMPAIGNS

In applications of the research discussed in this chapter for the design of persuasion campaigns, one issue to consider is whether the target audience has the capacity and motivation to engage in detailed processing of the arguments employed in the communication. If people lack the ability or motivation to comprehend, scrutinise, and evaluate the content of the communication, it is futile to expend great effort on developing a thoughtful, detailed argumentation. Instead, one should rely on mechanisms that do not depend on argumentation for their effectiveness. One could use classical conditioning, heuristic processing, and other mechanisms to influence the audience. It is no coincidence that most of the well-known advertisements for cigarettes, perfumes, or sunglasses rely heavily on this peripheral route to persuasion. If it can be assumed that members of the target audience are both motivated and able to assess the validity of more complex argumentation, it is advisable to develop a thoughtful and coherent argumentation that can stand up to this kind of scrutiny. Thus, the campaign against cigarette smoking made ample use of the scientific evidence on the health consequences of smoking.

Even if a communicator manages to produce the desired attitude change, this impact will not necessarily be translated into behaviour change. As we discussed earlier, there are many reasons why people might not act in accord with their attitudes. With communications urging preventive health behaviours, one of the main problems is that individuals usually have to give up some pleasurable activity (or engage in some unpleasant activity) in the here and now to avoid some negative consequences that might occur at a much later time. One way to bridge this time gap is the introduction of costs that are immediately effective; examples include imposing price increases or instituting legal restrictions and penalties.

The war against smoking was not fought only with arguments and scientific evidence. Increases in the price of cigarettes and legal restrictions on smoking made a significant contribution to the reduction in levels of smoking. Also, knowledge that smoking in enclosed environments endangers the health of others created strong social pressures against smoking (i.e., a subjective norm that countered smoking). This multi-process approach was no doubt essential to the striking success of the anti-smoking campaign.

FURTHER READING

Ajzen, I. (1988). *Attitudes, personality, and behavior*. Milton Keynes: Open University Press.

Eagly, A. H., & Chaiken, S. (1993). *The psychology of attitudes*. Forth Worth, TX: Harcourt Brace Jovanovich.

Fazio, R. H. (1990). Multiple processes by which attitudes guide behavior: The MODE model as an integrative framework. In M. P. Zanna (Ed.) *Advances in experimental social psychology* (vol. 23, pp. 75–109). San Diego, CA: Academic Press.

Petty, R. E., & Cacioppo, J. T. (1986). The elaboration likelihood model of persuasion. In L. Berkowitz (Ed.) *Advances in experimental social psychology* (vol. 19, pp. 123–205). San Diego, CA: Academic Press.

REFERENCES

Ajzen, I. (1988). *Attitudes personality, and behavior*. Milton Keynes: Open University Press.

Ajzen, I. (1991). The theory of planned behavior. *Organizational Behavior and Human Decision Processes, 50*, 179–211.

Ajzen, I., & Fishbein, M. (1977). Attitude–behavior relations: A theoretical analysis and review of empirical research. *Psychological Bulletin, 84*, 888–918.

Ajzen, I., & Fishbein, M. (1980). *Understanding attitudes and predicting social behavior*. Englewood Cliffs, NJ: Prentice-Hall.

Bandura, A. (1986). *Social foundations of thought and action: A social cognitive theory*. Englewood Cliffs, NJ: Prentice-Hall.

Bem, D. J. (1972). Self-perception theory. In L. Berkowitz (Ed.) *Advances in experimental social psychology* (vol. 6, pp. 1–62). San Diego, CA: Academic Press.

Chaiken, S. (1980). Heuristic versus systematic information processing and the use of source versus message cues in persuasion. *Journal of Personality and Social Psychology, 39*, 752–766.

Chaiken, S., Liberman, A., & Eagly, A. H. (1989). Heuristic and systematic processing within and beyond the persuasion context. In J. S. Uleman & J. A. Bargh (Eds) *Unintended thought* (pp. 212–252). New York: Guilford.

Eagly, A. H., & Chaiken, S. (1993). *The psychology of attitudes*. Fort Worth, TX: Harcourt Brace Jovanovich.

Fazio, R. H. (1986). How do attitudes guide behavior? In R. M. Sorrentino & E. T. Higgins (Eds) *Handbook of motivation and cognition: Foundations of social behavior* (pp. 204–243). New York: Guilford.

Fazio, R. H. (1990). Multiple processes by which attitudes guide behavior: The MODE model as an integrative framework. In M. P. Zanna (Ed.) *Advances in experimental social psychology* (vol. 23, pp. 75–109). San Diego, CA: Academic Press.

Festinger, L. (1957). *A theory of cognitive dissonance*. Evanston, IL: Row, Peterson.

Festinger, L., & Carlsmith, J. M. (1959). Cognitive consequences of forced compliance. *Journal of Abnormal and Social Psychology*, *58*, 203–210.

Fhanér, G., & Hane, M. (1979). Seat belts: Opinion effects of law-induced use. *Journal of Applied Psychology*, *64*, 205–212.

Fishbein, M., & Ajzen, I. (1974). Attitudes toward objects as predictors of single and multiple behavioral criteria. *Psychological Review*, *81*, 59–74.

Fishbein, M., & Ajzen, I. (1975). *Belief, attitude, intention and behavior: An introduction to theory and research*. Reading, MA: Addison-Wesley.

Greenwald, A. G. (1968). Cognitive learning, cognitive response to persuasion, and attitude change. In A. G. Greenwald, T. C. Brock, & T. M. Ostrom (Eds) *Psychological foundations of attitudes* (pp. 147–170). San Diego, CA: Academic Press.

Hildum, D. C., & Brown, R. W. (1956). Verbal reinforcement and interviewer bias. *Journal of Abnormal and Social Psychology*, *53*, 108–111.

Hovland, C. I., Janis, I. L., & Kelley, H. H. (1953). *Communication and persuasion: Psychological studies of opinion change*. New Haven, CT: Yale University Press.

Insko, C. A., & Cialdini, R. B. (1969). A test of three interpretations of attitudinal verbal reinforcement. *Journal of Personality and Social Psychology*, *12*, 333–341.

Johnson, J. A., & Oksanen, E. H. (1977). Estimation of demand for alcoholic beverages in Canada from pooled time series and cross sections. *Review of Economics and Statistics*, *59*, 113–118.

Lasswell, H. D. (1948). The structure and function of communication in society. In L. Bryson (Ed.) *The communication of ideas: Religion and civilization series* (pp. 37–51). New York: Harper & Row.

Lepper, M. R., Greene, D., & Nisbett, R. E. (1973). Undermining children's intrinsic interest with extrinsic reward: A test of the "overjustification" hypothesis. *Journal of Personality and Social Psychology*, *28*, 129–137.

Liska, A. E. (1984). A critical examination of the causal structure of the Fishbein/Ajzen attitude-behavior model. *Social Psychology Quarterly*, *47*, 61–74.

Lott, A. J., & Lott, B. E. (1968). A learning theory approach to interpersonal attitudes. In A. G. Greenwald, T. C. Brock, & T. M. Ostrom (Eds) *Psychological foundations of attitudes* (pp. 67–88). San Diego, CA: Academic Press.

McGuire, W. J. (1972). Attitude change: The information-processing paradigm. In C. G. McClintock (Ed.) *Experimental social psychology* (pp. 108–141). New York: Holt, Rinehart & Winston.

McGuire, W. J. (1985). Attitudes and attitude change. In G. Lindzey & E. Aronson (Eds) *Handbook of social psychology* (3rd edn, vol. 2, pp. 233–346). New York: Random House.

Moore, M. H., & Gerstein, D. R. (1981). *Alcohol and public policy: Beyond the shadow of prohibition*. Washington, DC: National Academy Press.

Novotny, T. E., Romano, R. A., Davis, R. M., & Mills, S. L. (1992). The public health practice of tobacco control: Lessons learned and directions for the States in the 1990s. *Annual Review of Public Health*, *13*, 287–318.

Page, M. M. (1969). Social psychology of a classical conditioning of attitudes experiment. *Journal of Personality and Social Psychology*, *11*, 177–186.

Pavlov, I. P. (1927). *Conditioned reflexes: An investigation of the physiological activity of the cerebral cortex*. New York: Oxford University Press.

Petty, R. E., & Cacioppo, J. T. (1986a). *Communication and persuasion: Central and peripheral routes to attitude change*. New York: Springer-Verlag.

Petty, R. E., & Cacioppo, J. T. (1986b). The elaboration likelihood model of persuasion. In L. Berkowitz (Ed.) *Advances in experimental social psychology* (vol. 19, pp. 123–205). San Diego, CA: Academic Press.

Petty, R. E., Cacioppo, J. T., & Goldman, R. (1981). Personal involvement as a determinant of argument-based persuasion. *Journal of Personality and Social Psychology*, *41*, 847–855.

Petty, R. E., Ostrom, T. M. & Brock, T. C. (Eds) (1981). *Cognitive responses in persuasion*. Hillsdale, NJ: Lawrence Erlbaum.

Petty, R. E., Wells, G. L., & Brock, T. C. (1976). Distraction can enhance or reduce yielding to propaganda: Thought disruption versus effort justification. *Journal of Personality and Social Psychology*, *34*, 874–884.

Rhodes, N., & Wood, W. (1992). Self-esteem and intelligence affect influenceability: The mediating role of message reception. *Psychological Bulletin*, *111*, 156–171.

Sheppard, B. H., Hartwick, J., & Warshaw, P. R. (1988). The theory of reasoned action: A meta-analysis of past research with recommendations for modifications and future research. *Journal of Consumer Research*, *15*, 325–343.

Skinner, B. F. (1957). *Verbal behavior*. New York: Appleton-Century-Crofts.

Staats, A. W., & Staats, C. K. (1958). Attitudes established by classical conditioning. *Journal of Abnormal and Social Psychology*, *57*, 37–40.

United States Surgeon-General's Advisory Committee on Smoking and Health (1964). *Smoking and health: Report of the Advisory Committee of the Surgeon General of the Public Health Service*. Princeton, NJ: Van Nostrand.

Verplanck, W. S. (1955). The control of the content of conversation: Reinforcement of statements of opinion. *Journal of Abnormal and Social Psychology*, *51*, 668–676.

Walsh, D. C., & Gordon, N. P. (1986). Legal approaches to smoking deterrence. *Annual Review of Public Health*, *7*, 127–149.

Webster's Third New International Dictionary of the English Language Unabridged (1986). Springfield, MA: Merriam-Webster.

Wicker, A. W. (1969). Attitude versus actions: The relationship of verbal and overt behavioral responses to attitude objects. *Journal of Social Issues*, *25*(4), 41–78.

Zanna, M. P., & Rempel, J. K. (1988). Attitudes: A new look at an old concept. In D. Bar-Tal & A. W. Kruglanski (Eds) *The social psychology of knowledge* (pp. 315–334). Cambridge: Cambridge University Press.

9.2

SOCIAL INFLUENCE PROCESSES

Peter B. Smith
University of Sussex, England

Most of the subject matter of social psychology could be said to be concerned with the way in which we influence the perceptions and the actions of one another. However, research into social psychology during the twentieth century has become increasingly focused into a series of discrete research areas whose interconnections are insufficiently explored. In this way, we have reached the point where two books on social influence by social psychologists (Cialdini, 1988; Turner, 1991) have virtually no shared content.

Studies of social influence divide most readily between those that consider how the mere presence of other people influences one's behaviour, and those that focus on situations where people actively try to influence one another. The first of these two areas has been most typically known as social facilitation, but includes the related effects referred to as the risky shift, group polarization, and social loafing. The second type of study has addressed phenomena such as leadership, obedience, persuasion, conformity, and minority influence.

SOCIAL FACILITATION EFFECTS

The very first social psychological experiment was undertaken in the 1880s by a French engineering professor named Ringelmann (Kravitz & Martin, 1986). He showed that the more members there were in a tug-of-war team, the less hard each member of the team pulled. Numerous other experiments have confirmed that while on some tasks the presence of others does indeed inhibit performance, on others performance is actually enhanced. Zajonc (1965) proposed that these mixed results may be explained by the proposition that the presence of others influences us to perform better on familiar tasks and worse on unfamiliar ones. This attempt at integration has proved difficult to test, since a task that is familiar to one person may well be unfamiliar to others.

A later series of studies has focused on some of the tasks where the presence of others does seem to inhibit performance, and promotes what Latané, Williams, and Harkins (1979) have dubbed "social loafing". Latané's thinking was based on the observation that bystanders become less likely to come to the aid of those in distress if there are others at hand. He devised a series of experimental tasks (for instance clapping or shouting as loudly as possible, alone or in the presence of others), which did consistently elicit social loafing, in a very similar manner to Ringelmann's original tug-of-war studies. Loud clapping and shouting are not on the whole a widespread activity of individuals on their own, but they are quite frequent in crowds. Zajonc's theory is therefore not much help in explaining social loafing. However, a number of other factors have been found to reduce or eliminate social loafing. For instance, Brickner, Ostrom and Harkins (1986) showed that social loafing occurred only where subjects thought that the task was unimportant and that no one else was watching their performance. When tasks with more everyday plausibility have been used, it has been found in more group-oriented countries such as China and Japan that social loafing effects are not merely eliminated but actually reversed. Here, the presence of others is found to enhance performance on the same tasks where a social loafing effect is found in more individualistic western countries (Smith & Bond, 1993). Evidently social facilitation is a function not only of the type of task, but also of the type of relationship existing between the individual, the group they are part of, and any other audience there may be.

These same issues have come to the fore in discussions of what is now known as group polarization. This is an effect occurring when experimental subjects are asked to make a series of group decisions on topics where they have already recorded individual preferences. It is reliably found that the group's decision will be more extreme, in one direction or the other, than the average of the individual group members' choices. Initially it was thought that the phenomenon occurred only with decisions involving risk, and that group decisions were more in favour of risk than was the average of

795

individual decisions. The effect thus became known for a time as the 'risky shift' (Stoner, 1961). However, it was subsequently found that on some decisions the group decision moves toward caution rather than risk, and that the polarization effect occurred on decisions that did not involve risk at all.

Numerous explanations of this effect have been proposed, and it appears that two of them have some validity (Brown, 1986). First, the additional time available to a group to reach their decisions after individual judgements have been made provides opportunities for members to exchange information on what choices others have made. If we presume that there is a socially desirable position that each group member would like to take up, then the exchange of information will reveal to some members that their initial choices are less desirable than they thought. When the topic involves risk and is one on which members would like to be seen as bold and adventurous, those who chose cautiously will move their choice toward risk. On topics where members would rather be seen as prudent and cautious, members who chose the riskiest options will move toward caution. Thus the mere exchange of information about who chose what can induce polarization.

A second explanation of polarization is also tenable (Brown, 1986). In discussion, group members may point out relevant information that others have missed and they may argue persuasively for its importance. Analyses of transcripts of group discussions show that this does occur.

Turner (1991) argues that, in addition to these explanations, polarized decisions are reached because group members wish to define their identity more positively and distinctively, in contrast to members of other groups whom they might expect to take up more average positions. Polarization does indeed become more extreme when groups are informed of the presumed decisions of other groups relevant to them (Doise, 1969).

Although the polarization effect has been of considerable interest to social psychologists, it is of limited practical importance, since it is found in groups where members have not met before and where no group leader is appointed. Where members do already know one another (Semin & Glendon, 1973), or where there is an established leader (Jesuino, 1986), polarization is not always found, and other types of social influence can be presumed to be more potent. Juries do, however, provide a practical instance in which polarization effects are likely to occur.

The interest aroused by the polarization studies most probably occurred because the effect that was found did not concur with the common-sense expectation that groups would make decisions that were close to the average of individuals' views. Had they done so, it would have been considered as an instance of conformity. It may well be that despite the different outcome of polarization studies, polarization and conformity are both explicable in similar ways. In order to consider this possibility we must now examine conformity studies.

CONFORMITY

Conformity is said to occur when group members move their opinions or behaviour towards that of the group's majority view, or else if uniformity already exists within a group. The classic study in this field was that of Asch (1951), who asked subjects to say which of several lines matched the length of a set of stimulus lines that he provided. Asch's experimental accomplices were also asked to make the judgements; although the task was easy, they gave the wrong response on about two-thirds of the trials. An example of one of the sets of lines used is shown in Figure 1. It was found that on around one-third of the crucial trials the experimental subject conformed to the erroneous majority.

It is by no means certain that this type of experiment captures the essence of conformity pressures in everyday social settings. One's judgements of aspects of the physical world such as line lengths may be governed by different factors than are the endorsement of particular attitudes or beliefs. For instance Allen and Levine (1968) showed that when judgements were asked for about matters of belief (such as the population of the United States), the presence of one judge giving correct answers did not inhibit some conformity toward the erroneous majority. In contrast, within the Asch experiments, even one accomplice responding correctly eliminates all conformity to the erroneous majority.

Despite these limitations on the validity of the Asch design, it has proved highly influential, and replications of the effect found have been widely published. Deutsch and Gerard (1955) proposed that there were two elements explaining the Asch effect, which they termed informational and normative social influence. Informational influence occurs in situations of ambiguity, where a person in doubt is likely to use others' responses as guideposts as to what is going on. Normative influence occurs in situations where a person wishes to give a good impression to others, or to avoid some type of sanction. The interviews conducted by Asch with his subjects indicated that both explanations were plausible. Some subjects denied that they had been aware of

Figure 1   An example of the Asch line judgement task: which of the lines on the right matches the one on the left?

797

giving incorrect responses – they had unwittingly used others as marker posts. But other subjects conceded that they had indeed given wrong responses, but had done so for fear of embarrassment from being out of line with everyone else's judgements.

The Asch experiments are frequently misinterpreted. As Friend, Rafferty, and Bramel (1990) point out, Asch actually found that on two-thirds of the judgements his subjects successfully resisted conformity pressures. At least in the case of judgements of unambiguous stimuli, conformity is thus the exception rather than the rule. However, Deutsch and Gerard were able to show that by introducing variations in experimental design, conformity rates would rise and fall in ways that they could predict. For instance, where a team prize was offered for correct responses, conformity rose, presumably because normative pressures were increased.

The explanations for conformity advanced by Deutsch and Gerard are rather similar to some of those put forward by investigators of group polarization. In both cases the exchange of information appears important as does the need of group members to present themselves in ways that gain social approval. Turner's reformulation of the polarization effect in terms of relations between groups rather than just within groups was touched on earlier. Abrams, Wetherell, Cochrane, Hogg, and Turner (1990) show that similar processes can also affect the rates of conformity in Asch-type conformity experiments. They found that information given to subjects as to who were the experimental accomplices giving the false answers made a good deal of difference to conformity rates. The accomplices were always described as fellow-students at a neighbouring prestigious university. However, when they were also stated to be students of psychology, conformity was high, whereas when they were described as students of ancient history, conformity was much lower. As Abrams and colleagues point out, there is no reason to expect that students of history would be any less able to judge line lengths than are students of psychology. The different conformity rates must be attributed to the fact that fellow-students of psychology were seen as more closely linked to the subjects and therefore as a group to which they would want to conform.

The misinterpretation of Asch's findings as showing that members of groups always conform to the majority has also been challenged by another group of researchers, based primarily in France. They argue that under certain circumstances influence may also be exerted by minorities within groups.

MINORITY INFLUENCE

Moscovici (1976) made a re-analysis of Asch's results, and succeeded in showing that conformity rates varied widely depending on the *proportion* of trials on which the accomplices had given incorrect answers. He concluded that in deciding whether or not to conform, subjects were paying attention to the *consistency* of others' judgements. From this point he went on to consider whether we might be influenced by those who made consistent judgements, regardless of whether they were a majority of group members or a minority.

Moscovici then conducted a series of experiments designed to illustrate how group minorities can, over time, change the views of the majority, by giving consistent responses. For instance in a colour judging task, a minority were instructed to consistently describe a blue-green colour as green. It was found that the views of majority subjects as to where the boundary might be drawn between the colours considered to be blue and those considered to be green was moved and that the effect persisted even when further judgements were required after the minority had withdrawn.

Moscovici (1980) subsequently developed his theory further to assert that the manner in which majorities and minorities achieve their influence differs. He proposes that majorities impose their views through a direct process of requiring compliance. On the other hand, minorities achieve their effect more indirectly, but they achieve a more lasting conversion of the majorities' views rather than mere overt compliance.

Findings in favour of minority influence have not always proved replicable, but this may be because Moscovici's complex and provocative hypotheses have several components. For instance, some studies have found that minorities do achieve influence, but only when they are willing to compromise, rather than adopting the consistently deviant position advocated in the original theory (e.g., Nemeth, Swedlund, & Kanki, 1974). It has also been repeatedly shown that the influence achieved by the minority depends on who they are. If they are identified as being similar to members of the majority, they are much more influential than if they differ by, for instance age, gender, or social category (Clark & Maass, 1988).

The studies of minority influence thus show that it is achieved not so much by a particular style of behaviour in the group, but more by a combination of attributes and behaviours that lead others to take note of their views. Whether such influence is more lasting than majority influence, as Moscovici proposed, is not yet clear. It may be that the influence achieved by members of a group derives more from their overall credibility and perceived commitment to the group than from their particular behavioural style or how many allies they have (Turner, 1991). This is nowhere more true than in the case of leaders, which we now consider.

LEADERSHIP

The capacity of one person to influence others has long been a subject of fascination, both popular and academic. While early researchers sought to identify the individual qualities that led particular persons to emerge as group leaders, subsequent attention has been given to the effectiveness of those who are appointed to a formal leadership role, usually within a large organization. Although the majority of such studies have been undertaken in business organizations, we may anticipate that substantially similar issues do also arise within schools, hospitals, universities, prisons, and government organizations.

The effectiveness of a leader at the very top of a large organization may sometimes be assessed on the basis of the whole organization's success. More usually effectiveness has been assessed by looking at the performance of the team or small group for whom the leader is responsible.

This shift of attention from leadership emergence to leadership effectiveness means that leadership study can no longer be thought of as the study of *all* kinds of social influence exerted by a single individual in a group, but only of those achievable by someone appointed or elected to a leadership role. Other types of influence by a single individual will certainly also occur in groups and these will be addressed in the rest of this chapter.

Obedience

The legitimacy accorded to someone's right to command others, simply because he or she has been appointed to a leadership role, was vividly illustrated by the work of Milgram (1974). Milgram created a situation in which experimental subjects found that they were being asked to administer what appeared to be increasingly dangerous levels of electric shocks to another person, as part of a programme of psychological research. Around two-thirds of his experimental subjects none the less continued to obey their instructions, right up to a level of shock that would in fact endanger life. These findings from the United States have been repeated in seven other countries (Smith & Bond, 1993), and are often used to illustrate the dangers of dictatorial or unscrupulous leadership. However, both Milgram and those who made similar studies in Germany, The Netherlands, and Australia found that under some circumstances obedience fell almost to zero. This happened when other experimental accomplices in the experimental setting refused to carry out their part in the administration of the shocks. In other words, the obedience demanded of the subjects was obtained only when there were no other dissenting group members present. Just as the studies of group polarization find effects that are much attenuated when a leader is present, so do the obedience studies find effects that are much weakened when other group members are present.

If we are to understand the effects attributable to leadership, we must therefore give most attention to settings in which both leaders and group members are actually present.

Leadership style

Leadership theorists have frequently attempted to identify particular patterns of leadership behaviour that are associated with successful team performance. In the early part of the twentieth century it was believed that such patterns, or leadership traits, were inborn qualities. The optimism of the 1950s and 1960s suggested instead that one could train leaders to adopt the styles of behaviour that were found to be most effective. A variety of leader styles were identified, many of them influenced by the distinction between an authoritarian or task-centred style and a more democratic or person-centred style.

Extensive research at the University of Michigan, for instance, provided an empirical base for the "human relations" school of management theorizing (Likert, 1961). By conducting surveys in a wide variety of organizations it was found that the supervisors of high-performing teams were perceived as more "employee-oriented", spending more time on planning and training and less on checking up on their teams. The breadth of data collected by the Michigan researchers was impressive, but its principal weakness lay in the fact that it all came from field surveys. As in the case of other types of correlational study, one cannot be sure whether there is a causal link between two variables found to be correlated. Subsequent researchers were able to show in laboratory experiments that by instructing workers who were experimental accomplices to work either slow or fast, it was quite possible to elicit different styles of leadership from their supervisors. So for instance in the Likert findings, the fact that a supervisor checked up less often on a particular team might not be the cause of that team's high performance, but rather a consequence of the fact that the supervisor already knew that this was a high-performing, trustworthy team.

Contingency theories

A second difficulty with the identification of effective leader styles has been that different research groups came up with differing answers as to which were the most effective styles. Several theorists have attempted to cope with this dilemma by formulating what have become known as contingency theories. These theories attempt to specify which type of leadership environment requires what style of leadership behaviour. The best known of these was Fiedler's (1967) theory, in which he proposed that the situations where leaders operated could be rank ordered in terms of their favourability in permitting the leader to exert influence.

In Fiedler's original model, the most favourable setting was one in which team members liked the leader, the task was a structured one and the leader's position carried the right to exert substantial power. Later, he acknowledged that other factors may also influence the favourability of the leader's situation. In contrast to the Michigan researchers, Fiedler believes that leaders have relatively poor capacity to modify their leadership styles, and that therefore the optimal procedure is to diagnose the leader's style, and ensure their placement in the type of setting where that style is effective (Fiedler & Chemers, 1984). His "LPC" measure of style uses a series of ratings completed by the leader, which evaluate the worst subordinate he or she has ever worked with. As one might expect, a more authoritarian or task-oriented leader tends to rate such a person negatively, whereas a more participative or relationship-oriented leader gives more moderate ratings. However, it appears that high and low LPC leaders' behaviour does in fact vary somewhat, depending on the situation in which they find themselves (Smith & Peterson, 1988). The predictions of Fiedler's theory are shown in Figure 2.

Both the validity of Fiedler's measure of leader style, and the capacity of his model to specify situation favourability have been strongly criticized (Schriesheim & Kerr, 1977). Despite this, the theory continues to attract adherents and Fiedler has progressively improved it by examining the contribution of additional leader qualities such as intelligence and prior experience (Fiedler & Garcia, 1987).

A second contingency theory of leadership is that advanced by Vroom and Yetton (1973). These authors see leaders as able to select the leadership style required for any particular specific decision. Their theory comes in the form of a series of questions a manager may ask as to the attributes of the

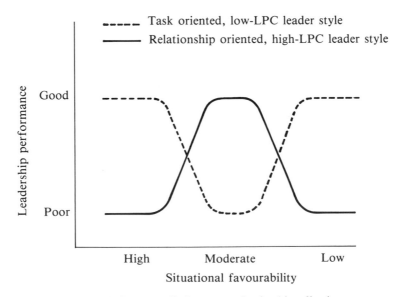

Figure 2 Fiedler's predictions as to leadership effectiveness

particular decision to be taken. Depending on answers to seven questions, the model will prescribe an appropriate style, ranging from autocratic decision-making to full team participation. Tests of the model have shown that where managers used the prescribed style, decisions are usually more effective (Vroom & Jago, 1988).

Rethinking the question: what is leadership?

Contingency theories were mostly formulated some time ago, and have not gained increasing adherence with the passage of time. In order to consider why this might be so, we must reflect on the overall changes occurring within the field of psychology since the early 1970s. From being a predominantly behaviourist enterprise, psychology has increasingly turned to investigating cognitive processes. From this perspective, it is easy to see that many of the conceptions of leadership held by theorists have been implicitly behaviourist. Leadership has been seen as something that a leader does to a subordinate, much in the way that behaviourists thought of stimuli as evoking responses. But thinking about relations between leaders and subordinates in this manner requires a great many simplifications of what happens in practical settings. As was noted earlier, subordinates are well able to influence their leaders. By working faster or slower, they can evoke predictable responses from their superiors. Thus, the leader's relation to the group must be thought of as a two-way rather than a one-way influence process. Attention is therefore required not only to the effects of a precise-sounding "leader style", but also to the manner in which leaders and their subordinates interpret the meaning of one another's actions. In line with this, many studies have explored such issues as how leaders choose between different possible responses to a subordinate who is, for instance, late for work or who does poor work.

A second simplification that leadership theorists have often found necessary can also be linked to the predominant emphases of psychology as a whole. Just as researchers in many fields sought to control extraneous influences by creating precisely defined experimental conditions, so leadership theorists have mostly examined only the links between leaders and their immediate subordinates. In practice, of course, leaders devote substantial amounts of time to their links with their own superiors, relevant colleagues and many others within and sometimes outside the organization in which they work. Long ago, Pelz (1951) showed that leaders' effectiveness as judged by their subordinates was strongly related to how well the leaders got on with their own superiors. Likert (1961) formulated what he termed a "linking pin theory" of leadership, which emphasised the leader's importance in linking the different groups within a large organization. Later theorists have developed this notion and reformulated the concept of leadership to emphasize the manner in which leader effectiveness can be thought of as the successful management of the conflicting needs and demands of the "role set" (Graen

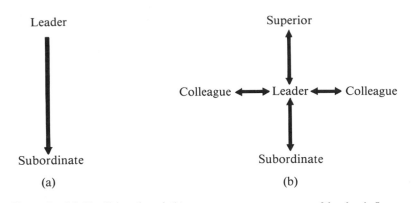

Figure 3 (a) Traditional and (b) contemporary patterns of leader influence

& Cashman, 1975; Smith & Peterson, 1988). The role set comprises all those people who make demands on the occupant of a particular role. This changing emphasis of leadership study is illustrated in Figure 3.

Such a reformulation provides a much more realistic model of the behaviour of leaders in organizations, but it poses additional problems for researchers. If we acknowledge that the different members of a leader's role set each have valid demands that they wish to make on the leader, how do we evaluate the leader's effectiveness? Since the various demands are likely to be at least partially incompatible, the various possible sources of evaluation are likely to give us different answers. Tsui's (1984) study of Californian managers showed that this problem was not insuperable. There was in fact some consensus among her sample of role set members as to which were the most effective managers.

Even though Tsui found that role set members may to some extent agree as to a leader's effectiveness or ineffectiveness, it is not likely that the leader will be displaying the same leader style toward them all. Once we relinquish the myth that leaders relate only to their subordinates we need to examine a fuller range of ways in which leaders might influence others around them.

CLASSIFICATION OF SOCIAL INFLUENCE STRATEGIES

French and Raven (1959) proposed that there are basically five ways in which we might influence one another. Later versions have added a sixth (Raven & Rubin, 1983). The classification provides three bases for distinguishing forms of social influence. First, it separates influence that depends on a continuing relationship with the influencing agent from that which does not. Second, it distinguishes influence based on continuing surveillance by the influence agent from that which is not. Finally, it distinguishes influence in the intended direction from that in which the effect is the opposite of that intended. A simplified version of the classification of these types is shown in Figure 4.

If we consider the application of the Raven-Rubin model to influence with a leader's role set, there are clearly some bases for influence that are available to a leader only for influencing subordinates. In particular, coercive power and legitimate power fall into this category. The power to coerce and to reward, and the legitimate right to give orders to subordinates, are inherent in the role definition of many appointed and elected leaders, although the use of these powers cannot necessarily be relied on to maximize leader effectiveness. However, in dealing with organizational colleagues and superiors, leaders must perforce rely mainly on the remaining three bases of influence. The term referent power describes influence based on the other's liking for oneself. Although such influence is no doubt widespread within (and outside of) organizations it is less likely to be openly acknowledged than is influence based on the provision of information and the demonstration of expertise.

The Raven and Rubin typology of social power has proved rather attractive to researchers, who have sought to delineate how widely each of the bases of social influence is employed in different settings. Unfortunately the questionnaire employed in many of these studies has major deficiencies (Podsakoff & Schriesheim, 1985). It yields scores that imply that the more one basis of influence is used, the less are the other bases used. Consequently, these studies do not provide reliable estimates of the frequencies of different types of social influence. However, Kipnis, Schmidt, and Wilkinson (1980) developed an alternative instrument (the "Profile of Organizational Influence Strategies") in which managers are asked to describe their influence strategies and with whom they use which strategy. These researchers distinguish seven types of influence: friendliness, reason, assertiveness, coalitions, higher authority, bargaining, and sanctions. Some of these overlap the Raven-Rubin model, but the inclusion of reason, bargaining, and the forming of coalitions

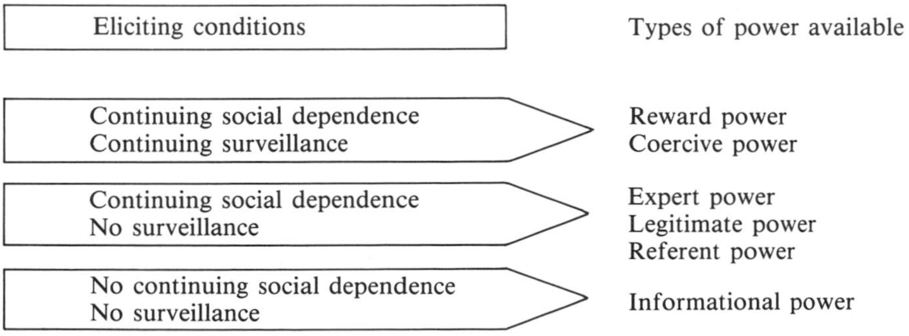

Eliciting conditions	Types of power available
Continuing social dependence Continuing surveillance	Reward power Coercive power
Continuing social dependence No surveillance	Expert power Legitimate power Referent power
No continuing social dependence No surveillance	Informational power

Figure 4 Raven and Rubin's typology of social influence processes

underlines the range of strategies likely to be used in influencing colleagues and superiors.

The formulation of these typologies thus represents an advance over the earlier excessive reliance on measures of leader style, because they allow for a rather fuller range of possibilities than those embedded in the style measures. It is of course plausible that leaders frequently also influence their subordinates through, for instance, reasoning with them and through the exercise of expertise, rather than through direct reliance on the powers given to them by those who appointed them. If this is so, then it becomes easier to see continuities between the results of traditional studies of leadership, and the rather broader range of studies that have looked at social influence in settings outside of organizations.

SOCIAL INFLUENCE IN INFORMAL SETTINGS

Christie and Geis (1970) attempted to analyse the techniques used by those who proved influential in informal and unstructured settings. For instance, they assembled groups of three and placed ten dollars on the table. They then stated that any two of the three people present could have the money, once they had agreed how the money would be divided between them. By definition, the third person got nothing. The experimental subjects who prospered under circumstances such as these were those whom Christie and Geis termed Machiavellians. Drawing on the prescriptions of the Renaissance master of intrigue and diplomacy, Machiavelli, they devised a questionnaire, which they named the "Mach" scale. This was intended to distinguish those who would behave in an equally ruthless manner within their experimental setting. As predicted, high Mach scorers did particularly well in gaining a large share of the money on the table. While Christie and Geis were thus successful in identifying Machiavellians, they did rather less well in identifying exactly what it was that they did that contributed to their success. Having examined Machiavellian behaviour in a dozen experiments they conclude that Machiavellian skill lies not so much in what is done as in the timing of Machiavellians' actions. The situations in which Machiavellians were found to do well were those in which people meet face-to-face, improvisation is at a premium, and the situation arouses what Christie and Geis call "irrelevant affect". Presumably the irrelevant affect experienced by low Machiavellians in the ten-dollar game would have to do with the unfairness of the third party getting nothing.

The exercise of Machiavellian skills is certainly not absent from life within many formal organizations, but the circumstances in which it is likely to be most favoured occur in more transient situations. Cialdini (1988) reviews social influence strategies in situations involving the selling of a product. Drawing on the findings of cognitive psychologists concerning the "mindlessness" of many of our everyday actions (Langer, 1978), he shows how salespeople are sometimes able to manipulate customers who are not on their guard. He proposes that influence can occur in any of six ways.

First, a salesperson may rely on the norm of reciprocity. By giving a free sample or a free survey of one's house, a sense of indebtedness is instilled, which the purchaser may feel should be repaid. Second, if the salesperson can obtain a small initial commitment, the purchaser will be more willing to make a greater commitment later. This "foot-in-the-door" effect was demonstrated experimentally by Freedman and Fraser (1966). Third, "social proof" may be drawn on, to establish that a product or service is good. This would be done through inviting conformity with the habits of others whom one might wish to emulate.

The fourth and fifth strategies rest on the findings established by leadership researchers and others that people accept influence from those whom they like and whom they see as authoritative. Salespeople therefore seek to establish their attractiveness, expertise, and similarity to the purchaser. Researchers into the process of ingratiation have identified some of the ways in which this may be done (Jones, 1964). For instance, ingratiators may compliment their target persons, emphasize the similarity of their views, and conceal their intentions to be influential. Pandey (1986) found that the ingratiation tactics favoured in India differed somewhat from Jones's US results. Name dropping and denigrating oneself were among the strategies favoured. Studies of the ways in which US managers exert upward influence over their own bosses also suggest that where reasoned argument fails many of these tactics of ingratiation will be employed (Porter, Allen, & Angle, 1981).

Finally, Cialdini (1988) points out that we frequently respond positively to the information that a product is scarce, forbidden, or about to be withdrawn.

Cialdini's list of types of influence strategy may be compared with those obtained by Kipnis et al. (1980) within organizations. There is clearly substantial overlap, but there are differences also. These may stem from the more transient relationship that some types of salesperson are likely to have with their customers. To the extent that a salesperson is concerned about maintaining the long-term satisfaction of customers, the range of available influence strategies will become increasingly similar to those found in organizations. Where a quick sale is all that counts, we may expect greatest use of Machiavellian strategies, such as those based on the creation of spurious indebtedness, the foot-in-the-door, and the exaggeration of scarcity.

Whatever effectiveness such sales techniques have rests on the fact that a sale is concluded on the spot. Where influence effectiveness is measured by its effect on longer-term behaviour, rates of compliance are likely to be very much weaker. Even in situations where an influence agent has substantial authority and expertise, they may not be very influential. For instance Ley (1982) has shown that less than half of the instructions given by doctors to take medicines or to modify behaviour in particular ways are subsequently carried out by the patients who consulted them.

CHARISMA

Our exploration of the diversity of influence strategies has left to one side a contrasting development in the study of leadership. The nineteenth-century sociologist Max Weber saw charisma as one possible basis for the influential powers of leaders. He saw charisma as an almost magical or religiously endowed quality through which certain leaders communicated a vision of the future or of the good life to their followers.

Some theorists of leadership have given new life to this concept (Bryman, 1992; Conger & Kanungo, 1988). Contrary to role-set theorists, who might seem to be arguing that all influence in organizations is to be thought of as leadership, these authors rely on the argument that leadership must be distinguished from management. Management is seen as routine administration, while the term leadership is reserved for those acts of influence that seek to create change and innovation. Such acts are more likely to be found at the very top of large organizations, or governments. It is suggested that effective leadership in this sense requires the types of charismatic skills that Weber had in mind. Case studies of some of the most charismatic business leaders are widely available (Bryman, 1992).

A somewhat different approach has been taken by Bass (1985), who has developed a questionnaire measure of perceived charismatic leader style. Bass sees charisma as having potential importance for leaders at all levels in organisations, not just at the top. However, all the current theorists of charisma would agree that the crucial distinction between their approach and earlier studies of leader style is that charismatic leaders establish an intense emotional bond with their followers that rests on a mutually shared vision. This contrasts with the earlier conception of leader style as a means of one-way downward influence, but it leaves relatively unexamined the manner in which the two-way bond is established.

SOCIAL INFLUENCE AS NEGOTIATION

The approaches to influence discussed earlier in this chapter imply that whether we are considering charisma, the way in which managers respond to their role set, or the activities of salespeople, it may be useful to think of all types of social influence as types of negotiation. Use of the word "negotiation" immediately implies that the process being considered is a two-way process. The type of negotiation implicit in influence need not entail overt bargaining, but will involve each party responding to the prior behaviours of the other. Hosking and Morley (1992) present an analysis of this kind, focused on the "social psychology of organizing". For them, the essence of social influence is the negotiation of what they call "order", by which term they mean a shared interpretation of events. Within this perspective, the manner in which all of the types of social influence surveyed in this chapter achieve their effect is by one or both parties changing the meaning they give to an event or an action. This can include the decision of an experimental subject as to the length of a line, the decision of a purchaser that something is worth buying, and the agreement between organization members as to how to handle a particular event. The virtue of this approach is that it offers to unify what has become a diverse field of inquiry, but it can do so only conceptually. If we wish to specify whether some participants in the negotiation of order are likely to be more powerful than others, then we must return to the issues addressed throughout this chapter. In their differing ways, each group of researchers has made proposals as to what it is that makes some of us more powerful or persuasive than others.

FURTHER READING

Bryman, A. (1992). *Charisma and leadership in organizations*. London: Sage.
Cialdini, R. B. (1988). *Influence: Science and practice*. Glenview, IL: Scott, Foresman.
Fiedler, F. E., & Garcia, J. E. (1987). *New approaches to effective leadership: Cognitive resources and organizational performance*. New York: Wiley.
Smith, P. B., & Peterson, M. F. (1988). *Leadership, organizations and culture*. London: Sage.
Turner, J. C. (1991). *Social influence*. Milton Keynes: Open University Press.

REFERENCES

Abrams, D., Wetherell, M., Cochrane, S., Hogg, M., & Turner, J. C. (1990). Knowing what to think by knowing who you are: Self-categorisation and the nature of norm formation, conformity and group polarisation. *British Journal of Social Psychology*, *29*, 97–119.
Allen, V., & Levine, J. M (1968). Social support, dissent and conformity. *Sociometry*, *31*, 138–149.
Asch, S. (1951). Effects of group pressure upon the modification and distortion of judgments. In H. Guetzkow (Ed.) *Groups, leadership and men* (pp. 177–190). Pittsburgh, PA: Carnegie.
Bass, B. M. (1985). *Leadership and performance beyond expectations*. New York: Free Press.
Brickner, M. A., Ostrom, T. M., & Harkins, S. G. (1986). Effects of personal involvement: Thought-provoking implications for social loafing. *Journal of Personality and Social Psychology*, *51*, 763–769.
Brown, R. (1986). *Social psychology: The second edition*. New York: Free Press.
Bryman, A. (1992). *Charisma and leadership in organizations*. London: Sage.
Christie, R., & Geis, F. (1970). *Studies in Machiavellianism*. New York: Academic Press.
Cialdini, R. B. (1988). *Influence: Science and practice*. Glenview, IL: Scott, Foresman.

Clark, R. D., & Maass, A. (1988). The role of social categorisation and perceived source credibility in minority influence. *European Journal of Social Psychology*, *18*, 381–394.

Conger, J. A., & Kanungo, R. N. (Eds) (1988). *Charismatic leadership: The elusive factor in organizational effectiveness*. San Francisco, CA: Jossey-Bass.

Deutsch, M., & Gerard, H. B. (1955). A study of normative and informational social influence. *Journal of Abnormal and Social Psychology*, *51*, 629–636.

Doise, W. (1969). Intergroup relations and polarization of individual and collective judgments. *Journal of Personality and Social Psychology*, *12*, 136–143.

Fiedler, F. E. (1967). *A theory of leadership effectiveness*. New York: McGraw-Hill.

Fiedler, F. E., & Chemers, M. (1984). *Improving leadership effectiveness: The leader match concept*. New York: Wiley.

Fiedler, F. E., & Garcia, J. E. (1987). *New approaches to effective leadership: Cognitive resources and organizational performance*. New York: Wiley.

Freedman, J. L., & Fraser, S. C. (1966). Compliance without pressure: The foot-in-the-door technique. *Journal of Personality and Social Psychology*, *4*, 195–202.

French, J. R. P., & Raven, B. H. (1959). The bases of social power. In D. Cartwright (Ed.) *Studies in social power* (pp. 150–167). Ann Arbor, MI: Institute for Social Research, University of Michigan.

Friend, R., Rafferty, Y., & Bramel, D. (1990). A puzzling misinterpretation of the Asch "conformity" study. *European Journal of Social Psychology*, *20*, 29–44.

Graen, G. B., & Cashman, J. F. (1975). A role-making model of leadership in formal organizations. In J. G. Hunt & L. L. Larson (Eds) *Leadership frontiers* (pp. 143–165). Kent, OH: Kent State University Press.

Hosking, D. M., & Morley, I. (1992). *The social psychology of organising*. London: Sage.

Jesuino, J. (1986). Influence of leadership processes on group polarisation. *European Journal of Social Psychology*, *16*, 413–424.

Jones, E. E. (1964). *Ingratiation: A social psychological analysis*. New York: Appleton-Century-Crofts.

Kipnis, D., Schmidt, S. M., & Wilkinson, I. (1980). Intraorganizational influence tactics: Explorations in getting one's way. *Journal of Applied Psychology*, *65*, 440–452.

Kravitz, D. A., & Martin B. (1986). Ringelmann rediscovered: The original article. *Journal of Personality and Social Psychology*, *50*, 936–941.

Langer, E. (1978). Rethinking the role of thought in social interaction. In J. H. Harvey, W. J. Ickes, & R. F. Kidd (Eds) *New directions in attribution research* (vol. 2, pp. 35–58). New York: Halstead.

Latané, B., Williams, K., & Harkins, S. G. (1979). Many hands make light work: The causes and consequences of social loafing. *Journal of Personality and Social Psychology*, *37*, 822–832.

Ley, P. (1982). Satisfaction, compliance and communication. *British Journal of Clinical Psychology*, *21*, 241–254.

Likert, R. (1961). *New patterns of management*. New York: McGraw-Hill.

Milgram, S. (1974). *Obedience to authority*. New York: Harper & Row.

Moscovici, S. (1976). *Social influence and social change*. London: Academic Press.

Moscovici, S. (1980). Towards a theory of conversion behavior. In L. Berkowitz (Ed.) *Advances in experimental social psychology*, *13*, 209–239.

Nemeth, C., Swedlund, M., & Kanki, B. (1974). Patterning of the minority's responses and their influence on the majority. *European Journal of Social Psychology*, *4*, 53–64.

Pandey, J. (1986). Sociocultural perspectives on ingratiation. In B. A. Maher & W. B. Maher (Eds) *Progress in experimental personality research*, *14*, 205–229.

Pelz, D. C. (1951). Leadership within a hierarchical organisation. *Journal of Social Issues*, *7*, 49–55.

Podsakoff, P. M., & Schriesheim, C. A. (1985). Field studies of French and Raven's bases of social power: Critique, reanalysis and suggestions for future research. *Psychological Bulletin*, *97*, 387–411.

Porter, L. W., Allen, R. W., & Angle, H. L. (1981). The politics of upward influence in organizations. In L. L. Cummings & B. M. Staw (Eds) *Research in Organizational Behavior*, *3*, 109–149.

Raven, B. H., & Rubin, J. Z. (1983). *Social psychology*. New York: Wiley.

Schriesheim, C. A., & Kerr, S. (1977). Theories and measures of leadership: A critical appraisal of current and future directions. In J. G. Hunt & L. L. Larson (Eds) *Leadership: The cutting edge* (pp. 9–45). Carbondale, IL: Southern Illinois University Press.

Semin, G., & Glendon, A. (1973). Polarisation and the established group. *British Journal of Social and Clinical Psychology*, *12*, 113–121.

Smith, P. B., & Bond, M. H. (1993). *Social psychology across cultures: Analysis and perspectives*. Hemel Hempstead: Harvester-Wheatsheaf.

Smith, P. B., & Peterson, M. F. (1988). *Leadership, organizations and culture*. London: Sage.

Stoner, J. A. F. (1961). *A comparison of individual and group decisions involving risk*. Unpublished master's thesis, Massachusetts Institute of Technology.

Tsui, A. S. (1984). A role set analysis of managerial reputation. *Organizational Behavior and Human Performance*, *34*, 64–96.

Turner, J. C. (1991). *Social influence*. Milton Keynes: Open University Press.

Vroom, V. H., & Jago, A. (1988). *The new leadership: Managing participation in organizations*. Englewood Cliffs, NJ: Prentice-Hall.

Vroom, V. H., & Yetton, P. W. (1973). *Leadership and decision-making*. Pittsburgh, PA: University of Pittsburgh Press.

Zajonc, R. B. (1965). Social facilitation. *Science*, *149*, 269–274.

9.3

ATTRIBUTION AND SOCIAL COGNITION

David J. Schneider

Rice University, Texas, USA

Social cognition may be defined as the study of how people understand their social worlds. It is, in short, the cognition of people, their behaviour, and the settings in which that behaviour occurs. This definition is broad enough to encompass all social cognition research and theory, but it is also vague. What exactly does social cognition cover?

It first concerns the perception of people, what has traditionally been called person perception (Schneider, Hastorf, & Ellsworth, 1979). There are three classic person perception problems. First, how do we interpret and describe the behaviour of self and others (attribution); more specifically, what do we infer about people from behaviour and whatever other information we may have? Second, how do we integrate that information into a coherent whole. Third, are our perceptions and inferences about others accurate?

The field of person perception has deep roots in social psychology; there has been speculation about our perceptions of self and others as long as there has been social analysis. Person perception reached its high flowering during the period from 1950 to 1980, and it was especially nourished by developments surrounding attribution theory, to be discussed shortly. Since the 1980s, however, the traditional areas of person perception have more or less been supplanted by what is called social cognition. Social cognition differs from the older field of person perception less in terms of phenomena under investigation as in the approach (see Fiske & Taylor, 1991; Ostrom, 1984; Schneider, 1991 for contrasting views).

Traditional person perception tended to take its lead from the larger area of social psychology which was concerned with the content of our thoughts about others on the reasonable assumption that this would help predict our behaviours toward them. Early studies dealt with the accuracy of our inferences about others, with factors affecting the evaluative nature of impressions, with how impressions were organized, with whether causes of behaviour were internal or external. That is not to say that process considerations were ignored, but only that they tended to be the tail wagged by the dog of emphasis on what people thought.

Social cognition, on the other hand, reverses this relative emphasis by focusing more heavily on how information is processed. Whereas inferences of evaluative traits or specific attributions used to be the dependent measures of choice, in the present day memory, reaction time, and other microscopically oriented process measures are favoured. That is in part because social cognition tends to ally itself with the larger field of cognitive psychology to such an extent that it is often quite impossible to know where one begins and the other leaves off. In this chapter we first discuss classic perception issues, and then we shall summarize some of the approaches taken by social cognition research.

ACCURACY

EMOTIONS

Whether people can be and are accurate in their perceptions of others is an obvious problem, and it was the first intensively studied issue in the person perception area. Early studies on accuracy of perception of emotional expression were stimulated by Darwin's speculations that emotional expression is evolutionarily determined and hence "hard-wired"; thus emotional expression should be cross-culturally invariant and presumably easily recognized. Early studies in this area (see Schneider et al., 1979) often found that people could not even agree on the precise labels to attach to emotional expression's let alone judge them accurately, but more careful contemporary work (Ekman & Friesen, 1975) has generally found a high degree of both agreement among perceivers and accuracy for six basic emotions (sadness, happiness, anger, fear, disgust, and surprise) judged from standard stimuli. That is not to suggest that every person conveys anger in exactly the same way or that all ways of expressing anger are easily recognized. Also some less central emotions such as wonderment or bewilderment or blends of emotions such as the horror and curiosity that might accompany seeing a grisly accident, may not be easily recognized. However, there are standard expressions of standard emotions, and these are easily recognized, as common sense would suggest.

TRAITS

Early studies of accuracy of perceptions of personality were also not particularly promising (Taft, 1955). In addition, it is now widely recognized that two major methodological problems plague this area. The first identified by Cronbach (1955) deals with the measurement of accuracy. Cronbach showed that when we measure accuracy as a departure of perceivers' judgements from a criterion (say, ratings of target's introversion), the differences may be due to many factors. For example, some perceivers may be inaccurate because they see everyone as being too introverted although they correctly see that Joseph is more introverted than Doris, who is in turn more introverted than Terry. Another perceiver might be quite accurate in the sense that she correctly sees that people are, on average, moderately introverted but cannot do a good job of discriminating how introverted individual targets are. Who is the more accurate? Simply calculating accuracy as a discrepancy of prediction from criterion might make the second perceiver more accurate, simply because her judgements are more in the "right ballpark", even though she doesn't have a clue as to which of several people is the more introverted. This does not seem quite right. Thus, there are many land-mines in the measurement of accuracy.

A second problem has come to be called the criterion problem (Schneider et al., 1979). How do we know how much hostility, self-esteem, extraversion, and so on people really have, especially when expression of these traits is likely to vary considerably over situations and encounters with individual perceivers? Not only do we not have objective, perfectly clear measures of traits such as introversion, but also most of us vary in how introverted we are from situation to situation.

For these and other reasons accuracy research declined during the 1960s and 1970s. However, during the 1980s, the area got a new lease on life. Swann (1984), Funder (1987), and others argued that people can be accurate if given a clear criterion (often behavioural) and rich information about the people they are judging. One interesting line of research shows that people tend to be more accurate for traits that are highly visible (e.g., extraversion) than for those which are less immediately visible (e.g., emotional stability) (Park & Judd, 1989; Watson, 1989).

ATTRIBUTION

THE CLASSIC HEIDER MODEL

Attribution theory deals with how we attribute traits, motives, and abilities to people from observations of their behaviour. Since the late 1960s, attribution models have been investigated extensively within social psychology and have been applied to problems not only in social psychology but also in clinical, personality, and developmental psychology.

Attribution theory was first proposed by Fritz Heider (1958). However, his version of the theory was not especially amenable to experimental test; it is unlikely that the theory would have become a dominating force in modern social cognition and social psychology more generally without "translations" by Jones & Davis (1965) and Kelley (1967). Heider's original formulation focused on how we attribute the causes of behaviour. In an analogy with the world of physical causality, he noted that objects behave the ways they do because of the joint influence of their own qualities that *dispose* them to behave in certain ways (dispositional qualities) and environmental forces. For example, the roundness of balls disposes them to roll when pushed, and the mass of large buildings does not dispose them to roll when force is applied. On the other hand, rubber balls may simply compress or disintegrate when a huge force is applied, whereas a tall building would sway. Heider argued that people are also disposed to behave in particular ways when various kinds of forces are applied to them. The dispositional properties of some people make them violent in the face of frustration while others would just cry. But even people who are dispositionally violent do not always hit and abuse; there must be a precipitating external force.

These two kinds of forces, sometimes called internal and external (mirroring an earlier distinction by Heider's friend, Kurt Lewin, between own and induced forces), must both be present for behaviour to occur. However, in a given situation, a perceiver may see behaviour as caused relatively more by one force or another. The behaviour of a violent criminal is likely to be seen as caused by dispositional forces ("He is a violent person"), whereas the ritualized behaviour of a groom at his wedding is more likely to be seen as caused by strong situational forces. So long as we remember that both kinds of forces are necessary for behaviour, it makes a certain amount of sense to see some behaviours as internally or dispositionally caused and others as having been influenced more by the situation. Roughly this corresponds to the common distinction between "She did it because she wanted to" vs "She did it because she had to".

The internal–external cause distinction is important because it allows us to predict and sometimes control the behaviour of others. If I know you are generally kind, I can predict that you will respond to my request for a loan favourably. However, if I know that you are kind only when you are in a good mood or when you are approached with a particularly strong external request, I may try to work on these external factors before hitting you up.

KELLEY'S MODEL

Types of information

The essential question of attribution theory is how we make those discriminations. Harold Kelley's (1967) theory has been the most influential guide. He argued that people look at three forms of information. Given that a person has performed a discrete behaviour or had a particular reaction (which is Kelley's starting-point), *consensus information* refers to how many other people performed the same behaviour. In other words, how unusual is the behaviour? If Janice orders fish at the restaurant (the *behaviour*), and most other people do the same, we would say that the consensus information for that behaviour is high. Conversely if she orders fish and is the only person to do so, consensus is low. Second, we might ask how consistent her behaviour is. Does she always order seafood in this restaurant? If so, the behaviour is consistent (high *consistency*), and if not her behaviour is inconsistent with past behaviour. Finally, we might ask about Janice's behaviour in other situations. Does she always order seafood, even when not in a seafood restaurant? Does she often buy fish at the local market. If her ordering seafood is restricted to this particular restaurant, her behaviour is distinctive (high *distinctiveness*), but if she shows a behavioural fondness for seafood in many situations, the distinctiveness of her present behaviour is low.

When one combines these three kinds of information, there are eight possible combinations. However, only two are directly relevant to the distinction between internal and external causality. According to Kelley internal, dispositional attributions (what he calls actor attributions) ought to be particularly high with a pattern of low consensus (Janice is the only person who orders fish), low distinctiveness (she almost always orders seafood wherever she is), and high consistency (she almost always orders fish at this restaurant). Janice must really love fish, and consequently she is disposed to order it. Conversely with high consensus (everyone orders fish), high distinctiveness (Janice almost never orders fish elsewhere), and high consistency (she always orders fish here), we would tend to think that Janice's behaviour is controlled mostly externally, by the situation – the fish is good.

Criticisms

This model has generated hundreds of empirical studies that confirm it in broad outline, but we might argue that it is unnecessarily complex. It requires that people have access to three different kinds of information and think in terms of patterns of information. Surely that is a bit too much to ask of people who, after all, must form their attributions on the fly and often without much reflection. A group of psychologists influenced by Jaspars (1983) has suggested that people really respond more simply.

The most fully worked out such model is that of Hilton and Slugoski (1986). They argue that each type of information is coordinated with a particular kind of attribution. For example, consensus information affects primarily internal attributions, distinctiveness information plays a major role in situation attributions, and consistency affects attributions to circumstance. People then make attributions to the information that seems to stand out, to be abnormal in the context. So if Janice is the only person to order fish, she stands out and the attribution will be to her dispositions. Conversely, if she orders fish only at this restaurant and never eats it elsewhere, the attribution would be to the restaurant and its way of fixing fish. The *abnormal conditions model* has the virtue of being simple, and it generally predicts attributions at least as well, and often better, than the more complex Kelley model.

Many other factors beyond those identified by Kelley affect the attribution process. For example, some traits and behaviours, typically those that are active, tend to be seen as dispositionally caused whereas emotional reactions tend to be seen as more often caused by external stimuli (Fiedler & Semin, 1988; Van Kleeck, Hillger, & Brown, 1988). Also the kinds of attributions that we make are highly sensitive to conversational norms and to what we assume other people know (McGill, 1989; Turnbull & Slugoski, 1988); "Why did John shout?" will be answered differently depending on whether these contextual factors focus attention on why John shouted as opposed to Jim, or why John shouted instead of leaving the situation.

ATTRIBUTIONAL BIAS

One problem with traditional attribution models has been that perceivers do not always follow them closely. It is not merely that predictions from the models do not always "come out"; if that were the case we might simply say that the models were wrong. Rather, the violations of the models tend to be systematic and biased. One kind of bias has been called egocentric; sometimes we attribute our behaviour and the behaviour of others in self-serving ways. For example, I may decide that poor student performance on my exams is due to their laziness or stupidity rather than to my poor teaching.

Such bias does occur (Hewstone, 1989), but the bias that has received the most research attention has been the tendency to downplay information about the situational causes of behaviour; this leads us to see the behaviour of others as less determined by situational forces that it should be, whereas own behaviour is more often seen as situationally determined (Jones & Nisbett, 1972). In general we assign too much dispositional impact to the behaviour of others, a feature that has come to be known as the fundamental attribution error.

Perhaps the most provocative explanation of this comes from Daniel Gilbert. Following research of Uleman and his students (Newman & Uleman, 1989) and of Trope (1986), Gilbert (1989) argues that perceivers first identify a bit of behaviour ("a kind act"), and then more or less automatically assume a dispositional explanation ("It was committed by a kind person"). Subsequently the perceiver may correct this dispositional inference by recognizing that everyone else in the situation also behaved kindly or that more generally there were strong situational forces encouraging kind behaviour. However, this correction requires some thought and can easily be disrupted by other demands on the person's thought processes. So in practice we often fail to perform the correction stage properly, and as a result we tend to see people as stronger authors of their behaviour than we ought.

INFORMATION INTEGRATION

After determining what other people are like, perceivers must integrate that diverse information about them. Sometimes this information is extended in time as when we observe the target's behaviour over a lengthy period. Sometimes the information is simultaneously presented as when we take into account information about what a person is saying as well as how she is saying it, her facial expressions, and the like.

THE WEIGHTED AVERAGING MODEL

Information weighting and averaging

While various models for how this information is integrated have been proposed, the most popular was proposed by Norman Anderson (1981), who argues that judgements are weighted averages of incoming information. So just as a final grade in a course is some average of all the exam, paper, and other grades accumulated throughout the course, so judgements about people's traits, likeability, job suitability, and so on, are assumed to be averages of relevant behaviours and other information. If I am trying to determine whether Jon will make a good research assistant, I may take into account his grades in classes, his demeanour, my observations of whether he shows up for appointments on time, even how he dresses.

Further, just as in a course some grades count more than others, so in life some kinds of information are seen as more diagnostic or important. In deciding about Jon, I might, for example, give more weight to behavioural information about his conscientiousness than to his dress or whether he wears glasses. Perceivers weight some information more than other because of perceived diagnosticity; negative information generally receives a higher weight than positive (Skowronski & Carlston, 1989) in part because it may be seen as more diagnostic. Also, information that captures attention more readily, such as unusual behaviour, may be weighted more heavily.

Primacy effects

One way in which this is important is in explaining primacy effects in impression formation. Research tends to confirm common wisdom that the first information we get about others is more important than the later. One reason for this is that the earlier information is weighted more heavily because it is assumed to be more important or because the perceiver pays less attention to later information because of boredom.

IMPLICIT PERSONALITY THEORY

Anderson's information integration model deals with how information is combined to reach a final decision, but people also have a sense of how information is interrelated. For example, most people assume that kind people are also warm, a not unreasonable assumption given that the two terms share a good deal of psychological and linguistic similarity. But why do people assume that intelligent people are happy or honest? Psychologically, intelligence and happiness seem to occupy different worlds. The fact that people have assumptions about what traits and other characteristics go with others has come to be known as implicit personality theory (Schneider, 1973). One reason people assume that intelligent people are happy is that in their experiences most of the intelligent people they have known are happy; it may even be that this is generally true. On the other hand, perceptions that these two traits go together may have more to do with our desires to see positive characteristics as going with other positive characteristics, a bias that has long been known as the halo effect (Nisbett & Wilson, 1977a).

INFORMATION PROCESSING

Since the late 1970s social cognition has been dominated by models, measures, and approaches largely imported from cognitive psychology. That is not to say that traffic between the two areas has been entirely one-sided. Social cognitive researchers have their insights which challenge revealed wisdom from the more basic cognitive psychology.

BASIC ASSUMPTIONS

Process is general

Several basic assumptions tend to guide research in social cognition. The first is that cognitive process is general across types of stimuli. While people and physical stimuli such as cars may have different features that attract attention, once one pays attention to one car as opposed to another, or this person rather than that, the consequences for further processing are likely to be the same. Similarly the same rules that govern how we encode, store, and recall information about cars should be the same rules that govern memory for people.

Schemata and knowledge structures

Knowledge structures are important in guiding our cognitive activities. Classically these knowledge structures were called schemata (singular schema) after the pioneering work of Bartlett (1932), but more recently they have also been called knowledge structures, frames, and stereotypes, among other terms. The basic idea is that our experience tends to be codified, made sensible, and stored in an organized fashion. Our knowledge base about people or most everything else does not merely consist of scraps of information filed away and accessible as dictionary entries. Rather it is more like a well-organized encyclopedia with headings for major topics and many cross-references among topics. I have a well-developed schema for college professor which suggests how people get to be professors, how they spend their days, and even what sorts of traits and other characteristics they are likely to have. I have theories that interrelate all these various kinds of information; for example, I understand that people who are highly extraverted are not likely to want to spend vast hours in musty libraries or smelly labs. I have many cross-references from my professor schema to my schemata of student, university, education in general and the like.

Such schemata affect how we process information. Schemata are rather imperialistic and bossy; our cognitive systems are built to give some priority to what we already know. Pragmatically, we would not want it otherwise. Most social situations represent too complex a stimulus array for us to have the energy or desire to process every single stimulus in its full glory.

Bias

The costs of efficiency

This deficiency, however, comes at a price: we are biased in what we experience and remember. Because we can never process all the information we encounter and because our schemata guide our processing, our knowledge is incomplete, biased, and sometimes dead wrong. Social cognition like cognitive psychology generally places a premium on showing that our cognitions are inherently biased. There have been three major traditions that have stimulated this research on cognitive bias in social cognition. First, as we have seen, attribution research has suggested that people do not follow what might be described as rational rules for the processing of behavioural information. Second, memory research during the 1970s and early 1980s documented a large number of memory errors produced by our tendencies to make incoming information consistent with our schemata. Much modern cognitive theory has assumed that the mind is a highly resource-limited "computer", one that needs to compress and abstract incoming information into schemata in the interests of preserving precious memory. Third, the provocative work of Tversky & Kahneman (1974) suggested that in an informationally rich world people must adopt simplified strategies (heuristics) for processing information, and these strategies, while often quite satisfactory and accurate, may in special circumstances produce biases and inaccuracies that cognizers may not fully appreciate.

Cognitive heuristics

There are many biases introduced by heuristic thinking, but I will list only a couple. One is our tendencies to judge present people or events on the basis of how well they fit known examples from the past. Normally this is a perfectly useful strategy − after all, we do want to benefit from past experience − but sometimes we use bad examples. So, we sometimes ascribe personality features to a person based on his or her physical resemblance to someone else (Lewicki, 1986) or judge whether to admit someone to a graduate programme

821

on the basis of whether he went to the same college as a recent successful or unsuccessful person in the present programme.

We sometimes judge how likely something is by how easy it is to retrieve relevant examples; this is called the availability heuristic. People see the risk of dying from accidents, cancer, and natural disasters as more likely than it actually is, in part because there is usually considerable publicity for such events and so it is easy to remember cases of people who die in these ways. On the other hand, we underestimate the prevalence of other less publicized risks such as emphysema and smallpox vaccination (Slovic, Fischhoff, & Lichtenstein, 1982). In short, we see as more likely those things for which we can find ready examples in memory, but underestimate those that are less salient in memory.

Automaticity

Some cognitive processes we have discussed may have seemed quite familiar: "Yes, I do that all the time". But with other processes you may have no relevant conscious experiences. In an important paper, Nisbett and Wilson (1977b) argued that we are generally not aware of how we think, of our cognitive processes, as opposed to what we think, the products of these processes. In this most general claim they are surely wrong. I am certainly aware of how I try to solve a complex chess problem, as I try out various moves and keep the results in my head for comparison. However, Nisbett and Wilson were correct in the more limited claim that we *often* do not know how we think. What goes through your head when you answer the question: "What is 2 + 2?" We can only hope nothing.

It is now widely recognized that many of our cognitive processes are so well practised that they become more or less automatic. This term has been used extensively, but it means different things to different psychologists. Generally, when we talk about automatic processes, we mean those that occur largely outside awareness, require few cognitive resources, and are hard if not impossible to control (Bargh, 1989). If I ask you your name, you will generally not be aware of how you retrieved it, you will answer quickly and without much effort, and while you might be able to inhibit actually saying your name aloud in answer to the question, there is probably nothing you could do short of destructive brain surgery to keep your name from popping into your mind.

Whether our cognitive processes are automatic or more controlled is important in everyday life. Suppose I am interviewing a physically handicapped person for a job. Can I ignore the fact that she is in a wheelchair? Probably not; I shall probably think of her as handicapped whether or not I want to do so. Now suppose I think that most handicapped people are hardworking. When I categorize this person as handicapped do I also more or less automatically see her as diligent? Devine (1989) has argued that stereotyping

822

in this way is fairly automatic, but that we can correct our initial, automatic judgements with more controlled thought processes. So I might say to myself that while most handicapped people work hard, this one seems to be on the lazy side. Unfortunately, we sometimes fail to make corrections based on behavioural data we have.

STAGES

Our processing of social and other information takes places in stages. Typically, one might think of attention, labelling and recognition, memory (itself composed of several well-defined stages), and inferential thinking as major stages.

Attention

Imagine that I have entered a crowed room, say a cocktail party. My attention will be guided in several ways. I shall probably look at the people rather than at the ceiling light fixtures or the carpeting. And as my gaze sweeps the room, it will pause on some people but not others. That handsome blond man in the Italian suit captures my attention, and so does the distinguished looking woman who seems to have an adoring crowd around her. I see an old friend across the room, and study him for a few seconds − he has put on weight, his hair is greyer, and for a moment I'm not sure that it is my friend. As I make my survey I focus not only on a relatively few people but also on individual features of the people at whom I look. As we all know, attention is highly labile and subject to many influences. If I am looking for a person serving drinks, I scan the room in a different way than if I am trying to find a particular friend.

Labelling and categorization

At the same time that my attention is landing here and there around the room, other processes are also going on. For one thing, I am implicitly (and sometimes explicitly) labelling and recognizing the things that I see. I know the difference between a man's suit and a dress, between grey and blonde hair. Sometimes that labelling and recognition is quite explicit (the woman with the adoring entourage seems to be powerful; I really should find out who she is), but more often than not it is simply implicit and done without conscious thought. I may also be actively seeking certain sorts of information which further guides attention and labelling. Is that man over there the chap I went to graduate school with 30 years ago? What should I look at to decide?

823

Category hierarchies

Before we can deal with any stimulus we must label it or place it into one of thousands of cognitive categories we keep available for just such purposes. Everything we encounter can be labelled and categorized in several ways. This thing before me is a computer screen, a part of my computer, an obstruction to my view out the window, a source of eyestrain, and so on. What is this thing? I am a male, a husband, a father, a professor, a psychology professor, a home-owner, grey-haired (very prematurely to be sure), an occasional squash player. Who am I?

One important question stimulated by the influential research of Eleanor Rosch (1978) concerns levels of categorization. The object before me could be described abstractly or relatively concretely as an object, a piece of equipment, a part of a computer, a monitor, an NEC monitor, an NEC 5FG, or an NEC 5FG with serial #XXX. Rosch has argued that there is a basic level of categorization, a level that maximizes the amount of information about uniqueness while giving us some general information. In the example just given "monitor" is probably the basic category. To say it is an object or a part of a computer does not really allow us to distinguish it usefully from the things I would want to see it as different from, but to say it is NEC #XXX is to be entirely too specific. A good but not infallible test of basic categories is what people would call the object without much thinking about it. I suspect that most people would call this piece of equipment a monitor. This might, of course, change. One would imagine that someone working in the NEC warehouse, might point and say "Please get me the 5FG" or (surrounded by similar models) the #XXX. "Get the monitor" would not, in this situation, communicate much.

Whether people, as stimuli, fall so neatly into this kind of framework is an open question. To be sure, the person before me is an animal, a mammal, a human, a male, but then things start to get a bit sticky. Do I proceed: young male, male who is 25, male who was born in July 1967? Or do I proceed: stockbroker, rising star, rising star with a Stanford MBA, rising star with a Stanford MBA working in bonds? This illustrates the simple fact that people are probably subject to quite a few alternative categorizations. Again: a lot depends on relevant contexts. Saying the young man is a father would not tell us much at a meeting of the local Parents' Organization for Better Teaching, but might among a group of other young males who do not have parental responsibilities.

Category use

Leaving aside the issue of how broad the categories are that we use, another important question is how we pick certain categories. Why do I see the Japanese businessman as Japanese rather than as a businessman? Why do I think of him as male but not necessarily in terms of his golfing prowess? As Brewer (1988) has argued, gender, age, and race are probably basic categories that we use for all people. It would seem strange indeed if after even a brief conversation with someone I could remember her eye colour but not whether she was male or female, old or young, Asian or Caucasian. Beyond that, many categories are given by our cultures. People from most western countries would tend to categorize people in terms of their marital or parental status, but we ordinarily pay little attention to whether an adult has living parents.

Obviously our own motives and goals can also play a role. When I interview people to be my research assistant, their race is much less important than whether they are good students. Our choice of categories is often influenced by which ones we habitually use or have used in the recent past (Smith, 1990). Categories that are "primed" are used more readily and more quickly. The dentist at a party may not be able to help herself from thinking about people in terms of their dental appearance. Physical fitness types may be more inclined to think of others in terms of their physique than I do, and I certainly am prone to categorize people quickly and often in terms of intelligence.

Exemplars and prototypes

We have been discussing alternative ways of categorizing basically familiar stimuli. But how do we classify things and people we have never seen before? As I walk across an unfamiliar university campus how do I know which people are students, which professors, and which visitors like myself? Advocates of the prototype view suggest that we have abstract representations of categories. When you think of some category, say college professor, you imagine the average professor, the prototypic one, and this prototype embodies the features common to most professors. You decide this new person you have met must be a professor if he or she matches that prototype.

Advocates of the exemplar view argue that we store many examples of each category, and we may even make some implicit decisions as to which are good or poor exemplars. So when you try to judge whether this man before you is a professor or a groundskeeper, you will quickly (and perhaps nonconsciously) think about as many professors and groundskeepers as you can and see whether this unknown person best fits with the exemplars from one or the other category. Those who espouse the exemplar view argue that we reason from individual cases and not from abstract summaries.

We use both exemplar and prototypic representations (Smith, 1990). However, the distinction is an important one for social cognition. I had better categorize this man approaching me late at night on a darkened street, and do so quickly. Is he a thug? A harmless, pathetic, homeless person, perhaps a policeman? One way I might decide is to compare him to the prototype of a thug. And where in my limited experience do I get such a prototype? Why, from newspapers and accounts from others. In short, I may use a stereotype of a thug to make my judgement, On the other hand, if I use exemplars, my recent experiences may play a larger role. The man approaching is large, has a dark complexion, is dressed shabbily, but as I try to find exemplars of such men I have encountered recently, I keep coming up with men I have recently met at a local shelter for alcoholics.

Memory

Memory is selective

While there have been many debates about how memory works, there has been general agreement on several basic facts. Perhaps the most central fact of our memory systems is that they are selective. We do not see and hear everything around us, and do not place into our memory storage all the things that register. Clearly we do not and probably cannot remember everything we have seen or heard, and that is surely useful. Would you want to clutter up your mind with everything that happened to you yesterday?

Sometimes we have trouble remembering because the information we require was never stored effectively. When students take exams, they may find that information they have read was never really incorporated into their store ▪ of useful information. Sometimes we have trouble remembering things because we can't retrieve the information. You may, for example, have trouble remembering the name of a childhood friend at the moment, but find the name comes easily when you visit your parents or childhood hang-outs.

Memory is biased

A second fact of memory is that it is sometimes not a faithful representation of experience. As we have suggested it leaves out many details that were never recorded or which have been forgotten. Beyond that, however, our memories are influenced by assumptions we make and inferences we draw. Having decided that the man before me is a criminal, I may remember him as bigger and more muscular than he really is.

Some of our "memories" are more or less conscious reconstructions of past events based on our schemata. So if I ask you what shoes you wore last Friday, you probably do not have a ready memory image at hand. However, you may reason that you wore your sneakers because you were shopping that day and you always wear sneakers to shop unless the weather is really bad.

However, even in cases where our memories are not based on conscious reconstructions, they may be biased by our knowledge about what we know must have happened. Research on eyewitness testimony has documented the fact that questions people are asked about events they have seen may bias what they remember (Loftus, 1979). For example, people who are asked how fast a car was going when it *smashed* into another car give higher estimates than those who are asked how fast the car was going when it *hit* the other car. We trust our memories (what other choice do we have?), but we should also be aware that they are sometimes wrong. In any event, we often remember information as particularly consistent with the schemata we used to understand and process that information.

Memory for inconsistent information

Schema theories argue that we should best remember information consistent with our schemata. However, if you stop and think about it, our mental lives would be in sorry shape if all we did was remember the ways things are like they are supposed to be. Taken to the extreme we could never recall any new information. Suppose you have a conversation with a professor. You will note the ways in which she fits the stereotype (schema) you have for a professor, but is that all you remember? Surely you also recall some of the things that make her different from other professors you know. Indeed, there is now good evidence that we do recall especially well information that is inconsistent with our schemata and expectations (Stangor & McMillan, 1992). This, of course, allows us to individuate our experiences.

Inferences

We all draw conclusions, lots of them, about what we have seen, heard, and remember. Because of our vast experience and many learning experiences, we all have a store of what might be called world-knowledge, that allows us to infer lots of things we never see. So at a party I normally assume that the people will understand my questions, that they have working hearts and auditory systems, and so on. This world knowledge is largely universal (at least within a given culture or group), and it represents the kinds of things we take for granted but which none the less guide our everyday behaviour at every step. I may also have more idiosyncratic knowledge that leads to other assumptions. I might assume that blond males who wear expensive suits have blue eyes and are taller than average; I may even assume that this blond man is less than optimally bright. I may assume that powerfully acting women are likely to be hard to talk to, that they will disdain my attempts at small talk, especially about sports.

These inferences are important inasmuch as they guide our interactions and our attempts to gather more information. If I assume that the blond man is deficient in IQ points I would initiate a conversation with him about the weather or vacations rather than the current state of the global warming controversy. I may, of course, be surprised to discover that he is a nuclear physicist. I may assume that the distinguished woman is also likely to be a business executive and interested in discussing the stock market only to discover that she is a famous cook or self-help author. Of course, sometimes our stereotypically guided inferences are perfectly accurate.

CONCLUSIONS

Nothing is as important to most of us as other people and their behaviour. Unfortunately the importance of social stimuli is more than matched by their complexity. The behaviour of others is dynamic, and it not only changes according to its own rules but also is responsive to the behaviour of perceivers who often find themselves trying to understand behaviour that they, themselves, have an ongoing role in creating. Unfortunately, we are a long way from understanding how we accomplish simple cognitive tasks such as reading prose or recognizing physical objects and even further from knowing how we understand the much more complex social world around us. Yet since the 1960s we have not only dramatically increased our scientific knowledge about social cognition, but also learned exciting new ways of studying it. There is every reason to believe that the study of social cognition will remain central to social and cognitive psychology, and that we will continue to learn even more about its mysteries.

FURTHER READING

Fiske, S. T., & Taylor S. E. (1991). *Social cognition* (2nd edn). New York: McGraw-Hill.

Hewstone, M. (1989). *Causal attribution: From cognitive processes to collective beliefs*. Oxford: Basil Blackwell.

Schneider, D. J., Hastorf, A. H., & Ellsworth, P. C. (1979). *Person perception* (2nd edn) Reading, MA: Addison-Wesley.

Uleman, J. S., & Bargh, J. A. (Eds) (1989). *Unintended thought*. New York: Guilford.

Wyer, R. S., Jr, & Srull, T. K. (1989). *Memory and cognition in its social context*. Hillsdale, NJ: Lawrence Erlbaum.

REFERENCES

Anderson, N. H. (1981). *Foundations of information integration theory*. New York: Academic Press.

Bargh, J. A. (1989). Conditional automaticity: Varieties of automatic influence in social perception and cognition. In J. S. Uleman & J. A. Bargh (Eds) *Unintended thought* (pp. 3–51). New York: Guilford.

Bartlett, F. C. (1932). *Remembering: A study in experimental social psychology*. Cambridge: Cambridge University Press.

Brewer, M. C. (1988). A dual process model of impression formation. In T. K. Srull & R. S. Wyer, Jr, (Eds) *Advances in social cognition* (vol. 1, pp. 1–36). Hillsdale, NJ: Lawrence Erlbaum.

Cronbach, L. J. (1955). Processes affecting scores on "understanding of others" and "assumed similarity". *Psychological Bulletin*, 52, 177–193.

Devine, P. G. (1989). Stereotypes and prejudice: Their automatic and controlled components. *Journal of Personality and Social Psychology*, 56, 5–18.

Ekman, P., & Friesen, W. V. (1975). *Unmasking the face.* Englewood Cliffs, NJ: Prentice-Hall.

Fiedler, K., & Semin, G. (1988). On the causal information conveyed by different interpersonal verbs: The role of implicit sentence context. *Social Cognition*, 6, 21–39.

Fiske, S. T., & Taylor, S. E. (1991). *Social cognition* (2nd edn). New York: McGraw-Hill.

Funder, D. C. (1987). Errors and mistakes: Evaluating the accuracy of social judgment. *Psychological Bulletin*, 101, 75–90.

Gilbert, D. T. (1989). Thinking lightly about others: Automatic components of the social inference process. In J. S. Uleman & J. A. Bargh (Eds) *Unintended thought* (pp. 189–211). New York: Guilford.

Heider, F. (1958). *The psychology of interpersonal relations.* New York: Wiley.

Hewstone, M. (1989) *Causal attribution: From cognitive processes to collective beliefs.* Oxford: Basil Blackwell.

Hilton D. J., & Slugoski, B. R. (1986). *Knowledge-based causal attribution: The abnormal conditions focus model. Psychological Review*, 93, 75–88.

Jaspars, J. M. F. (1983). The process of attribution in common sense In M. R. C. Hewstone (Ed.) *Attribution theory: Social and functional extensions* (pp. 28–44). Oxford: Basil Blackwell.

Jones, E. E., & Davis, K. E. (1965). From acts to dispositions: The attribution process in person perception. In L. Berkowitz (Ed.) *Advances in experimental social psychology* (vol. 2, pp. 219–276). New York: Academic Press.

Jones, E. E., & Nisbett, R. E. (1972). The actor and observer: Divergent perceptions of the causes of behavior. In E. E. Jones, D. Kanouse, H. H. Kelley, R. E. Nisbett, S. Valins, & B. Weiner (Eds) *Attribution: Perceiving the causes of behavior* (pp. 79–94). Morristown, NJ: General Learning Press.

Kelley, H. H. (1967). Attribution theory in social psychology. In *Nebraska Symposium on Motivation* (pp. 192–238). Lincoln, NB: University of Nebraska Press.

Lewicki, P. (1986). *Nonconscious social information processing.* New York: Academic Press.

Loftus, E. F. (1979). *Eyewitness testimony.* Cambridge, MA: Harvard University Press.

McGill, A. L. (1989). Context effects in judgments of causality. *Journal of Personality and Social Psychology*, 57, 189–200.

Newman, L. S., & Uleman, J. S. (1989). Spontaneous trait inference. In J. S. Uleman & J. A. Bargh (Eds) *Unintended thought* (pp. 155–188). New York: Guilford.

Nisbett, R. E., & Wilson, T. D. (1977a). The halo effect: Evidence for unconscious alteration of judgments. *Journal of Personality and Social Psychology*, 35, 250–256.

Nisbett, R. E., & Wilson, T. D. (1977b). Telling more than we can know: Verbal reports on mental processes. *Psychological Review*, 84, 231–259.

Ostrom, T. M. (1984). The sovereignty of social cognition. In R. S. Wyer & T. K. Srull (Eds) *Handbook of social cognition* (vol. 1, pp. 1–38). Hillsdale, NJ: Lawrence Erlbaum.

Park, B., & Judd, C. M. (1989). Agreement on initial impressions: Differences due to perceivers, trait dimensions, and target behaviors. *Journal of Personality and Social Psychology*, *56*, 493–505.

Rosch, E. H. (1978). Principles of categorization. In E. Rosch & B. B. Lloyd (Eds) *Cognition and categorization* (pp. 28–48). Hillsdale, NJ: Lawrence Erlbaum.

Schneider, D. J. (1973). Implicit personality theory. *Psychological Bulletin*, *79*, 294–309.

Schneider, D. J. (1991). Social cognition. *Annual Review of Psychology*, *42*, 527–561.

Schneider, D. J., Hastorf, A. H., & Ellsworth, P. C. (1979). *Person perception* (2nd edn) Reading, MA: Addison-Wesley.

Skowronski, J. J., & Carlston, D. E. (1989). Negativity and extremity biases in impression formation: A review of explanations. *Psychological Bulletin*, *105*, 131–142.

Slovic, P., Fischhoff, B., & Lichtenstein, S. (1982). Facts versus fears: Understanding perceived risk. In D. Kahneman, P. Slovic, & A. Tversky (Eds) *Judgment under uncertainty: Heuristics and biases* (pp. 463–489). Cambridge: Cambridge University Press.

Smith, E. R. (1990). Content and process specificity in the effects of prior experiences. In T. K. Srull & R. S. Wryer, Jr (Eds) *Advances in social cognition* (vol. 3, pp. 1–91). Hillsdale, NJ: Lawrence Erlbaum.

Stangor, C., & McMillan, D. (1992). Memory for expectancy-congruent and expectancy-incongruent information: A review of the social and social developmental literatures. *Psychological Bulletin*, *111*, 42–61.

Swann, W. B., Jr (1984). Quest for accuracy in person perception: A matter of pragmatics. *Psychological Review*, *91*, 457–477.

Taft, R. (1955). The ability to judge people. *Psychological Bulletin*, *52*, 1–23.

Trope, Y. (1986). Identification and inferential processes in dispositional attribution. *Psychological Review*, *93*, 239–257.

Turnbull, W., & Slugoski, B. R. (1988). Conversational and linguistic processes in causal attribution. In D. J. Hilton (Ed.) *Contemporary science and natural explanation: Commonsense perceptions of causality* (pp. 66–93). Brighton: Harvester.

Tversky, A., & Kahneman, D. (1974). Judgment under uncertainty: Heuristics and biases. *Science*, *185*, 1124–1131.

Van Kleeck, M., Hillger, L., & Brown, R. (1988). Pitting verbal schemes against information variables in attribution. *Social Cognition*, *6*, 89–106.

Watson, D. (1989). Strangers' ratings of the five robust personality factors: Evidence of a surprising convergence with self-report. *Journal of Personality and Social Psychology*, *57*, 120–128.

9.4

PREJUDICE AND INTERGROUP CONFLICT

James Vivian and Rupert Brown
University of Kent, England

Although there has been little discernible improvement in social relations across the globe, there have been considerable advances in our understanding of the causes of prejudice and intergroup conflict. In analysing the major contributions of social psychology to this topic it is possible to distinguish between three approaches: there are those that locate the cause of prejudice in the psychological make-up of the individual; there are approaches that emphasise the role that external or environmental factors play; and finally, there are approaches in which group membership itself is seen as critically important. Each of these different perspectives may be important to a full understanding of the causes of intergroup conflict and prejudice and the best strategies for their reduction.

By prejudice we mean the derogatory attitudes that members of one group may hold about another, and the discriminatory behaviour that is often associated with this. Although prejudice and intergroup conflict are conceptually distinct, they often coexist; wherever we find prejudice, we also find conflict, if only dormant. Prejudice, then, can be thought of as a special case of intergroup conflict.

Intergroup conflict occurs when people think or behave antagonistically towards another group or its members in terms of their group memberships and seem motivated by concerns relating to those groups (Sherif, 1966; Tajfel & Turner, 1986). Conversely, conflict is "interpersonal" to the extent that no reference to membership is made, and the issues dividing the participants are specific to those particular individuals. The distinction between these levels of social interaction is critical as behaviour is often qualitatively different between intergroup and interpersonal contexts. In spite of this dichotomy, most social relationships are recognized to be a mixture of both interpersonal and intergroup components, the relative importance of which may fluctuate over time and across situations.

PREJUDICE AS A FEATURE OF INDIVIDUAL PSYCHOLOGY

The prejudiced personality

Some psychologists believe that people who display prejudice differ in personality from non-prejudiced people. This notion was popularized by Adorno, Frenkel-Brunswick, Levinson, and Sanford (1950) in their analysis of the "authoritarian personality". These authors argued that a particularly strict upbringing by parents overly concerned with convention and conformity gives rise to an authoritarian personality, which is thought to predispose certain people to prejudice. According to this theory, the hostility felt towards such parents is repressed by the child, who then idealizes the parents and who subsequently displays a deferential and submissive attitude towards authority figures in general (who are presumed to symbolize the parents). Following from a presumed need to discharge the psychic energy that has accumulated from repression, the pent-up hostility is displaced on to less threatening, lower status targets who are normally other groups (e.g., foreigners, minority groups). These are seen as inherently defective or flawed in character and therefore deserving of contempt.

To measure authoritarianism, Adorno et al. (1950) developed the F-scale (tendency towards Fascism scale). Through detailed clinical interviews and projective tests of personality, Adorno and his colleagues were able to examine the relationships between F-scale responses, patterns of personality, and upbringing. Consistent with their theorizing, results seemed to indicate that highly authoritarian individuals tended to hold more ethnocentric (e.g., anti-Semitic, racist) attitudes and tended also to be those who had been subjected to stricter child rearing practices than their less authoritarian counterparts.

Following its publication, critics pointed to methodological flaws associated with the F-scale and the clinical interviews used to validate it (Brown, 1965). The major problem with the F-scale is that the items are coded in such a way that agreement with statements always implies an authoritarian attitude of one form or another (see Table 1). As a result, it is unclear whether those who score highly on the F-scale are actually more authoritarian than others or whether they are simply more inclined towards acquiescence with statements in general. Further, the clinical interviews used to validate the F-scale as a measure of authoritarianism were flawed because the interviewers were aware of the prior F-scale responses of their inter-viewees, thus possibly contaminating the interview in subtle ways.

But perhaps a more damning criticism of the theory relates to the problems associated with an "individual differences" (i.e., personality) approach to explaining prejudice and intergroup behaviour (Billig, 1976). The problem, very simply, is that an analysis of individual personalities cannot account for the large-scale social behaviour that normally characterizes prejudice and intergroup conflict more generally. If it were true that prejudice derived from a disorder in personality, then we would expect the expression of prejudice or discrimination within groups to vary as much as the personalities of members comprising the group. But in fact the evidence seems to indicate that prejudice within groups is often remarkably uniform. For example, Pet-tigrew (1958), while studying prejudice in South Africa and the United States, found that levels of prejudice between the countries differed markedly while

Table 1 Sample items from the F-scale

1	Obedience and respect for authority are the most important virtues that children should learn.
2	Young people sometimes get rebellious ideas, but as they grow up they ought to get over them and settle down.
3	What the youth needs most is strict discipline, rugged determination, and the will to work and fight for family and country.
4	An insult to our honour should always be punished.
5	Sex crimes, such as rape and attacks on children, deserve more than mere imprisonment; such criminals ought to be publicly whipped, or worse.
6	A person who has bad manners, habits, and breeding can hardly expect to get along with decent people.
7	Most of our social problems would be solved if we could somehow get rid of the immoral, crooked, and feeble-minded people.
8	If people would talk less and work more, everybody would be better off.
9	People can be divided into two distinct classes: the weak and the strong.
10	Human nature being what it is, there will always be war and conflict.

Source: Adorno, Frenkel-Brunswick, Levinson, and Sanford, 1950, pp. 255–257

levels of authoritarianism did not. As a result, he concluded that rather than seeing the prejudice as an expression of a personality disorder, it was more likely to be a result of the norms prevailing in society. The fact that all members are exposed to such cultural norms may thus account for the oft-observed uniformity of prejudice.

Additionally, if prejudice is rooted in individual personalities, which are, by definition, enduring characteristics, then one would expect consistency over time in the expression of prejudice. But the historical evidence seems to reveal patterns of prejudice that suddenly appear and disappear, depending on the relations between the groups in question. Thus, for example, the prejudice displayed by Americans during the Second World War that eventually led to the internment of thousands of Japanese living in the United States cannot plausibly be explained by the individual personalities of Americans suddenly becoming more authoritarian in the 1940s. It seems more likely that the rise in prejudice directed specifically at the Japanese was related to the change in the objective relations between the groups that followed the bombing of Pearl Harbor.

Belief similarity as an explanation of prejudice

As an alternative to a "personality explanation" of prejudice, Rokeach (1960) offered an account that emphasized the role of belief systems. He proposed that similarity or "congruence" of individuals' beliefs determine, in large part, their attitudes towards one another. Specifically, he reasoned that we are generally more attracted to those who share our beliefs and opinions because they validate and legitimize our own. Those who disagree with us, on the other hand, are less attractive because they invalidate our beliefs.

Rokeach made a direct application of these ideas to racial prejudice. According to belief congruence theory, racial prejudice is seen as an outcome of perceived differences in belief (belief incongruence) between members of different racial groups and, further, that these belief differences are ultimately more important than the differences in group membership. Thus, according to Rokeach, we are more likely to discriminate against someone in our own ethnic group who disagrees with us than against someone in another group with whom we concur.

In order to test the theory, Rokeach, Smith, and Evans (1960) developed what has come to be called the "Race-belief" paradigm whereby individual subjects are presented with "stimulus persons" who vary in terms of their attitudinal and ethnic similarity to the subject. With few exceptions, studies utilizing this paradigm have generally established that belief influences subjects' reported attitudes more than race. Thus, white subjects are usually more attracted to a black person with similar beliefs than a white person with different beliefs (Insko, Nacoste, & Moe, 1983). Field research has also provided results generally supportive of belief congruence theory. Other researchers, working in different cultural contexts, report relatively strong correlations between perceived cultural or linguistic similarity and attraction to different ethnic groups (e.g., Berry, Kalin, & Taylor, 1977; Brewer & Campbell, 1976).

As a further test of the hypothesized connection between similarity and intergroup attitudes, a number of experimental investigations have been conducted using methods that do not pit belief similarity directly against group membership. The evidence on this front is somewhat mixed. While certain studies offer support for the idea that similar outgroups are treated better than dissimilar ones (e.g., Brown, 1984), others do not (Diehl, 1988). In fact, there is some experimental evidence that actually contradicts belief congruence theory. Under certain conditions, such as where there is strong attitudinal consensus in the ingroup, unstable status discrepancies, or competition between groups, more discrimination can be found against a similar outgroup (Brown, 1984). These latter experimental findings thus challenge some of Rokeach's original claims.

How can these disparate results be accounted for? One explanation is offered by Brown and Turner (1981), who caution against the direct application of ideas developed to explain interpersonal behaviour to the realm of intergroup relations which are controlled, they argue, by different psychological processes. In a reconsideration of the race-belief literature, for example, they suggest that race may have had little impact because of the explicitly interpersonal, as opposed to intergroup, nature of the encounter. When race is made salient, they argue, the findings can be reversed, with race influencing judgements more than similarity. This argument has been supported by an experiment in which either interpersonal or intergroup similarity was made the main focus of people's attention (Diehl, 1988). As expected, in the former case, less discrimination was observed while the latter condition led to an increase in ingroup favouritism.

As a complete explanation of intergroup prejudice, then, belief-congruence theory is probably inadequate in its original form. In fact, Rokeach himself recognized the limitations of the theory and limited his claims to situations where prejudice or racism is not institutionalized as it was in South Africa under apartheid or where there is not significant social support for their expression (e.g., in certain areas in the southern United States).

Frustration, aggression, and prejudice

Predating both the authoritarian personality and belief-similarity theories was an ambitious attempt by Dollard, Doob, Miller, Mowrer, and Sears (1939) to explain aggressive behaviour between individuals and groups in society. Combining insights from traditional psychoanalytic and learning theories, Dollard et al. proposed that frustration, deriving from the blocking of basic needs, produces a "build-up of psychic energy" or an "instigation to aggress". Following a hydraulic model of human personality, such mounting pressure is alleged to be experienced as an aversive state of arousal that must eventually be relieved. Release of this energy restores balance or equilibrium and is thereby experienced as pleasurable or "cathartic". According to the theory, the release of such mounting tension normally takes the form of explicit or implicit acts of aggression that may be directed at the original source of the frustration or at alternative targets. Dollard and colleagues point out that the source of the frustration is often seen as relatively powerful or threatening (e.g., parents) and is sometimes difficult to identify at all, as when the impoverished consider the causes of their unfortunate position. Borrowing another psychoanalytic concept, Dollard et al. suggested that in cases like these, the aggression is displaced on to alternative targets who either share some surface similarity to the threatening source or are simply convenient scapegoats.

Dollard et al. (1939) used these ideas to explain prejudice, believing that they could account for both the pervasive character of prejudice and its apparent historical specificity. Prejudice is pervasive, they argued, because frustration is pervasive. In every culture at any point in time, most individuals are not having all of their needs met to their satisfaction. They may feel economically disadvantaged or unhappy with work or family life, but because almost nobody is perfectly contented, there exists at all times and places a certain "baseline" level of frustration and, consequently, of aggression. And because the sources of such frustration endemic to social life cannot be easily identified, the associated aggression is thereby displaced on to convenient targets, the targets of prejudice who are normally relatively powerless minority groups. Historical fluctuations can be explained, according to the theory, in terms of the frustrations associated with changing economic conditions (e.g., the rise of anti-Semitism in Germany following the First World War may have been due to the collapse of the German economy at this time). Evidence in support of this idea was offered by Hovland and Sears (1940) among others, who showed that lynchings of blacks in the southern United States in the late nineteenth and early twentieth centuries were related to the price of cotton, a major industry in this region during that time. As the economic standing of many declined along with the price of cotton, the number of lynchings increased. Presumably, the bleak economy produced feelings of frustration in those affected who vented their frustration in a particularly savage way on the convenient scapegoats of the day, the blacks. Some experimental studies have lent further support to the theory (e.g., Miller & Bugelski, 1948).

Despite its attractive simplicity and its empirical support, frustration-aggression theory may still be limited in its ability to explain intergroup prejudice. As with personality, the level of frustration experienced may vary from individual to individual and thus one would expect more variation in the expression of aggression or prejudice than is normally observed. Another major limitation relates to the choice of particular outgroups as targets of prejudice. Why, for example, did whites in the United States select blacks for lynchings rather than other disadvantaged minority groups? Finally, it has been established that frustration was neither necessary nor sufficient to produce aggression leading to a reformulation of the original theory (Berkowitz, 1962). However, even this revised version, based as it is on individual motivational states, is subject to some of the same criticisms that applied to the original theory offered by Dollard et al. (1939).

Individual cognitive processes underlying prejudice

Some theories of prejudice emphasize the role of cognitive processes in the formation and maintenance of negative group stereotypes. Stereotypes are preconceived ideas about entire classes of people and are thought to derive more from limitations in the ability to process information than from a disordered personality or individual needs or motivations. According to Tajfel (1959), we need to simplify the extraordinarily complex physical and social world that we inhabit by placing objects, events, and people (including the self) into various categories. Following from such categorical differentiation, Tajfel further showed that differences between separate categories of physical stimuli are overestimated (Tajfel & Wilkes, 1963). Similar effects have been obtained with social stimuli (people). Using children from Switzerland as subjects, Doise, Deschamps, and Meyer (1978) demonstrated how groups of boys and girls perceived greater differences between photographs of unknown boys and girls when the gender distinction was made explicit than when it was not. Further, the photographs of boys alone and girls alone were judged to be more similar under these same conditions. These results were repeated in a second study which involved judgements of Swiss linguistic groups. Thus, Doise et al. (1987) showed that both differences between and similarities within social categories are accentuated when intergroup categorizations are clear.

It is important to note, however, that the effects of social categorization are not symmetrical. While it appears that categorical distinctions tend to enhance the perception of within-category similarity, this effect is normally more pronounced for the outgroup which is seen as more internally homogeneous than the ingroup (e.g., Quattrone, 1986). For example, Jones, Wood, and Quattrone (1981) found when they asked members of university clubs to estimate the variability (of personalities) of members belonging to different clubs, that club members consistently perceived other clubs as more homogeneous than their own. With some important exceptions (e.g., Simon & Brown, 1987), similar results have been obtained in diverse contexts generally confirming the idea that group members tend to believe while "they" are all the same, "we" are different.

The cognitive process of social categorization may also lie at the heart of stereotype formation. It has been shown that when two distinctive (unusual) events co-occur, people come to believe that there is a correlation between them and that they go together (Chapman & Chapman, 1967). Hamilton and Gifford (1976) extended this notion to stereotypes by arguing, for example, that whites might perceive a correlation between criminality and black skin colour because the two events are unusual and therefore distinctive. To demonstrate this, they presented subjects with scenarios depicting desirable and undesirable actions of members of hypothetical groups. While one of the groups was twice as large as the other and, overall, there were more desirable than undesirable acts depicted, the proportion of desirable to undesirable behaviour within each group was held constant. So, for example, although there were twice as many undesirable acts emanating from the larger group, there were also twice as many people in that group, so there was no actual correlation between the nature of the act (desirable or undesirable) and group membership. Nevertheless, when asked to indicate which acts came from the larger and smaller groups, subjects overestimated the number of undesirable (less common) behaviours in the smaller (minority) group (see Table 2). Consistent with Hamilton's reasoning on the impact of distinctive stimuli, subjects thus perceived an "illusory correlation" between the possession of undesirable traits and minority group membership. This research provides some support, then, for the notion that distinctiveness explains why minorities are seen as having undesirable traits.

Although there is some evidence that people hold fewer derogatory stereotypes about traditionally oppressed groups than before (e.g., Campbell, 1971) later evidence seems to suggest that stereotypes persist even among liberally minded people. When more subtle measures are used (Crosby, Bromley, & Saxe, 1980) or when discriminatory attitudes cannot be unambiguously attributed to prejudice (Gaertner & Dovidio, 1986), a surprising

Table 2 Distinctive (infrequent) events as a source of illusory correlation

	Group	
	A (majority)	B (minority)
Actual distribution of behaviours between two groups		
Desirable	18 (67%)	9 (33%)
Undesirable	8 (67%)	4 (33%)
Distribution of behaviours between two groups as perceived by subjects		
Desirable	17.5 (65%)	9.5 (35%)
Undesirable	5.8 (48%)	6.2 (52%)

Source: Hamilton and Gifford, 1976, table 1
Note: Subjects overestimate the amount of undesirable behaviour emanating from the smaller (minority) group (Group B)

number of seemingly non-prejudiced people behave in characteristically prejudiced ways. Why is it that stereotypes are so resistant to change? One possibility is that people selectively attend to information that confirms their stereotypes. Thus, for example, Howard and Rothbart (1980) showed that even when ingroup and outgroup speakers make the same number of favourable and unfavourable remarks, subjects recall more unfavourable remarks coming from the outgroup. This selective memory together with the fact that unfavourable stereotypes are generally easier to acquire but more difficult to lose than favourable ones, probably contributes to the persistence of unflattering stereotypes of minority groups (Rothbart & Park, 1986).

Additionally, there is reason to believe that many of these cognitive processes may be outside of conscious control. Devine (1989) has proposed that most people share a knowledge of stereotypes and that this knowledge can affect, quite unconsciously, the processing of information. In one study Devine showed that a hypothetical person was viewed as more hostile (black stereotype) by subjects (both prejudiced and non-prejudiced) who had been previously exposed to stereotype-relevant words flashed so quickly that subjects could not recall their content. Presumably, the presentation of the stereotype-associated words activated the cultural stereotype which then had unconscious effects on subjects' assessments of the hypothetical person.

Although there is good reason to believe that individual cognitive processes play a role in the formation and maintenance of stereotypes, there is still reason to doubt that they can account for all of the stereotypes that we hold. If it were true, for example, that people tend to exaggerate the correlation between unusual events that sometimes co-occur, then minority groups should have as part of their stereotype both undesirable and unusually desirable traits (e.g., geniuses). Clearly, this is not the case as stereotypes of minority groups are normally derogatory. This fact highlights one of the important limitations of the purely cognitive explanation of prejudice phenomena: it cannot explain why categorical differentiation normally takes on an asymmetry that either favours the ingroup or derogates the outgroup. In addition, cognitive explanations are still individualistic in nature and thus have difficulty explaining widespread, collective behaviour which, it can be argued, are controlled by processes that differ from those operating at the individual psychological level.

PREJUDICE AS A RESULT OF INTERGROUP RELATIONSHIPS

Relative deprivation

Frustration-aggression theory subsequently evolved into a form which was more explicitly "intergroup" in focus and thus overcame some of the difficulties associated with the earlier version. Following Berkowitz's (1962) lead in emphasizing the subjective nature of frustration, others have argued that it is precisely when people feel deprived of something that they feel entitled to that they experience frustration. The discrepancy between our actual attainments (e.g., position in life) and our expectations (e.g., the position we feel we deserve) is referred to as "relative deprivation". Two types of relative deprivation can be distinguished (Runciman, 1966). One is "egoistic" relative deprivation which derives from comparisons made with other individuals who are seen as similar to oneself. Thus, if colleagues or peers are considerably better off in terms of wages or standard of living, one would be expected to feel deprived relative to these similar others. In "fraternalistic" relative deprivation, on the other hand, feelings of deprivation are thought to derive from comparisons between groups such as when members of particular ethnic or minority groups consider their standard of living in comparison to the dominant majority.

Runciman's discovery that intergroup comparisons could lead to relative deprivation has been confirmed in a number of studies. Vanneman and Pettigrew (1972) found that racist political attitudes were related to feelings of relative deprivation generally and that the most racist attitudes were found among those who reported being fraternally deprived. Further demonstrating the utility of distinguishing between egoistic and fraternalistic deprivation, Abeles (1976) and Walker and Mann (1987) have shown that blacks in the United States and unemployed workers in Australia were more likely to engage in social action when they felt that their group as a whole has not attained what they justly deserved relative to other groups. Abeles also points out that levels of militancy appear to be highest among blacks with higher socio-economic and educational status. This is consistent with Runciman's observation that leaders of collective movements are usually the least deprived members of their groups in an objective sense. Following from an understanding of frustration as a subjective phenomenon, it is likely that these individuals have higher expectations both for themselves and for their group and thus experience the perceived deprivation more acutely.

Relative deprivation theory is thus quite helpful in explaining when hostility will emerge between groups. When members of a given social group perceive a discrepancy between what they believe their group deserves and what they have actually attained, members share a sense of deprivation and a sense of injustice. Because notions of justice are socially determined in the sense that they reflect norms and values of a given culture, they are thought to apply equally across all members of the group. The shared sense of injustice then helps explain the uniformity of behaviour that normally characterizes intergroup relations generally and prejudice in particular.

Realistic conflict theory

Social scientists in various disciplines have long recognized that in addition to the needs, desires, or personalities of individual members, the goals or interests of groups are potent influences of behaviour. Thus, when members believe that another group can satisfy its desires only at their own group's expense (and vice versa), hostility develops between the groups along with the discriminatory and prejudiced behaviour that is commonly associated with such antagonistic intergroup relationships. According to this view, the attitudes and actions of members of different groups reflect the goal relations between those groups. This approach to intergroup relations is known as realistic conflict theory, as real (or perceived) conflicts of interest are presumed to underlie much of the prejudice and hostility often observed between groups.

The best known proponents of this approach have been Muzafer Sherif and his colleagues, who conducted some of the earliest empirical investigations of intergroup conflict. In these studies, they noted the relative ease with which groups of otherwise healthy, well-adjusted boys could be induced to display marked ingroup favouritism and openly hostile behaviour towards other groups of boys, simply as a result of introducing a competition between them (Sherif, 1966). Furthermore, they were able to reduce the tension by replacing the competitive arrangement, whereby one group succeeded at the other's expense, with a cooperative one, where both groups' success was contingent on cooperation between the groups. Based on these and other observations, Sherif suggested that conflict between groups, and the associated intergroup biases, develops through competition and can be reduced through intergroup cooperation in pursuit of superordinate goals.

Results similar to Sherif's have also been obtained among groups of adult managers in human relations workshops and among members of different cultures (e.g., Blake & Mouton, 1962; Diab, 1970). Nevertheless, subsequently, findings have begun to accumulate which suggest that while competition may be *sufficient for* the emergence of intergroup bias, it may not be *necessary*. In a series of what have come to be called "minimal group" experiments, where distinctions between groups are trivial (e.g., presumed aesthetic preferences) and members remain anonymous, the tendency to favour the ingroup either in evaluative judgements or the distribution of rewards has been clearly demonstrated (Rabbie & Horwitz, 1969; Tajfel, Flament, Billig, & Bundy, 1971). Additionally, though cooperative contact between groups in pursuit of "superordinate" goals generally improves relations between them, there are important exceptions when this is apparently not the case. For example, later research found that in order for the superordinate goals strategy to be effective, the cooperative effort must be successful and members of the groups must be able to preserve distinctive identities rather than being absorbed into a common culture (Brown & Wade, 1987; Worchel, Andreoli, & Folger, 1977). Otherwise, there is reason to believe that such contact can exacerbate rather than alleviate hostility.

PREJUDICE AS AN ASPECT OF GROUP MEMBERSHIP

Social identity theory

How can the "incipient hostility" that appears to emerge between groups even in the absence of explicit competition or conflicts of interest be explained? Further, why are comparisons between groups' material outcomes apparently so important in generating resentment and hostility? One influential theory which has been offered to explain these phenomena is one that emphasizes the role of cognitive and motivational processes in prejudice and intergroup relations; this explanation is now commonly known as social identity theory (Tajfel, 1978; Tajfel & Turner, 1986).

This theory starts with the assumption that the desire to understand and to evaluate oneself constitutes a primary motive underlying much of social behaviour. Joining two traditions in psychology, it proposes that we satisfy this desire through social categorization and social comparison. With social categorization, as noted, the complex social world is simplified by placing people, including the self, into various categories (e.g., gender, race, nationality, or political ideology). It is this process of self-categorization that defines what Tajfel called the social identity. Social identity theory hypothesizes that people are strongly motivated to understand and evaluate these group-based identities and, echoing an earlier theory (Festinger, 1954), it holds that this evaluative activity is primarily carried out through comparisons with other groups.

However, along with a need for self-evaluation and understanding, there may be a need for "self-enhancement". This added feature is necessary because while the dual processes of social categorization and social comparison can account for the tendency to compare and contrast groups, they cannot easily explain why, when the self is involved, the differentiation normally takes on an asymmetry that favours the groups to which one belongs (the ingroup). With this added concern for self-enhancement, it is argued that individuals are motivated not only by the desire to know and evaluate themselves, but also to evaluate themselves favourably relative to others. Comparisons between groups therefore often have the objective of attaining some distinctiveness from other groups in order to achieve or maintain a positive social identity. From this perspective, then, prejudice may be an expression of a basic motivation for a positive identity which is accomplished, in part, by positively distinguishing an ingroup from an outgroup.

There is abundant research evidence supporting the general claims of social identity theory. It is clear from the literature that intergroup bias (the tendency to favour the group to which one belongs over other groups) is an extraordinarily robust phenomenon which occurs in diverse contexts across a variety of group tasks (see Brewer, 1979). Consistent with the notion that people are motivated to attain positive social identities through intergroup comparisons, the evidence indicates that once groups are perceived to be meaningfully distinct from one another, intergroup bias often ensues in the form of discriminatory reward allocations, trait evaluations, or performance evaluations. In minimal group experiments especially, where the basis for group categorization is trivial, the results reveal a consistent pattern of in-group favouritism in the allocation of financial rewards that supports social identity theory. Even when alternative allocation strategies would have yielded higher profits for an anonymous ingroup member, participants in these experiments tended to prefer strategies that maximized the difference between the groups' outcomes in favour of the ingroup (Tajfel et al., 1971; see also Figure 1). Similar results were obtained in a field setting where Brown (1978) noted factory-workers' desire to maintain wage differentials between their own and other departments even at the expense of their own absolute wage levels.

Central to social identity theory is the idea that group members discriminate against outsiders in the service of the need to achieve, maintain, or enhance self-esteem. The evidence that relates to this hypothesis is mixed. Consistent with this idea, Oakes and Turner (1980) found that group members who were given the opportunity to discriminate reported higher levels of self-esteem afterwards than those who could not discriminate. Nevertheless, other evidence on this front indicates that the relationship between self-esteem and intergroup behaviour is not as straightforward as social identity theory would predict. In some cases, higher levels of self-esteem are associated with intergroup discrimination while in others, discrimination is actually associated with lower levels of self-esteem (Abrams & Hogg, 1988). Another problem for the theory stems from the supposed link between the strength of group identification and the amount of intergroup bias. While many studies report a consistent relationship between identification and intergroup bias, the magnitude of the relationships are relatively weak, and, in some cases, they are actually negative (see Hinkle & Brown, 1990). Additionally, it is clear that in certain cases, people favour the outgroup. It is commonly found, for example, that members of low-status

Ingroup member	7	8	9	10	11	12	13	14	15	16	17	18	19
Outgroup member	1	3	5	7	9	11	13	15	17	19	21	23	25

Figure 1 Sample matrix used in Tajfel et al. (1971). Subjects were instructed to allocate points (representing money) to anonymous members of their own and another group. Average responses were slightly to the left of the centre column (13, 13) suggesting that subjects were interested in allocating *more* money to the ingroup than to the outgroup member even at the expense of absolute profit for the ingroup member

groups exhibit outgroup favouritism to high-status outgroups (Mullen, Brown, & Smith, 1992). This does not fit simply with the theory's view that group members are attempting to create positive social identities by always engaging in ingroup-favouring behaviour.

Finally, and perhaps most importantly, it is not entirely clear whether social identity theory can account for intergroup prejudice if prejudice is defined as derogatory attitudes or behaviour directed at members of another group. Where the data are available, the majority of empirical studies concerned with intergroup bias report that differences in evaluations of ingroup and outgroup typically result from elevated ratings of the ingroup (Brewer, 1979). So while it is clear that members of groups often show favouritism to the group to which they belong, there is actually very little evidence that they derogate outgroups in the way that is characteristic of prejudice.

REDUCING PREJUDICE

The various approaches discussed above have direct implications for the reduction of prejudice and the resolution of conflict. The majority of programmes aimed at fostering harmonious relations between previously conflictual groups have operated under assumptions embodied in what has come to be known as the "contact hypothesis" (Allport, 1954). This hypothesis asserts attitudes and behaviour towards outgroups will become more positive after interaction with them. Although many studies conducted in diverse contexts support this idea, because many others were less encouraging, several qualifications to the original hypothesis were required. Thus, the effects of contact are greatly enhanced if it is sanctioned by institutional supports (e.g., law, custom), takes place between participants on an equal status footing in pursuit of common goals, and provided it is of a sort that leads to the perception of communality between the two groups (Amir, 1969).

In spite of the early awareness that these moderating conditions were necessary for the success of intergroup contact, many integration policies in the United States and elsewhere have gone forward somewhat blindly, ignoring the recommendations of social scientists. Contact between black and white children in US public (state) schools is a case in point. Early legislative action imposing desegregation was largely ineffective in the reduction of prejudice between these children probably because the interracial contact in the school setting did not satisfy the criteria necessary for successful intergroup contact. The contact was mostly involuntary and of a superficial nature between groups of markedly different statuses in communities which were often unsupportive of the contact to begin with (Schofield, 1986). Another interesting example of an attempt to reduce ethnic prejudice was described by Schwarzwald and Amir (1984). This study is concerned with efforts in Israel to deal with inter-ethnic tensions between those of middle eastern (North African and Asian) and western (European and American) descent; it documents an "asymmetry" in the patterns of acceptance and rejection between members of these two cultural groups. When asked to indicate social preferences, for example, westerners of all ages tended to accept and prefer other westerners over their eastern counterparts. At the same time, those of eastern descent appear also to prefer westerners, devaluing their own cultural heritage and social standing. This situation is not unlike some encounters between black and white Americans where it has been established that sometimes the minority group (blacks) adopt the majority evaluation of their group and consider themselves less worthy (Clark & Clark, 1947). As in the United States, the results of imposed ethnic integration within the Israeli schools were not very encouraging primarily because policy was rarely guided by scientific knowledge. Because the schools continued to "track" (i.e., to stream) their students, the clear status differentials remained, leaving a disproportionate number of middle easterners in the lower tracks (Schwarzwald & Amir, 1984).

These examples in the United States and Israel strongly suggest that contact itself is largely ineffective at reducing prejudice between cultural groups. More recent theoretical work has built on the original contact hypothesis in specifying additional conditions under which contact will successfully reduce prejudice and thereby improve relations between groups. It is generally agreed that intergroup contact is successful to the extent that diverse groups can coexist peacefully while maintaining distinctive identities. Such integration is the goal in any truly pluralistic society and should be distinguished from assimilation, another possible outcome of contact which is said to have occurred when previously differentiated groups are reduced into a common culture. In spite of efforts in numerous experimental and societal contexts, however, it remains to be seen how best to realize the goal of true integration.

To this end, two seemingly divergent positions have been advanced, both of which claim to offer the optimal strategy for facilitating integration between groups (Brewer and Miller, 1984; Hewstone & Brown, 1986). In their model of "de-categorization" Brewer and Miller propose that the goal of contact is "non-category-based" interaction. The major symptoms of category-based interaction, which prevents integration, include the depersonalization of outgroup members, who are treated as if they are part of a homogeneous or undifferentiated category. In order to achieve more harmonious relations, it follows that respective group memberships need to be made less salient during contact, the boundaries between groups less rigid, and social relations more interpersonally oriented. The assumption is that repeated interpersonal contact with members of the disliked group will produce stereotype-disconfirming experiences which encourage truly interpersonal as opposed to intergroup interactions. Miller, Brewer, and Edwards (1985) have provided some experimental evidence in favour of this approach.

They found that cooperative group interactions which emphasized interpersonal (rather than task) aspects of the situation generated more favourable intergroup attitudes and less discriminatory reward allocations.

Consistent with this view, several educational interventions have been developed which attempt to structure intergroup contact in a way that will weaken boundaries between groups by providing members with cooperative interpersonal experiences with members of a disliked group. One application of this strategy was offered by Aronson and his colleagues in their work with school-aged children of varying ethnic backgrounds in the United States (Aronson, Blaney, Stephan, Sikes, & Snapp, 1978). They devised a cooperative learning strategy referred to as the "jigsaw classroom". Classrooms employing this technique are comprised of racially mixed groups of students who are each responsible for mastering separate portions of material and for teaching this material to others in their group. Members thus depend on one another to achieve the common or superordinate goal of getting good marks in the class. Evidence indicates that students in jigsaw classes report liking classmates of other races more after the technique has been introduced than before. More generally, curricula which emphasize cooperative learning strategies seem to be effective in reducing intergroup tensions (Slavin, 1983).

The problem with many of these strategies that draw attention away from group memberships is that positive attitude changes are often restricted to the situation that produced them and to the members present in the original contact situation. Although the contact may provide stereotype-disconfirming experiences, the individuals present can be considered atypical or exceptions to the rule with respect to the group as a whole. As a result, attitudinal and behavioural changes achieved in the contact situation are often short-lived.

Hewstone and Brown (1986) addressed this problem of the lack of generalization associated with many intergroup contact efforts. Their model is based on the distinction between interpersonal and intergroup behaviour. Because the two levels of interaction may be controlled by different psychological processes, they argue that contact will produce generalized attitude change beyond the contact setting only when the interaction is construed as intergroup in nature, when members are seen as representative of their respective groups. In an experimental context, Wilder (1984) provided evidence in favour of this model. By varying the level of "prototypicality" of an outgroup member, he found that significant improvements in the evaluation of the outgroup as a whole, in this case a rival college, occurred only when there was a pleasant encounter with what was perceived to be a typical member of the outgroup (see Figure 2). In this case, a stereotype-confirming, yet pleasant experience with a typical outgroup member improved perceptions of rival groups.

846

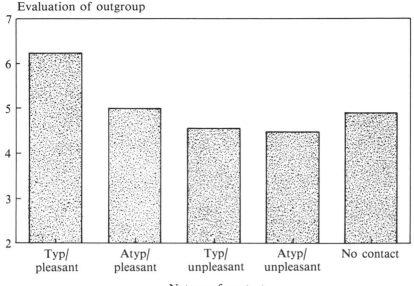

Figure 2 Evaluation of an outgroup after contact with a typical or atypical outgroup
member who behaved in either a pleasant or unpleasant manner
Source: Adapted from Wilder, 1984, Table 1

CONCLUSION

In this chapter several theories of prejudice and intergroup conflict have been
reviewed. It is clear that while each theory contributes to our understanding
of these phenomena, there are, nevertheless, important limitations to each.
It would thus appear that a complete understanding of prejudice and intergroup conflict requires multiple perspectives including those that focus on the
individual, those that focus on the group, and those that focus on the relations between groups in society. It is also clear from this review that only
under very specific conditions can we hope to eradicate prejudice and conflict. Such an important undertaking will undoubtedly require the continued
cooperation of specialists from diverse fields of endeavour.

FURTHER READING

Allport, G. W. (1954). *The nature of prejudice*. Reading, MA: Addison-Wesley.
Brown, R. J. (1988). *Group processes: Dynamics within and between groups*. Oxford:
Basil Blackwell.
Dovidio, J. F., & Gaertner, S. L. (Eds) (1986). *Prejudice, discrimination and racism*.
Orlando, FL: Academic Press.
Hamilton, D. L. (Ed.) (1981). *Cognitive processes in stereotyping and intergroup
behavior*. New York: Lawrence Erlbaum.

REFERENCES

Abeles, R. P. (1976). Relative deprivation, rising expectations and black militancy. *Journal of Social Issues*, *32*, 119–137.

Abrams, D., & Hogg, M. A. (1988). Comments on the motivational status of self-esteem in social identity and intergroup discrimination. *European Journal of Social Psychology*, *18*, 317–334.

Adorno, T. W., Frenkel-Brunswick, E., Levinson, D. J., & Sanford, R. N. (1950). *The authoritarian personality*. New York: Harper.

Allport, G. W. (1954). *The nature of prejudice*. Reading, MA: Addison-Wesley.

Amir, Y. (1969). Contact hypothesis in ethnic relations. *Psychological Bulletin*, *71*, 319–342.

Aronson, E., Blaney, N., Stephan, C., Sikes, J., & Snapp, M. (1978). *The jig-saw classroom*. London: Sage.

Berkowitz, L. (1962). *Aggression. A social psychological analysis*. New York: McGraw-Hill.

Berry, J. W., Kalin, R., & Taylor, D. M. (1977). *Multiculturalism and ethnic attitudes in Canada*. Ottawa: Supply and Services Canada.

Billig, M. G. (1976). *Social psychology and intergroup relations*. London: Academic Press.

Blake, R. R., & Mouton, J. S. (1962). Overevaluation of own group's product in intergroup competition. *Journal of Abnormal and Social Psychology*, *64*, 237–238.

Brewer, M. B. (1979). In-group bias in the minimal intergroup situation: A cognitive-motivational analysis. *Psychological Bulletin*, *86*, 307–324.

Brewer, M. B., & Campbell, D. T. (1976). *Ethnocentrism and intergroup attitudes. East African evidence*. New York: Sage.

Brewer, M. B., & Miller, N. (1984). Beyond the contact hypothesis: Theoretical perspectives on desegregation. In N. Miller & M. B. Brewer (Eds) *Groups in contact. The psychology of desegregation* (pp. 281–302). Orlando, FL: Academic Press.

Brown, R. (1965). *Social psychology*. New York: Macmillan.

Brown, R. J. (1978). Divided we fall: An analysis of relations between sections of a factory work-force. In H. Tajfel (Ed.) *Differentiation between social groups. Studies in the social psychology of intergroup relations* (pp. 395–429). London: Academic Press.

Brown, R. J. (1984). The role of similarity in intergroup relations. In H. Tajfel (Ed.) *The social dimension: European developments in social psychology* (pp. 603–623). Cambridge: Cambridge University Press.

Brown, R. J., & Abrams, D. (1986). The effects of intergroup similarity and goal interdependence on intergroup attitudes and task performance. *Journal of Experimental Social Psychology*, *22*, 78–92.

Brown, R. J., & Turner, J. C. (1981). Interpersonal and intergroup behaviour. In J. C. Turner & H. Giles (Eds) *Intergroup behaviour* (pp. 33–65). Oxford: Basil Blackwell.

Brown, R. J., & Wade, G. S. (1987). Superordinate goals and intergroup behaviour: The effects of role ambiguity and status on intergroup attitudes and task performance. *European Journal of Social Psychology*, *17*, 131–142.

Campbell, A. (1971). *White attitudes towards black people*. Ann Arbor, MI: Institute for Social Research.

Chapman, L. J., & Chapman, J. P. (1967). Genesis of popular but erroneous diagnostic observations. *Journal of Abnormal Psychology*, *72*, 193–204.

Clark, K. B., & Clark, M. P. (1947). Racial identification and preference in Negro children. In T. M. Newcomb & E. L. Hartley (Eds) *Readings in social psychology* (pp. 169–178). New York: Holt, Rinehart & Winston.

Crosby, F., Bromley, S., & Saxe, L. (1980). Recent unobtrusive studies of black and white discrimination and prejudice: A literature review. *Psychological Bulletin*, *87*, 546–563.

Devine, P. (1989). Stereotypes and prejudice: Their automatic and controlled components. *Journal of Personality and Social Psychology*, *56*, 5–18.

Diab, L. N. (1970). A study of intragroup and intergroup relations among experimentally produced small groups. *Genetic Psychology Monographs*, *82*, 49–82.

Diehl, M. (1988). Social identity and minimal groups: The effects of interpersonal and intergroup attitudinal similarity on intergroup discrimination. *British Journal of Social Psychology*, *27*, 289–300.

Doise, W., Deschamps, J.-C., & Meyer, G. (1978). The accentuation of intra-category similarities. In H. Tajfel (Ed.) *Differentiation between social groups. Studies in the social psychology of intergroup relations* (pp. 159–168). London: Academic Press.

Dollard, J., Doob, L. W., Miller, N. E., Mowrer, O. H., & Sears, R. R. (1939). *Frustration and aggression*, New Haven, CT: Yale University Press.

Festinger, L. (1954). A theory of social comparison processes. *Human Relations*, *7*, 117–140.

Gaertner, S. L., & Dovidio, J. F. (1986). The aversive form of racism. In J. F. Dovidio & S. L. Gaertner (Eds) *Prejudice, discrimination and racism* (pp. 61–89). Orlando, FL: Academic Press.

Hamilton, D. L. (1981). Illusory correlation as a basis for stereotyping. In D. L. Hamilton (Ed.) *Cognitive processes in stereotyping and intergroup behaviour* (pp. 115–144). New York: Lawrence Erlbaum.

Hamilton, D. L., & Gifford, R. K. (1976). Illusory correlation in interpersonal perception: A cognitive basis of stereotypic judgements. *Journal of Experimental Social Psychology*, *12*, 392–407.

Hewstone, M. R. C., & Brown, R. J. (1986). Contact is not enough: An intergroup perspective on the contact hypothesis. In M. R. C. Hewstone & R. J. Brown (Eds) *Contact and conflict in intergroup encounters* (pp. 1–44). Oxford: Basil Blackwell.

Hinkle, S., & Brown, R. (1990). Intergroup comparisons and social identity: Some links and lacunae. In D. Abrams & M. Hogg (Eds) *Social identity theory. Constructive and critical advances* (pp. 48–70). Hemel Hempstead: Harvester-Wheatsheaf.

Holland, C., & Sears, R. R. (1940). Minor studies in aggression: VI. Correlation of lynchings with economic indices. *Journal of Psychology*, *9*, 301–310.

Howard, J. W., & Rothbart, M. (1980). Social categorization and memory for ingroup and outgroup behavior. *Journal of Personality and Social Psychology*, *38*, 301–310.

Insko, C. A., Nacoste, R. W., & Moe, I. L. (1983). Belief congruence and racial discrimination: Review of the evidence and critical evaluation. *European Journal of Social Psychology*, *13*, 153–174.

Jones, E. E., Wood, G. C., & Quattrone, G. A. (1981). Perceived variability of personal characteristics in ingroups and outgroups: The role of knowledge and evaluation. *Personality and Social Psychology Bulletin*, *7*, 523–528.

Miller, N., & Brewer, M. B. (Eds) (1984). *Groups in contact. The psychology of desegregation*. New York: Academic Press.

Miller, N., Brewer, M. B., & Edwards, K. (1985). Cooperative interaction in desegregated settings: A laboratory analogue. *Journal of Social Issues*, *41*, 63–79.

Miller, N. E., & Bugelski, R. (1948). Minor studies in aggression: The influence of frustrations imposed by the ingroup on attitudes toward outgroups. *Journal of Psychology*, *25*, 437–442.

Mullen, B., Brown, R., & Smith, C. (1992). Ingroup bias as a function of salience, relevance, and status: An integration. *European Journal of Social Psychology*, *22*, 103–122.

Oakes, P. J., & Turner, J. C. (1980). Social categorization and intergroup behaviour: Does minimal intergroup discrimination make social identity more positive? *European Journal of Social Psychology*, *10*, 295–302.

Pettigrew, T. F. (1958). Personality and sociocultural factors in intergroup attitudes: A cross-national comparison. *Journal of Conflict Resolution*, *2*, 29–42.

Quattrone, G. A. (1986). On the perception of a group's variability. In S. Worchel & W. Austin (Eds) *The social psychology of intergroup relations* (2nd edn, pp. 25–48), Chicago, IL: Nelson Hall.

Rabbie, J. M., & Horwitz, M. (1969). Arousal of ingroup–outgroup bias by a chance win or loss. *Journal of Personality and Social Psychology*, *13*, 269–277.

Rokeach, M. (Ed.) (1960). *The open and closed mind*. New York: Basic Books.

Rokeach, M., Smith, P. W., & Evans, R. I. (1960). Two kinds of prejudice or one? In M. Rokeach (Ed.) *The open and closed mind* (pp. 132–168). New York: Basic Books.

Rothbart, M., & Park, B. (1986). On the confirmability and disconfirmability of trait concepts. *Journal of Personality and Social Psychology*, *50*, 131–142.

Runciman, W. G. (1966). *Relative deprivation and social justice*. London: Routledge & Kegan Paul.

Schofield, J. W. (1986). Black–white contact in desegregated schools. In M. Hewstone & R. J. Brown (Eds) *Contact and conflict in intergroup encounters* (pp. 79–92). Oxford: Basil Blackwell.

Schwarzwald, J., & Amir, Y. (1984). Interethnic relations and education: An Israeli perspective. In N. Miller & M. Brewer (Eds) *Groups in contact. The psychology of desegregation* (pp. 53–76). Orlando, FL: Academic Press.

Sherif, M. (1966). *Group conflict and co-operation*. London: Routledge & Kegan Paul.

Simon, B., & Brown, R. J. (1987). Perceived intragroup homogeneity in minority-majority contexts. *Journal of Personality and Social Psychology*, *53*, 703–711.

Slavin, R. E. (1983). When does cooperative learning increase student achievement? *Psychological Bulletin*, *94*, 429–445.

Tajfel, H. (1959). The anchoring effects of value in a scale of judgements. *British Journal of Psychology*, *50*, 294–304.

Tajfel, H. (Ed.) (1978). *Differentiation between social groups. Studies in the social psychology of intergroup relations*. London: Academic Press.

Tajfel, H., & Turner, J. C. (1986). The social identity theory of intergroup behavior. In S Worchel & W. Austin (Eds) *Psychology of intergroup relations* (pp. 7–24). Chicago: Nelson-Hall.

Tajfel, H., & Wilkes, A. L. (1963). Classification and quantitative judgement. *British Journal of Psychology*, *54*, 101–114.

Tajfel, H., Flament, C., Billig, M. G., & Bundy, R. P. (1971). Social categorization and intergroup behaviour. *European Journal of Social Psychology*, *1*, 149–178.

Vanneman, R. D., & Pettigrew, T. F. (1972). Race and relative deprivation in the urban United States. *Race*, *13*, 461–486.

Walker, L., & Mann, L. (1987). Unemployment, relative deprivation, and social protest. *Personality and Social Psychology Bulletin*, *13*, 275–283.

Wilder, D. A. (1984). Intergroup contact: The typical member and the exception to the rule. *Journal of Experimental Social Psychology, 20,* 177–194.

Worchel, S., Andreoli, V. A., & Folger, R. (1977). Intergroup cooperation and intergroup attraction: The effect of previous interaction and outcome of combined effort. *Journal of Experimental Social Psychology, 13,* 131–140.

NON-VERBAL COMMUNICATION

Peter Bull

University of York, England

Lesley Frederikson

Massey University, New Zealand

The role of non-verbal cues in social interaction	Interpersonal relationships
Emotion	**Practical applications of non-verbal communication research**
Body movement and speech	**Further reading**
Individual differences	**References**

There is nothing new in the belief that non-verbal communication is more powerful than speech. Alfred Adler (1870–1937), the neo-Freudian analyst, liked to quote an aphorism from the sixteenth-century Protestant reformer Martin Luther "not to watch a person's mouth but his fists". More recent decades have seen the growth of a popular literature which extols the significance and importance of "body language", while at the same time providing an underlying theme in the more sober pursuits of academic research. Within the rubric of such research can be considered investigations of facial expression, eye contact, pupil dilation, posture, gesture, and interpersonal distance. It can refer as well to communication through touch or smell, through various kinds of artifacts such as masks and clothes, or through formalized communication systems such as semaphore. Sometimes, it has also been used to refer to the vocal features of speech, such as intonation, stress, speech rate, accent, and loudness. Because the term "non-verbal" is a definition only by exclusion, the number of features that can be included under this term is virtually limitless.

The term communication also poses problems of definition, particularly with respect to what behaviours can be properly regarded as communicative. Some theorists have argued that all non-verbal behaviour should be regarded as communicative (e.g., Watzlawick, Beavin, & Jackson, 1968). Other theorists have argued that only those behaviours that are intended to be communicative should be regarded as such (e.g., Ekman & Friesen, 1969a). Both these viewpoints were criticized in an important theoretical paper by Wiener, Devoe, Robinson, and Geller (1972), who argued that for non-verbal behaviour to be regarded as non-verbal communication, it needs to be shown that information is both received and transmitted through non-verbal behaviour: in their terminology, that there is both systematic encoding and appropriate decoding.

Wiener et al. (1972) called their article "Nonverbal behaviour and non-verbal communication", and the distinction is important: not all non-verbal behaviour can be regarded as communicative. Communication can be said to occur only when information transmitted through non-verbal behaviour is accurately and appropriately interpreted by the decoder. Wiener et al. also challenge the view that the only non-verbal behaviours that can be regarded as communicative are those that are intended as such. They point out that the intentions of the encoder are irrelevant; it is often difficult to establish exactly what a person does intend to communicate and there is no basis in the behaviours themselves for deciding whether or not they should be regarded as intentional communications.

Indeed, non-verbal communication may take place even against the express intentions of the encoder. For example, Bull (1987) carried out a number of studies of the way in which listener attitudes and emotions are encoded in posture. They showed that boredom is systematically associated with leaning back, dropping the head, supporting the head on one hand and stretching out the legs (see Figure 1). A person in an audience may show these behaviours without any conscious intention to communicate boredom; nevertheless, this may well be the message that the speaker receives! The person in the audience may even try to suppress these tell-tale signs of boredom by trying hard to appear attentive, but still be incapable of suppressing the occasional yawn. To the speaker, the listener may still communicate that he or she is bored by the talk, despite the best intentions not to do so!

It is also our view that communication can occur without conscious awareness, in the sense that neither encoder nor decoder needs to be able to identify the specific non-verbal cues through which a particular message is transmitted. So, for example, people may be left with the feeling that someone was upset or angry without being able to specify exactly what cues were responsible for creating that impression. Indeed, it can be argued that a great deal of non-verbal communication takes this form, and that one task of the researcher is to try and identify more precisely the cues that are responsible for creating such impressions.

This view of communication can be nicely demonstrated from studies of

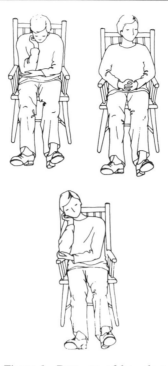

Figure 1 Postures of boredom
Source: Reproduced by permission from Bull, 1983

pupil dilation. Hess and Polt (1960) noticed that on viewing pictures of particular interest, the pupils of their subjects tended to dilate. So, for example, the pupils of women seemed to dilate when seeing a picture of a nude man and a picture of a mother and baby, while the pupils of men dilated when seeing a picture of a nude woman. (In this experiment there was an untested assumption that the subjects were heterosexual; the women's pupils did not dilate as much as the men's to the picture of the nude woman.) In another experiment, Hess (1965) showed a series of pictures to 20 young men, which included two photographs of an attractive young woman. The photos were touched up such that in one case the pupils of the young woman were extra large, and in the other case, extra small (see Figure 2). The pupils of the young men tended to dilate more on seeing the woman with the dilated pupils, although most of the men said the pictures were identical. Hess interpreted these findings as showing that the men found the woman with dilated pupils as more attractive, presumably because they felt she was more attracted to them. Hess (1975) also found that when asked to describe the two photos, they said that the woman with large pupils was "soft", "more feminine", or "pretty", while the same woman with constricted pupils was

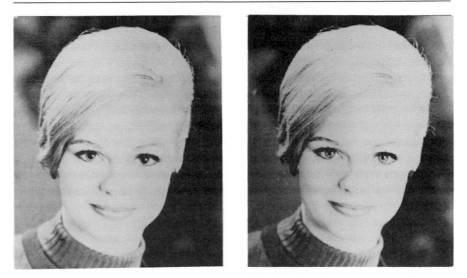

Figure 2 Photographs of a woman with dilated and constricted pupils
Source: Hess, 1965

described as being "hard", "selfish", or "cold". One of the interesting features of these studies is that none of the students seemed to be aware of the differences in pupil size; nevertheless, these differences appeared to have significant effects on the way in which the woman in the photograph was perceived. Another important feature of pupil dilation is that it is a response of the autonomic nervous system, and hence not under direct voluntary control; in that sense, it cannot be said to be an intentional form of communication (unless you apply belladonna to the eyes or dim the lights!).

But if people communicate unintended messages without awareness through pupil dilation, what is it that is being communicated? Hess (1965) proposed that the pupils dilate in response to stimuli we find attractive, and actually constrict in response to stimuli we find unattractive (the aversion-constriction hypothesis). In fact, this claim has proved to be extremely controversial. Other studies suggest that the pupils simply dilate in arousal, whether that arousal is positive or negative. For example, in one experiment by White and Maltzman (1978), the pupil sizes of students were measured while they were listening to passages read from a novel. One passage was intended to be erotic, another to be neutral, the third passage was an unpleasant description of a lynching mutilation. The authors found an immediate dilation at the beginning of each passage, with the erotic and mutilation passages maintaining pupil dilation for about 60 seconds. Thus, it seems that when aroused, the pupil dilates, although there is no intention to communicate, nor are people necessarily aware of pupil dilation.

THE ROLE OF NON-VERBAL CUES IN SOCIAL INTERACTION

Non-verbal cues can be said to communicate information about emotion, speech, individual differences, and interpersonal relationships; their significance also needs to be considered in specific social contexts (Bull, 1983).

Emotion

Particular importance is commonly ascribed to non-verbal cues in the communication of emotion, stemming from the observations of Charles Darwin (1872), who argued that the facial expressions of emotion constitute part of an innate, adaptive, physiological response. In fact, this view has proved to be extremely controversial. Its most explicit rejection came from Birdwhistell (1971), who described how he was initially influenced by Darwin's views, but came to recognize how both the incidence and meaning of, say, smiling might vary between different social groups. Birdwhistell reached the conclusion that "charts of smile frequency were not going to be very reliable as maps for the location of happy Americans". He rejected the view that smiles directly express underlying physiological states, arguing instead that meaning can be understood only within a particular social context.

Later research has provided support for Darwin's observations, although none of the evidence is conclusive. There are cross-cultural studies (e.g., Ekman, Friesen, & Ellsworth, 1972) which show that facial expressions associated with six emotions (happiness, sadness, anger, fear, disgust, surprise) are decoded in the same way by members of both literate and preliterate cultures. However, Russell (1991) has pointed out that the language used to describe emotion is by no means universal: neither the words for so-called basic emotions such as anger and sadness, nor even the word for emotion itself is found in every culture. He goes on to argue that experiments such as Ekman's, in which people are asked to identify facial expressions from a limited range of emotion categories, may well overestimate universality, because they obscure subtle and significant differences between cultures in the way in which they describe emotion. Moreover, even if one accepts the existence of universals in decoding, it is only necessary to hypothesize that whatever is responsible for common facial expressions is constant for all humankind: inheritance is one such factor, but learning experiences common to all humankind could equally well be another.

A second source of evidence comes from the study of children born deaf and blind. The ethologist Eibl-Eibesfeldt (1973) filmed a number of such children and claimed that they showed the same kinds of basic facial expressions in appropriate situational contexts as do non-handicapped children. Again, a likely explanation for these observations is that such expressions are inherited, but it is still possible that they may be learned through some form of behaviour shaping. Finally, Oster and Ekman (1977) have shown that all but one of the discrete muscle actions visible in the adult can be identified in newborn infants, both full-term and premature. Again, however, this does not prove that the association of particular facial expressions with particular emotions is innate. Smiling can be called a universal gesture in the sense that it is an expression that human beings are universally capable of producing, but this does not mean that it is innately associated with the emotion of happiness, nor that it has a universal meaning.

Thus, although the evidence is consistent with the view that certain facial expressions of emotion are innate, it is by no means conclusive. The rival positions have been neatly reconciled in what Ekman (1972) called his neuro-cultural model of emotional expression. He proposed that there are at least six fundamental emotions with innate expressions which can be modified through the learning of what he calls display rules; display rules refer to norms governing the expression of emotions in different contexts and may take the form of attenuation, amplification, substitution, or concealment of particular expressions. Ekman and Friesen (1986) also provided evidence for a seventh universal facial expression of contempt.

An experiment carried out by Ekman on cross-cultural differences clearly illustrates the use of this model. Ekman, Friesen, and Malmstrom (in Ekman et al., 1972) showed groups of Americans and Japanese a neutral and a stress-inducing film. They saw both films on their own, but their facial expressions were videotaped without their awareness. Both groups differed in their response to the neutral and stress films, but their facial expressions were highly similar. After seeing the stress film, a member of their own culture entered the room and conducted an interview about their experience. The Japanese appeared to engage in substitution by showing happy faces when interviewed by Japanese interviewers, whereas the Americans typically did not conceal signs of negative feelings when they talked with their American interviewer. The experiment nicely supports informal accounts of Japanese culture, where there is said to be a taboo governing the expression of negative emotions in public. The experiment also suggests that the fundamental emotional expressions were shown when the subjects watched the films on their own, but that culturally learned display rules came into operation when interviewed by a member of their own culture.

The neuro-cultural model of emotional expression has important implications for the significance we ascribe to facial expression in the communication of emotion. If there are at least seven innate expressions, then this would suggest that they constitute a particularly important means of communicating information about emotion. However, Ekman and Friesen also point out that we can learn control of our facial expressions through concealment, substitution, amplifications or attenuation. How then can we distinguish between expressions that are posed or spontaneous, between expressions that are faked or genuine? Ekman and Friesen (1982) suggest a number of ways in which spontaneous and false smiles can be distinguished.

In a genuinely felt smile, three action units are involved: raising the corners of the lips, raising the cheeks which may produce crows-feet wrinkles, and raising the lower eyelid. In a false or posed smile, the second and third action units may not be involved. They also suggest that timing may be a cue to posed smiles. A false smile may appear too early or too late. The apex of the smile may be too long – felt smiles seldom last more than 4 seconds. Onset may be too short, giving an abrupt appearance to the smile.

Another clue to the genuineness of an expression is its symmetry. Skinner and Mullen (1991) have published a meta-analysis of 14 studies of asymmetry, in which the authors investigated whether posed expressions are more asymmetrical than spontaneous expressions. Skinner and Mullen criticize earlier research for failing to make a distinction between emotional and neutral posed expressions. They conclude that the effect of asymmetry is much more pronounced for posed emotional expressions, which suggests that asymmetry may indeed be a useful cue in detecting insincere or deceitful expressions. Further cues to deception may come from what Ekman and Friesen call "non-verbal leakage" whereby information about deception is revealed more through body movement than facial expression. They argue that because of the greater repertoire of facial movement, people may be more careful to control their facial movements when trying to deceive others and hence are more likely to give themselves away inadvertently through bodily movements.

The proposal that facial expressions of emotion may be both innate and learned has important implications for the significance that we ascribe to facial expression in the communication of emotion. For example, it means that no simple answer is possible to the question of the relative importance of different cues in communicating information about emotion, since it may depend on whether we are discussing deliberate or spontaneous expressions. In terms of spontaneous expression, it still seems likely that the face constitutes the prime non-verbal source of information about emotion. Facial muscle changes are rapid, the face is usually clearly visible, and there are at least six universal expressions probably innately associated with different emotions. Conversely, the eyes and the pupils lack the same variety of movement as the face and are also less easily discernible. It has yet to be shown that pupil dilation or gaze enables us to distinguish between different emotions; instead, they probably convey information about intensity of emotion rather than the nature of emotion as such (Bull, 1983, pp. 2–9, 43–46). The evidence on posture and gesture is much less clear-cut; it is possible to distinguish between different emotions and attitudes on the basis of posture alone (Bull, 1987).

Body movement and speech

The central importance of non-verbal cues in the communication of emotion has led some writers to regard body movement as an alternative system to speech, offering a more reliable indicator of people's true feelings. This has been especially true of the popular literature on "body language", in which it seems to be suggested that it represents a kind of "royal road to the unconscious", providing a vital source of information about people's "real" feelings and attitudes. For example, Fast (1970) maintains that body language conveys an emotional message to the outside world that is more reliable than the spoken word: "if the spoken language is stripped away and the only communication left is body language, the truth will find some way of poking through" (Fast, 1970, p. 92).

One particular danger of this viewpoint is that it neglects the extent to which speech and body movement complement each other in communication; indeed, it may be the case that incidence in which non-verbal communication conflicts with speech are the exception rather than the rule. For example, Condon and Ogston (1966) described from a frame-by-frame analysis how the body of the speaker moves closely in time with his or her speech, a phenomenon which they called self-synchrony. Condon and Ogston's observations were not simply confined to hand gestures; it was movements of all parts of the body that they found to be closely synchronized with speech. At the same time, it does not appear to be the case that every bodily movement is related to discourse. Freedman and Hoffman (1967) found in a study of psychotherapy sessions that it was essentially non-contact hand movements (movements that do not involve touching the body) that were judged as related to speech. In a quite different context (that of political speech-making), Bull (1987) also found that it was primarily non-contact rather than contact hand movements that were related to vocal stress. In fact, non-verbal behaviour has been shown to be related to speech in terms of syntax (Lindenfeld, 1971), vocal stress (Pittenger, Hockett, and Danehy, 1960) and meaning (e.g., Scheflen, 1964).

If non-verbal behaviour is so clearly related to speech, what functions does it serve? Ekman and Friesen (1969a) distinguished three types of functions, which they termed emblems, illustrators, and regulators. The term "emblem" refers to those non-verbal acts that have a direct verbal translation, such as nodding the head when meaning "Yes", or shaking the head when meaning "No". Their function is communicative and explicitly recognized as such. Emblems are generally assumed to be specific to particular cultures or occupations, but there do appear to be pan-cultural emblems such as the "eyebrow flash", where a person raises the eyebrows for about one-sixth of a second as a greeting; Eibl-Eibesfeldt (1972) claims to have observed this in a wide number of differing cultures. Morris, Collett, Marsh, and O'Shaughnessy (1979) mapped the geographical distribution of 20 emblems across western and southern Europe and the Mediterranean. Their findings showed that some emblems were specific to one culture. In Italy, for example, pressing and rotating a straightened forefinger against the cheek

Figure 3 The cheek-screw
Source: Based on a photograph in Morris, Collett, Marsh, and Shaughnessy, 1979. Reproduced
by permission

(sometimes referred to as the cheek-screw) is a gesture of praise; it is,
however, little known elsewhere in Europe (see Figure 3).

The meaning of other emblems varies between cultures. A gesture that
Morris et al. (1979) call the ring, where the thumb and forefinger touch to
form a circle, means in Britain that something is good, in parts of France that
something is worthless, while in Sardinia it is an obscene sexual insult (see
Figure 4)!

Ekman and Friesen (1969a) argue that the particular importance of

Figure 4 The ring
Source: Based on a photograph in Morris et al., 1979. Reproduced by permission

emblems stems from the fact that they are often used when speech is difficult or impossible, and hence function as an alternative system to speech. So, for example, the police officer directing traffic on points duty can be said to be using emblems in a situation where speech is not possible. A number of the emblems described by Morris et al. (1979) are insults; the advantage of insulting people at a distance is presumably that it is more difficult for the insulted person to retaliate!

Regulators are movements that are assumed to guide and control the flow of conversation, for example, in the way in which people exchange speaking turns. The most intensive set of studies of turn-taking have been carried out by Duncan and his associates (e.g., Duncan & Fiske, 1985). Duncan found that attempts by the listener to take over the turn could be essentially eliminated by the speaker continuing to gesture; Duncan called this the attempt-suppressing signal. Duncan's observations also showed that ceasing to gesture was one of five turn-yielding cues, signals that offer a speaking turn to the other person. Duncan maintained that the effect of these five cues is additive: his observations showed a linear relationship between the number of turn-yielding cues displayed and a smooth switch between speakers. The other cues were the completion of a grammatical clause, a rise or fall in pitch at the end of a clause, a drawl on the final syllable, and the use of stereotyped expressions such as "you know".

Illustrators are movements that are directly tied to speech; it is maintained that they facilitate communication by amplifying and elaborating the verbal content of the message. Whether illustrators do in fact facilitate communication was tested in an experiment by Rogers (1978). Rogers prepared a silent film of various actions being performed, such as a car making a series of turns, or a tennis ball bouncing into a corner. Observers were asked to view these actions and to describe them to another person who was unable to see the film. These descriptions were videotaped and shown to a second group of observers either with sound and vision, sound only, or in a modified audio-visual condition where the contrast was reduced to obliterate facial information and hence prevent lip-reading. Comprehension was found to be significantly better in the modified audio-visual condition than in the audio condition only, thus suggesting that illustrators do facilitate speech comprehension independently of the information obtained from lip-reading.

Ekman and Friesen's (1969a) threefold distinction into emblems, illustrators, and regulators is useful in that it serves to highlight some of the different functions of gesture in relation to speech. However, a major implication of their typology is that gesture is essentially secondary to speech, either serving as a substitute form of communication when speech is difficult or impossible, or serving to support the spoken message. An alternative view stems from Kendon (1985), who points out that gesture as a silent, visual mode of expression has very different properties from those of speech, and consequently that it is suitable for a different range of communication tasks.

In fact, not only is gesture a visual means of communication, but also it is a highly visible means of communication, especially in comparison to facial expression or eye contact. Hence, gesture may be of particular value to an orator who is physically separated from the audience, such that other aspects of non-verbal communication may not be easily discernible (e.g., Bull, 1987). Again, gesture is extremely useful when seeking to attract someone's attention. Heath (1986) showed in a very interesting analysis of medical consultations that when the (male) doctor's attention was focused on his notes, patients would use more flamboyant gestures as a means of attracting his attention. In this context, gesture has the additional advantage of indirectness as well as visibility, avoiding the need to ask for attention from a higher-status figure like a doctor. This introduces another feature of gesture as a communication system, which is its lack of precision. In certain contexts this can be advantageous where something is too delicate to be put into words.

Not only is gesture a highly visible form of communication, but also there are differences in visibility between different forms of body movement. Scheflen (e.g., 1964) proposed that different sizes of movement are used to indicate structural units of differing importance in conversation. For example, he observed that American speakers change the position of their head and eyes every few sentences. Each of these shifts marks the end of a structural unit, which Scheflen calls a "point", because it corresponds roughly to making a point in a discussion. A sequence of several points go to make up a "position", which corresponds roughly to a point of view that a person may take in conversation. This is a much larger unit of speech and is indicated by a much larger body movement, typically by a gross postural shift involving at least half the body.

The value of emphasizing the distinctive properties of gesture is that it enables us to get a clearer sense of its distinctive role in communication. In fact, Kendon (1985) maintains that gesture is as fundamental as speech for the representation of meaning, that it is separate, in principle equal with speech, joined with speech only because it is used simultaneously for the same purpose. This is consistent with studies on language production, for example, McNeill (1985) has proposed that gestures and speech are part of the same psychological structure and share a common computational stage. The principal evidence for this, McNeill argues, is as follows. Gestures occur primarily during speech. They have semantic and pragmatic functions that parallel those of speech. They are synchronized with linguistic units in speech. They dissolve together with speech in aphasia. They develop together with speech in children.

Thus, gesture should be seen not as an alternative to speech, but as an additional resource, as part of a multichannel system of communication, which allows the skilled speaker further options through which to convey meaning.

Individual differences

Not only do non-verbal cues encode information about individual differences, but also there are individual differences concerning the extent to which people may transmit information through non-verbal cues: some people may transmit a great deal of information through non-verbal cues, others relatively little (Bull, 1985). For example, Hall (1979) reviewed twenty-six studies in which comparisons were made of sex differences in encoding: nine showed a significant gender difference, eight of which showed that women were clearer encoders. Hence, in this sense women can be seen as more expressive, that is, they transmit more information through non-verbal cues. Men and women also differ in the non-verbal behaviour they use. A review of the literature by Hall (1984) showed a number of consistent non-verbal sex differences. Women both smile more and gaze more at other people; they prefer closer interpersonal distances and are approached more closely than men; they also use smaller and less open body movements and positions. Given that people can make quite subtle judgements about the sex-role attitudes of others on the basis of their non-verbal behaviour alone (Lippa, 1978), it can be argued that such behaviours can be used as a code for communicating information about masculinity and femininity (Bull, 1985). Thus, not only do people differ in the extent to which they transmit information through non-verbal cues, but also the non-verbal cues they do employ may encode significant information about aspects of personality such as sex-role attitudes.

Individual differences in decoding constitute a second important theoretical issue. A number of studies have been carried out to investigate whether groups differ in their decoding ability, whether, for example, women are superior to men in this respect, or whether psychiatric patients are disadvantaged in comparison to the normal population. The importance of these findings is that although non-verbal cues may encode information about, say, emotion, speech, or individual differences, such information may not always be accurately decoded; if certain groups of people fail to decode non-verbal cues appropriately, then the significance of those cues as a form of communication must inevitably vary according to the sensitivity of the decoders.

Hall (1978) reviewed 75 studies of sex differences in decoding non-verbal cues. The majority of these studies made use of posed expressions, in which the decoders' task was to guess what emotions the actor was trying to convey. There were also studies of spontaneous expressions, in which encoders watched films or slides and the decoders' task was to guess from the non-verbal expressions which films or slides the encoders were watching. Of the 75 studies reviewed by Hall, 24 showed a significant sex difference, 23 of which were in favour of women – a proportion that is statistically highly significant. The sex of the encoders does not make any difference: women are better decoders whether they are judging men or other women. Sex differences in decoding are also unaffected by age. Girls are better decoders than boys, just as women are better decoders than men, and it makes no difference whether the encoder is a child or an adult. Subsequently, Hall (1984) analysed a further 50 studies of decoding: 11 of these showed a significant sex difference, 10 of which were in favour of women.

Smith, Archer, and Costanzo (1991) showed a further interesting sex difference in non-verbal cues. They used a test called the Interpersonal Perception Task, which poses questions about videotaped sequences of naturalistic behaviour; each question has an objectively correct answer. They found that, just as with previous research, men performed significantly worse on the task than did women. However, when they were asked to estimate the number of questions they had answered correctly, the men's estimates were significantly higher than the women's. This would suggest not only that women are better at decoding non-verbal cues, but also that either men overestimate their performance, or women underestimate their performance, or both.

Interpersonal relationships

Non-verbal behaviour varies as a function of the relationships between people. A number of experiments have been carried out in which observers are asked to make judgements about the identity of an unseen conversational partner on the basis of viewing the non-verbal behaviour of one of the conversationalists alone. For example, studies by Abramovitch (e.g., Abramovitch, 1977) have shown that even very young children are capable of accurately discerning the relationship between people from non-verbal cues alone. Benjamin and Creider (1975) showed that adult observers were able to perform this task successfully in terms of the age, sex, and acquaintanceship of the unseen conversational partner. From an analysis of the videotapes, they also identified certain differences in facial expression according to the type of the relationship. When adults talked to children, their muscle tonus was low, the skin beneath the eyes and over the cheek bones hanging loosely down except during broad smiles, whereas when adults talked to other adults, their skin was bunched and raised. There also appear to be significant differences in the activity rate between same-age and different-age conversations, conversations between people of the same age appearing to be much more animated. The significance of these studies is not only that non-verbal behaviour varies according to the nature of the relationship, but also that decoders can utilize such information to discern the relationship between people in terms of sex, age, and acquaintanceship.

One cue that appears to be of particular significance in interpersonal relationships is postural congruence. This refers to people imitating one another's postures, which Scheflen (1964) claimed indicates similarity in views or roles in a group; conversely, non-congruence of posture is used to indicate marked divergences in attitude or status. In a study based on

Scheflen's observations, Charny (1966) analysed a film of a psychotherapy session. Postures were categorized as congruent or non-congruent; a further distinction was made between mirror-image congruent postures, where one person's left side is equivalent to the other's right, and identical postures, where right matches right and left matches left (see Figure 5). Charny found that as the interview progressed, there was a significant trend towards spending more time in mirror-congruent postures. He also found that the speech associated with these postures was more positive, concluding that they may be taken as indicative of rapport or relatedness. Identical postures rarely occurred during the session, so were not included in the final analysis.

LaFrance investigated whether postural congruence is related to rapport in American college seminars. In one study, LaFrance and Broadbent (1976) found a significant positive correlation between mirror-congruent postures and a questionnaire intended to measure rapport, a significant negative correlation between non-congruent postures and rapport, and no significant relationship between identical postures and rapport. In a second study, LaFrance (1979) measured posture and rapport during the first week (time 1) and the final week (time 2) of a six-week seminar course to investigate the

Figure 5 Postural congruence. The pair in the foreground are showing identical postures, the pair in the background mirror-image postures
Source: Reproduced by permission from Bull, 1983

probable direction of causality between mirror-congruent postures and rapport, using a method of statistical analysis known as the cross-lag panel technique. The results suggested that it is postural congruence that may be influential in establishing rapport.

Thus, a number of encoding studies of postural congruence do show that it is related to rapport. Another way of investigating the phenomenon is to see how postural congruence is decoded. Trout and Rosenfeld (1980) set up an experiment to investigate the perception of postural congruency in simulated therapist–client interactions. They arranged for two male US graduate students to play the roles of therapist and client, and to adopt either mirror-congruent or non-congruent postures; there was no soundtrack, and the faces were blocked out of the tape. The results showed that the mirror-congruent postures were rated as indicating significantly more rapport than the non-congruent postures. Thus, given the evidence from studies of both encoding and decoding, it appears that postural congruence does communicate rapport.

Non-verbal communication also plays an important part in courtship: Grammer (1990) proposed that its function is both to enhance attractiveness and to show interest and availability. In fact, the very vagueness of non-verbal communication can be an advantage. Whereas direct verbal invitations require an explicit response, non-verbal invitations are not so binding and can be withdrawn, refused, or denied without giving offence or causing loss of self-esteem. Grammer has looked in detail at the non-verbal cues associated with sexual interest. He observed opposite-sex pairs of strangers in conversation, and correlated their non-verbal behaviour during laughter with ratings of sexual interest. He found that interest was significantly associated with a number of distinct body movements and postures but that it did not correlate with laughter. Postures of individual body parts can be combined to produce a total body posture which indicates an overall level of interest. In fact, Grammer found that the effect is additive: the more of the high-interest postures that are present the higher the level of expressed interest. This allows "fine-tuning" in signalling interest through various combinations of high and low interest postures.

Non-verbal behaviour can thus be used to identify the type of relationship between people, and it is also important within relationships. Studies of postural congruence have shown that the configuration of postures between people is important, while Grammer's (1990) study highlights the meaning of distinct signals communicated between members of the opposite sex.

PRACTICAL APPLICATIONS OF NON-VERBAL COMMUNI-CATION RESEARCH

There is no doubt that the systematic study of non-verbal behaviour does have considerable practical significance. According to the social skills model, social behaviour can be seen as a kind of motor skill involving the same kinds of processes as, for example, driving a car or playing a game of tennis (Argyle & Kendon, 1967). The advantage of this approach is that we can apply ideas and concepts developed in the study of motor skills to the study of social interaction.

One major implication of this model is that, if social behaviour is seen as a skill, then it is possible for people to improve their performance as with any other skill. This learning might take the form of a systematic course in social skills training, or it might be the case that simply reading a book on non-verbal communication may be sufficient to improve the quality of a person's social relationships (as is typically claimed in the popular literature on "body language"). One of the best known forms of social skills training is assertiveness training (e.g., Rakos, 1991). In fact, the two terms have sometimes been used interchangeably, although it is now recognized that assertiveness refers to a more limited set of interpersonal skills. Both these forms of training include specific instruction in non-verbal behaviour especially in the areas of encoding and decoding.

Social skills training has been used with a wide variety of populations for a wide variety of different problems. For example, it has been used as a way of improving people's ability to handle conversations, to improve their perceptiveness of others, and to improve people's performance in job interviews. It has also been used as a form of therapy for psychiatric patients experiencing a range of different problems. In addition, it has been used as a form of professional training with, for example, teachers, doctors, nurses, and police officers. In fact, the principles of social skills training can be applied to virtually any situation involving interpersonal communication. Wright (1989) cites the case of a disabled law student who was confined to a wheelchair and was also unable to produce a normal range of manual gestures. Her oral presentations were criticised for not appearing sufficiently aggressive, so she was encouraged (within the limits of her disability) to develop a range of head and shoulder movements and to utilise assertive pauses in the presentation to emphasize important points. The resulting communication was viewed as more assertive and better suited for the student's purpose.

One possible criticism of social skills training is the extent to which it may embody the prejudices and preconceptions of the social skills trainer. However, with advances in non-verbal communication research, it is now possible to use objective tests as a means of instruction, such as Costanzo and Archer's (1989) Interpersonal Perception Task (IPT) referred to earlier. This is an objective test of non-verbal perceptiveness, based on naturally occurring sequences of behaviour. Decoders are shown 30 brief scenes, each of which is paired with a multiple-choice question with two or three options. In every case, the answer to the question is completely objective. For example, two of the scenes show a woman talking on the telephone. In each scene, the decoders are asked to identify to whom she is talking. In the first scene (see Figure 6) the choice is between her mother, a female friend she has known for many years, or a male friend she has known for many years. In the second scene (see Figure 7) the choice is between her mother, a female friend, or her boyfriend.

The IPT has been used by Costanzo and Archer (1991) as a means of teaching about non-verbal communication; they found that a group instructed in this way performed significantly better than another group attending traditional lectures. The real value of the IPT is that it can be used not only to objectively assess skill in decoding but also as a means of improving non-verbal perceptiveness. However, perceptiveness is only one aspect of social skill; in terms of the social skills model, the selective perception of cues has to be transformed through central translation process into effective motor responses. Thus, it is perfectly possible for someone to be highly perceptive without being able to translate that perceptiveness into appropriate social behaviour. In this sense, we also need objective tests of encoding, which will be useful both as a means of assessing encoding skill and as a means of improving encoding performance.

Despite these reservations, the significance of advances in non-verbal communication research should not be underestimated. Studies since the 1960s have unquestionably demonstrated the importance of non-verbal behaviour in interpersonal communication; as a consequence, our concept of what constitutes communication has been substantially enhanced, while a more

Figure 6   Who is the woman talking to on the telephone?
Source: Reproduced by permission from Archer and Costanzo, 1988

Figure 7 Who is the woman talking to on the telephone?
Source: Reproduced by permission from Archer and Costanzo, 1988

profound and sophisticated understanding has been acquired of the processes
and practice of social interaction.

FURTHER READING

Argyle, M. (1988). *Bodily communication* (2nd edn). London: Methuen.
Bull, P. E. (1983). *Body movement and interpersonal communication*. Chichester:
Wiley.
Ekman, P., & Friesen, W. V. (1975). *Unmasking the Face*. Englewood Cliffs, NJ:
Prentice-Hall.
Rakos, R. F. (1991). *Assertive Behavior*. London: Routledge.
Smith, H. J., Archer, D., & Costanzo, M. (1991). "Just a hunch": Accuracy and
awareness in person perception. *Journal of Nonverbal Behavior*, *15*, 3–18.

REFERENCES

Abramovitch, R. (1977). Children's recognition of situational aspects of facial expres-
sion. *Child Development*, *48*, 459–463.
Archer, D., & Costanzo, M. (1988). *The Interpersonal Perception Task (IPT)*.
(Available from University of California Extension Center for Media and
Independent Learning, 2176 Shattuck Avenue, Berkeley, CA, 94704, USA.
Argyle, M., & Kendon, A. (1967). The experimental analysis of social performance.
In L. Berkowitz (Ed.) *Advances in Experimental Social Psychology* (vol. 3,
pp. 55–97). New York: Academic Press.
Benjamin, G. R., & Creider, C. A. (1975). Social distinctions in non-verbal behavior.
Semiotica, *14*, 52–60.

Birdwhistell, R. L. (1971). *Kinesics and context*. London: Allen Lane, The Penguin Press.

Bull, P. E. (1983). *Body movement and interpersonal communication*. Chichester: Wiley.

Bull, P. E. (1985). Individual differences in non-verbal communication. In B. D. Kirkcaldy (Ed.) *Individual differences in movement* (pp. 231–245). Lancaster: Medical and Technical Press.

Bull, P. E. (1987). *Posture and gesture*. Oxford: Pergamon.

Charny, E. J. (1966). Psychosomatic manifestations of rapport in psychotherapy. *Psychosomatic Medicine, 28*, 305–315.

Condon, W. S., & Ogston, W. D. (1966). Sound film analysis of normal and pathological behavior patterns. *Journal of Nervous and Mental Diseases, 143*, 338–347.

Costanzo, M., & Archer, D. (1989). Interpreting the expressive behavior of others: The Interpersonal Perception Task (IPT). *Journal of Nonverbal Behavior, 13*, 225–245.

Costanzo, M., & Archer, D. (1991). A method for teaching about verbal and non-verbal communication. *Teaching of Psychology, 18*, 223–226.

Darwin, C. (1872). *The expression of emotions in man and animals*. London: Murray.

Duncan, S., & Fiske, D. W. (1977). *Face-to-face interaction: Research and theory*. Hillsdale, NJ: Lawrence Erlbaum.

Duncan, S., & Fiske, D. W. (1985). *Interaction structure and strategy*. New York: Cambridge University Press.

Eibl-Eibesfeldt, I. (1972). Similarities and differences between cultures in expressive movements. In R. A. Hinde (Ed.) *Non-verbal communication* (pp. 297–311). Cambridge: Cambridge University Press.

Eibl-Eibesfeldt, I. (1973). The expressive behaviour of the deaf-and-blind born. In M. Von Cranach & I. Vine (Eds) *Social communication and movement* (pp. 163–194). London: Academic Press.

Ekman, P. (1972). Universal and cultural differences in facial expressions of emotion. In J. R. Cole (Ed.) *Nebraska symposium on motivation*, 1971 (pp. 207–283). Lincoln, NE: University of Nebraska Press.

Ekman, P., & Friesen, W. V. (1969a). The repertoire of nonverbal behavior: Categories, origins, usage and coding. *Semiotica, 1*, 49–98.

Ekman, P., & Friesen, W. V. (1969b) Non-verbal leakage and clues to deception. *Psychiatry, 32*, 88–106.

Ekman, P., & Friesen, W. V. (1982). Felt, false and miserable smiles. *Journal of Nonverbal Behavior, 6*, 238–252.

Ekman, P., & Friesen, W. V. (1986). A new pan-cultural facial expression of emotion. *Motivation and Emotion, 10*, 159–168.

Ekman, P., Friesen, W. V., & Ellsworth, P. (1972). *Emotion in the human face: Guidelines for research and an integration of findings*. New York: Pergamon.

Fast, J. (1970). *Body language*. New York: Evans.

Freedman, N., & Hoffman, S. P. (1967). Kinetic behavior in altered clinical states: Approach to objective analysis of motor behavior during clinical interviews. *Perceptual and Motor Skills, 24*, 527–539.

Grammer, K. (1990). Strangers meet: Laughter and nonverbal signs of interest in opposite-sex encounters. *Journal of Nonverbal Behavior, 14*, 209–236.

Hall, J. A. (1978). Gender effects in decoding non-verbal cues. *Psychological Bulletin, 85*, 845–857.

Hall, J. A. (1979). Gender, gender roles and non-verbal communication skills. In R. Rosenthal (Ed.) *Skill in non-verbal communication: Individual differences* (pp. 32–67). Cambridge, MA: Oelgeschlager, Gunn & Hain.

Hall, J. A. (1984). *Nonverbal sex differences: Communication accuracy and expressive style*. Baltimore, MD: Johns Hopkins University Press.

Heath, C. (1986). *Body movement and speech in medical interaction*. Cambridge: Cambridge University Press.

Hess, E. H. (1965). Attitude and pupil size. *Scientific American, 212*, 46–54.

Hess, E. H. (1975). The role of pupil size in communication. *Scientific American, 233*, 110–119.

Hess, E. H., & Polt, J. M. (1960). Pupil size as related to interest value of visual stimuli. *Science, 132*, 349–350.

Kendon, A. (1985). Some uses of gesture. In O. Tannen & M. Saville-Troike (Eds) *Perspectives on silence* (pp. 215–234). Norwood, NJ: Ablex.

LaFrance, M. (1979). Non-verbal synchrony and rapport: Analysis by the cross-lag panel technique. *Social Psychology Quarterly, 42*, 66–70.

LaFrance, M., & Broadbent, M. (1976). Group rapport: Posture sharing as a non-verbal indicator. *Group and Organisation Studies, 1*, 328–333.

Lindenfeld, J. (1971). Verbal and non-verbal elements in discourse. *Semiotica, 3*, 223–233.

Lippa, R. (1978). The naive perception of masculinity-femininity on the basis of expressive cues. *Journal of Research in Personality, 12*, 1–14.

McNeill, D. (1985). So you think gestures are nonverbal? *Psychological Review, 92*, 350–371.

Morris, D., Collett, P., Marsh, P., & O'Shaughnessy, M. (1979). *Gestures: Their origins and distribution*. London: Cape.

Oster, H., & Ekman, P. (1977). Facial behaviour in child development. In A. Collins (Ed.) *Minnesota symposium on child psychology vol. II* (pp. 231–276). Minneapolis, MN: Minnesota University Press.

Pittenger, R. E., Hockett, C. F., & Danehy, J. J. (1960). *The first five minutes: A sample of microscopic interview analysis*. Ithaca, NY: Martineau.

Rakos, R. F. (1991). *Assertive behavior*. London: Routledge.

Rogers, W. T. (1978). The contribution of kinesic illustrators toward the comprehension of verbal behaviour within utterances. *Human Comunication Research, 5*, 54–62.

Russell, J. A. (1991). Culture and the categorization of emotions. *Psychological Bulletin, 110*, 426–450.

Scheflen, A. E. (1964). The significance of posture in communication systems. *Psychiatry, 27*, 316–331.

Skinner, M., & Mullen, B. (1991). Facial asymmetry in emotional expression: A meta-analysis of research. *British Journal of Social Psychology, 30*, 113–124.

Smith, H. J., Archer, D., & Costanzo, M. (1991). "Just a hunch": Accuracy and awareness in person perception. *Journal of Nonverbal Behavior, 15*, 3–18.

Trout, D. L., & Rosenfeld, H. M. (1980). The effect of postural lean and body congruence on the judgment of psychotherapeutic rapport. *Journal of Nonverbal Behavior, 4*, 176–190.

Watzlawick, P., Beavin, J. H., & Jackson, D. D. (1968). *Pragmatics of human communication*. London: Faber & Faber.

White, G. L., & Maltzman, I. (1978). Pupillary activity while listening to verbal passages. *Journal of Research in Personality, 12*, 361–369.

Wiener, M., Devoe, S., Robinson, S., & Geller, J. (1972). Nonverbal behavior and nonverbal communication. *Psychological Review, 79*, 185–214.

Wright, G. (1989). The miscommunication of nonverbal behavior of persons with physical disabilities and the implications for vocational assessment. *Vocational Evaluation and Work Adjustment Bulletin*, Winter, 147–150.

10
ABNORMAL PSYCHOLOGY

INTRODUCTION

Abnormal psychology is devoted to the study of mental abnormalities. It is a branch of psychology concerned with research into the classification, aetiology (causation), diagnosis, treatment, and prevention of mental disorders; it is sometimes called psychopathology. It should be carefully distinguished from clinical psychology, which is a professional *practice* rather than an area of research and whose primary goal is practical help to people with mental disorders. Clinical psychology is discussed in detail in chapter 13.1 (Graham E. Powell).

The American Psychiatric Association's *Diagnostic and Statistical Manual of Mental Disorders*, which is referred to several times in this section, incorporates the most detailed classification system and diagnostic criteria for mental disorders in general use by psychologists as well as psychiatrists. The main categories of mental disorder in this classification are as follows: disorders usually first evident in infancy, childhood, or adolescence (including autistic disorder, which is discussed in chapter 10.3, and anorexia nervosa and bulimia nervosa, which are discussed in chapter 10.4); organic mental disorders (including senile and presenile dementia, which are touched on in chapter 8.5, John C. Cavanaugh); psychoactive substance use disorders (chapter 10.5); schizophrenia (chapter 10.2); delusional (paranoid) disorder (chapter 10.2); mood disorders (including the depressive disorders, discussed in chapters 10.1 and 10.2); anxiety disorders (including panic disorder, the phobias, obsessive-compulsive disorder, post-traumatic stress disorder, and generalized anxiety disorder, all of which are discussed in chapter 10.1); sexual disorders (touched on in chapter 6.4, John Bancroft); sleep disorders (touched on in chapter 2.4, J. Allan Hobson); somatoform disorders; dissociative disorders; and a few less specific rag-bag categories.

In more general terms, psychologists and psychiatrists commonly distinguish between two broad classes of mental disorders, which account for the majority of the cases requiring professional intervention, namely the psychoses (or psychotic disorders) and the neuroses (or neurotic disorders). Psychoses are characterized by gross impairment of self-insight, inability to meet some ordinary demands of life, and loss of contact with reality; in neurotic disorders, on the other hand, the symptoms are experienced as distressing and recognized by the individual as undesirable, but there is no gross impairment of functioning or loss of self-insight, and contact with reality is maintained. Chapter 10.1, by J. Mark G. Williams and Isabel R. Hargreaves, deals fairly comprehensively with the most common of the neurotic disorders, namely the depressive and anxiety disorders; chapter 10.2, by Chris Frith and Connie Cahill, deals equally comprehensively with the most common of the psychotic disorders, namely schizophrenia, the affective psychoses, and paranoia. Taken together, these two chapters cover the vast majority of people with mental disorders in society. Chapters 10.1 and 10.2 include discussions of the major symptoms and clinical features of the disorders, and their epidemiology (incidence, prevalence, and distribution), aetiology (causation), treatment, and prognosis.

In chapter 10.3 Simon Baron-Cohen summarizes the main features of infantile autism, one of the most severe, and also one of the most puzzling, of the mental disorders of young people. In chapter 10.4 Peter J. Cooper provides a comprehensive survey of the two major eating disorders, which are called anorexia nervosa and bulimia nervosa. Anorexia nervosa, sometimes misleadingly referred to in the popular press as "the slimmers' disease", involves a morbid fear of fatness and severe weight loss, and bulimia nervosa is usually associated with habitual bingeing followed by self-induced vomiting. Finally, in chapter 10.5, Geoffrey Lowe provides a wide-ranging survey of the whole field of alcohol and drug addiction.

A.M.C.

10.1

NEUROSES: DEPRESSIVE AND ANXIETY DISORDERS

J. Mark G. Williams and Isabel R. Hargreaves

University College of North Wales, Bangor, Wales

People vary in how much they are aware of their emotions, whether these are positive (such as happiness, joy, relaxation) or negative (such as anger, sadness, embarrassment, anxiety). This is partly because any emotion has a number of aspects, and people may feel or express their emotion in a variety of ways. First, there are the *subjective* aspects: we are consciously aware of certain feelings, even if we have difficulty in putting them into words. Second, there are the *behavioural* aspects. People who are anxious may pace up and down; people who are angry may clench their fists; people who are in despair may cry or hang their heads. Third, there are *bodily* aspects. The body undergoes various changes when an emotion is experienced. These may include changes in heart-rate, in muscle tension, in rate of perspiration (measured by small changes in electrical resistance across the surface of the skin), and in the electrical patterns in the brain (measured by electroencephalogram or EEG). Finally, there are the *cognitive* aspects. The ways in which the mind processes what is happening in the world and in the body (the perception, encoding, storage, and retrieval of information) becomes biased by emotional states. We shall see how such biases give rise to distortions in thinking, which cause even more emotional disturbance and further biased processing. That is, a vicious circle is set up from which it is difficult to escape. If this biasing has existed from childhood (often because of early stress), it gives rise to fixed attitudes and beliefs about oneself (e.g., "I am a failure") or about relationships ("No one would love me if they really knew me").

In this chapter, we shall describe the two most common emotional disorders: depressive and anxiety neuroses. The point at which normal emotion becomes abnormal is difficult to define. Anxiety and depression are a part of everyday living. It is only when they persist and become more severe that they cause problems for people or their families. We shall describe how symptoms of depression and anxiety tend to cluster together into different categories; and how a psychological understanding has helped in the development of new treatments.

DEPRESSION

DEPRESSION AND ITS SYMPTOMS

The term "depression" is used very often in our day-by-day conversation to describe a normal downswing of mood. Such downswings in mood may be adaptive. They may remind of losses and spur a person to find ways of re-engaging with activities or friends. But if the depression becomes more prolonged, it begins to cause more problems than it solves. Such people ruminate on negative themes, brooding about past unpleasantness and feeling pessimistic about the future. They feel resentful, irritable, or angry much of the time, feeling sorry for themselves, and constantly needing reassurance from someone.

If depression deepens still further, more symptoms are drawn in. These symptoms include further emotional changes (feelings of extreme sadness and hopelessness) cognitive changes (low self-esteem, guilt, memory and

Table 1   Symptoms of clinical depression

In order to be said to be suffering from clinical depression, a number of the following symptoms need to have occurred together over a period of time

A   Persistent low mood (for at least two weeks)

plus

B   At least five of the following symptoms

1   Poor appetite or weight loss, or increased appetite or weight gain (change of 1 lb a week over several weeks or 10 lb in a year when not dieting)
2   Sleep difficulty or sleeping too much
3   Loss of energy, fatigability, or tiredness
4   Body slowed down or agitated (not mere subjective feeling of restlessness or being slowed down but observable by others)
5   Loss of interest or pleasure in usual activities, including social contact or sex
6   Feelings of self-reproach, excessive or inappropriate guilt
7   Complaints or evidence of diminished ability to think or concentrate such as slowed thinking or indecisiveness
8   Recurrent thoughts of death or suicide, or any suicidal behaviour

Source: Spitzer, Endicott, and Robins, 1978

concentration difficulties); changes in behaviour (feeling agitated or slowed down, reduced interest in social or recreational activities) and bodily changes (sleep, eating, and sexual problems, aches and pains, loss of energy).

If the depression is intense enough to include five or more of the symptoms shown in Table 1 occurring together for more than a two-week period, it is usually thought to be a "clinical depression" which might benefit from some sort of psychological or medical help. At any one time, there are some 5 per cent of the population who are clinically depressed. Of these episodes of depression, 25 per cent last less than a month; a further 50 per cent recover in less than three months. However, depression tends to return, and within two years of recovering from one episode, around three-quarters will have suffered another episode of depression.

SEX DIFFERENCES IN DEPRESSION

Women are between two and three times as likely to become clinically depressed as are men. The reasons for this remain uncertain. Women with young children are particularly vulnerable; this has led some to suggest that women's disadvantaged role with regard to opportunities for paid employment and their increased responsibility for unpaid child-care is the major cause. The correlation between onset of depression, increase in life stress, and the absence of social support (Brown, 1989) supports this conclusion.

What is less clear is whether women are more vulnerable than men if they have never been depressed before. A large study in the United States surveyed 1,000 people in the community over an eight month period (Amenson & Lewinsohn, 1981). It found, as others have before and since, that depression was more common in women than men. But because the researchers followed the same people for a long period (rather than just taking a "snapshot" as other studies had done), they could count what proportion of men and women became depressed *for the first time* during the period of the study. Their results showed a balance between the sexes: 7.1 per cent of the men and 6.9 per cent of the women became depressed for the first time.

This implies that the sex difference arises because women who have had one episode of depression are more likely to become depressed again than are men who have had a similar episode. Of those women who had been depressed before the study began, 22 per cent became depressed again during the study, but only 13 per cent of men who had been depressed before became depressed again. We need to explain not the increased vulnerability of women to a single episode of depression, but their increased vulnerability to repeated episodes following a first episode. We have already mentioned the stresses and potential loneliness of a child-care role. This is clearly important. Another possibility is that the hormonal changes of a woman's menstrual cycle, though not enough to bring about clinical depression by itself, may nevertheless tend to reactivate memories and attitudes from a previous period of major depression once this has occurred for other reasons.

DISTINCTIONS BETWEEN DIFFERENT SORTS OF DEPRESSION

Many attempts have been made to identify different types of depression. The distinction that has aroused most controversy, yet become most firmly embedded within psychiatric thinking, is that between *endogenous* and *reactive* depressions. The term "endogenous" was originally intended to describe those whose depression arose "from the inside" (from biochemical disturbances in the brain). These were thought to be different from "reactive depression": those who were depressed because of some external stresses. Yet there are many more differences between "endogenous" and "reactive" depression than simply whether the person had been under stress. Indeed, it has been found that endogenous depression is preceded by stressful events as often as reactive depression (Paykel, 1989). The term "endogenous" (also called "biological" depression) is now used to describe a certain cluster of symptoms (see Table 2), and not to refer to how the depression was caused.

Table 2 Symptoms of endogenous-type depression

From group A and B a total of at least six symptoms are required before a definite diagnosis of endogenous-type depression is made; these six must include at least one symptom from group A

A 1 Distinct quality to depressed mood, that is, depressed mood is perceived as distinctly different from the kind of feeling (s)he would have or has had following the death of a loved one
   2 Lack of reactivity to environmental changes (once depressed doesn't feel better, even temporarily, when something good happens)
   3 Mood is regularly worse in the morning
   4 Loss of interest or pleasure which affects everything

B 1 Feelings of self-reproach or excessive or inappropriate guilt
   2 Early morning wakening or insomnia in the middle of the night
   3 Body is slowed down or agitated (more than mere subjective feeling of being slowed down or restless; rather the changes are large enough for others to notice)
   4 Poor appetite
   5 Weight loss (2 lb a week over several weeks or 20 lb in a year when not dieting)
   6 Loss of interest or pleasure in usual activities or decreased sexual drive

Source: Spitzer, Endicott, and Robins, 1978

PSYCHOLOGICAL THEORIES OF DEPRESSION

In order to deal effectively with depression, it is important to know what psychological factors may be causing and maintaining it. Two of the most prominent theories will be mentioned: first, that depression is caused and maintained by people's poor social skills, so that they become isolated from friends and family; and second, that depression is caused and maintained by negative attitudes and thoughts.

Problems in relating to others

Do depressed patients have problems in relating to others: do they have problems in their "social skills"? Early research seemed to show that depressed patients had problems in a number of areas including the extent to which they distribute their attention evenly around a group, slowness in responding to what another person has said, and the small number of times they "reward" other people with attentiveness and smiles. However, subsequent research has revealed a paradox. Depressed patients rate themselves (and are rated by others) as being socially unskilled. But when attempts are made to measure precisely what this social awkwardness might be, the evidence for it is weak. So how is it that patients and observers agree that there is something wrong with their social behaviour?

The question has been partly answered in a series of studies on the effect that a depressed person's behaviour has on other people. In one such study, psychologists recorded conversations between undergraduates and depressed patients. These were compared with conversations with patients who were not depressed (Coyne, 1976). They did not find any difference in the social skills of the depressed patients compared with non-depressed patients. However, when the undergraduates were asked about their own feelings after the conversations, they said that they felt more depressed, anxious, and hostile following the conversations with depressed patients than after the conversation with non-depressed patients. They were also more likely to say that they did not want any future contact with the depressed individuals. When the authors analysed the content of the depressed people's conversation, it was found that they spent more time giving personal information about themselves than the non-depressed person: they talked freely of deaths, marital infidelities, hysterectomies, family strife, and so on. It seems that the conversation of people when depressed may have an alienating effect on the person to whom they are talking. Early sympathy for the person is replaced by feelings of "not wanting to know" because of the depressing effect it has on the listener. The depressed person needs others to listen but may find that fewer and fewer people are available, which simply increases the feeling of desperation (see Figure 1).

So depressed people may find themselves (because of what they talk about) more often in situations that would exceed most people's capacities. It is

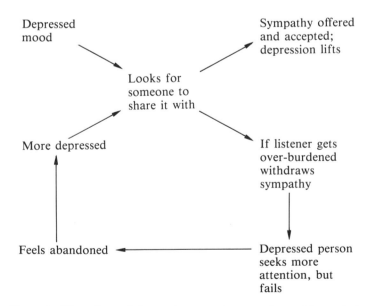

Figure 1 The effect of depression on other people: a vicious circle

hardly surprising that they withdraw altogether from such situations. If this is the case, the important thing for therapy to tackle is not social skills, but the person's negative and self-blameful way of thinking and talking to others. The second theory about the cause and maintenance of depression focuses on this negative attitude.

Depression and cognitive bias

We mentioned at the outset how emotion could affect the way information is processed. An important aspect of this is retrieval from memory. Many depressed people have had a number of stresses and traumas in their lives. Normally, people are quite adept at forgetting unpleasant things about the past. Depression reverses this tendency. As if it was not bad enough to remember the bad things that have happened, depression makes things even worse by reducing the person's ability to recall any good things that have occurred. Looking back on their lives, depressed people may see nothing but a series of disappointments and failures.

Researchers have studied this reversal by measuring the time taken to recall pleasant and unpleasant personal experiences (Lloyd & Lishman, 1975). Depressed patients were given common words as cues (e.g., table, house, wall) and asked to recall either a pleasant or unpleasant memory to each

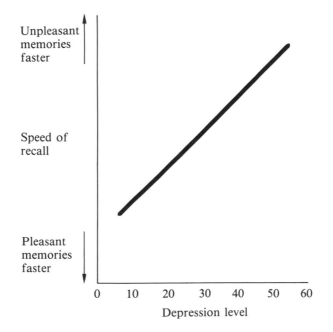

Figure 2 The effect of depression in memory biases

word. The ratio of time taken to recall unpleasant memories to the time taken to recall pleasant memories was calculated for each patient (see Figure 2). The results clearly showed that the more severe the depression the quicker the patient recalled an unpleasant memory relative to a pleasant memory.

That these results were not due to the more depressed patients having had more negative experiences in their life was shown by another study by Clark and Teasdale (1982) in Oxford. In this study, patients were asked about their memories when their mood was very low, and again when their depression was not so severe. They were again given words as cues and asked to respond with the first memory that came to mind. The results showed that happy memories were less probable and depressing memories more probable when patients were more depressed. This confirmed how the change in memory processes due to mood shifts may maintain depression by making the past seem even worse than it is (Clark & Teasdale, 1982).

What is the long-term effect of such bias? If a person has, since childhood, tended to recall unpleasant aspects of situations, then this will affect the way *new* events are explained. Successes will be discounted ("It was just good luck, the task was easy"). Failure will be seen as typical ("This confirms how useless I am"). Indeed, many researchers have found that people who are prone to depression differ in how they interpret events in just these ways. When an unpleasant event occurs, they attribute the cause to themselves (internal) rather than to other people or circumstances (external); and to factors that are unlikely to change (stable), rather than to changeable factors (unstable). Finally, they attribute the cause of the event to factors that affect a great many areas of their lives (global) rather than to factors that have only a restricted relevance (specific). For example, if depressed people fail an examination, they would tend to say that it was because they did not have the necessary ability (an internal, stable attribution) rather than that this particular examination was very difficult (external, unstable). Furthermore, they say that it is not just this particular subject at which they are poor, but that they are unsuccessful in exams in general. In this case they have made a global rather than a specific attribution. In the most extreme cases, they may conclude not only that all future attempts to take examinations will be hopeless but also that they are a failure as a person. It is not difficult to see that people who make attributions for failure to internal, stable, and global causes will tend to give up, will become more depressed, and might feel that it is not worth continuing with their education. If they make similar sorts of attributions in other areas of their lives (see Table 3), this will further increase their sense of despair and hopelessness about the future.

Table 3　First reactions

The different ways in which people interpret the same event can be assessed by asking for first reactions. The following items are taken from a questionnaire called the "Cognitive Style Test" by Ivy-Marie Blackburn. Look at these descriptions of everyday events. Imagine they are happening to you. What would your first reaction be?

You are unable to deal with a problem at work and have to ask for help

Would you think

(a)　I often find it difficult to cope with problems
(b)　I find it difficult to cope with some problems
(c)　I am a failure
(d)　These sorts of problems are always easier with help

A person you admire tells you he/she likes you

Would you think

(a)　I am glad she/he likes me
(b)　People sometimes say that without really meaning it
(c)　I am a very likeable person
(d)　I cannot believe that I am likeable

Now ask yourself how your reaction might have been different if you were overtired, or feeling down? How might it affect what you would do next? Psychologists have found that mood dramatically affects the way people interpret ambiguous events, causing further mood changes, and affecting how people behave (see Blackburn, 1987).

Source: Based on Blackburn, 1987

PSYCHOLOGICAL TREATMENT FOR DEPRESSION

Distortions in thinking which occur in people who are emotionally disturbed cannot be changed simply by telling them that they are wrong. New methods of treatment, called collectively "cognitive therapy", give guidelines on how to deal with the negative "self-propaganda" (thoughts, memories, and beliefs) that maintain depression and make the person vulnerable to future episodes. Cognitive techniques aim first at making patients reconceptualize their thoughts and memories as *simply* thoughts and memories which may have been susceptible to distortion, rather than as reflecting reality. It does this in three ways:

1 by eliciting the patient's thoughts, "self-talk", and interpretations of events (e.g., "I failed that exam because I am stupid");
2 by gathering, with the patient, evidence for or against the interpretation (e.g., "Are there any other reasons why I might have failed – e.g., difficult

exam, didn't revise correct material, ill on the day?" "Does failure in this subject imply that I am stupid?");

3 by setting up "experiments" (homeworks) to test out the truth of the interpretations and gather more data for discussion (Find out if others also failed; how do the teachers/lecturers explain what happened? Are resits allowed? What is the procedure for this?).

The major techniques used in cognitive therapy are listed in Table 4, together with a brief description of their purpose.

Many studies have shown that such cognitive therapy techniques are effective in reducing depression (Williams, 1992). They do so as rapidly and as effectively as antidepressant medication. They are more costly than drugs in the short term because each patient sees a therapist for an hour a week for up to 15 weeks, but cognitive therapy is suitable for those patients who cannot or do not want to take medication. More importantly, the chances of the depression returning following cognitive therapy are significantly lower than following antidepressant medication, so it may be better in the long term. These advances in the treatment of depression show the importance of understanding the psychological processes underlying such emotional problems, a theme which emerges strongly in the second emotion we discuss, namely anxiety.

Table 4 Five core techniques of cognitive therapy

Technique	Purpose
Thought catching	To teach the person to become aware of depressing thoughts as they occur
Task assignment	To encourage activities which the person has been avoiding (e.g., meeting a certain friend, attending a meeting of a club or society)
Reality testing	To select tasks which help to test out the truth of fixed negative thoughts or beliefs (e.g., phoning a friend to test out the idea that "no one will talk to me")
Cognitive rehearsal	To get the person to recount to the therapist all the stages involved in an activity he or she has been avoiding, together with the accompanying thoughts and feelings; the aim is to discover possible "roadblocks", what can be done about them, and to imagine eventual success
Alternative therapy	To instruct the person to imagine an upsetting situation and then generate strategies for coping

ANXIETY

ANXIETY AND ITS SYMPTOMS

Anxiety, like depression, is a normal part of everyday life for the majority of people. It serves the useful function of keeping us motivated to make the effort to overcome threatening situations. Take, for example, the common experience of becoming anxious prior to an interview. The fear that we shall do badly means that we work hard to prepare for it. However, it is also a common experience that anxiety can lead to worse performance. In other words, anxiety can become handicapping.

In evolutionary terms, anxiety can be viewed as a mechanism that has enabled animals and humans to deal with danger and threat. If an animal comes across a predator, a *survival reaction* occurs. Its body undergoes physiological changes which increase arousal levels, enabling enhanced performance to increase the chances of survival, either to stay and fight the threatening animal or to take rapid flight, the *fight/flight mechanism*.

The difference between adaptive anxiety and pathological anxiety is in the identification of threat. Whereas in adaptive anxiety the threat is all too clear (being mauled by a bear or the possibility of failing an exam), in pathological anxiety the threat is often either unidentified (the sufferer is only aware of fear, not what is feared) or out of proportion (for example, a fear of being embarrassed) or irrational (for example, anxiety about being severely ill despite all reassurance).

The result is that the bodily changes of the survival reaction occur in situations where there is no danger. Many of these symptoms are caused by the release of adrenaline (epinephrine) from the adrenal medulla located just at the top of the kidneys. On perception of threat, whether real or imagined, adrenaline is released into the body in order to allow the survival reaction to occur. All the symptoms of anxiety are by-products of bodily changes that would enhance performance in situations of real threat (see Figure 3). The problem with clinical anxiety is that because the threat is ill perceived, the anxious individual, for lack of an alternative focus, concentrates on bodily symptoms and discomforts. The symptoms of anxiety can be exceedingly unpleasant and frightening in themselves, and many people naturally conclude that there is something physically wrong with them. We shall list the symptoms first, then describe how they cluster together to form definable syndromes. Finally we shall describe how psychologists have approached anxiety and its treatment.

Symptoms of anxiety

The symptoms of anxiety are very diverse: dizziness, lightheadedness, blurred vision, hot flushes, dry mouth, tightness in the throat (often accompanied by a feeling of choking), muscular tension and pains, breathing difficulties, a pounding, racing heart, feelings of nausea, butterflies in the tummy, numbness in the limbs, pins and needles in the extremities, the urge to urinate and defecate, feeling cold, hot flushes, sweating, twitching, trembling, shaking, symptoms of vigilance and scanning such as feeling on edge, exaggerated startle response, poor concentration, trouble falling/staying asleep, and irritability. The number of symptoms and the severity varies from individual

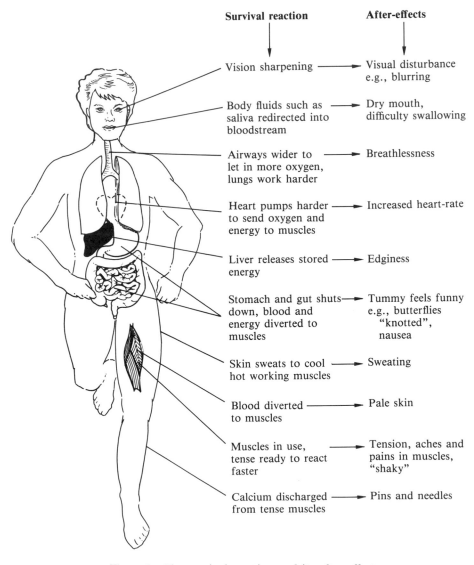

Survival reaction

After-effects

Vision sharpening ⟶ Visual disturbance e.g., blurring

Body fluids such as ⟶ Dry mouth, saliva redirected into difficulty swallowing bloodstream

Airways wider to ⟶ Breathlessness let in more oxygen, lungs work harder

Heart pumps harder ⟶ Increased heart-rate to send oxygen and energy to muscles

Liver releases stored ⟶ Edginess energy

Stomach and gut shuts⟶ Tummy feels funny down, blood and e.g., butterflies energy diverted to "knotted", muscles nausea

Skin sweats to cool ⟶ Sweating hot working muscles

Blood diverted ⟶ Pale skin to muscles

Muscles in use, ⟶ Tension, aches and tense ready to react pains in muscles, faster "shaky"

Calcium discharged ⟶ Pins and needles from tense muscles

Figure 3   The survival reaction and its after-effects

to individual. We shall now describe how these symptoms cluster together to form some of the more common problems, starting with the most common, generalized anxiety disorder.

COMMON TYPES OF ANXIETY DISORDERS

Generalized anxiety disorder

Generalized anxiety disorder is usually characterized by severe and disproportionate worry about life issues which persists more or less consistently for 6 or more months. In any one year, between 2 and 6.5 per cent of the general population suffer from generalized anxiety disorder. This makes it the most common form of anxiety neurosis. The most common forms of worry seem to be related to family issues (79 per cent in one study); overconcern about finances (50 per cent); work (43 per cent); and personal illness (14 per cent) (see Edelmann, 1992). In addition, most people report worrying about many other little things. As well as these worries, the anxious person shows muscle tension, hyperactivity in the autonomic nervous system (e.g., sweating), and is apprehensive for much of the time. Information processing is biased, but instead of the main bias being in memory (as in depression), the main problem is bias in attention. People are apt to be hypervigilant, scanning their environment for anything that might be a threat (Williams, Watts, Macleod, & Mathews, 1988).

Several experiments have demonstrated this hypervigilance in people who are anxious. In one study, mothers who were anxious because their children were soon to go into hospital to have their tonsils out were tested (Parkinson & Rachman, 1981). They listened to a tape recording of music in which were hidden words, recorded very quietly under the music. The words were either neutral (e.g. *newspaper*, *bird*) or threatening (*operation*, *bleeding*). Other women, whose children were not undergoing an operation, also listened to the tape. The results showed that, even when the unpleasant words were played at their quietest volume so that the other women could not hear them, the anxious mothers could hear them. This hypervigilance has been called "perceptual pop-out", and works for vision as well as for hearing (see Figure 4). Shortly after the operation, these mothers' attentional systems returned to normal. In severe anxiety states, however, the person suffers from such a bias almost all the time.

Panic disorder

Panic disorder is a more extreme form of anxiety than that found in generalized anxiety disorder. Panic disorder consists of recurrent panic attacks: time limited periods of extreme fear/discomfort. Panic attacks might last for a few minutes or, rarely, several hours. They usually occur unexpectedly, although

U	A	B	F	S	T	A	B	D
H	A	R	B	L	O	O	D	N
E	S	E	D	F	L	A	E	A
A	I	N	R	D	B	A	Z	N
L	G	I	T	S	E	R	D	E
T	C	A	N	C	E	R	B	M
H	D	D	O	Y	R	O	O	F

Figure 4 Perceptual pop-out. Anxious people may see threat words more quickly than non-threat words in an array of letters such as this

associations with situations and places may eventually develop, for example, crowded supermarkets. Such associations increase the likelihood of further panic attacks occurring because they are expected to happen. Any of the physical symptoms associated with anxiety can be experienced during a panic attack but at least four of the symptoms listed in Table 5 must be present for panic disorder to be diagnosed.

Panic attacks are very common in the general population. One study found that 34 per cent of young, normal adults experience an isolated panic attack in any twelve-month period. However, full-blown panic disorder is much rarer, estimated as being between 0.5 and 3 per cent in the general population.

Agoraphobia

Clinically, panic disorder is often associated with agoraphobia (fear of being in places or situations from which escape might be difficult). The literal

Table 5 Symptoms that may occur in panic disorder

Shortness of breath
Palpitations or accelerated heart-rate
Chest pain or discomfort
Choking or smothering sensations
Dizziness, unsteady feelings, or faintness
Trembling or shakiness
Tingling sensations
Sweating and hot and cold flushes
Fear of dying, going crazy, or doing something uncontrollable

meaning of the word "agoraphobia" is fear (Greek *phobos*) of the market-place (Greek *agora*). More generally, agoraphobia includes fear of busy streets, travelling on buses, trains, or cars, and standing in queues. It is now recognized that the onset and maintenance of agoraphobia is often due to the occurrence of panic attacks, and that these should be the primary focus of therapy.

Social phobia

Social phobia is the persistent fear of one or more social situations in which the individual feels exposed to the scrutiny of others. The fear then becomes one of embarrassing oneself. Social phobia includes fears such as speaking in public, eating in public, urinating in public conveniences, or writing in the presence of others. More general fears are of saying foolish things and being unable to respond to queries. The socially phobic individual usually avoids such situations wherever possible. In its mildest forms, social anxiety is very common. One UK study found 10 per cent of students had difficulty in or avoided social situations, and another US study put the figure at one-third. However, a social phobia of clinical proportions is rare, the prevalence in the general population being around 1 per cent.

Simple phobia

In simple phobia, the feared object is usually clearly defined: a fear of spiders, birds, snakes, mice, blood, closed spaces (claustrophobia), heights (acrophobia), or air travel. Being in the presence of the feared object produces the anxiety response but at all other times the person's anxiety level is normal. Because of this, and because the phobic object is often relatively easy to avoid, simple phobias are rarely handicapping. Surveys have reported that between 6 and 8 per cent of the general population report phobias but only 2 per cent of these find them disabling (Agras, Sylvester, & Oliveau, 1969).

Obsessive-compulsive disorder

Obsessive-compulsive disorder is characterized by persistent ideas, impulses, or images that are intrusive, seemingly useless and often distressing, and that interfere with daily life or relationships. Examples include the intrusive impulse of killing a much-loved child, shouting out swear-words in church, or thoughts to do with violence, contamination, and doubt. Compulsions are repetitive and apparently purposeless actions performed in a stereotyped fashion. For example, having to do things in a particular rigid sequence, repeatedly checking things, frequently handwashing, counting, and touching objects. The action usually serves the purpose of reducing anxiety and tension. It is not experienced as pleasurable, but resistance to a compulsion leads to mounting tension and anxiety. Studies show that up to 2.5 per cent of the population have suffered from this disorder at some point in their lives. In any six-month period, 1.5 per cent of the population can be found to have obsessive compulsive disorder. Men are equally likely to have the disorder as women, though the nature of the symptoms differ (see Edelmann, 1992). Women are more likely to be compulsive cleaners (86 per cent of compulsive cleaners are women). By contrast compulsive checkers are more likely to be men (73 per cent).

Post-traumatic stress disorder

Post-traumatic stress disorder (PTSD) is somewhat different from the rest of the anxiety disorders described so far. It is essentially a normal reaction to an abnormal situation. Symptoms develop following a highly distressing event, such as a threat to one's life (or the life of loved ones), the destruction of one's home/community, witnessing the death of others as the result of accident or physical violence, rape/assault, wartime experience, or torture. Typically in PTSD, the event is re-experienced in a number of ways. For example, the individual may experience intrusive thoughts and images relating to the event, dissociative states during which the event is re-lived, intense psychological distress as a result of other factors associated with the event (such as anniversaries, places), and recurrent nightmares about the event. Typically the PTSD sufferers will avoid circumstances associated with the trauma. However, sometimes PTSD can include amnesia for the event and feeling emotionally detached from the world. It is difficult to estimate how many people develop PTSD following a trauma, but some studies have found that up to 15 per cent do so. The proportion is higher in children, varying from 30 to 50 per cent (Yule, 1991).

PSYCHOLOGICAL THEORIES OF ANXIETY

We turn now to describe the two most commonly used theories and successful treatments of anxiety in psychology, the behavioural and cognitive approaches.

Behavioural theory

The behavioural theory of anxiety states that anxiety is a learned or classically conditioned response, produced at first by the association of fear with a certain situation/object. The second stage is finding that escaping from the situation produces relief. The final stage is the avoidance of anxiety by avoiding the particular situation or object altogether. Some psychologists have suggested that anxiety disorders may start as conditioned responses but then produce more obvious rewards and/or solve another problem. For example, an agoraphobic sufferer might find that the disorder produces benefits such as greater amounts of attention from an otherwise inattentive partner. If the agoraphobia is reduced, and the person becomes more independent, this change sometimes leads to a different and possibly more distressing problem such as interpersonal difficulties. Indeed, one study found that improving agoraphobic problems can lead to marital disharmony (Barlow, Mavissakalian, & Kay 1981).

Cognitive theory

The cognitive theory of anxiety disorders focuses on the thoughts individuals have about themselves, their symptoms, and the situations they are in. Pathologically anxious people are likely to make certain errors in thinking that lead them to overestimate the degree of danger/threat and underestimate their own ability to cope and the presence of rescue factors within the threatening situation. These errors are: catastrophization (fearing the worst will happen), personalization (assuming personal significance in negative events), overgeneralizing (assuming one negative event will affect everything), selective abstraction (taking one negative element and drawing negative conclusions), minimization (denying the importance of good events/coping skills) and maximization (exaggerating importance of negative events/non-adaptive skills).

For example, research on the cause of panic attacks by David Clark (1986) and his colleagues in Oxford has shown that panic attacks are the result of misinterpreting, in a catastrophic way, bodily reactions associated with anxiety such as increased heart-rate or dizziness. A person notices an increase in heart-rate (a normal symptom of anxiety which can cause no harm) and immediately concludes that he or she is about to suffer a fatal heart attack. The acute anxiety that this thought naturally creates causes further bodily symptoms (such as further increases in heart-rate) which serves only to confirm the initial "diagnosis". Such misinterpretations invariably lead to a further exacerbation of symptoms and hence a full-blown panic attack occurs (see Figure 5).

The proposal that catastrophic interpretations of bodily symptoms lead to panic attacks has had support from an experiment conducted by David Clark and his colleagues in Oxford (Clark et al. 1991). Panic patients were given sodium lactate, which has the effect of inducing symptoms very similar to those experienced during an attack. Patients were randomly assigned to two groups. Prior to the infusion of sodium lactate, all patients were told that sodium lactate is harmless and induces a specific set of symptoms and that they could stop the infusion at any time. One group were told no more than this. The other group were told that the sensations induced were similar to those produced by exercise or alcohol, that lactate is a natural substance produced by the body, that it was normal to experience intense sensations

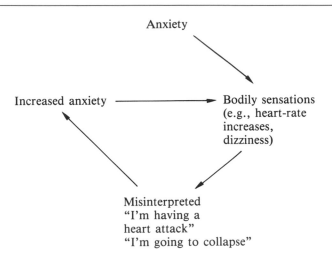

Figure 5   Vicious circle of anxiety and panic

during the infusion, and that these did not indicate an adverse reaction. The experimenters took measures of heart-rate, blood pressure, skin conductance, respiration rate, and anxiety self-ratings, before and throughout the infusion. Above all, the investigators wanted to know whether a panic attack had occurred or not so they arranged for an independent investigator to interview the patients about their experiences during the experiment. They found that very few of the patients who had been given the alternative explanation for their symptoms had a panic attack. By contrast, in the group that had been allowed to interpret their symptoms in their own (catastrophic) way, all patients experienced a panic attack during the infusion. These findings give very strong and compelling evidence in favour of a cognitive theory of panic disorder. They have led to the development of very effective techniques for treating panic and associated disorders. We shall describe some of these below, after mentioning several techniques that developed from behavioural theories.

PSYCHOLOGICAL TREATMENTS FOR ANXIETY

Behavioural treatment

One of the earliest behavioural treatment techniques was developed by Joseph Wolpe (1958) and is called systematic desensitization by reciprocal inhibition. Phobic patients are gradually faced with increasingly fearful and threatening situations or objects (either in actuality or imaginally) while at the same time putting into practice previously trained relaxation techniques. The theory behind this very successful technique was that by pairing the feared situation/object with a state of relaxation a new association is created and the anxiety reaction is inhibited from occurring. Others have argued that this technique works not because of the inhibiting effect of relaxation on anxiety but because of the exposure to the feared situation (Marks, 1973). Generally it is now assumed that the key to overcoming anxiety is through confronting or facing the fear. Exposure is the most effective way to achieve this – especially if it allows the person to disprove any predictions he or she is making that something awful will happen. Therapists usually use a gradual technique (graded exposure), building up the feared situations from week to week as therapy progresses. At the same time, the patient's sense of confidence to cope with exposure increases.

Cognitive treatment

The cognitive treatment of anxiety disorders involves tackling the way in which individuals think about the threatening situation (including their bodily symptoms) and how this affects the way they behave (see Beck & Emery, 1985). For example, as mentioned above, people with panic symptoms believe that if the panic attack is not curtailed rapidly, they will suffer from some physical catastrophe, so they attempt to escape the panic-provoking situation as soon as possible (Clark, 1986). Once escape has occurred, individuals lose the opportunity to establish whether their beliefs are justified or not since they are no longer able to put them to the test. The act of escaping leads to further faulty beliefs such as: "If I hadn't sat down I would definitely have fainted" or "If I hadn't got out I would definitely have had a fatal heart attack".

Like cognitive treatment for depression (see above) the treatment for anxiety aims initially to help the client to identify and recognize these thoughts and evaluate their influence on behaviour. Clients can then examine their status in the world of reality. Once these thoughts have been identified they can be re-evaluated and re-interpreted along more realistic lines. This impacts differently on the behaviour with the effect that the client is more able to cope with exposure to the feared situation. This gives the person further opportunity to discover that the predictions he or she was previously making were faulty.

CONCLUSION

This chapter has concentrated on anxiety and depression as problems in their own right, but it is important to realize that they occur in many other situations where people are disturbed or upset. Where they are present, one often finds that they cause avoidance of certain activities, which can then lead to further problems. Following bereavement, for example, some people find that even months afterwards, when they would like to be able to deal with the person's belongings, they cannot do so. If grief becomes "blocked" in this way, a combination of "cognitive rehearsal" and "graded exposure" can be used. The person first imagines him or herself going into that situation. Second, the person generates ways of coping with difficulties that might arise. Third, the person imagines as clearly as possible the potential benefits. Finally, the person sets a definite time when he or she is going to start the task, including a plan for what to do immediately afterwards.

Another way in which the ideas mentioned here have been extended is to help understand the attributional distortions in schoolchildren who persistently fail at reading or mathematics despite the fact that their level of intelligence should enable them to succeed. When they find work difficult, these children attribute their failure to internal, stable, and global factors, for example, that they are "stupid and incapable". Simply giving them experience of success to increase their self-esteem does not work. Psychologists found that this was because it did not teach them how to deal with failure (Dweck, 1975). They suggested instead that the children be allowed to fail as part of their remedial training so that their distorted attributions are made explicit and can be changed. The children were encouraged to think aloud as they attempted to do their work. When failure occurred, rather than seeing this as evidence of incompetence, the children were encouraged to interpret it as arising from things that could be changed (e.g., "I went too quickly", "I didn't concentrate hard enough in the middle"). The results showed that when the children met difficulty again in the real classroom, they persisted for longer and were more likely to succeed. The children had learned to cope with failure.

Psychological factors are important in determining the onset and course of anxiety and depression in many ways. First, habitual tendencies to interpret situations in a negative or threatening way can render the person vulnerable to stressors, such as a threatening life-event or a physical illness. Second, the psychological factors can act as precipitants which raise the level of stress experienced when a negative event occurs. Third, psychological factors contribute to the maintenance of emotional disturbance whatever the cause of the initial disturbance. Knowledge of underlying psychological processes have contributed much to the alleviation of these conditions. Note that "exposure" is an important element in the treatment of both depression and anxiety. However, in the case of anxiety, the emphasis has changed from focusing on the unpleasantness of the external environment to the fear of the internal environment, that is, bodily reactions. In both depression and anxiety, the emphasis has changed away from focusing on reactions to events in the world and towards how these events are interpreted.

FURTHER READING

Blackburn, I. M. (1987). *Coping with depression*. Edinburgh: Chambers.
Edelmann, R. J. (1992). *Anxiety: Theory, research and intervention in clinical and health psychology*. Chichester: Wiley.
Gotlib, I. H., & Hammen, C. L. (1992). *Psychological aspects of depression: Toward a cognitive interpersonal integration*. Chichester: Wiley.
Last, C., & Hersen, M. (Eds) (1987). *Handbook of anxiety disorders*. New York: Pergamon.
Williams, J. M. G. (1992). *The psychological treatment of depression: A guide to the theory and practice of cognitive behaviour therapy* (2nd edn). London: Routledge.

REFERENCES

Agras, W. S., Sylvester, D., & Oliveau, D. (1969). The epidemiology of common fears and phobia. *Comprehensive Psychiatry*, *10*, 151–161.
Amenson, C. S., & Lewinsohn, P. M. (1981). An investigation into the observed sex differences in prevalence of unipolar depression. *Journal of Abnormal Psychology*, *90*, 1–13.
Barlow, D., Mavissakalian, M., & Kay, L. (1981). Couples treatment of agoraphobia: Changes in marital satisfaction. *Behaviour Research and Therapy*, *19*, 245–255.
Barlow, D., O'Brien, G., & Last, C. (1988). Couples treatment of agoraphobia. *Behaviour Therapy*, *15*, 41–58.
Beck, A. T., & Emery, G. (1985). *Anxiety disorders and phobias*. New York: Basic Books.
Blackburn, I. M. (1987). *Coping with depression*. Edinburgh: Chambers.
Brown, G. W. (1989). Depression: A radical social perspective. In K. Herbst & E. S. Paykel (Eds) *Depression: An integrative approach* (pp. 21–44). Oxford: Heinemann Medical.
Clark, D. M. (1986). A cognitive approach to panic. *Behaviour Research and Therapy*, *24*, 461–470.
Clark, D. M., & Teasdale, J. D. (1982). Diurnal variation in clinical depression and accessibility of positive and negative experiences. *Journal of Abnormal Psychology*, *91*, 87–95.
Clark, D. M., Salkovskis, P. M., Gelder, M. G., Middleton, H., Anastasiades, P., & Hackmann, A. (1991). *Cognitive mediation of lactate induced panic*. Paper presented at the annual conference of the American Psychological Association, Washington, DC, August.
Coyne, J. C. (1976). Depression and the response of others. *Journal of Abnormal Psychology*, *85*, 186–193.
Dweck, C. S. (1975). The role of expectations and attributions in the alleviation of learned helplessness. *Journal of Personality and Social Psychology*, *31*, 674–685.
Edelmann, R. J. (1992). *Anxiety: Theory, research and intervention in clinical and health psychology*. Chichester: Wiley.
Lloyd, G. C., & Lishman, W. A. (1975). Effect of depression on the speed of recall of pleasant and unpleasant experiences. *Psychological Medicine*, *5*, 173–180.
Marks, I. M. (1973). The reduction of fear: Towards a unifying theory. *Journal of the Canadian Psychiatric Association*, *18*, 9–12.
Parkinson, L., & Rachman, S. (1981). Intrusive thoughts: The effects of an uncontrived stress. *Advances in Behaviour Research & Therapy*, *3*, 111–118.

Paykel, E. S. (1989). The background: Extent and nature of the disorder. In K. Herbst & E. S. Paykel (Eds) *Depression: An integrative approach* (pp. 3–20). London: Heinemann.

Spitzer, R. L., Endicott, J., & Robins, E. (1978). *Research Diagnostic Criteria (RDC) for a selected group of functional disorders* (3rd edn). New York: New York State Psychiatric Institute, Biometrics Research.

Williams, J. M. G. (1992). *The psychological treatment of depression: A guide to the theory and practice of cognitive behaviour therapy* (2nd edn). London: Routledge.

Williams, J. M. G., Watts, F. N., MacLeod, C., & Mathews, A. (1988). *Cognitive psychology and emotional disorders*. Chichester: Wiley.

Wolpe, J. (1958). *Psychotherapy by reciprocal inhibition*. Stanford, CA: Stanford University Press.

Yule, W. (1991). Working with children following disasters. In M. Herbert (Ed.), *Clinical child psychology* (pp. 349–364). Chichester: Wiley.

10.2

PSYCHOTIC DISORDERS: SCHIZOPHRENIA, AFFECTIVE PSYCHOSES, AND PARANOIA

Chris Frith and Connie Cahill

MRC Cyclotron Unit and University College London, England

Psychosis is the technical term for what non-psychologists call madness. In contrast to the symptoms of neurosis, psychotic symptoms are categorically outside the normal realm of experience, and as such they are beyond our common-sense powers of understanding and empathy. It is this aspect of psychotic symptoms that isolates persons experiencing them in "a world of their own". Schizophrenia is by far the most common of the psychoses. The lifetime risk of having a schizophrenic breakdown is estimated at between 0.5 per cent and 2 per cent; the risk for affective psychosis lies between approximately 0.6 per cent and 1.1 per cent. These disorders frequently strike in early adulthood, the average age of onset for schizophrenia being around 25 years in males and 30 years in females (Johnstone, 1991). The personal, social, and economic costs of these illnesses are great. Sufferers stand to lose their relationships, their jobs or careers, their homes, and ultimately their freedom. Families can be emotionally devastated by the shock of the changes wrought on their relative, as well as having to cope with the person's uncharacteristic or disturbing behaviour.

In the case of schizophrenia it has been estimated that the cost to the economy of the USA in terms of provision of treatment and care, and loss of earnings, is in the order of $15 billion annually (Gunderson & Mosher, 1975). This is roughly 2 per cent of the gross national product, suggesting a cost of £2 billion − £3 billion per year in the UK. The availability of antipsychotic drugs means that many sufferers today can obtain significant relief from symptoms. Unfortunately these drugs do not provide a cure, and approximately two-thirds of cases experience recurring episodes of illness. Although there is increasing evidence that psychotic illnesses are associated with brain abnormalities, the precise causes remain unknown.

THE DEVELOPMENT OF THE PSYCHOTIC DIAGNOSES

The history of our current concepts of the psychoses is very firmly rooted in the work of Emil Kraepelin (1896) and Eugen Bleuler (1913). Kraepelin was the first clinician to divide the huge and diverse concept that was "insanity" or "madness" into two major, distinct syndromes: "dementia praecox" and manic-depressive psychosis. He was steadfast in his belief that these were physical diseases like any other, and he distinguished the two disorders on the grounds of differential patterns of course and outcome. "Dementia praecox", he suggested, almost invariably resulted in a global deterioration of the patient's mental state: from dementia praecox there was no reprieve. Manic-depressive psychosis, on the other hand, was characterized by a remitting course, with the patient experiencing a restitution of function between psychotic episodes.

Bleuler, for his part, coined the term "schizophrenia" (from the Greek *schizein*, to split, and *phren*, mind) to describe not a "Jekyll and Hyde" syndrome as is the common misconception of the disorder, but a condition that took the form of a splitting up of different psychological faculties, such as emotion and language. Not surprisingly, when these conceptions were used as the basis of diagnosis, much confusion ensued. For a period during the 1950s and 1960s, diagnostic practices in Europe (where the Kraepelinian view prevailed) and the USA (where Bleulerian symptoms provided the focus) were markedly different. This situation has been greatly improved since the early 1980s with psychologists and psychiatrists around the world recognizing the need for greater cooperation and standardization in diagnostic procedures.

The two main classification systems in use today are the *International Classification of Diseases* (ICD-9) (World Health Organization, 1978) and the American Psychiatric Association's *Diagnostic and Statistical Manual of Mental Disorders* (DSM-IIIR) (American Psychiatric Association, 1987) — see Table 1. These diagnostic schemes are continuously under review and revised versions appear from time to time. Because we have no objective or biological marker for psychotic disorders, these diagnostic systems are largely based on the abnormal experiences and beliefs reported by the patient.

Paranoid psychosis can be seen as a variant of schizophrenia. In DSM-IIIR, Delusional (Paranoid) Disorder is diagnosed when patients have circumscribed, plausible delusions (for example, that they are being followed, or that their spouses are deceiving them), in the absence of bizarre behaviour or experiences.

Generally speaking, the diagnosis of affective psychosis is applied when a patient reports psychotic symptoms (that is, hallucinations and/or delusions)

Table 1 Summary of DSM-IIIR criteria for a diagnosis of schizophrenia

The patient must have

A   Characteristic psychotic symptoms for at least one week
B   Marked deterioration of functioning in self-care, work, or social relations
C   No major changes in mood (depression or elation)
D   Continuous signs of disturbance for at least six months
E   No evidence of organic factors (e.g., drug abuse)

Characteristic psychotic symptoms must include

1   two of the following:

(a) delusions
(b) prominent hallucinations
(c) incoherence or marked loosening of associations
(d) catatonic behaviour
(e) flat or grossly inappropriate affect

OR   2   bizarre delusions (e.g., thought broadcasting)
OR   3   prominent hallucinations of a voice

and also experiences pathological mood states (extreme elation or depression). Perris (1966) suggested that two distinct groups of these patients could be distinguished: those who suffer both manic and depressive episodes and those who experience *only* depressive psychosis. The terms *bipolar* and *unipolar* are often used to describe these two syndromes. There are also patients who meet DSM-IIIR criteria for schizophrenia and a major depressive or manic episode; these patients are classified as "schizo-affective".

PSYCHOTIC SIGNS AND SYMPTOMS

The experiences of persons in the grip of psychotic episodes recorded in centuries past are remarkably similar to the kinds of feelings and ideas described by sufferers today. Consider the extracts below. The first is from *The Life of the Reverend Mr George Trosse*, an autobiographical account of psychotic illness published in 1714. The second is from a letter written by a young man experiencing his first psychotic episode in 1992.

> Every person I saw seem'd to me to be an Executioner; and I thought every Thing either an instrument of, or a Preparation for, my Misery and Torture. I apprehended Self-Murther to be the only wise and charitable Act that I could do for my self, as the only Prevention of all expected and dreaded Torment. (Quoted in Peterson, 1982, p. 37)

> This ward is not a real one.... It is made up of black magic people.... It's horrific...I am to be eliminated soon.... Can you suggest a means of suicide?

The content, that is, the actual circumstance or subject referred to, is different, but the *form*, the way in which that content is processed or interpreted, is similar in both. The same process is reflected in the expression of symptoms in different cultures: whereas a patient in the Middle East may believe he is the direct descendant of the prophet Muhammad, his counterpart in Ireland might consider himself the new risen Christ.

Such ideas or beliefs would be classified as delusions – by far the most common of the psychotic symptoms. Jasper (1962) wrote: "Since time immemorial, delusion has been taken as the basic characteristic of madness. To be mad was to be deluded" (p. 93).

Delusions

Delusions may present as part of a complex of psychotic phenomena as in schizophrenia, mania, or psychotic depression, or as the lone, predominant psychotic feature of a paranoid psychosis. They may also occur in "organic" brain states, such as epilepsy. Jasper defined a "primary delusion" as follows: (1) it is held with extraordinary conviction, (2) it is impervious to other experiences and to compelling counter-argument, and (3) the content is incompatible with reality. Delusions are not, therefore, fleeting ideas; they are persistent, and they are experienced as true by the patient. Indeed, patients may be so convinced of the truth of their delusions that they will act on the basis of their content.

Curiously, certain themes appear to have an affinity for the delusional form. The belief that one is being persecuted by other people, watched by other people, the subject of some hateful plot, is the essence of what is perhaps the most common delusion – the delusion of persecution. Intimate relationships also feature in delusional content as in delusional or morbid jealousy, and the de Clerambault delusion, wherein the subject, typically a woman, believes a man with whom she has little or no real contact is actually her lover or husband. One such case known to the authors insisted that she had not actually married her real husband, writing to various registry offices making appointments to marry her "true lover". Delusions may, however, cover any topic, and they can be frankly bizarre: one patient informed us that "my friend Frank was actually Einstein in a previous life". Some patients present with one preoccupying delusion, while others may have a number of delusions which may be organised to greater or lesser degrees into a unified system of explanation (for example, "I am the son of God"; "I was born of a virgin mother"; "I have a special mission on earth the details of which God will communicate to me when the time comes").

Delusions can simply come "out of the blue": the patient will argue that he or she "just knew". In other cases they may rise out of a period during which the person feels the world, or the immediate surroundings, or people, have changed in some subtle, not obviously perceptible way; there is a feeling that something peculiar or sinister is going on and the patient, not surprisingly, may feel perplexed or anxious. This state is referred to as "delusional mood" or "delusional atmosphere". This period may last for days or weeks and almost invariably gives way to the formation of concrete, fully formed delusions, a process which usually has the effect of providing a release from the preceding state of tension. Once formed, delusions are likely to stay with the patient for a considerable time.

The delusions associated with the affective psychoses tend to have contents that are congruent with the mood of the patient. In a manic phase the patient will believe that he or she has superhuman abilities and is related to royalty, while when depressed he or she will feel responsible for all the troubles of the world.

Passivity experiences

Delusions, as pathological beliefs, obviously represent a disorder in the content of thought. However, a less apparent aspect of their character is the fact that they are also experienced, in the sense that one "feels" one knows something. At present we do not know whether or not a pathological process in this latter domain contributes to the formation or maintenance of delusions.

Certainly, abnormal "feelings" (by which we mean sensations) abound in the psychotic disorders.

In what is termed a "passivity phenomenon", patients report that their actions are not of their own doing but are in fact the actions of some other force which takes over control of their movements. Similarly patients will say that their thoughts are not their own but actually the thoughts of some external agency; again this is based on direct experience – the thoughts in my head do not feel like they are my thoughts. The opposite also occurs with patients reporting that they feel thoughts being physically withdrawn or "plucked" from their head. Because patients describe these experiences in terms of external forces or agencies, they have been called "delusions of control". However, what patients are describing here is an experience of their behaviour not being – or not feeling – generated, initiated, or maintained by themselves. In eliciting symptoms from a patient one must take great care to ascertain whether what the patient is reporting is simply a belief (for example, that people can put thoughts into other people's heads), or a belief based on an experience or sensation. Such experiences occur predominantly in schizophrenia (Schneider, 1959), but they can also occasionally be observed in manic patients.

Hallucinations

Among the most distressing of psychotic experiences are auditory hallucinations, that is, sounds, music, or "voices" experienced in the absence of an external stimulus. "Voices" coming through the ears (true hallucinations) or from inside the head (pseudo-hallucinations) are the most commonly experienced form. Those who experience such hallucinations think they are "real"; they are not, as far as the patients are concerned, imaginary. They may be unlikely, they may be odd, but they exist.

"Voices" may be male or female or "distorted". Some patients will identify them as the voices of individuals known or related to them. They are frequently interpreted in a manner consistent with concurrent delusions, so that the voice is construed as the voice of God or the devil, for instance. Typically, they enter the patients' consciousness in brief bursts over a period of time; in severe cases, however, they may be virtually continuous. The kinds of things that the voices say range from single words (for example, "go", "dirt") to complete sentences (for example, "You are unclean"). Schneider (1959) identified three distinct types of voices which he suggested are strongly associated with schizophrenia in particular: (1) two or more voices discussing the subject in the third person (e.g., "He is dishonest"); (2) voices commenting on the person or their actions (e.g., "He's opening the door now"); (3) voices repeating or anticipating the subject's own thoughts.

Occasionally, patients say they can have conversations with these voices; however, what they seem to be describing here takes the form of a "voice" commenting on events, to which the patient answers back, followed by another comment from the voice to which the patient again replies; this "conversation" does not have the quality of exchange of information that is usual in normal conversations.

While some patients say they can "ignore" the voices, many find their content and tone, which can be derogatory, accusatory, or obscene, very disturbing. Relentless voices of this kind, and those that instruct or demand the patient to commit acts that are unconscionable, reduce some patients to states of nothing less than torture and torment. During a psychotic depression, for example, patients may report hearing voices saying that they are worthless and should kill themselves.

Though much less common, hallucinations also occur in other sensory modalities: patients may report "visions"; unusual smells in a room or emanating from their own body; or physical sensations, as if someone was touching them, or even trying to have sexual intercourse with them. Again, as in delusional states, patients may feel compelled to act on the basis of these psychotic experiences.

Delusions, passivity phenomena, and hallucinations are subjective experiences. They are psychotic symptoms which we can infer only on the basis of the patient's verbal report. Other symptoms of this kind include "thought broadcasting", where the patient reports the experience of thoughts not being confined within his or her own mind but somehow managing to become available to others in their minds. There is also "thought echo" – the experience of one's thoughts being repeated or echoed inside one's head.

Thought disorder

While we can know about delusions and hallucinations only because the patient tells us about them, other psychotic symptoms are directly observable. The most dramatic of these is "formal thought disorder", a complex and ill-understood phenomenon whose defining characteristic is that the speech output of the patient is, in the severest case, almost entirely incomprehensible. This lack of comprehensibility can arise as a result of various combinations of abnormalities in the patient's attempts at communication. Andreasen (1979) has produced a scale for the assessment of these various abnormal features which include: derailment (that is, a lack of proper connection between phrases or ideas); incoherence (a lack of proper connection between words; loss of goal; failure to follow a chain of thought through to its natural conclusion); and tangentiality (oblique or irrelevant replies). The speech of patients with this symptom may also be dotted with neologisms (nonsense words, for example, "fancitung", "frowen") or clang associations (for example, "all the usual blah, la di da"). It is important to note that patients exhibiting "formal thought disorder" as manifest in their verbal utterances are not impaired in their understanding of speech. They do

903

understand statements directed at them; their problem lies purely in the domain of producing an adequate and appropriate response to that statement. Manic patients may also show incoherent speech. In addition they may also show "pressure of speech" in which words are produced at an abnormally high rate.

Expression of emotion

In fact, formal thought disorder occurs relatively infrequently; much more common are observable abnormalities in the expression of emotion. Blunting, flattening, and incongruity of affect are frequently observed in schizophrenia. Blunting refers to an apparent lack of emotional sensitivity; events or situations do not elicit the usual, normal emotional response. Flattening of affect describes a more pervasive, general absence of emotional expression. The patients appear devoid of emotional tone, presenting with minimal inflection in their speech (even though they may be recounting the most bizarre or disturbing experiences), and a lack of the normal variation of facial or bodily movements which convey feelings or emotions. Incongruity of affect, by contrast, is observed when the patient expresses emotions that are at odds with the circumstances. Thus, a patient may smile as she describes how she found her brother dead.

Poverty of behaviour

Also noted in schizophrenia are "poverty of speech" and "poverty of content of speech". The former refers to an extremely low level of speech output, such that the patient provides minimal, often monosyllabic responses in communication. The latter refers to an excessively low level of information in a normal rate of output; the patient expresses him/herself in a vague and repetitive manner. In addition to poverty of speech, poverty of thought and poverty of action may also be observed, especially when the illness has reached a chronic stage. Poverty of speech and action can also be observed in affective psychoses, but in these cases it would be associated with severe depression.

AETIOLOGY OF THE PSYCHOSES

Historically, the question of the aetiology of the psychoses has proved to be something of a "battleground" for the forces of psychological and medical science. Influential psychological explanations have propounded the role of deviant family relationships and patterns of communication, or stress, while biologically oriented researchers have argued forcefully for genetic or viral causes. However, psychological and biological explanation are not necessarily mutually exclusive. Increasingly, investigators in this field are coming to accept that each may have a contribution to make to the understanding of the aetiology of these disorders.

Evidence for a biological component in the aetiology of these disorders can be drawn from two main sources: epidemiological and genetic studies.

Epidemiological studies

The World Health Organization's series of epidemiological studies of schizophrenia have generated a database of over 3,000 clinically and socially documented cases in centres spanning Africa, Asia, Europe, and the Americas. Most importantly, patients enrolled in the initial study have been followed up and reassessed two and five years later (see Leff, Sartorius, Jablensky, Korten, & Ernberg, 1992). The results of this major initiative are quite clear-cut. First, the psychopathological syndromes considered to be characteristic of schizophrenia are present in all cultures and geographical areas studied. Second, when a "conservative" definition of schizophrenia is applied, the incidence rates across cultures vary to a very small degree: 0.7 per 10,000 in Aarhus (Denmark) to 1.4 per 10,000 in Nottingham (UK). Third, although the total cumulative risk for developing schizophrenia is about equal for women and men, in all cultures investigated there is a well-established difference in the age of onset of the disease, with men typically experiencing their first episode in their early 20s, women in their late 20s to early 30s. Finally, all centres reported a similar relationship between "mode of onset", meaning the manner in which the disorder developed from the first sign of a psychotic illness into the complete syndrome, and the subsequent course of the illness. The degree of similarity both in the incidence and the characteristics of the illness across very different cultures and geographical areas is striking and provides strong evidence for biological causal mechanisms.

The genetics of psychotic disorders

It is widely accepted that schizophrenia and manic-depressive psychosis are in some part genetically determined. Family studies have demonstrated that the risk of developing schizophrenia rises with the degree of genetic proximity to an affected individual (see Table 2).

Data obtained from adoption and twin studies have further consolidated the genetic interpretation of the results of these family studies (Gottesman & Shields, 1982). The results of similar kinds of studies of affective disorder also point to a significant degree of genetic determination in bipolar or manic-depressive disorder (see McGuffin & Katz, 1986).

Table 2 Lifetime expectancy of schizophrenia in the relatives of schizophrenic patients

Relative	% Schizophrenic
Parent	5.6
Sibling	10.1
Children (one parent affected)	16.7
Children (both parents affected)	46.3
Uncles/aunts/nephews/nieces	2.8
Unrelated	0.86

Source: Data abstracted from Gottesman and Shields, 1982

Other risk factors

Compelling as these data are in respect of the genetic hypothesis of the aetiology of psychotic disorders, they fall far short of being able to explain all instances of these illnesses: many monozygotic twins (who are genetically identical) are discordant for the illness (that is, only one twin is affected); the majority of diagnosed cases do not report a family history; and the modes of inheritance (that is, the precise mechanisms by which the putative abnormal genes are passed on to the next generation) remain elusive. Indeed, many investigators in the field are now of the opinion that the data gathered to date are most satisfactorily explained by a "multifactorial" model of these disorders. This kind of model posits that a number of genes may be involved in producing a continuum of liability, or predisposition, to developing the disorder, which may in turn interact with environmental factors before 'he illness is manifest. Environmental factors such as birth injury and viral infections during pregnancy are claimed to increase the risk of developing schizophrenia, but these effects seem to be small.

Evidence for a psychological component in aetiology

In studies of the aetiology of psychotic disorders, the only evidence for a psychological component that has managed to withstand methodological criticism concerns stress. Steinberg and Durrell (1968), for example, showed that the rate of schizophrenic breakdown in US army recruits was significantly higher in their first month of service than at any time in the following two years. They suggested that the transition from civilian life to army life, a time when one might expect an increase in the experience of stress, contributed to the occurrence of the illnesses. Further support for the "precipitating" role of stress comes from the work of Brown and Birley (1968), who found that schizophrenic patients had experienced significantly more life-events than controls drawn from the same neighbourhood in the 12 weeks preceding the onset of their illness. It is also plausible that the deleterious effects of high expressed emotion in patients' relatives (see below, on course and prognosis) in relation to relapse in schizophrenic patients could be mediated via increases in the level of stress.

BRAIN ABNORMALITIES AND THE PSYCHOSES

The mental abnormalities that define the psychoses are so severe that it seems not unreasonable to expect that associated brain abnormalities would be found. At the time that Kraepelin was studying dementia praecox, the characteristic neuropathological changes associated with organic dementias such as General Paralysis of the Insane (due to syphilis) and Alzheimer's disease had just been discovered. He expected that similar markers would be found for the psychoses. Nevertheless, the considerable effort expended by neuropathologists in this search met with surprisingly little success. More recently the picture has started to change. While no characteristic neuropathology has yet been found, we now have very strong clues available which are being vigorously pursued.

Functional brain abnormalities: dopamine and schizophrenia

In the 1950s a new class of drugs, the neuroleptics, which had dramatic effects on many psychotic symptoms, was discovered (see below, on treatment). A great many placebo controlled trials have been carried out (Davis & Garver, 1978) showing that these drugs can reduce the severity of the positive features of psychosis (hallucinations, delusions, thought disorder). It has also been shown that this therapeutic effectiveness depends on the extent to which the drug blocks dopamine receptors (Seeman, Lee, Chau-Wong, & Wong, 1976). Dopamine is a neurotransmitter. It is stored in certain neurons and is used to communicate between one neuron and another via dopamine receptors. Dopamine-blocking drugs prevent or reduce such communication. This observation among others lead to the dopamine theory of schizophrenia (Randrup & Munkvad, 1972). It was hypothesized that psychotic symptoms were associated with an excess of dopamine in the brain. More detailed observations suggest that this simple theory is not correct. Nevertheless it is clear that the dopamine system plays an important, though indirect, role in the production of psychotic symptoms. A great deal is known about the dopamine system. We know that dopamine-containing neurons are concentrated in the basal ganglia and in frontal cortex. These areas are concerned with the initiation and control of movement. Degeneration of the dopamine system is associated with Parkinson's disease. Sufferers from this disorder show a characteristic poverty of movement which bears a superficial resemblance to the motor retardation that can be observed in chronic schizophrenic patients and in patients with severe depression. These observations have important implications for developing a neuropsychology of psychosis (see, e.g., Robbins, 1990 and below, on mechanisms).

Structural brain abnormalities

The development of techniques for imaging the structure of the living brain has revolutionized the study of the psychoses. A large number of studies using these techniques have shown that the ventricles (the fluid spaces in the middle of the brain) are significantly enlarged in schizophrenic patients compared to controls (Gattaz, Kohlmeyer, & Gasser, 1991). This is by no means a change that is specific to the psychoses. Patients with degenerative brain disorders, such as Alzheimer's disease and Huntington's chorea, show considerably greater ventricular enlargement. Nevertheless, the result suggests that there is a lack of brain tissue in the psychoses, either because it has degenerated or because it failed to develop properly in the first place. Current opinion favours the hypothesis of developmental failure (e.g., Murray & Lewis, 1987). This is in part because there is no evidence that ventricle size increases with length of illness, and in part because there is little evidence for the gliosis (a kind of neural scar tissue) that is normally found in degenerative disorders. A number of investigations, particularly of post-mortem brains, have attempted to locate the missing and/or abnormal tissue. These results still remain somewhat inconclusive, but abnormalities of the medial temporal lobe in the region of the hippocampus have been reported in several independent studies (e.g., Brown et al., 1986).

MECHANISMS OF SIGNS AND SYMPTOMS

Psychotic patients have fundamental problems with behaviour, thought, and experience. Given that the brain serves to control behaviour and is the organ of thought, it is necessarily the case that these psychological abnormalities must be associated with parallel abnormalities of brain function. In principle, it should be possible to show that a particular symptom, such as an auditory hallucination, is associated with abnormal activity in a particular brain system. However, this does not mean that the hallucination is *caused* by this brain activity. Rather, the hallucination and the brain activity are two sides of the same coin. Likewise, the demonstration of relationships between symptoms and brain function does not mean that psychosis has a biological cause. Such demonstrations tell us nothing directly about aetiology.

Even if we had found specific neuropathological abnormalities in psychotic patients, we would still not understand why such patients heard non-existent voices or believed that alien forces were controlling their actions. In order to make a link between subjective experience and brain function we need a description of the relevant processes in cognitive terms.

Freud (1911) was probably the first to attempt an explanation of psychotic phenomena in terms of underlying cognitive processes, and Bleuler (1913) applied a similar approach to the study of schizophrenia. However, lacking the necessary methodology, these hypotheses were never tested experimentally. In this chapter we shall restrict our brief survey to accounts of psychotic signs and symptoms for which there is some empirical support.

Many different psychotic symptoms have been described, all of which could be studied separately. However, the very fact that these symptoms have all been classified as "psychotic" implies that they have something in common at the cognitive level of description. A number of studies have therefore searched for associations between signs and symptoms. The nature of the clusters revealed should tell us something about common underlying cognitive processes.

In studies of schizophrenia, the distinction made by Crow (1980) between positive and negative features has been particularly influential. Positive features are abnormal by their presence and include delusions, hallucinations, and incoherent speech. Negative features are abnormal through their absence and include poverty of speech, flattening of affect, and social withdrawal. Crow suggested that these two classes of symptoms were related to different pathological processes. Positive features are assumed to be associated with abnormal dopamine metabolism, and negative features with structural brain abnormalities. Subsequently, studies have been conducted which have refined Crow's description and have, with some consistency, revealed three clusters of features (Arndt, Alliger, & Andreasen, 1991). Liddle (1987) has named these "psycho-motor poverty" (poverty of speech, social withdrawal, flattening of affect), "disorganization" (incoherence of speech, incongruity of affect), and "reality distortion" (hallucinations, delusions). These clusters can also be observed in other types of psychoses. Psycho-motor poverty can be observed in depressed patients, and disorganization can be associated with mania. These three clusters provide a useful framework for considering the cognitive basis of psychotic features.

Poverty and disorganization

Typically patients with poverty of speech will answer questions put to them, but will use the minimum number of words with no spontaneous elaboration (see above, on signs and symptoms). Other areas of activity show the same pattern, in that patients respond appropriately in routine situations but produce no spontaneous activity of their own volition. These observations suggest a circumscribed deficit in the initiation of actions: spontaneous, "willed" actions are impaired, while routine actions elicited by appropriate circumstances (stimulus-driven acts) are not. Kraepelin (1896), in his original account of dementia praecox, concluded that this disorder was associated with a fundamental deficit of volition. Performance of patients with negative features on various experimental tasks are consistent with this hypothesis (Frith, 1992, chap. 4).

Shallice's Supervisory Attentional System (SAS) is a mechanism which can control the choice of actions in novel as well as routine situations and can account for the production of willed acts (Shallice, 1988, chap. 14). When this system is damaged, disorganization as well as poverty of action can occur, and thus impairments to such a mechanism could account for two different aspects of psychotic behaviour. Shallice's model was developed to explain abnormal behaviour after injury to the frontal lobes. A number of studies have shown that schizophrenic patients, particularly those with negative features, perform badly on "frontal lobe" tests, especially the Wisconsin Card Sorting Test (Corcoran & Frith, 1993).

This distinction between willed action and stimulus-driven action has also been made on the basis of neuro-physiological studies (for example, Goldberg, 1985). Goldberg has proposed that there is a motor system located in the medial part of the brain (including the prefrontal cortex, supplementary motor area, and the striatum) which is particularly concerned with the control of willed actions. He notes observations that patients with Parkinson's disease have much greater problems with willed acts than with stimulus-driven acts. On the basis of all these considerations, a number of authors have suggested that the negative features of schizophrenia are associated with abnormalities in a functional loop linking the frontal cortex and the striatum. This system is concerned with high-level control of action (for example, Robbins, 1990).

Reality distortion (hallucinations and delusions)

These phenomena are particularly difficult to study experimentally because they concern abnormal experiences which cannot be directly observed. Nevertheless, a number of accounts that are amenable to experimental investigation have been put forward.

Defective filter

One of the earliest insights of cognitive psychology was that we are all bombarded with a vast amount of information. A complex filtering mechanism ensures that most of this information remains in the "cognitive unconscious". Many positive features of psychosis can be explained as resulting from a breakdown in this filter (see e.g., Frith, 1979). For example, the patient becomes aware of irrelevant aspects of words such as their sound or alternative meanings. Such preoccupations can lead to incoherent speech, for example, a patient describing a light shade of green said, "Clean green. The one without the cream. Don't see this colour on planes. Looks like moss, boss" (Cohen, 1978). Likewise, patients who become aware of irrelevant stimuli in the environment may assume that these must be important and then develop complex delusional accounts as to why these stimuli are important to them. On this theory, delusions (false beliefs) are explained as occurring when normal logical arguments are applied to abnormal perceptions.

Gray and his colleagues (Gray, Feldon, Rawlins, Hemsley, & Smith, 1990) have put forward a detailed theory linking these kinds of psychological problems with impairments of a distributed brain mechanism involving the hippocampus and the dopamine system.

Self-monitoring

As yet there is no proven account of the mechanisms underlying auditory hallucinations. Currently, a popular notion is that auditory hallucinations are associated with the patient's own subvocal or "inner" speech. A few case studies have found hallucinating patients who were producing subvocal speech with the same content as their hallucinations (Gould, 1949). These observations imply that the hallucinating patient experiences his or her own inner speech or thought as alien and coming from some external source. This is an attractive idea since it could account for certain delusions (for example, the belief that my actions are being controlled by alien forces) as well as auditory hallucinations. Such delusions could arise if patients were unable to monitor their own intended actions and thus found themselves performing actions without being aware of any prior intention to do so. It is possible to study experimentally the ability to monitor our own actions, and there is some preliminary evidence that this ability is impaired in psychotic patients with delusions of alien control (Frith, 1992, chap. 5; Fritz & Done, 1989).

A simple physiological system which permits self-monitoring has been described in relation to eye movements and limb movements (Gallistel, 1980). Physiological studies that may have direct relevance to auditory hallucinations have shown that there are cells in the temporal cortex of the squirrel monkey that respond to vocalizations of other monkeys, but not to self-generated calls (Ploog, 1979). Defects in such a system could result in the monkey perceiving its own calls as emanating from another monkey and hence experiencing auditory hallucinations.

Abnormal inferences

Some researchers have suggested that delusions arise because processes of logic and inference are faulty (Garety, Hemsley, & Wesseley, 1991). There is some evidence that deluded patients reach conclusions on an abnormally small amount of evidence and then stick to these conclusions in the face of contradictory evidence. A major problem with this hypothesis is that most patients have circumscribed delusions. For example, the patient may believe that a small group of people is persecuting him or her. Application of logic

911

to the behaviour of other people would be perfectly normal as would reasoning in other spheres. These observations suggest that there is no general problem with making inferences. One proposal is that certain psychotic patients have a specific problem with making inferences about the beliefs and intentions of other people (Frith, 1992, chap. 7). Studies of autistic children have shown that the ability to make inferences about the mental states of other people can be specifically impaired while other abilities remain intact. A failure in this "mind reading" module could explain certain psychotic features. Paranoid delusions occur when patients falsely infer that others intend to do them harm. Delusions of reference occur when patients falsely infer that others intend to communicate with them.

As yet there are no physiological data concerning how the brain represents mental states. However, there are studies suggesting that there are circumscribed brain systems concerned with social interactions. The orbital frontal cortex and temporal cortex have been implicated in these systems (Brothers, 1990).

COURSE, PROGNOSIS, AND THERAPEUTIC INTERVENTIONS

At the time of Kraepelin and Bleuler the majority of psychotic patients became permanent invalids condemned to insanity, and hence an asylum, for life. Guttmann, Mayer-Gross, and Slater (1939) surveyed the outcome of 188 schizophrenic patients in the Maudsley Hospital during the 1930s and reported that although some 22 per cent made a complete recovery, over half remained more or less incapacitated by the disorder (some 80 per cent were still hospitalized at follow-up).

Schizophrenia

Research since the early 1960s indicates that this largely hopeless course for schizophrenia has been altered substantially. Johnstone (1991), for example, surveyed a cohort of some 530 schizophrenic patients discharged from psychiatric services over a period of ten years (1975–1985) and found that on average these patients spent only 13.7 of the 120 months between 1975 and 1985 in hospital; when contacted in 1990, less than 10 per cent of the patients were receiving continuing in-patient care. Symptoms such as hallucinations and incoherence were absent in the majority of cases, although 47.2 per cent were still found to have varying degrees of delusional belief. However, more than 90 per cent of patients were receiving medical and/or social support, and 45 per cent were still under the care of a psychiatrist.

This pattern of clinical and social outcomes reflects the advances and shortcomings inherent in current treatment regimes. While drugs such as chlorpromazine, the anti-psychotic properties of which were first demonstrated in the early 1950s, have had profound effects in terms of the alleviation of some of the most distressing symptoms, these compounds do not provide cures as such; they do not correct the abnormality (or abnormalities) causing the disorder. Consequently, to keep symptoms at bay, the majority of patients who experience psychotic episodes must continue to take medication. The "prophylactic" efficacy of continuous or "maintenance" medication has been demonstrated in numerous clinical trials. Goldberg, Schooler, Hogarty, and Roper (1977), for example, in a study of 400 newly discharged schizophrenic patients found that those receiving "maintenance" drug therapy had a relapse rate almost half that of those who received a placebo treatment (48 per cent compared to 80 per cent).

Relapse, however, is not a cut-and-dried issue, entirely dependent on drug treatment. A wide range of factors contribute to the possibility of the re-emergence of psychotic phenomena. Strauss and Carpenter (1977) demonstrated that outcome may be partially predicted from measures of the patients' pre-morbid (that is, prior to their becoming ill) level of functioning: those with a good pre-morbid level of functioning having a better outcome. Vaillant (1964) demonstrated that characteristics of the initial episode of illness, such as an acute onset, the occurrence of a stressful life-event or situation at the time of onset, and the lack of a family history of schizophrenia, also predicted a relatively good outcome. Social psychological research has shown that relapse may also be determined to some extent by the impact of life-events such as the death of a close relative or a change of accommodation (Brown & Birley, 1968) and by the patients' experience of highly emotionally strained relationships within the family (Vaughan & Leff, 1976).

These findings point to a role for psychological input in the prevention of relapse. Thus, Leff, Kuipers, Berkowitz, Everlein-Vreis, and Sturgeon (1982) reported that the introduction of a psychologically defined intervention consisting of giving information regarding the disorder (schizophrenia) to relatives, and conducting regular fortnightly group meetings with relatives and family therapy sessions, all designed to lower expressed emotion and face-to-face contact, resulted in a significantly lower relapse rate (50 per cent in those not receiving the package as against 9 per cent in those who were). In a similar vein, Falloon et al. (1985) have championed the cause of problem-oriented and behavioural therapy sessions in the prevention of relapse, reporting figures for their programme consistent with those of Leff et al. (1982). It should be stressed, however, that this programme has an adjunctive role; numerous clinical trials have demonstrated that psychological interventions alone make no impact on this disorder (Goldberg et al, 1977).

Unfortunately, despite the best efforts of clinicians, many schizophrenic patients are unable to resume "normal" levels of adult functioning. Johnstone (1991) found that at follow-up some 58 per cent of their cohort were unemployed, 60 per cent were single, and many lived alone. There is also a small minority of patients (approximately 7 per cent) for whom the drugs are of little benefit (e.g., Johnstone, 1991). For the majority it is still disappointing that the treatment regimes available provide varying degrees of control of positive symptoms but may have negligible impact on the negative symptoms. Thus, patients may not hear the voices as often as they used to, but they remain apathetic and withdrawn. There is the additional problem that anti-psychotic drugs have side-effects which not only are uncomfortable for the patient but also can compromise the patient's physical appearance (examples are weight gain, tremor, stiff gait). These problems, together with psychosocial factors, such as the strain imposed on relationships by the patient's behaviour during a psychotic episode, or the social stigma surrounding mental illness, preclude many from achieving stable or satisfying relationships or employment.

Affective psychoses

The outlook for patients suffering manic-depressive psychosis is not so bleak. As Kraepelin originally suggested, these patients typically make a good recovery from their psychotic episodes, although the episodes are likely to recur. Manic episodes of illness last approximately one to three months, whereas depressive episodes tend to be of longer duration generally, between three and eight months. The risk of recurrence of a manic episode is high, particularly if the person has his or her first episode before the age of 30. The time between bouts of illness is extremely variable, ranging from weeks to years.

Treatment of manic-depressive psychosis consists largely of drug therapies, the most appropriate form being determined by the current presentation. In depressive episodes patients are prescribed standard anti-depressive drug regimens, whereas patients in a manic state are likely to be treated initially with an anti-psychotic, following which lithium − a drug of unique value in the treatment of manic-depressive psychosis − may be introduced. The principal use of lithium is to prevent recurrence of mania and depressive episodes. How it achieves this is still unknown.

CONCLUSIONS

Psychotic disorders are associated with severe abnormalities in all the domains that reach their highest level of development in humans: emotion, will, consciousness, and the ability to interact with other minds. Currently the greatest challenge facing science is to explain how these mental entities can arise from a physical brain. Studies of psychotic illness will provide critical information for this endeavour. Such studies are also vital if we are to improve our ability to reduce the widespread suffering associated with these disorders.

FURTHER READING

Cutting, J. (1985). *The psychology of schizophrenia*. Edinburgh: Churchill Livingstone.

Frith, C. D. (1992). *The cognitive neuropsychology of schizophrenia*. Hove: Lawrence Erlbaum.

Gottesman, I. I., & Shields, J. (1982). *Schizophrenia: The epigenetic puzzle*. Cambridge: Cambridge University Press.

Sims, A. (1988). *Symptoms in the mind. An introduction to descriptive psychopathology*. London: Baillière Tindall.

Straube, E. R., & Oades, R. D. (1992). Schizophrenia: *Empirical research and findings*. London: Academic Press.

Wing, J. K., & Wing, L. (1982). *Handbook of psychiatry, vol. 3. Psychoses of uncertain aetiology*. Cambridge: Cambridge University Press.

REFERENCES

American Psychiatric Association (1987). *Diagnostic and statistical manual of mental disorders* (3rd edn, revised). Washington, DC: APA.

Andreasen, N. C. (1979). Thought, language and communication disorders. *Archives of General Psychiatry*, *36*, 1315–1321.

Arndt, S., Alliger, R. J., & Andreasen, N. C. (1991). The distinction of positive and negative symptoms: The failure of a two-dimensional model. *British Journal of Psychiatry*, *158*, 317–322.

Bleuler, E. (1913). *Dementia Praecox or the group of schizophrenias* (trans.). In J. Cutting & M. Shepherd (Eds) (1987). *The clinical routes of the schizophrenia concept* (pp. 59–74). Cambridge: Cambridge University Press.

Brothers, L. (1990). The social brain: A project for integrating primate behaviour and neurophysiology in a new domain. *Concepts in Neuroscience*, *1*, 27–51.

Brown, G. W., & Birley, J. L. T. (1968). Crises and life changes and the onset of schizophrenia. *Journal of Health and Social Behaviour*, *9*, 203–214.

Brown, R., Colter, N., Corsellis, J. A. N., Crow, T. J., Frith, C. D., Jagoe, R., Johnstone, E. C., & Marsh, L. (1986). Post-mortem evidence of structural brain changes in schizophrenia. *Archives of General Psychiatry*, *43*, 36–42.

Cohen, B. D. (1978). Referent communication disturbances in schizophrenia. In S. Schwartz (Ed.) *Language and cognition in schizophrenia* (pp. 1–34). Hillsdale, NJ: Lawrence Erlbaum.

Corcoran, R., & Frith, C. D. (1993). Neuropsychology and neurophysiology of schizophrenia. *Current Opinion in Psychiatry*, *6*, 74–79.

Crow, T. J. (1980). Molecular pathology of schizophrenia: More than one disease process? *British Medical Journal*, *280*, 66–68.

Davis, J. M., & Garver, D. L. (1978). Neuroleptics: Clinical use in psychiatry. In L. L. Iversen & S. D. Iversen (Eds) *Handbook of psychopharmacology* (vol. 10, pp. 129–164). New York: Plenum.

Falloon, I. R. H., Boyd, J. L., McGill, C. W., Williamson, M., Razani, J., Moss, H. B., Gilderman, A. M., & Simpson, G. M. (1985). Family management in the prevention of morbidity of schizophrenia. *Archives of General Psychiatry*, *42*, 887–896.

Freud, S. (1911). Psychoanalytic notes upon an autobiographical account of a case of paranoia (dementia paranoids). In S. Freud, *Collected papers* (J. Strachey, ed. and trans., vol. 3, pp. 387–470). London: Hogarth.

Frith, C. D. (1979). Consciousness, information processing and schizophrenia. *British Journal of Psychiatry*, *134*, 225–235.

Frith, C. D. (1992). *The cognitive neuropsychology of schizophrenia*. Hove: Lawrence Erlbaum.

Frith, C. D., & Done, D. J. (1989). Experiences of alien control in schizophrenia reflect a disorder in the central monitoring of action. *Psychological Medicine*, *19*, 359–363.

Gallistel, C. R. (1980). *Organization of action: A new synthesis*. New York: Lawrence Erlbaum.

Garety, P. A., Hemsley, D. R., & Wesseley, S. (1991). Reasoning in deluded and paranoid subjects: Biases in performance on a probabilistic inferencing task. *Journal of Nervous and Mental Disease*, *179*, 194–201.

Gattaz, W. F., Kohlmeyer, K., & Gasser, T. (1991). Computer tomographic studies in schizophrenia. In H. Hafner & W. F. Gattaz (Eds) *Search for the causes of schizophrenia* (vol. 2, pp. 242–256). Berlin: Springer.

Goldberg, G. (1985). Supplementary motor area structure and function: Review and hypotheses. *Behavioural and Brain Sciences*, *8*, 567–616.

Goldberg, S. C., Schooler, N. R., Hogarty, G. E., & Roper, M. (1977). Prediction of relapse in schizophrenic outpatients treated by drug and sociotherapy. *Archives of General Psychiatry*, *34*, 171–184.

Gottesman, I. I., & Shields, J. (1982). *Schizophrenia: The epigenetic puzzle*. Cambridge: Cambridge University Press.

Gould, L. N. (1949). Auditory hallucinations and subvocal speech. *Journal of Nervous and Mental Disease*, *109*, 418–427.

Gray, J., Feldon, J., Rawlins, J., Hemsley, D., & Smith, A. (1990). The neuropsychology of schizophrenia. *Behavioural and Brain Sciences*, *14*, 1–84.

Gunderson, J. G., & Mosher, L. R. (1975). The cost of schizophrenia. *American Journal of Psychiatry*, *132*, 901–906.

Guttmann, E., Mayer-Gross, W., & Slater, E. T. O. (1939). Short-distance prognosis of schizophrenia. *Journal of Neurology and Psychiatry*, *2*, 25–34.

Jaspers, K. (1962). *General psychopathology*. Manchester: Manchester University Press.

Johnstone, E. C. (Ed.) (1991). Disabilities and circumstances of schizophrenic patients: A follow-up study. *British Journal of Psychiatry*, *159*, suppl. 13.

Kraepelin, E. (1896) *Dementia Praecox* (trans.). In J. Cutting & M. Shepherd (Eds) (1987). *The clinical routes of the schizophrenia concept* (pp. 13–24). Cambridge: Cambridge University Press.

Leff, J., Kuipers, L., Berkowitz, R., Everlein-Vreis, R., & Sturgeon, D. A. (1982). A controlled trial of social intervention in the families of schizophrenic patients. *British Journal of Psychiatry*, *141*, 121–134.

Leff, J., Sartorius, N., Jablensky, A., Korten, A., & Ernberg, G. (1992). The international pilot study of schizophrenia: Five-year follow-up findings. *Psychological Medicine*, *22*, 131–145.

Liddle, P. F. (1987). The symptoms of chronic schizophrenia: A reexamination of the positive–negative dichotomy. *British Journal of Psychiatry*, *151*, 145–151.

McGuffin, P., & Katz, R. (1986). Nature, nurture and affective disorder. In J. F. W. Deakin (Ed.) *Biology of depression* (pp. 26–52). London: Gaskell and Royal College of Psychiatrists.

Murray, R. M., & Lewis, S. W. (1987). Is schizophrenia a developmental disorder? *British Medical Journal*, *295*, 681–682.

Perris, C. (1966). A study of bi-polar (manic-depressive) and unipolar recurrent depressive psychoses. *Acta Psychiatrica Scandinavica*, suppl. 194.

Peterson, D. (Ed.) (1982). *A mad people's history of madness*. Pittsburgh, PA: University of Pittsburgh Press.

Ploog, D. (1979). Phonation, emotion, cognition: With reference to the brain mechanisms involved. In G. Wolstenholme & M. O'Connor (Eds) *Brain and mind* (CIBA Foundation Symposium 69, pp. 79–98). Amsterdam: Elsevier/North-Holland.

Randrup, A., & Munkvad, I. (1972). Evidence indicating an association between schizophrenia and dopaminergic hyperactivity in the brain. *Orthomolecular Psychiatry*, *1*, 2–7.

Robbins, T. W. (1990). The case for a frontostriatal dysfunction in schizophrenia. *Schizophrenia Bulletin*, *16*, 391–402.

Schneider, K. (1959). *Clinical psychopathology*. New York: Grune & Stratton.

Seeman, P., Lee, T., Chau-Wong, M., & Wong, K. (1976). Antipsychotic drug doses and neuroleptic/dopamine receptors. *Nature* (London), *261*, 717–719.

Shallice, T. (1988). *From neuropsychology to mental structure*. Cambridge: Cambridge University Press.

Sims, A. (1988). *Symptoms in the mind. An introduction to descriptive psychopathology*. London: Baillière Tindall.

Steinberg, H. R., & Durrell, J. (1968). A stressful situation as a precipitant of schizophrenic symptoms: An epidemiological study. *British Journal of Psychiatry*, *114*, 1097–1105.

Strauss, J. S., & Carpenter, W. T. (1977). The prediction of outcome in schizophrenia: III. Five-year outcome and its predictors. *Archives of General Psychiatry*, *34*, 159–163.

Vaillant, G. E. (1964). Prospective prediction of schizophrenic remission. *Archives of General Psychiatry*, *11*, 509–518.

Vaughan, C. E., & Leff, J. P. (1976). Influence of family and social factors on the course of psychiatric illness. *British Journal of Psychiatry*, *129*, 125–138.

World Health Organization (1978). *Mental disorders: Glossary and guide to their classification in accordance with the ninth revision of the International Classification of Diseases*. Geneva: WHO.

10.3

INFANTILE AUTISM

Simon Baron-Cohen
University of London Institute of Psychiatry, England

Autism is often described as the most severe of all of the child psychiatric disorders. Why should this be? Surely each disability is severe in its own way? Autism has gained this reputation because, unlike all other childhood disorders, people with autism appear to be virtually cut off from other people − "in a world of their own". It is in this sense that autism is sometimes also categorized as a psychosis: like schizophrenia, autism appears to be qualitatively unlike anything in the normal range of experience. In contrast, neurotic disorders (such as anxiety or depression) seem closer to experiences in the normal range.

Even the other communication disorders of childhood do not leave the sufferer isolated to quite the same degree as occurs in autism. Thus, although dysphasic disorders of childhood include language comprehension or expression deficits, somehow the social contact between the sufferer and other people is not severed: children with various dysphasias still find some way of making and developing relationships with others. They may use sign-language, impoverished speech, or even simply eye-contact and gesture. This is not true of children with autism. For them, even understanding *what*

918

communication is for seems to be missing. Why? As I shall describe, this is part of the *social* difficulties that lie at the core of autism.

WHAT IS AUTISM?

Autism is a psychiatric disorder which begins during the first three years of life (American Psychiatric Association, 1987). It affects approximately 4 children in every 10,000, although some studies have suggested it may be as common as 15–20 per 10,000 (Frith, 1989). Boys are affected three times as often as girls; two-thirds of children with the condition have learning difficulties in addition to the problems specific to autism. That is, two-thirds of children with autism have an IQ (or measured intelligence) below the average range (Rutter, 1985). Even those whose intelligence is in the normal range show an unusual pattern of skills, with visuo-spatial intelligence usually being superior to verbal abilities (Frith, 1989).

Various sets of diagnostic criteria exist (American Psychiatric Association, 1987; Rutter, 1985), but all of these share an emphasis on three key symptoms. First, the child fails to make normal social relationships, or to develop socially in the normal way. Instead, social interests tend to be one-sided, non-reciprocal, and exist only to satisfy the child's immediate wishes. Missing are any genuinely social games (or turn-taking), any attempt to share interests through *joint-attention behaviours* (such as using the pointing gesture to indicate things of interest to people, or showing people things of interest), normal use of eye-contact, or any friendship beyond the most superficial acquaintance. A lack of empathy is often identified as the central feature of the social deficit (Baron-Cohen, 1988; Hobson, 1986, 1993; Kanner, 1943).

Second, the child fails to develop language or communication in the normal way. This symptom can include a multitude of anomalies. For example, some children with autism are functionally completely mute, while others are slow learning to speak, and their language development severely limited. Yet others can speak in full sentences, but nevertheless show a range of speech abnormalities, and fail to use their speech appropriately to achieve communication or to use gesture in a normal way. These abnormalities are described in detail below.

The final symptom is repetitive behaviour, in conjunction with a lack of normal imagination. Thus, children with autism often carry out the same action over and over again, becoming quite distressed if other people attempt to prevent them from carrying out their repetitive rituals, and their play is often devoid of any apparent creativity or imagination (Baron-Cohen, 1987). During play, for example, children with autism often simply arrange objects in strict geometric patterns in the same way every day, rather than transforming objects into *pretend* or symbolic play, as normal children do even from the age of about 18 months (Leslie, 1987).

Tragically, while the symptoms may change in form as people with autism get older, and while with age a considerable amount of learning may be possible, autism appears to be a lifelong condition (Frith, 1989). Some claims of "cures" have been reported, but in none of these cases has recovery to a *normal* state been verified, and in the majority of cases individuals remain "odd" and obviously disabled in adulthood.

CAUSES

Various possible causes of autism have been identified, all biological, and all of these are assumed to disturb the normal development of the central nervous system (Gillberg, 1990). The major causes for which there is scientific evidence are genetic, perinatal, viral, and a variety of medical conditions.

The genetic evidence centres on the higher concordance rate for autism among monozygotic (genetically identical) twins, where one has autism, than among dizygotic (genetically non-identical) twins, where one has autism (Bolton & Rutter, 1990). In addition, some 2–3 per cent of the siblings of children with autism also develop autism, and this is approximately 50 times higher than one would expect from chance alone (Bolton & Rutter, 1990). The perinatal evidence centres on the increased risk for autism produced by a range of complications during pregnancy and labour. The viral evidence centres on the statistically significant association between autism and infection by the rubella (German measles) virus during pregnancy (Wing, 1969).

Finally, the range of medical conditions associated with autism (and assumed to be causal) include genetic disorders (such as Fragile X Syndrome, phenylketonuria, tuberous sclerosis, neurofibromatosis, and other chromosomal anomalies); metabolic disorders (such as histidinaemia, abnormalities of purine synthesis and of carbohydrate metabolism); and congenital anomaly syndromes (such as Cornelia de Lange Syndrome, Noonan Syndrome, Coffin-Siris Syndrome, Williams Syndrome, Biedl-Bardet Syndrome, Moebius' Syndrome, and Leber's Amaurosis). These are reviewed by Gillberg (1990).

No single cause has been identified for all cases, and current theories suggest that there may instead be several separate causes of autism, any of which may affect the part of the brain that produces the condition. This view has come to be known as the *final common pathway* hypothesis. Using neuro-imaging techniques, brain abnormalities have been found in various regions of the brain in different cases, but again none of these is consistent across all individuals with autism (George, Costa, Kouris, Ring, & Ell, 1993). The exception to this is the finding that the cerebellum may show specific atrophy in all cases (Courchesne, Yeung-Courchesne, Press, Hesselink, & Jernigan, 1988). This work remains to be replicated. But the clearest evidence that there is brain dysfunction in autism stems from the fact that some 30 per cent of people with autism also develop epilepsy at some stage in their lives (Rutter,

1985). Finally, autism has not been demonstrated to be associated with either poor parenting, or social factors such as class. This last statement rules out some early theories of autism. For example, Bettelheim (1968) had proposed that the mothers of children with autism gave inadequate emotional input to their children, preventing the formation of the primary bond between mother and child, and thus preventing further social development or development of the child's concept of self. Tinbergen and Tinbergen (1983) argued for a similar characterization of autism, emphasizing traumatic factors that might have prevented the primary mother–child attachment relationship from forming. Finally, Kanner (1943) emphasized the predominantly intellectual, upper-middle-class nature of the parents of children with autism, implying that a lack of emotion in the parents may have caused the child's autism. None of these claims has been supported by subsequent work (Frith, 1989).

WHAT ARE THE LANGUAGE ABNORMALITIES IN AUTISM?

Language abnormalities exist in all of the subsystems of language. In syntax, for example, there can be considerable delays in rate of acquisition of syntactical forms, although longitudinal studies show that the order of acquisition does not differ from that found either in normal children or in children with learning difficulties (Tager-Flusberg et al., 1990). Thus, children with autism who develop speech usually go through a one-word and a two-word phase, their *mean length of utterance* (MLU) usually increases in normal ways, and the syntactical forms used seem to appear in the same order as in normal development. In phonology, intonation can sometimes be rather monotonous and "mechanical" sounding, but otherwise is often normal, if not superior. Thus, when children with autism produce *echolalia*, echoing someone else's speech, it is often with identical intonation to the person who first uttered it.

In semantics, words are clearly referential, but neologisms may be present. Thus, the child may use a word that is not a conventional one, but which nevertheless has a meaning for that child. For example, one boy with autism referred to a cat as a "milk outside". When the origin of such neologisms is traced, they are often found to derive from incomplete learning during the first usage of the term. In the example above, the boy's mother often used to say "Let's put the milk outside for the cat". Kanner, the psychiatrist who first described autism in 1943, characterized such neologisms in the speech of children with autism as "metaphorical", although it is worth stressing that these do not conform to cases of true metaphor. Indeed, semantic abnormalities in the speech of people with autism include difficulties in understanding or creating true metaphors and other forms of figurative language, such as irony or sarcasm (Happé, 1992).

Other semantic abnormalities are seen in the production of echolalia – either *immediate*, where the person with autism repeats straight back what the other person has just said, or *delayed*, where the person repeats back a segment of conversation that was overheard some time before. In delayed echolalia, the speech echoed may be part of a television jingle, or lyrics from a song, and often testifies to excellent long-term memory in people with autism.

But of all the language abnormalities in autism, the most severe are in the pragmatics of speech. By pragmatics is meant the rules governing the appropriate *use* of language in specific social contexts, and the rules for inferring a speaker's intended meaning. Almost every aspect of pragmatics that has been studied in people with autism has been found to be abnormal (see Baron-Cohen, 1988, for a review). Thus, the range of *speech acts* that they produce is quite limited – requests being the most frequent, informative or humorous speech acts being quite rare. They also appear not to realize how to use language in a way that is sensitive to the social context. For example, they tend to say things that are rude, not because of any wilful desire to offend, but simply because they are blind to the polite/rude distinction (e.g., one child with autism correctly noticed but then said out loud "That woman has dyed her moustache!"). Furthermore, they often do not distinguish old and new information in a conversation, failing to take into account what the listener already knows or does not know. For example, they may repeat things they have already told the listener, or they may refer to things that the listener could not possibly know about, without explaining these. It is also rare for them to introduce their topic so that the listener can appreciate its relevance (e.g., by using phrases such as "You know I was in France for my holidays, well . . .").

Another instance of the pragmatic deficit in the language of people with autism is seen in the lack of normal turn-taking in conversation. Instead, they may talk at the same time as the other person, or deliver extended monologues, or simply not reply at all when a reply is expected. This can appear as a failure to recognize the intention behind a question. For example, when asked "Can you pass the salt?", a person with autism may simply reply "Yes". Such a limited reply is not a sign of wilful rudeness, but simply due to a failure to recognize the question as a request for an object.

The pragmatic deficit is also seen in the use of a pedantic style of language that is inappropriate for the social situation. For example, one girl with autism asked "Do you travel to work on a driver-only-operated number 68 bus?" Also, many people with autism do not establish eye contact with the listener before speaking, or use eye contact to regulate any conversational turn-taking. Finally, some studies have shown that they tend to ask questions to which they already know the answers, thus violating conventional uses of different parts of speech.

RELATIONSHIP BETWEEN THE LANGUAGE AND THE SOCIAL ABNORMALITIES

During the 1960s and early 1970s one major theory of autism argued that the social abnormalities in this disorder were secondary to the language problems (Rutter, 1985). This theory lost credibility when studies compared children with dysphasia and children with autism. Such studies demonstrated that language disabilities did not inevitably produce social disabilities, in that children with even severe dysphasia nevertheless often showed surprisingly intact social skills and sensitivities. In contrast, more recent psychological theories suggest that language delay is an entirely independent disability which may co-occur in autism, while the abnormalities in pragmatic competence are an inevitable consequence of the social disability in people with autism, and are seen in all cases. One such psychological theory is elaborated below.

THE MIND-BLINDNESS THEORY

Experiments have demonstrated that people with autism are severely impaired in their understanding of mental states, such as beliefs and thoughts, and in their appreciation of how mental states govern behaviour (Baron-Cohen, Leslie, & Frith, 1985; Baron-Cohen, 1993). This ability in normal people has been referred to as a "theory of mind" (Premack & Woodruff, 1978) because of how we use our concepts of people's mental states to explain their behaviour. Attributing mental states such as thoughts, desires, intentions, and so on to other people allows us to understand why people do what they do, and in keeping track of both other people's mental states and our own, we can mesh flexibly in social interaction.

Apart from using a theory of mind to make sense of the social world, and to participate in it (Dennett, 1978), a second key function of a theory of mind in normal people is to make sense of communication, and to communicate with others (Grice, 1975). In computing the meaning and relevance of another person's speech we constantly take into account their background mental states, and in making our speech meaningful and relevant to our listener, we do the same (Sperber & Wilson, 1986).

Given these two functions of a theory of mind, it is clear that, if people with autism are unable to appreciate that other people have different mental states, this would severely impair their ability not only to understand and participate in social interaction, but also communication itself. It is in this sense that the deficits they show in pragmatics are thought to be intimately entwined with their social deficits. A number of experiments have demonstrated specific difficulties for people with autism in understanding the mental states of belief, knowledge, pretence, and intention (Baron-Cohen et al., 1985; Leslie & Frith, 1988; Goodhart & Baron-Cohen, 1992; Phillips, 1993).

One example of a test of understanding belief is shown in Figure 1. This core inability to appreciate other people's mental states has been termed "mind-blindness" (Baron-Cohen, 1990). Current research is elucidating whether this problem constitutes a case of *specific developmental delay*, in that some children with autism do eventually develop a theory of mind, *years* after it emerges in normal development (Baron-Cohen, 1989a), and what the origins of their mind-blindness might be (Baron-Cohen, 1989b; Baron-Cohen, 1993; Hobson, 1993).

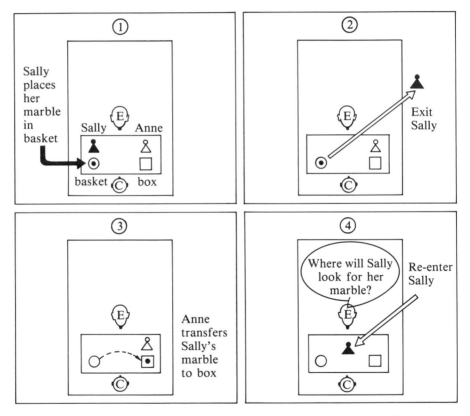

Figure 1   A test of children's understanding of belief. The story: *Sally puts her marble in the basket. Then she goes out. Anne takes Sally's marble, and puts it into her box. Then Sally comes back from her walk. Where will she look for her marble?* Normal 4-year-old children have no difficulty in correctly pointing to the basket, in answer to this question. In contrast, children with autism usually point (incorrectly) to the box

Source: Taken from Baron-Cohen, Leslie, and Frith, 1985, with permission

924

COGNITIVE MECHANISMS

The failure to develop a normal theory of mind in autism has been explained by several theories. Perhaps the most detailed account to date has been advanced by Leslie (1987; Leslie & Roth, 1993) who argues that in the normal case there is a specialized module called the *theory of mind mechanism* (ToMM) which matures around 12–18 months of age, and which processes information in the form of *metarepresentations*. These are essentially representations of mental representations, or representations of propositional attitudes. Leslie argues that this module for processing metarepresentations is not the same as a general capacity for representing *any* representation (such as a drawing, or a map, or a photograph). Rather, it is a highly specialized mechanism for representing *mental* representations. Evidence in favour of this specialized function comes from experiments showing that children with autism are able to represent non-mental representations such as photographs (Leekam & Perner, 1991) and drawings (Charman & Baron-Cohen, 1992), despite failing tasks of representing beliefs.

A second proposal, suggested by Frith (1989), is that the theory of mind deficit is just one part of a larger deficit in cognition, in the capacity for finding "central coherence": by this, she means the ability to use context to relate otherwise disparate sets of information. In the normal case, this ability to find central coherence can be seen in the non-social domain in our tendency to be distracted by overall *meaning* when perceiving a scene, rather than focusing on individual parts in the scene. Her work has shown that children with autism are more accurate in tasks such as the Children's Embedded Figures Test, in which the subject has to identify a target shape among a more complex, meaningful design (Shah & Frith, 1983), for example, identifying the triangle within the picture of the pram (depicted in Figure 2). By extension, she argues that in the social domain, theory of mind is par excellence an illustration of how we normally find central coherence. Rather than focusing on the myriad of individual behaviours, we focus on inferred mental states that we assume must underlie these behaviours. In Frith's theory, the superiority of children with autism on tasks like the Embedded Figures Test, and their deficits on theory of mind tasks, can be explained by reference to this single impairment in finding central coherence. Note that this explanation is opposed to Leslie's account, in that his account is highly modular, while hers is not. Frith's theory also predicts that children with autism should have difficulties in building *any* theory about some aspect of the world, not just a theory of mind. Tests of whether children with autism develop theories of biology would, for example, provide data with which to evaluate the coherence theory.

A third account that has been proposed is that the theory of mind deficits in autism may be secondary to deficits in *executive function* (Hughes, Russell and Robbins, 1993). By "executive function" is meant the ability to

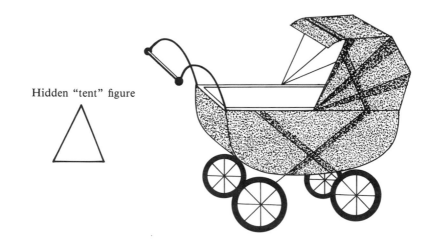

Hidden "tent" figure

Figure 2   An example of an item from the Children's Embedded Figures Test
Source: Described by Shah and Frith, 1983; reprinted with permission

inhibit responses to salient stimuli in the here-and-now, in favour of representations of objects, plans, or events that are not currently present. Individuals with autism, like many patients with frontal lobe damage, show impairments in tests of executive functioning (Hughes, Russell & Robbins, 1993; Ozonoff, Pennington, & Rogers, 1991), and this is the main evidence in favour of this account. An alternative possibility is that there is not a *single* cognitive deficit in autism, but rather there are several. It may be that the brain damage responsible for theory of mind impairments is localized in the same area of the brain that can also produce executive function deficits, namely, in the frontal lobe (Baron-Cohen et al., 1993). On this view, executive function and theory of mind deficits may be independent of one another, but tend to co-occur in the autistic syndrome by virtue of their neural proximity to each other. Testing the independence of these deficits is an important question for research in this area.

EARLY DIAGNOSIS

Leaving the question of the nature of the cognitive mechanism underlying the theory of mind deficit to one side, another area of research has been exploring developmental *precursors* to the theory of mind deficit in autism, partly towards understanding the ontogenesis of this psychological deficit, and partly to test if abnormalities in these precursors might be useful in the early diagnosis of autism. Candidate precursors of theory of mind are joint-attention skills (Baron-Cohen, 1989c, 1993) and pretend play (Leslie, 1987). Not only have these been found to be absent or impoverished in older children with autism (Baron-Cohen, 1987; Sigman, Mundy, Ungerer, & Sherman, 1986), but their absence in a sample of 18 month olds at raised genetic risk for autism predicted which children were undiagnosed infants with autism (Baron-Cohen, Allen, & Gillberg, 1992).

TREATMENT

Currently, treatment centres on special education for children with autism, and the most effective techniques seem to include highly structured, individually tailored behaviour therapy, aimed at skill-building, reducing difficult behaviours, and facilitation of educational achievements (Howlin & Rutter, 1987). Other specialist therapies also play important roles, and these include speech and music therapies. Sign-languages, such as Makaton or Paget-Gorman, are also used with some children with autism, if speech is particularly limited. However, none of these treatments claims any dramatic success in removing the core social abnormalities, although these may become less intrusive and disabling over time. Medical treatments exist for specific difficulties, such as epilepsy and hyperactivity, but at present there are no medical treatments which are useful in ameliorating the language or social difficulties in people with autism. Current and future research is aiming to find the links between the behavioural, psychological, and biological abnormalities in this condition, as well as aiming at developing more effective treatment and diagnostic methods.

ACKNOWLEDGEMENTS

This work was written while the author was in receipt of grants from the Medical Research Council, the British Council, the Royal Society, and the Mental Health Foundation. Parts of this chapter appeared in J. Cooper (Ed.) (1992). *The Encylopaedia of Language and Linguistics*. Oxford: Pergamon and Aberdeen University Press. Permission to reprint these parts is gratefully acknowledged.

FURTHER READING

Baron-Cohen, S., Tager-Flusberg, H., & Cohen, D. J. (Eds) (1993). *Understanding other minds: Perspectives from autism*. Oxford: Oxford University Press.
Frith, U. (1989). *Autism: Explaining the enigma*. Oxford: Basil Blackwell.
Howlin, P., & Rutter, M. (1987). *Treatment of autistic children*. Chichester: Wiley.
Schopler, E., & Mesibov, L. (1988). *Neurobiological issues in autism*. New York: Plenum.

REFERENCES

American Psychiatric Association (1987). *Diagnostic and statistical manual of mental disorders* (3rd edn). Washington, DC: APA.

Baron-Cohen, S. (1987). Autism and symbolic play. *British Journal of Developmental Psychology, 5*, 139–148.

Baron-Cohen, S. (1988). Social and pragmatic deficits in autism: Cognitive or affective? *Journal of Autism and Developmental Disorders, 18*, 379–402.

Baron-Cohen, S. (1989a). The autistic child's theory of mind: A case of specific developmental delay. *Journal of Child Psychology and Psychiatry, 30*, 285–298.

Baron-Cohen, S. (1989b). Are autistic children behaviourists? An examination of their mental–physical and appearance–reality distinctions. *Journal of Autism and Developmental Disorders, 19*, 579–600.

Baron-Cohen, S. (1989c). Perceptual role-taking and protodeclarative pointing in autism. *British Journal of Developmental Psychology, 7*, 113–127.

Baron-Cohen, S. (1990). Autism: A specific cognitive disorder of "mind-blindness". *International Review of Psychiatry, 2*, 79–88.

Baron-Cohen, S. (1993). From attention-goal psychology to belief-desire psychology: The development of a theory of mind and its dysfunction. In S. Baron-Cohen, H. Tager-Flusberg, & D. J. Cohen (Eds) *Understanding other minds: Perspectives from autism*. Oxford: Oxford University Press.

Baron-Cohen, S., Allen, J., & Gillberg, C. (1992). Can autism be detected at 18 months? The needle, the haystack, and the CHAT. *British Journal of Psychiatry, 161*, 839–843.

Baron-Cohen, S., Leslie, A.M., & Frith, U. (1985). Does the autistic child have a "theory of mind"? *Cognition, 21*, 37–46.

Baron-Cohen, S., Ring, H., Moriarty, J., Schmitz, B., Costa, D., & Ell, P. (1993). *The role of the orbito-frontal region of the brain*. Unpublished manuscript, Institute of Psychiatry, University of London.

Bettelheim, B. (1968). *The empty fortress*. Chicago: Free Press.

Bolton, P., & Rutter, M. (1990). Genetic influences in autism. *International Review of Psychiatry, 2*, 67–80.

Charman, T., & Baron-Cohen, S. (1992). Understanding beliefs and drawings: A further test of the metarepresentation theory of autism. *Journal of Child Psychology and Psychiatry, 33*, 1105–1112.

Courchesne, E., Yeung-Courchesne, R., Press, G., Hesselink, J., & Jernigan, T. (1988). Hypoplasia of cerebellar vernal lobules VI and VII in infantile autism. *New England Journal of Medicine, 318*, 1349–1354.

Dennett, D. (1978). *Brainstorms: Philosophical essays on mind and psychology*. Sussex: Harvester.

Frith, U. (1989). *Autism: Explaining the enigma*. Oxford: Basil Blackwell.

George, M., Costa, D., Kouris, K., Ring, H., & Ell, P. (1993). Cerebral blood flow abnormalities in adults with infantile autism. *Journal of Nervous and Mental Diseases*.

Gillberg, C. (1990). What is autism? *International Review of Psychiatry, 2*, 61–66.

Goodhart, F., & Baron-Cohen, S. (1992). *Do children with autism understand how knowledge is acquired?* Unpublished manuscript, Institute of Psychiatry, University of London.

Grice, H. P. (1975). Logic and conversation. In R. Cole & J. Morgan (Eds) *Syntax and semantics: Speech acts*. New York: Academic Press (original work published in 1967).

Happé, F. (1992). *A test of Relevance Theory: Communicative competence and theory of mind in autism*. Unpublished manuscript, MRC Cognitive Development Unit, London.

Hobson, R.P. (1986). The autistic child's appraisal of expressions of emotion. *Journal of Child Psychology and Psychiatry, 27*, 321–342.

Hobson, R. P. (1993). Understanding persons: The role of affect. In S. Baron-Cohen, H. Tager-Flusberg, & D. J. Cohen, (Eds) *Understanding other minds: Perspectives from autism*. Oxford: Oxford University Press.

Howlin, P., & Rutter, M. (1987). *Treatment of autistic children*. Chichester: Wiley.

Hughes, C., Russell, J., and Robbins, T. (1993). Autistic children's difficulty with mental disengagement from an object: Its implications for theories of autism. *Developmental Psychology*.

Kanner, L. (1943). Autistic disturbance of affective contact. *Nervous Child, 2*, 217–250. Reprinted in L. Kanner (1973). *Childhood psychosis: Initial studies and new insights*. New York: Wiley.

Leekam, S., & Perner, J. (1991). Does the autistic child have a metarepresentational deficit? *Cognition, 40*, 203–218.

Leslie, A. M., (1987). Pretence and representation: The origins of "theory of mind". *Psychological Review, 94*, 412–426.

Leslie, A. M., & Frith, U. (1988) Autistic children's understanding of seeing, knowing, and believing. *British Journal of Developmental Psychology, 6*, 315–324.

Leslie, A. M., & Roth, D. (1993). What autism teaches us about metarepresentation. In S. Baron-Cohen, H. Tager-Flusberg, & D. J. Cohen (Eds) *Understanding other minds: Perspectives from autism*. Oxford: Oxford University Press.

Ozonoff, S., Pennington, B., & Rogers, S. (1991). Executive function deficits in high-functioning autistic children: Relationship to theory of mind. *Journal of Child Psychology and Psychiatry, 32*, 1081–1106.

Phillips, W. (1992). *Comprehension of desires and intentions by children with autism*. Unpublished PhD thesis, Institute of Psychiatry, University of London.

Premack, D., & Woodruff, G. (1978). Does the chimpanzee have a "theory of mind"? *Behavioral and Brain Sciences, 4*, 515–526.

Rutter, M. (1985). Infantile autism and other pervasive developmental disorders. In M. Rutter & L. Hersov (Eds) *Child and adolescent psychiatry*. Oxford: Basil Blackwell.

Shah, A., & Frith, U. (1983). An islet of ability in autism: A research note. *Journal of Child Psychology and Psychiatry, 24*, 613–620.

Sigman, M., Mundy, P., Ungerer, J., & Sherman, T. (1986). Social interactions of autistic, mentally retarded, and normal children and their caregivers. *Journal of Child Psychology and Psychiatry, 27*, 647–656.

Sperber, D., & Wilson, D. (1986). *Relevance: Communication and cognition*. Oxford: Basil Blackwell.

Tager-Flusberg, H., Calkins, S., Nolin, T., Baumberger, T., Anderson, M., & Chadwick-Dias, A. (1990). A longitudinal study of language acquisition in autistic and Down's Syndrome children. *Journal of Autism and Developmental Disorders, 20*, 1–22.

Tinbergen, N., & Tinbergen, E. (1983). *Autistic children: New hope for a cure*. Oxford: Pergamon.

Wing, L. (1969). The handicaps of autistic children: A comparative study. *Journal of Child Psychology and Psychiatry, 10*, 1–40.

10.4

EATING DISORDERS

Peter J. Cooper
University of Cambridge, England

Accounts of self-induced weight loss can be traced back to the Middle Ages. However, the first clinical description of anorexia nervosa was provided in 1694 by an English physician, Richard Morton. He suggested the name *phthisis nervosa* for a disorder he had encountered in two of his patients involving food avoidance, extreme emaciation, amenorrhoea (cessation of menstrual periods), and overactivity. Morton regarded the disorder as neurological in origin, but recognized the influence of psychological factors. He reported that one of these patients, a "skeleton only clad with skin", died from "a multitude of cares and passions of the mind". The term *anorexia nervosa* was introduced into the medical literature in 1874 by Sir William Gull, Physician Extraordinary to Queen Victoria. Gull described a "peculiar form of disease" occurring mostly in young women, and characterized by extreme emaciation. He clearly regarded anorexia nervosa as essentially a psychological disorder. In 1914, the German pathologist Morris Simmonds reported a case of emaciation and amenorrhoea in a girl whose pituitary gland had atrophied. For the next 24 years most cases of anorexia nervosa were thought to be suffering from Simmonds' disease and were treated with pituitary extracts. Eventually it became clear that the pituitary disorder produces symptoms not found in anorexia nervosa and the two disorders were recognized as distinct. In the 1940s and 1950s theories of psychological causality flourished, the most influential early writer being Hilda Bruch (1973). Since then, there has been a remarkable consistency in the conceptualization of the disorder, with authorities in the field of varying theoretical orientations presenting accounts of the central psychopathological features in very similar terms (Crisp, 1967; Garfinkel & Garner, 1982; Russell, 1970).

Bulimia nervosa is a far newer clinical concept. Although there were a few early reports, it was towards the end of the 1970s that a number of clinical accounts began to emerge of people with a disorder characterized principally by episodes of uncontrolled eating. They closely resembled patients with anorexia nervosa in terms of their psychopathological features but were generally of normal weight. The disorder attracted a variety of names, but the two terms that gained widest acceptance were *bulimia nervosa* (Russell, 1979) and *bulimia* (American Psychiatric Association, 1980). The use of the term *bulimia* to refer to the disorder was unfortunate because it confused a behaviour (gross overeating) with a constellation of psychological characteristics in which bulimic episodes invariably occur. The revised version of the third edition of the American Psychiatric Association's (1987) *Diagnostic and Statistical Manual of Mental Disorders* (DSM-III-R) removed this ambiguity by adopting the term *bulimia nervosa*.

DIAGNOSTIC CRITERIA

Since Russell's (1970) seminal account of anorexia nervosa, there has been little disagreement about the necessary diagnostic criteria, which in itself is a testimony to the clarity with which the disorder presents itself. Table 1 shows the criteria proposed for the DSM-IV (American Psychiatric Association, 1991). Criterion A specifies a minimum degree of weight loss. This is presented in terms of a refusal to maintain a weight above 15 per cent below that expected (that is, for age, sex, and height). Criteria B and C specify the core psychological disturbance, sometimes referred to as the specific psychopathology of the disorder. The formulation of these criteria constitutes the first time any formal diagnostic system has explicitly included as a necessary criterion the notion of an overvalued idea about body shape and weight (embedded within Criterion C), although this has frequently been alluded to in the past in such terms as "a morbid fear of fatness" (Russell, 1970), "a pursuit of thinness" (Bruch, 1973), and a "weight phobia" (Crisp, 1967). The inclusion of amenorrhoea as a necessary condition (Criterion D) is intended to pick out the "secondary endocrine disorder" (Garfinkel & Garner, 1982). However, it is doubtful whether those who fulfil only Criteria A, B, and C differ in terms of their psychopathology from those who fulfil all four criteria. The proposed DSM-IV criteria include a "sub-typing" of anorexia nervosa into "bulimic type" and "non-bulimic type". This is

Table 1 Proposed criteria for DSM-IV for anorexia nervosa and bulimia nervosa

Anorexia nervosa

A Refusal to maintain body weight over a minimal normal weight for age and height (e.g., weight loss leading to maintenance of body weight 15% below that expected; or failure to make expected weight gain during period of growth, leading to body weight 15% below that expected).

B Intense fear of gaining weight or becoming fat, even though underweight.

C Disturbance in the way in which one's body weight or shape is experienced, undue influence of body shape and weight on self-evaluation, or denial of the seriousness of current low body weight.

D In females, absence of at least three consecutive menstrual cycles when otherwise expected to occur (primary or secondary amenorrhea). (A woman is considered to have amenorrhea if her periods occur only following hormone, e.g. oestrogen, administration.)

Specify type:

Bulimic type: During the episode of anorexia nervosa, the person engages recurrent episodes of binge eating.

Non-bulimic type: During the episode of anorexia nervosa, the person does not engage in recurrent episodes of binge eating.

Bulimia nervosa

A Recurrent episodes of binge eating. An episode of binge eating is characterized by both of the following:

 1 Eating, in a discrete period of time (e.g., within any two-hour period), an amount of food that is definitely larger than most people would eat during a similar period of time;
 2 A sense of lack of control over eating during the episode (e.g., a feeling that one cannot stop eating or control what or how much one is eating).

B Recurrent inappropriate compensatory behaviour in order to prevent weight gain, such as: self-induced vomiting; misuse of laxatives, diuretics or other medications; fasting; or excessive exercise.

C A minimum average of two binge-eating episodes a week for at least three months.

D Self-evaluation is unduly influenced by body shape and weight.

E The disturbance does not occur exclusively during episodes of anorexia nervosa.

Specify type:

Purging type: Regularly engages in self-induced vomiting or the use of laxatives or diuretics.

Non-purging type: Use of strict dieting, fasting, or vigorous exercise, but does not regularly engage in purging.

Source: American Psychiatric Association, 1991

sensible given the established differences between these two groups of patients in terms of a wide range of clinical features (Garfinkel, Modlofsky, & Garner, 1980).

The specification of diagnostic criteria for bulimia nervosa has generated rather more disagreement. The criteria proposed for DSM-IV (American Psychiatric Association, 1991), shown in Table 1, go a long way towards resolving earlier differences of opinion. Bulimic episodes, accepted by all previous criteria as a necessary condition, are clearly defined. Criterion B specifies the presence of one of a range of extreme or inappropriate measures to compensate for overeating or control weight. Criterion D (as was the case for Criterion C for anorexia nervosa) is an explicit recognition that a central feature of this disorder is an overvalued idea about shape and weight. Criterion C, the threshold criterion, is intended to exclude subclinical or partial cases. Criterion E, the exclusion criterion, is necessary because criteria A to D could be met by a patient fulfilling criteria for anorexia nervosa ("bulimic" sub-type). The proposed DSM-IV criteria include a sub-typing of bulimia nervosa into a "purging type" and a "non-purging type". This too is sensible given that most research into the disorder has been conducted on patients who purge and they may differ from those who do not purge but, say, fast is weak.

EPIDEMIOLOGY

Studies of the incidence and prevalence of anorexia nervosa are beset with methodological difficulties. Uncertainties concerning the definition of a "case", and the fact that many people with frank anorexia nervosa do not regard themselves as having a problem, make it difficult to derive accurate prevalence figures for anorexia nervosa from the community studies. Case register studies are difficult to interpret because they do not include mild cases that have escaped detection and because they are contaminated by the vicissitudes of diagnostic and referral practices. The latter point is well illustrated by a case-register study covering three distinct geographical areas: north-east Scotland, Munroe County in New York, and Camberwell in London (Kendell, Hall, Hailey, & Babigian, 1973). The estimates of incidence of anorexia nervosa varied from 0.37 per 100,000 per year in Munroe County to 1.6 per 100,000 per year in north-east Scotland. A consistent finding of the case-register studies is that there has been a sharp rise in the number of cases coming to specialist attention during the 1970s and 1980s. For example, Szmukler, McCance, McCrone, and Hunter (1986) reported that the rate of anorexia nervosa in north-east Scotland, based on records of contacts with the in-patient and out-patient psychiatric services, had risen from 1.60 per 100,000 per year for the period 1966 to 1969 to 4.06 per 100,000 per year for the period 1978 to 1982. A similar increase has been observed in the USA. It is likely that these well-documented changes in the number of cases being referred for treatment reflect a genuine increase in the incidence of the disorder. This conclusion is supported by a community-based epidemiological study in which the medical records of over 13,000 residents of Rochester (Minnesota) were examined for the period 1935 to 1984: over this 50-year timespan the age-adjusted incidence of anorexia nervosa among young women rose from 7.0 per 100,000 person years to 26.3 per 100,000 (Lucas, Beard, O'Fallon, & Kurland, 1991).

There have been several community studies of the prevalence of anorexia nervosa. In Britain, Crisp, Palmer, and Kalucy (1976) conducted a five-to-six-year retrospective survey of nine schools, seven private and two state run. Their estimate of prevalence was one case of anorexia nervosa per 100 girls aged over 16 in the private schools, and roughly one-fifth this rate among the girls in the state schools. A later survey has largely confirmed these findings (Mann et al., 1983). In this study the estimated prevalence of anorexia nervosa in six private schools was one case per 90 girls aged 16–18. A similar difference between state and private schools to that reported by Crisp and colleagues was found. A further finding of this study was that, among the girls in the private schools, in addition to the cases of anorexia nervosa, 5 per cent had sub-threshold disorders or "partial syndromes". A particularly notable prevalence study is that reported by Rastam, Gillberg, and Garton (1989), in that the total population of 15-year-old schoolchildren in Göteborg, Sweden, was screened using questionnaires, growth charts, and individual school nurse reports. After full clinical assessment and interviews with the mothers, 23 of the 4,291 children were found to have an eating disorder, and the prevalence of anorexia nervosa among the girls was 0.84 per cent. This figure must be regarded as an underestimate of the true rate in the community, given that girls over the age of 15 were not included in this survey.

Anorexia nervosa is a disorder that predominantly affects young women, only 5–10 per cent of cases being male. The most common ages of onset are 14 and 16, although cases with a considerably earlier onset do arise (Lask & Bryant-Waugh, 1992), as do some with an onset well into adult life. The disorder is over-represented in girls from upper socio-economic families. There is a striking elevation of prevalence of anorexia nervosa among those for whom a slim body shape has special significance, such as ballet and modelling students (Garfinkel & Garner, 1982). The disorder arises predominantly in western countries and developed non-western societies such as Japan. It is extremely rare in other cultures. The disorder also used to be rare among American blacks, but it appears to be increasing in this group (Hsu, 1990).

Little is known of the incidence of bulimia nervosa. The diagnostic concept is too new for case-register studies to be of use, and there have been no community studies that could cast light on the inception rate. Nevertheless, it is generally accepted that the incidence of the disorder has increased dramatically since the early 1980s. Although individual case histories can be found in the annals of psychiatry, and patients with 20–30-year histories are sometimes seen, it was only towards the end of the 1970s that reports began to emerge of large numbers of these patients presenting for treatment.

There have been a number of attempts to estimate the prevalence of bulimia nervosa and its constituent components (Fairburn & Beglin, 1991). This work has produced conflicting findings, largely because of weaknesses in method. In particular, the great majority of the surveys have used simple self-report questionnaires with key concepts inadequately defined. Those studies that have used two-stage designs, with a clinical interview following a phase of screening by questionnaire, have been compromised by high attrition rates. Despite these difficulties, a consensus has emerged: among young adult women, bulimia nervosa appears to have a prevalence of 1–2 per cent (e.g., Cooper, Charnock, & Taylor, 1987; Schotte & Stunkard, 1987). Bulimia nervosa is largely confined to women; fewer than 5 per cent of cases presenting for treatment are men (Carlat & Camargo, 1991). The age of patients at presentation is somewhat older than those with anorexia nervosa, most being in their 20s, although a wide age range is affected. The social class distribution of patients has not been systematically studied, but it appears to be broader than that of patients with anorexia nervosa.

CLINICAL FEATURES

The clinical features of anorexia nervosa have been clearly described by numerous authorities in the field, such as Bruch (1973), Crisp (1967), Garfinkel and Garner (1982), and Russell (1970). There is wide agreement about the central features. More uncertainty has surrounded the core disturbance in bulimia nervosa. The clinical features of the eating disorders comprise features specific to these disorders and features more generally associated with psychological disturbance.

Specific psychopathology

Eating habits

Patients with anorexia nervosa markedly restrict their food intake. This involves a selective avoidance of food regarded as "fattening", generally leading to a high-protein low-carbohydrate diet. Frequently they monitor their calorie intake closely and set a rigid limit, usually in the region of 600–800 calories per day. The term "anorexia" is a misnomer because, except in long-standing cases, appetite for food persists. There is often an obsessional component to these patients' eating habits: they may eat exactly the same food every day, cut up their food into very small pieces, or engage in other ritualistic practices surrounding eating. Associated with the efforts to restrict food intake there is a preoccupation with food and eating. Patients frequently spend hours poring over recipe books, cook elaborate meals for others, or choose jobs that involve working with food.

About half of those with anorexia nervosa alternate between episodes of dietary restriction and bulimic episodes. During such bulimic episodes food that is normally avoided tends to be consumed, sometimes in large quantities. The episodes lead to considerable distress and are a source of profound guilt and shame. Usually bulimic episodes are followed by self-induced vomiting. A number of consistent differences have been found between the bulimic and the restricting subgroups of patients with anorexia nervosa as regards presenting symptoms and history (Garfinkel, Modlofsky, & Garner, 1980). Patients with anorexia nervosa engage in a variety of weight control measures in addition to dietary restriction. Many induce vomiting, some abuse laxatives, diuretics, and appetite suppressants, and many exercise vigorously.

The principal complaint of patients with bulimia nervosa is that they have lost control of their eating. Thus they report episodes of gross overeating that are experienced as outside of voluntary control. The frequency of bulimic episodes varies between patients, but in one patient series, at presentation, half the patients reported that such episodes were occurring at least daily (Fairburn & Cooper, 1984). It is not unusual to see patients who are experiencing bulimic episodes many times a day. The proportion of protein, fat, and carbohydrate consumed in a bulimic episode is typically the same as that consumed by people with normal eating habits during an ordinary evening meal (Walsh, Kissileff, Cassidy, & Danzic, 1989).

Bulimic episodes are fairly uniform in nature. They are invariably secret, and food is usually eaten quickly with little attention being paid to its taste. They tend to consist of those foods that patients are at other times attempting to exclude from their diet. Typically, patients alternate between bulimic episodes and attempts to maintain a rigid diet. Strict dieting may be disrupted by dysphoric mood states and boredom, and by the belief that some dietary rule has been transgressed.

The body weight of patients with bulimia nervosa is usually within the normal range, reflecting a balance between the episodes of overeating and various compensatory behaviours designed to counteract the effects of bulimic episodes. The most common method of weight control is self-induced vomiting, which frequently terminates bulimic episodes. Vomiting is generally accomplished by inducing the gag reflex with the fingers, but around a quarter of these patients learn to vomit spontaneously. Vomiting is a source of considerable guilt and self-disgust and is almost always practised secretly. It may go undetected for many years. Self-induced vomiting is habit-forming. While it relieves the abdominal discomfort that results from overeating and lessens the risk of weight gain, it also appears to encourage overeating and therefore further vomiting. Purgatives are also used by some patients to control their weight. Like vomiting, purgative use can become habit-forming and, since tolerance develops, some patients increase their consumption progressively. As in anorexia nervosa, a variety of other methods of weight control are also practised by some patients.

Beliefs and attitudes

A central feature of the eating disorders is certain overvalued ideas concerning the importance of shape and weight. Thus, patients with anorexia nervosa place an abnormal degree of significance on the pursuit of a thin body shape, and they have an exaggerated fear of weight gain. Accompanying these extreme concerns, there is often a complete denial that they have any problems. Since Bruch (1973) first declared that a disturbance of body image was pathognomonic in anorexia nervosa, there has been a considerable amount of empirical work concerned with establishing whether patients with eating disorders overestimate their body size (Garfinkel & Garner, 1982). Two main methods of assessment have been used: the movable calliper technique, which provides data on particular body regions; and an image distorting technique, which provides data on patients' perception of their whole body. Using both techniques, as a group patients have usually been found to overestimate their body size, and in most studies this overestimation has been greater than that found in controls. However, many patients have been found to be accurate in their estimation of their body size and some have been found to underestimate their size. Moreover, many people with no eating disorder have been found to overestimate their size. Marked overestimation in patients has been found to be rare.

Patients with bulimia nervosa display similar concerns about their shape and weight to those with anorexia nervosa. In patients with bulimia nervosa the discrepancy between their actual body weight and desired weight is generally no greater than among normal young women; however, the discrepancy between their estimation of their body size and their desired size is substantial and significantly greater than among a control population (Cooper & Taylor, 1988). Thus, they tend both to overestimate their body size significantly more than do controls, and to have a desired size significantly smaller than that of controls.

General psychopathology

General neurotic symptoms are common in anorexia nervosa. Depressive symptoms are particularly prominent, with the level of depression positively associated with the degree of disturbance in eating habits and attitudes. Other symptoms present in anorexia nervosa are lability of mood, obsessional symptoms, and anxiety symptoms related to situations that involve eating. In more chronic cases hopelessness and suicidal ideation are sometimes present. Suicide is the most likely cause of death among those who die prematurely because of the disorder (Hsu, 1990).

The nature, frequency, and severity of the neurotic symptoms occurring in patients with bulimia nervosa has been systematically studied (Cooper & Fairburn, 1986; Fairburn & Cooper, 1984). A wide range of symptoms occur. Depressive and anxiety symptoms are particularly common. Studies in which the psychopathological profile of patients with bulimia nervosa have been compared with depressed and anxious patients (Cooper & Fairburn, 1986; Steere, Butler, & Cooper, 1990) reveal differences of clear diagnostic significance: the affective symptoms are predominantly secondary to the core eating disturbance in the patients with bulimia nervosa who present with more anxiety symptoms than depressed patients and more depressive symptoms than anxious patients.

Physical factors

One of the most striking features of anorexia nervosa is these patients' state of semi-starvation. This emaciation has wide-ranging effects on patients' physiology and also on their physical health (Mitchell, 1986a). Low body temperature, low blood pressure, and rapid heartbeat are common, as is lanugo hair on the back and face. Amenorrhoea is a *sine qua non*, arising from the low levels of gonadotrophins and gonadal steroids. Some patients have raised carotene and cholesterol levels. Starvation carries a marked risk of numerous complications including osteoporosis (reduction or atrophy of bone matter), liver function abnormalities, a low white blood cell count and a low platelet count, and impaired cardiac function. Some of the consequences of the emaciation interact with the central psychological disturbances. For example, slow gastric emptying, arising from low weight and reduced caloric consumption, leads patients to complain of fullness, bloating, and abdominal pain; and these symptoms are taken by them as evidence of the need for further dietary restriction. It has been argued that many aspects of the psychopathology of anorexia nervosa could be a direct result of starvation (Garner, Rockert, Olmsted, Johnson, & Coscina, 1985).

There are a number of physiological abnormalities and medical complications in bulimia nervosa (Mitchell, 1986b). Unlike anorexia nervosa, where most of these disturbances are the result of emaciation, most of those seen in bulimia nervosa result from specific behaviours, such as vomiting, purgative abuse, and the bulimic episodes themselves. Thus, the vomiting often leads to erosion of dental enamel and can lead to damage of the oesophageal sphincter; bulimic episodes frequently cause swelling of the parotid glands and, rarely, lead to acute dilation of the stomach. Complications associated with laxative abuse include profound constipation on laxative withdrawal and, in rare cases, permanent impairment of colonic function. Gastro-intestinal bleeding, malabsorption, and protein-losing gastric problems have also been described. Electrolyte abnormalities are common in these patients, the most significant being low potassium levels. Most of these physical disturbances are reversed by the restoration of normal eating habits.

AETIOLOGY AND MAINTENANCE

While the aetiology of the eating disorders is not known, it is widely accepted that a combination of biological, psychological, and social factors are of importance (Garfinkel & Garner, 1982). There has been a considerable amount written about the significant aetiological factors but there are few firm data to support the theoretical speculations.

A number of factors broadly related to personality have been suggested as predisposing individuals to anorexia nervosa. One of these, especially emphasized by Bruch (1973), is difficulty in autonomous functioning and an associated sense of ineffectiveness. Crisp (1967) has emphasized how those predisposed to develop anorexia nervosa are unprepared for maturity and how the symptoms of the disorder represent a flight from adolescent concerns and responsibilities. However, problems with autonomy and with coming to terms with adult sexuality are by no means unique to patients with anorexia nervosa; indeed, they may reflect no more than a general predisposition to psychological disorder. Both Bruch and Crisp also emphasize the compliant, perfectionist, and dependent nature of these patients' personalities. However, as Garfinkel and Garner (1982) note, it is difficult to draw meaningful conclusions about premorbid personality characteristics in a disorder with such significant and wide-ranging physical and psychological repercussions.

Eating disorders run in families. Thus the prevalence of these disorders in the relatives of patients with eating disorders has been found to be significantly higher than the expected rate in the general population (Strober & Humphrey, 1987). Gershon, Schreiber, and Hamovit (1984) found a 6 per cent lifetime morbid risk for eating disorders in the first-degree relatives of 24 patients with anorexia nervosa, compared with a 1 per cent risk in the families of normal controls. Similarly, Strober and Katz (1987) found a significant excess of eating disorders in the first- and second-degree relatives of patients with anorexia nervosa compared with non-anorexic psychiatric controls: indeed, a case of anorexia nervosa or bulimia was found in 27 per cent of the families of the patients with anorexia nervosa, compared with 6 per cent of the control families. There are also a number of reports, reviewed by Garfinkel and Garner (1982), of anorexia occurring in twins. In one rigorously conducted study of 34 pairs of twins and one set of triplets with anorexia nervosa (Holland, Hall, Murray, Russell, & Crisp, 1984), a 55 per cent concordance rate was found for identical twins compared with 7 per cent concordance for non-identical twins. In another study, a 23 per cent concordance for bulimia nervosa was found in identical twins compared to 8.7 per cent in non-identical twins (Kendler et al., 1991).

The family aggregation findings are explicable in both genetic and environmental terms. The data on the pathogenesis of family influences in the eating disorders have been reviewed by Strober and Humphrey (1987). A major problem with this work is that the findings are derived exclusively from families of patients and, as such, it is not possible to conclude anything about the causal role of any family disturbances identified. The mothers of patients with eating disorders have been described as particularly intrusive and overprotective, anxious and perfectionist, and the fathers as passive, obsessional, and ineffectual. These impressions have little empirical basis, because it has not been demonstrated that these characteristics are specific to the parents of those with eating disorders; nor, indeed, that they are present in these parents to any significant degree. Although some systematic examinations of the families of patients with bulimia have found that they perceive their families as more disturbed in various ways than do controls, it has not been shown that these perceptions are related to the eating disorder rather than to the non-specific psychological disturbance as might be found in a group of young patients with other psychological disorders. Indeed, unless some practicable means of conducting prospective research can be developed, it is unlikely that studies of the family functioning of patients with eating disorders will reveal anything significant about the aetiology of the disorder. They may well, of course, produce important findings relevant to the maintenance of these conditions and to their treatment. It has been argued that patients with eating disorders are especially likely to have had a history of sexual abuse in childhood. However, it has been found that the rate of such abuse is no greater among these patients than among patients with other psychiatric disorders.

A family history of affective disorder is common among patients with eating disorders. Thus the rate of affective disorder among the relatives of patients with anorexia nervosa is as high as among relatives of patients with depression. Preliminary evidence indicates that this association also obtains for patients with bulimia nervosa (Strober & Katz, 1987). Patients with eating disorders are also commonly found to have a personal history of affective disorder. However, a major problem with the interpretation of the findings of the latter studies is that the chronology of symptoms in patients with eating disorders is not always clear; in many cases depressive symptoms may arise as a secondary response to disturbances in eating. Nevertheless, some studies have made particularly careful analysis of the order in which symptoms have arisen. For example, Piran, Kennedy, Garfinkel, and Owens (1985) reported that among 18 patients with anorexia nervosa with a lifetime history of major depression, affective symptoms post-dated the onset of the eating disorder in 34 per cent, occurred within the same year in 22 per cent, and preceded the emergence of the eating disorder by at least one year in 44 per cent. Comparable analyses have been made with similar results in patients with bulimia (e.g. Walsh, Roose, Glassman, Gladis, & Sadik, 1985). Thus,

940

It appears that a vulnerability to depression may increase predisposition to eating disorders, and an episode of depression may contribute to the initiation of its symptoms.

As noted above, eating disorders are especially prevalent in social subgroups where a particularly high value is placed on slim body shape. This observation, together with other related evidence, has led to considerable speculation about the role of societal pressures in the aetiology of the eating disorders (Striegel-Moore, Silbertstein, & Rodin, 1986). Indeed, the shift in societal preference towards a thinner female body shape has been offered as a possible explanation for the increasing prevalence of anorexia nervosa by leading to greater numbers of young women dieting (Garfinkel & Garner, 1982). While this explanation is highly persuasive, it is obviously not complete. Not all ballet dancers, modelling students, or young women who diet to be slim develop eating disorders, and as yet the factors that render dieters vulnerable to developing anorexia nervosa or bulimia nervosa have not been systematically investigated.

Attempts to account for the maintenance of eating disorders have proved more profitable than attempts to account for aetiology. Two views of maintenance can be distinguished. The first regards eating disorders as "closely related to" or "a form of" affective disorder. Several lines of evidence have been advanced to support this contention (Hudson, Pope, Jonas, & Yurgelun-Todd, 1983), relating to the course of these disorders, their response to certain biological tests, their phenomenology, the raised family history of affective disorder, and these patients' response to antidepressant medication. None of these lines of evidence stands up to close scrutiny (Cooper & Cooper, 1988) and there is little basis for the affective disorder view of eating disorders. There is, of course, a strong association between eating disorders and depression. However, the data suggest that a vulnerability to affective disorder may predispose individuals to develop an eating disorder, or it may contribute to its maintenance; but they do not support the idea that the eating disorders are in some sense a manifestation of an affective disorder.

The second view of maintenance derives from a cognitive behavioural conceptualization of the eating disorders. The argument for such a view of anorexia nervosa and bulimia nervosa has been extensively elaborated in earlier reviews (Fairburn, Cooper, & Cooper 1986; Garner & Bemis, 1982). The essential tenet of this view is that the central psychopathological disturbance in these patients is the overvalued ideas about weight and shape. Indeed, it is argued, most of the other clinical features of these disorders can be understood in terms of this core psychopathology. According to this view, the belief that shape and weight are of fundamental importance and must be kept under strict control is not merely symptomatic of these disorders but is of primary importance in their maintenance. The specific features of eating disorders, such as frequent weighing, sensitivity to changes in shape and weight, extreme dieting, self-induced vomiting and purgative abuse, and abnormal attitudes towards food and eating, are also presented as comprehensible given these core beliefs concerning shape and weight.

The cognitive behavioural account of eating disorders regards the relatively uniform beliefs and values of these patients as implicit unarticulated rules by which they assign meaning and value to their experience. The way they evaluate themselves and their behaviour, their perceptions, and aspirations, are regarded as being determined by these values. Thus their self-worth is seen as being evaluated largely in terms of their shape and weight: they view fatness as odious and reprehensible, they see slimness as attractive and desirable, and the maintenance of self-control is of prime importance. In addition, some attach extreme importance to weight loss. It is clear that such beliefs are not radically different from views that are widely held and reinforced by prevailing social values. They differ from these more generally held attitudes by being exaggerated, rigidly held and imbued with great personal significance; it is these qualities, it is argued, which make them dysfunctional. It is further argued that the absolute and exaggerated nature of these concerns about shape and weight reflects the operation of certain dysfunctional styles of reasoning, similar to those described as operating in depression. The cognitive behavioural conceptualization of eating disorders has considerable prima facie validity, but there is little direct evidence to support it.

Bulimic episodes present two problems for a cognitive behavioural view of eating disorders. First, given these patients' implicit values concerning shape and weight, it would be predicted that their fear of weight gain would simply lead to constant dieting, with success reinforcing further dietary restriction. Second, it would be predicted that, if for some reason a patient did break the diet, the patient would simply recommence dieting. The clinical features of bulimia nervosa and of the bulimic subgroup of patients with anorexia nervosa are not consistent with either of these predictions. These patients do not successfully adhere to their dietary regimes, and when their diets are broken, rather than minimizing the indiscretion, they go to the other extreme and overeat. It has been argued that it is dietary restriction itself that is responsible for the episodes of loss of control over eating, and that the link between dieting and bulimic episodes is a cognitive one (Polivy & Herman, 1985). It has been found in laboratory research that, under certain predictable circumstances, subjects who are restricting their food intake will overeat or "counter-regulate". One such circumstance is the belief that certain dietary rules have been transgressed: that is, in contrast to unrestrained eaters, restrained eaters tend to eat more following the prior consumption of a large number of calories than following a small number of calories. This effect has also been produced by simply manipulating the subjects' beliefs about the calorie content of the previously consumed food. Other factors found to produce counter-regulation in dieters are dysphoric mood states and the consumption of alcohol. Once the cognitive constraints on eating are removed by some disinhibiting factor, hunger and other physiological forces aimed at correcting the deprivation take over and lead to overeating. This essentially laboratory phenomenon has been presented as an analogy for bulimic episodes. Despite the intuitive appeal of this analogy, there is no clear and direct evidence to support the causal role of dietary restraint in the aetiology of bulimic episodes, and it remains wholly unclear what the conditions are that render individuals vulnerable to dietary disinhibition and bulimic episodes (Cooper & Charnock, 1990).

TREATMENT

Although much has been written about the treatment of anorexia nervosa, there has been little controlled research into the management of this disorder. Such research that has been done has produced largely negative findings. Thus, both the appetite-stimulating antihistamine drug cyproheptadine and the tricyclic antidepressant amitryptyline have been shown to add nothing in terms of weight gain to routine nursing care (Halmi, Eckert, LaDu, & Cohen, 1986), and the antidepressant clomipramine has been shown to be equally unhelpful (Lacey & Crisp, 1980). Similarly negative conclusions have emerged from studies of psychological methods of intervention. Thus, a behaviour modification regime has been found to confer no benefit to short-term weight gain when compared to milieu therapy (Eckert, Goldberg, Halmi, Casper, & Davis, 1979); and, similarly, a strict operant regime has been shown to be no better at promoting weight gain than a more lenient regime (Touyz, Beumont, & Glaun, 1984). The single exception to these negative conclusions derives from an investigation of family therapy (Russell, Szmuckler, Dare, & Eisler, 1987). In a study in which, following a period of inpatient weight restoration, patients received one year of either family therapy or individual therapy, the family therapy was found to be superior, especially for non-chronic patients with an early age of onset.

The mainstay of treatment for anorexia nervosa has been hospitalization and nursing care (Crisp, 1965; Garfinkel & Garner, 1982; Russell, 1970). Essentially these treatments involve the re-feeding of patients coupled with nutritional education. All the authorities cited catalogue a number of strategies for dealing with particular aspects of these patients' care, such as their tendency to induce vomiting, hide food, engage in secret exercising, and so on. The short-term results of such an approach are good and most patients can be restored to a healthy body weight within three or four months. However, improvement in other aspects of the disorder is less impressive. In the Maudsley study cited above (Russell et al., 1987), after inpatient weight restoration and a year of therapy (family or individual) only 23 per cent were classified as having a good outcome and 60 per cent as having a poor outcome. The Maudsley is a tertiary referral centre and these disappointing figures are not typical. Thus, a two-year follow-up of patients treated in the

Toronto General Hospital revealed that 50 per cent of the patients had a good outcome and only 16 per cent a poor outcome (Kennedy, Kaplan, & Garfinkel, 1992).

An innovation in the management of anorexia nervosa has been the description of a day-patient treatment programme (Piran & Kaplan, 1990). There are both clinical and financial advantages to such an outpatient setting. A detailed programme has been specified and preliminary accounts of its efficacy are encouraging: close to 70 per cent of patients demonstrate at least a moderate outcome and clinical gains appear to be well maintained six months following discharge.

Despite the fact that bulimia nervosa was not identified as a distinct disorder until the end of the 1970s, there have been a remarkable number of systematic evaluations of specific forms of treatment (Fairburn et al., 1991). Two lines of work have gone on largely independently. The first has concerned the efficacy of medication. A number of double-blind controlled trials have been conducted of the efficacy of a variety of antidepressant drugs. The studies have involved mainly standard tricyclic medication such as imipramine and desipramine. These studies have all been rather restricted in scope in that only a limited range of the psychopathology has been assessed, and rarely has attention been paid to the maintenance of change and the effects of discontinuation of drug treatment. There are four principal conclusions that can be drawn from the studies (Fairburn et al., 1992). First, antidepressant drugs are superior to placebo (inactive dummy pills) at reducing the frequency of bulimic episodes and improving related clinical features; they also have a beneficial effect on the general psychopathology. Second, the clinical impact of drugs is modest: although most patients reduce the frequency of bulimic episodes, at the end of a course of treatment most are still experiencing bulimic episodes and few could be regarded as eating normally. Third, no consistent predictors of response have been identified and, in particular, the level of depressive symptomatology does not predict outcome. Finally, the two studies that have examined maintenance of change on medication and response to discontinuation (Pyle et al., 1990; Walsh, Hadigan, Devlin, Gladis, & Roose, 1991) have revealed that relapse is common, even with patients continuing to take the medication. There has been interest in the efficacy of the new generation of antidepressants, the selective serotonin re-uptake inhibitors. It is clear that this class of drugs has a significant positive clinical effect in these patients. However, this effect appears to be no greater than that obtained using far less expensive tricyclic medication; and there is no evidence suggesting that it is especially appropriate for patients with a particular clinical profile.

The second line of research has concerned the efficacy of certain psychological treatments. Most of the studies have involved an assessment of a cognitive behavioural approach to the management of bulimia nervosa. This form of treatment, which has been comprehensively described (Fairburn &

Cooper, 1989), is generally delivered on an individual basis to outpatients over the course of four to five months. A consistent finding of the treatment studies is that this treatment produces marked reductions in the frequency of episodes of bulimia and purging. In addition, there is an improvement in the other aspects of the specific psychopathology, such as attitudes to shape and weight and dietary restraint, as well as improvements in general mental state and social functioning. Maintenance of change, at least up to one year, is good (Fairburn, Kirk, O'Connor, & Cooper, 1986; Fairburn et al., 1991). Longer-term maintenance has not yet been reported. Cognitive behaviour therapy for bulimia nervosa has been compared with other forms of brief psychological management. Comparisons with a purely behavioural approach have consistently favoured the cognitive behavioural condition. However, in two studies other focal psychotherapies emerged as just as effective (Fairburn, Kirk, O'Connor, & Cooper, 1986; Fairburn et al., 1991), notably a form of interpersonal psychotherapy.

There have been only two reports in which cognitive behaviour therapy has been compared with antidepressant medication in the treatment of bulimia nervosa (Agras et al., 1992; Mitchell et al., 1990). In both, psychological treatment alone was markedly superior to the drug alone. Both studies included a combined treatment condition. In the Minneapolis study (Mitchell et al., 1990), the outcome of patients receiving both the psychological treatment and imipramine was the same as for those who only received the psychological treatment; but in the Stanford study (Agras et al., 1992), there was some benefit from combining the two treatments. It is unclear what accounts for this difference and further studies of combination treatment are required. An important clinical question, particularly since cognitive behaviour therapy is an expensive specialist treatment, is whether an antidepressant could enhance a cheaper simpler treatment. Indeed, it has been suggested that cognitive behaviour therapy may well constitute overtreatment for many patients and, in view of this, a stepped care approach has been recommended. This has yet to be evaluated.

COURSE AND OUTCOME

A number of studies have been conducted of the course and outcome of anorexia nervosa. The overall findings indicate that about one-third of patients recover completely, one-third have a moderate outcome, and one-third remain severely ill (Hsu, 1990). The results have been published of a 20-year follow-up study of 41 patients treated for anorexia nervosa at the Maudsley hospital between 1959 and 1966 (Ratnasuria, Eisler, Szmukler, & Russell, 1991). This study highlights the very serious nature of the disorder when it takes a chronic course. After 20 years, almost 40 per cent of the patients were still gravely incapacitated by the illness or had died. Indeed, an alarming and consistent finding of the outcome studies is that the mortality rate for anorexia nervosa is around 15 per cent (Hsu, 1990). In the Maudsley sample all the deaths (i.e., 14.6 per cent), with one exception, were attributable to anorexia nervosa. Of these, half were due to suicide and the remainder to complications of the illness associated with electrolyte imbalance. Factors associated with a poor prognosis were a later age of onset of the disorder, a history of neurotic and personality disturbances, disturbed relationships in the family and a longer duration of illness. The outcome of mild cases of the disorder is unknown but likely to be considerably more favourable.

Little is known about the course and outcome of bulimia nervosa. There have been no systematic studies of the natural history of the disorder. The reports of outcome following treatment have been limited in that the full range of psychopathological disturbance has rarely been reported and follow-up has been short term. As noted, two studies have revealed that relapse is the likely outcome when tricyclic medication is withdrawn and, indeed, even when patients are maintained on medication (Pyle et al., 1990; Walsh et al., 1991). There have been more encouraging reports of the short-term outcome following a relatively brief course of psychological treatment (e.g. Fairburn, Kirk, O'Connor, & Cooper, 1986; Fairburn et al., 1993). In a review of the outcome studies, Hsu (1990) has noted that, while outcome varies considerably across samples, overall at least two-thirds of patients receiving treatment no longer fulfil the diagnostic criteria at one-year follow-up. The population of patients with bulimia nervosa appears to be heterogeneous with respect to prognosis, and longitudinal clinical and epidemiological research is required to determine the profile of outcomes of these patients and to identify prognostic indicators.

FURTHER READING

Garfinkel, P. E., & Garner, D. M. (1982). *Anorexia nervosa: A multidimensional perspective*. New York: Basic Books.

Garner, D. M., & Garfinkel, P. E. (1985). *Handbook of psychotherapy for anorexia nervosa and bulimia nervosa*. New York: Guilford.

Hsu, L. K. (1990). *Eating disorders*. New York: Guilford.

Russell, G. F. M. (1979). Bulimia nervosa: An ominous variant of anorexia nervosa. *Psychological Medicine*, *9*, 429–448.

REFERENCES

Agras, W. S., Rossiter, E. M., Arnow, B., Schneider, J. A., Telch, C. F., Raeburn, S. D., Bruce, B., Perl, M., & Koran, L. M. (1992). Pharmacologic and cognitive-behavioral treatment for bulimia nervosa: A controlled trial. *American Journal of Psychiatry*, *149*, 82–87.

American Psychiatric Association (1980). *Diagnostic and statistical manual of mental disorders* (3rd edn). Washington, DC: APA.

American Psychiatric Association (1987). *Diagnostic and statistical manual of mental disorders* (3rd edn, revised). Washington, DC: APA.

American Psychiatric Association (1991). *DSM-IV Options Book: Diagnostic and statistical manual of mental disorders*. Washington, DC: APA.

Bruch, H. (1973). *Eating disorders. Obesity, anorexia nervosa, and the person within*. New York: Basic Books.

Carlat, D. J., & Camargo, C. A. (1991). Review of bulimia nervosa in males. *American Journal of Psychiatry*, *148*, 831–843.

Cooper, P. J. (1993). *Bulimia nervosa: A guide to recovery*. London: Robinson.

Cooper, P. J., & Charnock, D. (1990). From restraint to bulimic episodes: A problem of some loose connections. *Appetite*, *14*, 120–122.

Cooper, P. J., & Cooper, Z. (1988). Eating disorders. In E. Miller & P. J. Cooper (Eds) *Adult abnormal psychology* (pp. 268–298). Edinburgh: Churchill Livingstone.

Cooper, P. J., & Fairburn, C. G. (1986). The depressive symptoms of bulimia nervosa. *British Journal of Psychiatry*, *148*, 268–274.

Cooper, P. J., & Taylor, M. J. (1988). Body image disturbance in bulimia nervosa. *British Journal of Psychiatry*, *153*, 32–36.

Cooper, P. J., Charnock, D. J., & Taylor, M. J. (1987). The prevalence of bulimia nervosa: A replication study. *British Journal of Psychiatry*, *151*, 684–686.

Crisp, A. H. (1965). A treatment regime for anorexia nervosa. *British Journal of Psychiatry*, *30*, 279–286.

Crisp, A. H. (1967). Anorexia nervosa. *Hospital Medicine*, *1*, 713–718.

Crisp, A. H., Palmer, R. L., & Kalucy, R. S. (1976). How common is anorexia nervosa? A prevalence study. *British Journal of Psychiatry*, *128*, 548–549.

Eckert, E. D., Goldberg, S. C., Halmi, K. A., Casper, R. C., & Davis, J. M. (1979). Behaviour therapy in anorexia nervosa. *British Journal of Psychiatry*, *134*, 55–59.

Fairburn, C. G., & Beglin, S. (1991). Studies of the epidemiology of bulimia nervosa. *American Journal of Psychiatry*, *147*, 401–408.

Fairburn, C. G., & Cooper, P. J. (1984). The clinical features of bulimia nervosa. *British Journal of Psychiatry*, *144*, 238–246.

Fairburn, C. G., & Cooper, P. J. (1989). The cognitive-behavioural treatment of eating disorders. In K. Hawton, P. Salkovskis, J. Kirk, & D. M. Clark (Eds) *Cognitive-behavioural approaches to adult psychiatric disorders. A practical guide* (pp. 277–314). Oxford: Oxford University Press.

Fairburn, C. G., Agras, W. S., & Wilson, G. T. (1992). The research on the treatment of bulimia nervosa: Practical and theoretical implications. In G. H. Anderson & S. H. Kennedy (Eds) *The biology of feast and famine. Relevance to eating disorders* (pp. 317–340). New York: Academic Press.

Fairburn, C. G., Cooper, Z., & Cooper, P. J. (1986). The clinical features and maintenance of bulimia nervosa. In K. D. Brownell & J. P. Foreyt (Eds) *Handbook of eating disorders. Physiology, psychology and treatment of eating disorders* (pp. 389–404). New York: Basic Books.

Fairburn, C. G., Kirk, J., O'Connor, M., & Cooper, P. J. (1986). A comparison of two psychological treatments for bulimia nervosa. *Behaviour Research and Therapy*, *24*, 629–643.

Fairburn, C. G., Jones, R., Peveler, R. C., Carr, S. J., Solomon, R. A., O'Connor, M. E., Burton, J., & Hope, R. A. (1991). Three psychological treatments for bulimia nervosa: A comparative trial. *Archives of General Psychiatry*, *48*, 463–469.

Garfinkel, P. E., & Garner, D. M. (1982). *Anorexia nervosa. A multidimensional perspective*. New York: Basic Books.

947

Garfinkel, P. E., Modlofsky, H., & Garner, D. M. (1980). The heterogeneity of anorexia nervosa. *Archives of General Psychiatry, 37*, 1036–1040.

Garner, D. M., & Bemis, K. M. (1982). A cognitive behavior approach to anorexia nervosa. *Cognitive Therapy and Research, 6*, 1–27.

Garner, D. M., Rockert, W., Olmsted, M. P., Johnson, C., & Coscina, D. V. (1985). Psychoeducational principles in the treatment of bulimia and anorexia nervosa. In D. M. Garner & P. E. Garfinkel (Eds) *Handbook of psychotherapy for anorexia nervosa and bulimia nervosa* (pp. 513–572). New York: Guilford.

Gershon, E. S., Schreiber, J. L., & Hamovit, J. R. (1984). Clinical findings in patients with anorexia nervosa and affective illness and their relatives. *American Journal of Psychiatry, 141*, 1419–1422.

Halmi, K. A., Eckert, E., LaDu, T. J., & Cohen J. (1986). Anorexia nervosa; Treatment efficacy of cyproheptadine and amitriptyline. *Archives of General Psychiatry, 43*, 177–181.

Holland, A. J., Hall, A., Murray, R., Russell, G. F. M., & Crisp, A. H. (1984). Anorexia nervosa: A study of 34 twin pairs and one set of triplets. *British Journal of Psychiatry, 145*, 414–418.

Hsu, L. K. (1990). *Eating disorders.* New York: Guilford.

Hudson, J. I., Pope, H. G., Jonas, J. M., & Yurgelun-Todd, D. (1983). Family history study of anorexia nervosa and bulimia. *British Journal of Psychiatry, 142*, 133–138.

Kendell, R. E., Hall, D. J., Hailey, A., & Babigian, H. M. (1973). The epidemiology of anorexia nervosa. *Psychological Medicine, 3*, 200–203.

Kendler, K. S., McLean, C., Neale, M., Kessler, R., Heath, A., & Eaves, L. (1991). The genetic epidemiology of bulimia nervosa. *American Journal of Psychiatry, 148*, 1627–1637.

Kennedy, S., Kaplan, A., & Garfinkel, P. (1992). Intensive hospital treatment for anorexia nervosa and bulimia. In P. J. Cooper & A. Stein (Eds) *Monographs in clinical paediatrics. Feeding problems and eating disorders in children and adolescents* (pp. 161–181). New York: Harwood.

Lacey, J. H., & Crisp, A. H. (1980). Hunger, food intake and weight: The impact of clomipramine on a refeeding anorexia nervosa population. *Postgraduate Medical Journal, 56*, 79–85.

Lask, B., & Bryant-Waugh, R. (1992). Childhood onset anorexia nervosa and related eating disorders. *Journal of Child Psychology and Psychiatry, 3*, 281–300.

Lucas, A. R., Beard, C. M., O'Fallon, W. M., & Kurland, L. T. (1991). 50-year trends in the incidence of anorexia nervosa in Rochester, Minneapolis: A population based study. *American Journal of Psychiatry, 148*, 917–922.

Mann, A. H., Wakeling, A., Wood, U., Monck, E., Dobbs, R., & Szmukler, G. I. (1983). Screening for abnormal eating attitudes of psychiatric morbidity in an unselected population of 15 year old school girls. *Psychological Medicine, 13*, 573–580.

Mitchell, J. E. (1986a). Anorexia nervosa: Medical and physiological aspects. In K. D. Brownell & J. P. Foreyt (Eds) *Handbook of eating disorders. Physiology, psychology and treatment of obesity, anorexia and bulimia* (pp. 247–265). New York: Basic Books.

Mitchell, J. E. (1986b). Bulimia: Medical and physiological aspects. In K. D. Brownell & J. P. Foreyt (Eds) *Handbook of eating disorders: Physiology, psychology and treatment of obesity, anorexia and bulimia* (pp. 379–388). New York: Basic Books.

Mitchell, J. E., Pyle, R. L., Eckert, E. D., Hatsukami, D., Pomeroy, C., & Zimmerman, R. (1990). A comparison study of antidepressants and structured intensive group psychotherapy in the treatment of bulimia nervosa. *Archives of General Psychiatry, 47,* 149–157.

Piran, N., & Kaplan, A. S. (1990). *A day hospital group treatment program for anorexia nervosa and bulimia nervosa.* New York: Brunner/Mazel.

Piran, N., Kennedy, S., Garfinkel, P. E., & Owens, M. (1985). Affective disturbance in eating disorders. *Journal of Nervous and Mental Disease, 173,* 395–400.

Polivy, J., & Herman, C. P. (1985). Dieting and tingeing: Causal analysis. *American Psychologist, 40,* 193–201.

Pyle, R. L., Mitchell, J. E., Eckert, E. D., Hatsukami, D., Pomeroy, C., & Zimmerman, R. (1990). Maintenance treatment and six month outcome for bulimia patients who respond to initial treatment. *American Journal of Psychiatry, 147,* 871–875.

Rastam, M., Gillberg, C., & Garton, M. (1989). Anorexia nervosa in a Swedish urban region: A population based study. *British Journal of Psychiatry, 155,* 642–646.

Ratnasuria, R. H., Eisler, I., Szmukler, G., & Russell, G. F. M. (1991). Anorexia nervosa: Outcome and prognostic factors after 20 years. *British Journal of Psychiatry, 158,* 495–502.

Russell, G. F. M. (1970). Anorexia nervosa: Its identity as an illness and its treatment. In J. H Price (Ed.) *Modern trends in psychological medicine* (pp. 131–164). London: Butterworths.

Russell, G. F. M. (1979). Bulimia nervosa: An ominous variant of anorexia nervosa. *Psychological Medicine, 9,* 429–448.

Russell, G. F. M., Szmuckler, G. I., Dare, C., & Eisler, I. (1987). An evaluation of family therapy in anorexia nervosa and bulimia nervosa. *Archives of General Psychiatry, 44,* 1047–1056.

Schotte, D. E., & Stunkard, A. J. (1987). Bulimia vs bulimic behaviors on a college campus. *Journal of the American Medical Association, 258,* 1213–1215.

Steere, J. A., Butler, G., & Cooper, P. J. (1990). The anxiety symptoms of bulimia nervosa: A comparative study. *International Journal of Eating Disorders, 9,* 293–301.

Striegel-Moore, R. H., Silbertstein, L. R., & Rodin, J. (1986). Toward an understanding of risk factors for bulimia. *American Psychologist, 41,* 246–265.

Strober, M., & Humphrey, L. (1987). Familial contributions to the etiology and course of anorexia nervosa and bulimia. *Journal of Consulting and Clinical Psychology, 55,* 656–659.

Strober, M., & Katz, J. L. (1987). Do eating disorders and affective disorders share a common etiology? *International Journal of Eating Disorders, 6,* 171–180.

Szmukler, G. I., McCance, C., McCrone, L., & Hunter, D. (1986). A psychiatric case register study from Aberdeen. *Psychological Medicine, 16,* 49–58.

Touyz, S. W., Beumont, P. J. V., & Glaun, D. (1984). A comparison of lenient and strict operant conditioning programmes in refeeding patients with anorexia nervosa. *British Journal of Psychiatry, 144,* 517–520.

Walsh, B. T., Hadigan, C. M., Devlin, M. J., Gladis, M., & Roose, S. P. (1991). Long-term outcome of anti-depressant treatment for bulimia nervosa. *American Journal of Psychiatry, 148,* 1206–1212.

Walsh, B. T., Kissileff, H. R., Cassidy, S. M., & Danzic, S. (1989). Eating behavior of women with bulimia. *Archives of General Psychiatry, 46,* 54–58.

Walsh, B. T., Roose, S. P., Glassman, A. H., Gladis, M. A., & Sadik, C. (1985). Depression and bulimia. *Psychosomatic Medicine, 47,* 123–131.

10.5

ALCOHOL AND DRUG ADDICTION

Geoffrey Lowe

University of Hull, England

Psychology and its allied behavioural disciplines have been increasingly recognized for their contributions in helping to understand addiction and its treatment. In these research programmes we have seen an emerging integration of biological, psychological, and sociological approaches to aetiology and treatment. In this chapter I shall highlight this biopsychosocial model, together with perspectives based on social-learning theory and on cognitive principles.

950

Does addiction to various drugs involve different processes, each specific to a particular drug type (that is, individual theories)? Or is there some general process that different drug addictions have in common (that is, a unitary theory)? Many theories embrace a commonalities approach for a variety of addictive behaviours, but emphasize alcohol abuse and alcoholism – the most costly of addiction problems in terms of frequency of abuse and potential for harm.

I shall proceed by first looking at alcohol as a major psychoactive drug. Many of the basic observations about alcohol-behaviour interactions have implications for dependence (or alcoholism). Next I shall consider various approaches to the specific aetiology of alcoholism and its treatment, before looking at drug dependence in general as an addictive process.

ALCOHOL

Alcohol is the major social drug, with interesting psychoactive properties. One of its first effects is on the central nervous system, the higher centres related to judgement, inhibition, and the like. What is more important is what this feels like, how it is experienced. With mild intoxication comes relaxation, a more carefree feeling. It is generally experienced as a plus, a high; pre-existing tensions are relieved. A good mood can be accentuated: alcohol is experienced as a mood changer in a positive direction. This capacity of alcohol is one factor to remember in trying to understand use sufficient for addiction.

In the field of psychopharmacology, researchers have found the effects of alcohol a useful tool in the study of fundamental psychological mechanisms, while others have been interested in such research for clinical reasons. Consequently, the psychopharmacology of alcohol as a research area has expanded rapidly in breadth and depth. Certainly the experimental investigation of alcohol's effects on the central nervous system and behaviour, and of the alcohol dependence process, has achieved a good measure of scientific respectability.

ALCOHOL INTOXICATION

Alcohol is a depressant agent, capable of impairing, retarding, and disorganizing the functions of the central nervous system (CNS). Nevertheless, many of the overt behavioural effects of alcohol are stimulant. The behaviourally arousing effects of alcohol arise partly because CNS inhibitory processes tend to be more susceptible to disruption than the excitatory processes. A further contribution to the behavioural stimulation caused by alcohol is a compensatory response, counteracting the depressant drug effect.

Subjective reports of intoxication are important because they provide

Table 1 Typical effects at different levels of blood-alcohol concentration (BAC)

BAC (mg/100 ml)	Psychological/clinical effects*
20	Negligible
30	Possible slight flushing and a little more talkative than usual
50	Relaxation, lowering of inhibitions; impaired attention, impaired vigilance
60–99	Impaired sensory function; motor incoordination; changes in mood and behaviour (mild euphoria, self-satisfaction, louder profuse speech); impaired mental activity
100	Significant feelings of intoxication; impaired short-term memory
150	Staggering; lengthened reaction time; marked impairment on mental and psycho-motor tests; slurred speech
200	Insensitivity to stimuli; extreme clumsiness; nausea and vomiting
250	Marked tendency to pass out
300	Hypothermia; amnesia; anaesthesia; slow, heavy breathing
400	Comatose
500	Breathing abolished; death

Note: *These approximations are given for determinations obtained during *rising* BACs. During this period the mental effects are more pronounced and the mood tends to be more euphoric. On the other hand, as BAC declines, at equivalent levels the mental effects are less pronounced, and more negative feeling tones are experienced

access to the subjective cues that govern drinking behaviour in a single drinking session. However, the meaning or intensity of subjective intoxication varies greatly according to dose level and drinking habits. Although subjective ratings (SR) and BAC (blood-alcohol concentration) correspond quite closely while BAC is rising, as BAC decreases the disparity between BAC and SR becomes marked, with SR declining much faster. This means that people may *feel* quite sober, even when they still have significant BACs.

EFFECTS ON HUMAN PERFORMANCE

There is little doubt that alcohol can affect various aspects of human performance. But when we ask more precise questions about which kinds of tasks, under what conditions, and under what dosages, then a whole variety of factors come into play. These include differences in subject population (for example, sex, weight, age, and type of drinker); differences in methods of alcohol administration; different types of alcohol; temporal variations (for example, consumption period, time of day, time between ingestion and testing); and different tasks and demand characteristics.

In general, cognitive and perceptual-sensory performances are most disrupted by alcohol; psycho-motor tasks seem to be more resistant, although measurable decrements are usually observed. Moskowitz (1979) and others have reported the sensitivity of attention, perception, and information processing to moderate and even low doses of alcohol and related drugs. Since these are the areas of crucial importance for skills performance in complex human–machine interactions, such findings explain why activities such as driving are so susceptible to alcohol-induced disruption.

Alcohol intoxication also interferes with memory and learning processes. The most severe memory disturbance is the alcoholic "blackout", an inability to recall events that happened during a drinking episode, even though consciousness was neither significantly clouded nor lost. We may observe poorer recall at BACs of 40 mg/dl, and it seems to worsen in a linear fashion as BAC rises.

One of the major difficulties in determining and explaining these memory deficits is that the effects of acute intoxication wear off after a few hours, leaving the person in a different physiological state. What is learned while intoxicated is not so well recalled when tested under a sober state (and vice versa). Retention is, however, greater when the original drug state is reinstated (Lowe, 1981, 1988). *State-dependent learning* (SDL) is the term used to describe this phenomenon. Such "dissociation" of learning between drunk and sober states has led to the speculation that SDL may be a factor in the aetiology of alcoholism (see below).

ALCOHOLISM

There is no single definition of alcoholism, but several behavioural criteria taken together enable one to judge the severity of a drinking problem. Among these criteria are "loss-of-control" (of drinking behaviour); psychological dependence ("needs a drink" to get anything done); loss of job(s), family, or friends because of drinking; blackouts; increasing tolerance for alcohol; withdrawal symptoms upon stopping drinking (physical dependence).

Most psychologists prefer the terms *alcohol dependence* or *problem drinking* to refer to the excessive and compulsive use of alcohol, since the label "alcoholism" is too closely associated with a simple disease model (see below). But for convenience I shall use these terms interchangeably to refer to a condition determined by a host of influences rather than a static all-or-none entity.

We need to understand how chronic and excessive alcohol drinking is generated, as well as the conditions under which such over-indulgence can be attenuated and prevented.

Why do people drink?

Any useful theoretical model for drinking behaviour must address at least three questions. First, why do people start drinking? Second, what factors maintain drinking? Third, why do some drink so much as to develop serious problems?

Psychological approaches

Psychological formulations of dependence, like the definitions of the World Health Organization (WHO) and the American Psychiatric Association's DSM-III (*Diagnostic and Statistical Manual of Mental Disorders*), generally imply that dependence is a mental or behavioural disorder whose origins are as much environmental as they are physical (Babor & Lauerman, 1986). Three definitions that convey some of the variety of psychological approaches to dependence are those proposed by psychoanalysts, behaviourists, and family interaction theorists.

In the *psychoanalytic model*, dependence is seen as a symptom of some underlying psychological conflict or pre-alcoholic personality type. *Behavioural* definitions, on the other hand, emphasize the environmental conditions that initiate and maintain drinking behaviour, avoiding assumptions about physical or psychological causes of a disease process. *Family interaction* theorists define dependence as a family illness, and give primary emphasis to the alcohol or drug user's interpersonal relationships.

The tension-reduction hypothesis

Historically one of the first models proposed to explain drinking was termed the tension-reduction hypothesis, or TRH (Conger, 1956), which holds that people drink alcohol primarily because of its tension-reducing effects. This hypothesis has much intuitive appeal, because alcohol is a sedative drug that leads to relaxation and slowed reactions.

However, alcohol's effects on physiological processes are not simple, which creates difficulties for a simple version of the TRH. Moreover, in a longitudinal study of a heavy social drinker, Rohsenow (1982) found that drinking occurred for reasons of attaining a positive state of affect rather than avoiding a negative state of tension.

Two reformulations of the TRH seem to be more viable. Sher and Levenson (1982) discovered that high levels of alcohol consumption decrease the strength of responses to stress. This decrease was termed the *stress-response-dampening* (SRD) effect. It was found that people who had been drinking did not respond as strongly as non-drinking subjects to either physiological or psychological stresses. So that, rather than tension reduction, alcohol may produce tension avoidance, and that high-risk drinkers are more likely to experience this effect than others.

A second reformulation, proposed by Hull (1981), is based on social psychological theories of self-awareness. He suggests that alcohol can interfere with cognition to make thought more superficial and decrease negative self-feedback that would otherwise produce tension.

The disease model

The most influential model during much of the twentieth century has been the disease conception of alcoholism. Among psychiatric and other medically oriented treatment programmes, this model still predominates, although since the early 1980s the disease model has become much less influential among psychologically based treatment programmes.

Throughout history, isolated attempts have been made to describe alcohol intoxication as a disease, but not until the late 1930s and early 1940s did this view become popular. The disease model of alcoholism was elevated to scientific respectability by the pioneering work of E. M. Jellinek, who defined alcoholism as "any use of alcoholic beverages that causes any damage to the individual or society or both" (1960). Damage was conceived broadly as physiological, psychological, social, or even financial. This sweeping conception of alcoholism enabled Jellinek to identify several different "species" or types of alcoholism.

The distinguishing mark of gamma alcoholism is loss of control. In addition, gamma alcoholism is characterised by increased tissue tolerance, adaptive cell metabolism, and withdrawal symptoms. These four elements add up to physical dependency and, ultimately, serious organic damage.

Delta alcoholism also features the latter three elements but there is no loss of control and the pattern of drinking is different. Rather than losing control, the delta alcoholic has an inability to abstain.

The alcohol dependence syndrome

A later conception of the disease model is the alcohol dependence syndrome (Edwards, 1986). This model grew out of some dissatisfaction with the term "alcoholism" and with the traditional concept of alcoholism as a disease. The word "syndrome" adds flexibility to the disease model because it suggests a group of concurrent behaviours that accompany alcohol dependence. The behaviours need not always be observed in an individual, nor do they need to be observable to the same degree in everyone who is alcohol dependent. Thus the concepts of loss of control and inability to abstain, with their all-or-none connotation, do not apply to the alcohol dependence syndrome. Instead, the term "impaired control" is used to suggest that people drink heavily because, at certain times and for a variety of psychological and physiological reasons, they choose not to exercise control.

There are seven essential elements in the alcohol dependence syndrome. First is a narrowing of drinking repertoire. The dependent person gradually begins to drink the same, whether it is a workday, a weekend, or a holiday, whether in a depressed or happy mood. Second is a salience of drink-seeking behaviour, meaning that drinking begins to take top priority over all other aspects of life. A third element is increased tolerance. Alcohol does not produce as much tolerance as some other drugs, but the dependent person often becomes accustomed to going about his or her business at drug levels that would incapacitate the non-tolerant drinker.

A fourth element of the alcohol dependence syndrome is withdrawal symptoms – depending on length and amount of use. Fifth is the relief or avoidance of withdrawal symptoms by further drinking. Sixth is the subjective awareness of the compulsion to drink. Dependent drinkers may fight against the compulsion, but they drink anyway. A final element of the alcohol dependence syndrome is reinstatement of dependence after abstinence. When drinking cues are removed, as in a treatment centre, patients often find abstinence surprisingly easy. However, if abstinence is broken, dependency is reinstated. Time of reinstatement is inversely related to degree of dependence, meaning that moderately dependent drinkers may take months, while severely dependent patients may resume full dependency in as little as three days.

Simple disease models have now been largely replaced by a more complex set of working hypotheses based, not on irreversible physiological processes, but on learning and conditioning, motivation and self-regulation, expectations and attributions.

The social learning model

Many psychologists have accepted social learning theory as offering the most useful explanation for why people begin to drink, continue in moderation, or drink in a harmful manner. Social learning theory conceives of problem drinking as a multiply determined, learned behaviour disorder. It can be understood best through the empirically derived principles of social learning, cognitive psychology, and behaviour therapies.

People begin to drink, according to social learning theory, for at least three reasons. First, the taste of alcohol and/or its immediate effect may be pleasurable (positive reinforcement); second, a person may decide earlier that drinking alcohol is consistent with personal standards (cognitive mediation); and third, one may learn to drink through observing others (modelling). Any one or combination of these factors is sufficient to initiate and control drinking behaviour.

The social learning model also offers several explanations for why people drink too much. Excessive drinking may serve as a coping response. In other words, although alcohol acts as a depressant, the initial effect of small doses is often interpreted by drinkers as a means of strengthening their ability to cope. This response to alcohol gives drinkers a sense of power and also a feeling of avoiding responsibility or minimizing stress. People will then continue to drink as long as they perceive the desirable effects of alcohol.

Modelling also provides an explanation for heavy drinking. Heavy-drinking models do produce increased consumption – especially in drinkers with a prior history of heavy drinking.

A third explanation for excessive drinking offered by the social learning model is based on the principles of *negative reinforcement*. Most heavy drinkers have learned that they can avoid or reduce the painful effects of withdrawal symptoms by maintaining blood-alcohol concentrations at a particular level. As this level begins to drop, the alcohol addict feels the discomfort of withdrawal. These symptoms can be avoided by ingesting more alcohol; thus negative reinforcement increases the likelihood that heavy drinking will be continued.

The cognitive social learning approach

The cognitive social learning approach (Marlatt & Donovan, 1982) additionally emphasizes cognitive processes and expectations (see also Hodgson, 1990). The individual's expectancies about alcohol and its anticipated effects can influence drinking and a number of related behaviours (Brown, Goldman, & Christiansen, 1985). Such cognitive expectancies appear to override the pharmacologic effects of alcohol for a variety of human behaviours in which one's beliefs about alcohol are influential (Critchlow, 1986; Goldman, Brown, & Christiansen, 1987; Lowe, 1990).

The behavioural perspectives of these social learning theories not only provide explanations for why people drink, but also suggest a variety of treatment techniques to help people overcome excessive drinking habits. Since drinking behaviour is learned, it can be unlearned or relearned. People can learn to abstain from alcohol completely, or they can learn to moderate their intake. The social learning model therefore is not tied to the goal of abstinence, but can accommodate either controlled drinking or abstinence as a treatment goal. Useful interventions could be directed towards the development of social skills, both generalized and specific, to high-risk drinking situations, perceived control and enhanced personal efficacy, and relapse-prevention techniques.

Is alcoholism hereditary?

The notion that alcoholism is hereditary dates back at least to the eighteenth and nineteenth centuries when the belief among doctors and the general public was that a "constitutional weakness" ran in families and that this weakness produced alcoholics. With the growth of the temperance movement came an emphasis on the environmental causes and consequences of drinking. The issue of environment versus heredity now produces heated debate in the area of alcohol abuse. It is a complex issue, mostly addressed by studies of twins and adopted children, but few clear-cut findings are emerging. It seems safest to conclude that both factors play a role in the development of alcohol abuse and that the people most likely to become alcoholics have both a genetic and an environmental risk. However, another relevant question is "Why do the overwhelming majority of people who have both a genetic and an environmental risk never become alcoholics?" Nevertheless, a significant minority do, and we next need to consider why some people are more "vulnerable" than others.

Vulnerability and risk factors

It is likely that cognitive and behavioural disturbances may presage alcoholism (Tarter & Edwards, 1988). The findings implicating psychological disturbances are based on longitudinal investigations of children followed into adulthood who subsequently became alcohol-dependent, alcoholics' retrospective descriptions of their behaviour during childhood and adolescence, children at high risk for becoming alcoholic, twins discordant for drinking behaviour, and adolescents who present early signs of problem drinking. Much of this research effort has focused primarily on males.

In as much as alcoholism tends to run in families, the particular feature comprising the vulnerability may be more frequently or more strongly present in individuals with a family history of alcoholism.

Risk (for the development of alcohol abuse) has also been defined on the basis of sensation seeking, left-handedness, and Type A personality. Other vulnerability characteristics for substance abuse include poor school performance, perceived use of drugs by parents and other adults, psychological disorders (for example, depression and behaviour disturbance), low self-esteem, low religious involvement conflict with parents, lack of sense of purpose, a reduced sense of social responsibility, and childhood hyperactivity. However, each characteristic by itself is not a powerful predictor of outcome. Rather, it is typically the total number of factors that best predicts outcome.

It should be stressed that the presence of psychological features in childhood alone is not assumed to be sufficient to lead to an alcoholism outcome. This depends on a facilitating environment impacting on a person with a vulnerability to develop this condition: only a small proportion of these cases turn out to be "alcoholic".

Once the cognitive and behavioural characteristics of alcoholism vulnerability are more fully clarified, it will be feasible to implement targeted prevention procedures. For example, social skill disturbances, impulsivity, and anxiety symptoms are among the vulnerability traits that have been tentatively found to presage alcoholism. The rationale of such intervention strategies is that by improving the behaviours that presage alcoholism, the risk for developing this disorder is attenuated.

Can dissociation cause alcohol dependence?

State-dependent learning (SDL) or "dissociation" may be partially responsible for poor recall of events that take place during drinking (Lowe, 1988). This could, indeed, constitute the basis for "loss of control". After a few drinks, the alcoholic "forgets" the (negative) consequences of heavy drinking – consequences usually experienced in a relatively sober state.

The relevance of state-dependent learning to alcoholism also arises from the possibility of conditioned reactions to alcohol, as distinct from its unconditioned pharmacological effects. Alcoholics may drink to obtain access to behavioural or emotional repertoires that have become conditioned to the presence of alcohol, rather than to obtain any of the intrinsic effects of alcohol. Or intoxication may alter the user's sensitivity to social reinforcement so that reinforcing contingencies are effectively changed even in the absence of any real change in the external environment. Thus, in so far as the drinker has developed drug state behaviours that are more reinforcing than sober behaviours, the drug state will have acquired more positive aspects than it initially possessed, by virtue of its conditioned associations.

There is, incidentally, nothing about this argument that uniquely applies to alcoholism. It appears equally relevant to other substances with strong stimulus properties, such as nicotine, cannabis, and heroin (Overton, 1987).

CONCLUSION

Excessive and chronic alcohol ingestion would seem to be best viewed as a set of behaviours for which others might have been substituted, and intermittently are, rather than as a highly specific disorder or disease. Some aetiological, preventive, and therapeutic orientations emphasize the role of physical dependence and favour genetic influences as strong determinants of alcohol-related disorders. But many psychologists believe that severe dependence is the result of learning and conditioning. Psychological treatments are therefore being developed that reverse or modify this process. It is important to recognise that problem drinking is malleable, waxing and then entering periods of remission. Alcohol drinking, even in severely dependent individuals, remains susceptible to control by both antecedent and consequential environmental events.

DRUG ADDICTION

The human body is capable of tolerating and eliminating small quantities of virtually any substance or drug with no permanent or harmful effects. However, if large doses are ingested or if a drug is used frequently even though in small quantities, harmful effects on the person's physical or mental health may begin to appear. Generally, any use of a drug to a point where one's health is adversely affected or one's ability to function in society is impaired can be defined as *drug abuse*.

DEPENDENCE AND TOLERANCE

Physical dependence

The dangers of using a particular drug are often associated with the drug's potential to cause addiction, or physical dependence as it is commonly referred to. Many legal drugs, including barbiturates, tranquillizers, analgesics, opiates, alcohol, and tobacco, have this potential, and abusers can become physically dependent. Among the illegal drugs, only heroin leads to severe physical dependence, which means that complex physiological changes result from using the drug, so that *withdrawal symptoms* will occur if the addict abstains from using it. The withdrawal from a physically addicting drug invariably causes moderate to severe physical and mental symptoms.

The relationship between a withdrawal syndrome and drug dependence is complex. There are drugs which, if given repeatedly over a long period, produce physical dependence and therefore a withdrawal syndrome when they are discontinued. But for many of these drugs the syndrome is not necessarily accompanied by severe discomfort, anxiety, or even a marked desire to get more of the drug. So physical dependence need not equal "addiction" or "psychological dependence". A good example of this is the drug imipramine, which is used in the treatment of depression. When it is stopped after prolonged administration, there may be nausea, muscle aches, anxiety, and difficulty in sleeping but never a compulsion to resume the use of the drug (Jaffe, 1975).

Besides physical dependence, drugs can lead to habituation, and a second kind of physiological condition referred to as tolerance. Some people speak of "psychological" dependence, but this term has little scientific meaning beyond the notion that some activities, including drug taking, become part of one's habitual behaviour. Giving up the activity is accomplished only through much difficulty because the person has become habituated to it.

Habituation

Habituation is the repeated use of a drug because the user finds that each use increases pleasurable feelings or reduces feelings of anxiety, fear, or stress. Habituation becomes problematic when the person becomes so consumed by the need for the drug-altered state of consciousness that all of his or her energies are directed to compulsive drug-seeking behaviour. Physically addicting drugs such as heroin and alcohol typically produce habituation as well, so that the person is trapped into using all of his or her energies and resources for obtaining the drug. As a consequence of this compulsive drug-seeking behaviour, relationships, jobs, and families can be destroyed. Many of the widely used recreational drugs, including cannabis (marijuana), cocaine, LSD (lysergic acid diethylamide), PCP (phencyclidine, commonly called "angel dust"), and MDMA (methylenedioxymethamphetamine, also known as "Ecstasy") do *not* create physical dependence, but people do become habituated to their use. There are no physical symptoms of withdrawal from stopping use of these drugs, but people may experience uncomfortable psychological symptoms because of the habituation.

Tolerance

Drug tolerance is an adaptation of the body to a drug such that ever larger doses are needed to gain the same effect. The more tolerance potential a drug has, the more potentially dangerous it is. Because not all regions of the body become tolerant to the same degree, these higher doses may cause harmful side-effects to some parts of the body. For example, a heroin or barbiturate user can become tolerant to the psychological effects of the drug, but the brain's respiratory centre, which controls breathing, does not. If the dose of heroin, barbiturate, or other depressant becomes high enough, the brain's respiratory centre ceases to function and the person stops breathing.

There is a physiological component in dependence. It is usually called neurological adaptation, the state in which the brain adapts to the presence of alcohol (or other drugs). This state results in tolerance and also withdrawal symptoms when blood-drug levels decline. It is important to emphasize that neurological adaptation does not always lead to psychological dependence or habituation. For this reason the term *neuro-adaptation* is preferable to the term physical dependence. Neurological adaptation can be conditioned so that it is aroused by signals or associated stimuli in the absence of drugs. This leads to *behavioural tolerance* and conditioned withdrawal (Corfield-Sumner & Stolerman, 1978).

Siegel (1988) has demonstrated that tolerance to a drug's effect can best be understood in terms of an *anticipatory response* to this effect. Compensatory classically conditioned adaptive responses oppose a drug's action and these can be triggered by any cue that enables the individual to anticipate that the drug is imminent: that is, with a drug that the person has previously experienced. These responses may be triggered by environmental as well as internal stimuli.

Tolerance and dependence are independent properties. It is possible for a drug to produce tolerance but no dependence, and it is also possible that dependence can develop to a drug that has little or no tolerance potential. In addition, some drugs have both a tolerance and a dependency potential. Moreover, tolerance and dependence are not inevitable consequences of

961

taking drugs. Not everyone who drinks alcohol, for instance, does so with sufficient frequency and in sufficient quantity to develop a tolerance, and most drinkers do not become dependent.

COMMONALITIES ACROSS ADDICTIVE BEHAVIOUR

"Addiction" is a complex, progressive behaviour pattern having biological, psychological, sociological, and behavioural components. What sets this behaviour pattern apart from others is the individual's overwhelmingly pathological involvement in or attachment to it, subjective compulsion to continue it, and reduced ability to exert personal control over it.

A distinction can be made between the "object of addiction" and the "addictive process" (Peele, 1985). The compulsive involvement in a behaviour pattern represents the addictive process. It is this process, along with its multidimensional determinants, that is comparable across different drugs of addiction (Lang, 1983).

The possibility that addiction to different drugs involves a common mechanism has considerable appeal. There is no presumption that addictions to all classes of drugs are identical: there are obvious differences among addictions to different drugs, and even individual cases involving the same drug can display marked differences. However, certain elements of addiction seem to be shared across distinctively different drugs and behaviour, and these similarities provide the impetus for developing unifying theories of addiction (Orford, 1985).

First, the addictive experience provides a potent and rapid means of changing one's mood and sensations because of both direct physiological effects and learned expectations (Peele, 1985). The individual engages in a form of self-indulgence for short-term pleasure or satisfaction, despite an awareness of the long-term negative consequences (Miller, 1980).

A second, and related, feature is that various physical and psychological states such as general arousal, stress, pain, or negative moods tend to be associated with and to influence the likelihood of engaging in the addictive behaviour. Alcohol and drug abusers typically use such substances co-occurrently or interchangeably (Istvan & Matarazzo, 1984). Moreover, coming off one substance often results in the abuse of another. In particular, alcohol and the benzodiazepines (minor tranquillizers) have been linked in this regard.

A third feature is the role of both classical and instrumental conditioning in the addictive process. The changes that are induced when the individual engages in the addictive behaviour serve as an unconditioned stimulus. Through repeated association with these changes, a wide variety of other stimuli acquire the power of conditioned stimuli. The latter may include mood states, cognitive expectations, and levels of physiological arousal, as well as more specific features of the social and physical environment in which the behaviour typically occurs. The presence of such conditioned stimuli may elicit changes that the individual interprets as a strong desire or craving for the addictive experience, and may also contribute to the contextual events that predict engaging in that behaviour.

Another commonality across addictions is the high rate of *relapse* following a period of abstinence (Marlatt & Gordon, 1985). It appears that a number of cognitive-expectational, emotional, and behavioural factors make comparable contributions to the relapse process in drinking, smoking, and drug use (Gossop, 1989).

Common "high risk" situations include negative emotional states such as anxiety, depression, boredom, and loneliness; interpersonal conflicts typically resulting in feelings of frustration, anger, and resentment; and social pressure associated with being in a physical, social or emotional context in which substance use has occurred in the past and is being directly encouraged by peers (Marlatt & Gordon, 1985).

An additional risk of relapse is the possibility of "triggering" a return to the target substance by engaging in alternative behaviour strongly linked with the target behaviour (Miller, 1980). This risk is high among multi-drug users.

Different functions

Although there are many who advocate a general mechanism underlying addiction to different drugs, others do not subscribe to this unitary theory. An extreme variation of the opposing multiple theory approach might assert that the cause of addiction to even a single drug varies with each individual. So we would need unique explanations for every case of addiction.

Psychopharmacologists have also shown that (potentially) addictive drugs may serve a number of different functions. And if the social context is taken into account, the list of such functions becomes potentially varied and vast.

For instance, in the smoking research area, Warburton (1988) suggests that the psychological effects of nicotine are much more subtle than those of other drugs, such as alcohol or heroin. He reviews evidence indicating that the psychological effects of nicotine are crucial to the maintenance of the smoking habit. He also suggests that the mechanisms by which the drug achieves this effect are quite different from those underlying other habitual substance use.

THEORETICAL APPROACHES

The field of addictive behaviour has previously been dominated by contributions from disciplines other than psychology – particularly from medicine and the neurosciences. A glut of popular and non-expert books has also appeared on the topic of addiction, many written by individuals who are themselves recovering from addictions. The frequent discrepancies between the approaches have added fuel to ongoing debates and have contributed to the divisive nature of the field.

Since the early 1970s there have been numerous publications in the biomedical and social sciences. Because of a parallel improvement in methodology, this research has produced a wealth of empirical data and theoretical insights. There has been a gradually growing conviction that the causes of dependency cannot be found within the limits of one single discipline. The various scientific search routes for explanations can be taken without interfering with one another, and each can contribute to unravelling the complexity of addictive behaviours. It is now generally agreed that addictive behaviours are multiply determined phenomena, and should be considered as biopsychosocial entities.

The biopsychosocial model

A major development in the addictions field since the early 1980s has been a move away from reductionist thinking and towards more integrative theories. Addiction is seen as being determined by the interaction of psychological, environmental, and physiological factors (Peele, 1985). This formulation is consistent with a biopsychosocial approach to health and illness (Schwartz, 1982).

Thus, addiction is a total experience involving physiological changes in individuals (some of whom may be genetically and/or psychologically predisposed). These changes are interpreted and given meaning by the individual within the sociocultural context in which the addictive behaviour occurs (Zinberg, 1981).

Within the biopsychosocial perspective, psychologists focus on the behaviour of individuals. This is in contrast with biomedical orientations, which focus on biological deviances (including constitutional or genetic aspects). Sociologists and cultural anthropologists, on the other hand, search for social and cultural factors, such as norms and cultural beliefs. Epidemiologists examine the social and economic factors that influence the spreading of addictive behaviours in groups or nations. Until the 1970s the interest of psychology in the subject of addiction had been scarce. Since then, however, developments have been impressive (e.g., Sobell & Sobell, 1987). This applies to questions of causation, to treatment possibilities, as well as to the function of assessment (Blane & Leonard, 1987; Donovan & Marlatt, 1988; Hester & Miller, 1989).

THE "ADDICTIVE" PERSONALITY?

Many studies of the addictive personality have been carried out in trying to find characteristics typical of the addictive individual. But convincing evidence has eluded researchers. The idea that a unitary set of personality factors precedes and results in the development of addictive disorders has not been widely accepted in alcohol and drug treatment research and theory. Indeed, some researchers minimize any causal role for personality factors in substance use.

In general, addictive populations appear to differ from non-addictive populations in that they show more deviancy. But specific addictive subgroups hardly differ from each other.

DRUGS AS REINFORCERS

Since the mid-1960s, powerful procedures have been developed to analyse the behavioural aspects of drug dependence in animals. This analysis is based on conditioning principles widely used by experimental psychologists and behavioural pharmacologists. For the analysis of drug-seeking behaviour, conditions are arranged so that a behavioural response is followed by the administration of a drug. If the response increases in frequency, then the drug is defined as a positive reinforcer for that behaviour.

A drug seems to be the ultimate reinforcer in that it is often quick-acting. If delivered in a very quick and intense way (for example, inhaling tobacco smoke or injecting heroin) its effects are certain and predictable. It affects basic reward mechanisms in the brain. A wide variety of psychoactive drugs have been shown to serve as positive reinforcers in both rats and monkeys. In general, drugs that serve as positive reinforcers in animals are those that produce dependence in humans.

Developments based on this methodology have led to a description of drug addiction as an extreme case of compulsive drug use associated with strong motivational effects of the drug (Bozarth, 1990). The "addiction potential" of a drug is derived from its ability to activate brain mechanisms involved in the control of normal behaviour – to such an extent that it can disrupt the individual's normal motivational hierarchy. This effect has been termed *motivational toxicity*.

At some point in the drug-use cycle there is a shift in control from intrapersonal and sociological to pharmacological factors in governing drug-taking behaviour. This is concomitant with a marked increase in the motivational strength of the drug and with a progression from casual to compulsive drug use and ultimately to drug addiction. This may occur quite rapidly for some drugs, such as heroin or free-base cocaine, and much more slowly for other drugs, such as alcohol.

CONCLUSION

Many feel that the incidence and prevalence of drug addictive behaviours are increasing and that these problems are affecting a broad spectrum of individuals. At the same time there is an increase in interdisciplinary approaches to investigating the addictions. Addictions are best viewed as behaviours developed and maintained by multiple sources: they are multiply determined and multidimensional in nature. The most useful explanatory models take into account biological, psychological, and social components. Within the psychological components, (social) learning theory and cognitive-behavioural approaches have been particularly effective. The emergence of a biopsychosocial model in the areas of health psychology and behavioural medicine is another landmark. As applied specifically to the area of alcohol and drug addiction, an interactive biopsychosocial model provides a bridge across the varying perspectives of different disciplines, ideologies, and paradigms.

FURTHER READING

Edwards, G., & Lader, M. (Eds) (1990). *The nature of drug dependence.* Oxford: Oxford University Press.

Galizio, M., & Maisto, S. A. (Eds) (1985). *Determinants of substance abuse: Biological, psychological, and environmental factors.* New York: Plenum.

Lowe, G. (1984). Alcohol and alcoholism. In D. J. Sanger & D. E. Blackman (Eds) *Aspects of psychopharmacology* (pp. 84–109). London: Methuen.

Marlatt, G. A., Baer, J. S., Donovan, D. M., & Kivlahan, D. R. (1988). Addictive behaviors: Aetiology and treatment. *Annual Review of Psychology, 39,* 223–252.

Miller, W. R., & Heather, N. (Eds) (1986). *Treating addictive behaviors: Processes of change.* New York: Plenum.

REFERENCES

Babor, T. F., & Lauerman, R. J. (1986). Classification and forms of inebriety: Historical antecedents of alcoholic typologies. In M. Galanter (Ed.) *Recent developments in alcoholism* (vol. 4, pp. 13–144). New York: Plenum.

Blake, H. T., & Leonard, K. E. (Eds) (1987). *Psychological theories of drinking and alcoholism.* New York: Guilford.

Bozarth, M. A. (1990). Drug addiction as a psychobiological process. In D. M. Warburton (Ed.) *Addiction controversies* (pp. 112–134). London: Harwood Academic.

Brown, S. A., Goldman, M. S., & Christiansen, B. A. (1985). Do alcohol expectancies mediate drinking patterns of adults? *Journal of Consulting and Clinical Psychology, 53,* 512–519.

Conger, J. (1956). Reinforcement theory and the dynamics of alcoholism. *Quarterly Journal of Studies on Alcohol, 17,* 296–305.

Corfield-Sumner, P. K., & Stolerman, I.P. (1978). Behavioral tolerance. In D. E. Blackman & D. J. Sanger (Eds) *Contemporary research in behavioral pharmacology* (pp. 391–448). New York: Plenum.

Critchlow, B. (1986). The powers of John Barleycorn. *American Psychologist, 41,* 751–764.

Donovan, D. M., & Marlatt, G. A. (Eds) (1988). *Assessment of addictive behaviors.* New York: Guilford.

Edwards, G. (1986). The alcohol dependence syndrome: A concept as stimulus to enquiry. *British Journal of Addiction, 81,* 71–84.

Goldman, M. S., Brown, S. A., & Christiansen, B. A. (1987). Expectancy theory: Thinking and drinking. In II. T. Blane & K. E. Leonard (Eds) *Psychological theories of drinking and alcoholism* (pp. 181–226). New York: Guilford.

Gossop, M. (1989). *Relapse and addictive behaviour*. London: Tavistock/Routledge.

Hester, R. K., & Miller, W. R. (1989). *Handbook of alcoholism treatment approaches*. New York: Pergamon.

Hodgson, R. J. (1990). Cognitions and desire. In D. M. Warburton (Ed.) *Addiction controversies* (pp. 223–235). London: Harwood Academic.

Hull, J. G. (1981). A self-awareness model of the causes and effects of alcohol and consumption. *Journal of Abnormal Psychology, 90*, 586–600.

Istvan, J., & Matarazzo, J. D. (1984). Tobacco, alcohol, and caffeine use: A review of their interrelationships. *Psychological Bulletin, 95*, 301–326.

Jaffe, J. H. (1975) Drug addiction and drug abuse. In L. S. Goodman & A. Gilman (Eds) *The pharmacological basis of therapeutics* (pp. 284–324). New York: Macmillan.

Jellinek, E. M. (1960). *The disease concept of alcoholism*. New Brunswick, NJ: Hillhouse.

Lang, A. (1983). Addictive personality: A viable construct? In P. Levinson, D. Gerstein, & R. Maloff (Eds) *Commonalities in substance use and habitual behavior* (pp. 157–236). Lexington, MA: Lexington Books.

Lowe, G. (1981). State-dependent recall decrements with moderate doses of alcohol. *Current Psychological Research, 1*, 3–8.

Lowe, G. (1988). State-dependent retrieval effects with social drugs. *British Journal of Addiction, 83*, 99–103.

Lowe, G. (1990). Alcohol: A positive enhancer of pleasurable expectancies? In D. M. Warburton (Ed.) *Addiction controversies* (pp. 53–65). London: Harwood Academic.

Marlatt, G. A., & Donovan, D. M. (1982). Behavioral psychology approaches to alcoholism. In E. M. Pattison & E. Kaufman (Eds) *Encyclopaedic handbook of alcoholism* (pp. 560–576). New York: Gardner.

Marlatt, G. A., & Gordon, J. R. (Eds) (1985). *Relapse prevention: Maintenance strategies in addictive behavior change*. New York: Guilford.

Miller, W. R. (Ed.) (1980). *The addictive behaviors*. New York: Pergamon.

Moskowitz, H. (1979). The effects of alcohol and other drugs on skills performance and information processing. In G. Olive (Ed.) *Drug-action modifications: Comparative pharmacology. Advances in Pharmacology and Therapeutics, 8*, 211–221.

Orford, J. (1985). *Excessive appetites: A psychological view of addictions*. New York: Wiley.

Overton, D. A. (1987). Applications and limitations of the drug discrimination method for the study of drug abuse. In M. A. Bozarth (Ed.) *Methods of assessing the reinforcing properties of abused drugs* (pp. 291–340). Heidelberg: Springer-Verlag.

Peele, S. (1985). *The meaning of addiction: compulsive experience and its interpretation*. Lexington, MA: Lexington Books.

Rohsenow, D. J. (1982). Social anxiety, daily moods, and alcohol use over time among heavy social drinking men. *Addictive Behaviors, 7*, 311–315.

Schwartz, G. E. (1982). Testing the biopsychosocial model: The ultimate challenge facing behavioral medicine. *Journal of Consulting and Clinical Psychology, 50*, 1040–1053.

Sher, K. E., & Levenson, R. W. (1982). Risk for alcoholism and individual differences in the stress-response-dampening effect of alcohol. *Journal of Abnormal Psychology, 91*, 350–367.

Siegel, S. (1988). Drug anticipation and drug tolerance. In M. H. Lader (Ed.) *The psychopharmacology of addiction* (pp. 73–96). Oxford: Oxford University Press.

Sobell, L. C., & Sobell, M. B. (Eds) (1987). Two decades of behavioral research in the alcohol field: Change, challenge, and controversy (special issue). *Advances in Behavioral Research and Therapy*, *9*, 59–72.

Tarter, R. E., & Edwards, K. (1988). Psychological factors associated with the risk for alcoholism. *Alcoholism: Clinical and Experimental Research*, *12*, 471–480.

Warburton, D. M. (1988). The puzzle of nicotine use. In M. Lader (Ed.) *The psychopharmacology of addiction* (pp. 27–49). Oxford: Oxford University Press.

Zinberg, N. E. (1981). Social interactions, drug use, and drug research. In J. H. Lowinson & P. Ruiz (Eds) *Substance abuse: Clinical problems and perspectives*. Baltimore, MD: Williams & Wilkins.

11
SPECIAL TOPICS

INTRODUCTION

This section is truly a mixed bag; it contains chapters on fields of psychological research that are sufficiently important to be included but that could not, without distortion, be shoehorned into any of the other sections of the encyclopedia.

Susan Blackmore deals with parapsychology (from the Greek *para*, beside or beyond, + psychology) in chapter 11.1. This is a small but active field of research focusing on psychological phenomena that appear to be paranormal (that is, beyond the normal). This chapter traces the historical development of parapsychology and then summarizes and provides a balanced evaluation of the evidence regarding ESP (extra-sensory perception, or perception without the use of normal sensory processes), PK (psychokinesis, or the movement or change of physical objects by purely mental processes), psychic experiences, out-of-body experiences, and survival after death.

In chapter 11.2 Graham F. Wagstaff discusses hypnosis and the controversy surrounding the interpretation of the various strange phenomena associated with hypnotic behaviour. Wagstaff deals critically with the debate about whether or not hypnosis is (or entails) an altered state of consciousness, the physiology of hypnosis, its apparently transcendent properties, and its major phenomena, including trance logic, hypnotic amnesia, hypnotic analgesia, and hypnotic susceptibility, together with its clinical applications. Hypnosis has occasionally been applied in an attempt to elicit more or better evidence from witnesses in criminal trials; research in that area is discussed in chapter 11.4 in connection with psychology and the law.

In chapter 11.3 Mary Crawford and Rhoda K. Unger provide an expansive survey of various lines of research that converge on gender issues in psychology. Many contemporary psychologists, including the authors of this chapter, distinguish between sex differences, which are the genetically determined biological differences between male and female, and gender differences, which are the products of psychological, social, and cultural influences acting on sex differences. This chapter examines a number of conceptual and methodological issues surrounding research in this area before focusing on gender and development throughout the lifespan, "doing gender" (the effects of cognitive categories based on sex on gender-characteristic patterns of interpersonal interaction), and sexuality and relationships in sociocultural context. Some additional comments on gender issues in psychology, focusing specifically on ethical issues, are contained in chapter 12.6 (Anthony Gale).

In chapter 11.4 Robert T. Croyle and Elizabeth F. Loftus survey all major aspects of psychology and the law. Most of the research in this area has focused on aspects of criminal trials, especially the validity of eyewitness testimony and various aspects of jury decision-making. Croyle and Loftus review research in these areas and several others broadly related to aspects of psychology and the law. Many of the research issues raised are directly relevant to the professional practice of forensic (criminological) psychology, which is discussed in depth in chapter 13.4 (Clive R. Hollin).

Finally, chapter 11.5, by John Weinman, is on health psychology. This is an area of research that is concerned with psychological factors relevant to the promotion and maintenance of health and the prevention and treatment of illness, and the identification of psychological causes and correlates of health and illness. This chapter covers all main aspects of research on health psychology, including the relationship between stress and health, which is also discussed in chapter 6.5 (Robert J. Gatchel).

A.M.C.

11.1

PARAPSYCHOLOGY

Susan Blackmore

University of the West of England, Bristol, England

Parapsychology has been a controversial science since its inception, with experimenters claiming results that cannot be explained by chance and critics arguing that the best explanations are methodological flaws, statistical errors, or outright fraud. Methods have gradually improved, but the goal of a conclusively convincing demonstration or a repeatable experiment has not been achieved. Fully automated experiments have provided new evidence, and meta-analyses have revealed consistent features in whole areas of research.

PSYCHICAL RESEARCH AND SPIRITUALISM

The origins of parapsychology are often traced back to the start of spiritualism, a Christian faith with the added dimension of spirit communication through mediumship. Kate and Margaretta Fox are usually credited with being the first mediums. As children in 1848 in the little New York town of Hydesville, they heard raps and banging apparently from the spirit of a man buried beneath their wooden house. Neighbours and visitors wanted to communicate with the spirits themselves and soon the Fox sisters began giving public demonstrations.

From the start there was controversy, with some investigators arguing that the girls were clicking their joints to produce the noises. In a dramatic public confession in 1888 they demonstrated just this and said they had been cheating all along, but later they retracted. Critics accept the confessions as the end of the matter while supporters argue that the sisters were by then penniless and alcoholic and were bribed to confess (Brandon, 1983; Podmore, 1902).

By this time thousands of mediums were practising across Europe and the USA. Spirits were heard speaking through floating trumpets, cold breezes and touches were felt, music mysteriously played, and "ectoplasm", a substance supposedly exuded from the bodies of certain mediums, "materialized" in the form of spirits. In "table tipping", sitters placed their hands on a table's surface and the spirits answered their questions by tipping the table up or banging its legs on the floor. In one of the first experimental studies, the physicist Michael Faraday (1791–1867) tried to determine where the force came from. He stuck pieces of card to the table, under the sitters' fingers, and showed that they slipped along in the direction of the table's movement. It was not the table (pulled by the spirits) but the sitters' hands that moved first. He suggested that the sitters were not frauds but used "unconscious muscular action" (Faraday, 1853).

For him this was the end of the matter, but mediumship continued to grow. Among many famous mediums was Eusapia Palladino, who began her mediumistic career as an orphan in Naples and apparently levitated, materialized extra limbs, caused inexplicable noises, and made furniture glide about. In 1895 she was caught cheating, but some researchers were convinced that she had produced genuine phenomena under controlled conditions (Gauld, 1968). Mediums could readily purchase equipment for augmenting their acts, such as muslin drapes, luminous paint, slates on which spirits could mysteriously reply to questions, and trumpets which could float around unaided in the dark. Whether any mediums operated entirely without such aids has never been resolved. Some argue that any medium who is caught cheating once must be presumed always to be cheating, while others argue that the pressures on even the best of mediums mean that they may resort to fraud in exceptional circumstances. This issue still appears in the arguments about special subjects such as Uri Geller (Randi, 1975).

It is often claimed that one medium, Daniel Dunglas Home (pronounced Hume), was never caught cheating. He worked in reasonably well-lit rooms, unlike many mediums who preferred total darkness. He apparently handled live coals without burning, materialized glowing hands, levitated heavy tables, and even floated out of one window and into the next (Gauld, 1968). The famous chemist, Sir William Crookes, was convinced that his powers implied a new form of energy (Gauld, 1968; Grattan-Guinness, 1982).

Of course, if claims like these were genuine they would present a direct challenge to science. In this late Victorian era physics was enormously successful and Darwinism had come as a threat to many people's beliefs. Evolution in particular and the materialist view in general were strongly opposed by the Church, and some saw spiritualism as providing the evidence they needed to refute them. If the spirits of the dead could appear and speak, then materialism was false. Scientists and scholars began to take the claims seriously and to investigate them. It was in this context that, in 1882, the Society for Psychical Research (SPR) was founded in London.

Among its founder members were Edmund Gurney, Frederick Myers, and Henry Sidgwick, Fellow of Trinity College, Cambridge, and the SPR's first president. They established their objectives, now enshrined in every issue of the *Journal of the Society for Psychical Research*, as "to examine without prejudice or prepossession and in a scientific spirit those faculties of man, real or supposed, which appear to be inexplicable on any generally recognized hypothesis". They established committees to study thought transference, mesmerism, apparitions and haunted houses, and physical phenomena of mediumship.

One of their major motivations was to determine whether there is life after death, or survival. In an enormous project, the "Census of Hallucinations", 17,000 people were asked whether they had ever seen or felt something, or heard a voice, that was not due to any physical cause. Among the recognizable hallucinations of people, far more than could be expected occurred within twelve hours either way of that person's death. It seemed to be evidence for apparitions of the dying. Thousands of accounts of spontaneous experiences were collected and published, including telepathy, psychic dreams, apparitions, and collective hallucinations (Gurney, Myers, & Podmore, 1886).

The problems of drawing conclusions from spontaneous cases were obvious, and many preferred to carry out experiments. The first experiments into thought transference, or telepathy as it became known after 1882 (Grattan-Guinness, 1982), used what would now be called "free-response" methods. For example, the percipient or receiver tried to draw the picture the agent or sender was looking at. Although many striking hits were obtained, it is difficult to assess how many would be expected by chance. However, even in the 1880s statistical methods for estimating probabilities of guessing at playing cards or numbers were being developed, though the first large-scale experiments of this kind were probably those carried out in 1912 by John Coover (1917). This laid the foundation on which parapsychology was to be built.

THE FOUNDING OF PARAPSYCHOLOGY

Two people were almost entirely responsible for the founding of parapsychology in the 1930s – J. B. Rhine and his wife Louisa (Mauskopf & McVaugh, 1980). Trained as biologists they, like the psychical researchers before them, wanted to find evidence against a purely materialist view of human nature. Indeed the laboratory which now continues the work they began at Duke University in Durham, North Carolina, is called the Foundation for Research on the Nature of Man. Although their aims were the same, they wanted to get right away from any associations with spiritualism and bring their new science firmly into the laboratory. They renamed it parapsychology, began to develop experimental methods, and defined their terms operationally. Throughout their long research careers J. B. Rhine concentrated more on the experimental methods and Louisa Rhine on the collection of spontaneous cases (L. E. Rhine, 1981). He preferred to tackle the problem of verification by using statistical and experimental techniques; she preferred to collect large numbers of cases, hoping that they would teach us something about the nature of psychic phenomena even if many could never be verified.

In 1934 J. B. Rhine's first book launched the term "extrasensory perception" (ESP). This was a general term used to cover three types of communication supposedly occurring without the use of the senses: telepathy, in which the information comes from another person; clairvoyance, in which it comes from distant objects or events; and precognition, in which the information comes from the future (see Figure 1).

In the early telepathy experiments a receiver or percipient had to guess the identity of a target being looked at by an agent or sender. To make the task as easy as possible, a set of simple symbols was developed and made into cards called Zener cards (after their designer) or ESP cards. They consisted of a circle, square, cross, star, and wavy lines – 5 of each in a pack of 25 cards (see Figure 2). The order of the cards was determined initially by shuffling and later by the use of random number tables or other methods. It is extremely important for targets in ESP experiments to be properly

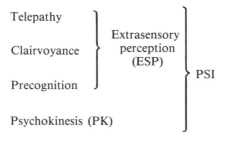

Figure 1   The four types of psi

Figure 2 The five symbols on traditional Zener cards. A pack consists of 25 cards, five of each symbol. They were designed to be simple and easy to distinguish but are tedious to use

randomized so that the results cannot be affected by systematic biases of any kind. Shuffling is not an adequate method.

In clairvoyance experiments the pack was randomized out of sight of anyone, and in precognition experiments its order was decided only *after* the guesses had been made. To obtain significant results, even with a very weak ESP effect, long series of guesses were made. The technique appeared to be successful, and the Rhines reported results that were far beyond what could be expected by chance.

Also in 1934 they began another controversial step, research into psychokinesis (PK). Many of their subjects claimed to be able to affect things at a distance by the power of the mind, and a gambler suggested they might test whether he could influence the roll of dice. Rhine subsequently turned this into an experimental method, first using hand-thrown dice and then a

975

dice-throwing machine. The results were not as impressive as the ESP results but nevertheless seemed to suggest some paranormal ability, or "psi" power (J. B. Rhine, 1947). The term "psi" came to be used as a general term to cover any paranormal phenomena or the hypothesized mechanism underlying them. It includes both ESP and PK (see Figure 1).

The development of these definitions was an important step, but the definitions themselves are problematic (Alcock, 1981). All are negative in the sense that they depend on ruling out "normal" communication before the paranormal can be assumed. Progress in parapsychology's experimental methods has necessarily been designed to exclude the "normal" ever more securely. However, this inevitably leaves it open for critics to argue for ever more devious ways in which sensory communication or outright fraud might occur. Another consequence of some definitions is that the field of parapsychology is ever-shrinking. For example, hypnosis used to be considered part of psychical research, as did hallucinations and lucid dreams, until psychologists made progress in understanding them. As the psychologist Edwin Boring (1966) put it, a scientific success is a failure for psychical research. This is inevitable if parapsychology is defined as the study of the paranormal (e.g., Thalbourne, 1982) and this may be one reason why some parapsychologists now prefer to define their subject matter in terms of psychic *experiences*, without commitment to a particular explanation (e.g., Broughton, 1991).

THE DEVELOPMENT OF PARAPSYCHOLOGY

The controversy provoked by the Rhines spread around the world. Early problems in methodology and experimental design were detected, such as being able to read the symbols from the back of the cards, inadequate shuffling of the cards, biased dice, incomplete separation of the subjects, or the possibility of recording errors. When these were ironed out, some significant results continued. Their statistics were also criticized until in 1937 the President of the American Institute of Mathematical Statistics declared that if the experiments were properly performed, the statistical analysis was essentially valid (J. B. Rhine, 1947). Soon others, appreciating the importance of these findings, if they were true, tried to replicate them.

Among these was S. G. Soal, a mathematician at Queen Mary College, London, who spent five unsuccessful years trying. Another researcher, Whateley Carington, had been successful using objects on his mantelpiece as targets and had found that sometimes his subjects guessed the object before or after the one they were supposed to be guessing, a phenomenon that later became known as the "displacement effect" (J. B. Rhine, 1969). Following Carington's suggestions, Soal checked for guessing targets ahead and behind. In the results of one subject, Basil Shackleton, he found significant scores and went on to use Shackleton in what became his most famous experiments.

The odds against the results he obtained occurring by chance were astronomical (Soal & Bateman, 1954). To ensure that Shackleton could not be cheating, rigid controls were employed and other scientists used as observers throughout. These experiments, along with Rhine's, became the mainstay of the evidence for ESP (West, 1954).

As so often happens with significant results, accusations of fraud abounded. One of Soal's agents claimed that she had seen Soal changing figures in the target list. This provoked a series of many re-analyses and investigations of Soal's work, none of which could conclusively incriminate or exonerate him. In 1978 Betty Markwick, a member of the Society for Psychical Research in London, hoped to clear Soal's name by using a computer to search through the voluminous log tables he claimed to have used to decide his targets. She failed to find them. Only a tedious hand search revealed some repeated sequences and then the odd discovery that some sequences had numbers added in. All of these corresponded to hits, and when they were removed the results fell to chance (Markwick, 1978). It had taken a quarter of a century to solve the mystery and prove that Soal had cheated, and in that time thousands of people had been convinced that this evidence for ESP was genuine. As in many other cases, finding out whether he had cheated required at least as much work as the original experiments.

Meanwhile, research in parapsychology continued. In addition to finding subjects who could score higher than chance expectation, some subjects scored significantly *below* chance expectation, that is, psi missing. A decline effect was also found, whereby results tended to decline from the start of an experiment or session, as though novelty or freshness was required for success. These "signs of psi" added to the evidence but still did not reveal much, if anything, about the new phenomena that supposedly had been found. Some researchers tired of simply seeking more and more evidence to convince the critics and wanted to find out more about psi itself, in what would now be called "process oriented" rather than "proof oriented" research.

One of the best known of the early findings was the "sheep–goat" effect. Gertrude Schmeidler divided subjects into believers, whom she called sheep, and disbelievers or goats. She found that sheep consistently scored higher than goats, who often psi-missed (Schmeidler & McConnell, 1958). A review of sheep–goat experiments many years later indicated that the effect is widespread across many experiments (Palmer, 1971) suggesting that belief or motivation might be important in psi ability.

If experimenters needed these qualities too, it might explain the failure of some replication attempts. In a famous two-experimenter study, Donald West of Cambridge University obtained null results while his colleague, Fisk, was successful (West, 1954). There have been many suggestions that some experimenters are psi-inhibitory while others have the necessary attitudes or beliefs. That is, there could be a psi-mediated experimenter effect in addition to the more usual effect of the experimenter's personality or way of handling the subjects (Irwin, 1989; White, 1977). Critics argue that the differences are because some experimenters are more careful or carry out better experiments than others and that some experimenters cheat.

This parallels another long-standing issue in parapsychology – whether it is better to use special subjects who can produce powerful effects unpredictably and have to be guarded carefully for fraud, or many ordinary subjects who may produce weak effects over many experiments. There have been many famous special subjects, such as Pavel Stepanek, who could guess the colours of concealed cards, Malcolm Bessent, who took part in many kinds of experiments, Ted Serios, who apparently affected unexposed film, and Uri Geller, whose speciality was bending metal. However, most of the standard methods of contemporary experimental research in parapsychology now use unselected subjects. The most important of these are the free-response ESP techniques and PK with random number generators (RNGs).

FREE-RESPONSE ESP RESEARCH

One of the constraints of the early Rhine work was that guessing long series of cards was exceedingly boring. Even when results kept coming, the subjects did not enjoy it and more often results were poor. By contrast, reports of psychic dreams, premonitions, and real-life ESP abounded. The challenge was to capture this in the lab.

One of the best known attempts was the ESP-dream research begun by Montague Ullman in 1960. With the development of electroencephalograph (EEG) recording it became possible to detect when a sleeping person was likely to be dreaming. In experiments at the Maimonides Medical Center in New York the subject slept while an agent looked at a randomly chosen target (Ullman, Krippner, & Vaughan, 1973). Unlike the card-guessing experiments, the targets used could be anything from interesting and colourful pictures to multisensory environments. Sometimes dramatic correspondences were found between the dreams the subject reported and the target. Just as in the early thought transference experiments, this presented a problem of assessment. With such a large amount of material and complex targets, some stunning correspondences are only to be expected, but how many? The solution, and one which has been used in many forms since, was to provide a set of possible targets, only one of which was the actual target. On the basis of the dream, the subject or an independent judge could match up the dream imagery with each of the set and try to identify the true target. In this way the results of a free-response experiment could be subjected to simple statistical tests.

In the case of the dream experiments the results for many subjects were better than would be expected by chance. However, other laboratories did not successfully replicate these findings, possibly because it is very time-consuming and expensive to use a dream laboratory, and the method was dropped.

Instead, other free-response methods were developed. One was "remote viewing". In this case one experimenter goes to a randomly selected remote location and stays there, observing or walking about, for a specified length of time. Meanwhile the subject sits comfortably and relaxes, reporting any impressions or images that arise. Afterwards the subject, or an independent judge, tries to match up the impressions with a set of possible target locations and pick the right one. This method was used by Russell Targ and Harold Puthoff (1977) at the Stanford Research Institute in California and was apparently highly successful. However, two psychologists, David Marks and Richard Kammann, failed to replicate the findings and argued that the previous success had been because the transcripts contained clues as to which previous targets had already been used, increasing the chances of a hit. This lead to a controversy in the prestigious journal *Nature* and attempts by others to confirm or refute the relevance of these clues, a controversy which was never entirely resolved (Marks & Kammann, 1980).

Since then others have claimed success with the remote viewing technique and new methods of analysis have been developed including the use of fuzzy sets. It is often argued that if psi is a real power it ought to have practical applications. Betting seems never to have been one of them, and skeptics have pointed out that casinos reliably continue to make money. However, remote viewing has been used in "psychic archaeology" to find lost sites and, in its most controversial application, to predict price fluctuations of silver futures on the stock market. This attempt, by a group called Delphi Associates, initially produced nine consecutive hits and a hefty profit, but subsequent attempts were not so lucrative.

Since then the most successful of the free-response methods has undoubtedly been the *Ganzfeld* technique, first used for psi experiments in 1974 by Charles Honorton. He argued that the reason ESP occurs in dreams, meditation, and reverie is because they are all states of reduced sensory input and increased internal attention. He tried to find a way to produce such a "psi-conducive state" without the expense of a dream laboratory. His answer was to tape halved ping-pong balls over the subjects' eyes and play soothing sea-sounds or hissing "white noise" through headphones while they lay on a comfortable couch or reclining chair. This is not total sensory deprivation in complete darkness and silence but does deprive the person of patterned input and encourages internal imagery. This, argued Honorton, would be conducive to ESP.

It appeared to be highly successful. He and his team at the Psychophysical Research Laboratories in Princeton, New Jersey, put many subjects into *Ganzfeld* while an agent looked at a randomly chosen target picture. The subjects were able to pick the correct target picture from a set of others more often than would be predicted by chance. Although several other researchers were unable to replicate the findings, some succeeded, and a replication rate of over 50 per cent was claimed for the technique. Given the problem of replication in parapsychology this appeared to be something of a breakthrough.

In 1982 the "*Ganzfeld* Debate" was launched at a conference marking the centenary of the founding of the Society for Psychical Research. Psychologist Ray Hyman reviewed the entire database and carried out a meta-analysis (in which the results of many similar studies are analysed together). He argued that the replication rate was actually far lower and that there were problems of over-analysis, bias, and many procedural flaws in the experiments. He also found that the most successful studies were those with the most flaws: claims which suggested the entire effect was an artifact (Hyman, 1985). Honorton responded with his own meta-analysis, finding no correlation between the number of flaws and the outcome. In addition, he found that the large effect size was distributed throughout the database and was not dependent on the outstanding results of any one experimenter (Honorton, 1985).

Like many controversies in parapsychology, this one has also never been resolved. However, it led directly to sceptics and parapsychologists coming together to decide what they considered to be serious flaws and what would constitute an acceptable experiment. In the light of these ideas Honorton went on to design a fully automated *Ganzfeld* experiment in which there was little room for any human errors or deliberate fraud. The results of several such experiments were statistically significant and showed consistently better performance using dynamic targets than static ones. When compared to the results of previous meta-analyses, a similar effect size was found and there were better results using senders and receivers who knew each other and who had previous experience of *Ganzfeld* (Honorton et al., 1990). These appear to be consistent and meaningful results that present a real challenge to present-day critics.

Meta-analysis has also been applied to forced-choice studies of precognition. Analysing over 300 studies carried out during a 50-year period, Honorton and Ferrari (1989) found a much smaller effect size than with *Ganzfeld*, but again it was consistent throughout the database and not dependent on study quality. Selective reporting could not explain the effect since they calculated that for each reported study it would need 46 unreported failures to reduce the effect to statistical non-significance. In addition they found that the best results were obtained with short time intervals and with preselected subjects, tested individually and given feedback on their scores.

These findings might suggest that the failure of so many ESP experiments is not because there is no psi but because they have used the easier forced-choice techniques with unselected subjects, tested in groups. The use of meta-analysis constitutes significant progress in that the claims cannot be refuted by finding a single flaw or isolated instance of fraud. They could be undermined only by finding widespread undetected flaws, wholesale cheating, or problems with the meta-analytic techniques themselves.

PK AND RANDOM EVENTS

Psychokinesis (PK) research has come a long way since the studies of table-tipping and levitation. Some have still involved large systems, or macro-PK, such as the attempts to get a purely invented "imaginary ghost" called Philip to levitate tables like an old-fashioned spirit (Owen & Sparrow, 1976); or studies of metal bending with Uri Geller and the many children who emulated him; and studies of the influence on biological systems by William Braud at the Mind Science Foundation in Texas (Braud & Schlitz, 1989). However, by far the majority of research has turned to micro-PK, the supposed effect of the human mind on microscopic, quantum mechanical, or probabilistic systems.

In 1970, Helmut Schmidt, at the Durham Institute for Parapsychology, began work with a new kind of PK machine. The subject's task was to watch a circle of nine lamps and make whichever lamp was lit move clockwise or anti-clockwise. Although the subject did not need to know anything about the mechanism, it actually used a strontium-90 radioactive source emitting particles at random intervals and a Geiger counter to detect them. Since then many other kinds of PK machine have been used and have made it possible to tackle some tricky questions.

For example, what is the difference between PK and precognition? Whenever subjects successfully predict an outcome it is possible to say that instead of using precognition they have actually used PK and brought the event about. This may seem impossible or just unacceptable if the event is a natural disaster or a plane crash, but in experimental situations it seems quite plausible. Schmidt designed a special experiment in which the random number generator was wired up in different ways to test either precognition or PK but the difference could not be detected by the subject (Schmidt & Pantas, 1972). In other experiments the link between the particles emitted and the display that the subject saw was either simple or complex. In either case it seemed to make no difference. Psi seemed to be goal-oriented rather than dependent on the nature of the underlying task.

Another concerned the moment at which the psi is supposed to occur. According to one type of theory, the observational theories, it is the moment of feedback to the subject that is important, not the moment at which the particles are emitted. The display the subject sees and the motivation or concentration at that time are what counts. If this were so it should be possible to delay feedback and still get PK effects. In 1976 Schmidt reported successful results with pre-recorded targets. A radioactive source was used to generate random numbers, and these were converted into clicks on an audio tape or movements of a needle. The subject had to try to influence the clicks to be more in the left or right ear, more strong or weak clicks, or whatever. The strange thing was that the tapes had been made hours, days, or even weeks before. To refute the possibility that subjects might be actually changing the tape by PK, copies of the original output were kept, unseen by anyone, and compared after the experiment was completed. Even more extraordinary was that when some subjects were given the same targets four times over, the effect was stronger, again implying that it was the feedback to the subjects that was important (Schmidt, 1976).

If time-displaced PK seems impossible or nonsensical it is worth bearing in mind that all forms of psi are, from some perspectives, impossible, and this is why the controversies over psi have been so heated and apparently insoluble. The micro-PK experiments have never been so successful with experimenters other than Schmidt, leading some to reject them, but recently Schmidt has designed a PK experiment in which outside observers are needed for crucial phases. This ensures that he alone could not product significant results by cheating. It would need all the people involved to be in collusion. The first experiment of this kind produced a fairly small, but still significant, effect (Schmidt, Morris, & Rudolph, 1986).

Although other PK researchers have not replicated Schmidt's findings, they have developed related machines to act as random event generators (REGs). At the Princeton Engineering Anomalies Research Lab (PEAR) Bob Jahn and his colleagues have collected enormous amounts of data using quantum mechanical REGs. Subjects have some trials in which they have to influence the REG in one direction, some in the opposite direction, and others baseline or resting trials. This allows for comparisons to rule out any bias in the machine itself; all the data ever collected are automatically recorded so that data selection cannot influence the results. The results have produced a tiny, but apparently reliable, deviation from chance expectation.

It is difficult to know how to interpret results such as these. They do not appear to be anything like the classic idea of a mental influence on a physical system, and if they are it must be an extremely weak one. Some parapsychologists interpret it as a mental effect that changes the probabilities of quantum mechanical events. Another approach is that psi is used to bring about desired outcomes, both in ordinary life and experiments, through a "psi-mediated instrumental response" (Stanford, 1990). Ed May at Stanford Research Institute has developed the theory of "intuitive data sorting", which suggests that subjects obtain the desired outcome by selecting the right starting-point for a series of trials rather than influencing each random event in turn. These theories each lead to different testable predictions about the distribution of scores in psi experiments (Walker, 1987).

Critics argue that the effects are very weak, confined to a few investigators, and are probably statistical or experimental artifacts and not paranormal at all. As in the case of the *Ganzfeld*, meta-analysis has been applied. Dean Radin and Roger Nelson (1989) analysed the results of over 800 studies and found chance results in control conditions but deviations from chance in experimental conditions. This effect, though exceedingly small in size, was consistent throughout the database, not related to methodological quality and not dependent on the work of just a few investigators. They conclude that there is an effect of consciousness on physical systems. This connection to consciousness seems unwarranted as yet and it might better be described as an effect of intention.

Alternatively, it could be argued that the relevant flaws have not been found, the chance model with which the effects are compared is inappropriate, or even that an anomaly without a firm theoretical basis is not of interest. Whatever its explanation turns out to be, there does at least seem to be an anomaly in need of explanation, and this is generally the conclusion drawn from other meta-analyses in parapsychology (Utts, 1991).

PSYCHIC EXPERIENCES

The other major areas of parapsychology deal mainly with experiences outside the laboratory. Some odd experiences are not usually considered part of parapsychology, such as sightings of UFOs or strange creatures, earth mysteries, hypnotic regression, fire-walking, astrology, and fortune telling, although some of these have attracted serious study (Frazier, 1991). Those which do form part of parapsychology include spontaneous cases of apparent telepathy, clairvoyance or precognition; psychic dreams and premonitions; poltergeists, apparitions, and hauntings; and out-of-body and near-death experiences.

SPONTANEOUS CASES

Spontaneous cases of telepathy or precognition are notoriously difficult to verify convincingly. The problems of memory distortions and relying on witnesses' reports have been known since the early days and never entirely overcome; perhaps this is why such investigations are rare in modern parapsychology. Attempts have been made to establish premonitions bureaux to which people could send their predictions before they come true, but these have not produced strong evidence of successful prediction. However, many people continue to report apparently psychic experiences. Indeed, personal experience is often given as the main reason for believing in the paranormal, and surveys show that about 50 per cent of the population believe in ESP (Gallup & Newport, 1991).

Possibly this belief reflects the occurrence of genuine psychic events, but other alternatives have been studied. For example Susan Blackmore has suggested that the fact that people underestimate chance probabilities underlies their tendency to interpret ordinary coincidences as psychic events and so bolster their belief. In line with this she found that sheep were more biased in their probability judgements than goats, a finding subsequently confirmed by others (Blackmore & Troscianko, 1985; Brugger, Landis, & Regard, 1990). Other studies have found poorer reasoning skills in believers (Wierzbicki, 1985). Another approach relates psychic and mystical experiences to instability in the temporal lobes. Several studies have found that people with more temporal lobe epileptic signs also report more subjective paranormal experiences (Neppe, 1990; Persinger & Makarec, 1987). Possibly this is due to an increase in a spurious sense of familiarity (as in *déjà vu*) or of emotional salience associated with temporal lobe activity.

Poltergeists have been a traditional area for field research. They are distinguished from apparitions, in which spirits of the dead, or sometimes the living, are apparently seen, and hauntings, in which odd phenomena occur in specific locations.

Parapsychologists have come to regard poltergeists as caused not by the spirits of the dead but by the living, and hence they are sometimes referred to as recurrent spontaneous psychokinesis (RSPK). A review of 500 cases, going back to the sixteenth century, shows features they have in common, in particular the unexplained movements of objects (Gauld & Cornell, 1979). Objects are sometimes seen actually flying around, though the beginning of the movement is rarely observed. Often there are unexplained noises, doors opening and closing, and occasionally, as in the Enfield case in north London, levitation of people. Often, but not invariably, the focus of activity is a teenager or sometimes younger children. In the famous Rosenheim case in Germany, an 18-year-old secretary in a lawyer's office was apparently the centre of extraordinary movements of objects, explosions in the light fittings and fuses, and a total disruption of the telephone system. Electricians and telephone engineers were unable to discover the cause of the disturbance. In another well-known case a Miami novelty warehouse was plagued by movements and breakages centring on a 19-year-old Cuban refugee. Although he was said to be unhappy and had been arrested for shop-lifting, and was naturally under suspicion, he was never observed throwing the souvenirs himself (Gauld & Cornell, 1979).

Poltergeist focuses are often said to be unstable, suffering psychological conflict, or living in difficult family situations. A connection to epilepsy has also been suggested, but poltergeists are hard to study and the data far from conclusive. Of course in many putative poltergeist cases the children or adult focus are suspected of fraud, and in some, such as one instance in Cleveland, Ohio, they are caught red-handed. In this case it was a journalist's films which revealed the child throwing a telephone across the room when no one was looking (Randi, 1985). There has been a long history of fraudulent children in psychical research (Nicol, 1985). It is certain that many otherwise astute scientists have been duped by such tricks and that it is not always possible to detect them. Whether all poltergeists are due to trickery is very much a matter of dispute.

OUT-OF-BODY EXPERIENCES

Another phenomenon traditionally studied by parapsychologists but now increasingly becoming part of psychology, is the out-of-body experience (OBE). About 10 per cent of the population claims to have had this experience at least once in their life. Typically they seem to be viewing the world from a location outside their body. It feels as though they, their "spirit", "soul", or "centre of consciousness", has temporarily left the body and is able to travel around without it. OBEs often occur in times of stress, sensory deprivation, deep relaxation, or when close to death. They are often very brief, although some people can learn to induce them at will and take control. The world seen during an OBE is extremely vivid and realistic, and OBEs sometimes claim to see things at a distance that they could not possibly have known about (Blackmore, 1982).

Traditionally, these experiences have been described as "astral projection" in which the astral body leaves the physical. Parapsychologists have tried with little success to find evidence that this other body is detectable or can actually see things. Alternative psychological theories have recently been developed to try to account for the experience in terms of changes in the body image or reconstructions from memory and imagination (Blackmore, 1993; Irwin, 1985).

SURVIVAL OF DEATH

Research into apparitions at the moment of death, mediumistic communication, and other apparent forms of evidence for survival still continue, but not to the extent they did in the early days of psychical research. One problem that has never been resolved is known as the super-ESP hypothesis. If the possibility of ESP and PK is admitted then any evidence that purports to come from a discarnate being could alternatively be said to come from the psi powers of the living. This may have to entail ridiculously complex or powerful forms of ESP, unlike anything seen in the lab (hence the name super-ESP), nevertheless it is always an alternative which makes finding evidence for survival next to impossible.

Attempts have been made to get round this. In the famous "cross-correspondences", during the first three decades of the twentieth century, several mediums independently produced allusions to the same things at the same time, purportedly coming from Frederick Myers (see above) among others, and including obscure but meaningful literary references (Gauld, 1982). Communications like this do not seem to happen today. However, some people are still trying to prove survival. One method is to leave behind a combination lock which can be opened only when the correct number is communicated through a medium. Another is to create a coded message for which the cipher is known to only one person. So far these techniques have not produced any successes.

Another kind of evidence, sometimes said to indicate survival, comes from near-death experiences (NDEs). These are experiences reported by people who have been close to death but have survived. NDErs typically feel peaceful and even joyful. They often seem to float or rush quickly down a dark tunnel with a bright light at the end. The light is warm and even friendly. It may seem like a person greeting them or asking questions to help them evaluate their life and its meaning. Often the experience includes an OBE in which the person seems to observe attempts at resuscitation, or whatever else is going on, from a distance. In the longest or deepest NDEs people may enter other worlds of love and beauty, meet dead friends or relatives, and have experiences which seem to be of mystical understanding and acceptance. Often they report being changed for the better, becoming more caring and less materialistic afterwards.

NDEs were first described in detail by the American physician Raymond Moody (1975), although many isolated cases had been reported before that. Subsequently, more detailed research has confirmed that the experiences take a consistent form and are independent of the cause of the close brush with death or the drugs taken at the time. Indeed it is possible to have all the features of the NDE without being physically close to death, for example in climbers who fall but land safely, or people who think they are about to die but in fact are not. Some researchers argue that the NDE is a glimpse of the afterlife or an alternative reality (Ring, 1980). If something leaves the body in out-of-body experiences, it is argued, that "something" might survive after the physical body is truly dead.

Others argue that the experience is a product of the dying brain. For example drugs such as LSD or even nitrous oxide can induce comparable experiences; the tunnel can be explained by the random firing that occurs in the visual cortex as the brain dies, the blissful feelings may be related to the release of endorphin (a natural opiate in the brain) under stress, and the OBE can be understood in psychological terms (Blackmore, 1993). Many of the phenomena are similar to those induced by temporal lobe stimulation, and it is known that the endorphins released during fear and stress can lead to temporal lobe seizures. Evidence against such explanations is the claim that people during NDEs are able to see things they could not possibly have heard or known about. However, there are very few cases of this kind and even these are very hard to substantiate (Blackmore, 1993). As has occurred in many other areas, what looked like evidence for life after death can be interpreted in alternative ways, in this case ways that also increase our understanding of brain function. Evidence for survival, though often claimed, is elusive.

CRITICISM AND SCEPTICISM

Right from the start of parapsychology there have been constructive critics who have helped it develop the necessary methodological rigour, and extreme critics who have made unwarranted accusations and preferred any alternative to the possibility of the paranormal. Many of the first critics in the 1940s were silenced by the progressing research, but in 1955 a paper in the prestigious journal *Science* argued that "just one good experiment" was still needed (Price, 1955). In the mid-1960s the Swansea psychologist Mark Hansel (1966) argued that most of the impressive results so far could have been obtained by fraud, and he suggested how subjects or experimenters could have looked through windows, used trap doors, or in other ways circumvented the experimental controls. Many parapsychologists felt that these suggestions were far-fetched, but the subsequent exposure of Soal's trickery showed how carefully experiments need to be evaluated.

During the 1970s the issues were argued in the pages of a psychology journal (Moss & Butler, 1978; Rao, 1979), and in the 1980s in the peer review journal, *Behavioral and Brain Sciences* (Alcock, 1987). As well as the British and American Societies for Psychical Research, and the professional Parapsychological Association, there is also now a powerful sceptical organization called the Committee for the Scientific Investigation of Claims of the Paranormal (CSICOP) and many local sceptical groups. Although many of the best researchers are not interested in taking sides and actively encourage cooperation between researchers and critics, the arguments do not appear to be dying down.

After over a century of research into the paranormal, there are very few definite conclusions to be drawn. The methods used have become increasingly sophisticated, as have the types of criticism required. Meta-analyses of large areas of research claim to have found consistent, if weak, effects. We have yet to see whether these herald a new era of progress for this controversial science.

FURTHER READING

Alcock, J. E. (1981). *Parapsychology: Science or magic?* Oxford: Pergamon.
Broughton, R. S. (1991). *Parapsychology: The controversial science.* New York: Ballantine.
Edge, H. L., Morris, R. L., Palmer, J., & Rush, J. H. (1986). *Foundations of parapsychology: Exploring the boundaries of human capability.* London: Routledge & Kegan Paul.
Irwin, H. J. (1989). *An introduction to parapsychology.* Jefferson, NC: McFarland.
Kurtz, P. (1985). *A skeptic's handbook of parapsychology.* Buffalo, NY: Prometheus.

REFERENCES

Alcock, J. E. (1981). *Parapsychology: Science or magic?* Oxford: Pergamon.

Alcock, J. E. (1987). Parapsychology: Science of the anomalous or search for the soul? *Behavioral and Brain Sciences*, *10*, 553–643 (including commentary by other authors).

Blackmore, S. J. (1982). *Beyond the body: An investigation of out-of-the-body experiences.* London: Heinemann.

Blackmore, S. J. (1993). *Dying to live: Science and the near-death experience.* London: Grafton.

Blackmore, S. J., & Troscianko, T. S. (1985). Belief in the paranormal: Probability judgements, illusory control, and the "chance baseline shift". *British Journal of Psychology*, *76*, 459–468.

Boring, E. G. (1966). Introduction. In C. E. M. Hansel, *ESP: A scientific evaluation* (pp. xiii–xxi). New York: Scribners.

Brandon, R. (1983). *The spiritualists.* London: Weidenfeld & Nicolson.

Braud, W., & Schlitz, M. (1989). A methodology for the objective study of transpersonal imagery. *Journal of Scientific Exploration*, *3*, 43–63.

Broughton, R. S. (1991). *Parapsychology: The controversial science.* New York: Ballantine.

Brugger, P., Landis, T., & Regard, M. (1990). A "sheep-goat effect" in repetition avoidance: Extra-sensory perception as an effect of subjective probability? *British Journal of Psychology*, *81*, 455–468.

Coover, J. E. (1917). *Experiments in psychical research at Leland Stanford Junior University*, Psychical Research Monograph, Stanford, CA: Leland Stanford University Publications.

Faraday, M. (1853). Experimental investigation of table-moving. *The Athenaeum*, July, 801–803.

Frazier, K. (Ed.) (1991). *The hundredth monkey and other paradigms of the paranormal.* Buffalo, NY: Prometheus.

Gallup, G. H., & Newport, F. (1991). Belief in paranormal phenomena among adult Americans. *Skeptical Inquirer*, *15*, 137–146.

Gauld, A. (1968). *The founders of psychical research.* London: Routledge & Kegan Paul.

Gauld, A. (1982). *Mediumship and survival: A century of investigations.* London: Heinemann.

Gauld, A., & Cornell, A. D. (1979). *Poltergeists.* London: Routledge & Kegan Paul.

Grattan-Guinness, I. (1982). *Psychical research: A guide to its history, principles and practices.* Wellingborough, Northants: Aquarian.

Gurney, E., Myers, F. W. H., & Podmore, F. (1886). *Phantasms of the living.* London: Trubner.

Hansel, C. E. M. (1966). *ESP: A scientific evaluation.* New York: Scribners.

Honorton, H. (1985). A meta-analysis of psi ganzfeld research: A response to Hyman. *Journal of Parapsychology*, *49*, 51–91.

Honorton, C., & Ferrari, D. C. (1989). "Future telling": A meta-analysis of forced-choice precognition experiments, 1935–1987. *Journal of Parapsychology*, *53*, 281–308.

Honorton, H., Berger, R. E., Varvoglis, M. P., Quant, M., Derr, P. Schechter, E. I., & Ferrari, D. C. (1990). Psi communication in the ganzfeld: Experiments with an automated testing system and a comparison with a meta-analysis of earlier studies. *Journal of Parapsychology*, *54*, 99–139.

Hyman, R. (1985). The Ganzfeld psi experiment: A critical appraisal. *Journal of Parapsychology*, *49*, 3–49.

Irwin, H. J. (1985). *Flight of mind: A psychological study of the out-of-body experience*. Metuchen, NJ: Scarecrow.

Irwin, H. J. (1989). *An introduction to parapsychology*. Jefferson, NC: McFarland.

Marks, D., & Kammann, R. (1980). *The psychology of the psychic*. Buffalo, NY: Prometheus.

Markwick, B. (1978). The Soal-Goldney experiments with Basil Shackleton: New evidence of data manipulation. *Proceedings of the Society for Psychical Research*, *56*, 250–281.

Mauskopf, S. H., & McVaugh, M. R. (1980). *The elusive science: Origins of experimental psychical research*. Baltimore, MD: Johns Hopkins University Press.

Moody, R. (1975). *Life after life*. Covinda, GA: Mockingbird.

Moss, S., & Butler, D. C. (1978). The scientific credibility of ESP. *Perceptual and Motor Skills*, *46*, 1063–1079.

Neppe, V. M. (1990). Anomalistic experience and the cerebral cortex. In S. Krippner (Ed.) *Advances in parapsychological research* (vol. 6, pp. 168–183). Jefferson, NC: McFarland.

Nicol, J. F. (1985). Fraudulent children in psychical research. In P. Kurtz (Ed.) *A skeptic's handbook of parapsychology* (pp. 275–286). Buffalo, NY: Prometheus.

Owen, I. M., & Sparrow, M. (1976). *Conjuring up Philip: An adventure in psychokinesis*. Toronto: Fitzhenry & Whiteside.

Palmer, J. (1971). Scoring in ESP tests as a function of belief in ESP. Part 1: The sheep–goat effect. *Journal of the American Society for Psychical Research*, *65*, 373–408.

Persinger, M. A., & Makarec, K. (1987). Temporal lobe epileptic signs and correlative behaviours displayed by normal populations. *Journal of General Psychology*, *114*, 179–195.

Podmore, F. (1902). *Modern spiritualism: A history and a criticism*. London: Methuen.

Price, G. R. (1955). Science and the supernatural. *Science*, *122*, 359–367.

Radin, D. I., & Nelson, R. D. (1989). Evidence for consciousness-related anomalies in random physical systems. *Foundations of Physics*, *19*, 1499–1514.

Randi, J. (1975). *The truth about Uri Geller*. Buffalo, NY: Prometheus.

Randi, J. (1985). The Columbus poltergeist case: Part 1. *Skeptical Inquirer*, *9*, 221–235.

Rao, K. R. (1979). On "The scientific credibility of ESP". *Perceptual and Motor Skills*, *49*, 415–429.

Rhine, J. B. (1934). *Extrasensory perception*. Boston, MA: Bruce Humphries.

Rhine, J. B. (1947). *The reach of the mind*. New York: Sloane.

Rhine, J. B. (1969). Position effects in psi test results. *Journal of Parapsychology*, *33*, 136–157.

Rhine, L. E. (1981). *The invisible picture: A study of psychic experiences*. Jefferson, NC: McFarland.

Ring, K. (1980). *Life at death*. New York: Coward, McCann & Geoghegan.

Schmeidler, G. R., & McConnell, R. A. (1958). *ESP and personality patterns*. New Haven, CT: Yale University Press.

Schmidt, H. (1976). PK effect on pre-recorded targets. *Journal of the American Society for Psychical Research*, *70*, 267–292.

Schmidt, H., & Pantas, L. (1972). PK tests with internally different machines. *Journal of Parapsychology*, *36*, 222–232.

Schmidt, H., Morris, R., & Rudolph, L. (1986). Channeling evidence for a PK effect to independent observers. *Journal of Parapsychology, 50*, 1–15.

Soal, S. G., & Bateman, F. (1954). *Modern experiments in telepathy*. London: Faber & Faber.

Stanford, R. (1990). An experimentally testable model for spontaneous psi events: A review of related evidence and concepts from parapsychology and other sciences. In S. Krippner (Ed.) *Advances in parapsychological research* (vol. 6, pp. 54–167). Jefferson, NC: McFarland.

Targ, R., & Puthoff, H. (1977). *Mind-reach*. New York: Delacorte.

Thalbourne, M. A. (1982). *A glossary of terms used in parapsychology*. London: Heinemann.

Ullman, M., Krippner, S., & Vaughan, A. (1973). *Dream telepathy*. London: Turnstone.

Utts, J. (1991). Replication and meta-analysis in parapsychology. *Statistical Science, 6*, 363–403 (with comments by other authors).

Walker, E. H. (1987). A comparison of the intuitive data sorting and quantum mechanical observer theories. *Journal of Parapsychology, 51*, 217–227.

West, D. (1954). *Psychical research today*. London: Duckworth.

White, R. A. (1977). The influence of the experimenter motivation, attitudes and methods of handling subjects in psi test results. In B. Wolman (Ed.) *Handbook of parapsychology* (pp. 273–303). Jefferson, NC: McFarland.

Wierzbicki, M. (1985). Reasoning errors and belief in the paranormal. *Journal of Social Psychology, 125*, 489–494.

11.2

HYPNOSIS

Graham F. Wagstaff
University of Liverpool, England

Although some writers, claim that hypnotic techniques can be traced back to ancient times, it is more often assumed that the origins of modern hypnosis are to be found in the practitioners of "magnetic medicine", in particular Franz Anton Mesmer (1734–1815). Mesmer proposed that the human body was filled with a magnetic fluid, that disease resulted from a disequilibrium in this fluid, and that by using techniques with his patients, such as making passes over them, touching them, and staring into their eyes, he could correct this disequilibrium and effect cures. However, in 1784 two commissions were appointed to investigate Mesmer's activities, they concluded that the alleged magnetic phenomena were simply the result of imagination (Wagstaff, 1981).

The coining of the term "hypnosis" itself (derived from the Greek *hypnos* or sleep) is usually attributed to the Manchester surgeon James Braid (1795–1860), although the term "hypnotism" is to be found in French dictionaries published several decades before Braid's principal work (Gravitz & Gerton, 1984). Braid, like some previous observers of mesmerism, had concluded that mesmerized subjects had fallen into a sleep-like state. This idea was then developed most notably by the French neurologist Jean Charcot (1825–1893), who asserted that the hypnotic state was an hysterical condition that involved three stages, lethargy, catalepsy, and somnambulism. A famous and very vigorous disagreement then arose between Charcot and his followers at the Salpêtrière hospital, and Hippolyte Bernheim (1840–1919) and his followers at the University of Nancy. Bernheim proposed that hypnosis is a non-pathological state and that hypnotic phenomena are primarily the result of suggestion; indeed, he argued that the hypnotic induction ritual does not necessarily enhance the effectiveness of suggestion.

The role of imagination and suggestion in hypnosis has continued to be a source of considerable controversy, to the extent that some contemporary theorists contend that to explain hypnotic phenomena we do not need to postulate an hypnotic state at all. As a result a continuing debate exists between those theorists, often loosely referred to as "state" theorists, who adhere to the notion of hypnosis as an altered state of consciousness, and "non-state" theorists, who reject this notion (Fellows, 1990).

HYPNOSIS AS AN ALTERED STATE

According to the classic state view, hypnosis is seen as an altered state of consciousness with various depths, such that the deeper one enters the hypnotic state the more likely one is to manifest hypnotic phenomena (Bowers, 1983). This state is alleged by some to occur spontaneously, but it is normally brought about through induction procedures, such as eye fixation and vocal suggestions for sleep and relaxation. In academic research, susceptibility to hypnosis is usually measured by means of standardized scales; commonly used are the Stanford Hypnotic Susceptibility Scale (forms A, B, and C), and the Harvard Group Scale of Hypnotic Susceptibility. This scales usually start off with an induction ritual followed by various suggestions, such as hand lowering ("Your hand is heavy and falling"), amnesia ("You will find it difficult to remember"), and sometimes an hallucination ("There is a fly buzzing round your head").

Most modern state theorists contend that hypnosis is an altered state of consciousness that enables subjects to release the "dissociative" capacities that lie within them (see e.g., J. Barber, 1991). Of these approaches, undoubtedly the most influential is Hilgard's "neo-dissociation theory" (Hilgard, 1986, 1991). Basing his ideas on those of the early dissociationists such as Prince and Janet, Hilgard argues that there exist multiple systems of control that are not all conscious at the same time. Normally these cognitive control systems are under the influence of a central control structure, or "executive ego", that controls and monitors the other systems; but when a subject enters hypnosis, the hypnotist takes away much of the normal control and monitoring such that, in response to suggestion, motor movements are experienced as involuntary, memory and perception are distorted, and hallucinations are perceived as real. To demonstrate this principle, Hilgard frequently refers to the "hidden-observer" phenomenon, whereby a subject is "hypnotized" and given the following instruction:

> When I place my hand on your shoulder, I shall be able to talk to a hidden part of you that knows things are going on in your body, things that are unknown to the part of you to which I am now talking. The part to which I am now talking will not know what you are telling me or even that you are talking.... You will remember that there is a part of you that knows many things that are going on that may be hidden from either your normal consciousness or the hypnotized part of you. (Knox, Morgan, & Hilgard, 1974, p. 842)

Hilgard and his associates claim that, using this technique on "hypnotized" subjects, they are able to access, or talk to, other control systems of which the subject might otherwise be unaware.

The concept at dissociation is particularly useful for state theorists as it provides a possible explanation for two of the fundamental assumptions of the traditional view of hypnosis: first, when "under hypnosis", subjects typically experience suggested effects as involuntary "happenings", not as deliberate, voluntary activities, and second, hypnotic performance can transcend normal waking performance, or at least hypnotic procedures enable subjects to experience effects in a unique or unusual way; thus, for example, most state theorists accept that hypnotized subjects possess a special capacity to control pain and can experience amnesia and hallucinations in a unique way (Bowers, 1983; Bowers & Davidson, 1991; Hilgard & Hilgard, 1983).

The state view has tended to dominate the popular conception of hypnosis, and perhaps one of the major reasons for this is the dramatic nature of many hypnotic phenomena; for example, "hypnotized" subjects can allegedly tolerate surgery without pain, regress back to childhood with great accuracy, be made deaf, blind, and amnesic, hallucinate objects and people "as real as real", and perform complex tasks without awareness of doing so. Such phenomena might suggest that some rather exotic process is at work in hypnosis. However, the idea of hypnosis as an altered state has been subject to a concerted attack from those who deny that any special process is involved.

THE NON-STATE APPROACH

Scepticism concerning the notion of hypnosis as an altered state has mounted since the 1960s (see, e.g., T. X. Barber, 1969; Sarbin & Coe, 1972; Spanos, 1991; Wagstaff, 1981). Although they differ in their emphases, non-state theorists argue that hypnotic phenomena are readily explicable in terms of more mundane psychological concepts, mainly from the areas of social and cognitive psychology, such as attitudes, expectancies, beliefs, compliance, imagination, attention, concentration, distraction, and relaxation.

To many non-state theorists the hypnotic situation is best seen as a social interaction in which both hypnotist and subject enact roles; the role of the hypnotic subjects being to present themselves as "hypnotized" according to previous expectations and cues available in the immediate situation. This does not mean that hypnotic behaviours are necessarily faked or sham (though some may be); the subject may become very involved in the role and may use a variety of strategies to successfully bring about the desired effects. For example, in response to an arm-lowering suggestion, subjects may try to imagine weights on the arm, or if amnesia is suggested, they may try to forget by employing a distraction strategy. In fact, Wagstaff (1991) has proposed that hypnotic responding may involve three stages. First, the subject figures out what is expected on the basis of previous experience and the hypnotist's instructions. Second, the subject employs imaginative or other strategies to try to bring about the suggested effects, and third, if the strategies fail, or are judged to be inappropriate, the subject either gives up, or reverts to behavioural compliance or faking. Non-state theorists thus question the assumption that hypnotic behaviour is automatic; for example, according to Wagstaff (1981) much alleged involuntary behaviour may simply be a pretence, and Spanos (1986a, 1991) argues that, because non-volition is implied in hypnotic suggestions, subjects may try to actively redefine what is in fact voluntary behaviour as involuntary. Non-state theorists also reject the notion that hypnotic behaviour can transcend "waking" behaviour.

The problem of compliance, or faking, in hypnosis is one recognized by both state and non-state theorists, largely as a result of the pioneering work of Orne (1959, 1966), who emphasized the extent to which subjects in any experimental context may modify their behaviour in an attempt to please the experimenter, save themselves from embarrassment, or bolster their self-image. However, to some non-state theorists compliance is not just an annoyance in hypnosis research, it may be seen as an integral component of much hypnotic responding (Spanos, 1991; Wagstaff, 1991). Such ideas raise some difficult semantic issues; for instance, are non-state theorists saying that "hypnosis" actually does not exist? There is no simple answer to this question; however, most non-state theorists continue to use the words "hypnosis" or "hypnotic" operationally, to refer to any context defined by those participating in it as "hypnosis". Thus a "hypnotic" group would be one that has been given a hypnotic induction procedure, and "hypnotized" or "hypnotically susceptible" subjects are those who tend to respond positively to suggestions in what is defined as a hypnotic context. From this non-state perspective, therefore, "hypnosis" does exist, but as a label for a context rather than as an altered state of consciousness (see, e.g., Spanos, 1989; Wagstaff, 1991).

The methodological problems involved in deciding between the state and non-state viewpoints are immense and have given rise to some highly innovative experimental research designs. The basic approach has been to compare subjects who have been given an hypnotic induction procedure with various control groups designed to test alternative non-state explanations. At the forefront has been Orne's (1979) "real-simulator" design, in which "hypnotized" subjects are compared with subjects instructed to fake excellent hypnotic subjects, but without any explicit instructions as to how this is to be accomplished. Another popular control group has been T. X. Barber's (1969) "task-motivated" group; in this subjects are told to try hard to imagine and experience hypnotic suggestions, but without a formal induction procedure. The logic behind these approaches is that if no differences emerge between the hypnotic and control groups, then it is not necessary to propose a special hypnotic process, or state, to explain the responses of the hypnotic subjects; on the other hand, if differences do occur, it may be reasonable to assume that hypnotic induction may add a special element.

THE PHYSIOLOGY OF HYPNOSIS

If hypnosis is a special state of consciousness, perhaps related to sleep, it would be useful to know whether "hypnotized" subjects would manifest any physiological changes not shown by non-hypnotic control subjects. A wide variety of measures have been investigated, including EEG, blood pressure and chemistry, respiration rate, and skin temperature and resistance. Although the search continues (see, e.g., Gruzelier, 1988), most researchers of both state and non-state persuasion now seem to agree that the quest to find a unique correlate of the hypnotic state has not been very successful. Physiological changes do often occur following hypnotic induction or hypnotic suggestions, but they seem to be explicable in other ways; for example, they may be due simply to normal changes in attention (Jones & Flynn, 1989), or the achievement of a relaxed state (Edmonston, 1991). This latter finding invites an obvious question; is hypnosis simply a state of relaxation? At first it would seem that hypnosis and relaxation are not equivalent because subjects can appear "hypnotized" when involved in strenuous activities, such as pedalling an exercise bike (Malott, 1984). Nevertheless, Edmonston (1991) has argued that one can still be relaxed (cognitively) even when engaged in physical activity. However, perhaps the main problem with the notion that hypnosis is just relaxation is that it does not adequately explain how various hypnotic phenomena, such as hallucinations and amnesia, arise (Fellows, 1990).

TRANSCENDENT PROPERTIES OF HYPNOSIS

Part of the popular conception of hypnosis is that it enables individuals to transcend their normal capacities. Some early claims were very dramatic; for example, it was once believed that hypnotic subjects could see with the backs of their heads, see through the skin to the internal organs, and communicate with the dead (Spanos, 1982). It has also been claimed that hypnosis can enable people to relive past lives (Wagstaff, 1981). Although such dramatic claims tend not to be taken seriously by academic researchers, less exaggerated claims continue to be made. For instance, claims have been made that hypnosis may be particularly valuable in the forensic context for helping victims and eyewitnesses to remember details of crimes; however, most evidence suggests that hypnosis does not facilitate memory more than other procedures that encourage the vivid recollection of details; in fact, sometimes hypnosis may simply encourage witnesses to confabulate, or make up details (Wagstaff, 1989).

Work in this area has emphasized many of the pitfalls in research into hypnosis. Often observers of demonstrations of hypnosis are unaware of the capacities of the average person, which go untested; for example, most people are quite able to perform the apparent transcendent feats in stage demonstrations of hypnosis without any attempt to employ an hypnotic procedure (T. X. Barber, Spanos, & Chaves, 1974); these include not showing outward expressions of pain in response to a noxious stimulus, and the ability of a subject to support the weight of one or even two individuals while suspended between two chairs – one under the shoulders, the other under the calves. In experimental and clinical research an important difficulty arises when attempts are made to compare the performance of the *same* subjects in both hypnotic and non-hypnotic conditions; in these circumstances subjects may tend to underperform or "hold back" in the non-hypnotic condition so that when they are "hypnotized" their performance will appear to have improved (Wagstaff, 1981). Using more appropriate experimental designs, such as using independent groups of simulators or task-motivated subjects, some of the earlier claims for hypnosis seem to be unsubstantiated; for example, there is no conclusive evidence that hypnotic subjects are superior to suitably motivated non-hypnotic subjects on a range of tasks including appearing deaf, blind, and colour blind, acting like a child and recalling events from childhood, producing perceptual effects while "hallucinating", lifting weights and other athletic tasks, showing improvements in eyesight, and learning and remembering (T. X. Barber, 1969; Jacobs & Gotthelf, 1986; Jones & Flynn, 1989; Wagstaff, 1981). Even when tasks involve dangerous or antisocial activities, subjects simulating hypnosis are just as likely, and occasionally more likely, to perform them than hypnotic or "real" subjects; such tasks have included picking up a poisonous snake, putting one's hand into a glass of concentrated acid and throwing the acid at the experimenter, peddling heroin, mutilating the Bible, and making slanderous statements (Wagstaff, 1981, 1989).

As attempts to demonstrate that hypnosis enables individuals to transcend their normal capacities have generally failed or been inconclusive, researchers have turned their attention to more subtle differences between hypnotic and non-hypnotic behaviour and experience. For example, one possible way of determining whether hypnotic behaviours are influenced by experimental demands would be to see if they still occur when the hypnotist is not present. In one investigation, Orne, Sheehan, and Evans (1968) found that some hypnotic subjects continued to respond to a posthypnotic suggestion (to touch their foreheads on hearing the word "experiment"), even when the hypnotist was not present, whereas simulators stopped responding in the absence of the hypnotist. However, other investigators have found that when subjects are tested totally outside the experimental setting, by someone who ostensibly has nothing whatsoever to do with the experiment, the post-hypnotic responses disappear entirely (Spanos, Menary, Brett, Cross, & Ahmed, 1987). The latter finding appears to fit well with the non-state view, but other phenomena seem less easily dismissed.

TRANCE LOGIC

One of the most controversial issues is that of "trance logic". This term was devised by Orne (1959, 1979) to refer to the observation that "hypnotized" individuals, unlike simulators, appear to have little need for logical consistency and can tolerate illogical responses. Four phenomena, in particular, have been identified as key examples of trance logic. First, when hypnotic subjects ("reals") view a person, and at the same time receive a suggestion to hallucinate the person standing in a different place, they tend to report seeing *both* the actual person and the hallucinated image; however, hardly any simulators do this. Orne (1959) termed this the "double hallucination" response. Second, when hypnotic subjects are shown an empty chair and it is suggested to them that a person is sitting on it, they will tend to report that the image is transparent; that is, they can see the chair through the person. Simulators, however, tend to report an opaque or solid image; they say they cannot see the back of the chair. Third, when given a suggestion to regress back to childhood, some hypnotic subjects will report, alternately or simultaneously, that they felt both like an adult *and* a child. Fourth, unlike a child, they will correctly write a complex sentence; simulators, on the other hand, will tend to report feeling like a child all the time, and will write the sentence incorrectly, as would a child. These phenomena have been termed "duality" and "incongruous writing" respectively (Nogrady, McConkey, Laurence, & Perry, 1983). In terms of neo-dissociation theory, all of these examples of trance logic could reflect the possibility that, during hypnosis, different "parts" of consciousness are being accessed alternately or simultaneously. It should be noted, however, that not all hypnotically susceptible "reals" display trance logic.

Further research into these phenomena has produced mixed results. According to de Groot and Gwynn (1989), at least nine studies have failed to demonstrate a difference between "reals" and simulators on the double hallucination response; nevertheless, a number of researchers have found that "reals" are indeed more likely to proffer a transparent hallucination response, and display duality and incongruous writing, than simulators. However, non-state theorists have questioned whether these differences between "reals" and simulators are evidence for hypnosis as a special state.

One of the difficulties with the traditional real-simulator design is that the two groups operate under different instructions; the simulators are told specifically to behave like *excellent* subjects, whereas the "reals" are not; the latter can behave as "hypnotized" as they wish, and report as honestly as they wish. It could be the case, therefore, that because they are trying to behave like excellent subjects, simulators are more likely to act in an extreme way (Wagstaff, 1981); hence, just like some of the highly susceptible "reals" who do *not* display trance logic, simulators, when asked to hallucinate, will tend to report complete solid hallucinations, and when given suggestions to regress, will report feeling like a child all of the time, and will write like a child. On the other hand, perhaps the "trance-logical reals" use a different strategy; they may simply be exercising their imagination, or offering a less complete or less extreme response. To test this hypothesis, some researchers have used control groups who have been instructed to imagine the various effects, or have been given the same suggestions without hypnotic induction; using these controls no differences have been found between the hypnotic and non-hypnotic groups on the various measures of trance logic (de Groot & Gwynn, 1989; Spanos, 1986a). It has been proposed by state theorists that the non-hypnotic controls in these studies might have inadvertently "slipped into an hypnotic state", but apart from the general difficulty of arguing that, in their everyday lives, people must slip in and out of an hypnotic state whenever they use their imagination, typically imagination controls do not report experiences of being "hypnotized" (Obstoj & Sheehan, 1977).

In opposition to the non-state view on this topic, however, is the finding that hypnotic subjects who display trance logic are also more likely to show the "hidden-observer" effect (Nogrady et al., 1983). If trance logic is simply an incomplete response, or reflects the use of everyday imagination, it seems difficult to see why it should relate to hidden-observer responding; this finding would seem to fit better with a neo-dissociation explanation, in that both trance logic and the production of a "hidden observer" could be construed as examples of the capacity for dissociation under hypnosis. Nevertheless, Spanos, de Groot, Tiller, Weekes, and Bertrand (1985) have failed to replicate this finding, so the issue remains unresolved.

The idea that when hypnotic subjects report transparent hallucinations they may simply be saying they "imagined" what was suggested to them raises the general question of the validity of hypnotic hallucinations. State theorists seem in little doubt that hypnotic subjects can experience hallucinations "as real as real" (Bowers, 1983). Non-state theorists are more sceptical; for example, Spanos (1982) reports that, if given the option, hypnotic subjects will prefer to say their hallucinations were "imagined" rather than seen, and though some subjects continue to maintain they have "seen" suggested hallucinations, so do an equivalent proportion of task-motivated subjects. However, Bowers (1983) argues that, when asked to be honest, task-motivated subjects report less vivid hallucinations than hypnotic subjects.

One of the most extraordinary hypnotic phenomena is the *negative* hallucination, whereby hypnotic subjects maintain that they *cannot* see something placed plainly before their open eyes. According to some state theorists, the visual stimulus is "seen" by one "part" of the mind, but it is somehow blocked from awareness (Zamansky & Bartis, 1985). To some non-state theorists, however, the explanation for this phenomenon is rather more simple: the subjects are lying (Wagstaff, 1991).

HYPNOTIC AMNESIA

Another hotly debated phenomenon is hypnotic amnesia. Typically, if hypnotic subjects are given some suggestions to perform, or a word list to learn, and are told they will forget what they have done or learned, they will show either total or partial forgetting, until a release signal, such as "Now you can remember", is given. It is commonly accepted that hypnotic amnesia is not equivalent to normal forgetting, because some or all of the "forgotten" material can be recovered immediately following the release signal. According to neo-dissociation theory, this happens because temporarily, during hypnosis, the memories are dissociated from conscious control and cannot be accessed voluntarily. Thus, no matter how hard they try, hypnotic subjects cannot remember the material until the release signal is given and normal control is restored (Bowers, 1983; Hilgard, 1986).

Non-state theorists tend to explain hypnotic amnesia differently; they argue that hypnotic subjects interpret the amnesia suggestion as an instruction to avoid remembering. Hence, when they have apparently forgotten, hypnotic subjects are not engaging in fruitless attempts to remember, rather they are deliberately trying *not* to remember. To do this subjects may adopt a number of different strategies; for example, they may simply pretend that they cannot remember, or they may try to avoid remembering by distracting themselves, or making no effort to think about the material (Spanos, 1986a; Wagstaff, 1981).

If the non-state theorists are correct, then presumably it should be possible to "breach" hypnotic amnesia by instructing subjects to tell the truth, or to actively attend to the material. However, Kihlstrom, Evans, Orne, and Orne (1980) found that some hypnotic subjects continued to display amnesia despite such instructions. In response, non-state theorists have argued that some subjects may have such an investment in displaying amnesia that they would "lose face" if they started to remember as a result of such instructions; consequently, to breach amnesia, subjects need either a more powerful stimulus to remember, or to be able to remember without discrediting themselves. In support of this view it has been shown that, in the vast majority of subjects, amnesia can be breached when subjects are asked to be honest, rigged up to a lie detector, and shown a videotape of their performance (Coe, 1989). Wagstaff (1977) demonstrated that amnesia can be eliminated

999

completely if subjects are given an opportunity to say they were "role-playing", rather than in a hypnotic "trance". The fact remains, however, that hypnotic amnesia is difficult to breach entirely, and state theorists can argue that these breaching techniques effectively destroy the influence of the hypnotic state.

A number of other amnesia effects have been investigated. For example, when hypnotic subjects are presented with items in sequence or categories, and are asked to forget them, they sometimes recall them in a disorganized fashion (out of sequence or not in categories); this is unlike normal memory (Kihlstrom & Wilson, 1984). However, in accordance with the non-state position, similar disorganization effects can be shown by subjects who have been instructed to "pretend to forget", or to "attend away" from the material (Spanos, 1986a; Wagstaff, 1982). It has also been proposed that "reals" and simulators differ in the extent to which they show "source amnesia"; that is, after a session of hypnosis, unlike simulators, "reals" will sometimes recall information given to them when they were "hypnotized", but they say they cannot remember where they learned this information (Evans, 1979). However, Wagstaff (1981) suggests that one reason why simulators may fail to show source amnesia is that, in trying to be excellent subjects, they show total amnesia, that is, amnesia for both the information to be recalled and the source. Later studies have supported this interpretation and have shown that non-hypnotic task-motivated subjects and simulators instructed to show partial amnesia also display source amnesia (Coe, 1989).

Nevertheless, state theorists remain unconvinced that the mechanisms proposed by non-state theorists can account adequately for hypnotic amnesia (see, e.g., Bowers & Davidson, 1991), so this debate will continue.

HYPNOTIC ANALGESIA

On first consideration, the fact that hypnosis can enable patients to endure surgery with little or no pain (hypnotic analgesia) might seem incompatible with a non-state viewpoint, and a number of theorists adhere to this opinion. However, non-state theorists insist that it is possible to explain hypnotic analgesia in terms of "ordinary" psychological processes, and argue the following: first, cases of surgery with hypnosis alone are rare, and some individuals can tolerate pain without medication or hypnosis; second, much major surgery is actually less painful than is commonly expected; and third, pain is a complex sensation that can be alleviated through relaxation, the reduction of stress and anxiety, and the use of strategies such as distraction and the reinterpretation of noxious stimulation; all of which are frequently involved in cases of hypnotic surgery (Chaves, 1989; Spanos & Chaves, 1989).

Because of the difficulties involved in the interpretation of clinical cases researchers have turned to laboratory studies of pain in an attempt to test the state and non-state explanations of hypnotic analgesia. In these studies pain is most usually induced by plunging the subject's hand into ice cold water, or applying a pressure stimulus. According to state theorists, laboratory studies show that suggestions for analgesia can be more effective when given in the hypnotic state than in the "waking" state (Hilgard, 1986; Hilgard & Hilgard, 1983). However, non-state theorists point to the fact that many of the studies supportive of this view have tended to use the same subjects in both the hypnotic and non-hypnotic conditions and are thus vulnerable to the criticism that, to fulfil the demands of the experimental situation, subjects may not have used pain-reducing and coping strategies in the non-hypnotic situation; in some cases, subjects may even have faked an absence of pain in the hypnotic situation (Wagstaff, 1981). In support of this interpretation, Spanos and his associates report that hypnotic analgesia is more, less, or equally as effective as non-hypnotic analgesia, depending on the expectations conveyed to the subjects; moreover, for subjects who are not hypnotically susceptible, hypnotic suggestions seem to be less effective than other pain-reducing strategies, such as distraction (Spanos, 1986a, 1989). Nevertheless, some state theorists continue to report that hypnotic suggestions for analgesia are superior to non-hypnotic interventions (Bowers & Davidson, 1991).

Some of the most interesting results on hypnotic analgesia have come from "hidden observer" reports. Hilgard (1986) found that, following suggestions for analgesia, hypnotic subjects typically report pain relief; however, when the "hidden observer" is contacted (by placing a hand on the subject's shoulder), the "hidden part" reports higher levels of pain only slightly less than those reported in the normal "waking" state. Hilgard argues that this occurs because pain *is* experienced during hypnotic analgesia, but the "part" experiencing pain is dissociated from awareness by an "amnesic barrier". In contrast, non-state theorists argue that the reports of the "hidden observer" simply reflect what subjects think they are expected to say as implied by the experimental instructions (Spanos, 1989; Wagstaff, 1981).

Not surprisingly Hilgard's supporters disagree with the view that one can explain his finding solely in terms of subjects reporting what they think they ought to report. For example, Nogrady et al. (1983) found that if "reals" and simulators are given only a hint that higher pain reports are expected from the "hidden observer", then some "reals" show the classic "hidden observer" effect, where as no simulators show it. But in reply, Spanos, Gywnn, and Stam (1983) argue that the reason why the simulators had failed in this study to respond like the "reals" was because, trying to act like excellent subjects and not give themselves, away, they had acted conservatively in the face of ambiguous instructions; so, to test this idea further, they ran a study in which they removed the subtle hint for higher pain reports from the "hidden observer"; as they predicted, the standard "hidden observer" effect was then virtually eliminated. Spanos (1989) argue, that this latter finding is inconsistent with the view that hypnotic analgesia occurs because the actual pain is "held" in a separate cognitive subsystem behind an amnesic barrier. To add further support for the non-state view, Spanos and his associates have found that "hidden observers" will report greater, the same, or less pain than the ordinary "hypnotized" part, if these expectations are conveyed to them (Spanos, 1989).

Also somewhat disquieting to the state view of hypnotic analgesia is apparent support for Wagstaff's (1981, 1991) contention that reports of hypnotic analgesia may be inflated by compliance or faking. Thus Spanos, Perlini, Patrick, Bell, and Gwynn (1990) found that, if *after* receiving a painful stimulus, it is implied to hypnotic subjects that they were, or were not, "hypnotized" at the time they were experiencing the stimulus, they will report pain relief, or not, accordingly.

Disagreements about the mechanisms involved in hypnotic pain control are as rife as ever, but perhaps the most fascinating outcome of research in this area is the realization that human beings have a considerable capacity to control and tolerate pain without chemical analgesics.

CLINICAL HYPNOSIS

There is little doubt that hypnotic techniques have been used successfully in the clinical field for the treatment of many problems other than pain. For example, successful outcomes have been reported in the treatment of problems such as insomnia, obesity, mild phobias, smoking, and dental stress (Heap & Dryden, 1991; Wadden & Anderton, 1982). However, once again, difficulties arise in deciding whether it is necessary to postulate an "hypnotic state" to explain such effects. Hypnotic techniques typically involve a variety of factors that are not unique to hypnosis, and could account for the improvements; these include social support, relaxation, covert modelling, and even social compliance (Wadden & Anderton, 1982; Wagstaff, 1981). A number of claims have been made that hypnosis may be useful in the treatment of physical symptoms such as skin problems and even cancer. Unfortunately it seems that, as yet, research in these areas has not been sufficiently rigorous to isolate the factors involved in treatment success, or, in some cases, to decide even whether the treatment was successful (Johnson, 1989; Stam, 1989).

Clearly, regardless, of whether one believes in the notion of an hypnotic state, the area of clinical hypnosis remains a rich source of data on the psychological influences on physical illness, and one that should bear fruit as research into hypnosis continues.

HYPNOTIC SUSCEPTIBILITY

Are some people more susceptible to hypnotic suggestions than others; if so, why? Research indicates that people differ widely in their susceptibility to hypnotic suggestions; but state and non-state theorists tend to differ in their explanations of these differences. Various attempt have been made to relate hypnotic susceptibility to a number of physiological and performance parameters including attentional skills, EEG activity, right brain hemisphere processing, and eye movements, but, on the whole, such attempts have been inconclusive (Spanos, 1982). In contrast, both state and non-state theorists seem to agree that the tendency to become absorbed in imaginings is one of the main correlates of hypnotic susceptibility. However, they differ in their interpretations of this finding. According to state theorists, the reason why this relationship occurs is because absorption in imaginings may reflect a capacity to dissociate, and at the heart of hypnotic responding is the capacity for dissociation (see, e.g., Bowers, 1983). Non-state theorists argue that it would not be surprising if a propensity to fantasize and become involved in imaginings should correlate with hypnotic susceptibility as this would facilitate the enactment of the role of the "hypnotized" individual, but they do not see why this relationship should be viewed as evidence for differences in the ability to enter an altered state of consciousness.

Non-state theorists also argue that there are a number of other factors that have been found to correlate with hypnotic susceptibility and can be seen as supportive of their view; these include social conformity, acting or drama skills, and possessing appropriate attitudes and expectancies (Spanos, 1986b; Wagstaff, 1986, 1991). Indeed, if hypnotic susceptibility is seen as not a fixed ability or trait, but a strategic response to a particular context, then by modifying subjects' attitudes and expectancies, and training them how to use their imaginations to pass suggestions, it should be possible to change "low" hypnotic responders into "highs". This is exactly what Spanos and his colleagues have claimed to have done (Bertrand, 1989). However, critics have argued that such training techniques may encourage subjects to fake rather than evoke genuine changes in hypnotic susceptibility (Bowers & Davidson, 1991).

CONCLUSION

Research and debate in hypnosis obviously flourishes, but in over one hundred years we seem to be no further forward in deciding whether there is an altered state of consciousness that we can call "hypnosis". However, the lessons that this controversy has taught us are many. We have accumulated valuable knowledge about the problems associated with experiments on human beings, lessons valuable not only to psychology but also to other disciplines, and we have learned much about the capacities and vulnerabilities of ordinary people.

Traditionally, it seems that hypnosis has almost been viewed as an embarrassment to psychologists — something better left to psychiatrists or parapsychologists. However, the high standard of research in this area makes such a view untenable; perhaps now is the time for the topic of hypnosis to be placed firmly where it belongs, on the mainstream psychology syllabus.

FURTHER READING

Bowers, K. S. (1983). *Hypnosis for the seriously curious*. New York: Norton.

Hilgard, E. R. (1986). *Divided consciousness: Multiple controls in human thought and action* (expanded edn). New York: Wiley.

Lynn, S. J., & Rhue, J. W. (Eds) (1991). *Theories of hypnosis: Current models and perspectives*. New York: Guilford.

Spanos, N. P. (1986). Hypnotic behavior: A social psychological interpretation of amnesia, analgesia and trance logic. *Behavioral and Brain Sciences, 9*, 449–467.

Spanos, N. P., & Chaves, J. F. (Eds) (1989). *Hypnosis: The cognitive-behavioral perspective*. Buffalo, NY: Prometheus.

REFERENCES

Barber, J. (1991). The locksmith model: Accessing hypnotic responsiveness. In S. J. Lynn & J. W. Rhue (Eds) *Theories of hypnosis: Current models and perspectives* (pp. 241–274). New York: Guilford.

Barber, T. X. (1969). *Hypnosis: A scientific approach*. New York: Van Nostrand.

Barber, T. X., Spanos, N. P., & Chaves, J. F. (1974). *Hypnosis, imagination, and human potentialities*. Elmsford, NY: Pergamon.

Bertrand, L. D. (1989). The assessment and modification of hypnotic susceptibility. In N. P. Spanos & J. F. Chaves (Eds) *Hypnosis: The cognitive-behavioral perspective* (pp. 18–31). Buffalo, NY: Prometheus.

Bowers, K. S. (1983). *Hypnosis for the seriously curious*. New York: Norton.

Bowers, K. S., & Davidson, T. M. (1991). A neo-dissociative critique of Spanos's Social-Psychological model of hypnosis. In S. J. Lynn & J. W. Rhue (Eds) *Theories of hypnosis: Current models and perspectives* (pp. 105–143). New York: Guilford.

Chaves, J. F. (1989). Hypnotic control of clinical pain. In N. P. Spanos & J. F. Chaves (Eds) *Hypnosis: The cognitive-behavioral perspective* (pp. 242–271). Buffalo, NY: Prometheus.

Coe, W. C. (1989). Post-hypnotic amnesia. Theory and research. In N. P. Spanos & J. F. Chaves (Eds) *Hypnosis: The cognitive-behavioral perspective* (pp. 110–148). Buffalo, NY: Prometheus.

de Groot, H. P. & Gwynn, M. I. (1989). Trance logic, duality, and hidden-observer responding. In N. P. Spanos & J. F. Chaves (Eds) *Hypnosis: The cognitive-behavioral perspective* (pp. 187–205). Buffalo, NY: Prometheus.

Edmonston, W. E. (1991). Anesis. In S. J. Lynn & J. W. Rhue (Eds) *Theories of hypnosis: Current models and perspectives* (pp. 197–240). New York: Guilford.

Evans, F. J. (1979). Contextual forgetting: Post-hypnotic source amnesia. *Journal of Abnormal Psychology, 88*, 556–563.

Fellows, B. J. (1990). Current theories of hypnosis: A critical overview. *British Journal of Experimental and Clinical Hypnosis, 7*, 81–92.

Gravitz, M. A., & Gerton, M. I. (1984). Origins of the term hypnotism prior to Braid. *American Journal of Clinical Hypnosis, 27*, 107–110.

Gruzelier, J. (1988). The neuropsychology of hypnosis. In M. Heap (Ed.) *Hypnosis: Current clinical, experimental and forensic practices* (pp. 68–76). London: Croom Helm.

Heap, M., & Dryden, W. (1991). *Hypnotherapy: A handbook*. Milton Keynes: Open University Press.

Hilgard, E. R. (1986). *Divided consciousness: Multiple controls in human thought and action* (expanded edn). New York: Wiley.

Hilgard, E. R. (1991). A neodissociation interpretation of hypnosis. In S. J. Lynn & J. W. Rhue (Eds) *Theories of hypnosis: Current models and perspectives* (pp. 83–104). New York: Guilford.

Hilgard, E. R., & Hilgard, J. R. (1983). *Hypnosis in the relief of pain*. Los Altos, CA: Wiulliam Kaufmann.

Jacobs, S., & Gotthelf, C. (1986). Effects of hypnosis on physical and athletic performance. In F. A. De Piano & H. C. Salzberg (Eds) *Clinical applications of hypnosis* (pp. 157–173). Norwood, NJ: Ablex.

Johnson, R. F. Q. (1989). Hypnosis, suggestion, and dermatological changes: A consideration of the production and diminution of dermatological entities. In N. P. Spanos & J. F. Chaves (Eds) *Hypnosis: The cognitive-behavioral perspective* (pp. 297–312). Buffalo, NY: Prometheus.

Jones, W. J., & Flynn, D. M. (1989). Methodological and theoretical considerations in the study of "hypnotic" effects in perception. In N. P. Spanos & J. F. Chaves (Eds) *Hypnosis: The cognitive-behavioral perspective* (pp. 149–174). Buffalo, NY: Prometheus.

Kihlstrom, J. F., & Wilson, L. (1984). Temporal organization of recall during posthypnotic amnesia. *Journal of Abnormal Psychology*, *93*, 200–208.

Kihlstrom, J. F., Evans, F. J., Orne, E. C., & Orne, M. T. (1980). Attempting to breach posthypnotic amnesia. *Journal of Abnormal Psychology*, *89*, 603–616.

Knox, J. V., Morgan, A. H., & Hilgard, E. R. (1974). Pain and suffering in ischemia: The paradox of hypnotically suggested anesthesia as contradicted by reports from the "hidden-observer". *Archives of General Psychiatry*, *30*, 840–847.

Malott, J. M. (1984). Active-alert hypnosis. Replication and extension of previous research. *Journal of Abnormal Psychology*, *93*, 246–249.

Nogrady, H., McConkey, K. M., Laurence, J. R., & Perry, C. (1983). Dissociation, duality, and demand characteristics in hypnosis. *Journal of Abnormal Psychology*, *92*, 223–235.

Obstoj, J., & Sheehan, P. W. (1977). Aptitude for trance, task generalizability and incongruity response in hypnosis. *Journal of Abnormal Psychology*, *86*, 543–552.

Orne, M. T. (1959). The nature of hypnosis: Artifact and essence. *Journal of Abnormal and Social Psychology*, *58*, 277–299.

Orne, M. T. (1966). Hypnosis, motivation and compliance. *American Journal of Psychiatry*, *122*, 721–726.

Orne, M. T. (1979). On the simulating subject as quasi-control group in hypnosis research: what, why, and how? In E. Fromm & R. E. Shor (Eds) *Hypnosis: Research developments and perspectives* (pp. 519–565). New York: Aldine.

Orne, M. T., Sheehan, P. W., & Evans, F. J. (1968). The occurrence of posthypnotic behavior outside the experimental setting. *Journal of Personality and Social Psychology*, *26*, 217–221.

Sarbin, T. R., & Coe, W. C. (1972). *Hypnosis: A social psychological analysis of influence communication*. New York: Holt, Rinehart & Winston.

Spanos, N. P. (1982). A social psychological approach to hypnotic behavior. In G. Weary & H. L. Mirels (Eds) *Integrations of clinical and social psychology* (pp. 231–271). New York: Oxford University Press.

Spanos, N. P. (1986a). Hypnotic behavior: A social psychological interpretation of amnesia, analgesia and trance logic. *Behavioral and Brain Sciences, 9,* 449–467.

Spanos, N. P. (1986b). Hypnosis and the modification of hypnotic susceptibility: A social psychological perspective. In P. L. N. Naish (Ed.) *What is hypnosis?* (pp. 85–120). Philadelphia, PA: Open University Press.

Spanos, N. P. (1989). Experimental research on hypnotic analgesia. In N. P. Spanos & J. F. Chaves (Eds) *Hypnosis: The cognitive-behavioral perspective* (pp. 206–241). Buffalo, NY: Prometheus.

Spanos, N. P. (1991). A sociocognitive approach to hypnosis. In S. J. Lynn & J. W. Rhue (Eds) *Theories of hypnosis: Current models and perspectives* (pp. 324–362). New York: Guilford.

Spanos, N. P., & Chaves, J. F. (1989). Hypnotic analgesia and surgery: In defence of the social-psychological position. *British Journal of Experimental and Clinical Hypnosis, 6,* 131–139.

Spanos, N. P., Gwynn, M. I., & Stam, H. J. (1983). Instructional demands and ratings of overt and hidden pain during hypnotic analgesia. *Journal of Abnormal Psychology, 92,* 479–488.

Spanos, N. P., de Groot, H. P., Tiller, D. K., Weekes, J. R., & Bertrand, L. D. (1985). "Trance logic" duality and hidden observer responding in hypnotic, imagination control and simulating subjects. *Journal of Abnormal Psychology, 94,* 611–623.

Spanos, N. P., Menary, E., Brett, P. J., Cross, W., & Ahmed, Q. (1987). Failure of posthypnotic responding to occur outside the experimental setting. *Journal of Abnormal Psychology, 96,* 52–57.

Spanos, N. P., Perlini, A. H., Patrick, L., Bell, S., & Gwynn, M. I. (1990). The role of compliance in hypnotic and nonhypnotic analgesia. *Journal of Research in Personality, 24,* 433–453.

Stam, H. J. (1989). From symptom relief to cure. Hypnotic interventions in cancer. In N. P. Spanos & J. F. Chaves (Eds) *Hypnosis: The cognitive-behavioral perspective* (pp. 313–339). Buffalo, NY: Prometheus.

Wadden, T., & Anderton, C. H. (1982). The clinical use of hypnosis. *Psychological Bulletin, 91,* 215–243.

Wagstaff, G. F. (1977). An experimental study of compliance and post-hypnotic amnesia. *British Journal of Social and Clinical Psychology, 16,* 225–228.

Wagstaff, G. F. (1981). *Hypnosis, compliance, and belief.* Brighton: Harvester.

Wagstaff, G. F. (1982). Disorganized recall, suggested amnesia, and compliance. *Psychological Reports, 51,* 1255–1258.

Wagstaff, G. F. (1989). Forensic aspects of hypnosis. In N. P. Spanos & J. F. Chaves (Eds) *Hypnosis: The cognitive-behavioral perspective* (pp. 340–359). Buffalo, NY: Prometheus.

Wagstaff, G. F. (1991). Compliance, belief and semantics in hypnosis: A non-state sociocognitive perspective. In S. J. Lynn & J. W. Rhue (Eds) *Theories of hypnosis: Current models and perspectives* (pp. 362–396). New York: Guilford.

Zamansky, H. S., & Bartis, S. P. (1985). The dissociation of an experience: The hidden observer observed. *Journal of Abnormal Psychology, 94,* 243–248.

11.3

GENDER ISSUES IN PSYCHOLOGY

Mary Crawford

University of South Carolina, Pennsylvania, USA

Rhoda K. Unger

Montclair State College, New Jersey, USA

Since the late 1960s, scholars and practitioners in psychology have engaged in sustained evaluation of the discipline's representation of women and gender. This critique has developed in a social context of changing roles and opportunities for women and the emergence of a feminist social movement.

Of course, the women's movement originating in the late 1960s was not the first. A previous women's rights initiative had reached its peak over a hundred years earlier. At the turn of the century, many of the first generation of scientifically trained women psychologists, perhaps influenced by the earlier movement, devoted their research efforts to examining accepted wisdom about the extent and nature of sex differences. Determined to demonstrate women's capacity to contribute to science on an equal basis with men, they laboured to refute hypotheses that they themselves did not find credible and that they did not believe could account for the inferior social position of women (Unger, 1979). While some achieved a measure of professional success, as group they succeeded neither in legitimizing nor institutionalizing the study of women and gender (Rosenberg 1982; Scarborough & Furumoto, 1987).

Psychology's interest in sex differences and gender waned with the rise of behaviourism. Gender would not return to the research agenda until the 1970s, and it was only in the mid-1980s that an *Annual Review of Psychology* article could state that it was an idea whose time had come (Deaux, 1985). As psychologists have once again begun to examine psychology's understandings of women, problems and inadequacies have been catalogued:

> There was widespread agreement about [psychology's] faults: that women were infrequently studied; that theories were constructed from a male-as-normative viewpoint and that women's behavior was explained as deviation from the male standard; that the stereotype of women was considered an accurate portrayal of women's behavior; that women who fulfilled the dictates of the gender stereotype were viewed as healthy and happy; that differences in the behaviors of women and men were attributed to differences in anatomy and physiology; and that the social context which often shapes behavior was ignored in the case of women. (Kahn & Jean, 1983, p. 660)

Unlike its earlier counterpart, the new psychology of women and gender has become institutionalized. Before 1968, there were virtually no psychology departments offering courses in the psychology of women and/or gender; in the early 1990s about half of all US psychology departments provided them. Psychology of women courses are often connected to, and have contributed to, the rapid growth of women's studies programmes, which in the 1990s exist on over 450 US college and university campuses (Stimpson, 1986). The new field has its own journals, which are important resources for scholars and students: *Sex Roles*, which began publishing in 1975, *Psychology of Women Quarterly*, since 1977, and *Feminism & Psychology*, a UK addition in 1991.

Women psychologists and men who support their goals have worked toward an improved status for women within psychology. They first formed the Association for Women in Psychology (AWP) in 1969, then lobbied the American Psychological Association (APA) to form a division of the Psychology of Women. This division, officially approved in 1973, is now one of the larger divisions of the APA, with over 3,000 members. A similar pattern of progress in incorporating women occurred among Canadian psychologists, and (more recently) within the British Psychological Society. These organizational changes have acknowledged the presence of women in psychology and helped enhance their professional identity (O'Connell & Russo, 1991; Scarborough & Furumoto, 1987).

The new psychology of women and gender is rich and varied. Virtually every intellectual framework from Freudian theory to cognitive psychology has been used in developing new theories and approaches. Virtually every area of psychology, from developmental to social, has been affected (Crawford & Marecek, 1989). In this chapter we shall examine first some conceptual and methodological issues, and then provide reviews of selected research topics. Throughout, we shall note connections to clinical/practice issues.

CONCEPTUAL AND METHODOLOGICAL ISSUES

Gender: more than just sex

Feminist psychology makes a conceptual distinction between sex and gender (Unger, 1979). *Sex* is defined as biological differences in genetic composition and reproductive anatomy and function. *Gender* is what culture makes out of the "raw material" of biological sex. All known societies recognize biological differentiation and use it as the basis for social distinctions. In North American society, the process of creating gendered human beings starts at birth. When a baby is born, the presence of a vagina or penis represents sex – but the pink or blue blanket that soon enfolds the baby represents gender. The blanket serves as a cue that this infant is to be treated as girl or boy, not as a "generic human", from the start.

The influence of gender-based social distinctions is pervasive. Gender-related processes influence behaviour, thoughts, and feelings in individuals; they affect interactions among individuals; and they help determine the structure of social institutions. The processes by which differences are created and power is allocated can be understood by considering how gender is played out at three levels: societal, interpersonal, and individual.

The social structural level: gender as a system of power relations

In the broadest sense, gender is a classification system that shapes the relations among women and men. For example, virtually all societies label some tasks as "men's" and others as "women's" work. While there is a great deal of variability in tasks assigned to each sex across societies, whatever is labelled "women's work" is usually seen as less important and desirable. Not only women's work but also women themselves are devalued. Thus gender can be viewed as a system of social classification that influences access to power and resources (Crawford & Marecek, 1989; Sherif, 1982).

The interpersonal level: gender as a cue

In every society, certain traits, behaviours, and interests are associated with each sex and assumed to be appropriate for people of that sex. Since there are only two sexes, gender is also assumed to be dichotomous: a person can be classified as either "masculine" or "feminine", but not both. Although many traits, interests, behaviours, and even physical characteristics are ascribed to women *or* men, in reality, people often show characteristics ascribed to the other sex. Thus gender, as it is usually framed, reflects a form of stereotyping (Deaux & Major, 1987; Unger & Crawford, 1992).

Gender stereotypes are brought to bear in social interaction, where the influence of sex and gender interact. Not only do people use gender cues to make inferences about sex, but also they use perceived sex to make inferences about gender. Gender cues are used to tell us how to behave towards others in social interactions. Although much sex-differential treatment happens outside awareness, research confirms its occurrence. For example, observations in elementary or primary school classrooms show that, although teachers believe that they are treating boys and girls the same, boys receive more attention, both positive and negative, than girls do. Boys are yelled at and criticized more in front of their classmates. Moreover, in some classes, a few boys are allowed to dominate class time by interacting constantly with the teacher, while most students remain silent (Eccles, 1989).

Research shows that the behaviour of men and boys is often evaluated more positively than the behaviour of women and girls. Even when a woman and a man behave in identical ways, their behaviour may be interpreted differently (Porter & Geis, 1981; Wallstrom & O'Leary, 1981; Wiley & Eskilson, 1982; Yarkin, Town, & Wallston, 1982). Moreover, sexual categorization is not only a way of seeing differences, but also a way of creating differences. When men and women are treated differently in ordinary daily interactions, they may come to behave differently in return. These processes will be discussed later (see below, "Doing gender").

The individual level: gender as masculinity and femininity

To a greater or lesser extent, women and men come to accept gender distinctions visible at the structural level and enacted at the interpersonal level as part of the self-concept. They become *gender-typed*, ascribing to themselves the traits, behaviours, and roles normative for people of their sex in their culture. Women, moreover, internalize their devaluation and subordination. Feminist theories of personality development (e.g., Miller, 1986) stress that "feminine" characteristics such as passivity, excessive concern with pleasing others, lack of initiative, and dependency are psychological consequences of subordination. Members of subordinate social groups who adopt such characteristics are considered well adjusted; those who do not are controlled by psychiatric diagnosis, violence or the threat of violence, and social ostracism.

Much of the psychology of women and gender has consisted of documenting the effects of internalized subordination. Laboratory and field research, as well as clinical experience, attest that, compared to boys and men, girls and women lack a sense of personal entitlement (Apfelbaum, 1986; Major, McFarlin, & Gagnon, 1984), pay themselves less for comparable work (Major & Deaux, 1982), are equally satisfied with their employment, even though they are paid significantly less than men (Crosby, 1982), lose self-esteem and confidence in their academic ability, especially in mathematics and science, as they progress through the educational system (Chipman & Wilson, 1985; Eccles (Parsons) et al., 1985), and are more likely to suffer from disturbances of body image, eating disorders, and depression (McGrath, Keita, Strickland, & Russo, 1990; McCauley, Mintz, & Glenn, 1988; Hesse-Biber, 1989).

Gender at the social structural level has traditionally been the province of sociology and anthropology, while the interactional level has been encompassed by social psychology and the individual level by clinical, developmental, and personality psychology. In studying women and gender it is necessary to focus on one level while keeping sight of the system as a whole. Just as clinicians who treat the effects of internalized subordination must conceptualize and respond to structural aspects of clients' problems (Greenspan, 1983), researchers in the psychology of gender must place their work in the context of gendered social structures. Both clinicians and researchers share conceptual and methodological concerns with those attempting to understand other systems of social classification such as age, "race", and class (Brown & Root, 1990).

Methodological innovations and epistemological debates

The psychology of women and gender has generated substantial critique of psychology's traditional methods of research; selection of research participants has been a major area of contention. Many feminist researchers have examined the biases produced by ignoring the sex of the participants, by studying men more than women, and/or by examining one sex more than the other in certain situational contexts, such as affiliation among women or aggressiveness among men (cf. Grady, 1981; McHugh, Koeske, & Frieze, 1986; Wallston & Grady, 1985).

Feminist researchers have also raised similar questions about the exclusion of race and ethnicity, social class, and sexual orientation (Denmark, Russo, Frieze, & Sechzer, 1988). This kind of exclusion may lead to overgeneralizations about women as a global category similar to earlier overgeneralizations about human beings based largely on studies of men.

Others have raised more basic questions about the way research questions are generated and the values reflected by the way questions are asked. For example, much research has focused on whether mothers' outside employment endangers their children's psychological welfare. There is much less research, however, on whether fathers' work commitments harm their children or whether mothers' employment might be beneficial (Hare-Mustin & Marecek, 1990). Similar questions have been raised about comparison groups in psychological research; for example, when a biomedical study includes both sexes, should the two samples be matched on physical or social criteria (Parlee, 1981)?

The most intense debates in the area of research methodology have been about whether and how to conduct research on sex differences (cf., Unger, 1979, 1990; Unger & Crawford, 1992, chap. 3). Issues raised include whether researchers should stress similarities rather than differences since every psychological trait studied shows large overlaps between females and males; confusions between description and explanation; and problems associated with using biological rather than social explanations for the differences found. Despite cogent criticisms of specific problems in this kind of research (cf. Jacklin, 1981), dubious practices continue. Researchers using meta-analysis have questioned the stability and permanence of so-called sex differences (Hyde & Linn, 1986).

Despite the critiques, few methodological alternatives have emerged thus far (Fine & Gordon, 1989). Peplau and Conrad (1989) have examined feminist methodological issues and concluded that all methods can be used or abused. Thus, while the experimental method not only is inherently hierarchical, can result in context stripping and may be ecologically invalid, it can on the other hand result in the elucidation of psychological mechanisms that are difficult to detect in a normal environment. Similarly, so-called feminine qualitative methodology can be used for or against women. For example, Freud used qualitative methodology, but has frequently been accused of an anti-female bias.

One of the great innovations in feminist research has been to make values and politics explicit. Personal experience sensitizes people to different aspects of problems. Because the values of dominant groups in society are normative, they are not always recognized as values. When others – women or minorities, for example – question the assumptions of the dominant group, the underlying values are made more visible (Unger, 1983).

Using innovative techniques, some feminist researchers have explored value contradictions between groups of women. For example, Fine (1983–1984) showed how white middle-class assumptions about effective coping following a rape may not be helpful for poor black women. Lykes (1989) found that her use of a written signed consent form was seen as a violation of personal trust by the Guatemalan Indian women with whom she worked. Feminist clinicians have explored how similarities and differences in group membership and values between therapist and client can affect the course of therapy (Lerman & Porter, 1990).

The psychology of women and gender is not unique in being influenced by societal factors. Values and beliefs about the way the world works have been found to be related more to political and religious identity than to sex (Unger, 1992). These data question theories that stress a unique female epistemology or moral orientation. Feminist theorists have also argued that values and beliefs help to create reality rather than simply bias what aspects of reality we perceive (cf., Hare-Mustin & Marecek, 1990). Evidence for the social construction of reality has been provided by mainstream cognitive researchers as well as by feminists (Unger & Crawford, 1992).

Because psychology is part of our culture, doing psychological research is inevitably a political act (Crawford & Marecek, 1989). Feminist research is, therefore, explicitly political. It is particularly concerned with the impact of differential distinctions on individuals who regularly receive lower evaluations because of their social category. The topics in this chapter were chosen partially because they illuminate such phenomena as well as being representative of current research and practice in the field.

GENDER AND DEVELOPMENT THROUGH THE LIFESPAN

The area of gender development has been of great interest to psychologists for many years. Attention has now shifted away from concern with the socialization of gender in childhood to more interactive lifespan perspectives. According to such interactive models of social development, gender-related perceptions and behaviours change throughout the lifespan both because society's demands change with people's age and because people interpret seemingly identical messages about gender differently as they mature.

Childhood: becoming gendered

Current research on childhood has continued to find evidence that gender-characteristic traits in children of both sexes are shaped by parental attitudes and behaviours. Data ranging from sex-selective abortion practices to behavioural observations of the treatment of newborn infants show that males remain the preferred sex (Unger & Crawford, 1992, chap. 7). Pressure for gender-role conformity is stronger for boys than girls at an earlier age. Differential parental treatment tends to produce gender stereotypic traits of independence and efficacy in boys and emotional sensitivity, nurturance, and helplessness in girls. Parents appear largely unaware that they treat daughters and sons differently.

Children are not merely the passive recipients of gender socialization but active participants in it. By the nursery school years, girls and boys have different preferences in play and toys (Maccoby, 1988). In this age group, the choice of toy determines the sex of one's playmates rather than the other way around (Roopnarine, 1984). By the primary school years, girls and boys have formed sex-segregated social networks based on these preferences (Maccoby, 1988). Such sex segregation is greatest in situations that have *not* been structured by adults.

Sex segregation persists until adolescence, maintained by social control mechanisms such as teasing (Thorne & Luria, 1986). In same-sex peer interaction, boys and girls learn different styles of social influence and norms for aggression. These gender-characteristic patterns are not equally effective in mixed sex groups. For example, the physical dominance tactics used by boys to influence each other appear to be more effective in mixed sex situations than are the verbal persuasion techniques more frequently used by girls (Charlesworth & Dzur, 1987).

As children acquire cultural norms for stereotyping they become more intolerant of peers who deviate from these norms (Carter & McCloskey, 1984). Pressure for conformity is stronger for boys than for girls, as a quick scrutiny of the differential connotations of "tomboy" versus "sissy" easily demonstrates. Ironically, girls and women are probably permitted more latitude because boys and men are seen as the more valuable sex and, thus, as requiring greater attention to their socialization.

Short-term interventions designed by adults to help children unlearn gender typing are relatively ineffective because of peer pressures (Carpenter, Huston, & Holt, 1986). However, some girls resist gender typing and actively participate in sports, mathematics, and science. Familial factors related to this type of positive social deviance include active parental encouragement and the absence of brothers. Social class and "racial" differences are also important, but require further investigation.

Puberty and adolescence: gendered transitions

Puberty adds complexity to the processes underlying gender development. Biological, social, and cultural processes are interrelated in the transition from girlhood to womanhood. Researchers have moved beyond simple physiological mechanisms to explanations involving the social and cultural meaning of pubertal changes (cf., Brooks-Gunn, 1987; Martin, 1987; Ussher, 1989).

A major area of attention is the social implications of increasing bodily differences between boys and girls. Probably because of the subjective meaning of bodily change, puberty appears to be a more difficult transition for girls than for boys. For example, puberty involves a greater increase in body fat composition for girls than for boys (who gain muscle mass). Western society has, however, developed increasingly stringent norms for thinness in women (Silverstein, Perdue, Peterson, & Kelley, 1986). Girls' dissatisfaction with their looks begins during puberty, along with a decline in self-esteem.

Comparisons between early- and late-maturing girls indicate that dissatisfaction with one's looks is associated with the rapid and normal weight gain that is part of growing up (Attie & Brooks-Gunn, 1989). In comparison to late-maturing girls, early-maturing girls have less positive body images despite the fact that they date more. This seeming paradox highlights the contradictions produced by the differential meaning of mature physical development in females as compared to males. An attractive appearance is stressed more for young women than men despite the fact that excessive thinness is physiologically more abnormal for them. Sexual activity is also more problematic for women than men because of still existing double standards and differential responsibility in the event of pregnancy. In contrast, physical maturation in males carries with it unambiguous social advantages including opportunities for enhanced athletic prowess, leadership roles, and expectations for occupational success (Unger & Crawford, 1992).

Research on puberty has also focused on differences within groups of women; this research indicates that causal effects should be looked for at the level of physiological and social interactions. But, it also suggests that ignoring cultural norms such as the meaning of physical appearance may lead to the omission of important explanatory variables. For example, studies of ethnicity and the development of eating disorders among young women suggest that women of colour have a lower risk of anorexia nervosa and bulimia nervosa than white women (Root, 1990). Ironically, women of colour may be protected from eating disorders because white standards of beauty are not applied to them and they are less subject to social demands for low body weight.

Social constructions of developmental events

Cross-racial and cross-cultural research on gender and development are particularly useful in disentangling physiological and social influences. It has been suggested, for example, that menstruation has different meanings for black and for white women (Martin, 1987). Similarly, menopause as a developmental transition seems to be associated with the status of ageing women in different cultures. The depressive symptoms associated with menopause in the United States do not appear to exist in non-western cultures where women gain status and political power as they age (Kaiser, 1990). These women are freed from taboos involving ideas about menstrual pollution, they gain seniority in their domestic unit, and they acquire new role opportunities. In contrast, images of ageing women in the USA are almost uniformly negative (Kimmel, 1988).

Research on reproductive events unique to women – such as pregnancy and childbirth, menarche and menstruation, and menopause – emphasizes the social construction of meaning around these normal developmental processes. Normal events are medicalized and evoked as clinical diagnoses and explanations (cf. Ussher, 1989), and become reified in the official diagnostic manual (Hamilton & Gallant, 1988). This emphasis on physiological causality may have led previous researchers to ignore sociocultural context and exaggerate differences between women and men (Unger & Crawford, 1992). Newer research examining cross-cultural and intra-cultural differences among groups of women is valuable for setting the limits of biological explanation.

DOING GENDER

One of the most interesting areas of research is one that some psychologists and sociologists refer to as "doing gender" (Unger, 1988; West & Zimmerman, 1987). This kind of research focuses more on the interpersonal aspects of gender than its intra-psychic characteristics; it analyses the way cognitive categories based on sex as a social cue influence people's behaviour and elicit gender-characteristic patterns of interaction. Thus, it conceptualizes gender as a process through which social inequalities are created and maintained (Crawford & Marecek, 1989).

Sex is a salient social category. Distinctions based on the sex of target persons influence a wide variety of behaviours. For example, in remembering "who said what" in a conversation, people make more within-sex than between-sex errors. All women (or men) seem to "look alike". People also tend to minimize differences within groups and exaggerate differences between them. This process is particularly noticeable when individuals of that social category are present as a small minority. Under these conditions, their characteristics are seen as more stereotypic. Thus, people see women as more feminine and men as more masculine when there are few other members of their sex present in a group. Women and men do not differ in their tendency to categorize and make social judgements based on the sex of the minority group. Parallel effects have been found when "race", rather than sex, is the salient category (Taylor, Fiske, Etcoff, & Ruderman, 1978).

Other cognitive mechanisms are also influenced by the sex of stimulus persons. For example, people "remember" different (and stereotypic) information about the same individual based on her sexual (lesbian or heterosexual) or occupational (librarian or waitress) label (Snyder & Uranowitz, 1978). They evaluate the same material differently depending upon whether it is associated with a male, female, or ambiguously named person (Paludi & Strayer, 1985). Many researchers have found different causal attributions based on cues associated with gender (e.g., Wallston & O'Leary, 1981).

People also alter their self-presentation strategies to confirm others' gender-related expectations. For example, when women believed that they were to be interviewed by a male chauvinist rather than a non-sexist potential employer, they wore more frilly clothing, jewellery, and perfume to the interview. The process by which people act in a way that confirms other people's expectations about them is known as a self-fulfilling prophecy (e.g., Towson, Zanna, & MacDonald, 1989).

Self-fulfilling prophecies have been found in areas associated with gender such as physical attractiveness and some personality traits. One of the most dramatic demonstrations of the way self-fulfilling prophecies contribute to the perpetuation of gender stereotypes is a study by Skrypnek and Snyder (1982). Unacquainted pairs of women and men were asked to negotiate a division of labour on a series of work-related tasks that differed in their gender-role connotations. Individuals in each pair were located in a different room and communicated by means of a signalling system. Although each male participant was actually interacting with a female partner, some of the men were told that they were interacting with a male, some with a female partner, and some were not informed about the sex of their partner. During the first part of the study, men were given the opportunity to make the choices. Men were more likely to choose the more masculine tasks when they believed their partner was a woman than when they believed she was a man or had no information about her sex. Their partners provided behavioural confirmation of their beliefs. "Males" chose more masculine tasks whereas "females" chose more feminine tasks. The sex of assignment influenced their behaviour more than their actual sex did. Even after their male partners no longer had the opportunity to control the negotiations, many of the women continued to maintain "gender-appropriate behaviours" – appropriate for the sex to which they had been assigned.

Many gender-typed social behaviours are associated with status and power differences. Henley (1977) pioneered the study of the relationship between non-verbal behaviours associated with status and the behaviours of women and men. In many aspects of non-verbal behaviour women behave in a manner similar to men with low status and power and are treated by others as if they possess such subordinate status. Females' politeness, smiling, emotional responsiveness, smaller personal space, less frequent initiation of touching, and greater frequency of being interrupted all reflect subordinate status.

Researchers have manipulated assigned roles or levels of achievement to see if the way men customarily behave toward women is due more to gender or status. They have found that both men and women who are assigned higher social roles (e.g., teacher rather than student) or greater power tend to display non-verbal behaviours that are considered more characteristic of males. They claim more personal space, touch their partners more, and visually dominate their partners more than do women and men who have been granted less status and power in the experimental setting (Dovidio, Ellyson, Keating, Heltman, & Brown, 1988; Leffler, Gillespie, & Conaty, 1982). Non-verbal cues connoting status and power are readily decoded, but both men and women appear reluctant to use such cues to confer leadership on women (Porter & Geis, 1981).

The use of "masculine" forms of power by women is associated with a variety of social sanctions. For example, in mixed-sex groups men are more influenced by a woman who speaks tentatively than one who speaks assertively (Carli, 1990). Women who use expert power are rated by experienced managers as far colder than men using identical power strategies (Wiley & Eskilson, 1982).

A number of studies have also found that women are expected to be less competent as well as less powerful in groups (Dion, 1985). These perceptions are difficult to change. One set of researchers could change perceptions about male superiority on spatial tasks only by rigging the situation so that the women performed significantly better than did the men (Pugh & Wahrman, 1983). However, even these higher-performing women never gained a meaningful advantage over their male partners.

People use gender to infer power and status. For example, when students were given no information (other than their sex) about a man or a woman who were trying to influence each other in either a bank or a supermarket setting, they assumed the man had higher status and would be more successful in his influence attempts. When, however, job titles such as bank vice-president and teller were added to denote relative status, students used titles rather than gender to predict compliance (Eagly & Wood, 1982).

Gender-linked assumptions about power and powerlessness influence not only beliefs and attitudes but also behavioural interactions. Dovidio and Gaertner (1983) have provided a clever demonstration of the behavioural consequences of upsetting the customary relationship between sex and status. Male and female college students interacted with a male or female confederate who was introduced either as their superior or subordinate and who was purportedly of higher or lower ability than themselves. The confederate then had an "accident" in which a container of pencils was knocked to the floor. Status but not ability influenced the extent to which women were helped, whereas ability, not status, influenced the extent to which men were helped. Both sexes helped high- and low-ability women equally, but helped high-ability men more often than low-ability men. They helped women supervisors less than women subordinates, but did not differentiate in their assistance to men based on their rank.

This study demonstrates how customary status/sex confounds are maintained. Individuals who deviated from traditional expectations were penalized by receiving less assistance from others. The researchers found a parallel effect when superiors and subordinates differed in "race" rather than sex. Participants did not appear to realize that sexism or racism played a role in their helping behaviour.

These studies indicate the way that behaviours associated with masculinity and femininity are constructed in our society. Differential inferences and expectations based on sex as a social category lead to gender-differentiated behaviours to which target individuals respond. These behavioural responses confirm gender-stereotypic belief patterns. What begins in the minds of individuals becomes social reality.

SEXUALITY AND RELATIONSHIPS IN SOCIOCULTURAL CONTEXT

The development of sexual identity, sexual norms and behaviours, and the dynamics of intimate relationships are of clinical and theoretical concern to researchers in women and gender. Although sexual behaviour takes place between individuals, it is learned about and interpreted in the context of cultural institutions. Sexuality, the most intimate aspect of the self and the most private of experiences, is shaped by a social order where issues of status, dominance, and power affect that which is personal (Travis, 1990). Sexual desire, like gender itself, is a social construct, developed within the individual in the context of a particular time in history, social class and ethnic group, religion, and prevailing set of gender roles (Foucault, 1978; Rubin, 1984).

The repertoire of sexual acts that is recognized by a particular social group, together with the rules or guidelines for expected behaviour, and the expected punishments for violating the rules, form the basis of sexual scripts (Laws & Schwartz, 1977). Sexual scripts can be thought of as schemas for sexual concepts and events. They represent both pre-formed ways of understanding and interpreting potentially sex-relevant situations, and plans for action that people bring to such situations. Sexual scripts for practices such as dating (Rose & Frieze, 1989) mesh with norms and laws that govern the institution of marriage (Blumstein & Schwartz, 1983).

Content, vehicles, and consequences of sexual scripts

Popular culture provides many agents for the learning of sexual scripts. These include advertising, television programming, popular magazines, sex manuals, and romance novels (Altman, 1984; Jackson, 1987; Radway, 1984; Signorielli, 1989; Soley & Kurzbard, 1986).

The content of prevailing scripts on sexuality and relationships is almost exclusively heterosexual, focuses on male agency and control, and perpetuates a double standard for sexual activity that allows males a greater variety of sexual behaviours and partners (Unger & Crawford, 1992, chap. 9). Girls and women are rarely presented as active sexual agents, whether the medium is school sex education materials (Fine, 1988), adult sex manuals (Altman, 1984; Jackson, 1987), rock videos, or genre novels (Radway, 1984). The cultural muting of female sexual desire and agency – the "missing discourse of desire" (Fine, 1988) – has been related to clinical sexual dysfunction in women (Radlove, 1983; Tevlin & Leiblum, 1983). The emphasis on male pleasure and control, and the resulting difficulties for women in asserting a claim to safer sex, have been implicated in the increasing rate of

HIV infection, especially among women of colour. Finally, acceptance of scripts which encode women as passive and coy and men as conquerors has been related to the use of coercion by males in date and acquaintance rape and dating abuse (Muehlenhard & Linton, 1987; Russell, 1984).

Another aspect of sexual scripts is that youth, slimness, and conventional female attractiveness are presented as central dimensions of the schema for femininity and sexual desirability. Enhancing attractiveness thus becomes a central way of enacting sexuality for many women (Chapkis, 1986; Freedman, 1986; Ussher, 1989).

Much research has analysed cultural pressures for slimness. The representation of standards of female beauty has become more restrictive in the second half of the twentieth century; for example, the ideal body shape has (literally) narrowed, and the weight of movie actresses and models in women's magazines has been declining since about 1950 (Garner, Garfinkel, Schwartz, & Thompson, 1980). Popular media encode the message that women should stay slim (ads for diet foods occur at a 63:1 ratio in women's vs men's magazines) while at the same time stressing preoccupation with food (ads for sweets and snacks occur at a 359:1 ratio) (Silverstein, Perdue, Peterson, Vogel, & Fantini, 1986). The negative evaluation of normal female bodily shape has been related to psychological distress, low self-esteem, and negative body image in women (Freedman, 1986; Jackson, Sullivan, & Rostker, 1988; Stake & Lauer, 1987; Ussher, 1989).

Many groups are marginalized by the prevailing discourse of sexuality: lesbian and bisexual women and homosexual men (Boston Lesbian Psychologies Collective, 1987), women of colour (Espin, 1986), older women (Bell, 1989), and people with disabilities (Fine & Asch, 1988).

Power and roles in intimate relationships

The study of power and roles in marriage has a long history in psychology and sociology. Marriages have been categorized as traditional, modern, egalitarian, dual-earner, or dual-career based on the allocation of authority, degree of role differentiation, patterns of shared activities, and economic contributions (Peplau & Gordon, 1985). In most marriages, husbands have greater power than wives, due to a variety of social factors (Blumstein & Schwartz, 1983; Steil & Weltman, 1991). Marital satisfaction is affected by power differentials and flucuates over the life cycle, with the child-rearing years least satisfying (Rhyne, 1981; Ruble, Fleming, Hackel, & Stangor, 1988; Steinberg & Silverberg, 1987). Increasingly, researchers are studying the interplay of roles (spouse, parent, and paid worker), ongoing role negotiation in both sexes, and committed relationships other than heterosexual marriage (e.g., Crosby, 1987). Although research on gay and lesbian couples is compromised by sampling biases, it suggests that equality is more likely in lesbian relationships than heterosexual marriage, and that satisfaction is related to many of the same variables (Blumstein & Schwartz, 1983; Peplau & Gordon, 1985).

Researchers are beginning to compare mixed-sex and same-sex couples in efforts to untangle individual-level gender-effects (e.g., socialized differences) from interactional (e.g., role expectations) and structural effects (e.g., greater male access to external resources such as money). An interesting example is research on influence strategies. Gender stereotypes are clear: women are believed to use indirect, manipulative strategies (sulking, crying, alleging insensitivity in the partner) and men are believed to use direct strategies (expressing anger, calling for a rational discussion). Dating partners report that they believe such stereotypes and also that their own behaviour is congruent with them (Kelley et al., 1978).

If influence strategies are due to childhood socialization for females to be more emotional and males more task-oriented, both partners in a lesbian couple should use tactics such as withdrawal and emotionality; among gay men, both partners should use more direct tactics. However, in a study of self-reported influence strategies in lesbians, gay men, and heterosexuals, sex affected the type of strategy employed only among the heterosexuals. In all groups, the individual who saw him/herself as the more powerful partner used direct, interactive strategies and the less-powerful partner used indirect and non-interactional tactics (Falbo & Peplau, 1980). Thus, "sex-related" strategies may be more accurately considered "power-related" strategies. This interpretation is supported by cross-cultural research showing that women from the United States use more direct influence tactics than women from Mexico, who have relatively less economic and social power (Belk, Garcia-Falconi, Hernandez-Sanchez, & Snell, 1988).

CONCLUSION

The new psychology of women and gender encompasses virtually every subfield within the discipline. The revisionist work of feminist psychologists holds the possibility of transforming the discipline into a true psychology of people. In addition to the selected topics reviewed here, there is a great deal of research on interactions of multiple roles such as spouse, parent, and worker; the causes, incidence, and effects of forms of violence against women; personality development across the lifespan; the psychology of pregnancy and mothering; masculinity and male roles; stereotypes; sexual differentiation, variation, and the social construction of sexual dichotomy; work and achievement. The volumes suggested below invite the reader to participate in the rich knowledge and ongoing debates of this emerging field.

FURTHER READING

Basow, S. A. (1992). *Gender stereotypes and roles* (3rd edn) Pacific Grove, CA: Brooks/Cole.

Crosby, F. (Ed.) (1987). *Spouse, parent, worker: On gender and multiple roles*. New Haven, CT: Yale University Press.

Hare-Mustin, R. T., & Marecek, J. (Eds) (1990). *Making a difference: Psychology and the construction of gender*. New Haven: Yale University Press.

Kimmel, M. S. (Ed.) (1987). *Changing men: New directions in research on men and masculinity*. Newbury Park, CA: Sage.

Unger, R. K., & Crawford, M. (1992). *Women and gender: A feminist psychology*. New York and Philadelphia, PA: McGraw-Hill and Temple University Press.

Wilkinson, S. A. (Ed.) (1986). *Feminist social psychology*. Milton Keynes: Open University Press.

REFERENCES

Altman, M. (1984). Everything they always wanted you to know. In C. S. Vance (Ed.) *Pleasure and danger: Exploring female sexuality* (pp. 115–130). Boston, MA: Routledge & Kegan Paul.

Apfelbaum, E. (1986). *Women in leadership positions*. Henry Tajfel Memorial Lecture presented at the annual conference of the British Psychological Society, University of Sussex.

Attie, I., & Brooks-Gunn, J. (1989). The development of eating problems in adolescent girls: A longitudinal study. *Developmental Psychology*, *25*, 70–79.

Belk, S. S., Garcia-Falconi, R., Hernandez-Sanchez, J., & Snell, W. E. (1988). Avoidance strategy use in the intimate relationships of women and men from Mexico and the United States. *Psychology of Women Quarterly*, *12*, 165–174.

Bell, I. P. (1989). The double standard: Age. In J. Freeman (Ed.) *Women: A feminist perspective* (4th edn, pp. 236–244). Mountain View, CA: Mayfield.

Blumstein, P., & Schwartz, P. (1983). *American couples*. New York: William Morrow.

Boston Lesbian Psychologies Collective (Eds) (1987). *Lesbian psychologies: Explorations and challenges*. Urbana, IL: University of Illinois.

Brooks-Gunn, J. (1987). The impact of puberty and sexual activity upon the health and education of adolescent girls and boys. *Peabody Journal of Education*, *64*, 88–112.

Brown, L., & Root, M. (Eds) (1990). *Diversity and complexity in feminist therapy*. New York: Harrington Park Press.

Carli, L. L. (1990). Gender, language, and influence. *Journal of Personality and Social Psychology*, *59*, 941–951.

Carpenter, C. J., Huston, A. C., & Holt, W. (1986). Modification of pre-school sex-typed behaviors by participation in adult-structured activities. *Sex Roles*, *14*, 603–615.

Carter, D. B., & McCloskey, L. A. (1984). Peers and the maintenance of sex-typed behavior: The development of children's conceptions of cross-gender behavior in their peers. *Social Cognition*, *2*, 294–314.

Chapkis, W. (1986). *Beauty secrets: Women and the politics of appearance*. Boston, MA: South End.

Charlesworth, W. R., & Dzur, C. (1987). Gender comparisons of pre-schoolers' behavior and resource utilization in group problem-solving. *Child Development*, *58*, 191–200.

Chipman, S. F., & Wilson, D. M. (1985). Understanding mathematics course enrollment and mathematics achievement: A synthesis of the research. In S. F. Chipman, L. R. Brush, & D. M. Wilson (Eds) *Women and mathematics: Balancing the equation* (pp. 275–328). Hillsdale, NJ: Lawrence Erlbaum.

Crawford, M., & Marecek, J. (1989). Psychology reconstructs the female. *Psychology of Women Quarterly*, *13*, 147–166.

Crosby, F. (1982). *Relative deprivation and working women*. New York: Oxford University Press.

Crosby, F. (Ed.) (1987). *Spouse, parent, worker: On gender and multiple roles*. New Haven, CT: Yale University Press.

Deaux, K. (1985). Sex and gender. *Annual Review of Psychology*, *36*, 49–81.

Deaux, K., & Major, B. (1987). Putting gender into context: An interactive model of gender-related behavior. *Psychological Review*, *94*, 369–389.

Denmark, F., Russo, N. F., Frieze, I. H., & Sechzer, J. A. (1988). Guidelines for avoiding sexism in psychological research: A report of the ad hoc committee on nonsexist research. *American Psychologist*, *43*, 582–585.

Dion, K. L. (1985). Sex, gender, and groups. In V. E. O'Leary, R. K. Unger, & B. S. Wallston (Eds) *Women, gender, and social psychology*, Hillsdale, NJ: Lawrence Erlbaum.

Dovidio, J. F., & Gaertner, S. L. (1983). The effects of sex, status, and ability on helping behavior. *Journal of Applied Social Psychology*, *13*, 191–205.

Dovidio, J. F., Ellyson, S. L., Keating, C. F., Heltman, K., & Brown, C. E. (1988). The relationship of social power to visual displays of dominance between men and women. *Journal of Personality and Social Psychology*, *54*, 233–242.

Eagly, A. H., & Wood, W. (1982). Inferred sex differences in status as a determinant of gender stereotypes about social influence. *Journal of Personality and Social Psychology*, *43*, 915–928.

Eccles, J. S. (1989). Bringing young women to math and science. In M. Crawford & M. Gentry (Eds) *Gender and thought: Psychological perspectives* (pp. 36–58). New York: Springer-Verlag.

Eccles (Parsons), J. S., Adler, T. F., Futterman, R., Goff, S. B., Kaczala, C. M., Meece, J. L., & Midgley, C. (1985). Self-perceptions, task perceptions, socializing influences, and the decision to enroll in mathematics. In S. F. Chipman, L. R. Brush, & D. M. Wilson (Eds) *Women and mathematics: Balancing the equation* (pp. 95–122). Hillsdale, NJ: Lawrence Erlbaum.

Espin, O. M. (1986). Cultural and historical influences on sexuality in Hispanic/Latin women. In J. Cole (Ed.) *All American women: Lines that divide, ties that bind* (pp. 272–284). New York: Free Press (Macmillan).

Falbo, T., & Peplau, L. A. (1980). Power strategies in intimate relationships. *Journal of Personality and Social Psychology*, *38*, 618–628.

Fine, M. (1983–1984). Coping with rape: Critical perspectives on consciousness. *Imagination, Cognition, and Personality*, *3*, 249–267.

Fine, M. (1988). Sexuality, schooling, and adolescent females: The missing discourse of desire. *Harvard Educational Review*, *58*, 29–53.

Fine, M., & Asch, A. (1988). *Women with disabilities: Essays in psychology, culture, and politics*. Philadelphia, PA: Temple University Press.

Fine, M., & Gordon, S. M. (1989). Feminist transformations of/despite psychology. In M. Crawford and M. Gentry (Eds) *Gender and thought: Psychological Perspectives*. New York: Springer-Verlag.

Foucault, M. (1978). *The history of sexuality*. New York: Pantheon.

Freedman, R. (1986). *Beauty bound*. Lexington, MA: D. C. Heath.

Garner, D. M., Garfinkel, P. E., Schwartz, D., & Thompson, M. (1980). Cultural expectations of thinness in women. *Psychological Reports, 47*, 483–491.

Grady, K. E. (1981). Sex bias in research design. *Psychology of Women Quarterly, 5*, 628–636.

Greenspan, M. (1983). *A new approach to women and therapy*. New York: McGraw-Hill.

Hamilton, J. A., & Gallant (Alagna), S. J. (1988). On a premenstrual psychiatric diagnosis: What's in a name? *Professional Psychology: Research and Practice, 19*, 271–278.

Hare-Mustin, R. T., & Marecek, J. (Eds) (1990). *Making a difference: Psychology and the construction of gender*. New Haven, CT: Yale University Press.

Henley, N. M. (1977). *Body politics: Power, sex, and nonverbal communication*. Englewood Cliffs, NJ: Prentice-Hall.

Hesse-Biber, S. (1989). Eating patterns and disorders in a college population: Are college women's eating problems a new phenomenon? *Sex Roles, 20*, 71–89.

Hyde, J. S., & Linn, M. C. (Eds) (1986). *The psychology of gender: Advances through meta-analysis*. Baltimore, MD: Johns Hopkins University Press.

Jacklin, C. N. (1981). Methodological issues in the study of sex-related differences. *Developmental Review, 1*, 266–273.

Jackson, L. A., Sullivan, L. A., & Rostker, R. (1988). Gender, gender role, and body image. *Sex Roles, 19*, 429–443.

Jackson, M. (1987). "Facts of life" or the eroticization of women's oppression? Sexology and the social construction of heterosexuality. In P. Caplan (Ed.) *The cultural construction of sexuality* (pp. 52–81). London: Tavistock.

Kahn, A. S., & Jean, P. J. (1983). Integration and elimination or separation and redefinition: The future of the psychology of women. *Signs: Journal of Women in Culture and Society, 8*, 659–670.

Kaiser, K. (1990). Cross-cultural perspectives on menopause. In M. Flint, F. Kronenberg, & W. H. Utian (Eds) *Multidisciplinary perspectives on menopause. Annals of the New York Academy of Sciences, 592*, 430–432.

Kelley, H. H., Cunningham, J. D., Grisham, J. A., Lefebvre, L. M., Sink, C. R., & Yablon, G. (1978). Sex differences in comments made during conflict within close heterosexual pairs. *Sex Roles, 4*, 473–491.

Kimmel, D. C. (1988). Ageism, psychology, and public policy. *American Psychologist, 43*, 175–178.

Laws, J. L., & Schwartz, P. (1977). *Sexual scripts*. Hinsdale, IL: Dryden.

Leffler, A., Gillespie, D. L., & Conaty, J. C. (1982). The effects of status differentiation on nonverbal behavior. *Social Psychology Quarterly, 45*, 153–161.

Lerman, H., & Porter, N. (1990). The contribution of feminism to ethics in psychotherapy. In H. Lerman & N. Porter (Eds) *Feminist ethics in psychotherapy* (pp. 5–13). New York: Springer.

Lykes, M. B. (1989). Dialogue with Guatemalan Indian women: Critical perspectives on constructing collaborative research. In R. K. Unger (Ed.) *Representations: Social constructions of gender* (pp. 167–186). Amityville, NY: Baywood.

McCaulay, M., Mintz, L., & Glenn, A. A. (1988). Body image, self-esteem, and depression-proneness: Closing the gender gap. *Sex Roles, 18*, 381–391.

Maccoby, E. E. (1988). Gender as a social category. *Developmental Psychology, 24*, 755–765.

McGrath, E., Keita, G. P., Strickland, B. R., & Russo, N. F. (1990). *Women and depression: Risk factors and treatment issues*. Washington, DC: American Psychological Association.

McHugh, M. D., Koeske, R. D., & Frieze, I. H. (1986). Issues to consider in conducting nonsexist psychological research: A guide for researchers. *American Psychologist, 41*, 879–890.

Major, B., & Deaux, K. (1982). Individual differences in justice behavior. In J. Greenberg & R. L. Cohen (Eds) *Equity and justice in social behavior*. New York: Academic Press.

Major, B., McFarlin, D. B., & Gagnon, D. (1984). Overworked and underpaid: On the nature of gender differences in personal entitlement. *Journal of Personality and Social Psychology, 47*, 1399–1412.

Martin, E. (1987). *The woman in the body: A cultural analysis of reproduction*. Boston, MA: Beacon.

Miller, J. B. (1986). *Toward a new psychology of women*. Boston, MA: Beacon (originally published 1976).

Muehlenhard, C. L., & Linton, M. A. (1987). Date rape and sexual aggression in dating situations: Incidence and risk factors. *Journal of Counseling Psychology, 34*, 186–196.

O'Connell, A. N., & Russo, N. F. (1991). Special issue: Women's heritage in psychology: Origins, development, and future directions. *Psychology of Women Quarterly, 15*(4).

Paludi, M. A., & Strayer, L. A. (1984). What's in an author's name? Differential evaluations of performance as a function of author's name. *Sex Roles, 10*, 353–361.

Parlee, M. B. (1981). Appropriate control groups in feminist research. *Psychology of Women Quarterly, 5*, 637–644.

Peplau, L. A., & Conrad, E. (1989). Beyond nonsexist research: The perils of feminist methods in psychology. *Psychology of Women Quarterly, 13*, 379–400.

Peplau, L. A., & Gordon, S. L. (1985). Women and men in love: Gender differences in close heterosexual relationships. In V. E. O'Leary, R. K. Unger, & B. S. Wallston (Eds) *Women, gender, and social psychology* (pp. 257–292). Hillsdale, NJ: Lawrence Erlbaum.

Porter, N., & Geis, F. (1981). Women and nonverbal leadership cues: When seeing is not believing. In C. Mayo & N. Henley (Eds) *Gender and nonverbal behavior*. New York: Springer-Verlag.

Pugh, M. D., & Wahrman, R. (1983). Neutralizing sexism in mixed-sex groups: Do women have to be better than men? *American Journal of Sociology, 88*, 746–762.

Radlove, S. (1983). Sexual response and gender roles. In E. R. Allgeier & N. B. McCormick (Eds) *Changing boundaries: Gender roles and sexual behavior* (pp. 87–105). Palo Alto, CA: Mayfield.

Radway, J. (1984). *Reading the romance: Women, patriarchy, and popular literature*. Chapel Hill, NC: University of North Carolina Press.

Rhyne, D. (1981). Bases of marital satisfaction among men and women. *Journal of Marriage and the Family, 43*, 941–955.

Roopnarine, J. L. (1984). Sex-typed socialization in mixed-age preschool classrooms. *Child Development, 55*, 1078–1084.

Root, M. P. P. (1990). Disordered eating in women of color. *Sex Roles, 22*, 525–536.

Rose, S. A., & Frieze, I. H. (1989). Young singles' scripts for a first date. *Gender & Society, 3*, 258–268.

Rosenberg, R. (1982). *Beyond separate spheres: The intellectual roots of modern feminism*. New Haven, CT: Yale University Press.

Rubin, G. (1984). Thinking sex: Notes for a radical theory of the politics of sexuality. In C. S. Vance (Ed.) *Pleasure and danger: Exploring female sexuality* (pp. 267–319). Boston, MA: Routledge & Kegan Paul.

Ruble, D. N., Fleming, A. S., Hackel, L. S., & Stangor, C. (1988). Changes in the marital relationship during the transition to first time motherhood: Effects of violated expectations concerning division of household labor. *Journal of Personality and Social Psychology*, *85*, 78–87.

Russell, D. E. H. (1984). *Sexual exploitation: Rape, child sexual abuse, and workplace harassment*. Beverly Hills, CA: Sage.

Scarborough, E., & Furumoto, L. (1987). *Untold lives: The first generation of American women psychologists*. New York: Columbia University Press.

Sherif, C. W. (1982). Needed concepts in the study of gender identity. *Psychology of Women Quarterly*, *6*, 375–398.

Signorielli, N. (1989). Television and conceptions about sex roles: Maintaining conventionality and the status quo. *Sex Roles*, *21*, 341–360.

Silverstein, B., Perdue, L., Peterson, B., & Kelley, E. (1986). The role of the mass media in promoting a thin standard of bodily attractiveness for women. *Sex Roles*, *14*, 519–532.

Silverstein, B., Perdue, L., Peterson, B., Vogel, L., & Fantini, D. A. (1986). Some possible causes of the thin standard of bodily attractiveness for women. *International Journal of Eating Disorders*, *5*, 907–916.

Skrypnek, B. J., & Snyder, M. (1982). On the self-perpetuating nature of stereotypes about women and men. *Journal of Experimental Social Psychology*, *18*, 277–291.

Snyder, M., & Uranowitz, S. W. (1978). Reconstructing the past: some cognitive consequences of person perception. *Journal of Personality and Social Psychology*, *36*, 941–950.

Soley, L. C., & Kurzbard, G. (1986). Sex in advertising: A comparison of 1964 and 1984 magazine advertisements. *Journal of Advertising*, *15*, 46–64.

Stake, J., & Lauer, M. L. (1987). The consequences of being overweight: A controlled study of gender differences. *Sex Roles*, *17*, 31–37.

Steil, J. M., & Weltman, K. (1991). Marital inequality: The importance of resources, personal attributes, and social norms on career valuing and the allocation of domestic responsibilities. *Sex Roles*, *24*, 161–179.

Steinberg, L., & Silverberg, S. B. (1987). Influences on marital satisfaction during the middle stages of the family life cycle. *Journal of Marriage and the Family*, *49*, 751–760.

Stimpson, C. R. (1986). *Women's studies in the United States*. New York: Ford Foundation.

Taylor, S. E., Fiske, S. T., Etcoff, N. L., & Ruderman, A. J. (1978). Categorical and contextual bases of person memory and stereotyping. *Journal of Personality and Social Psychology*, *36*, 778–793.

Tevlin, H. E., & Leiblum, S. R. (1983). Sex-role stereotypes and female sexual dysfunction. In V. Franks & E. Rothblum (Eds) *Stereotyping of women: Its effects on mental health* (pp. 129–148). New York: Springer.

Thorne, B., & Luria, Z. (1986). Sexuality and gender in children's daily worlds. *Social Problems*, *33*, 176–190.

Towson, S. M. J., Zanna, M. P., & MacDonald, G. (1989). Self-fulfilling prophecy: Sex-role stereotypes and expectations for behavior. In R. K. Unger (Ed.) *Representations: Social constructions of gender* (pp. 97–107). Amityville, NY: Baywood.

Travis, C. (1990). *The social construction of women's sexuality*. Paper presented at the annual conference of the American Psychological Association, Boston, MA, August.

Unger, R. K. (1979). *Female and male*. New York: Harper & Row.

Unger, R. K. (1983). Through the looking glass: No Wonderland yet! (The reciprocal relationship between methodology and models of reality). *Psychology of Women Quarterly*, *8*, 9–32.

Unger, R. K. (1988). Psychological, feminist, and personal epistemology. In M. M. Gergen (Ed.) *Feminist thought and the structure of knowledge* (pp. 124–141). New York: New York University Press.

Unger, R. K. (1990). Imperfect reflections of reality. In R. I. Hare-Mustin & J. Marecek (Eds) *Making a difference: Psychology and the construction of gender* (pp. 102–149). New Haven, CT: Yale University Press.

Unger, R. K. (1992). Will the real sex difference please stand up? *Feminism & Psychology*, *2*, 231–238.

Unger, R. K., & Crawford, M. (1992). *Women and gender: A feminist psychology*. New York and Philadelphia, PA: McGraw-Hill and Temple University Press.

Ussher, J. (1989). *The psychology of the female body*. London: Routledge.

Wallston, B. S., & Grady, K. E. (1985). Integrating the feminist critique and the crisis in social psychology: Another look at research methods. In V. E. O'Leary, R. K. Unger, & B. S. Wallston (Eds) *Women, gender and social psychology* (pp. 7–34). Hillsdale, NJ: Lawrence Erlbaum.

Wallston, B. S., & O'Leary, V. E. (1981). Sex makes a difference: Differential perceptions of women and men. In L. Wheeler (Ed.) *Review of personality and social psychology* (vol. 2). Beverly Hill, CA: Sage.

West, C., & Zimmerman, D. H. (1987). Doing gender. *Gender & Society*, *1*, 125–151.

Wiley, M. G., & Eskilson, A. (1982). Coping in the corporation: Sex role constraints. *Journal of Applied Social Psychology*, *12*, 1–11.

Yarkin, K. L., Town, J. P., & Wallston, B. S. (1982). Blacks and women must try harder: Stimulus persons' race and sex and attributions of causality. *Personality and Social Psychology Bulletin*, *8*, 21–24.

11.4

PSYCHOLOGY AND THE LAW

Robert T. Croyle

University of Utah, USA

Elizabeth F. Loftus

University of Washington, USA

Barriers to acceptance	Psychologists as expert
Pre-trial	witnesses
Pre-trial publicity	Participants: decision-makers
Alternatives to a formal trial	**Sentencing and incarceration**
Trial	Juries
Procedures	Judges
Participants: information	Prison confinement
suppliers	**Conclusion**
Eyewitness testimony	**Further reading**
Assessing and improving	**References**
the validity of testimony	

Every legal system is, in part, a way to evaluate and manage human behaviour. Hence the law makes a number of assumptions, often unstated, about human psychology. The overlap of psychology and the law has always interested psychologists. The 1908 publication of Hugo Münsterberg's *On the Witness Stand* marks the beginning of systematic psychological research on the legal system of the United States. More recently, the rise of social psychology in the 1960s led to comprehensive books and papers that rejuvenated interest in psychology and the law (Kalven & Zeisel, 1966; Tapp, 1969). Research since then has tended to focus on issues of criminal jury trials, despite the small number of such trials compared to other legal actions.

BARRIERS TO ACCEPTANCE

There are differences in the method of inquiry of the two disciplines: the law relies on doctrine and precedent, whereas psychology relies on empirical support for theory-bound hypotheses. As a result, legal judgments are clinical and diagnostic, and data from psychological research are mainly probabilistic and statistical (Doyle, 1989). Understandably, there are barriers to the law's acceptance of empirical psychology. Sometimes personal biases surface. The trial, to some psychologists, is an arena where attorneys defend preconceptions in the face of constant debate, where actual guilt or innocence is not the point. On the other hand, some lawyers believe that psychologists are inclined by temperament and training to mitigate the rigour of the law (e.g., Cederbaums & Arnold, 1975). Despite these differences, psychological studies are used more and more as evidence in trials, and as support in written court opinions (Vollrath & Davis, 1980).

Although the bulk of research deals with criminal trials, virtually every area of the legal process that touches on psychology has been investigated. It is useful to organize research by relating findings to the legal process itself. The first major phase of the judicial process involves pre-trial activities, such as influences on criminal behaviour, pre-trial publicity, and alternative methods of resolving disputes. The second phase is the trial, where research follows procedures and participants, to paraphrase the classification suggested by Thibaut and Walker (1975). Trial procedures involve the organization of the trial and competence to stand trial. Participants include information suppliers such as witnesses, and judges and juries as decision-makers. Finally, research on sentencing and incarceration includes sentencing disparity and prison confinement.

PRE-TRIAL

Pre-trial publicity

Often the media report details of a crime before it comes to trial; potential jurors may have knowledge and opinions about a case before hearing any evidence in trial. The prejudicial impact of pre-trial publicity operates in a number of specific ways. Some researchers distinguish between factual publicity, which might include incriminating evidence, and emotional publicity, which usually takes the form of a dramatic appeal to the emotions. For both of these types of publicity, the more that witnesses have been exposed to such information, the more they will tend to favour the prosecution in trial. Judges' instructions have no appreciable effect on biases from pre-trial publicity, and deliberation usually strengthens these publicity biases. Although most jurors who have been exposed to "anti-defence" publicity do not report any partiality, they perceive the defendant as being more guilty than do jurors who have not been exposed (Kramer, Kerr, & Carroll, 1990). Even gossip may have a role in prejudicial publicity: testimony following discussion of the facts of a case includes false information at a much greater rate than testimony with no prior discussion. This result did not, however, hold for narrative recall of simple information (Hollin & Clifford, 1983).

Alternatives to a formal trial

Alternatives to trial decisions arose primarily during the 1970s in the United States as a method of reducing backlog and delay in the court system. One method was the Summary Jury Trial, which utilized a videotape of trial proceedings, edited for clarity by the judge. The resulting jury verdict took on the character of advice to the court rather than a binding decision such as a jury verdict. Experimental confirmation of the utility of the Summary Jury Trial is mixed and sparse.

TRIAL

Procedures

Research related specifically to the process of the trial involves issues with the trial's procedures or participants. This distinction is pragmatic only, and not clear-cut in every instance.

Research indicates that European and American subjects tend to think of their native judicial system as more fair, regardless of whether their countries employ an adversary or non-adversary system. The adversary system somewhat reduces expectancy biases, but increases the chance that pertinent information will not reach the trier of fact (Walker & Lind, 1984). Other procedural research suggests that the chronological order in which jurors receive information affects their judgement about defendants. For example, if attorneys present charges against a defendant in reverse order of severity, then juries are more inclined to find against the defendant. These relationships hold both for mock juries (groups who deliberate about a decision) and for mock jurors (individuals) (Davis, 1989). Multiple charges against a defendant in a single trial may increase the rate of guilty verdicts, over the rate found with independent consideration of the charges. In addition, experienced jurors may be more likely than uninitiated jurors to convict a suspect (Davis, Tindale, Nagao, Hinsz, & Robertson, 1984).

Participants: information suppliers

Eyewitness testimony

Eyewitness testimony is a highly popular area of psychology and law research. Generally, memory for the events of a crime involves the same issues as does memory for any other event. The process of memory roughly comprises the acquisition, retention, and retrieval stages. For memory acquisition, some factors relate directly to the criminal act. For example, witnesses tend drastically to overestimate crime duration, a phenomenon typical of memory for complex or rapid events. Victims also tend to remember fewer details, especially peripheral details, as the violence of the crime increases. Other research on event factors covers lighting conditions, speed, distance, and colour vision (Loftus, Greene, & Doyle, 1989).

Characteristics of the witness have also been related to memory acquisition. For instance, most studies conclude that memory for everyday facts does not improve with a witness's training or experience. Although women are better than men at recognizing faces in some laboratory studies, this does not seem to be the case in the eyewitness context (Loftus, Banaji, Schooler, & Foster, 1987). Finally, when witnesses have different preconceptions or prior expectations relating to some element of a crime, their recall of events may vary widely.

The role of age in an eyewitness's accuracy has also been examined. Adult memory performance declines with advancing age, on the average. Children often recall less than adults, although they can be quite accurate in what they do recall. Children tend to make more errors when responding to specific questions, and young children tend to be more suggestible than adults (Doris, 1991).

Stress and arousal during a crime can influence recall in a number of ways. The Yerkes-Dodson Law states that performance is best at a certain optimum level of stress, and that an increase or decrease in stress from this level will accompany a decline in performance (Yerkes & Dodson, 1908). Tolerance for stress varies from person to person. Experimental research findings tend to agree with this model, although one field study found that reported stress did not impair accurate memory (Yuille & Cutshall, 1986). The relation between stress and accurate memory is hard to evaluate, but it seems clear that stress restricts attention. In particular, witnesses to crimes with weapons often experience "weapon focus" – concentration on a visible weapon to the exclusion of other details of the situation. Chronic stress on a person, such as is brought on by the loss of a job or death in the family, can also reduce memory (Loftus, Greene, & Doyle, 1989).

Memory retention is influenced by time and by post-event information. Ebbinghaus's forgetting curve suggests that memory declines rapidly soon after an event, and then declines gradually. Many studies support this trend for eyewitness memory (e.g., Cash & Moss, 1972). Beyond the effect of time, the stress of a violent or emotional event may motivate a witness to "forget" an unpleasant incident. Memory is also malleable and subject to distortions. Information that may not be true about a crime reaches witnesses through

1031

Figure 1 Materials used in memory experiment. These photographs were used in an experiment designed to test the accuracy of recollection of two groups of subjects. The only difference between the two photos is that there is a stop sign in one and a yield (give way) sign in the other
Source: Loftus, Miller, and Burns, 1978

conversation, newspapers, and television, and even through questions about the crime posed to them by the authorities.

Additional information, true or false, can supplement or distort true memories. Loftus, Miller, and Burns (1978) showed subjects a series of colour slides depicting an accident. A red car was shown approaching an intersection. After turning a corner, the car knocked down a pedestrian who was crossing the street. One of the slides was varied (see Figure 1). Half of the subjects saw the slide with the stop sign, whereas others saw the slide with the yield (give way) sign. Immediately afterward, some subjects were asked a series of questions that included, "Did another car pass the red Datsun while it was stopped at the stop sign?" On a later memory test, subjects who answered this question after seeing the slide with a yield sign were more likely to remember seeing a stop sign. These effects of false information grow as the original memory fades in time. Warning a witness about the possibility of misleading information reduces the chance of memory distortion.

Legal procedures require witnesses to retrieve all kinds of information from memory. Witnesses might identify particular objects or people, or simply give general impressions. As the Loftus et al. (1978) study described above illustrates, the method of eliciting information plays a large role in accuracy. The most fruitful interview strategy is for the witness first to report freely about the crime and then to answer specific questions. Even small differences in question wording can produce different answers. For example, researchers found that asking, "Did you see the broken headlight?" led to more wrong affirmations than did the question, "Did you see a broken head-light?" The greater the perceived credibility of the questioner, the more easily witnesses can be misled. Laws of procedure are intended to prevent the court-room use of many types of leading questions. Nevertheless, many interviews take place before the witness is in court. The importance of unbiased interviews and identification procedures prior to trial cannot be overstated (Wells, 1993).

Jurors are often impressed with witnesses who are conspicuously confident or detailed about their own testimonies. Unfortunately, most research findings conclude that the relationship between confidence and accuracy in testimony is not a strong one. When a single witness is partly confident and partly hesitant in testimony, the confidently stated information is slightly more likely to be correct (Loftus et al., 1989). The relation of confidence to accuracy is positively strengthened when witnesses watch videotapes of them-selves making an identification, and then rate their confidence in their identi-fications (Kassin, 1985).

Assessing and improving the validity of testimony

Social scientists and legal professionals have developed several interview methods with a view to maximizing recall accuracy. Most research has been devoted to the hypnosis, cognitive, and polygraph interview methods. The phenomenon of hypnosis is complex and not thoroughly understood (Sigman, Philips, & Clifford, 1985). Dramatic cases exist where hypnosis interviews appeared to enhance recall for otherwise inaccessible information, but the method is not considered reliable by many court jurisdictions in the USA. Common misunderstandings about the nature of hypnosis and conflicting research results hinder its acceptance. For instance, popular films often depict hypnotists as able to control their hypnotized subjects' minds. No research finding supports this belief. Another misunderstanding is that hypnotized subjects *ipso facto* tell the truth; actually there is no medical or psychological method known to ensure truthfulness. Hypersuggestibility is sometimes attributed to subjects in a hypnosis interview (Reiser, 1989). Other commentators maintain that hypnosis interviews increase in reported testimony the amount of confabulation, or the filling in of memory gaps with invented information, in testimony. In addition, hypnotized witnesses can later become overconfident of their memories (Wrightsman, 1991).

The close similarity between part of the hypnosis interview and the cognitive interview format prompted some researchers to investigate the comparative utility of the two methods. The cognitive interview was developed to help standardize and improve the interviewing skills of law enforcers. Cognitive interviews use the same general format as a "standard" interview: free recall followed by specific questions, but it also contains certain general memory enhancement features. The close similarity of the preparation steps for the hypnosis interview and the cognitive interview itself may be responsible for a large part of improved memory under hypnosis, rather than the hypnotic state itself (Yuille & Kim, 1987). At the beginning of an interview, a witness receives instructions on these techniques. For example, a common version of the cognitive interview includes instructions to reinstate the crime's context, be complete, recall information in varying sequences, and change perspectives. Mentally reconstructing the crime's context helps to make recall more complete, and may be better than actually revisiting the crime scene since the scene may have changed. Such context reinstatement is a particular aid in accurate memory for facial details (Davies & Milne, 1985). Enjoining witnesses to be complete keeps them from withholding information that they think is not important, and may increase mental associations. Changing perspectives involves thinking about the incident from different points of view, and may help recall for details. Generally, cognitive interviews produce more correct information than standard interviews, and with no accompanying increase in incorrect recall. There is some evidence that cognitive interviews may help reduce the effects of leading questions relative to a standard interview. The cognitive interview can be applied to adults and children (Geiselman & Fisher, 1989).

Perhaps the most notorious forensic interview method is the polygraph interview (the "lie-detector test"). Polygraphy had an inauspicious start in the time of Münsterberg, and evolved to measuring blood pressure and respiratory changes in the 1930s. In the 1990s polygraph devices measure these two variables and electrodermal response, perspiration, and peripheral vascular activity. Polygraph relies on physiological responses to psychological changes. The fact that such responses exist seems obvious – blushing, nervous perspiration, and so on – but many emotions such as anger, excitement, fear, or guilt produce similar physiological responses. The problem for polygraph is to tease out the effects of particular emotions while controlling for the effects of any others. The ability of polygraph to isolate and distinguish these effects is a matter of wide debate (Wrightsman, 1991).

There are two types of polygraph techniques. The first type is the deception test, where a person is overtly tested for deceit. The second is the information test, where a person is tested for knowledge of or involvement in a particular crime. Questions on deception tests must refer only to information for which a person has clear memory, and must be phrased in such a way that the person can answer only yes or no. Questions should not ask for interpretations or conclusions. One type of deception test is the relevant-irrelevant test, which is composed of neutral questions such as, "Is today March 15th?" and relevant questions such as, "Did you take the diamonds from the jewellery case?" The basis for scoring the test is the assumption that guilty people will conceal their involvement in a crime, and will answer "no" to relevant questions. Although they answer no, the polygraph will detect an involuntary autonomic response that the polygrapher can compare to the neutral question responses. Validity for relevant-irrelevant questions is low for two reasons: innocent subjects can be very anxious when presented relevant questions, and people with unusual reactivity in general confuse the test (Raskin, 1989).

A second type of deception test is the control question test. The control question test compares reactions to relevant questions with reactions to control questions. Control questions ask about acts that most people have engaged in but are motivated to conceal during a proper polygraph interview. For example, a control question might be, "In the first 25 years of your life, did you ever take something that did not belong to you?" The polygrapher reviews these questions with the subject before the actual polygraph interview in such a way that the subject will answer them in the negative (even when this is not true). The basis for scoring the control question test is the assumption that innocent subjects will produce noticeably stronger reactions to control questions than to relevant questions, and that the opposite will hold for guilty subjects (Kircher & Raskin, 1992).

Experimental tests of polygraph validity have the advantage of knowing whether a subject was truthful or deceptive, while field studies must infer this information from confessions. In experimental studies, rates of correct classification for guilty and innocent subjects range from 50 per cent to nearly 100 per cent. A reason for these divergent findings may be the difficulty of recreating the strong emotional atmosphere of a real polygraph interview (Wrightsman, 1991). Field studies show consistently higher rates of correct classification. Even computerized scoring methods have been introduced to polygraph. Regardless of these findings, polygraph evidence is admitted in court either with strong stipulations, or not at all (Kircher & Raskin, 1992).

Information tests assess not deception, but the likelihood of a subject's knowledge of certain information. The most frequently used information test is the concealed knowledge test, originally referred to as the guilty knowledge test. This format requires the polygrapher to have information about a crime that is not known to the public. The subject's electrodermal responses to multiple-choice questions such as, "Regarding the weapon used to stab the victim, do you know if it was: (a) a bread knife, (b) an icepick, or (c) a screw-driver?" The assumption underlying this approach is that the electrodermal response will be strongest in response to the correct item for individuals with knowledge about the crime. Experimental research on concealed knowledge tests is encouraging, but there are no published attempts to replicate these findings in field settings (Raskin, 1989).

Opponents of polygraphy and deception tests cite the enormous complexity of human physiological responses. The ostensible accuracy rate of the polygraph is an artifact, they argue, stemming from the individual's likelihood of confessing in the face of a "deceptive" polygraph result, regardless of whether the person is actually responsible for the crime. An argument against the use of control question polygraphy is that the method relies on certain interpersonal abilities of the polygrapher, such as the polygrapher's ability to consistently deceive the person taking the examination. Research on the validity of polygraphy is difficult to interpret for a number of reasons. First, experimental settings with volunteer subjects may not recreate the same level of emotional arousal found in someone accused of a crime. Second, studies involving real defendants often cannot be validated by subsequent confessions, for reasons just mentioned (Lykken, 1992).

Besides witnesses, videotapes of crime scenes have been studied as information suppliers to the courtroom process. Findings of mock jury studies suggest that videotapes of crime scenes can prejudice criminal trials. In one study, mock jurors viewed videotapes of a murder victim and the scene of the crime. Other mock jurors saw a videotape from an unrelated case, and a third group saw no videotape at all. Two days later at a mock trial, jurors who saw the first videotape set lower standards of evidentiary proof and showed stronger juror biases than did jurors from the other two groups (e.g., Kassin & Garfield, 1991).

Psychologists as expert witnesses

Psychologists participate in trials in two ways. First, clinical psychologists may offer testimony regarding some set of symptoms displayed by a particular victim or defendant. Such testimony can take the form of a competency evaluation based on diagnostic tests. A second sort of testimony offered by psychologists is "social framework" testimony, where a psychologist presents statistical analyses and findings of relevant scientific research. Testimony of this latter type is often restricted to broad topics such as the psychological effects of discrimination in the workplace (Loftus, 1991).

When presenting this second sort of testimony, psychologists are acting as "expert witnesses". In 1975 the United States Congress codified the Federal Rules of Evidence. Rule 702 requires that expert witnesses "assist the trier of fact to understand the evidence or to determine a fact in issue". The *Frye* decision of 1923 set criteria for admissibility of expert testimony that augment the Federal Rules of Evidence. Experts must confine their testimony to theory that is generally accepted by psychologists, and their testimony must be such that its probative value is not outweighed by its prejudicial value in the eyes of the court. Judges interpret the wording of these guidelines of admissibility on a case-by-case basis (Goodman & Loftus, 1992).

Clearly expert psychological testimony can bear on matters crucial to the disposition of a case, such as the accuracy of eyewitness testimony. The law has, in effect, a series of screens designed to eliminate unreliable evidence. In addition to the Federal Rules of Evidence and the *Frye* criteria, judges can admit or reject evidence based on various legal idiosyncrasies that a particular case might pose. The role of the expert psychological witness is to be part of this screen for evidence, especially on the issues of perception, memory, and extenuating circumstances. The use of psychologists as expert witnesses appears to be increasing, and accompanying this increase is legal and psychological debate about the efficacy of their testimony.

Many legal arguments against psychological experts relate to the possible reaction of juries. A common warning is that juries may be overpersuaded by a testifying psychologist and assume that the expert testimony is infallible. In fact, experimental evidence suggests that expert testimony may cause juries to deliberate longer. One study reported that expert testimony accounts for only 3 per cent of the variance in jury verdicts (Hosch, Beck, & McIntyre, 1980). In addition, people tend to favour clinical, specific, and personal details of a situation over statistical data when making decisions, even if they are told beforehand that decisions based on statistical information have been preferable in the past. Psychological experts are also subjected to rigorous cross-examination in trials; their testimony does not pass unchallenged (Doyle, 1989).

A second variety of legal argument against experts is that the information in their testimony can be conveyed to the court without them. For example, an expert might testify that eyewitness confidence has a very small correlation with eyewitness accuracy. An attorney instead might introduce research summaries as part of a proposed instruction to the jury. Opponents of this objection claim that judges and lawyers cannot be familiar with *all* the relevant research. Some Supreme Court decisions have drawn conclusions about witness behaviour that stand in opposition to established psychological findings

(Goodman & Loftus, 1992). Even where written court opinions have made reference to psychological studies, these studies are sometimes misinterpreted (Davis, 1989).

A third legal argument against psychological experts is that jurors will misinterpret the role of the expert in court. The jury may expect testimony to be specific to the parties in trial. Jury members may therefore wrongly think that framework testimony about, say, the general unreliability of time estimates from eyewitnesses directly refutes the estimate of a particular eyewitness whose testimony is germane to the case's disposition. Federal Rule of Evidence 704 allows expert opinion testimony on the particular "ultimate issue" to be decided in a case, but such testimony might not conform to the parameters of accepted methods of scientific inference.

Opposition to social framework testimony from psychologists rests on a belief in the incompatibility of empirical psychology and formal jurisprudence. The reason for this incompatibility may be that scientific findings cannot apply to issues in single cases with particular defendants, from either ungeneralizable experimental methods or conflicting results in similar studies. A second reason is that the adversary legal system may be by nature unsuited to the rigorous and candid pursuit of facts. For example, the forgetting curve of memory has a certain shape: memory falls off rapidly after an event and then levels off. Yet the rate at which memory drops is different for different people, and different for various memories within an individual. Therefore, the argument runs, confidence in expert witness testimony on this subject is unwarranted.

There are several options in conveying psychological findings to courts. Besides expert witnesses, there are *amicus curiae* (friend of the court) briefs written by psychologists for judges. Such briefs allow summaries of psychological data. Some psychologists argue that research findings should not be treated as testimony, but as legal precedent (e.g., Monahan & Walker, 1988). Another option is to write instructions for the jury regarding relevant studies. Drawbacks of these options are that instructions may be hard to interpret or weigh properly, and that with such written information there is no opportunity for cross-examination (Goodman & Loftus, 1992).

As the debate has continued, courts have broadened the acceptability of expert testimony by psychologists in both criminal and civil cases. Courts are increasingly willing to admit expert testimony that does not purport to refer directly to parties involved in the case at hand (framework testimony); for example, psychologists have provided testimony that describes both general research findings as well as their application to the specific case at hand (Colman, 1991; Fiske, Bersoff, Borgida, Deaux, & Heilman, 1991; Goodman & Croyle, 1989). The United States Supreme Court, for example, accepted the testimony of a social psychologist in an important sex discrimination case (Fiske et al., 1991). In that case, the expert provided testimony concerning research on stereotyping, as well as opinions regarding the role of stereotyping in the evaluation of a woman under consideration for promotion.

Participants: decision-makers

Relatively few trials, civil or criminal, require juries. None the less, a large body of research exists on jury decision-making. Jury members, ideally, must weigh evidence without prejudice and reach a legal decision about human actions. Many times a jury makes decisions of importance to the community. Psychological research aims to evaluate just how well the jury performs its role. Jury decisions have been shown to relate to characteristics of the jurors themselves, and also to constraints of the legal system.

The law assumes that jurors can put aside personal biases when in court. Yet despite screening methods devised to eliminate prejudiced jurors, often jurors show bias during trial deliberations. Research into demographic characteristics of jurors has been inconclusive. Race, gender, age, religion, and education do not appear to be strongly linked with verdicts. Not even combinations of these factors can produce particularly reliable information about jury decisions. Research into juror personality characteristics shows some predictive power. First, research into locus of control shows that jurors with internal locus of control form negative attitudes more readily against defendants than do externals. Yet, locus of control seems to be unrelated to verdicts. Similarly, belief in a just world, as defined by Lerner (1980), predicts attitudes towards trial material but not legal decisions. The context of the trial, the mass of information and legal constraints, appear to outweigh these personal characteristics.

Somewhat stronger relationships hold in studies of "authoritarianism". Authoritarians are characterized by a rigid adherence to traditional middle-class values and a submissive attitude toward authority figures. High scorers on scales measuring authoritarianism are more likely to vote guilty both before and after group deliberation. Yet there are important contextual factors. For example, a juror with an authoritarian personality is less punitive towards police officers or dutiful military personnel. Thus personality characteristics do not operate without reference to the information of the particular case in question (Gerbasi, Zuckerman, & Reis, 1977). Another attitude that is relevant concerns the amount of money available for compensation. Some studies have found that plaintiffs are generally awarded more money if injured by a corporation than an individual. In addition, awards for plaintiffs are larger for defendants who are covered by insurance.

Jurors must assess the credibility of other participants and information providers in a trial (e.g. Williams, Bourgeois, Croyle, in press). Non-evidentiary factors such as facial expressions play a large role in evaluations of credibility. Even in the methodical atmosphere of the courtroom, such factors are essentially "commonsensical" and are moderately accurate at best.

Research suggests that jurors focus their attention automatically on the facial expressions of witnesses, apparently looking for cues to the unconscious content of a verbal message. Unfortunately, since people pay most attention to their facial expressions when under scrutiny, the face is fairly uninformative about truth or deception. Body, hand, and foot movement can be more reliable indicators, as can be tone of voice and hesitations in speech. These findings suggest that if a witness cannot be present to offer testimony during a trial, a videotaped deposition is superior to a message read by a court official.

Factors such as the attractiveness of the defendant play a role in jury verdicts. For example, jurors are more likely to find an unattractive defendant guilty when the victim is attractive than vice versa, even when the facts of the cases are identical. Even small changes in facial features to make an unconscious appeal to impressions of honesty, such as large eyes and high eyebrows, can affect the jury's verdict (Berry & Zebrowitz-McArthur, 1988).

Juries display common patterns of group interaction during deliberation. Although the ideal is for each juror to participate equally without domination of other jury members, in reality some jurors emerge as leaders of their group's opinions. Factors relating to opinion leadership include gender, employment and socio-economic status, and prior jury experience. Most jury leaders are male, hold jobs with more prestige than their fellows, and those with jury experience are selected as forepersons at a higher-than-normal rate. Even such arbitrary factors as seating position exert a strong influence on group leadership: jurors seated at the head of a rectangular table tend to dominate discussion during deliberation.

The deliberation process generally produces a more lenient attitude toward defendants on the part of the jury (MacCoun & Kerr, 1988). Since the majority opinion usually prevails, the collective opinions of the jurors before deliberation generally predict the verdict. In addition, some studies show that the verdict is predictable from the jurors' mid-trial opinions. Fortunately, jurors seem more receptive to new relevant information than to pressure to conform.

The legal system also strongly influences jury behaviour – overtly and covertly. Three areas of research into systemic factors in jury verdicts are the process of juror selection, the inclusion of non-evidence in the trial proceedings, and judges' instructions to juries. When selecting jurors, trial lawyers employ a variety of intuitive criteria that may have nothing to do with the legally sanctioned disposition of a case, such as the emotional impact of facial features or favouritism towards certain sports teams. Findings on the effectiveness of these methods are mixed, and there is considerable variation in the accuracy of different lawyers when screening potential jurors. Scientific jury selection, to be effective, must focus very narrowly on the specific facts of the case at hand. Demographic information of this sort is so specific that often no helpful research exists.

During the trial juries are exposed to information that is not admissible as evidence, information that none the less can affect verdicts. For example, lawyers' opening and closing statements can include recapitulations of evidence, interpretations of evidence, and alternative explanations of the crime. Jurors must be able to weed out the relevant evidence from the possibly self-interested formulations of lawyers, since the legal system permits such non-evidence in trial. A special case of non-evidence exists in testimony that is ruled inadmissible by the judge. Research shows that forbidding a jury to use some bit of evidence can have exactly the opposite effect (Wolf & Montgomery, 1977). The reason for this paradoxical effect seems not to be because of deceit or rebelliousness, but rather because jurors find such information much more salient after instructions to disregard it.

Judges sometimes give other instructions to juries, regarding the application of points of law to the evidence of the case at hand. The timing of these instructions relative to presentation of evidence is crucial. When juries received instructions before hearing evidence, the instructions had a beneficial impact on their ability to integrate facts and law (Smith, 1991). There seems to be very little difference in verdicts between juries that had no instructions and juries that received instructions after the evidence was presented. Juries provided with written or videotaped instructions from the judge seem to benefit from a clarification of the issues in a case (Kassin & Wrightsman, 1988).

SENTENCING AND INCARCERATION

Juries

Jurors weigh a large number of factors when choosing sentences for convicted defendants. Nevertheless, three factors have emerged from research as predictors of sentence severity. The first factor, prior experience on a jury, has long been suspected by attorneys as having an impact on sentencing. In an archival study of 143 criminal trials resulting in convictions, Himelein, Nietzel, and Dillehay (1991) found that more experienced juries gave significantly more severe sentences than did the less experienced juries. Whether the prior experience was on a criminal or civil case did not matter.

Wrightsman (1991) has summarized evidence indicating that women receive less severe sentences than men. When cases are matched on a number of factors, however, this difference diminishes. The same author notes evidence that American offenders convicted of murdering whites are more likely to receive the death penalty than those convicted of murdering blacks.

Judges

Like juries, judges can vary in their interpretation of the law. Sometimes disagreements among judges are quite wide, and include differences on the question of whether a criminal should be incarcerated at all. Sentences vary from state to state, court to court, and judge to judge. Studies into alternative methods of trial management and disposition, for instance review panels, also show considerable disparity. In accounting for different sentences imposed by different judges, the factor that accounts for most of the variability is the different value of legal objectives held by each judge. Less important but still prominent factors comprise the facts of the case and the political party of the judge. Special methodological problems exist in studying sources of sentencing variability. Years of special legal experience cannot be duplicated in a controlled experimental setting by lay subjects. In addition, studies involving appellate decisions are seriously confounded by different evidence and circumstances between the original and appellate trials (Palys & Divorski, 1986).

Prison confinement

There are both psychological and physiological effects to confinement in prison. Although there is no evidence for changes in cognitive functioning while in prison, inmates report being unable clearly to visualize the future beyond their prison sentences. Crowding in prisons is associated with increases in suicides, disciplinary infractions, and commitments to psychiatric wards. There are also personal factors that influence an inmate's adjustment to prison. For example, inmates who come from large families have an easier time adjusting to prison life. Other characteristics that help adjustment include previous prison experience and upbringing in an urban area. Higher educational attainment, higher socio-economic status, and being in a minority relative to the prison population are all characteristics that relate to negative reactions to prison and poorer adjustment to prison life (Paulus, 1988).

The study of physiological effects of prison confinement is complex. On the face of it, prisoners seem to have more medical problems than comparable populations outside. Prisoners have a higher-than-normal incidence of alcoholism and drug addiction on entry into prison. In addition, medical care is more readily available to prisoners than to a large percentage of the non-incarcerated population (e.g., Paulus & Dzindolet, 1992).

CONCLUSION

Given the short history of empirical research on psychological aspects of legal systems, the significant progress of this subfield is impressive. As the body of research continues to grow, so will the pressures to reform the system in a manner consistent with social scientific knowledge. Many of the goals of modern legal systems and scientific psychology are compatible, and psychologists are well equipped to assist in the development of methods to further the fair and effective application of the law. What remains to be seen, however, is whether the contributions of psychology to criminal law and procedure will be complemented by equally substantial contributions to civil law.

FURTHER READING

Davis, J. H. (1989). Psychology and law: The last 15 years. *Journal of Applied Social Psychology, 19,* 199–230.
Raskin, D. C. (Ed.) (1989). *Psychological methods in criminal investigation and evidence.* New York: Springer.
Kassin, S. M., & Wrightsman, L. S. (1988). *The American jury on trial: Psychological perspectives.* New York: Hemisphere.
Wrightsman, L. S. (1991). *Psychology and the legal system.* Belmont, CA: Wadsworth.

REFERENCES

Berry, D. S., & Zebrowitz-McArthur, L. (1988). What's in a face: Facial maturity and the attribution of legal responsibility. *Personality and Social Psychology Bulletin, 14,* 23–33.
Cash, W. S., & Moss, A. J. (1972). Optimum recall period for reporting persons injured in motor vehicle accidents (*DHEW – HSM Publication no. 72-1050*). Washington, DC: US Government Printing Office.
Cederbaums, J., & Arnold, S. (1975). *Scientific and expert evidence in criminal advocacy.* New York: Practicing Law Institute.
Coleman, A. M. (1991). Crowd psychology in South African murder trials. *American Psychologist, 46,* 1071–1079.
Davies, G., & Milne, A. (1985). Eyewitness composite production: A function of mental or physical reinstatement of context. *Criminal Justice and Behavior 12,* 209–220.
Davis, J. H. (1989). Psychology and law: The last 15 years. *Journal of Applied Social Psychology, 19,* 199–230.
Davis, J. H., Tindale, R. S., Nagao, D. H., Hinsz, V. B., & Robertson, B. (1984). Order effects in multiple decisions by group: A demonstration with mock juries and trial procedures. *Journal of Personality and Social Psychology, 47,* 1003–1012.
Doris, J. (Ed.) (1991). *The suggestibility of children's recollections: Implications for eyewitness testimony.* Washington, DC: American Psychological Association.
Doyle, J. M. (1989). Legal issues in eyewitness evidence. In D. C. Raskin (Ed.) *Psychological methods in criminal investigation and evidence* (pp. 125–147). New York: Springer.
Fiske, S. T., Bersoff, D. N., Borgida, E., Deaux, K., & Heilman, M. E. (1991). Social science research on trial: Use of sex stereotyping research in *Price Waterhouse v. Hopkins. American Psychologist, 46,* 1049–1060.
Geiselman, R. E., & Fisher, R. P. (1989). The cognitive interview technique for victims and witnesses of crime. In D. C. Raskin (Ed.) *Psychological methods in criminal investigation and evidence* (pp. 191–215). New York: Springer.
Gerbasi, K. C., Zuckerman, M., & Reis, H. T. (1977). Justice needs a new blindfold: A review of mock jury research. *Psychological Bulletin, 84,* 323–345.

Goodman, J., & Croyle, R. T. (1989). Social framework testimony in employment discrimination cases. *Behavioral Sciences and the Law*, *7*, 227–241.

Goodman, J., & Loftus, E. F. (1992). Judgement and memory: The role of expert psychological testimony on eyewitness accuracy. In P. Suedfeld & P. Tetlock (Eds) *Psychology and social policy* (pp. 267–282). New York: Hemisphere.

Himelein, M. J., Nietzel, M. T., & Dillehay, R. C. (1991). Effects of prior juror experience on jury sentencing. *Behavioral Sciences and the Law*, *9*, 97–106.

Hollin, C. R., & Clifford, B. R. (1983). Eyewitness testimony: The effects of discussion on recall accuracy and agreement. *Journal of Applied Social Psychology*, *13*, 234–244.

Hosch, H. M., Beck, E. L., & McIntyre, P. (1980). Influence of expert testimony regarding eyewitness accuracy on jury decisions. *Law and Human Behavior*, *4*, 287–296.

Kalven, H., & Zeisel, H. (1966). *The American jury*. Boston, MA: Little, Brown.

Kassin, S. M. (1985). Eyewitness identification: Retrospective self-awareness and the accuracy-confidence correlation. *Journal of Personality and Social Psychology*, *49*, 878–893.

Kassin, S. M., & Garfield, D. A. (1991). Blood and guts: General and trial-specific effects of videotaped crime scenes on mock jurors. *Journal of Applied Social Psychology*, *21*, 1459–1472.

Kassin, S. M., & Wrightsman, L. S. (1988). *The American jury on trial: Psychological perspectives*. New York: Hemisphere.

Kircher, J. C., & Raskin, D. C. (1992). Polygraph techniques: History, controversies, and prospects. In P. Suedfeld & P. Tetlock (Eds) *Psychology and social policy* (pp. 295–308). New York: Hemisphere.

Kramer, G. P., Kerr, N. L., & Carroll, J. S. (1990). Pretrial publicity, judicial remedies, and jury bias. Special issue: Law and the media. *Law and Human Behavior*, *14*, 409–438.

Lerner, M. J. (1980). *The belief in a just world: A fundamental delusion*. New York: Plenum.

Loftus, E. F. (1991). Resolving legal questions with psychological data. *American Psychologist*, *46*, 1046–1048.

Loftus, E. F., Greene. E. L., & Doyle, J. M. (1989). The psychology of expert testimony. In D. C. Raskin (Ed.) *Psychological methods in criminal investigation and evidence* (pp. 3–45). New York: Springer.

Loftus, E. F., Miller, D. G., & Burns, H. J. (1978). Semantic integration of verbal information into a visual memory. *Journal of Experimental Psychology: Human Learning and Memory*, *4*, 19–31.

Loftus, E. F., Banaji, M. R., Schooler, J. W., & Foster, R. A. (1987). Who remembers what? Gender differences in memory. *Michigan Quarterly Review*, *26*, 64–85.

Lykken, D. T. (1992). Controversy: The fight-or-flight response in *Homo scientificus*. In P. Suedfeld & P. Tetlock (Eds) *Psychology and social policy* (pp. 309–325). New York: Hemisphere.

MacCoun, R. J., & Kerr, N. L. (1988). Asymmetric influence in mock jury deliberation: Jurors' bias for leniency. *Journal of Personality and Social Psychology*, *54*, 21–33.

Monahan, J., & Walker, L. (1988). Social science research in law. *American Psychologist*, *43*, 465–472.

Münsterberg, H. (1908). *On the witness stand*. New York: Little, Brown.

Palys, T. S., & Divorski, S. (1986). Explaining sentence disparity. *Canadian Journal of Criminology*, *28*, 347–362.

Paulus, P. B. (1988). *Prison crowding: A psychological perspective.* New York: Springer-Verlag.

Paulus, P. B., & Dzindolet, M. T. (1992). The effects of prison confinement. In P. Suedfeld & P. Tetlock (Eds) *Psychology and social policy* (pp. 327–354). New York: Hemisphere.

Raskin, D. C. (1989). Polygraph techniques for the detection of deception. In D. C. Raskin (Ed.) *Psychological methods in criminal investigation and evidence* (pp. 247–296). New York: Springer.

Reiser, M. (1989). Investigative hypnosis. In D. C. Raskin (Ed.) *Psychological methods in criminal investigation and evidence* (pp. 151–190). New York: Springer.

Sigman, A., Philips, K. C., & Clifford, B. R. (1985). Attentional concomitants of hypnotic susceptibility. *British Journal of Experimental and Clinical Hypnosis, 2,* 69–75.

Smith, V. L. (1991). Impact of pretrial instruction on jurors' information processing and decision making. *Journal of Applied Psychology, 76,* 220–228.

Tapp, J. L. (1969). Psychology and the law: The dilemma. *Psychology Today, 2,* 16–22.

Thibaut, J., & Walker, L. (1975). *Procedural justice: A psychological analysis.* Hillsdale, NJ: Lawrence Erlbaum.

Vollrath, D. A., & Davis, J. H. (1980). Jury size and decision rule. In R. J. Simon, (Ed.) *The jury: Its role in American society.* Lexington, MA: Lexington Books.

Walker, L., & Lind, E. A. (1984). Psychological studies of procedural models. In G. M. Stephenson & J. H. Davis (Eds) *Progress in applied social psychology* (vol. 2). Chichester: Wiley.

Wells, G. L. (1993). What do we know about eyewitness identification? *American Psychologist, 48,* 553–571.

Williams, K. D., Bourgeois, M. J., & Croyle, R. T. (in press). The effects of stealing thunder in criminal and civil trials. *Law and Human Behavior.*

Wolf, S., & Montgomery, D. A. (1977). Effects of inadmissible evidence and level of judicial admonishment to disregard on the judgments of mock jurors. *Journal of Applied Social Psychology, 7,* 205–219.

Wrightsman, L. S. (1991). *Psychology and the legal system.* Belmont, CA: Wadsworth.

Yerkes, R. M., & Dodson, J. D. (1908). The relation of strength of stimulus to rapdity of habit-formation. *Journal of Comparative Neurology and Psychology, 18,* 459–482.

Yuille, J. C., & Cutshall, J. L. (1986). A case study of eyewitness memory of a crime. *Journal of Applied Psychology, 71,* 291–301.

Yuille, J. C., & Kim, C. K. (1987). A field study of the forensic use of hypnosis. *Canadian Journal of Behavioural Science, 19,* 418–429.

11.5

HEALTH PSYCHOLOGY

John Weinman

Guy's Hospital, London, England

The emergence of health psychology	Psychological responses to investigations and treatments
Behavioural factors influencing health	**Explaining health-related behaviour: social-cognitive approaches**
Stress and health	Specific models of health-related behaviour
Personality and health	Perceptions of cause and control
Lifestyle and health	
Psychological aspects of illness and health care	**Conclusions**
Coping and social support	**Further reading**
Communication	**References**
Adherence to treatment	

Health psychology is concerned with understanding human behaviour in the context of health and illness. The most widely used definition of the field has been provided by Matarazzo (1982), who described health psychology as the

> aggregate of specific educational, scientific, and professional contributions of the discipline of psychology to the promotion and maintenance of health, the prevention and treatment of illness, and the identification of etiologic and diagnostic correlates of health, illness, and related dysfunction. (p. 4)

Thus health psychologists study the psychological factors that influence how people stay healthy, why they become ill, and how they respond to illness and treatment. This chapter will overview each of these areas to illustrate the breadth and variety of work.

As with many other areas of psychology, there are three types of health psychology research, namely descriptive, explanatory, and intervention-based. Although a great deal of current research is descriptive, there are increasing attempts to develop explanatory approaches. For example, instead of providing a description of a health-related behaviour (e.g., dietary choice; adhering to medication) and perhaps relating it to an outcome (e.g., health status), more studies are using models to explain health-related behaviours or to predict their outcomes. The development of models is obviously important in any field since they add strength to the design and interpretation of research. For this reason, a separate section is included on a selection of widely used models of health-related behaviour.

THE EMERGENCE OF HEALTH PSYCHOLOGY

Health psychology emerged as a separate discipline in the 1970s, and there are many reasons for this and for its rapid development. An important background factor is the major change in the nature of health problems in industrialized societies during the twentieth century. Until the 1900s, the primary causes of illness and death were pneumonia, influenza, tuberculosis, and other infectious diseases. Since that time, chronic illnesses such as heart disease and cancer have become the leading causes of death (see Table 1). These are diseases for which social and psychological factors have been shown to be important as causal agents and in determining how individuals cope with the diseases and respond to their treatment. The provision of health care has

Table 1 The changes in leading causes of death in the USA, 1900–1980

Cause of death	1900	1980
Pneumonia/influenza	1	6
TB	2	
Diarrhoea and other gastro-intestinal disease	3	
Heart disease	4	1
Intra-cranial vascular lesions	5	
Nephritis	6	
Accidents	7	4
Cancer	8	2
Senility	9	
Diphtheria	10	
Diabetes		7
Cardiovascular disease		3
Chronic obstructive pulmonary disease		5
Cirrhosis of the liver		8
Atherosclerosis		9
Suicide		10

Source: Based on Matarazzo and Leckliter, 1988

grown enormously and there is an increased emphasis on good communication as a central ingredient of medical treatment, an awareness of the importance of patient satisfaction and of quality of life as a key outcome in evaluating the efficacy of medical interventions (Fallowfield, 1990).

In view of all these changes, there has been a shift from an exclusively biomedical model of health towards a much broader "biopsychosocial" one (Engel, 1977). Whereas the biomedical approach reduces the explanation of illness to biological malfunction, a biopsychosocial approach recognizes the complex, multifactorial nature of illness causation and outcome, as well as the concept of health as a positive state (i.e., not merely the absence of illness). Similarly, whereas biomedical treatments will typically involve physical methods (e.g., medication, surgery, etc.) to reduce or eliminate physical symptoms, health psychology shows us not only that it is possible to use psychological approaches to prevention and treatment but also that the efficacy of any treatment depends on a variety of psychological and social factors, including the quality of the relationship between practitioner and patient. Moreover, the important criteria for judging treatment success not only may be in terms of changes in physical symptoms but also will be reflected in psychological and social outcomes such as coping, mood, and quality or life (see Kaplan, 1990).

BEHAVIOURAL FACTORS INFLUENCING HEALTH

A wide range of behaviours can influence health. In broad terms these have been classified in positive and negative terms as health-protective or health-risk behaviours, and many of these are described later in the chapter (see below, on lifestyle and health). Risk-increasing behaviours have been referred to as *behavioural pathogens*, whereas health-enhancing or protective behaviours have been referred to as *behavioural immunogens* (see Matarazzo & Leckliter, 1988). The influence of these behaviours on health has been established from epidemiological studies of populations which examine the factors associated with the incidence of different diseases. Thus they reflect a statistical correlation and do not necessarily show how or why the behaviour concerned has an effect on health status. We begin with an overview of a number of different behavioural factors that affect health. First, there is a focus on the topic of stress and its effects. There is then a consideration of personality factors that can influence health and health behaviour. Finally, there is an outline of so-called "lifestyle" factors that can have both positive and negative health consequences.

Stress and health

The links between stress, health, and disease are complex and need to be examined carefully. Stress is usually used to describe situations in which

Figure 1   Stress and disease: direct and indirect effects

individuals are faced with demands that exceed their immediate ability to cope (Lazarus & Folkman, 1984). Stressful situations are typically those that are novel, unpredictable, and uncontrollable as well as those involving change or loss. Very often, these situations produce adverse psychological and physiological changes which, in turn, may result in disease.

However, a major problem for health psychologists is to understand the way in which stress is associated with the development of illness. Two broad possibilities have been proposed; these have been referred to as "indirect" and "direct" effects (see Figure 1). Thus stress may have indirect effects on health by increasing levels of risk behaviour (e.g., smoking, alcohol consumption), or may have direct effects on specific physiological mechanisms (e.g., increases in blood pressure) as well as affecting the individual's resistance to disease through suppression of the immune system, or by exacerbating or triggering a disease process in an already vulnerable individual.

A range of behavioural responses are shown by individuals as they attempt to cope with stressful situations and the associated emotions. At the same time there are neuroendocrine and immunological changes resulting from acute or chronic stressful episodes. During stressful episodes, releasing factors from the brain cause the pituitary to release adrenocorticotropic hormone (ACTH) which gives rise to the release of corticosteroids from the cortex of the adrenal glands. In addition to producing a number of well-known changes associated with the mobilization of both short and longer-term physical resources (e.g., release of adrenalin or noradrenaline; release of glucose; activation of endorphins/encephalins; etc.), these steroids can also have effects on the immune system. Thus fairly acute stressors, such as exams, and more chronic stressors, such as caring for a dependent elderly relative, can lead to deleterious immunological changes and increased incidence of illness (see Kiecolt-Glaser & Glaser, 1987).

Personality and health

Older studies attempting to link psychological factors with specific diseases gave rise to the rather misleading idea that different types of diseases are experienced by individuals with certain sorts of personality. In general this research, often based on psychodynamic theories and the idea that certain sorts of subconscious conflict result in specific patterns of disease, has not received support from subsequent research. However, there is growing evidence from different, more credible sources, that personality can influence health and play a role in determining illness in other ways.

Probably the best known work in this area concerns the link between the so-called "Type A" personality and coronary heart disease (Friedman & Rosenman, 1974). The Type A personality was characterized by competitiveness, time urgency, hostility, and related behavioural factors which were associated with a significantly increased risk of coronary heart disease. Although the earlier studies in the 1960s and 1970s were very encouraging, subsequent work has complicated the picture. Some studies have notably failed to find any relation between Type A and heart disease; it is now thought that only certain components (e.g., anger and hostility) of the original Type A formulation are "pathogenic".

How is the Type A behaviour pattern associated with increased levels of heart disease? As was discussed above, there are almost certainly direct and indirect effects of Type A behaviour on health. Type A individuals show a greater physiological reactivity (e.g., in blood pressure and heart-rate) to environmental demands and may even generate more demands by their style of behaviour. Thus the more frequent elevations in blood pressure and higher levels of hormonal change linked to stress responses may eventually cause adverse physical changes to the heart and blood vessels. Also, Type A individuals are more likely to engage in unhealthy behaviours since they drink more alcohol than Type B individuals and, if they smoke, they inhale their cigarette smoke for a longer time. They are less likely to relax and more often push themselves to their physical limits.

Type A behaviour is the most extensively investigated personality factor in current health psychology research, and there have been impressive interventions developed to change the behaviour pattern, with positive health outcomes (see Thoresen, Friedman, Powell, Gill, & Ulmer, 1985). However there is other research investigating personality in relation to disease-proneness and to health behaviours. For example Temoshok and colleagues have investigated the role of Type C personality in relation to cancer (Temoshok, 1987). The Type C personality is characterized by a difficulty in the expression of emotion and by the tendency to suppress or inhibit emotions, particularly negative emotions such as anger. Some psychologists have proposed that these aspects of personality can play a causal role in cancer but, as yet, there are no convincing data on this (see Fox, 1988). However, there are clearer indications that these kinds of factors may influence the progression of cancer and hence the survival time of individuals with cancer. Currently, interventions that encourage positive patterns of responding emotionally are being evaluated in cancer patients and it remains to be seen whether these can be effective.

Personality variables can influence health in a variety of ways, and a broad distinction can be made between those with a positive relation to health and health behaviour and those with an adverse relation. In contrast to the adverse effects of Type A and Type C, other personality variables can be protective in various ways. One which has generated a great deal of interest is the concept of *hardiness* (Kobasa, 1979) which describes individuals with a high sense of personal control over events in their lives, with a strong sense of commitment or involvement, together with a tendency to see environmental demands or changes as challenges.

Hardy individuals are thought to be less affected by stress: there is some evidence for this, even though there are problems in measuring hardiness. Other related aspects of personality have also shown to be health-protective. One example is that of *optimism* (Scheier, Weintraub, & Carver, 1986) which describes a tendency towards positive expectations in life and which enables individuals to cope better with stressors and engage in healthier lifestyles.

Finally, there is emerging evidence that general patterns of positive or negative emotional responses, associated with personality, can influence various aspects of health (Watson & Pennebaker, 1991). Individuals who are high in negative affect (i.e., experience more negative emotions, particularly anxiety) do not seem to be more prone to disease, but they are more likely to notice bodily changes and symptoms and consequently seek medical help more frequently. In contrast, those individuals high in positive affect, as reflected by a more engaged and enthusiastic approach to life, are less likely to report health problems or to seek medical help. Watson and Pennebaker provide interesting evidence to indicate that these styles of emotional responding are very much personality-related and may possibly be genetically determined.

The role of personality factors in health is obviously complex (see Friedman & Booth-Kewley, 1987). Older ideas about particular patterns of personality and emotional conflict being associated with particular diseases have not been supported. However, there is important evidence that aspects of personality may make individuals more or less vulnerable to the effects of stress and can influence both health and illness behaviours.

Lifestyle and health

One very obvious way in which behaviour can influence health comes from research on lifestyle, which has identified a number of behaviours that can have both positive and negative effects on health status. The word "lifestyle" is usually applied to the coherent and consistent use of a range of different health behaviours (Nutbeam, Aaro, & Wold, 1991). However, individuals are not always entirely consistent across different health behaviours, and so we shall focus on separate behaviours and their effects on health rather than on the more generic concept of lifestyle.

The effects on health of behaviours such as smoking and high alcohol use are well documented. There is overwhelming evidence that smokers not only are much more likely to die from lung cancer and other cancers but also have much higher rates of cardiovascular disease and chronic respiratory disorders, particularly emphysema and chronic bronchitis. Moreover the disease risk is dose-related in that higher levels of smoking are more strongly associated with all these diseases. With sustained high levels of alcohol use a different but equally unpleasant spectrum of health problems can be seen. Drinking is a major cause of accidents particularly motoring accidents and can cause liver damage as well as having detrimental effects on brain functioning.

For health psychologists, the key questions about health-risk behaviours concern their origin, their maintenance, and their prevention or treatment. There are diverse determinants of both behaviours since both may start as ways of coping with stress, in response to peer pressure, for pleasure, and for a number of other reasons. Similarly, they will be maintained by a variety of psychological, social, and biological factors. Even though their effects on health are physical and dramatic it is nevertheless important to remember that they are behaviours and that the routes to limiting their effects are through prevention and behaviour change.

There are many other risky behaviours that cannot be discussed in detail in an overview; these include drug abuse, poor diet, and accidents, and the health effects of all these are also well documented. Although health psychology has an important role to play in describing, explaining, and intervening in all risk behaviours, it is very important not to think of these problems exclusively in individual, behavioural terms since they often reflect adverse social circumstances or particular cultural contexts.

The same caveats about the influence of social and cultural factors must also be applied to the understanding of health-protective or health-enhancing behaviours. The behavioural factors (seven or eight hours' sleep; eating three regular meals each day, including breakfast; moderate body weight; not smoking; limited alcohol intake; regular physical activity) identified by the Alameda County study (Breslow & Enstrom, 1980) provide some indicators of basic behaviours that can have a positive (or negative) influence on health. This study showed that the adoption of all or most of these health practices was associated with significantly lower mortality in the following five- and ten-year follow-up periods.

There is now a growing body of evidence to indicate that regular exercise has a beneficial effect on physical and psychological health (Haskell, 1984). Exercise can reduce the incidence of physical health problems in elderly people and facilitate recovery from heart attack. However, there can be significant problems in ensuring that exercise and other health-promoting activities are adhered to (Dishman, 1982). Thus interventions need to be carefully planned and delivered by appropriately skilled individuals since it has been found to be extremely hard to give up risky behaviours and to adopt more healthy lifestyles. Providing information is usually insufficient to promote change, since it is necessary to alter cognitions (see below, on explaining health behaviour) and to influence social networks as a basis for bringing about changes in health-related behaviour.

PSYCHOLOGICAL ASPECTS OF ILLNESS AND HEALTH CARE

Coping and social support

There is now a great deal of interest in the way patients respond to chronic illness. Much of this work has been concerned with understanding the way patients cope with the different demands of their illnesses. Whereas older work assumed that the demands depended primarily on the illness, more recent studies show that coping depends very much on the individual's perception of the threats and demands as well as on the social circumstances in which the illness is experienced (Burish & Bradley, 1983).

Coping is a general term that describes the wide range of responses used by individuals to deal with their health problems. Although the concept of coping seems straightforward, there is still disagreement about its nature and measurement as well as about its effects on emotional and physical outcomes (Cohen, 1987). It is generally agreed that coping is not a static process in the context of chronic illness since it can change over time as the perceptions, demands, and social implications of the illness change. Some researchers prefer to use very broad dimensions of behaviour (e.g., approach vs avoidance) to characterize individual differences in coping behaviour, whereas others focus on much more specific behaviours in order to describe the wide range of responses shown by patients. It is also unclear whether coping determines psychological or physical well-being or whether this relationship is a more two-way process. A great deal of the coping research has been based on the assumption that coping determines various outcomes, such as emotional state, but there are increasing indications that coping can also be a consequence of emotional state (Fillip, Kauer, Freudenberg, & Ferring, 1990).

The individual's social circumstances are also of particular importance in determining the way in which patients cope and in the degree of success that coping strategies can have in regulating their well-being. The most widely used concept here is that of *social support* which refers not only to the access one has to other individuals but also to their perceived value or adequacy in actually providing support. As with coping, there are conceptual and methodological issues associated with social support. Social support does not always produce a beneficial outcome (see Schwarzer & Leppin, 1989) and it is important to understand the relationship between different types and sources of support and different physical and psychological outcomes for the patient. Nevertheless, social support can have significant direct and indirect effects on the well-being of individuals with chronic illnesses and disabilities. Thus those individuals with little or no effective social support are more likely to show a poorer response to illness or treatment.

The increasing understanding of the nature and role of such processes as coping and social support are particularly important for developing interventions in this area. General training for health professionals in communication and listening skills (see below) can provide a basis for understanding more about patients' needs. More specific psychological interventions have been developed for helping patients cope better with certain aspects of their illness. There is now a range of psychological approaches for the management of chronic pain which is a very common component of chronic or disabling conditions (Pearce & Erskine, 1989).

Communication

Many studies have examined aspects of communication between health-care professionals (HCPs), particularly doctors and patients, in order to explain the all-too-often disappointing outcomes (see Ley, 1988). These have shown that patients complain frequently that they are not given sufficient information or that their doctors do not seem interested or concerned. Moreover, it has been found that patients may find it difficult to understand or remember information that they have been given. Not surprisingly therefore, there is quite widespread evidence of patient dissatisfaction with communication.

A number of problems have been described in the outcomes of medical encounters and, of these, the two most widely investigated have been the low levels of patient satisfaction and the low rates of adherence to advice or treatment (see below). Causes of these problems are quite diverse but many relate to aspects of the communication process and the failure of the HCP to attend to and discuss the needs and concerns of the patient. This has led to a number of psychological interventions in this area, including communication skills training for HCPs, particularly during their early training (Weinman & Armstrong, 1988). Some of these training interventions have aimed to improve general communication skills, whereas others have been designed for work with particular types of patients or particular situations (e.g., giving "bad news").

Adherence to treatment

The term "adherence" describes the extent to which an individual follows recommended treatment or advice. Older studies tended to use the term "compliance" but adherence is now preferred for a number of reasons. It refers to a broad range of behaviours including taking medication and following advice about health-related behaviour change such as dietary change, quitting smoking, or increasing levels of exercise. Thus adherence can be seen as a potentially health-enhancing behaviour, but more typically non-adherence or low adherence is a potential health-risk behaviour.

High levels of non-adherence have been found across a range of treatments and treatment settings (Meichenbaum & Turk, 1987). Very typically, findings are that some 40–50 per cent of patients do not adhere to treatment or advice in a way that is clinically significant. The level of adherence is affected by treatment and illness factors, since the lowest rates of adherence are found in patients with chronic conditions and in those taking medication for preventive purposes. In contrast, patients receiving such treatments as chemotherapy for cancer generally show very high levels of adherence, even though the treatments may produce unpleasant side-effects.

Although factors associated with the nature of the illness and the demands of the treatment influence patient adherence, many studies have also identified the contribution of communication and patients' beliefs. The quality of communication between doctor and patient has a strong influence on patient satisfaction, which in turn plays a role in determining adherence levels. As was discussed earlier, quality of communication depends not only on the doctor's ability to listen and respond effectively to the patient's problems, but also on the way information is presented.

Much early work on adherence pointed to the importance of the health beliefs (described below). If patients perceive their condition as serious and believe in the efficacy of the treatment, they are more likely to adhere to it. For adherence to recommendations to avoid or reduce health-risk behaviours such as smoking, or to adopt potentially health-protective behaviours such as "safe sex" practices, there is increasing evidence that "normative beliefs" are particularly important. These are the beliefs held by individuals about the views or attitudes held by their social peers.

Health psychologists have devised a variety of interventions to facilitate adherence (see Meichenbaum & Turk, 1987). Some of these are based on communication training for health professionals in order to improve their basic communication skills including their ability to present information concerning treatment. More focused interventions encourage the doctor to share decision-making and treatment planning with the patient in order to agree treatment goals and anticipate any barriers.

Psychological responses to investigations and treatments

Many studies have demonstrated the stressfulness associated with admission to hospital and with various medical investigative or treatment procedures. As a result, psychologists have provided a range of interventions to prepare patients for hospitalization generally, or for a specific unpleasant procedure within the hospital setting. Preparation for hospital admission has mostly been confined to work with children (Eiser, 1988), but preparations for stressful procedures have been developed for both children and adults. These interventions work at a number of levels. Some essentially provide information as to what will happen to the patient, in terms of the nature of the procedure and its likely effects. Others are designed to reduce anxiety, either generally using relaxation training or by helping the patient to identify and cope with specific fears or concerns. For children there are videotapes of other children undergoing the same investigations or treatment: these allow children to model themselves on the child in the video.

The interventions have had a mixed success in helping patients cope with the procedures and in improving the outcome (Weinman & Johnston, 1988). There are many different sorts of outcome that can be affected (e.g., pain, anxiety, speed of recovery, etc.) and some interventions are clearly better for achieving particular outcomes. Overall it would appear that cognitive-behavioural approaches produce better outcomes than other types of interventions on both behavioural and self-report measures. It may also be necessary to match the type of intervention to the patient's coping style and informational needs.

Health psychologists have also been concerned with understanding how health-care professionals are affected by their work environment. There are widespread reports of job stress among HCPs and a number of factors appear to contribute to this. These include the stressfulness of the work, the lack of support, and the working conditions and long hours worked by many HCPs (Herbert, 1990). As a result various psychological interventions have been developed for the management of job stress in HCPs (Sutherland, 1990).

EXPLAINING HEALTH-RELATED BEHAVIOUR: SOCIAL-COGNITIVE APPROACHES

We shall now outline some models and approaches that are concerned with the cognition (beliefs, attitudes, perceptions, etc.) underlying health-related behaviours. At present, these are the most widely used explanatory models and frameworks in health psychology and have been applied as explanations of health-risk behaviours (e.g., Croog & Richards, 1977), preventive or protective behaviours, and in explaining differential responses to stress. They are also used to explain the nature of psychological responses to illness (e.g., Affleck, Tennen, Croog, & Levine, 1987) and the extent of behaviours such as adherence to medication or recommended lifestyle change (e.g., Meichenbaum & Turk, 1987). Despite their popularity, these models still do not provide complete explanations of specific health or illness behaviours. This may partly be because they were not all originally developed to explain health-related behaviours and may not reflect the ways that individuals think about their own health or illness. It may also be because many aspects of health are determined or shaped by social and cultural factors (see Blaxter, 1990) as well as individual cognitions.

Specific models of health-related behaviour

The most established model of health-related behaviour is the *Health Belief Model* (HBM: Janz & Becker, 1984), which proposes that, in response to a cue or action, such as the experience of a symptom or invitation to attend a health check, individuals will act on the basis of their beliefs about the threat of a potential health problem, as well as their beliefs about the advantages and disadvantages of taking a particular course of action. Their perception of the threat will depend on their beliefs about its seriousness and their susceptibility or vulnerability to it.

Thus for individuals to engage in a specific health-related behaviour (e.g., "safe" sexual behaviour), they must consider not only that they may be vulnerable to the possible consequences of not engaging in that behaviour (being infected by HIV) but also that the consequences are serious. Moreover they need to believe that the advantages of engaging in that behaviour outweigh the disadvantages of doing so. Thus for some health-related behaviours (e.g., "safe" sexual behaviour) individuals may acknowledge the seriousness of the associated health threat but may not see themselves as being vulnerable. In contrast, for behaviours such as dental health care, individuals may well acknowledge their susceptibility to the health threat (caries or gum disease) but may not regard it as sufficiently serious to take the appropriate preventive action.

The HBM has been extensively used for studies of health-related behaviour, particularly those concerned with prevention. It has not been entirely successful and, as a result, other variables (e.g., efficacy beliefs – see below) have been added to increase its explanatory power. Even with these, the overall results are still quite modest; this may partly reflect the general problem of trying to predict behaviour from attitudes, as well as the more specific problem that people may not necessarily think about health issues in the way suggested by the HBM.

A less widely used but more successful model is the *Theory of Reasoned Action* (TRA: Ajzen & Fishbein, 1980), which proposes that the best predictors of individuals' voluntary actions are their behavioural *intentions*, which are determined by two factors. The first is their *attitude* regarding the behaviour; this is based on two types of *behavioural beliefs* – beliefs about the likely outcomes of behaviour (e.g., "If I exercise, I will improve my health") and evaluations of these outcomes (e.g., "Being healthy is important to me"). The second determinant of intentions is the *subjective norm* concerning the behaviour, which is based on two *normative beliefs* – beliefs regarding others' opinions about the behaviour (e.g., "My family and friends think I should exercise") and the motivation to comply with these opinions (e.g., "I wish to do what they want").

The TRA proposes that the subjective norm and attitude regarding the behaviour combine to produce an intention, which leads to performance of the behaviour. The theory has been developed as the *Theory of Planned Behaviour* (Ajzen, 1985) which adds other variables, including perceived behavioural control and perceived barriers.

Both the HBM and the TRA conceptualize health-related behaviour as a rational process based on the interplay and weighing up of organized beliefs. Unfortunately, health behaviours may not be like this in all individuals since some may occur for reasons other than health. For example, dieting or good dental hygiene may be carried out for primarily cosmetic reasons rather than for avoiding long-term health consequences. Also, specific health beliefs are far more likely to be useful in predicting health behaviours in those who attach a high value to health (Lau, Hartman, & Ware, 1986). Thus the concept of health value and the relative priority given to health in comparison with other factors (e.g., wealth, happiness, appearance, etc.) is an important general cognitive variable to take account of in explaining health behaviours.

Perceptions of cause and control

An individual's motivation or willingness to engage in a health-related behaviour not only depends on beliefs about the health issue concerned but also will be influenced by a belief in the ability to carry out the behaviour concerned. This has been referred to as a self-efficacy expectancy or belief and has been proposed by Bandura (1986) as a key determinant of all behaviour including health-behaviour. Bandura has developed a general theory of behaviour change which distinguishes two important related beliefs: *self-efficacy*, which refers to the belief that an individual can succeed at a particular task or with a particular behaviour (e.g., giving up smoking); and *outcome efficacy*, which refers to the belief that the behaviour will result in a valued outcome (e.g., that the treatment will be successful).

Self-efficacy beliefs are based on the previous experiences of individuals and on their observations of the behaviour of others in equivalent situations. Individuals with a high level of self-efficacy will probably attribute previous successes to their own efforts or abilities rather than to the help of others or to chance factors. Similarly, they will be more likely to have a high *internal locus of control* belief. Both of these concepts (attributions, locus of control) are also used to explain health and illness behaviours.

The concept of *health locus of control* has been developed by Wallston, Wallston, South, and Dobbins (Wallston et al., 1987) and identifies three distinct sources of control over health behaviours, namely self (internal control), powerful others (doctors, etc.), and chance factors. In general those with high internal locus of control beliefs are more likely to carry out preventive and other health actions. However, it is usually necessary to specify the type of health-behaviour (e.g., control over diabetes) in order for these control beliefs to be useful as predictors.

Attribution theory (see Turnquist, Harvey, & Anderson, 1988) is concerned with people's explanations for events and has shown that these can be described in terms of a number of important dimensions (due to oneself or external factors, due to a temporary or more long-lasting factor: due to a specific or a more global cause; etc.). The types of causal attributions that people make for illnesses and accidents have been found to influence their subsequent adjustment and psychological well-being (e.g., Affleck et al., 1987).

Attribution theory has also been used to describe more long-term or personality-related aspects of causal thinking. These are referred to as attributional styles and they assume that people show a consistency in the types of attributions they make over time and in different situations. This has been mainly applied to the study of the role of cognitions in depression (Peterson & Seligman, 1984) but later work suggests the possibility of attributional styles in the perception of symptoms (Robbins & Kirmayer, 1991).

Illness representation models (Lau, Bernard, & Hartman, 1989; Meyer, Leventhal, & Guttman, 1985) are concerned with the way patients conceptualize or make sense of illness or health threats. Leventhal and colleagues propose that there are three stages which regulate the adaptive behaviours during an illness (Meyer et al., 1985). The stages are cognitive representation, action planning or coping, and appraisal. The first involves the individual developing a model or representation of what is going wrong and of the causes and consequences of this. The second stage involves plans to deal with the problem; the efficacy of these is evaluated during the third stage, which in turn may result in changes in the representation and/or in the coping plans.

Five components of illness representations have been identified:

1 *Identity* which comprises both an abstract label (e.g., hypertension) as well as concrete signs and symptoms that are experienced or associated. This is very much the individual's own idea as what the disease is.
2 *Consequences* the individual's ideas about the short-term and longer-term consequences of the disease.
3 *Time-line* the individual's perceived time-frame for the development and duration of the disease or health threat. Typically illnesses are initially thought of as having an acute or short-term time-line, and it may take considerable time before the chronicity of a condition is accurately understood.
4 *Causes* the perceived causes of the disease (see above, on attribution theory).
5 *Cure* the individual's ideas about the possibilities of cures and their likely impact.

Although research in this area is still at an early stage, it has shown that many responses to illness (e,g., the type of coping, adherence to medication) are determined by the individual's own representation or understanding of the illness (see Skelton & Croyle, 1991).

CONCLUSIONS

This selective overview of health psychology has attempted to demonstrate the range of psychological processes in health and health care. At the present time, it is a disciplinary area of psychology with an emphasis on research into health and illness behaviour. However, many interventions have been developed for healthy individuals, patients, and health-care staff. Thus there is a very important practitioner component to health psychology, and this may well result in specific professional developments in the near future. In the USA, professional postgraduate training in health psychology is developing quite rapidly; in other countries (e.g., Canada, The Netherlands, and the United Kingdom) postgraduate programmes began to emerge in the early 1990s (see Jansen & Weinman, 1991).

Health psychology has established itself very rapidly but still has a long way to go. Future research must provide greater insights into the ways in which psychological processes can influence the biological mechanisms in health and disease. Also, a much clearer understanding and better theoretical models are needed for all aspects of health and illness behaviour. All this will inevitably result in the more widespread use of psychological interventions for preventing and treating health problems, and for the effective delivery of health care.

FURTHER READING

Bennett, P., Weinman, J., & Spurgeon, P. (Eds) (1990). *Current developments in health psychology*. London: Harwood Academic.
Gatchel, R. J., Baum, A., & Krantz, D. (1989). *An Introduction to health psychology* (2nd edn). New York: Random House.
Sarafino, E. P. (1990). *Health psychology: Biopsychosocial interactions*. New York: Wiley.
Taylor, S. E. (1990). *Health psychology* (2nd edn). New York: Random House.

REFERENCES

Affleck, G., Tennen, H., Croog, S., & Levine, S. (1987). Causal attribution, perceived control and recovery from a heart attack. *Journal of Social and Clinical Psychology*, *5*, 356–364.
Ajzen, I. (1985). *From intentions to actions: A theory of planned behavior*. Englewood Cliffs, NJ: Prentice-Hall.
Ajzen, I., & Fishbein, M. (1980). *Understanding attitudes and predicting social behavior*. Englewood Cliffs, NJ: Prentice-Hall.

Bandura, A. (1986). *Social foundations of thought and action: Social cognitive theory.* Englewood Cliffs, NJ: Prentice-Hall.

Blaxter, M. (1990). *Health and lifestyle.* London: Tavistock.

Breslow, L., & Enstrom, J. (1980). Persistence of health habits and their relationship to mortality. *Preventive Medicine, 9,* 469–483.

Burish, T. C., & Bradley, L. A. (Eds) (1983). *Coping with chronic disease: Research and applications.* New York: Academic Press.

Cohen, F. (1987). Measurement of coping. In S. V. Kasl & C. L. Cooper (Eds) *Stress and health: Issues in research methodology* (pp. 283–305). Chichester: Wiley.

Croog, S., & Richards, N. P. (1977). Health beliefs and smoking patterns in heart patients and their wives: A longitudinal study. *American Journal of Public Health, 67,* 921–993.

Dishman, R. K. (1982). Compliance/adherence in health-related exercise. *Health Psychology, 1,* 237–267.

Eiser, C. (1988). Do children benefit from psychological preparation for hospitalisation? *Psychology and Health, 2,* 107–132.

Engel, G. L. (1977). The need for a new medical model: A challenge for biomedicine. *Science, 196,* 129–136.

Fallowfield, L. (1990). *The quality of life: The missing measurement in health care.* London: Souvenir.

Fillip, S.-H., Kauer, T., Freudenberg, E., & Ferring, D. (1990). The regulation of subjective well-being in cancer patients: An analysis of coping effectiveness. *Psychology and Health, 4,* 305–318.

Fox, B. H. (1988). Psychogenic factors in cancer, especially its incidence. In S. Maes, C. D. Spielberger, P. B. Defares, & I. G. Sarason (Eds) *Topics in health psychology* (pp. 37–55). Chichester: Wiley.

Friedman, H. S., & Booth-Kewley, S. (1987). The disease-prone personality: A meta-analytic view of the construct. *American Psychologist, 42*(6), 539–555.

Friedman, M., & Rosenman, R. H. (1974). *Type A behaviour and your heart.* New York: Knopf.

Haskell, W. L. (1984). Overview: Health benefits of exercise. In J. D. Matarazzo, S. M. Weiss, J. A. Herd, N. E. Miller, & S. M. Weiss (Eds) *Behavioral Health* (pp. 409–423). New York: Wiley.

Herbert, M. (1990). Healthcare workers in adverse environments. In P. Bennett, J. Weinman, & P. Spurgeon (Eds) *Current developments in health psychology* (pp. 277–304). London: Harwood Academic.

Jansen, M., & Weinman, J. (Eds) (1991). *The international development of health psychology.* London: Harwood Academic.

Janz, N. K., & Becker, M. (1984). The health belief model: A decade later. *Health Education Quarterly, 11,* 1–47.

Kaplan, R. M. (1990). Behavior as the central outcome in health care. *American Psychologist, 45*(11), 1211–1220.

Kiecolt-Glaser, J. K., & Glazer, R. (1987). Psychological moderators of immune function. *Annals of Behavioural Medicine, 9*(2), 16–20.

Kobasa, S. C. (1979). Stressful events and health: An enquiry into hardiness. *Journal of Personality and Social Psychology, 37,* 1–11.

Lau, R. R., Bernard, T. M., & Hartman, K. A. (1989). Further explorations of common sense representations of common illnesses. *Health Psychology, 8,* 195–219.

Lau, R. R., Hartman, K. A. & Ware, J. E. (1986). Health as value: Methodological and theoretical considerations. *Health Psychology, 5,* 25–43.

Lazarus, R. S., & Folkman, S. (1984). *Stress, appraisal and coping.* New York: Springer.

Ley, P. (1988). *Communicating with patients: Improving communication, satisfaction and compliance*. London: Croom Helm.

Matarazzo, J. D. (1982). Behavioral health's challenge to academic, scientific and professional psychology. *American Psychologist*, *37*, 1–14.

Matarazzo, J. D., & Leckliter, I. N. (1988). Behavioral health: The role of good and bad habits in health and illness. In S. Maes, C. D. Spielberger, P. B. Defares, & I. G. Sarason (Eds) *Topics in health psychology* (pp. 3–18). Chichester: Wiley.

Meichenbaum, D., & Turk, D. C. (1987). *Facilitating treatment adherence: A practitioner's guidebook*. New York: Plenum.

Meyer, D., Leventhal, H., & Guttman, M. (1985). Common-sense models of illness: The example of hypertension. *Health Psychology*, *4*, 115–135.

Nutbeam, D., Aaro, L., & Wold, B. (1991). The lifestyle concept and health education for young people. *World Health Statistics Quarterly*, *44*, 55–61.

Pearce, S., & Erskine, A. (1989). Chronic pain. In S. Pearce & J. Wardle (Eds) *The practice of behavioural medicine* (pp. 427–442). Oxford: Oxford University Press.

Peterson, C., & Seligman, M. E. P. (1984). Causal explanations as a risk factor for depression: Theory and evidence. *Psychological Review*, *91*, 347–374.

Robbins, J. M., & Kirmayer, L. J. (1991). Attributions of common somatic symptoms. *Psychological Medicine*, *21*, 1029–1045.

Scheier, M. F., Weintraub, J. K., & Carver, C. S. (1986). Coping with stress: Divergent strategies of optimists and pessimists. *Journal of Personality and Social Psychology*, *51*, 1257–1264.

Schwarzer, R., & Leppin, A. (1989). Social support and health: A meta-analysis. *Psychology and Health*, *3*, 1–16.

Skelton, J. A., & Croyle, R. T. (Eds) (1991). *Mental representation in health and illness*. New York: Springer-Verlag.

Stone, G. C., Weiss, S. M., & Matarazzo, J. D. (Eds) (1987). *Health psychology: A discipline and a profession*. Chicago, IL: University of Chicago Press.

Sutherland, V. (1990) . Managing stress at the worksite. In P. Bennett, J. Weinman, & P. Spurgeon (Eds) *Current developments in health psychology* (pp. 305–330). London: Harwood Academic.

Temoshok, L. (1987). Personality, copying style, emotions and cancer: Towards an integrative model. *Cancer Surveys*, *6*, 545–567.

Thoresen, C., Friedman, M., Powell, L. H., Gill, J. J., & Ulmer, D. (1985). Altering the Type A behavior pattern in postinfarction patients. *Journal of Cardiopulmonary Rehabilitation*, *5*, 258–266.

Turnquist, D. C., Harvey, J. H., & Anderson, B. L. (1988). Attributions and adjustment to life-threatening disease. *British Journal of Clinical Psychology*, *27*, 55–65.

Wallston, K. A., Wallston, B. S., South, S., & Dobbins, C. J. (1987). Perceived control and health. *Current Psychological Research and Reviews*, *6*, 5–25.

Watson, D., & Pennebaker, J. W. (1991). Situational, dispositional and genetic bases of symptom reporting. In J. A. Skelton & R. T. Croyle (Eds) *Mental representation in health and illness* (pp. 60–84). New York: Springer-Verlag.

Weinman, J., & Armstrong, D. (1988). Using interview training as a preparation for behavioural science teaching. In J. Aldridge-Smith, A. Butler, H. Dent, & R. H. S. Mindham (Eds) *Proceedings of first conference of behavioural sciences in medical undergraduate education* (pp. 20–29). Leeds: Leeds University Press.

Weinman, J., & Johnston, M. (1988). Stressful medical procedures: An analysis of the effects of psychological interventions and of the stressfulness of the procedures. In S. Maes, C. D. Spielberger, P. B. Defares, & I. G. Sarason (Eds) *Topics in health psychology* (pp. 205–217). Chichester: Wiley.

12
RESEARCH METHODS AND STATISTICS

INTRODUCTION

Given a clearly formulated empirical question about some aspect of behaviour or mental experience that can be tackled by collecting objective evidence, how do psychologists go about planning and carrying out empirical research to answer it? And, after the data have been collected, how do the researchers analyse and interpret the findings? The chapters in this section are devoted to these closely interconnected problems.

The section opens with chapter 12.1, by David D. Stretch, on experimental design. In a controlled experiment, the experimenter controls one or a small number of variables that might influence the responses of the experimental subjects and simultaneously controls potentially confounding extraneous variables. Stretch explains, from first principles, the fundamental ideas behind experimental design in psychology and the major problems encountered by experimenters in designing their research and interpreting their findings. Controlled experimentation is by no means the only research method used in psychology, but it is the most powerful because it enables firm conclusions to be drawn about cause–effect relationships, and it is usually the method of choice where it is feasible. In chapter 12.2 Brian S. Everitt focuses in more detail on analysis of variance designs, which are by far the most common experimental designs in contemporary psychology.

In chapter 12.3 A. W. MacRae deals with descriptive and inferential statistics. Methods of descriptive statistics, as the name suggests, are used for summarizing data in ways that make them more easily interpretable. The techniques of inferential statistics are used for drawing inferences from the data, specifically to help decide whether the results are statistically significant or whether they could have arisen purely by chance. MacRae explains the ideas behind all of the most important statistical techniques used by psychologists. Among the methods of descriptive statistics dealt with in this chapter is correlation; for more on correlation, see chapters 12.1 and 12.4.

In chapter 12.4 Michael L. Raulin and Anthony M. Graziano discuss quasi-experiments and correlational studies. Quasi-experiments are research studies that are not strictly experimental but that resemble controlled experiments in some ways; correlational studies involve no experimental manipulation and are concerned essentially with the way in which two or more variables are "co-related". This chapter provides a comprehensive survey of all of the major quasi-experimental methods (including time-series methods) and correlational methods used in psychological research. For more on correlational methods, see chapters 12.1 and 12.3.

In chapter 12.5 Francis C. Dane discusses survey methods, naturalistic observations, and case studies. Survey methods are used for investigating the distribution of attitudes, opinions, beliefs, and other psychological attributes in specific sections of a population or in different populations; naturalistic observations involve careful observations and recordings of behaviour in natural habitats; case studies are confined to detailed investigations of single individuals, or occasionally single social organizations. Dane explains all of these methods and discusses the opportunities and problems that they present to the researcher.

Finally, chapter 12.6, by Anthony Gale, is on ethical issues in psychological research. This chapter includes a comparison and critical analysis of the ethical guidelines for the conduct of research issued by the American Psychological Association and the British Psychological Society, the two largest psychological associations in the world. It also ranges over many issues of ethical significance, including ageism (see also chapter 8.5, John C. Cavanaugh) and gender as a psychological variable (see also chapter 11.3, Mary Crawford and Rhoda K. Unger).

A.M.C.

12.1

EXPERIMENTAL DESIGN

David D. Stretch

University of Leicester, England

Experiments involve comparisons	Forward planning
Experimental control and causes of behaviour	Alternative explanations
Populations, samples, randomization, and representativeness	The methods of measuring and the meaning of psychological variables
Interpretability, plausibility, generalizability, and communicability	Optimum strategy in experimental design
	Further reading
	References

This chapter deals with experimental design in psychology. Experimental design has a close relationship with statistics and statistical analysis, as it is usually via statistical analysis that we interpret and understand the evidence provided for us by the experiments we carry out. However, statistical analysis is not the only aspect of experimental design that is important, and it is some of these other aspects that will be discussed here.

EXPERIMENTS INVOLVE COMPARISONS

It is usual that experiments involve comparing conditions, groups of people, or situations on various measures, for example, rather than determining "absolute" values of a single group on one or more measures. So, if we have a theory that states, say, that speech is lateralized in the left hemisphere of the brain in right-handed people, then in order to investigate this hypothesis, we have to frame a research question that involves a comparison of some sort that sheds light on the theory. Similarly, if we have a theory that states that the environmental situation in which people learn information can be used as a cue for later recall of that information, then this needs to be similarly framed as a research question that involves comparisons. Finally, if we consider a theory that rewards and punishments are powerful modifiers of behaviour, we can derive from this theory a research question that asks a comparative question.

To make this clear, the following list of statements can be looked upon as research questions suitable for experimental investigation because they involve comparisons. They may not yet be in a form that can be directly used to frame an experiment, but they are certainly immediate candidates for experimental investigation:

1 Do right-handed people have more difficulty speaking if their left hemisphere is slightly anaesthetized rather than their right hemisphere?
2 Can people remember more information than they otherwise would if they attempt to recall that information in similar environmental situations to those in which it was learned?
3 Does immediate reward of appropriate behaviour in children result in more episodes of appropriate behaviour?

The following are questions that, as they stand, ask about "absolutes". Consequently, they are not immediately available as ready-made research questions that can be investigated by means of experiments.

4 Do people who practise "sleep hygiene" sleep well?
5 Are psychologists closed-minded?

They can, however, be altered so that they do ask about comparisons, though it will be seen that the altered questions are rather different in the kinds of things they are asking about:

4' Does the imposition of a regime of "sleep hygiene" in people who suffer from insomnia cause them to have better quality sleep than they might otherwise experience?
5' Are psychologists more closed-minded than physicists?

Of the two questions 4' and 5', the former more easily allows us to make inferences about potential causes of behaviour than the latter. This is the case even though both pose comparative questions; we shall now discuss the reason for this.

EXPERIMENTAL CONTROL AND CAUSES OF BEHAVIOUR

The reason why question 5' above does not logically allow statements to be made about the possible cause of any observed differences in behaviour is that the question is asking about the association that exists between pre-existing attributes of people and observable behaviour. As such, then, the study does not exhibit experimental control.

In question 5′, the pre-existing attribute is the occupation of the people under study (whether they are psychologists or physicists), and although we could speculate that it was solely being a psychologist or a physicist that caused the observed difference in closed-mindedness, it could equally well be another (unobserved) factor or variable that led them to choose a course in psychology or physics as well as causing them to have particular levels of closed-mindedness.

Question 4′, however, involves us causing some change in people who suffer from insomnia (i.e., imposing a regime of sleep hygiene on them), and seeing if a corresponding change in behaviour is observed (i.e., an improved quality of sleep). In these circumstances, we are said to impose a treatment, and so we can have greater confidence in concluding what may have caused the observed difference in behaviour.

Question 4′ leads to what is often termed a true experiment whereas question 5′ leads to what is known as a correlational study. Now, if it were ethically possible to alter question 5′ above, to something like this

5″ Are people who would otherwise possess equal degrees of closed-mindedness affected by the kind of degree course attended so that a psychology course results in *less* closed-mindedness than a physics course?

then this is a research question that would be in a suitable form for a true experiment, because we would essentially be imposing a treatment on people (attendance at either a psychology or physics course), and seeing if this treatment caused a difference in the degree to which they were closed-minded. Of course, issues of plausibility or sensibility and ethical issues would still need to be considered.

The treatments or attributes are usually called independent variables or explanatory variables, whereas the behaviour in which we are attempting to explain the observed differences is usually called the dependent variable or response variable. For complicated experiments, there may be more than one dependent variable, or it may well happen that a variable is both an independent variable and a dependent variable, depending on context. This is particularly prone to happen when investigating proposed networks of causal influences in path analysis (Kenny, 1979), or structural equation modelling (Bollen, 1989; Everitt, 1984; Long, 1983a, 1983b).

Of course, experiments involve more things than are mentioned in the above discussion, but the examples have served to illustrate what is involved in the experimental control of variables. As has been shown, experimental control is quite an important aspect of experiments as it provides a way of identifying or confirming, from all the potential causes of the behaviour under investigation, a sub-set of causes that have a more dominant role in determining the behaviour being studied. If experimental control is particularly good, and our subject-matter for research is particularly well circumscribed, it may well be that we can discover that the total number of potential causes is quite small, but the nature of psychology is such that all behaviour is probably influenced by a very great number of other factors or causes, and so this is not often found to be achievable.

Although experimental control is usually associated with true experiments, this does not mean that it can never be present in any of the other empirical methods. For example, experimental control can be present to a greater or lesser extent in quasi-experiments (Campbell & Stanley, 1966). If case-studies in clinical psychology (say) are designed in a particular way, perhaps by making use of some of the single-case experimental designs mentioned in Barlow and Hersen (1984), experimental control is certainly present. Hence causes of behaviour can potentially be identified from such studies. Similarly, hypothesized networks of causal influences can be investigated in correlational studies by making use of the modelling technique of path analysis (Kenny, 1979), or, for the more adventurous, structural equation modelling or analysis of covariance structures (Bollen, 1989; Everitt, 1984; Long, 1983a, 1983b).

POPULATIONS, SAMPLES, RANDOMIZATION, AND REPRESENTATIVENESS

There is another feature of experiments that should also be mentioned at this stage: randomization. This term is more usually associated with statistics, but it is necessary to mention it here as there are issues that are tackled when designing an experiment that are most effectively explained by using concepts commonly employed within statistics. Closely bound to the idea of randomization are the ideas of populations, samples, and representativeness, and it is difficult to explain randomization without also using the latter three terms.

A population is the entire set of things about which we hope the experiment will allow us to make inferential statements. Thus, if we want to investigate degrees of closed-mindedness among psychologists, the population is the entire set of psychologists. (Although logically this should also include all psychologists who have ever lived, and are yet to live and become psychologists, it is almost always impractical to include literally everyone when planning and designing our experiments.) Similarly, if we want to investigate whether the aromas of lemon and pine can reduce the number of keyboard errors committed by people when working at a computer, then the population consists of all work sessions when people are using a computer keyboard.

We do not usually have the time to observe all elements of a population, and so we arrange to observe only a sample. If we choose random samples, using a suitable randomization technique, then we have some confidence that we can extrapolate or generalize the results we find from studying the sample to the entire population. Selecting a random sample is a very good way of ensuring that the sample is representative of the entire population of interest; consequently we can have confidence in being able to extrapolate or generalise any results based on this random sample. We shall see (below) that generalizability has been identified as being of high importance in psychological research, and so it is clear that random samples and representativeness need to be considered carefully. A random sample from a population can be constructed by ensuring that every member of the population has an equal chance of being picked as a member of the sample.

Constructing a random sample is often very difficult to arrange, but it is a worthwhile goal to achieve. The issue of representativeness has already been mentioned. Another benefit, arguably the greatest, of using an appropriate randomization technique concerns the random assignment of subjects to one or more experimental groups or conditions. This results in the subsequent experimental control of all ways in which the groups could differ, other than the ways the experimenter imposes by manipulation of the independent variable.

So, if we take our random sample, and then assign its units (usually subjects) to the experimental groups or conditions so that the final sizes of the experimental groups are equal, we will, on average, control every possible way in which the experimental groups could differ in terms of pre-existing attributes. This will, of course, not include the difference we are investigating in the experiment, which is not an attribute, but an imposed treatment. The principle of randomization was first expounded by the statistician Ronald A. Fisher in 1926 and popularized by his later textbook (Fisher, 1966); the principle proves to be one of the crucial aspects of true experiments. Note that the experimental groups ideally must be of the same size in order for this result or property of randomization to hold. Thus, if groups are unequal in size, either through poor planning, or subject attrition or drop-out (i.e., subjects failing for any reason to complete the experiment, resulting in groups of different size), then alternative explanations of any differences among the experimental groups may become viable; these alternative explanations will hinge on the different compositions of the groups, based on other, unmeasured features or attributes of the subjects. Furthermore, the more unequal the sizes of the experimental groups, the greater is the chance that alternative explanations become viable, and indeed they may become the most plausible explanation of an experiment's results.

It is therefore clear that if one wants to keep to a minimum the possibility that alternative explanations can explain the results of one's experiments, then ensuring that the experimental groups are of the same size is a useful first step to take. Furthermore, if subject attrition or drop-out occurs, it is useful to see if the remaining experimental groups differ in some attribute or attributes of the subjects. If they do, an alternative explanation of any differences among the groups may be possible in which the differences are explained in terms of the attribute differences among the experimental groups.

Even if the groups are of equal size, though, there is still a chance that the experimental groups will differ in some pre-existing attribute, because the principle of randomization will work only in the long run. In order to rule out these kinds of alternative explanations, sometimes extensive numbers of additional subject attributes will have to be measured, and this becomes very time-consuming. Consequently, ensuring equally sized groups and minimizing subject attrition are advisable in true experiments. Furthermore, if there is a suspicion that the groups are likely to differ on any pre-existing attribute that could form the basis of a plausible alternative explanation, then, even if the groups are of equal size, measurements of the attributes identified and their incorporation into any subsequent statistical analysis (such as analysis of covariance, and suchlike) will often help.

To illustrate some problems of random sampling, suppose we want to investigate by experiment whether people are better able to write down an address if a radio announcer reads out the complete address a number of times, or whether it is better for each line to be read out a number of times before the announcer moves on to the next line of address. (That is, if the lines of addresses are represented by the letters ABCD, the first method would correspond to people hearing ABCDABCDABCD, whereas the second method would correspond to AAABBBCCCDDD.) In the UK, the BBC usually has its announcers reading out entire addresses a number of times, but there was a short period when announcers repeated each line a number of times before moving on to the next line.

Now, we could ask for volunteers who would participate in this experiment. However, we would not then be constructing a strictly random sample, as the people who are unwilling to come forward and volunteer would never be picked. And, because some people would never be picked as members of the sample, our sample is at great risk of not being representative of everybody because it may contain a disproportionate number of people who share or possess a particular attribute. In this example, it could be that people who tend to volunteer are those who have found the current method of reading out addresses on the radio very difficult to follow, and so may be better able to write the addresses down if the second method of delivery was employed. One explanation of how this may have come about might be that they are rather irritated by the current method of reading out addresses, and may therefore have a slightly greater inclination to volunteer for the study. If such people were more prone to volunteer, then the resulting sample would not be representative of the entire population we originally wanted to generalize our results to, and any such generalization would consequently be subject to bias.

Given that we are ethically obliged to avoid deception of subjects who participate in experiments, a great deal of psychological research could be biased in a way similar to the above example. The reason is that we cannot be sure that we can justifiably generalize from our sample to the entire population because of sampling bias. The situation could be retrieved somewhat by narrowing the population to which we generalize, so that our sample would be more representative (Coombs, 1983, 1984). Another way of tackling this potential problem would be to change the way in which the sample is drawn up and constructed so that it is more representative of the original population of interest. Finally, we could leave the design unchanged, but exercise great care and caution in generalizing the results.

INTERPRETABILITY, PLAUSIBILITY, GENERALIZABILITY, AND COMMUNICABILITY

Now is a suitable point at which to introduce four key features of any experiment (or, indeed, any other type of psychological research). The four most important features are those of interpretability, plausibility, generalizability, and communicability.

First, we must design experiments whose results we can easily interpret. One way of improving the interpretability of an experiment is to strive towards simplicity and clarity without descending into triviality. This can be very difficult to attain as Nature does not usually work in a simple manner. However, one should not overcomplicate experiments by, for example, collecting additional observations because they "could" be useful in an as-yet unspecified manner. A simple, clear research question, with an experiment closely focused on answering just that simple, clear question is best. Furthermore, a great help in attaining interpretability is to design experiments in which all alternative explanations of the results, apart from the one relevant to the research question, are eliminated. This subsidiary goal is discussed further below.

Second, an experiment must be designed so as to be a plausible way of investigating the research question. Similarly, the explanations that emerge from the results should also be plausible. Once again, simplicity, clarity, and closely focused research are likely to succeed in attaining plausibility, as well as attention to the elimination of alternative explanations.

Third, we must ensure that the results of the experiment are generalizable in the way we want: we need to be able to state with justification that the conclusions to which we come, based on the sample we used in the experiment, apply to the population from which the sample was drawn.

Finally, since psychological research is really part of a collective effort, we need to be able to communicate our results and conclusions effectively to our fellow researchers. Once again, simplicity, clarity, and closely focused research will facilitate communicability.

The above points have been introduced by Levy (1981). The message can best be summed up with the following sentence:

Keep things as simple, clear, and focused as possible, because they will always turn out to be more complicated than you imagine.

There are a number of strategies that can be adopted to ensure that experiments have the features mentioned above, and one of these (constructing a representative sample of the population of interest) has already been mentioned. A strategy that underlies most of the others, though, is forward planning.

FORWARD PLANNING

To maximize our chances of completing experiments that possess the characteristics introduced above, a period of extremely careful planning preceding any collection of observations is often helpful. This forward planning will be easier to accomplish if we consider a number of subsidiary goals along the way (mentioned below). The advisability of planning is so important that its message can be summed up simply:

If you fail to plan, you are planning to fail.

Informal evidence from my colleagues who also give research advice to people shows that inadequate planning occurs frequently. As Levy (1981) notes, failure to plan leads to situations where researchers have collected uninterpretable observations and data. Additionally, the sample used may not be representative of the population about which inferences are to be made. Often, the researcher consults someone who has expertise in research design or statistical analysis only after the observations have been gathered – and this is too late. Usually, a large amount of time and effort will be involved in rescuing an inadequately planned experiment, and this rescue bid is not bound to succeed. In these circumstances, the only advice that ought to be given to the researcher is to throw away the observations and start again properly – making sure that sufficient forward planning is carried out before any move is made to gather observations. Careful forward planning can drastically reduce the resulting waste of time and resources. Hand & Everitt (1987a), Greenfield (1987), and Barnett (1987) (all contained in Hand & Everitt, 1987b) discuss this issue from the point of view of statisticians.

Finally, too much emphasis is placed on checking that the data emerging from an experiment can be (statistically) analysed. The conditions that determine whether a statistical test can be justifiably applied to a set of data do not necessarily include or require that the data are appropriate for the substantive psychological research question: this issue is assumed to have been dealt with beforehand in the forward planning stage. It is much more important to determine that the experiment is interpretable (Levy, 1981). Although Kenny (1979) was writing about path analysis and causal modelling, a sentence of his, with a minor addition, is very relevant here: "Good ideas do not come out of computer packages [or statistical tests], but from people's heads" (p. 8). Instead, the planning needs to concentrate on maximizing the interpretability, plausibility, generalizability, and communicability of the experiment, because if they are maximized, it is almost always the case that the resulting data can be statistically analysed.

ALTERNATIVE EXPLANATIONS

If we tackle a number of subsidiary issues or goals in the forward planning stage, it becomes easier to design experiments that attain the four goals of interpretability, plausibility, generalizability, and communicability. One of these subsidiary issues is that we must eliminate, as far as possible, any alternative explanations of the results we could obtain. So, the research must be designed in such a way that, when any necessary statistical analyses have been completed, an interpretation of the results remains that makes use of only those explanations of relevance to the original research question.

From what has been written earlier about experimental control, it should be obvious that a good way of minimizing the chance of alternative explanations being offered for experimental results is to use experimental control of variables, and hence design and carry out "true experiments". (Note, however, that there are alternative points of view to the one offered here, some of which are discussed in Bickhard, 1992.) Furthermore, if sampling is done with care, possible alternative explanations which rely on the samples used being unrepresentative of the population of interest cannot be proposed. (This issue was discussed above.) Coombs talks about a decision having to be made about "saying more about less, or less about more" (Coombs, 1983, 1984), and this is clearly related to the matter under discussion here.

It is important to become skilled at identifying the potential alternative explanations for results of experiments, because, once identified, the design of the experiments can be modified to try to eliminate them. This must be done in the planning stage, otherwise much time and effort is wasted in carrying out and completing flawed research. Huck and Sandler (1979) devote an entire book to giving examples of psychological research where the reader is invited to identify, with justifications, alternative explanations for the results the researchers report.

The following example comes from their book. The Pepsi-Cola Company carried out research to determine whether people tended to prefer Pepsi Cola to Coca Cola. Participants were asked to taste and then state which of two glasses of cola they preferred. The two glasses were not labelled "Pepsi" or "Coke" for obvious reasons. Instead, the Coke glass was labelled Q and the Pepsi glass was labelled M. The results showed that "more than half chose Pepsi over Coke" (Huck & Sandler, 1979, p. 11). Are there any explanations for this difference other than the taste of the two drinks? One alternative explanation mentioned was the systematic bias that was introduced into the study by always using letter Q for Coke and M for Pepsi. When the Coca Cola Company conducted another study where Coke was put into *both* glasses, one labelled M and the other Q, the results showed that a majority of people chose the glass labelled M in preference to the glass labelled Q. Since the taste of cola in the two glasses was presumably the same in this second study, the original conclusion (people prefer Pepsi to Coke) could not be upheld, and another alternative explanation of the results, based on letter preferences, could be offered instead. (Of course, there are still more alternative interpretations – for example, did people always taste the cola in glass M before the cola in glass Q? If so, would this affect the results?)

Possible alternative explanations of an experiment's results, like the above example, should be considered at the planning stage, and if they exist and are important, the design of the experiment should be changed to rule them out. It may not always be possible to do this, but, even so, the attempt should be made.

Consider another example, not directly taken from Huck and Sandler (1979). Suppose we want to determine whether taking a particular drug affects people's reaction times. To investigate this, we might take a large number of people and assign each person to one of two groups at random. Both groups would then complete a simple reaction time task so that we could derive a typical score on that task for each person. In one group we would administer the drug in tablet form, and in the other group we would administer a placebo, which in this case would be a tablet, identical to the tablet in the first group, except that it would not contain the drug. If the resulting statistical analysis of the reaction times showed a difference in the typical scores of the two groups (for example, if the drug group overall had shorter reaction times than the placebo group), we could conclude that the difference between the two groups in the design (drug vs no drug) *caused* the difference in the typical scores.

It may be possible to identify alternative explanations that would explain the results. Most of these alternative explanations would not explain the difference in the reaction times in terms of the drug, but would rely on the discovery of other ways in which the two groups differ. This is obviously an issue to do with random sampling and representativeness (discussed above), and using those ideas would ensure that the two groups were unlikely to differ in any characteristic other than whether they were given a drug or a placebo. If alternative explanations are easy to discover, and they take the form of discovering further ways in which the two groups differ, then this may indicate that not enough care was taken in randomly allocating the people to the two groups. This would be another example of insufficient forward planning.

In particular, note that if we assigned people to the drug and the placebo groups not at random, but according to whether they were already taking the drug in question or not, then the taking of the drug or the placebo would no longer be a treatment applied to each person, but would rather be an attribute of each person. Consequently, there could quite likely be many ways in which the two groups differed other than the mere taking of the drug or not; for example, the group of people taking the drug could already have a particular illness. Alternative explanations could be offered that explained any difference in reaction times in terms of whether the people had these illnesses or not rather than whether they were taking the drug or the placebo.

There are a number of standard experimental designs that can be used to control variables and, at the same time, determine whether possible alternative explanations can be ruled out. Details of some of these can be found in Spector (1981). Additionally, there is an entire class of statistical analyses, known as analysis of variance, that has been developed to allow various kinds of alternative explanations to be ruled out at the same time as providing a coherent and consistent approach to statistical analysis (as long as certain assumptions can be made about independence of scores from each other, and the way random error can affect these scores). Good sources for these kinds of approaches are Fleiss (1986), Myers (1979), and Pedhazur and Schmelkin (1991).

THE METHODS OF MEASURING AND THE MEANING OF PSYCHOLOGICAL VARIABLES

Another subsidiary goal that must be considered is the careful examination of the meaning and the method of measurement of the psychological variables relevant to the experiment. If this is not done, we may find that the measures we use are very different (in a way that has not been clearly justified) from other similar experiments, thus making the integration of different experiments in the same research area very difficult. However, a more serious problem is that another experiment, identical to the first apart from the particular way of measuring the psychological variables, may yield quite different results, and it is important to know to what extent the results obtained reflect the particular method of measuring things, rather than the way in which the underlying psychological processes work. These kinds of issues are often labelled "methodological problems" in psychology, but they are almost always substantive psychological issues in their own right. Consequently, they are worthy of being researched in their own right, rather than being treated as mere annoyances. In fact, most of the "problems" of psychological measurement mentioned here are researched within psychology quite extensively. However, the research (some of which is known as *Axiomatic Measurement Theory*) can be highly mathematical in nature and is therefore not easily accessible to many psychologists. For those who wish to see some of this material, Krantz, Luce, Suppes, and Tversky (1971), Luce, Krantz, Suppes, and Tversky (1990), and Suppes, Krantz, Luce, and Tversky (1989) are the main sources. More accessible sources are Falmagne

(1985), French (1981), Levelt, Riemersma, and Bunt (1972), and van der Ven (1980, chap. 10).

The meaning of psychological terms, and hence the measurement of them, is a particular problem in psychology because psychologists sometimes have no widely agreed method of measuring psychological concepts like depression, intelligence, pain, performance, memory, or learning. The usual tactic used in psychology to overcome this problem is to make use of operational definitions. A definition of a psychological construct is an operational definition if it consists of a description of the operations that are performed to measure the psychological construct. So, in an experiment investigating speed of information processing, performance may be operationally defined as the reaction times people have to certain stimuli. Similarly, the degree of depression may be operationally defined to be the scores that people obtain when they complete a depression questionnaire.

There is obviously a problem with these kinds of definitions if they are used in an unthinking way, because the definitions are entirely circular. A psychological construct is defined in terms of the operations necessary to measure it, and the measurements are defined to be measures of the psychological construct! In fact, the originator of operational definitions (Percy Bridgman, a physicist) never intended them to be the *sole* definitions offered for a construct, and details of the history of operational definitions are available in a number of sources (Bickhard, 1992; Green, 1992; Koch, 1992). However, we are left with a problem of what to do if we can no longer use operational definitions to help us define psychological constructs. Psychologists may sometimes not make sufficient use of good dictionaries, constructed by lexicographers, as a means to help them determine the "standard" meaning of some constructs, although this does not always provide a satisfactory solution. A useful rule of thumb is to consider many different ways of measuring the psychological construct of interest and determine the extent to which each method could yield different experimental results. If you find that the measurement techniques radically affect the results that emerge, this should indicate that more work is needed on developing the underlying psychological and measurement models to explain these effects. Axiomatic measurement theory (mentioned above) is potentially useful here, though most researchers would find it difficult to work with. Concentration on the purpose and the meaning of the measurements often helps.

For example, in measuring change in psychological variables, a simple way of assessing changes is to take the straightforward difference between scores obtained on repeated administration of the same instrument as a measure of change, but this can sometimes lead to difficulties that are conceptual rather than statistical. If we take simple difference scores, we are assuming that we are measuring the same psychological attributes, but if the measures are of something that is subject to developmental processes this may not be justifiable. If we administered a simple addition and subtraction test to 5-year-old children, and then administered the same test to the children when they were 16, the first score is likely to measure the extent to which the children have acquired the skills of addition and subtraction, whereas the second score may be more likely to measure the efficiency with which the children can apply the already-acquired skills of addition and subtraction. Depending on what one wanted to do, the simple difference score approach could be appropriate or inappropriate. This matter is discussed in Plewis (1985), who gives alternative methods of analysing data from such studies, as does Goldstein (1979).

However, the most striking example of the problem of ambiguous psychological terms is best left to the end. This example clearly shows the necessity of careful thought and analysis of experiments. The possible solutions will not be easy for most psychologists to grapple with, but in order to build a solid and plausible set of psychological sciences, they must be confronted. Possible means of dealing with these issues are either purely statistical, or involve the use of axiomatic measurement theory ideas. However, greater mathematical and statistical understanding and expertise will be required for psychologists to master and hence make proper use of these techniques.

If one wishes to determine, for right-handed people, in which hemisphere speech is lateralized, one could get people to balance a rod vertically on the end of the index finger. Subjects would do this separately for right and left hands when either speaking or silent. The time taken from the start of balancing each rod until it fell from the finger would be observed. Thus we would take observations from people balancing rods in four different situations: balancing in the right hand when silent, balancing in the right hand when speaking, balancing in the left hand when silent, and balancing in the left hand when speaking. A graph which might be typically obtained of mean performance in the $2 \times 2 = 4$ experimental conditions is shown in Figure 1: better performance for balancing with right hands rather than left hands; better performance when silent rather than speaking; and a greater difference between silent and speaking performance in the right-handed than the left-handed condition.

Because there is contralateral control of movement by the two hemispheres of the brain, right-handed balancing is controlled by the left hemisphere, and left-handed balancing is controlled by the right hemisphere. Given that the disadvantage of speaking compared with being silent is greater when balancing with the right hand rather than the left hand, this suggests that speech is lateralized in the left hemisphere. This conclusion relies on the assumption that it is usually more difficult for a hemisphere to control two things at the same time rather than one. (For more details of experiments like this one, see Hicks, 1975; Kinsbourne and Cook, 1971.)

However, the data for performance need not be analysed as a time-based measure of mean seconds per rod, as in Figure 1. Instead, a speed-based measure of rods per second can be derived from the same observations by taking the reciprocal of the performance points shown in Figure 1. No change

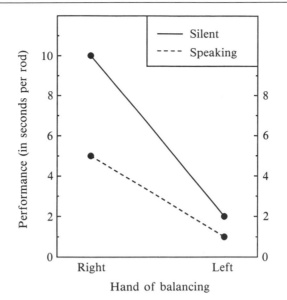

Figure 1 Graph showing hypothetical results from the rod-balancing experiment using a time-based measure of performance. This shows an interaction between hand of balancing and the speaking and silent conditions that would lead one to conclude that speech was lateralized in the left hemisphere
Source: Results based on work by Kinsbourne and Cook, 1971, and Hicks, 1975

to the treatment of the observations or of the interpretation of the results occurs other than this re-scaling of the dependent variable. Figure 2 shows the identical observations re-scaled in this way.

This figure shows that the nature of the interaction has been reversed by this simple re-scaling of the observations. Using the same arguments and assumptions that were used to interpret Figure 1, we can interpret Figure 2 as follows: better performance for balancing with right hands rather than left hands; better performance when silent rather than speaking; and a greater difference between silent and speaking performance in the left-handed than the right-handed condition. (Note that the re-scaling is such that low scores indicate better performance than high scores when performance is measured in rods per second.) Given that the disadvantage of speaking compared with being silent is greater when balancing with the left hand rather than the right hand, this suggests that speech is lateralized in the right hemisphere. This conclusion also relies on the assumption that it is usually more difficult for a hemisphere to control two things at the same time rather than one.

So, by re-scaling the observations, quite legitimately, from a time-based measure to a speed-based measure and by using exactly the same assumptions to interpret the resulting graph, we come to opposite conclusions about the hemisphere in which speech is lateralized. Unless there are very good grounds

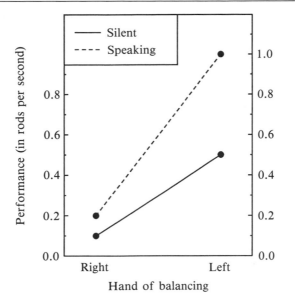

Figure 2 Graph showing hypothetical results from the rod-balancing experiment using a speed-based measure of performance derived from the identical observations used in Figure 1. This shows an interaction between hand of balancing and the speaking and silent conditions that would lead one to conclude that speech was lateralized in the right hemisphere

Source: Results based on work by Kinsbourne and Cook, 1971, and Hicks, 1975

for choosing one form of measure over another, any monotonic transform of the dependent variable can be justified. So, results like those shown above cannot allow us to decide with certainty in which hemisphere speech is lateralized. In this case, there are alternative sources of evidence that allow us to decide in which hemisphere of the brain speech is lateralized, but in many cases within psychology this will not be the case. It should be clear that a greater emphasis on the meaning, method, and understanding of the psychological measurements one is making is required. And to do this, greater expertise among psychologists of the ideas explored in axiomatic approaches to psychological measurement is needed.

OPTIMUM STRATEGY IN EXPERIMENTAL DESIGN

Many issues have been mentioned that need to be considered when designing experiments. These issues have to be thought about and decisions made *before* the collection of observations begins. It may be difficult to remember all the issues, and so the following strategy may help ensure that any flaws in a planned experiment have a good chance of being detected before observations have been gathered.

If the proposed experiment is written up during the planning stage, as if the research has already been completed, it will help to highlight any areas that may need further consideration. This will often be helped if, in the results section, a number of alternative sets of dummy results that could plausibly be obtained are described. Thus, the issues of interpretability, plausibility, generalizability, and communicability will be considered in the planning stage. Furthermore, by considering a number of plausible sets of results, attention is placed upon possible alternative explanations.

A useful side-effect of this strategy is that the actual paper or final report is largely written by the time the observations have been collected. Thus, the phase of research that is often seen as the most tedious − writing up after the analysis has been completed, often under time pressure − will have its undesirable qualities reduced somewhat.

FURTHER READING

Coombs, C. H. (1983). *Psychology and mathematics*. Ann Arbor, MI: University of Michigan Press.

Huck, S. W., & Sandler, H. M. (1979). *Rival hypotheses: Alternative interpretations of data based conclusions*. New York: Harper & Row.

Kenny, D. A. (1979). *Correlation and causality*. New York: Wiley.

Levy, P. (1981). On the relation between method and substance in psychology. *Bulletin of the British Psychological Society*, *34*, 265–270.

van der Ven, A. H. G. S. (1980). *Introduction to scaling*. Chichester: Wiley.

REFERENCES

Barlow, D. H., & Hersen, M. (1984). *Single case experimental designs: Strategies for studying behavior change* (2nd edn). New York: Pergamon.

Barnett, V. (1987). Straight consulting. In D. J. Hand & B. S. Everitt (Eds) *The statistical consultant in action* (chap. 3, pp. 26–41). Cambridge: Cambridge University Press.

Bickhard, M. H. (1992). Myths of science. *Theory and Psychology*, *2*(3), 321–337.

Bollen, K. A. (1989). *Structural equations with latent variables*. New York: Wiley.

Campbell, D. T., & Stanley, J. C. (1966). *Experimental and quasi-experimental designs for research*. Chicago, IL: Rand McNally.

Combs, C. H. (1983). *Psychology and mathematics*. Ann Arbor, MI: University of Michigan Press.

Combs, C. H. (1984). *Theory and experiment in psychology* (transcript of talk presented to the European Mathematical Psychology Group, 29 March 1983, at the University of Hamburg, FRG).

Everitt, B. S. (1984). *An introduction to latent variable models*. London: Chapman & Hall.

Falmagne, J.-C. (1985). *Elements of psychophysical theory*. Oxford: Clarendon.

Fisher, R. A. (1926). The arrangement of field experiments. *Journal of the Ministry of Agriculture*, *33*, 503–513.

Fisher, R. A. (1966). *The design of experiments* (8th edn). London: Oliver & Boyd (1st edn published 1938).

Fleiss, J. L. (1986). *The design and analysis of clinical experiments*. New York: Wiley.

French, S. (1981). Measurement theory and examinations. *British Journal of Mathematical and Statistical Psychology*, *34*, 38–49.

Goldstein, H. (1979). *The design and analysis of longitudinal studies: Their role in the measurement of change*. London: Academic Press.

Green, C. D. (1992). Of immortal mythological beasts. *Theory and Psychology*, *2*(3), 291–320.

Greenfield, T. (1987). Consultants' cameos: A chapter of encounters. In D. J. Hand & B. S. Everitt (Eds) *The statistical consultant in action* (chap. 2, pp. 11–25). Cambridge: Cambridge University Press.

Hand, D. J., & Everitt, B. S. (1987a). Statistical consultancy. In D. J. Hand & B. S. Everitt (Eds) *The statistical consultant in action* (chap. 1, pp. 1–10). Cambridge: Cambridge University Press.

Hand, D. J., & Everitt, B. S. (1987b). *The statistical consultant in action*. Cambridge: Cambridge University Press.

Hicks, R. E. (1975). Intrahemispheric response competition between vocal and unimanual performance in normal adult human males. *Journal of Comparative and Physiological Psychology*, *89*(1), 50–60.

Huck, S. W., & Sandler, H. M. (1979). *Rival hypotheses: Alternative interpretations of data based conclusions*. New York: Harper & Row.

Kenny, D. A. (1979). *Correlation and causality*. New York: Wiley.

Kinsbourne, M., & Cook, J. (1971). Generalized and lateralized effects of concurrent verbalization on a unimanual skill. *Quarterly Journal of Experimental Psychology*, *23*, 341–345.

Koch, S. (1992). Psychology's Bridgman *vs*. Bridgman's Bridgman. *Theory and Psychology*, *2*(3), 261–290.

Krantz, D. H., Luce, R. D., Suppes, P., & Tversky, A. (1971). *Additive and polynomial representations* (vol. 1 of *Foundations of measurement*). New York: Academic Press.

Levelt, W. J., Riemersma, J. B., & Bunt, A. A. (1972). Binaural additivity of loudness. *British Journal of Mathematical and Statistical Psychology*, *25*, 51–68.

Levy, P. (1981). On the relation between method and substance in psychology. *Bulletin of the British Psychological Society*, *34*, 265–270.

Long, J. S. (1983a). *Confirmatory factor analysis*. Beverly Hills, CA: Sage.

Long, J. S. (1983b). *Covariance structure models: An introduction to LISREL*. Beverly Hills, CA: Sage.

Luce, R. D., Krantz, D. H., Suppes, P., & Tversky, A. (1990). *Representation, axiomatization, and invariance* (vol. 3 of *Foundations of measurement*). San Diego, CA: Academic Press.

Myers, J. L. (1979). *Fundamentals of experimental design* (3rd edn). Boston, MA: Allyn & Bacon.

Pedhazur, E. J., & Schmelkin, L. P. (1991). *Measurement, design and analysis: an integrated approach*. Hillsdale, NJ: Lawrence Erlbaum.

Plewis, I. (1985). *Analyzing change*. Chichester: Wiley.

Spector, P. E. (1981). *Research designs*. Beverly Hills, CA: Sage.

Suppes, P., Krantz, D. H., Luce, R. D., & Tversky, A. (1989). *Geometrical, threshold, and probabilistic representations* (vol. 2 of *Foundations of measurement*). San Diego, CA: Academic Press.

van der Ven, A. H. G. S. (1980). *Introduction to scaling*. Chichester: Wiley.

12.2

ANALYSIS OF VARIANCE DESIGNS

Brian S. Everitt

University of London Institute of Psychiatry, England

It is said that when Gertrude Stein lay dying, she roused briefly and asked her assembled friends, "Well, what's the answer?" They remained uncomfortably quiet at which she sighed, "in that case, what's the question?"

Research in psychology, and in science in general, is about searching for the answers to particular questions of interest. Do politicians have higher IQ scores than academics? Do men have faster reaction times than women? Should phobic patients be treated by psychotherapy or by a behavioural treatment such as flooding? Do children who are abused have more problems later in life than children who are not abused? Do children of divorced parents suffer more marital breakdowns themselves than children from more stable family backgrounds? Other questions, for example "Does God exist?" and "Is marriage bad?" are, however, *not* the province of the research psychologist or of science in general. Why not? Why are such questions fundamentally different from the kind listed earlier.

The acid test by which scientific questions may be divided from the nonscientific is that the former must be falsifiable, that is, capable in principle of being proved false by scientific investigation. From the scientists' point of view, the strongest theories are those which allow the most opportunities to falsify them, but which withstand all such attempts. In science, this does not mean that a particular theory or hypothesis has been confirmed: hypotheses can never be proved to be true however much the current weight of evidence is in their favour (consider, for example, Newton's theory of gravitation); they can only be shown to be worth retaining and perhaps subjecting to further and more rigorous testing.

Having decided that a question is scientific, however, does not necessarily mean that its investigation will be straightforward. Careful planning will almost certainly be required, using well-established principles from the statistical theory of design. Statistical primarily because of the inherent variability in observations on human and animal subjects. Consider the question "Do British politicians have higher IQs than British academics?" Suppose ten politicians allow their IQs to be measured (this is after all a hypothetical example!), and similarly ten academics, with the results shown in Table 1. Clearly some politicians have higher scores than some academics and vice versa. But what about the difference in average or mean IQ in the two groups? From Table 1 it is seen that for these two particular sets of samples the average IQ of academics is higher than that of politicians. But if we took further samples would this always be so? Can anything be concluded about the difference in average IQ of all British politicians and all British academics from the result found in this particular sample? Drawing conclusions about a population on the basis of observations on a sample of values is the role of inferential statistics.

In any serious study of the IQs of politicians and academics, of course, many other aspects of the design would need to be considered. For example, should only people of the same sex be considered? Or only politicians of a particular party? Or only academics from a particular discipline? And should

Table 1 IQ scores of samples of British academics and politicians

	Academics	*Politicians*
	106	110
	99	112
	122	115
	128	105
	105	128
	107	127
	131	109
	119	99
	99	110
	132	104
Mean	114.80	111.90
SD	13.06	9.36

age be taken into account? Perhaps even more fundamental are considerations of the IQ measurements involved, are they, for example, reliable and valid?

MEASUREMENT

Measurement taken during scientific investigations should be objective, precise, and reproducible. Clearly not all measurement is the same. Measuring an individual's weight is qualitatively different from measuring his or her response to some treatment in terms such as "improved" or "not improved". Measurement scales are differentiated according to the degree of precision in the measurement. The comment that a woman is tall is not as accurate as specifying that her height is 1.88 metres. Certain characteristics of interest are more amenable to precise measurement than others. Given an accurate thermometer, an individual's temperature can be measured very precisely. Quantifying the level of anxiety or depression of patients, or assessing their degree of pain, are, however, far more difficult measurement tasks. Measurement scales may be classified into a hierarchy ranging from categorical through ordinal to interval and finally ratio scales. Details of the characteristics of each type of scale are given in Everitt (1989).

An important component of many scientific investigations is the assessment of the reliability and consideration of the validity of the measurements to be made. In very general terms, reliability concerns the variability in repeated measurements made on the same material by the same measuring instrument, and validity expresses the extent to which a measuring instrument measures the characteristic it purports to measure. (Both terms are explained in more detail in Schontz, 1986.) But one characteristic of many behavioural and social measurements that distinguishes them from physical measurements is that they are obtained from the responses to several different questions or test items. The weight of an object is given by a single instrument reading whereas an intelligence quotient may be calculated from answers given to 50 or 100 individual tests (items) of cognitive ability. For such measures the reliability of the total test score is estimated using the subtotals obtained from splitting the test into two equal sized groups of comparable items. The result is what is generally known as the *split-half reliability*. (For details see Dunn, 1989.)

In many areas of research the observer, interviewer, or rater is an obvious source of measurement error, and reliability studies are often required to investigate the measurement procedures to be used for collecting the data of interest. Details of how such studies should be conducted are given in Dunn (1989). That such studies are crucial is emphasized by the following quotation from Fleiss (1986).

The most elegant design of a study will not overcome the damage caused by unreliable or imprecise measurement. The requirement that one's data be of high quality is at least an important component of a proper study design as the requirement for randomization, double blinding, controlling where necessary for prognostic factors, and so on. Larger sample sizes than otherwise necessary, biased estimates, and even biased samples are some of the untoward consequences of unreliable measurements that can be demonstrated. (p. 1)

OBSERVATIONAL AND EXPERIMENTAL STUDIES

Research studies can be divided roughly into those that are observational and those that are experimental. Both generally involve the comparison of two (or more) groups of subjects, one group which has received the new treatment or been exposed to a particular risk factor or whatever, and another group which has received only the normal treatment as a placebo or has not been exposed to the risk factor. (Studies in which, for example, all patients are given a new treatment are generally neither scientifically nor ethically acceptable.) The basic differences between the two types of studies is the amount of control which the investigator has over the way in which the groups of subjects to be compared are constructed. In an observational study there is essentially no control and in an experimental study usually complete control, although there are types of studies which fall somewhere between these two extremes (see below). In an investigation into the relationship between smoking and systolic blood pressure, for example, the researcher cannot allocate subjects to be smokers and non-smokers; instead the systolic blood pressure of naturally occurring groups of individuals who smoke and those who do not would be compared. In such a study any difference found between the blood pressure of the two groups would be open to three possible explanations.

1 Smoking causes a change in systolic blood pressure.
2 Level of blood pressure has a tendency to encourage or discourage smoking.
3 Some unidentified factors play a part in determining both the level of blood pressure and whether or not a person smokes.

In contrast, in an experimental study, investigators may allocate subjects to groups in a way of their choosing. For example, in a comparison of a new treatment with one used previously, the researcher would have complete control over which subjects received which treatment. The manner in which this control is exercised is, of course, crucial to the acceptability or otherwise of the study. If, for example, subjects who are first to volunteer are all allocated to the new treatment, then the two groups may differ in level of motivation and so subsequently in performance. Observed treatment differences would be confounded with differences produced by the allocation procedure.

The method most often used to overcome such problems is random allocation of subjects to treatments. Whether a subject receives the new or the old treatment is decided, for example, by the toss of a coin. The primary benefit that randomization has is the chance (and therefore impartial) assignment of extraneous influences among the groups to be compared and it offers this control over such influences whether or not they are known by the experimenter to exist. Note that randomization does not claim to render the two samples equal with regard to these influences. If, however, the same procedure were applied in repeated samplings, equality would be achieved in the long run. Thus randomization ensures a lack of bias, whereas other methods of assignment may not, and the interpretation of an observed group difference in an experiment is largely unambiguous: its cause is the different treatments or conditions received by the two groups. (Many forms of randomization might be employed in designing an experiment, apart from the simple "flipping-a-coin" variety mentioned above; for details see Altman, 1991.)

Randomization alone does not necessarily prevent biased comparisons. Observer judgements may, for example, be affected by knowing the treatment that a subject is getting. This problem is particularly relevant in clinical trials, where it is generally essential to keep both patients and assessors in ignorance of the treatment given, a procedure known as blinding (see Pocock, 1983; for details).

Somewhere between the observational study and the laboratory experiment come studies which attempt to alter the state of affairs in a non-laboratory environment. An example might be, an educational programme designed to prevent smoking, introduced into one school but not another. After a suitable time interval, the programme might be assessed by comparing the two schools on say an outcome measure derived from pupils' responses to a questionnaire that asks how often they smoke. This is not a rigorous experiment since it leaves many conditions uncontrolled, for example, possible differences between the backgrounds of the children who attend the two schools. Nevertheless, because such investigations are designed to come as close as possible to the ideal of a laboratory experiment they are generally termed quasi-experimental.

DESIGNS FOR EXPERIMENTS

"There are only a handful of ways to do a study properly but a thousand ways to do it wrong" (Sackett, 1986, p. 1328). The issue of the variability of observations made on human and animal subjects was briefly touched upon above. It is such variability that necessitates a statistical approach both to the design and analysis of data from psychological experiments. Many of the principles of experimental design are aimed at trying to control sources of variation that are not of primary interest, so that attention can be focused on variability that is of concern. Some sources of variability may be known, or suspected, but often much remains unexplained. Altman (1991) gives an example involving variability in birth weight. Several variables are known which affect birth weight, including length of gestation, foetal sex, parity, maternal smoking, height above sea level, and so on, but statistical models incorporating such information explain only about one-quarter of the variability in birth weight. While there are undoubtedly other factors not yet identified that contribute to the variability, it is most unlikely that any important factors remain unidentified. The bulk of the observed variability must therefore be considered unexplanable; it is what is known as random variation. Such variation might be considered "background noise" against which it is hoped to detect some effect of interest. The simple, two-group design (see above), for example, attempts to detect a between group difference among the inherent variability of the individual observations. A simple extension of this type of design to more than two groups is one of the simplest experimental procedures used by psychologists. It may be used to illustrate many points concerning the design and subsequent analysis of experiments.

One-way designs

Suppose an investigator is interested in evaluating the effectiveness of three methods of teaching a given course. Thirty subjects are available who are considered to be a representative sample from the population of interest (important when drawing inferences about the population from the results found in the sample). Three subgroups of ten subjects each are formed at random, and each subgroup taught by one of the three methods. Upon completion of the course, each subject is given the same test covering the material in the course. A possible set of test scores are given in Table 2. How can these scores be used to shed light on whether or not the three teaching methods are equally effective?

The answer involves the comparison of two variances, one of which measures variation between the observations within the three groups, the

Table 2 Teaching methods data

Method 1	Method 2	Method 3
10	8	7
12	9	6
11	10	5
8	12	9
13	11	10
7	8	9
14	12	10
11	11	10
6	7	10
12	8	7

other of which assesses the variation between the group means. It can be shown that, if the teaching methods are equally effective, then both these sample variances estimate the same population value, so should, within the limits of random sampling, be equal. A statistical test (*F test*) is available which allows the investigator to judge whether or not it is reasonable to assume that the two variances, are estimates of the same population value and hence to conclude whether or not the teaching methods are equally effective. The procedure is a simple example of a technique known as analysis of variance, introduced by Ronald A. Fisher in the 1920s. Table 3 sets out the relevant results for the data in Table 2. The various terms in Table 3, for example, DF (degrees of freedom), MS (mean square), and so on, are explained in more detail in Weiner (1971).

Essentially what the analysis reported in Table 3 has achieved is a partition of the total variation in the observations into two parts: the first, due to differences between the mean scores for the three teaching methods and the second, due to random variation. If the former is "large" compared to the latter, a group difference is claimed (where "large" is assessed formally by means of the *F* test). The results here suggest that there is no difference between the teaching methods, since the relevant *F* statistic is not significant.

The validity of the *F* test used here is based on certain assumptions which should be briefly mentioned. The first is that the test scores follow a normal distribution and the second is that the variation of these test scores is the same for each of the teaching methods – the homogeneity of variance assumption. If these assumptions are not met then the *F* test is not strictly correct. There is considerable evidence however, that the test is robust to moderate departures from both assumptions.

If the hypothesis that the teaching methods are equally effective had been rejected, it would not necessarily imply that they all differ, and further analyses may be required to examine the differences in more detail. Such analyses often involve multiple comparison tests described in Bruning and Kintz

Table 3 Analysis of variance table for teaching methods data in Table 2

Source	SS	DF	MS	F	p
Method	22.47	2	11.23	2.43	0.11
Error	124.90	27	4.62		

Notes:
SS = sum of squares (the sum of the squared deviations of scores from their means)
DF = degrees of freedom (the number of squared deviations minus one)
MS = mean square (the sum of squares divided by the corresponding degrees of freedom)
F = the ratio of the mean square associated with the method divided by the mean square associated with the error
p = the probability of an F ratio at least as large occurring by chance alone, if the methods are equally effective

(1977, pt 3) Weiner (1971, chap. 3), and in detail by Hochberg and Tamhane (1987).

Factorial designs

Experiments in psychology frequently involve more than a single grouping variable. In the teaching methods example, for instance, it may be thought that age has some effect, and the experimenter may wish to consider separately subjects in the age ranges 10–12 years, 13–15 years, and 16–18 years. The two experimental factors, teaching method and age group, could be considered independently of each other using the procedure outlined above. This would, however, shed no light on their combined effect, which may not be simply the sum of their separate effects. In such cases a factorial design can be used to evaluate possible interaction effects between the grouping factors.

Suppose, for example, fifteen children from each age group are available, five might be randomly assigned to each teaching method and then test scores

Table 4 Teaching methods and age group data

	Method 1	*Method 2*	*Method 3*
10–12 years	10	8	9
	8	7	10
	9	7	12
	8	9	14
	10	10	12
13–15 years	11	9	8
	10	8	9
	10	8	11
	15	10	12
	9	11	11
16–18 years	13	8	7
	12	7	8
	14	6	5
	10	9	7
	15	10	8

Analysis of variance table

Source	*SS*	*DF*	*MS*	*F*	*p*
Age	5.91	2	2.95	1.10	0.34
Method	45.91	2	22.95	8.57	< 0.001
Age × method	86.09	4	21.52	8.04	< 0.001
Error	96.40	36	2.68		

Note: For abbreviations see Table 3

recorded as in the previous example. A possible set of results is shown in Table 4. Again using the analysis of variance procedure the total variation in the observations can be separated into components representing variation between age group means, variation between teaching method means, variation due to the age group/teaching method interaction, and random error variation. Each of these may be used in an F test to assess whether the data suggest equivalent population effects. Here the analysis of variance indicates the presence of a statistically significant interaction effect, and it is important to consider exactly what this implies.

The simplest method for interpreting an interaction effect is by plotting a graph of appropriate mean values. The relevant plot for the teaching styles/age group example is shown in Figure 1. Examining this plot it can be seen that, for the younger age group, teaching method 3 produces the best results, but for the oldest age group, it leads to the lowest mean value. Because of the presence of this significant interaction, the significant main effect of method seen in the analysis of variance table is largely ignored. The

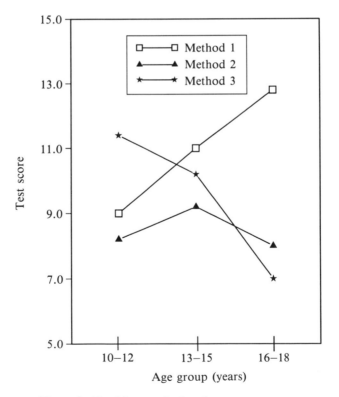

Figure 1   Teaching method and age group means

finding of most consequence is that which teaching method is best depends on the age group of the children being taught.

Factorial designs are not restricted to two grouping variables. In the teaching styles, study for example, the investigator may have some a priori evidence (from previous work, etc.) that the sex of a student may need to be

Table 5 Teaching method, age group, and sex data

		Method 1	Method 2	Method 3
Male	10–12 years	10	6	8
		8	7	12
		6	8	13
		9	9	14
	13–15 years	6	8	7
		8	7	9
		9	8	12
		8	10	12
	16–18 years	7	12	11
		6	12	10
		8	10	9
		7	9	9
Female	10–12 years	11	8	9
		9	9	8
		8	7	8
		12	12	10
	13–15 years	6	9	12
		8	12	11
		7	13	9
		10	12	12
	16–18 years	12	12	14
		8	7	12
		7	14	6
		13	11	10

Analysis of variance table

Source	SS	DF	MS	F	p
Age	5.02	2	2.51	0.64	0.53
Method	41.69	2	20.85	5.34	0.01
Sex	16.05	1	16.05	4.11	0.05
Age × method	31.22	4	7.80	2.00	0.11
Age × sex	6.69	2	3.35	0.86	0.43
Method × sex	16.69	2	8.35	2.14	0.13
Age × method × sex	31.55	4	7.89	2.02	0.10
Error	211.00	54	3.91		

Note: For abbreviations see Table 3

considered. Consequently, sex could be added to give a three-way factorial design. A possible data set and corresponding analysis of variance table is shown in Table 5. Here the division of the total variation in the observations is into quite a large number of components corresponding to what are usually termed main effects (age, method, and sex), first-order interactions (age × method, age × sex, and method × sex), and second-order interactions (age × sex × method). Several graphs might be needed in the interpretation of significant interaction effects.

Clearly factorial designs become increasingly complex as the number of factors is increased. A further problem is that the number of subjects required for a complete factorial design quickly become prohibitively large so that alternative designs need to be considered which are more economical in terms of subjects. Perhaps the most common of these is the latin-square (described in detail in Winer, 1971, chap. 10). Here economy in number of subjects required is achieved by assuming a priori that there are no interactions between the factors.

Within-subject repeated-measure designs

In the discussion of the differences between experimental and observational studies, the advantages of random allocation in the former were described: foremost among these was the balance achieved in the groups on differences between subjects existing prior to the experiment. An alternative approach to eliminating individual differences is to use the same subjects for all conditions. Such studies are known as within-subjects or repeated-measure designs. In such designs any individual peculiarities are equalized out over all conditions.

To illustrate this type of design consider a study in which ten phobic patients are each given three possible treatments and their level of anxiety then recorded. A possible set of data is shown in Table 6.

The analysis of such designs poses more problems than these considered earlier since, to the extent that characteristics of individual subjects remain constant in the different conditions, pairs of observations on the same subject will tend to be correlated rather than independent as assumed previously. Unless these correlations conform to a particular pattern, the usual F tests are no longer applicable. Alternative tests and analysis procedures are described in Greenhouse and Geisser (1959), Hand and Taylor (1987), and Huynh and Feldt (1970).

In the example shown in Table 6, a number of other features of good design need comment. It would, for example, not be sensible to administer the treatments in the same order to each subject, since then the effect of occasion would be confounded with the treatment effect. The order in which a subject is administered the treatments is instead randomized. It would also be important to allow sufficient time between the administration of each

Table 6 Simple example of a repeated-measures design

Subject	Treatment 1	Treatment 2	Treatment 3
1	3	5	5
2	4	7	6
3	2	3	3
4	5	4	6
5	3	6	7
6	2	4	5
7	2	3	5
8	6	7	9
9	3	6	7
10	4	4	5

treatment to avoid the possible effects of one treatment on the effect of subsequent treatments.

Such possible carry-over effects are particular important in the commonly used 2×2 crossover design, in which two treatments are to be compared. Here subjects are randomly allocated to one of two groups: in one group the subjects receive treatment A followed by treatment B, in the other group subjects receive the treatments in the reverse order. Note that this design has both a between-subjects component, the different orders of administration of the two treatments, and a within-subjects component, the measurements made on each subject for both treatments. An example of the practical application of such a design is provided by Broota (1989), where an experimenter is interested in testing the effect of caffeine on a tracking task. Two doses of caffeine are used (5 mg and 10 mg), each subject being observed under each dose, and scored on a measure of dexterity. The experiment was conducted at two different periods of the day (morning and evening) five subjects being randomly assigned to the order 5 mg, 10 mg, and a further five to 10 mg, 5 mg. The data are shown in Table 7.

There are several difficult issues involved in the analysis of what appears to be a relatively simple design. They are discussed in detail in Armitage and Hills (1982), Brown (1980), and Jones and Kenward (1989). Major problems are the detection of possible carry-over effects and their impact on the assessment of the treatment effect. In general the design can be used with confidence only when a carry-over effect can be discounted a priori. In the caffeine experiment, for example, the interval between the two tests was considered large enough to dissipate the effect of the earlier dose. The appropriate analysis of variance table for the data in Table 7 is shown in Table 8. Here the test for group differences in the between subjects section is equivalent to testing for a carry-over effect. The result confirms that for these data there is no such effect. In the within-subjects section it is seen that the occasion effect is non-significant and the group × occasion interaction is highly

Table 7 2 × 2 crossover study: two doses of caffeine

	Subject	Morning	Evening
Group 1 (5 mg, 10 mg)	1	15	24
	2	16	25
	3	17	24
	4	14	22
	5	16	22
Group 2 (10 mg, 5 mg)	6	22	18
	7	23	15
	8	21	17
	9	22	18
	10	25	17

Table 8 Analysis of variance for crossover data

Analysis of variance table

Source	SS	DF	MS	F	p
Between subjects					
Group	0.45	1	0.45	0.23	0.63
Error	14.60	8	1.83		
Within subjects					
Occasion	6.05	1	6.05	3.71	0.09
Group × occasion (caffeine)	224.45	1	224.45	137.70	< 0.0001
Error	13.00	8	1.63		

Note: For abbreviations see Table 3

significant. With this type of design the test for this interaction corresponds to a test of the treatment main effect, in this case a test of the difference in the two doses of caffeine. Here the higher dose of caffeine clearly produces higher dexterity scores on the tracking task.

ANALYSIS OF COVARIANCE

In the 1930s Fisher introduced the technique known as the analysis of covariance as a means of reducing error variation and increasing the sensitivity of an analysis of variance for detecting mean differences. The method depends upon identifying one or more measurements known as covariates, which are related to the response variable but not to the experimental treatment condition. (This is most often assured by measuring the covariate prior to the administration of the treatment.) By including such concomitant measures in the analysis, residual variation can be reduced by the extent to which it is attributable to the covariates. As an example, consider again the teaching methods experiment. Here a useful covariate might be a test score for each subject recorded before the experiment began. (Such a data set is given in Table 9.) A possible method for introducing this covariate into the analysis of the data would be to simply subtract it from the test score observed at the completion of the experiment. The one-way analysis of variance would then be applied to the difference scores (see Table 10). A more formal procedure is to assume that the dependent variable is related to the covariate in some way and use this assumed relationship for the purpose of adjustment. Details of such models are given in Winer (1971). An appropriate analysis for the data in Table 9 is shown in Table 11. The analyses in Tables 10 and 11 do not change the original conclusion that the teaching methods do not differ. In each case, however, the error mean square is much lower than in the simple analysis of variance shown in Table 3. Note also that the error term in the analysis of covariance has lost a degree of freedom due to the estimation of the relationship between final and initial scores.

When the analysis of variance procedure is used in experiments involving random allocation of subjects to groups it is generally a completely acceptable approach to deriving more sensitive tests. Unfortunately it is often used by psychologists in the hope of overcoming the disadvantages of studies

Table 9   Teaching methods data-initial and final scores

Method 1		Method 2		Method 3	
Initial	Final	Initial	Final	Initial	Final
7	10	6	8	4	7
9	12	5	9	5	6
9	11	7	10	5	5
8	8	11	12	6	9
12	13	10	11	6	10
8	7	6	8	7	9
11	14	12	12	9	10
10	11	9	11	10	10
3	6	5	7	9	10
8	12	7	8	7	7

Table 10   Analysis of variance for differences between final and initial scores in Table 9

Source	SS	DF	MS	F	p
Methods	0.87	2	0.43	0.22	0.80
Error	53.00	27	1.96		

Note: For abbreviations see Table 3

1095

Table 11 Analysis of covariance for teaching methods data-initial score used as covariate

Source	SS	DF	MS	F	p
Method	3.30	2	1.65	0.99	0.38
Error	43.27	26	1.66		

Note: For abbreviations see Table 3

where randomization is not possible. An investigator may, for example, be interested in determining whether normal subjects have different reaction times from those diagnosed as schizophrenic and those diagnosed as depressed. A variable which clearly affects reaction time is age, and this may be introduced as a covariate, and analysis of covariance used to adjust the comparisons of reaction time across the three groups for the possibly different group age distributions.

Although such an approach may be helpful in particular instances there are possible problems. First, there may be variables other than the observed covariate, age, that affect reaction time. Unless age acts as a surrogate for all of these the comparison between groups could still be misleading. Second, after performing the analysis of covariance the investigator will have an answer to the question, "Conditional on having the same age, does the reaction time of normals, schizophrenics, and depressives differ?" In some circumstances, however, this might not be a sensible question: suppose, for example, that patients diagnosed as schizophrenic were always younger than those with the diagnosis, depression? Such difficulties are discussed in detail in Fleiss and Tanur (1972).

CONCLUSION

The good design of experiments in psychology is essential if valid conclusions are to be drawn. One of the corner-stones of a well-designed experiment is randomization, a procedure which can only partially be replaced by methods such as analysis of covariance which purport to offer some form of statistical control. In situations where randomization is not an option, the quasi-experimental approach might be used. A feature of designing experiments not mentioned in this chapter is that concerning the number of subjects needed in a study; this important problem is dealt with in detail by Pocock (1983).

Psychologists need to be familiar with the basics of experimental design and with methods of analysis such as analysis of variance. Nowadays, of course, they need not be familiar with the arithmetic of such procedures, since the ubiquitous personal computer can perform even the most complex analyses in a few seconds. This is not, however, without potential dangers and experimental psychologists need to ensure that they are familiar with exactly what type of analysis has been performed. A visit to a statistician may often be necessary!

FURTHER READING

Campbell, D. T., & Stanley, J. C. (1963). *Experimental and quasi-experimental designs for research*. Chicago, IL: Rand McNally.
Cox, D. R. (1958). *Planning of experiments*. New York: Wiley.
Mead, R. (1989). *The design of experiments*. Cambridge: Cambridge University Press.
Myers, A. (1980). *Experimental psychology*. New York: Van Norstrand.

REFERENCES

Altman, D. G. (1991). *Practical statistics for medical research*. London: Chapman & Hall.
Armitage, P., & Hills, M. (1982). The two-period crossover trial. *The Statistician, 31*, 119–131.
Broota, K. D. (1989). *Experimental design in behavioural research*. New Delhi: Wiley.
Brown, B. W. (1980). The crossover experiment for clinical trials. *Biometrics, 36*, 69–79.
Bruning, J. L., & Kintz, R. L. (1977). *Comparative handbook of statistics* (2nd edn). Glenview, IL: Scott, Foresman.
Dunn, G. (1989). *Design and analysis of reliability studies*. Sevenoaks: Edward Arnold.
Everitt, B. S. (1989). *Statistical methods for medical investigations*. Sevenoaks: Edward Arnold.
Fleiss, J. L. (1986). *The design and analysis of clinical experiments*. New York: Wiley.
Fleiss, J. L., & Tanur, J. M. (1972). The analysis of covariance in psychopathology. In M. Hammer, K. Salzinger, & S. Sutton (Eds) *Psychopathology: Contributions from the social, behavioural and biological sciences* (pp. 509–527). New York: Wiley.
Greenhouse, S. W., & Geisser, S. (1959). On the methods in the analysis of profile data. *Psychometrika, 24*, 95–112.
Hand, D. J. & Taylor, C. C. (1987). *Multivariate analysis of variance and repeated measures*. London: Chapman & Hall.
Hochberg, Y., & Tamhane, A. C. (1987). *Multiple comparison procedures*. New York: Wiley.
Huynh, H., & Feldt, L. S. (1970). Conditions under which mean square ratios in repeated measurement designs have exact F distributions. *Journal of the American Statistical Association, 65*, 1582–1589.
Jones, B., & Kenward, M. G. (1989). *Design and analysis of cross-over trials*. London: Chapman & Hall.
Pocock, S. J. (1983). *Clinical trials*. Chichester: Wiley.
Sackett, D. L. (1986). Rational therapy in the neurosciences: The role of the randomized trial. *Stroke, 17*, 1323–1329.

Schontz, F. C. (1986). *Funadmentals of research in the behavioral Sciences.* Washington, DC: American Psychiatric Press.

Winer, B. J. (1971). *Statistical principles in experimental design.* New York: McGraw-Hill.

12.3

DESCRIPTIVE AND INFERENTIAL STATISTICS

A. W. MacRae

University of Birmingham, England

When we have a body of data – numbers that describe some aspect of the world that interests us – and hope to learn something useful from it, two approaches are available: descriptive and inferential statistics. For example, if we have information about 100 children we may want to say things about the particular individuals studied, so we quantify their abilities, classify their social interactions, and so on. These are descriptions (using descriptive statistics) which summarize the data we actually obtained; that may be useful when advising these children or their parents but does not tell us anything about other children. Alternatively, we might perform an experiment to evaluate a teaching method. We then want the data to tell us something about the response of children in general. Because we cannot try out the method with all children we must do so with a sample of children – perhaps 100 again. Our analysis now uses the information from the sample to make inferences (using inferential statistics) about what to expect from the much larger group of children we have not studied. A wider group to which we hope to generalize our results is called a population.

DESCRIPTIVE STATISTICS

Even small collections of data can be hard to understand until they are simplified by organizing the original numbers to make their overall pattern clearer or summarizing them by calculating a few numbers that capture as much as possible of the original information.

A stem-and-leaf diagram organizes a collection of numbers with no loss of information. The two sets of numbers in Table 1 contain exactly the same information, but in the stem-and-leaf diagram (1b) the first two digits of the number are represented by a row in the table. For example, the number 137 contributes to the row labelled "13". The third digit of each number is written in the appropriate row. For example, the top row of 1b represents the numbers 105, 107, 107, 108, and 109. When organized in that way, it becomes obvious that numbers between 155 and 170 did not occur, whereas that fact (which might be quite important when dealing with real measurements) is not at all obvious in the unorganized list of numbers in 1a.

Table 1 Organizing data without losing any information can reveal attributes originally hidden

1a Raw data as originally obtained					*1b The same data organized in a stem-and-leaf diagram*
137	111	134	147	110	
185	173	183	115	185	10 57789
114	113	137	187	126	11 00011233455568
110	112	121	175	171	12 0011345679
147	192	110	179	125	13 3347788
183	190	116	191	115	14 47799
177	185	183	154	107	15 1444
149	109	184	191	149	16
138	120	178	154	173	17 11233356789
144	176	184	113	120	18 00222333444555578
182	182	184	188	151	19 0111223
171	154	129	115	121	
185	105	182	107	138	
180	118	108	191	172	
173	123	124	133	193	
111	127	192	133	180	

A box-and-whisker plot is a pictorial summary of data, where the "box" indicates the range of scores that omits the highest 25 per cent and lowest 25 per cent of all scores, the mid-line indicates the median (the score exceeded by exactly 50 per cent of all the scores) while the whiskers indicate the extreme range of high and low scores. Unlike the stem-and-leaf diagram, a box-and-whisker plot is just a summary which does not allow us to identify all the original numbers because it captures only some of their attributes. However, what it captures may be all we need, and because it is a very simplified representation of the original table it may be good for comparing several sets of data. Figure 1 shows box-and-whisker plots of the data in Table 1. Each column is shown by a different plot − which would be appropriate if each was obtained from a different condition in an experiment, say. They allow us to see that all the columns have much the same range of scores (roughly 105 to 190) but column 2 is noticeably different from the others in having a very low median. That is, half the scores in column 2 lie below 125 whereas only about a quarter of those in columns 1, 3, 4, and 5 do. The strange distribution of values in Table 1 is hinted at by the two halves of the "box" being longer than the two "whiskers" in every case, whereas in a distribution having a peak near the centre, the whiskers would be longer than the box. Other differences between columns can also be seen.

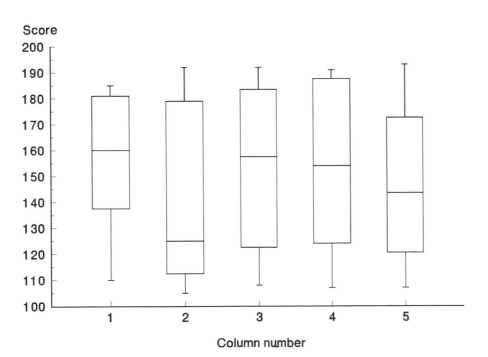

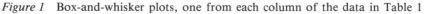

Figure 1 Box-and-whisker plots, one from each column of the data in Table 1

Techniques for organizing and summarizing data have been described by Tukey (1977), under the name of "Exploratory Data Analysis" (EDA). They are often the best way to start because representing the same data in various ways often lets us see "what is really happening".

Types of data

We use data to represent aspects of the world by symbols that we can manipulate, tabulate, and so on. (The "aspects of the world" that interest psychologists may be attributes of individuals that are not directly observable.) Often, numerical data result from measurement, but we must distinguish between the numbers and the things we really want to know about. The numbers may allow us to make inferences and predictions about aspects of the world,but they are of little interest in themselves. Levy (1981) comments that when people have what they think is a "statistical" problem it is usually because of uncertainty about how the numbers relate to the question being investigated.

Figure 2 shows one way of classifying types of data. The first division is into "frequencies" and "measures". Frequencies are counts of the number of cases of a particular kind, and obviously must be whole numbers. Measures are numbers that express the amount of something. They may be whole numbers but need not be. (In fact, the frequency of occurrence of something may be treated as a measure, though a measure should not be treated as a frequency.) Distributions of frequencies occur when various values of a single attribute

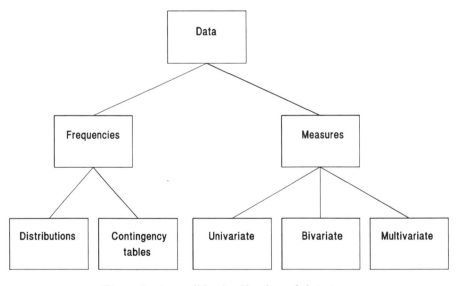

Figure 2 A possible classification of data types

1102

are used to divide up the cases into their various categories – for example, if we count the number of children with black, brown, red, or fair hair. Contingency tables (also known as cross-classifications) are generated when two or more attributes are used to divide up the cases – for example, if we classify children as high, medium, and low in anxiety and simultaneously separate them out by hair colour as above, giving twelve categories in all.

Univariate measures vary in only one respect. Examples of univariate data are age, score on a test, family size, and time taken to solve a problem. Multivariate measures vary in several respects. For example, for each individual in our sample we might know the age, the family size, and the score made on a test. That collection of information about the individual is multivariate. Each measure is univariate when considered on its own, but the set of measures is multivariate if we think of them as a composite description of the individual. Of course we can treat such an assembly of measures as multivariate only if they are related together in some way, for example if each measure comes from a single individual. Bivariate data are just a special kind of multivariate data with exactly two measures per individual.

Questionnaires are often best thought of as multivariate measures because each respondent is free to give any pattern of answers and each pattern may have a different meaning. Sometimes all the questions assess the same thing (all are comparable indicators of some political attitude, say) and then you might take no interest in which particular questions received positive answers but count only the number that did. A total score obtained in that way would be univariate. Thus the distinction between these types of data is not clear-cut and is more an expression of opinion about the meaning of the data than a matter of actual fact. However, if we take the view that our data are multivariate, we need different statistical techniques from those used with univariate data. Another source of multivariate information is an experiment where more than one type of result is recorded on each trial – for example, the time taken to respond and also the accuracy of the response made. In some experiments, we may need dozens of separate measures to describe the outcome of each trial and a multivariate analysis should be used.

Scales of measurement

The classification of data types by Stevens (1946, 1951) describes the relationship between the numbers constituting the data and the "true" value of the thing measured. The numbers are said to conform to a measurement scale which is nominal, ordinal, interval, ratio, or absolute. In a nominal scale, there is no relationship between the size of a number and the value of the thing "measured" by it. A No. 14 bus need not exceed a No. 7 bus in any way – and you would certainly not think of catching two No. 7s if you really wanted a No. 14! All that you can tell from the numbers is whether two things are equivalent in some respect (because they have the same number) or are different (because they have different numbers). In an ordinal scale, the order of sizes of the numbers tells us the order of sizes of the things measured. If item A is assigned a larger number than item B, then A has more of the thing measured. For example, we can often be pretty confident that Arthur is happier than Bernard (though both are quite happy) and Carol is happier than Diana (though both are unhappy). But we probably have no way to decide if the difference in happiness between Arthur and Bernard is greater or smaller than the difference in happiness between Carol and Diana. If we can put such differences in order, we have an ordered metric scale (a fairly common type which is not often mentioned in psychology). If, in addition, we can say when differences are equal we have an interval scale. True interval scales are rather rare because if we can compare differences between pairs of large values and pairs of small values well enough to say if they are equal or not, we usually also know when the thing measured is completely absent, and then we have a ratio scale. In a ratio scale, the number zero denotes absence of the thing measured and equal increases in number denote equal increases in the thing measured. If so, equal ratios between numbers must denote equal ratios in the thing measured, so it makes sense to talk about one measurement being twice as great as another, for example. Most of the familiar measures of daily life, for example weights or distances, are ratio scales, but they are rare for psychological variables. An absolute scale has no freedom to change even the units of measurement and for all practical purposes occurs only when we count things rather than measure them.

In my classification, frequency data correspond to absolute scales while different types of measures correspond to ordinal, interval, ordered metric, or ratio scales. Most numbers used in psychology relate to the relevant aspect of the world by either an absolute scale (counting) or an ordinal scale (measuring). Proving that a psychological measurement is on an interval or ratio scale is more difficult than it is for most physical scales, such as those of length or weight. For the latter, we can easily take a standard unit (a rod 10 mm long, say) and hold it against various sections of a tape measure to show that the difference between 20 and 30 mm is the same as that between 80 and 90 mm. Nothing comparable can be done for measures of most psychological attributes, but for many practical purposes people are willing to assume that measurement is on an interval, or even a ratio, scale and that the difference between levels of ability indicated by scores of 20 and 30 is equivalent to that between scores of 80 and 90 on some well-constructed test.

Some people consider that a scale type being ordinal or interval determines the kinds of statistical treatment that may be appropriate, but I think that view is very often exaggerated (see MacRae, 1988). The distinction between scale types affects the interpretation of numerical results, but is less relevant to the choice of significance test (discussed later). However, the distinction between univariate and multivariate data does affect the type of statistical analysis needed.

Graphical descriptions

There are many ways to graph one variable against another, each method emphasizing different properties of the relationship and using the power of the human eye and brain to see patterns that might not be detectable in a table of numbers Cleveland (1985) and Tufte (1983) advise on ways to assist the process, with an overview by Cleveland and McGill (1985). Numerical summaries are less trouble to produce, take up less space and can be conveyed orally if necessary, so there is a place for both approaches.

A bar chart shows on one axis the frequency of occurrence of each score (or group of scores) displayed along the other axis. Bar charts can easily be compared if the same units are used in each, and thus can reveal the differences among two or more sets of results. A histogram is a bar chart where the scores have a natural order, that is, they are univariate measures on at least an ordinal scale. A histogram displays the frequency distribution of the measure, from which we can easily see the highest and lowest values that occurred and get a good idea of which scores were frequent and which were rare.

Cross-tabulated frequencies may not be easy to graph. Even if there are only two dimensions of cross-classification, the resulting frequency must be expressed on a third dimension. It is possible to draw a perspective view of a 3D histogram where each slice is a normal histogram or (if the frequencies vary smoothly) it may be useful to draw contour plots, using the conventions of map-making to represent the frequency as though it were a height. Alternatively, the frequency can be expressed as a number of dots, with the two classification dimensions forming the axes of a grid. When there are more than two dimensions of classification it will usually be necessary to draw multiple graphs to represent the data adequately.

Bivariate measures arise when each individual is measured in two different ways. For example, we might give all applicants for a job a test that is designed to predict how well they will perform it, and later assess how well they did in fact perform in their first year. Each individual thus obtains a "Test Score" and later a "Performance Score". The relationship between the two can be expressed in a scatter plot (also called a scattergram) in which each individual appears as a single point. The scales are chosen to give about the same spread on each axis so that the outline of the graph is approximately square.

In each of Figures 3a, 3b, and 3c, we see a tendency for the performance scores to be high if scores on the test were high. In 3a the relationship is very close so it is possible to be fairly confident about the performance to be expected if we know the test score. Figure 3b shows a much weaker relationship. Knowing the test score improves our prediction of performance − our best estimate is higher if the test score high and is lower if the test score is low − but many exceptions occur. In 3c, there is again a strong relationship

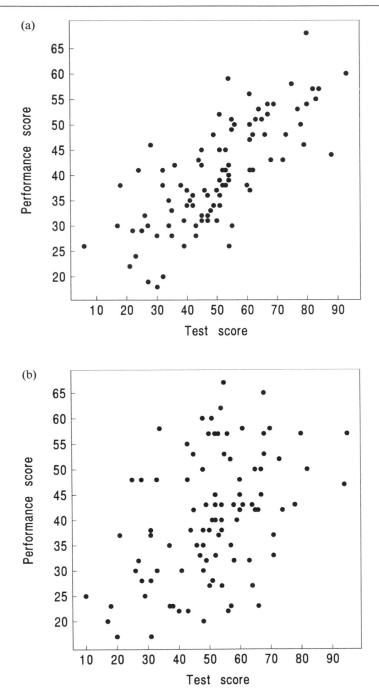

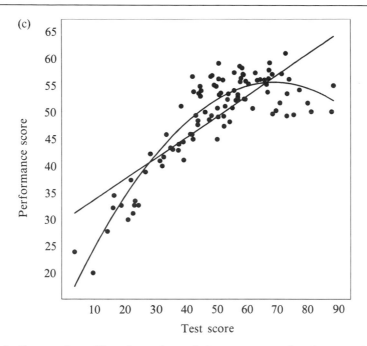

Figure 3 Scatter plots of imaginary data relating a measure of performance in a job to the score obtained by the same individual in an earlier selection test

but it does not follow a straight line. For test scores above about 40, there is little further increase in the typical performance score. In Figure 3c, the best-fitting straight line and the best-fitting quadratic (curved) line are plotted through the data points and we see that the curved line passes close to more points than does the straight one and so provides a better description of the relationship present in these results.

Multivariate measures can take advantage of our ability to extract patterns visually from complex diagrams if each component is represented by some attribute of a pattern which can then be recognized as a whole. Chernoff (1973) proposed the use of faces, where one component might alter the size of the face, another the curvature of the mouth, another the spacing of the eyes, and so on. There are problems of avoiding undue emphasis on particular components and inappropriate patterns, such as a smiling face to indicate a distressing combination of symptoms, but the approach is interesting. Advice on multivariate graphs can be found in Cleveland (1985), Everitt (1978), and Wainer and Thissen (1981).

Numerical summaries

Numerical summaries reduce many numbers to just a few which describe the general nature of the results. With frequency distributions and univariate measures, a mean (symbol $\overline{X}$), expressing a typical value, and a standard deviation (symbol SD), expressing the spread of the scores, may be enough to give a good idea of the sorts of numbers that occur. The mean is calculated by adding all the scores and dividing by the number of scores, so it is the measure usually thought of as the "average" value. One formula expressing the SD is

$$SD = \sqrt{\frac{\Sigma(X - \overline{X})^2}{N - 1}}$$

The symbol Σ is the Greek capital letter sigma, and is an instruction to add up all the values of the expression that follows it. The formula can be interpreted as a sequence of instructions, thus: find the difference between each score (X) and the mean ($\overline{X}$) (that is, its deviation); square each deviation; add up the results; divide the answer by ($N - 1$), where N is the number of scores in the collection; take the square root of the answer.

How much can be deduced about the original numbers from their mean and standard deviation depends on what we know about the way the numbers are distributed. If we have no idea of the distribution, the summary given by a mean and standard deviation may not be very useful, but the median (midpoint of the distribution) and inter-quartile range (the spread of the middle 50 per cent of the scores) give a description that can always be interpreted. (It is these, together with the highest and lowest scores, that are displayed in box-and-whisker plots.)

Descriptive methods for cross-tabulated frequencies usually concern relationships between the categories forming the rows and columns of the table. In the example of hair colour and anxiety proposed earlier, we might be interested in discovering if those with one hair colour are more likely than those with another to be rated high on anxiety. Another example would be where two clinicians make independent assessments of the same clients. We might then be interested in characterizing the extent of their agreement. Various measures can be used for each of these purposes, all with somewhat different meanings (Leach, 1979).

The product-moment correlation (r) also known as Pearson correlation, is a measure of how well bivariate data fit a straight-line plot on a scattergram. If the line slopes up, as in Figures 3a, 3b, and 3c, the value of r will be positive. If it slopes down, r will be negative. If there is no trend up or down, r will be zero. There are several ways to calculate r, including this one

$$r = \frac{\Sigma(X - \overline{X})(Y - \overline{Y})}{\sqrt{\Sigma(X - \overline{X})^2 \Sigma(Y - \overline{Y})^2}}$$

In this formula, X represents scores on one of the variables and Y represents corresponding scores on the other.

The value of r does not measure any other kind of relationship than a straight line, so it should not be interpreted as measuring relatedness in general. We must not interpret a small or zero correlation as showing that there is little relationship between the variables – it may be close but not linear, as in Figure 3c.

If we believe that product-moment correlation underestimates relatedness because the variables are related in a non-linear way, we may use a variant called multiple correlation (or multiple regression) to express curvilinear relatedness. It can also be used to express the way that a single variable is related to several others. For example, success in a course might be separately predictable from intelligence, time spent studying, ambition to succeed, and previous knowledge of the subject. Knowing an individual's score on all four of these predictors would surely permit better prediction than any one of them on its own, and the multiple correlation of all the predictors with success would express the closeness of the agreement between prediction and outcome.

INFERENTIAL STATISTICS

There are several styles of statistical inference, but the dominant one, referred to as "classical" statistics, draws conclusions about "statistical significance". These inferences invoke the notion of probability. That is, we do not conclude that something is true or false but that there is some chance of it being true or false, which can be described by a number between 0 and 1, where 0 indicates that there is no chance and 1 indicates certainty. The chance that a fair coin will fall heads when tossed is .5 because there are two possible outcomes and both are equally likely.

The methods of classical statistics evaluate the possibility that when a result looks interesting, it is merely the uninteresting variability in the measurements that has caused it. To eliminate that disappointing explanation, significance tests calculate the probability of obtaining results like those actually obtained if chance alone is the true explanation. If the probability is small, then the explanation that chance alone is responsible seems less reasonable. If it is small enough, the result is said to be statistically significant. By convention, results are usually considered significant if the probability is no larger than .05 (1 in 20), and for some purposes other levels such as .01 and .001 may be quoted. Note however that showing a result to be significant only disposes of chance as an acceptable explanation for result: a significance test does not endorse any other explanation in particular. It is the task of experimental design to ensure that just one satisfactory explanation is left after chance is eliminated.

The logic of classical statistical inference

Consider the following (non-statistical) hypotheses, H_a and H_b, that you

1109

might be entertaining about my possible location at this moment and two alternative items of information I might give you (possible observations, O_c and O_d) to help you to decide where I am:

H_a: I am at the top of a mountain in Wales
H_b: I am *not* at the top of a mountain in Wales
O_c: I can see a double-decker bus within ten yards of me
O_d: I can *not* see a double-decker bus within ten yards of me.

One or other of the hypotheses must be true, and also one or other of the observations must occur. Now consider what each of the possible observations tells you about the truth of each of the hypotheses. If I give you information O_c, you should feel very inclined to reject hypothesis H_a – you probably think it most unlikely that I should see a double-decker bus at the top of a mountain. If so, you will be pretty confident that H_b is true, so in this case you make a decision in favour of one hypothesis out of two that between them cover all the possibilities.

However, if the information I give you is O_d, reporting that I can *not* see a double-decker bus, you are certainly not obliged to conclude that I am on a Welsh mountain! This time, the information does not induce you to reject one hypothesis and accept the other. Thus there may be a lack of symmetry about the sorts of inference that observations allow us to make about hypotheses. The difference between H_a and H_b is that the first is very specific and the second is very general: it excludes absolutely nothing except the one possibility mentioned by H_a. The null hypothesis invoked in classical statistics is also very specific: it declares that the true difference between groups is exactly zero. The alternative hypothesis includes absolutely every other possibility, including the possibility that there is some real but very tiny difference. For that reason, there is a lack of symmetry about the inferences to be made about the null hypothesis too.

The probability given by a test of significance is thus the probability of obtaining such results if the null hypothesis is exactly true and chance is the only explanation for the observations. But that is not the probability that chance is the only explanation. To clarify that point, consider the following probabilities:

(a) Probability that (I visit Westminster Abbey) if (I am in London) = .01
(b) Probability that (I am in London) if (I visit Westminster Abbey) = 1.00

For everyone, (b), the probability of being in London when visiting Westminster Abbey, is 1.00. The probability (a) of visiting Westminster Abbey when in London will be different for each person, and will hardly ever be 1.00.

Therefore, the probabilities described by (a) and (b) are different, even though the phrases look rather similar. Now consider the following:

(c) Probability that (I get such results) if (the null hypothesis is true) = .05
(d) Probability that (the null hypothesis is true) if (I get such results) = ?

The probabilities (a) and (b) are different, but the relationship between (a) and (b) is exactly the same as that between (c) and (d), so the probabilities described by (c) and (d) are different also. A test of significance gives us a value for (c) but does not tell us the value of (d), so we do not know how likely it is that the null hypothesis is true.

Now suppose our result is non-significant, that is, the probability of obtaining results like ours is *greater* than .05. Even if we find that the probability of obtaining such results when chance is the only cause is very high, say .9, *we should not conclude that chance is likely to be the only cause.* The significance test shows that chance *can* easily explain the results but it does not estimate the probability that it *did* give us the results. In fact, a conventional test of significance lets us conclude nothing useful if the result is not significant.

If the aim of our study is to show that two treatments differ, then a significant result is helpful, because it makes mere chance unattractive as an explanation. (Telling you that I can see a bus makes a Welsh mountaintop an unlikely location.) If our aim is to show that they are *not* different, a non-significant result is of no real help. (Telling you that I can not see a bus gives you hardly any information about my location since it can be true practically anywhere.) That limitation on the inferences to be drawn from significance tests is a serious one, and too little attention is paid in psychology to the main ways of dealing with the problem: classical confidence intervals (discussed later) and Bayesian inference.

Bayesian inference

Bayesian methods address the question we really want to answer when faced with data that may support an interesting conclusion: "How likely is it that the interesting conclusion is correct?" Compared with the huge number of books and papers about classical methods, there are few about Bayesian methods and only one textbook for psychologists (Phillips, 1973).

Bayesian methods evaluate the probabilities of observing the data, D, if Hypothesis A is correct, written $p(D|H_A)$, and if possibility B is correct, written $p(D|H_B)$. These correspond to the calculations in classical inference of the probability of obtaining the data given that the null hypothesis, H_O, is correct. But Bayesian methods invoke an additional relationship named

"Bayes Rule" after the eighteenth-century Revd Thomas Bayes, who wrote about it:

$$p(H_A|D) = p(H_A) \frac{p(D|H_A)}{p(D)}$$

It signifies that the probability of Hypothesis A being true, given the observed data, is found by multiplying the probability of Hypothesis A being true anyway, $p(H_A)$, by the probability of obtaining the data if Hypothesis A is true, $p(D|H_A)$, and dividing the answer by the probability of obtaining the data without stating what hypothesis is true, $p(D)$.

In that form, the result is not very useful, since the probability of obtaining the data can be calculated only when we have adopted a particular hypothesis. However, if the analogous expression is calculated for the probability of Hypothesis B being true, and the first expression is divided by the second, we obtain the more useful result where the unknown probability, $p(D)$, is cancelled out:

$$\frac{p(H_A|D)}{p(H_B|D)} = \frac{p(H_A)}{p(H_B)} \frac{p(D|H_A)}{p(D|H_B)}$$

On the left of the equation, the relative probabilities of Hypotheses A and B being correct in the light of the data is calculated from (on the right of the equation) their relative probabilities before obtaining the data and the relative probabilities of the data under Hypotheses A and B respectively. The calculations and data thus alter our previous opinion about the relative probabilities of hypotheses A and B. If we are at first strongly convinced that A is correct, we need strong evidence to persuade us that B is the correct explanation and the evidence consists of the relative probabilities of obtaining these results when A is true and when B is true. The data need not be *likely* if B is the true explanation – only much *less* likely if A is true.

Considering in this way the hypotheses about my location, the information that I can see a bus is not particularly likely at any time. We can write that as $p(O_c|H_b) = .001$, say, to indicate that the probability, that I can see a bus, O_c, is one in a thousand even on the hypothesis, H_b, that I am not on a mountain. But the probability of seeing a bus, O_c, is very much smaller if I *am* on a mountain, H_a – surely not more than 1 in 1 million, so $p(O_c|H_a) = .000001$. The ratio of $p(O_c|H_b)$ to $p(O_c|H_a)$ is thus at least 1,000 to 1, so whatever prior ratio of probabilities you had for me being on a mountain as opposed to not being on a mountain, it is decreased by a factor of at least 1,000 after you are told that I can see a bus.

Had the data indicated that I can *not* see a bus, O_d, the information has little effect. That result has very high likelihood (.99999) if I am on a mountain, but is almost as high (.99000) if I am not on a mountain, so it causes hardly any increase (the ratio is only 1.01 to 1) in what was originally a very small likelihood of being on a Welsh mountaintop.

Bayesian or classical methods?

Some people dislike the Bayesian style of argument because it explicitly refers to our prior beliefs about the relative likelihoods of the theories under test, but that is a mistaken objection. Classical methods focus on a precise null hypothesis and see if the results have a probability under it that is small enough to be significant. That appears not to invoke prior beliefs, but if we ask what counts as "significant" we find that it depends on the plausibility of the alternative hypotheses available. For example, we may be convinced that one training method is better than another if a result is significant at the .05 level, but if an experiment is so well done that chance is the only alternative, many people would still prefer to believe in chance than accept .05 significance as proof of extrasensory perception. Similarly, people usually consider a result that is significant at the .01 level more convincing than one significant at the .05 level. That way of thinking is quite contrary to the logical structure of classical statistics because the latter views a set of results as falling into one or other of two categories of outcome: a rejection region, and a non-rejection region. The range of possible outcomes constituting the rejection region is decided in advance and the probability of falling in it by chance alone – of falling anywhere in it – is the significance level of the result. That is the formal structure, but, (as noted above) most of those who use it do not follow it in detail. Rather, they reach conclusions in a way that is approximately Bayesian.

There have been interesting developments in France using Bayesian logic. Most of the publications are in French, but there are some in English (e.g., Rouanet & Lecoutre, 1983; Rouanet, Lépine, & Pelnard-Considère, 1976). The approach may allow psychologists to address directly the questions they usually want to ask, that is, to decide how likely a particular conclusion is in the light of the data rather than following the back-to-front classical approach of testing a null hypothesis they do not believe in the first place with a view to rejecting it.

Inferential statistics for different types of data

Frequencies

In the case of distributions, we are almost bound to be concerned with measures of agreement: does the distribution conform to some theoretical prediction? In the case of contingency tables we may likewise want to evaluate agreement with a theoretical prediction, but are more likely to want to test independence. In the latter case, we see if the distribution on one variable is different for different values of another variable. Significance tests assess the probability of obtaining the results under either of these hypotheses.

1113

A style of significance testing found in all basic texts calculates a statistic called χ^2 (Chi-squared) which is found by applying the formula

$$\chi^2 = \Sigma \frac{(O - E)^2}{E}$$

where E is the expected frequency of occurrence if the null hypothesis is true, O is the frequency actually observed, and Σ is an instruction to carry out the calculation for each pair of frequencies (one observed and one expected) and sum the results.

The calculations are easy and the main problem is to decide on the expected frequencies, E, that correspond to the null hypothesis under test. Validity of the answers depends on certain conditions being met, principally independence of the scores and having an adequate amount of data. (Other methods allowing exact calculation of probabilities can be used if there are few observations.) It is, however, a serious error to apply these calculations to data that are not independent or not frequencies. The commonest cause of non-independence is having an individual contribute more than one unit to the count of frequencies, so it is a good rule of thumb that the total of the observed frequencies should equal the number of individuals. Another useful rule is that the total of "expected" frequencies in the calculation of any χ^2 must equal the total of the "observed" frequencies.

Another style of analysis is called log-linear modelling. It is more versatile but less well known than applications of Chi-squared. There is an introduction by Upton (1986), and books by Everitt (1977) and Upton (1978).

Univariate measures

For measurements, the most developed set of methods is called analysis of variance (ANOVA) (Iversen and Norpoth, 1987). It differs from other methods mainly in complexity. For example, it allows one to test the existence of several different effects in the same set of data simultaneously and it can also evaluate the extent to which one effect depends on (or interacts with) another. The price of its versatility is that it can be trusted only when certain assumptions are met, but these assumptions are not very restrictive; in any case it is often possible to transform data before analysis so as to conform better to the requirements of ANOVA. A version of ANOVA for comparing just two sets of scores, called the t-test, was one of the first significance tests to become known in psychology and has been very prominent ever since. Because of its versatility, several efficient types of experimental designs have been developed specifically with a view to analysis by ANOVA.

Bivariate measures

The correlation coefficient (r), discussed as a descriptive technique for bivariate data, is conceptually related to ANOVA and the square of r estimates the proportion of variance in one variable that can be predicted from knowledge of the other. It is not a test of significance, but its significance can be tested. Our calculated r is a description of the data, but we can use a form of ANOVA or t-test to ask if the true value of r in the population we are sampling from might plausibly be zero. We can also ask if two values of r obtained from different samples might plausibly have been drawn from populations having the same value of r by means of Fisher's z transform.

If we want to know whether the relationship between two variables is or is not linear, we must not merely look for a significant linear relationship. A curved relationship usually contains a linear relationship, as in Figure 3c, so that r is not zero. The linear component of a curved relationship may be highly significant,so a significant linear component does not demonstrate absence of curvature. If a curved line fits significantly better than a straight one, we have shown that the relationship is curved, not straight. Unfortunately, that does not work in reverse — we can never prove that a straight line is the best description of the data because allowing curvature *always* improves the fit! But if we can show that the improvement in fit is no more than would be expected by chance we can conclude that a linear relationship is an adequate description. We can also calculate confidence intervals for the amount of curvature present.

Multivariate measures

When data are multivariate, quite different analyses are required. The essential problem is that the number of possible *patterns* increases rapidly when the number of measures increases. Even if responses are only "yes" and "no", there are over a thousand possible patterns from ten questions and over a million patterns with only twenty questions. If all of these patterns potentially mean different things, it is difficult to obtain enough data to sample them adequately. Furthermore, it is difficult or impossible to *represent* them in any way that can be comprehended, so we must summarize the results drastically.

Among the possible multivariate analyses are discriminant analysis, multivariate analysts of variance (MANOVA), principal components analysis (PCA), and factor analysis. The one general principle that I shall state is that it is almost always invalid to embark on a multivariate analysis unless the number of individuals is substantially greater than the number of components in each multivariate measure. I shall not offer any detailed guidance but just give an alert to the nature of multivariate data and the need to seek advice if you want to analyse it in any way that needs a computer. As a first step, you could consult Harris (1985) or Tabachnick and Fidell (1989).

Nonparametric statistics

All significance tests propose a "statistical model" to explain the observed data and evaluate the probability of obtaining such results if the model is valid. The methods described so far are parametric methods because they determine which elements (parameters) of the model are needed to explain the data. When a new parameter is included the model always fits better and the test determines if the improvement is more than would be expected by chance. If so, we can conclude that the parameter is needed for a good explanation of the data. Bradley (1968), Leach (1979), Mosteller and Rourke (1973), and others recommend the use of nonparametric methods in some circumstances, because we cannot always be confident that the models invoked by parametric methods are justified. Essentially, what they argue for is not specifically *nonparametric* methods but robust or distribution-free methods – what Mosteller and Rourke call "sturdy statistics", whose answers do not depend much on assumptions.

Individual values departing considerably from the rest of the data can have a marked effect on some statistical calculations. Such exceptional scores sometimes have different origins from the others with which they have been grouped and may be considered to be outliers, that is, scores that do not properly belong with the others. If so, it is usually best to treat each as a special case and omit it from the calculation. There are no firm rules for identifying outliers, but see Lovie (1986) and Tukey (1977).

Another possibility is to replace each score by its rank, so that out of N scores, the smallest has rank 1 and the largest has rank N. Methods using ranks can be used for descriptive and inferential statistics and are not much affected by outliers among the original scores. The best known rank methods lack the ability of ANOVA and its relatives to deal in an integrated way with very complex data, but if your data and questions are appropriate, rank methods may serve your needs well, as Meddis (1984) shows. A product-moment correlation calculated from ranks is called a Spearman correlation, whose symbol is ρ (the Greek letter rho).

Since the early 1980s there has been expansion in nonparametric methods based on a technique called randomization (Edgington, 1980) which usually requires a computer but can achieve something like the versatility of ANOVA without its assumptions.

Directional and non-directional tests

When only two groups are being compared, there are three different null hypotheses we might consider when trying to reach a conclusion about the populations the groups are drawn from. One is that there is no difference between the populations, with the alternative hypothesis that there is some difference (in either direction). If we test that one, we have a non-directional test, also called a two-tailed test. A second null hypothesis is that Population A scores at least as high as Population B, with the alternative hypothesis that Population B scores higher than Population A. The third is like the second, but transposing A and B. These are directional or one-tailed tests. A given size of difference in a directional test results in a smaller probability of occurrence by chance than in a non-directional test if the outcome is in the direction implied by the alternative hypothesis. If it is in the opposite direction, the same size of difference gives no reason to reject the null hypothesis so the result is not significant. It is often said that in order to use a directional test we need to predict the direction of the difference before observing the data. But in fact, that is not sufficient. To invoke a directional null hypothesis, we must be prepared to say that any outcome in the direction opposite to the one predicted will be interpreted as a chance result, *however great the effect turns out to be.*

Multiple comparisons: planned and unplanned

It is not valid to apply a method designed to compare two sets of scores to a situation where there are really several sets. If you measure two groups on twenty independent attributes you should not be surprised if one of the comparisons reaches the .05 level of significance – you expect one case in twenty to reach it by chance alone. If you intend to make twenty comparisons you must test a null hypothesis that takes account of that intention.

For the example just stated the procedure might be multivariate, but the problem can arise with univariate data too. Suppose you have completed an experiment with four different conditions and have carried out an ANOVA which has not proved significant. Nevertheless you observe that condition 2 has resulted in generally low scores while condition 4 has produced high ones. You compare conditions 2 and 4 using a *t*-test and find that the difference *is* significant. What has gone wrong?

The problem is that if you have two sets of data, as supposed by the *t*-test, there is only one comparison that can be made and the test tells you the probability of obtaining such results from that comparison. When you have four sets of data, there are six pairs you might consider: 1–2, 1–3, 1–4, 2–3, 2–4, and 3–4. The probability that at least one out of these six comparisons will produce such results by chance is clearly higher than the probability that one particular comparison will do so. Thus the result is more likely than the *t*-test suggests and the result is not really significant.

The situation may be even worse, because there are yet other comparisons such as $1 - (2 + 3)$ or $1 - (2 + 3 + 4)$. A technique that evaluates a true significance level where all possible comparisons can be considered is the Scheffé test. If you are not interested in comparing groups of conditions with others but only pairs of single conditions, the Scheffé test is much too cautious. Tests such as Newman-Keuls, Duncan, and Tukey can be used instead.

Dunnett's test is appropriate if all the comparisons are with a single condition, for example if four experimental groups are each compared with the same control group. Hsu's test can be used if you want to discover if one out of a set of conditions is significantly better (or worse) than all of the others. These and other multiple comparison tests are explained in statistical textbooks such as those of Howell (1989) and Iversen and Norpoth (1987).

The situation is different again if you know before looking at the data that you will be interested in particular comparisons. Provided that the comparisons are orthogonal (the outcome of one does not help us to predict another) the significance given by a standard test, such as a t-test, can be interpreted without adjustment, in fact ANOVA can be thought of as a set of such planned comparisons. The essential difference is between comparisons selected on the basis of the data and comparisons selected on the basis of the design of the investigation. In the former case, if the data had turned out differently, other comparisons would have been made, giving other ways of obtaining a result of the size you have, whereas in the latter case there is only one way to obtain it.

PARAMETER ESTIMATION AND CONFIDENCE INTERVALS

There is a regrettable tendency in psychological statistics to focus on the *significance* of results rather than on their *importance* — a distinction nicely captured by Bolles (1962). It is true that unless you have managed to demonstrate significance (cast doubt on chance as an explanation for your results) it will be difficult to get others to take them seriously. However, your results may be highly significant and yet not important, even if the topic is an important one. The reason is that with a large amount of data, significance can be demonstrated even for a very weak effect. Thus in addition to significance, we must pay attention to magnitude of effect (see especially Cohen, 1977; Howell, 1987). Various measures have been devised to describe the magnitude of effects, but an appealing one is the proposal by Levy (1967) to characterize an effect in terms of the proportion of individuals who are correctly classified if the effect is used for the sorting.

The descriptive approach called parameter estimation focuses on the size of effect rather than on significance. Parameters are hypothetical characteristics of the population and they are estimated from the data. Parameter estimates should not change systematically as the sample size changes but significance does. It is the parameter estimates that show the *importance* of an effect, because they describe the differences among the sets of scores being compared. The degree of success in deducing group membership from scores depends on these differences and not on the *significance* of the effect.

A confidence interval is a hybrid of a descriptive statistic and a significance test. The idea is that when you estimate a parameter, for example a population mean or correlation, you also calculate a range of values (a confidence interval) within which you are reasonably confident that its true value lies. (There is no uncertainty about the mean of your sample of data but you are uncertain about the mean of the population.) If you have a large amount of consistent data, the interval will be narrow and you will be sure of the value of the measure. If you have less data, or if the results are less consistent, the interval will be wider and you will be more uncertain about the true value of the measure.

Confidence intervals are particularly useful if your purpose is to show that treatments or groups do not differ. If the confidence interval for an estimate of the true difference includes zero, the upper and lower bounds estimate respectively the largest positive and negative difference that can reasonably exist. If the data are consistent and plentiful, the interval will be narrow so any difference between the treatments must be small.

As with tests of significance, the answer is not definite but acknowledges that there is a finite probability of error. The upper bound of the .95 confidence interval is that value for the population parameter which, if it were the true value, would allow by chance an estimate at least as *low* as that obtained on 2.5 per cent of occasions. The lower bound is the value which would allow a result at least as *high* as the one observed on 2.5 per cent of occasions.

Confidence intervals are described in the better textbooks of psychological statistics, but less prominently than significance tests. When they are discussed it is usually in connection with ANOVA, perhaps because these are the easiest confidence intervals to calculate, but they can be calculated for virtually any statistical result, such as a correlation coefficient or an estimate of the proportion of people who answer a question in a certain way.

FURTHER READING

Ferguson, G. A., & Takane, Y. (1989). *Statistical analysis in psychology and education* (6th edn). New York: McGraw-Hill

Hays, W. L. (1988). *Statistics* (4th edn). New York: Holt, Rinehart & Winston.

Hoaglin, D. C., Mosteller, F., & Tukey, J. W. (Eds) (1983). *Understanding robust and exploratory data analysis*. Chichester: Wiley.

Howell, D. C. (1989). *Fundamental statistics for the behavioral sciences* (2nd edn). Boston, MA: PWS-Kent.

Pagano, R. R. (1990). *Understanding statistics in the behavioural sciences* (3rd edn). St Paul, MN: West.

REFERENCES

Bolles, R. C. (1962). The difference between statistical hypotheses and scientific hypotheses. *Psychological Reports*, *11*, 639–645.

Bradley, J. V. (1968). Distribution-free statistical tests. Englewood Cliffs, NJ: Prentice-Hall.

Chernoff, H. (1973). The use of faces to represent points in k-dimensional space graphically. *Journal of the American Statistical Association*, *68*, 361–368.

Cleveland, W. S. (1985). *The elements of graphing data*. Monterey, CA: Wadsworth.

Cleveland, W. S., & McGill, R. (1985). Graphical perception and graphical methods for analyzing scientific data. *Science, 229*, 828.

Cohen, J. (1977). *Statistical power analysis for the behavioral sciences*. New York: Academic Press.

Edgington, E. S. (1980). Randomization tests. New York: Marcel Dekker.

Everitt, B. S. (1977). *The analysis of contingency tables*. London: Chapman & Hall.

Everitt, B. S. (1978). *Graphical techniques for multivariate data*. London: Heinemann.

Harris, R. J. (1985). *A primer of multivariate statistics* (2nd edn). New York: Academic Press.

Howell, D. C. (1987). *Statistical methods for psychology* (2nd edn). Boston, MA: Duxbury.

Howell, D. C. (1989). *Fundamental statistics for the behavioral sciences* (2nd edn). Boston, MA: PWS-Kent.

Iversen, G. R., & Norpoth, H. (1987). *Analysis of variance* (2nd edn) Newbury Park, CA: Sage.

Leach, C. (1979). *Introduction to statistics: A nonparametric approach for the social sciences*. Chichester: Wiley.

Levy, P. M. (1967). Substantive significance of significant differences between two groups. *Psychological Bulletin, 67*, 37–40.

Levy, P. M. (1981). On the relation between method and substance in psychology. *Bulletin of the British Psychological Society, 34*, 265–270.

Lovie, P. (1986). Identifying outliers. In A. D. Lovie (Ed.) *New developments in statistics for psychology and the social sciences* (pp. 44–69). London: British Psychological Society/Routledge.

McGuigan, F. J. (1983). *Experimental psychology: Methods of research* (4th edn). Englewood Cliffs, NJ: Prentice-Hall.

MacRae, A. W. (1988). Measurement scales and statistics: What can significance tests tell us about the world? *British Journal of Psychology, 79*, 161–171.

Meddis, R. (1984). *Statistics using ranks: A unified approach*. Oxford: Basil Blackwell.

Mosteller, F., & Rourke, R. E. K. (1973). *Sturdy statistics: Nonparametrics and order statistics*. Reading, MA: Addison-Wesley.

Phillips, L. D. (1973). *Bayesian statistics for social scientists*. London: Nelson.

Rouanet, H., & Lecoutre, B. (1983). Specific inference in ANOVA: From significance tests to Bayesian procedures. *British Journal of Mathematical and Statistical Psychology, 36*, 252–268.

Rouanet, H., Lépine, D., & Pelnard-Considère, J. (1976). Bayes-fiducial procedures as practical substitutes for misplaced significance testing: An application to educational data. In D. N. M. de Gruijter & L. J. Th. van der Kamp (Eds) *Advances in psychological and educational measurement* (pp. 33–50). New York: Wiley.

Stevens, S. S. (1946). On the theory of scales of measurement. *Science, 103*, 677–680.

Stevens, S. S. (1951). Mathematics, measurement and psychophysics. In S. S. Stevens (Ed.) *Handbook of experimental psychology* (pp. 1–49) New York: Wiley.

Tabachnick, B. G., & Fidell, L. S. (1989). *Using multivariate statistics* (2nd edn). New York: Harper & Row.

Tufte, E. R. (1983). *The visual display of quantitative information*. Cheshire, CT: Graphics Press.

Tukey, J. W. (1977). *Exploratory data analysis*. Reading, MA: Addison-Wesley.

Upton, G. J. G. (1978). *The analysis of cross-tabulated data*. Chichester: Wiley.

Upton, G. J. G. (1986). Cross-classified data. In A. D. Lovie (Ed.) *New developments in statistics for psychology and the social sciences* (pp. 70–92). Leicester: British Psychological Society.

Wainer, H., & Thissen, D. (1981). Graphical data analysis. *Annual Review of Psychology, 32,* 191–241.

12.4

QUASI-EXPERIMENTS AND CORRELATIONAL STUDIES

Michael L. Raulin and Anthony M. Graziano
State University of New York at Buffalo, USA

<table>
<tr><td>

Experimental research
Quasi-experimental procedures
  Non-equivalent control-group
    designs
  Differential research designs
  Interrupted time-series designs
  Single-subject designs
    Reversal (ABA) design
    Multiple baseline design
    Single-subject, randomized,
      time-series design

</td><td>

Correlational approaches
  Simple correlations
  Advanced correlational
    techniques
  Simple linear regression
  Advanced regression
    techniques
  Path analysis
Conclusion
Further reading
References

</td></tr>
</table>

Scientific research is a process of inquiry – sequences of asking and answering questions about the nature of relationships among variables (e.g., How does A affect B? Do A and B vary together? Is A significantly different from B? and so on). Scientific research is carried out at many levels that differ in the types of questions asked and, therefore, in the procedures used to answer them. Thus, the choice of which methods to use in research is largely determined by the kinds of questions that are asked.

In research, there are four basic questions about the relationships among variables: causality, differences between groups, direction and strength of relationships, and contingencies. This chapter will focus primarily on three of them: methods applied to questions of causality (experiments and quasi-experiments), methods to address questions about group differences (differential research), and methods used to answer questions about the direction and strength of relationships among variables (correlations). (For more detail on these topics see Graziano and Raulin, 1993.)

EXPERIMENTAL RESEARCH

Experiments are the most effective way to address questions of causality — does one variable have an effect upon another (e.g., Does a new drug X reduce anxiety?). A precise and well-controlled experiment eliminates alternative explanations of results. If a well-designed experiment indicates that anxiety decreases when drug X is given, we shall have high confidence that it was drug X, and not some other factor, that brought about the decrease.

In an experiment, the causal hypothesis (that X, the independent variable, will affect Y, the dependent variable) is tested by manipulating X and observing Y. In the simplest experiment, the independent variable is manipulated by presenting it to one group of subjects and not presenting it to another group. The two groups must be comparable prior to the manipulation so that any post-manipulation group difference is clearly due to the independent variable and not to some other, extraneous variable. If an uncontrolled, extraneous variable may have affected the outcome, then we have an alternative explanation of the results. Consequently, we cannot be sure which variables were actually responsible for the effects. Comparability of groups before the manipulation is assured by assigning subjects randomly to the groups.

Well-designed experiments have sufficient controls to eliminate alternative explanations, allowing us to draw causal conclusions. Uncontrolled variables threaten the validity of the experiment and our conclusions. For example, suppose you develop a headache while working for hours at your computer. You stop, go into another room, and take two aspirin. After about 15 minutes your headache is gone and you return to work. Like most people, you would probably conclude that the aspirin eliminated the headache, that is, you would infer a causal relationship between variable X (aspirin) and variable Y (headache). But other variables besides the aspirin might have been responsible for the improvement. You stopped working for awhile. You left the room and stretched your legs. You may have closed your eyes for a few minutes and rubbed your temples. You took a cool drink of water when you swallowed the aspirin. Mostly, you took a break from the intensive work and relaxed for a few minutes. All of those variables are potential contributors to the observed effect; they are confounding factors in the research. Therefore, it is not clear that it was the aspirin alone that reduced the headache. To be confident of a causal relationship between the aspirin and headache reduction, one would have to carry out an experiment designed to control these confounding factors and to eliminate the alternative explanations.

The discussion above refers to one of the most important concepts in experimentation – validity. A research study has good validity when it controls confounding factors and thus eliminates rival explanations, allowing a causal conclusion. To state it another way, uncontrolled extraneous variables threaten the validity of experiments.

QUASI-EXPERIMENTAL PROCEDURES

Experiments allow us to draw causal inferences with the greatest confidence. However, there are conditions under which we cannot meet all demands of a true experiment but still want to address causal questions. In these situations we can use quasi-experimental designs. Using quasi-experiments in clinical and field situations to draw cautious causal inferences is preferable to not experimenting at all.

Quasi-experimental designs resemble experiments but are weak on some of the characteristics. Quasi-experiments include a comparison of at least two levels of an independent variable, but the manipulation is not always under the experimenter's control. For example, suppose we are interested in the health effects of a natural disaster such as a destructive tornado. We cannot manipulate the tornado but we can compare those who experienced the tornado with a group of people who did not. Likewise, in many field situations we cannot assign subjects to groups in an unbiased manner. Indeed, we often cannot assign subjects at all, but must accept the natural groups as they exist. Thus, in quasi-experimental designs:

1 We state a causal hypothesis.
2 We include at least two levels of the independent variable, although we may not manipulate it.
3 We usually cannot assign subjects to groups, but must accept existing groups.
4 We include specific procedures for testing hypotheses.
5 We include some controls for threats to validity.

Compare this list with the characteristics of a *true* experiment:

1 We state a causal hypothesis.
2 We manipulate the independent variable.
3 We assign subjects randomly to groups.
4 We use systematic procedures to test the hypothesized causal relationships.
5 We use specific controls to reduce threats to validity.

There are a number of basic quasi-experimental designs, but we shall focus on four of the most important: non-equivalent control-group designs, differential research designs, interrupted time-series designs, and single-subject designs.

Non-equivalent control-group designs

We can test causal hypotheses with confidence if we randomly assign subjects to groups, because such groups are likely to be equivalent at the beginning of the study. However, sometimes subjects cannot be assigned randomly to groups, and the groups may not be equivalent on some variables at the beginning of the study. Campbell and Stanley (1966) popularized the non-equivalent control-group design by suggesting that already existing groups can be similar to one another on most relevant variables even though there is no systematic assignment of subjects to groups. The more similar natural groups are to one another, the closer the design approximates a true experiment. Furthermore, Cook and Campbell (1979) showed that it is sometimes possible to draw strong conclusions from non-equivalent control-group studies, even when the groups are different, provided the researcher carefully evaluates all potential threats to validity.

There are two problems with non-equivalent groups: groups may be different on the dependent measure(s) at the start of the study, and there may be other differences between groups. To address the first issue, we include a pre-test measure. The pre-test tells us how similar the groups are on the dependent variable(s) at the beginning of the study. The more similar the groups are, the greater control we have. To address the second issue – that groups may differ on variables other than the dependent variable – it is important to rule out each potential confounding variable. To do this, we must first identify potential confounding variables, measure them, and carefully rule them out. Figure 1 shows six possible outcomes of a non-equivalent control-group design. In Figures 1(a), 1(b), and 1(c) the pattern of scores for the experimental and control groups suggests no effect of the independent variable. In Figure 1(a), neither group changes; the pre-test scores suggest that the group differences existed prior to the independent variable manipulation. Both Figures 1(b) and 1(c) show an equivalent increase in the groups on the dependent measure from pre-test to post-test, suggesting that there is no effect of the independent variable. Again, the pre-test in 1(b) allows us to rule out the hypothesis that the group post-test differences are due to the independent variable. In Figure 1(d), groups equivalent at the beginning of the study diverge; there does appear to be an effect of the independent variable. In both Figures 1(e) and 1(f), the groups differ on the dependent measure at pre-test, and the experimental group changes more than the control group after the manipulation. Figure 1(f) shows a slight change in the control group but a marked change in the experimental group, suggesting an effect of the independent variable. However, there is still the potentially confounding factor of regression to the mean. Regression is a potential source of confounding whenever we begin an experiment with extreme scores. The marked pre-test difference between groups in Figure 1(f) may represent extreme scores for the experimental group. In the course of the experiment the scores for the group may have returned to the mean level represented by the control group. Consequently, we cannot be confident in attributing the results to the causal effects of the independent variable. In Figure 1(e), the control group does not change but the experimental group changes markedly in the predicted direction, even going far beyond the level of the control group. This is called a crossover effect. The results give us considerable confidence in a causal inference. Maturation (normal changes in subjects over time) and history (changes in subjects during the study due to events other than the independent variable manipulation) are unlikely alternative hypotheses because the control group should also have been affected by these factors. Regression to the mean is also an unlikely alternative hypothesis because the experimental group increased not only to the mean of the control group but also beyond it. With these results a quasi-experimental design gives us fairly good confidence in a causal inference.

These examples are reasonably interpretable. Other situations described by Cook and Campbell (1979) are more difficult, or even impossible, to

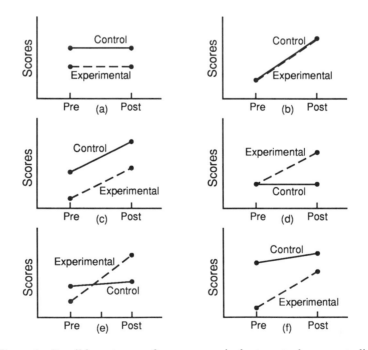

Figure 1 Possible outcomes from non-equivalent control group studies

interpret. Using non-equivalent control group designs appropriately requires considerable expertise.

Differential research designs

In differential research, pre-existing groups (e.g., diagnostic groups) are compared on one or more dependent measures. There is no random assignment to groups; subjects are classified into groups and measured on the dependent variable. In essence, the researcher measures two variables (the variable defining the group and the dependent variable). Consequently, many researchers classify differential research as a variation of correlational research. We believe that differential research designs can employ control procedures not available in straight correlational research and therefore should be conceptualized as somewhere between quasi-experimental and correlational designs. We cannot draw causal conclusions from differential research, but we can test for differences between groups.

A typical differential research study might compare depressed and non-depressed subjects. The dependent variable is selected for its theoretical significance. For example, we might measure people's judgment of the probability of succeeding on a test of skill, as Alloy and Abramson (1979) did. They hypothesized that depressed subjects would be more likely to expect failure. This hypothesis was based on a causal model of depression that suggested that one's attributional style would affect the risk for depression. This causal model could not be tested directly with a differential research design, but the data from this study could test the plausibility of the model. If there were attributional differences in depressed and non-depressed subjects, then it is plausible that these differences predated the depression, perhaps even contributing to the development of depression.

One could think of a differential research study as including an implicit manipulation that occurs prior to data collection – a manipulation that created the defining characteristic of the groups. This would be equivalent to comparing a group of people who lived through a tornado and a group who had never experienced one. The groups are defined by an event that predated the research study. However, the exposure to a tornado is likely a random event, so this comparison is conceptually close to an experiment. The subjects are assigned randomly, although not by the researcher; one group experiences the independent variable (i.e., the tornado), although again not controlled by the researcher; dependent measures are taken after the manipulation. We would classify such a study as a strong quasi-experimental design and would feel justified in drawing rather strong causal conclusions on the basis of our group comparisons. However, when the manipulation is something less likely to be random, such as becoming depressed or not, the possibility of confounding is greatly increased.

Whenever you start with pre-existing groups, the groups are likely to differ on many variables other than the variable that defines the groups. For example, if we compare schizophrenic patients with a randomly selected non-patient control sample, the groups would differ not only on diagnosis, but probably also on social class, education level, average IQ, amount of hospitalization, history of medication use, and the social stigma associated with a psychiatric diagnosis. Any difference between our schizophrenic and control samples could be due to the disease or any of the other differences listed above. These variables are all confounded with the diagnosis of the subjects. It is impossible to draw a strong conclusion.

Confounding is the norm in differential research, even in cases where you might not expect it. For example, if we compare children of various ages in a cross-sectional developmental study, we might expect that the children made it into the various groups by the random factor of when they were born. That may be true, but there are likely to be differences between the groups that are a function of historical factors unique to a given age range of children. These might include major historical events occurring at critical ages, differences in economic conditions that affect what resources are available to the children at any given age, differences in school systems that may be the result of budget issues or political pressures, or even the impact of a single teacher. (Note that most samples of subjects for research come from accessible populations from a narrow geographic area. Therefore, it is possible that a single teacher could differentially affect the results.) Differences between age groups that are the result of a different set of historical experiences are known as cohort effects.

The ideal control group in differential research is identical to the experimental group on everything except the variable that defines the groups. This ideal often is impossible. Therefore, researchers attempt to equate the groups on critical variables, that is, variables that could confound the interpretation of the results. A variable can confound the results, first, if it has an effect on the dependent variable, and second, if there is a mean difference on the variable in the groups being compared. For example, IQ might confound results in a study of cognitive styles, but hair colour is unlikely to because hair colour is probably unrelated to cognitive styles. However, even though IQ is a potential confounding variable, it cannot confound the results *unless* there is a mean difference between the groups. In differential research, it is common to include control groups that are matched on one or more of these critical variables to avoid confounding. For more discussion of this strategy, see Chapman and Chapman (1973) and Graziano and Raulin (1993).

Interrupted time-series designs

In interrupted time-series designs, a single group of subjects is measured several times both before and after some event or manipulation. The multiple measures over time strengthen the design considerably over a simple pre-post design, controlling many potential confounding factors. A major potential confounding factor in the simple pre-post study is regression to the mean. Behaviour fluctuates over time, displaying considerable variability. The intervention might be applied only at a high point in that natural variation, just before the behaviour decreased again. Thus, the observed changes in behaviour may not be due to the treatment at all but only to the natural variability of behaviour. The same reduction might have been observed even if we had not applied the treatment. The multiple measures of the interrupted time-series design give several points of comparison, allowing us to rule out the effects of regression to the mean. We can see the natural variability and can see if the post-treatment change exceeds the natural variability.

Figure 2 shows the results of an interrupted time-series study of disruption in autistic children (Graziano, 1974). Disruptive behaviour of four autistic children was monitored for a full year before the treatment (relaxation training) was introduced and a year following the treatment. Note that the variability during baseline disappears after treatment, with disruptive behaviour dropping to zero and remaining there for a full year. Such results are not likely due to normal fluctuation or regression to the mean. They also seem unlikely to be due to maturation of all subjects during the same period of time. With time-series designs, however, there are still two potentially confounding factors – history and instrumentation. History can confound results in any procedure that requires a fairly long period of time because other events might account for changes in the dependent variable. Thus, when using the interrupted time-series design, the experimenter must identify potential confounding due to history and carefully rule it out. Instrumentation is another potential threat to validity. When new programmes are started there may be accompanying changes in the way records are kept. The

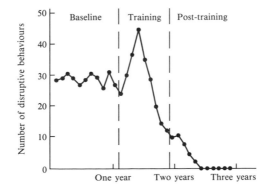

Figure 2   An interrupted time-series design showing the effects of relaxation treatment on disruptive behaviour in autistic children

researcher must be careful to determine that an apparent change is not due to changes in record-keeping.

The interrupted time-series design is useful in clinical or naturalistic settings where the effects of some event, naturally occurring or manipulated, can be assessed by taking multiple measurements both before and after the event. It can also be used in studies where the presumed causal event occurs to all members of a population. For example, the effects of a policy change (e.g., a change in the speed limit) could be evaluated with an interrupted time-series design using routinely gathered data (e.g., traffic fatality counts).

The interrupted time-series design can be improved by adding one or more comparison groups. In our hypothetical study of the effects of a change in speed limit on the number of fatalities, we could use comparable data from a neighbouring state that did not reduce the speed limit. Such a comparison would help to control for potentially confounding factors such as history and maturation.

Graphical presentations of data in the interrupted time-series design can provide considerable information. In a time-series study, the change in the time graph must be sharp to be interpreted as anything other than only a normal fluctuation. Slight or gradual changes are difficult to interpret. But in a time-series design, simply inspecting the graph is not enough. Testing the statistical significance of pre-post differences in time-series designs requires sophisticated procedures, which are beyond the scope of this chapter (see Glass, Willson, & Gottman, 1975; or Kazdin, 1992).

Single-subject designs

Single-subject designs were developed early in the history of experimental psychology and were used in both human and animal learning studies. Since the early 1960s they have become popular in clinical psychology. With single-subject designs we are able to manipulate independent variables, to observe their effects on dependent variables, to draw causal inferences, and to do so with a single subject. Modern clinical psychology is now heavily reliant on behaviour modification treatment methods, and behaviour modification research utilizes single-subject research designs refined from the work of B. F. Skinner. For more information on single-subject designs, consult Barlow and Hersen (1984), Kratochwill (1978), and Sidman (1960).

Single-subject designs are variations of time-series designs. The same subject is exposed to all manipulations, and we take dependent measurements of the same subject at different points in time. This allows us to compare measures taken before and after some naturally occurring event or an experimental manipulation. The basic comparison is between the same subject's own pre-treatment and post-treatment responses. Note that at its simplest level, this resembles the pre-test–post-test comparison – a relatively weak non-experimental design. A control group would strengthen a pre-test

– post-test design, but a control group is not possible when we have only one subject. Single-subject designs improve on the pre-post design, not by adding a control group, but by adding more conditions to the experiment. If the dependent variable changes in the predicted direction at each manipulation, we can have reasonable confidence that the manipulation is responsible for the observed change in the dependent variable. There are several single-subject designs, including reversal or ABA designs, multiple baseline designs, and single-subject, randomized, time-series designs.

Reversal (ABA) design

In reversal or ABA designs, the effects of an independent variable on a dependent variable are demonstrated by measuring the dependent variable at three or four points in time. There is a no-treatment baseline period during which the dependent behaviour is only observed, a treatment period in which the manipulation is carried out, and a return or reversal to the no-treatment condition. The effects of the independent variable (the treatment) on the dependent variable (the behaviour to be changed) is demonstrated if the behaviour changes in the predicted direction whenever the conditions are reversed. We often strengthen the design by measuring the dependent variable several times during each condition. A hypothetical study will help to describe the general format used. The study concerns self-stimulatory behaviour of a retarded child, Terry. After observing Terry in the classroom, a psychologist forms the tentative hypothesis that the teacher's attention is reinforcing the self-stimulatory behaviour. That is, whenever Terry begins her self-stimulatory activity, the teacher tries to soothe and comfort her. The teacher does not realize that it may be her efforts to help Terry control the behaviour that are actually helping to maintain it.

To test the hypothesis the psychologist sets up an ABA design, in which condition A, the baseline, involves the teacher's usual approach of attending to Terry whenever she displays the self-stimulatory behaviour. Condition B is the treatment – a differential reinforcement procedure in which the teacher provides attention and support for Terry whenever she refrains from the self-stimulatory behaviour, but withdraws attention when Terry engages in self-stipulatory behaviour. Precise observations are carried out for one hour at the same time each day. The graph in Figure 3 shows the behavioural changes as the A and B conditions are sequentially reversed. The graph suggests that there may be a causal relationship between teacher attention and Terry's self-stimulatory behaviour. Notice that the psychologist has not limited the approach to only three conditions, ABA, but has added another reversal at the end for an ABAB procedure. The ABA sequence is sufficient to suggest causality, but the demonstration of a casual link creates an ethical demand to return Terry to the optimal state.

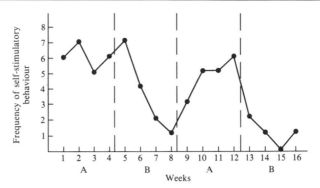

Figure 3   A reversal design showing the effects of contingent reinforcement on self-stimulatory behaviour of a single child

Multiple baseline design

Although the ABA design can provide a powerful demonstration of the effect of one variable on another, there are situations in which reversal procedures are not feasible or ethical. For example, suppose in our example of Terry above, the self-stimulatory behaviour was injurious, such as severe head-banging. We would be unwilling to reverse conditions once we achieved improved functioning because it could risk injury. Instead, we could use a multiple baseline design.

In the multiple baseline design, the effects of the treatment are demonstrated on different behaviours successively. To illustrate, we shall use an example similar to the previous example. Suppose that a fifth-grade boy (about 10 years old) is doing poorly in school, although he appears to have the ability to achieve at a high level. He also disrupts class frequently and often fights with other students. A psychologist spends several hours observing the class and notes some apparent contingencies regarding the boy's behaviour. The teacher, attempting to control the boy, pays more attention to him when he is disruptive – scolding, correcting, lecturing him, and making him stand in a corner whenever he is caught fighting. The psychologist notes that the boy seems to enjoy the attention. However, on those rare occasions when he does his academic work quietly and well, the teacher ignores him completely. "When he is working, I leave well enough alone," the teacher says. "I don't want to risk stirring him up." Based on these observed contingencies, the psychologist forms the tentative hypothesis that the contingent teacher attention to the boy's disruptive behaviour and fighting may be a major factor in maintaining these behaviours, whereas the teacher's failure to reward the boy's good academic work may account for its low occurrence. The psychologist sets up a multiple-baseline design to test the hypothesis about the importance of teacher attention on disruptive

1132

behaviour, fighting, and academic performance. The independent variable here is teacher attention.

Figure 4 shows the sequence of phases of the hypothetical study. During Phase 1 all three dependent variables are measured while the teacher continues the usual procedure of trying to punish the disruption and fighting while ignoring the positive academic behaviour. As seen in Figure 4, disruptive behaviour and fighting are high and academic performance is low. In Phase 2, the teacher's attention to fighting is withdrawn and positive attention is made contingent on academic work. In Phase 3, these procedures continue and the teacher withdraws attention for disruption as well as for fighting. The measured changes in the dependent variables associated with the independent variable manipulations provide evidence for the hypothesis that contingent teacher attention is an important controlling factor in the child's behaviour.

Single-subject, randomized, time-series design

When a reversal design is not appropriate and a multiple baseline procedure is not feasible because we want to study only one behaviour, the single-subject, randomized, time-series design can be used. This design is an interrupted time-series design for a single subject with one additional element — the randomized assignment of the manipulation in the time-series.

The single-subject, randomized, time-series design could be applied in the example above, but let us take another example. Suppose that Joey, another child in the special class, does not complete his daily work. During lesson periods, when he should be responding to a workbook lesson, Joey looks around the room or just closes his eyes and does no work. Reminders from

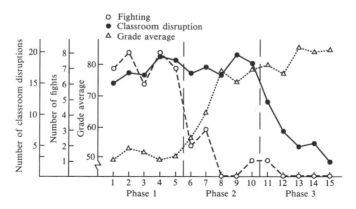

Figure 4 A multiple baseline design showing improvement in disruptive behaviour, fighting, and academic performance for a single child contingent upon teacher attention

the teacher have little effect. An effective motivational intervention with children is a token reinforcement system in which paper or plastic tokens are given to the child whenever he engages in the desired behaviour. The tokens serve as immediate secondary reinforcement for the desired behaviour. They are saved by the child and cashed in for items and privileges. If we were to employ a single-subject, randomized, time-series design, we might decide to measure the child's homework achievement for 6 weeks (30 school days). We might decide that we want at least 5 days before and after the implementation of the treatment. This ensures adequate pre-treatment and post-treatment measures. We then use a table of random numbers to select randomly one of the middle 20 days as our point for introducing the manipulation. The manipulation is the use of token reinforcement for homework achievement. Suppose we randomly select the ninth day as the point for introducing the token reinforcement programme. The beginning of the manipulation is preceded by 8 days of baseline measurement followed by 22 days of measurements of the dependent variable under the token reinforcement condition. If the time graph shows a marked improvement in homework achievement coincident with the ninth measurement, we have a convincing illustration of the effects of the token reinforcement. Note that it is unlikely that such marked improvement would occur by chance, or because of maturational or historical factors, at exactly the point at which we have randomly introduced the treatment.

CORRELATIONAL APPROACHES

Like quasi-experimental designs, correlation designs are used in situations in which the manipulation of an independent variable is either impossible or unethical. Because there is no experimental manipulation, one must be cautious in drawing causal conclusions. In fact, most correlational procedures are not powerful enough to justify causal interpretations.

Simple correlations

The correlation coefficient is probably the single most widely computed statistic in psychology. In many research studies, the purpose of the study is to produce measures of relationships between variables (i.e., correlations). Even in experimental designs or other designs, it is common to compute numerous correlation coefficients to help interpret the data. These correlation coefficients may or may not be reported in the final paper, but they are often routinely computed. Correlations between demographic variables and performance on the dependent measure often help us to identify potential confounding variables in a current study or in a future study that might be run.

The most commonly used correlation coefficient is the Pearson product-moment correlation. This coefficient is used when both variables are measured on an interval or ratio scale. A Spearman rank-order correlation is preferred if at least one of the two variables is measured on an ordinal scale. Computational procedures for either of these coefficients are readily available in almost any undergraduate statistics textbook. There are other correlation coefficients available as well, which we shall discuss shortly. The range for both the Pearson and Spearman correlations is -1.00 to $+1.00$. A correlation of $+1.00$ indicates a perfect positive relationship (i.e., as one variable increases the other increases by a predictable amount). A correlation of -1.00 indicates a perfect negative relationship (i.e., as one variable increases the other variable decreases by a predictable amount). The sign indicates the direction of the relationship and the absolute size of the correlation indicates the strength of the relationship.

Correlations are most easily visualized in a scatter plot. Each person is plotted in a coordinate system in which their location is determined by the scores on variables X and Y. Figure 5 gives several examples of scatter plots, each indicating a particular degree of relationship. The actual product-moment correlation is indicated next to each scatter plot. Figures 5(a) and 5(b) illustrate scatter plots for strong positive and negative correlations, respectively. Figures 5(c) and 5(d) illustrate zero correlations. Note a zero correlation is often described as circular scatter plot. The scatter plot is circular, however, only if the variance on variables X and Y are equal, something that rarely occurs. Figure 5(d), for example, illustrates a zero correlation where variable X has a greater variance than variable Y. In this situation, the circular correlation is elongated horizontally. Figure 5(e) shows a perfect positive relationship with all the points clearly lining up on a straight line. Figure 5(f) shows the powerful effect of a single deviant score, especially when you have a small sample. In this case, 14 of the 15 data points clearly seem to show a zero correlation, but the correlation when you include the fifteenth point (at 10, 10) is .77. Finally, scatter plots shown in Figure 5(g) and 5(h) illustrate non-linear correlations. The product-moment correlation is sensitive only to the linear component. In Figure 5(g), the correlation is essentially zero, whereas in Figure 5(h), the correlation is somewhat positive. In both Figure 5(g) and 5(h), the product-moment correlation is an inappropriate measure of relationship. Simple product-moment correlation should be used only in situations where you anticipate a linear relationship between variables X and Y.

As mentioned earlier, the strength of the relationship between X and Y is illustrated by the size of the correlation regardless of the sign. A commonly used index is the square of the correlation, which can be interpreted as the proportion of variability in one variable that is predictable on the basis of knowing the scores on the second variable. This statement is usually shortened to "the proportion of variance accounted for".

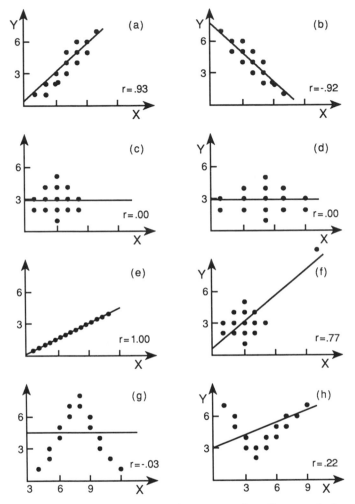

Figure 5 Several examples of scatter plots, regression lines, and the product-moment correlations that each plot represents

Advanced correlational techniques

More sophisticated correlational procedures are also available. You can correlate one variable with an entire set of variables (multiple correlation) or one set of variables with another set of variables (canonical correlation). It is also possible to correlate one variable with another after statistically removing the effects of a third variable (partial correlation). Discussion of these procedures is beyond the scope of this chapter, but the interested reader is referred to Nunnally (1976) for a more detailed discussion.

Simple linear regression

Regression techniques utilize the observed relationship between two or more variables to make predictions. The simplest regression technique is linear regression, with one variable being predicted on the basis of scores on a second variable. The equation below shows the general form for the prediction equation.

Predicted Y score $= (b \times X) + a$

The values of the slope b and the intercept a in the above equation are a function of the observed correlation and the variances for both the X and Y variables. The computational detail can be found in virtually any undergraduate statistics text (e.g., Shavelson, 1988). In each of the eight scatter plots shown in Figure 5, the regression line for predicting Y from X has been drawn. When the correlation is zero the regression line is horizontal with an intercept at the mean for Y. In other words, if X and Y are unrelated to one another the mean of the Y distribution is the best prediction of Y, regardless of the value of X.

Advanced regression techniques

It is possible to use the relationships of several variables to the variable that you wish to predict in a procedure known as multiple regression. Multiple regression is also a linear regression technique, except that instead of working in the two-dimensional space indicated in Figure 5, we are now working in N-dimensional space, where N is equal to the number of predictor variables plus one. For example, if you have two predictor measures and one criterion measure, the prediction equation would be represented by a line in the three-dimensional space defined by these measures. If you have several predictor measures, visualizing multiple regression is difficult, even though the procedure is conceptually straightforward.

Although it is possible to put all of the predictor variables into the regression equation, it is often unnecessary to do so in order to get accurate predictions. The most commonly used procedure for a regression analysis is a procedure called stepwise regression, which uses a complex algorithm to enter variables into the equation one at a time. The algorithm starts by entering the variable that has the strongest relationship with the variable that you want to predict, and then selects additional variables on the basis of the incremental improvement in prediction that each variable provides. The computational procedures for stepwise regression are too complex to be done without the use of a statistical analysis program such as SPSS or SPSS/PC + (Norusis, 1990b).

All of the regression models discussed above assume linear regression. In Figure 5(g) and 5(h), the scatter plot suggests that there is a non-linear relationship between variables X and Y. When a non-linear relationship exists, there are non-linear statistical procedures for fitting a curve to the data. These procedures are well beyond the scope of this chapter: the interested reader is referred to Norusis (1990a).

Path analysis

A procedure that is rapidly becoming the standard for analysis of correlational data is path analysis. Path analysis is one of several regression procedures that fall under the general category of latent variable models. All latent variable models make the assumption that the observed data are due to a set of unobserved (i.e., latent) variables. Factor analysis is probably the most widely used of the latent variable models.

Path analysis seeks to test the viability of a specified causal model by factoring the matrix of correlations between variables within the constraints of the model. This process is best illustrated with an example. Suppose that we had three variables (A, B, and C) that we hypothesize are causally related to another variable (E). Further, we hypothesize that the causal effects of variables B and C on variable E are indirect – that is, variables B and C are causally related to a variable D which in turn is causally related to variable E. This model is illustrated in Figure 6. Straight lines in a path model represent hypothesized causal connections, while curved lines represent potential correlations that are not hypothesized to be causal. To make our example more intuitive, we shall present a scenario where such a model might make sense. We shall assume that we are studying high-risk sexual behaviour (i.e., sexual behaviour that increases the risk of HIV infection). Variable E in this model is *safe-sex behaviour in heterosexual college students*. We are hypothesizing that safe-sex behaviour is a function of *knowledge of safe-sex procedures* (variable D) and how *vulnerable* one feels (variable A). Whether one obtains knowledge of safe-sex procedures is hypothesized to be a function of *whether such information is available to people* (variable B) and *whether one believes that AIDS is not just a disease found in gay men or IV drug users* (variable C). In our model, we are suggesting that simply making information about safe-sex procedures available will not lead to the practice of safe sex unless (1) the information is learned, which will occur only if (2) the person believes that heterosexual sex represents a risk. Even if the person knows about safe sex procedures, the behaviour will not be practised unless (3) the person feels vulnerable to AIDS at the time of engaging in sex. We could expand this model by adding other variables if we wanted. For example, we might hypothesize that vulnerability is increased if the person knows people with HIV infection and is temporarily decreased if the person has been drinking (i.e., additional variables F and G are causally related to variable A). However, we shall restrict our model to the five variables shown in Figure 6 to illustrate the procedures.

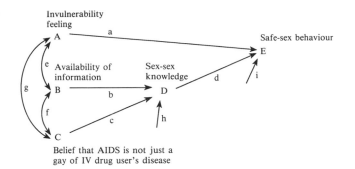

Figure 6 A hypothetical example of a path analysis

We have labelled the various paths in Figure 6 with lower-case letters. We shall solve for the strength of path coefficients for each of these paths. We have also included residual arrows for variables *D* and *E*. These residual arrows will have a strength that represents the unexplained variance in our model. Technically, all variables would have residual arrows, but it is customary not to include them with the initial variables (i.e., variables *A*, *B*, and *C* in our model). These variables represent our starting-point; our model does not address the question of what factors cause these initial states.

To evaluate the feasibility of our causal model, we need measures of the variables on a large sample of subjects. We need not have measures of all of the variables to do the computation; some variables may be unseen (latent). We start by computing a correlation matrix from which the path coefficients are computed. The actual path coefficient computations are beyond the scope of this chapter (the interested reader is referred to Loehlin, 1992). Path analysis tests the feasibility of a hypothesized causal model. If the absolute value of the path coefficients in the model are generally large and the residual coefficients are generally small, the model is feasible. You strive to create as parsimonious a path model as possible. Generally, as you include more paths, you will explain more of the variance, but you also run the risk of capitalizing on chance variance.

CONCLUSION

If given a choice, a researcher should use an experimental design. Manipulating variables and observing their effects on other variables, coupled with the other controls that are a part of experimental research, gives us the greatest confidence that the observed relationship is causal. However, there are many circumstances in which experimental research is impractical or unethical. This chapter has described some of the many quasi-experimental and correlational designs available for these situations. Data from these designs should be interpreted with caution because the possibility of confounding is much larger than with experimental designs. However, these designs have proved their value in psychological research.

FURTHER READING

Barlow, D. H., & Hersen, M. (1984). *Single case experimental designs: Strategies for studying behaviour change* (2nd edn). New York: Pergamon.

Campbell, D. T., & Stanley, J. C. (1966). *Experimental and quasi-experimental designs for research on teaching*. Chicago, IL: Rand McNally.

Cook, T. D., & Campbell, D. T. (1979). *Quasi experimentation: Design and analysis issues for field studies*. Chicago, IL: Rand McNally.

Graziano, A. M., & Raulin, M. L. (1993). *Research methods: A process of inquiry* (2nd edn). New York: Harper Collins.

Kazdin, A. E. (1992). *Research design in clinical psychology* (2nd edn). New York: Macmillan.

Loehlin, J. C. (1992). *Latent variable models: An introduction to factor, path, and structural analyses* (2nd edn). Hillsdale, NJ: Lawrence Erlbaum.

REFERENCES

Alloy, L. B., & Abramson, L. Y. (1979). Judgment of contingencies in depressed and nondepressed subjects: Sadder but wiser? *Journal of Experimental Psychology: General, 108*, 447–485.

Barlow, D. H., & Hersen, M. (1984). *Single case experimental designs: Strategies for studying behaviour change* (2nd edn). New York: Pergamon.

Campbell, D. T., & Stanley, J. C. (1966). *Experimental and quasi-experimental designs for research on teaching*. Chicago, IL: Rand McNally.

Chapman, L. J., & Chapman, J. P. (1973). *Disordered thought in schizophrenia*. Englewood Cliffs, NJ: Prentice-Hall.

Cook, T. D., & Campbell, D. T. (1979). *Quasi experimentation: Design and analysis issues for field studies*. Chicago, IL: Rand McNally.

Glass, G. V., Willson, V. L., & Gottman, J. M. (1975). *Design and analysis of time series*. Boulder, CO: Laboratory of Educational Research Press.

Graziano, A. M. (1974). *Child without tomorrow*. Elmsford, NY: Pergamon.

Graziano, A. M., & Raulin, M. L. (1993). *Research methods: A process of inquiry* (2nd edn). New York: Harper Collins.

Kazdin, A. E. (1992). *Research design in clinical psychology* (2nd edn). New York: Macmillan.

Kratochwill, T. R. (Ed.) (1978). *Single-subject research: Strategies for evaluating change*. New York: Academic Press.

Loehlin, J. C. (1992). *Latent variable models: An introduction to factor, path, and structural analyses* (2nd edn). Hillsdale, NJ: Lawrence Erlbaum.

Norusis, M. J. (1990a). *SPSS-PC+ Advanced Statistics 4.0*. Chicago, IL: Statistical Package for the Social Sciences.

Norusis, M. J. (1990b). *SPSS-PC+ Statistics 4.0*. Chicago, IL: Statistical Package for the Social Sciences.

Nunnally, J. C. (1976). *Psychometric theory* (2nd edn). New York: McGraw-Hill.

Shavelson, R. J. (1988). *Statistical reasoning for the behavioral sciences* (2nd edn). Boston: Allyn & Bacon.

Sidman, M. (1960). *Tactics of scientific research: Evaluating scientific data in psychology*. New York: Basic Books.

12.5

SURVEY METHODS, NATURALISTIC OBSERVATIONS, AND CASE-STUDIES

Francis C. Dane
Mercer University, Georgia, USA

Survey methods	Probability sampling
Survey content	Non-probability sampling
Categorical information	**Naturalistic observation**
Self-reports of past	Intrusion
behaviour	Selecting events
Opinions, beliefs, attitudes,	Coding
and values	**Case-studies**
Self-reports of intentions	Sampling
Sensitive information	Hypothesis testing
Administration mode	**Further reading**
Sampling	**References**

The purpose of this chapter is to provide an overview of survey methods, naturalistic observations, and case-studies as they are used in psychology. Like all research techniques, these methods are appropriate for some, but not all, research purposes. Surveys, for example, are appropriate when one wants to discover what people are willing to report about themselves and others. Naturalistic observation, in contrast, is most appropriate for monitoring the behaviour of others. Case-studies are appropriate for both of these purposes, but only when one wishes to obtain a great deal of information about one or a few people or events.

SURVEY METHODS

Survey methods are based on the simple discovery "that asking questions is a remarkably efficient way to obtain information from and about people" (Schuman & Kalton, 1985, p. 635). The number of people may vary from a hundred to hundreds of millions, but the hallmark of surveys is that the researcher presents specific questions or items (the survey instrument) to which people (the respondents) provide answers or reactions (the responses). Thus, surveys involve an exchange of information between researcher and respondent; the researcher identifies topics of interest, and the respondent provides knowledge or opinions about those topics. Depending upon the length and content of the survey as well as the facilities available, this exchange can be accomplished via written questionnaires, in-person interviews, or telephone conversations.

In practice, the exchange of information is not always smooth. One must first decide what information is to be obtained and construct an instrument that will prompt objective responses. Questions, for example, must be phrased such that prospective respondents will understand what is being asked without introducing any bias. Then one must find the appropriate respondents and convince them to participate. Even with properly phrased questions, respondents may not know or may be unwilling to provide the requested information. Finally, depending upon the questions asked, responses may need to be coded before being analysed.

Survey content

Traditionally, survey content has been divided into two types: fact and opinion. This dichotomy was used to acknowledge the researcher's ability to verify some information, such as age, sex, or marital status, but not other information, such as private behaviours or attitudes. Schumann & Kalton (1985), however, argued that the dichotomous distinction is overly simple and proposed the following divisions for survey content: categorical information; self-reports of past behaviour; opinions, beliefs, attitudes, and values; self-reports of intentions concerning behaviour; and sensitive information dealing with the past, present, or future. This break from the traditional, objective/subjective dichotomy reflected the increasing complexity of survey content and presaged theoretical developments concerning how people think about and report social behaviour (e.g., Fiske & Taylor, 1991). Of course, which content one includes in a specific survey instrument depends primarily upon one's research objectives. One general rule is to include only items that are relevant to the topic of interest and to avoid asking questions for which one has no explicit reason for asking.

1143

Categorical information

Surveys are an extremely efficient means by which to obtain categorical information, the dimensions that people use to describe themselves: age, education level, employment status, and so on. Although one does not always obtain accurate categorical information (Weaver & Swanson, 1974), the margin of error is generally small. There also exist attempts to establish standardized categories for use in surveys (e.g., Van Drusen & Zill, 1975). For example, Feldman (1990) used categorical information in a survey of 1,648 people employed in Denver, Colorado, to assess the concept of settlement identity – psychological bonds with the type of community in which one was raised. She used a priori response categories in which respondents were asked to categorize themselves as either a "city person", a "suburbanite", a "small-town person", or a "country/mountain" person. Additional items requested respondents to use the same categories to indicate past settlements, current settlement, and any intended future settlements.

Feldman found that the self-identification of the majority of the respondents was consistent with their history of residential experiences. For example, those who identified themselves as a "city person" were most likely to have lived in, currently lived in, and planned to continue to live in downtown areas or city neighbourhoods.

Self-reports of past behaviour

Reports of past behaviour, too, can be easily obtained through survey methods, provided respondents understand what one is asking, can remember their past behaviour, and are willing to divulge such information. Seemingly straightforward questions are not always understood (Skogan, 1981). For example, Metts (1989) explored deception in close relationships with the question "Please describe in as much detail as possible a situation in which you were not completely truthful with [your partner]". Despite the apparent clarity of the item, about 1 per cent of the responses were too vague to be analysed. Thus, survey instruments should be pre-tested to ensure that prospective respondents will understand what is being asked of them.

Memory, too, plays a role in reporting behaviours. Survey respondents are subject to the same memory biases as other people, including the representativeness heuristic and the availability heuristic (Tversky & Kahneman, 1974, 1980). When using the former heuristic, people are more likely to report behaviours that are consistent with their self-images or stereotypes about others, while the latter heuristic involves a tendency to report more recent or more salient events. Thus, even respondents who had been victims of a crime tended to be less likely to report being victimized as the number of months between the incident and the time at which the survey was completed increased (Turner, 1972). Clear instructions and an emphasis on complete-ness and accuracy, combined with information about why the information is being asked, appear to overcome problems related to these heuristics (Cannell, Miller, & Oksenberg, 1981).

Opinions, beliefs, attitudes, and values

Although how one asks any question partially determines the response that one obtains, response format is particularly important when one is asking about attitudes. For example, merely being asked to provide an opinion on a given topic is sufficient to create an opinion where none existed (Fazio, Lenn, & Effrein, 1983/1984). Thus, failure to allow an explicit option for "don't know" or "no opinion" may produce inflated estimates of people's opinions by forcing them to espouse an attitude that did not exist prior to their being surveyed (Bishop, Oldendick, & Tuchfarber, 1983). Similar results have been obtained when no "neutral" response alternative is provided (Kalton, Roberts, & Holt, 1980). Respondents are likely to assume that the provided response options are the only ones in which the researcher is interested, and tailor their responses to the format presented to them.

Wording, too, is important when attempting to measure attitudes. One should always avoid double-barrelled items, which are items that contain two or more questions or statements. To do so, however, requires one to write simple items, and even seemingly trivial changes in the wording of a simple item can have a substantial impact on responses. Thus, whenever possible one should employ pre-existing measures of attitudes or pre-test a new measure to determine its level of reliability and construct validity.

Self-reports of intentions

Reports of behavioural intentions can be understood as a combination of attitudes towards the behaviour, subjective norms or beliefs about what one is expected to do, and perceived control over the behaviour (Ajzen & Madden, 1986). Thus, to predict forthcoming behaviour one needs to deter-mine all three aspects of intention. Although a complete discussion is beyond the scope of this chapter, research has shown that prediction is more reliable when respondents have prior experience with (Fazio & Zanna, 1981) and have more knowledge about (Kallgren & Wood, 1986) the behaviour for which intentions are stated.

Agreement between reports of intentions and completed intentions also depend upon the amount of time between the stated intention and the oppor-tunity to engage in the behaviour (Schwartz, 1978). As the delay between the stated intention and the opportunity to fulfil it increases, the probability that the original intention will be implemented decreases. Simply put, circum-stances change and greater delay allows greater change.

Sensitive information

Any of the above types of survey content may include sensitive information – any information that, if revealed to another, would threaten a respondent's public image. Exactly what type of information may be sensitive depends, of course, on one's respondents, and preliminary research may be required to determine whether items contained in an instrument involve sensitive information. Schuman and Kalton (1985), however, argue that concern about the accuracy of responses regarding sensitive information may be overestimated because respondents tend to assume others' beliefs and behaviours are similar to their own (e.g., Ross, Greene, & House, 1977) and are therefore not reluctant to share such information.

Research on self-disclosure and privacy (e.g., Altman, 1975; Jourard, 1971) clearly indicates that one must first establish rapport with an individual before one can obtain sensitive information. Bradburn and Sudman (1979), for example, discuss a variety of strategies that can be used to increase both response rates and response accuracy when dealing with sensitive information, and all of these strategies involve gaining the trust of the respondent. Thus, tactics such as placing sensitive questions towards the end of an instrument may be effective simply because respondents, if they have cooperated to that point, have done because they already trust the researcher.

Administration mode

One cannot state categorically that one of the three modes of survey administration – face-to-face, telephone, and mail – is better than any other in every situation. Each has its advantages and disadvantages, and each is better suited to a specific research situation.

Administering a survey through face-to-face interviewing is time-consuming and expensive, and requires well-trained interviewers. Despite the drawbacks, it remains the best mode for administering a lengthy, complicated survey instrument that contains numerous items for which responses may generate follow-up questions. Face-to-face interviews are sometimes the only way to obtain reactions to specific materials.

The proportion of residences with telephones in most industrialized countries is so high that telephone interviews may well be the most preferred survey administration mode. The ability to employ computers to dial numbers, structure questions, and immediately record responses provides additional advantages. The use of random digit dialling enables one to contact individuals with unlisted telephone numbers, and precludes the need for a priori identification of prospective respondents. With the obvious exception of presenting visual material, telephone interviews provide few disadvantages relative to personal interviews (Groves & Kahn, 1979).

Mailing instruments to respondents is the least expensive mode for a lengthy instrument, but response rates for postal surveys tend to be lower than those for telephone or personal interviews. However, when effort is expended to convince prospective respondents that the survey is worthwhile, response rates can be very high (Dillman, 1978). Enclosing monetary and other incentives also increases response rates, as do secondary and tertiary mailings for tardy respondents. The two major disadvantages to mailed surveys is that one must have a list of prospective addresses and one cannot be certain who at that address actually completed the survey.

Sampling

Typically, one purpose of survey research is to use the results to make inferences about the probable responses of those who were not included in the group of respondents. That is, one wishes to use the sample of respondents to make predictions about the population, the group of all prospective respondents. For example, the purpose of an exit poll of voters is to predict the outcome of the election, in which case the population is all voters. Similarly, the purpose of a marketing survey is to predict consumers' responses to a new product; the population is all consumers. The extent to which survey data can be used to make such predictions validly depends upon the sampling procedures, the manner in which the actual respondents have been selected from the group of all possible respondents.

In general, there are two types of sampling procedures: probability and non-probability. Probability sampling includes all procedures for which the probability of any prospective respondent's inclusion in the sample can be estimated and is known to be non-zero. That is, every prospective respondent has at least some estimable chance of being included in the survey. Non-probability sampling includes all other procedures, that is, procedures in which some prospective respondents have a zero probability of being chosen or in which the probability of being selected cannot be estimated.

Probability sampling

All procedures for obtaining a probability sample are, essentially, variations of placing identical slips of paper, each of which contains a name, in a hat, closing one's eyes, and plucking slips from the hat until one has the desired number of slips. This procedure is known as simple random sampling (SRS), and provides each prospective respondent with an equal chance of being selected. Thus, the key to probability sampling is the existence of a sampling frame, a list of prospective respondents (Kish, 1965). Without a sampling frame, one cannot know the number of prospective respondents, and therefore cannot determine the probability of a single respondent being selected. For example, to select a probability sample of students at University X one must obtain a listing of all students enrolled at X.

When subgroups such as race, gender, religion, nationality, and so on, exist within the population, SRS may produce an unrepresentative sample. For example, a SRS based on geographic location might produce relatively few, if any, residents from rural areas. In such cases, stratified random sampling is the preferred procedure. Essentially, one treats each subgroup *as though* it were a population and employs SRS within the subgroups. The sub-samples selected from each subgroup are then combined to form the survey sample. The number of respondents selected from each subgroup may be proportional to their representation in the population, in which case stratified random sampling is equivalent to an ideal SRS. For a variety of reasons, however, a disproportionate stratified sample may be preferable. If the number of rural residents in the population is relatively small, one may need to select a disproportionately large sample of rural residents to obtain reliable estimates of the opinions of the population of rural residents.

Stratified sampling procedures are used to increase the extent to which the sample represents a heterogeneous population. For economy, however, one may choose to employ cluster sampling, a procedure in which groupings (clusters) of prospective respondents are randomly selected and then respondents are randomly selected from within the selected clusters. For example, a sample of university students could be selected by first obtaining a random sample of universities and then using SRS to select specific students from each selected university. In this case, the cluster is university. Variants of cluster sampling include multiple stages, such as selecting students within colleges within universities within countries.

Non-probability sampling

Non-probability sampling procedures generally base selection on availability or convenience. The commonality is that they do not provide any means by which to make valid inferences from the selected sample because one cannot determine sampling error. For example, accidental sampling involves "selecting" whoever is willing to respond to one's survey, a procedure that led editors of the *Literary Digest* to predict that Alf Landon would win the US presidential election in 1936; Franklin D. Roosevelt obtained 63 per cent of the votes. Similarly, quota sampling, non-randomly choosing respondents on the basis of categorical membership, in the 1948 US presidential election led to the infamous DEWEY DEFEATS TRUMAN headline.

There are, however, research purposes for which non-probability sampling is appropriate. For example, Abdalla (1991) attempted to explore gender differences in uses of social support to relieve job stress in Kuwait. Because no previous research on this topic had been conducted in Arab cultures, Abdalla was more interested in whether any gender differences could be identified than in how such differences could be used to predict males' and females' reactions to job stress. Thus, a non-probability sample of middle-level managers in Kuwait was sufficient for the research goal. In general, non-probability samples are appropriate whenever one does not wish to generalize beyond the specific sample of respondents.

NATURALISTIC OBSERVATION

Whereas survey methods involve an interaction between the researcher and the respondent, naturalistic observation involves methods designed to examine behaviour without actually being a part of it, to avoid as much as possible interfering with what is being observed. Naturalistic observation typically involves collecting data in order to form new hypotheses and is particularly suited to exploratory and descriptive research purposes (Butler, Rice, & Wagstaff, 1963).

Intrusion

If one is to observe events as they unfold, one must avoid intrusion, defined as anything that lessens the participants' perception of an event as natural (Tunnell, 1977). Intrusion can involve any aspect of an event; the behaviours that comprise the event, the setting in which it takes place, and the treatment of the participant by the researcher. With respect to behaviours, the key element is the degree to which those being observed are aware that they are being observed. The degree of intrusion into the setting is determined by the extent to which the event takes place in an environment the participant believes is a research setting. Natural settings include those normally frequented for purposes other than participating in research. Intrusion with respect to treatment refers to the extent to which the event could have occurred without the researcher's presence or influence.

The naturalness of the events being studied is a continuum rather than a dichotomy. Participants' perceptions of naturalness can vary from one end of the continuum to the other. Also, the mixture of behaviour, setting, and treatment makes some events more or less natural than others. Natural behaviours do not always occur in natural settings; they can arise from intrusive treatments, or arise under unusual settings, and so forth. The key to determining the naturalness of an event is attempting to understand what is going on from the participant's point of view.

Selecting events

When selecting events, one must first decide which events are of interest, and then decide how to sample the specific events. The first decision, of course, depends on the hypotheses to be examined. Weick (1968) has categorized events on the basis of behaviours in which researchers are most often interested: non-verbal, spatial, extra linguistic, and linguistic.

Non-verbal behaviours are body movements that convey information. They may include facial expressions, eye contact, hand movements, posture, and so on. Spatial behaviours involve maintaining or altering distances among people or between people and objects; again, such behaviours convey information or reactions to another's behaviour. Extralinguistic behaviours include rate, tone, volume, and other similar characteristics of speech. Finally, linguistic behaviours refer to the content of speech or written material.

Deciding which behaviours from among an entire behavioural sequence to observe involves the general principles of sampling described for survey methods above, but there are a few aspects specific to naturalistic observation. Generally, sampling events involves either time or event sampling. Time sampling, as the term implies, refers to selecting a specific interval of time during which observations will be made. One may sample continuously, that is observe the entire behavioural sequence, but such extensive selection clearly must be reserved for sequences of short duration. Alternatively, one may employ time-point sampling, in which one selects a specific time such as the top of every hour and observes whatever occurs at that moment, or employ time-interval sampling, in which one selects a specific interval such as the last five minutes of every hour and observes ongoing behaviours during the interval. Event sampling involves observing one behaviour contingent upon the presence of another behaviour and is usually used for hypotheses about relationships between two variables or when knowing the duration of the behaviour is not necessary. Event sampling provides only relative information; only continuous time sampling enables absolute measurements of the behaviour.

Coding

Coding involves interpreting what has been recorded, and it is very often accomplished at the same time as recording. It may be used to represent behaviour. For example, Leventhal and Sharp (1965) developed an elaborate system of symbols used to record facial expressions, and LaFrance (1979) developed a similar system for arm positions. The symbols used are a shorthand for the actual behaviour, but they don't necessarily ascribe any meaning to the behaviour.

More often than not, however, coding involves both recording and interpreting an observation. The best known of such systems is the interaction process analysis (IPA) system developed by Bales (1970). IPA allows observers to record inferred meanings for linguistic, extralinguistic, and non-verbal behaviours among groups. The IPA is one of many examples of check-list coding schemes. Barker (1963) developed an elaborate check-list of social behaviours, while Benjamin's (1979) system deals with interpersonal motivations.

An alternative to check-list systems is the unstructured or ethological system, also known as natural history. The ethological system involves a detailed and comprehensive recording of behaviours with little or no inferred meaning. For example, McGrew (1972) used an ethological system to categorize 110 different behaviours of nursery schoolchildren's social interactions. Although use of an ethological system does not preclude the eventual interpretation of one's observations, it does preclude mixing recording with interpretation.

When the behaviour being observed is linguistic, content analysis is usually the coding mechanism (Holsti, 1968; Lasswell, Lerner, & Pool, 1952). One may use content analysis to establish authorship (Rokeach, Homant, & Penner, 1970), authors' attitudes (Seider, 1974), cultural beliefs (Zimbardo & Meadow, 1974), persuasion tactics (McHugh, Lanzetta, Sullivan, Masters, & Englis, 1985), social learning (Kounin & Gump, 1961), and social motivation (Runyan, 1982).

There are two major types of content that one may analyse – manifest and latent. Manifest content is the physical or non-inferential material that makes up a message, and is usually coded in terms of words or letters in written material, words and pauses in audio material, concrete actions in visual material, and so forth. It is relatively easy to code reliably; few people would disagree about the presence or absence of a word or an action in an observation. Latent content refers to inferred, underlying, or hidden meaning in material. It may be coded in terms of words or actions, and it usually involves inferences from sentences, paragraphs, facial expressions, and tone of voice, as well as other indications of meaning. Because coding latent content involves making inferences about the manifest content of an archive, latent content is generally less reliable than manifest content. On the other hand, latent content may be the only way to operationalize some concepts. Evaluative assertion analysis (Osgood, 1959) is frequently used for coding latent content.

When check-lists or rating scales are used to simultaneously record and code actions, at least some interpretation occurs before any observations are made. Choosing the categories to be included on the check-list, or choosing an existing check-list, involves interpreting what will and will not be important before any observation occurs. Gellert (1955) has noted that the number of different categories and the number of coding errors are directly related. Similarly, category abstractness and error are directly related: the more a coder/recorder must do in terms of interpretation, the more likely it is that he or she will make a mistake.

Dunnette (1966) described four sources of error that reduce reliability: inadequate sampling, chance response tendencies, changes in the participant, and changes in the situation. Inadequate sampling occurs when only a subset of events is recorded and the sampling process is not systematic. That is, errors occur when observers do not have or fail to follow a system for selecting observations. Chance response tendencies involve replacing formal category definitions with idiosyncratic definitions. Poorly trained or inadequately motivated observers are often the sources of such errors, but not the only sources. For example, chance response tendencies are more likely to occur when using abstract categories in a check-list system. Assessing interobserver reliability enables one to estimate the extent of sampling and chance response errors. The latter types of errors are more difficult to detect, and may in fact not be considered errors at all. That is, changes in the individual(s) or situation(s) being observed may result from reactivity, or they may be part of the natural progression of the event. The use of unobtrusive measures (e.g. Webb, Campbell, Schwartz, & Sechrest, 1966) is the most effective way to avoid reactivity.

CASE-STUDIES

Case-studies involve intensive research of a single individual or event. For the former, one can employ survey methods or naturalistic observation, adapted, of course, for the much smaller sample size. For the latter, one must employ participant observation, an observational method in which the researcher becomes part of the events being observed (Liebow, 1967). In participant observation, recording equipment includes little more than paper and pencil (and perhaps a word processor). The research tool of greatest importance is the field journal or notebook into which observations are entered.

Sampling

Whereas naturalistic observation involves selecting behaviours, participant observation is more likely to involve selecting a setting in which to observe the event(s) of interest. Sampling in participant observation involves first selecting the group of people to be observed and then locating settings in which those people can be found. This can sometimes be accomplished via informants, who often provide the information necessary to employ one of three types of sampling suggested by McCall and Simmons (1969): quota, snowball, and deviant case.

Quota sampling, selecting sampling elements on the basis of categories assumed to exist within the population, involves purposefully searching out participants who fit the research requirements. Snowball sampling involves obtaining suggestions for other participants from those one has already observed. Also called key informant sampling, snowball sampling is analogous to a salesperson asking the most recent customer for names of prospective customers. Deviant case sampling involves observing individuals who do not seem to fit some pattern exhibited by others. Insights into reasons for engaging in an activity often can be discovered from those who choose not to engage in the activity.

Hypothesis testing

Testing hypotheses in case-studies typically involves negative case analysis, which includes searching for data that disconfirm a tentative hypothesis, revising the hypothesis to include the disconfirming data, searching for more data, and so on. Whatever hypothesis survives this procedure is very likely to contain both necessary and sufficient causes. The depth with which one can test a hypothesis using negative case analysis often makes up for the fact that the results of case-studies can rarely be generalized beyond the individual(s) or event(s) studied.

FURTHER READING

Dane, F. C. (1990). *Research methods*. Pacific Grove, CA: Brooks/Cole.
Fassnacht, G. (1982). *Theory and practice of observing behaviour* (trans. C. Bryant). London: Academic Press.
Fowler, F. J., Jr (1988). *Survey research methods*. Newbury Park, CA: Sage.
Miller, D. C. (1991). *Handbook of research design and social measurement*. Newbury Park, CA: Sage.
Yin, R. K. (1989). *Case study research: Design and methods*. Newbury Park, CA: Sage.

REFERENCES

Abdalla, I. A. (1991). Social support and gender responses to job stress in an Arab culture. *Journal of Social Behavior and Personality, 6*(7), 273–288.
Ajzen, I., & Madden, T. J. (1986). Prediction of goal-directed behavior: Attitudes, intentions, and perceived behavioral control. *Journal of Experimental Social Psychology, 22*, 453–474.
Altman, I. (1975). *The environment and social behavior: Privacy, personal space, territory, and crowding*. Pacific Grove, CA: Brooks/Cole.
Bales, R. F. (1970). *Personality and interpersonal behavior*. New York: Holt, Rinehart & Winston.
Barker, R. G. (Ed.) (1963). *The stream of behavior*. New York: Appleton-Century-Crofts.
Benjamin, L. S. (1979). Use of structural analysis of social behavior (SASB) and Markov chains to study dyadic interactions. *Journal of Abnormal Psychology, 88*, 303–319.
Bishop, G. F., Oldendick, R. W., & Tuchfarber, A. J. (1983). Effects of filler questions in public opinion surveys. *Public Opinion Quarterly, 47*, 528–546.
Bradburn, N. M., & Sudman, S. (1979). *Improving interview method and questionnaire design*. San Francisco, CA: Jossey-Bass.
Butler, J. M., Rice, L. N., & Wagstaff, A. K. (1963). *Quantitative naturalistic research*. Englewood Cliffs, NJ: Prentice-Hall.

Cannell, C. F., Miller, P. V., & Oksenberg, L. (1981). Research on interviewing techniques. In S. Leinhardt (Ed.) *Sociological methodology* (pp. 389–437). San Francisco, CA: Jossey-Bass.

Dillman, D. A. (1978). *Mail and telephone surveys: The total design method.* New York: Wiley.

Dunnette, M. D. (1966). *Personnel selection and placement.* Belmont, CA: Wadsworth.

Fazio, R. H., & Zanna, M. P. (1981). Direct experience and attitude-behavior consistency. *Advances in Experimental Social Psychology, 14,* 161–202.

Fazio, R. H., Lenn, T. M., & Effrein, E. A. (1983/1984). Spontaneous attitude formation. *Social Cognition, 2,* 217–234.

Feldman, R. M. (1990). Settlement-identity: Psychological bonds with home place in a mobile society. *Environment and Behaviour, 22*(2), 183–229.

Fiske, S. T., & Taylor, S. E. (1991). *Social cognition* (2nd edn). New York: McGraw-Hill.

Gellert, E. (1955). Systematic observation: A method in child study. *Harvard Educational Review, 25,* 179–195.

Groves, R. M., & Kahn, R. L. (1979). *Surveys by telephone: A national comparison with personal interviews.* New York: Academic Press.

Holsti, O. R. (1968). Content analysis. In G. Lindzey & E. Aronson (Eds) *The handbook of social psychology* (pp. 596–692). Menlo Park, CA: Addison-Wesley.

Jourard, S. M. (1971). *Self-disclosure.* New York: Wiley.

Kallgren, C. A., & Wood, W. (1986). Access to attitude-relevant information in memory as a determinant of attitude-behavior consistency. *Journal of Experimental Social Psychology, 22,* 328–338.

Kalton, G., Roberts, J., & Holt, D. (1980). The effects of offering a middle response option with opinion questions. *Statistician, 29,* 11–24.

Kish, L. (1965). *Survey sampling.* New York: Wiley.

Kounin, J., & Gump, P. (1961). The comparative influence of punitive and non-punitive teachers upon children's concepts of school misconduct. *Journal of Educational Psychology, 52,* 44–49.

LaFrance, M. (1979). Nonverbal synchrony and rapport: Analysis by the cross-lagged panel technique. *Social Psychology Quarterly, 42,* 66–70.

Lasswell, H. D., Lerner, D., & Pool, I. de S. (1952). *The comparative study of symbols.* Stanford, CA: Stanford University Press.

Leventhal, H., & Sharp, E. (1965). Facial expressions as indicators of distress. In S. Thompkins & C. Izard (Eds) *Affect, cognition, and personality* (pp. 296–318). New York: Springer.

Liebow, E. (1967). *Tally's corner.* Boston, MA: Little, Brown.

Literary Digest (1936). Landon, 1,293,669: Roosevelt, 972,897. *Literary Digest,* 31 October, pp. 5–6.

McCall, G. C., & Simmons, J. L. (Eds) (1969). *Issues in participant observation.* Reading, MA: Addison-Wesley.

McGrew, W. C. (1972). *An ethological study of children's behavior.* New York: Academic Press.

McHugo, G. J., Lanzetta, J. T., Sullivan, D. G., Masters, R. D., & Englis, B. G. (1985). Emotional reactivity to a political leader's expressive displays. *Journal of Personality and Social Psychology, 49,* 1513–1529.

Metts, S. (1989). An exploratory investigation of deception in close relationships. *Journal of Social and Personal Relationships, 6,* 159–179.

Osgood, C. E. (1959). The representational model and relevant research methods. In I. de S. Pool (Ed.) *Trends in content analysis* (pp. 33–88). Urbana, IL: University of Illinois Press.

Rokeach, M., Homant, R., & Penner, L. (1970). A value analysis of the disputed federalist papers. *Journal of Personality and Social Psychology*, *16*, 245–250.

Ross, L., Greene, D., & House, P. (1977). The "false consensus effect": An egocentric bias in social perception and attribution processes. *Journal of Experimental Social Psychology*, *13*, 279–301.

Runyan, W. M. (1982). *Life histories and psychobiography: Explorations in theory and method*. New York: Oxford University Press.

Schuman, H., & Kalton, G. (1985) Survey methods. In G. Lindzey & E. Aronson (Eds) *Handbook of social psychology* (3rd edn, vol. 1, pp. 635–697). Reading, MA: Addison-Wesley.

Schwartz, S. H. (1978). Temporal instability as a moderator of the attitude–behavior relationship. *Journal of Personality and Social Psychology*, *36*, 715–724.

Seider, M. S. (1974). American big business ideology: A content analysis of executive speeches. *American Sociological Review*, *39*, 802–815.

Skogan, W. G. (1981). *Issues in the measurement of victimization*. Washington, DC: Bureau of Justice Statistics, US Department of Justice (NCJ-74682).

Tunnell, G. B. (1977). Three dimensions of naturalness: An expanded definition of field research. *Psychological Bulletin*, *84*, 426–437.

Turner, A. G. (1972). *The San Jose methods test of known crime victims*. Washington, DC: National Criminal Justice Information and Statistics Service, US Department of Justice.

Tversky, A., & Kahneman, D. (1974). Judgment under uncertainty: Heuristics and biases. *Science*, *815*, 1124–1131.

Tversky, A., & Kahneman, D. (1980). Causal schemes in judgments under uncertainty. In M. Fishbein (Ed.) *Progress in social psychology* (vol. 1, pp. 49–72) Hillsdale, NJ: Lawrence Erlbaum.

Van Drusen, R. A., & Zill, N. (Eds) (1975). *Basic background items for U.S. household surveys*. Washington, DC: Center for Coordination of Research on Social Indicators, Social Science Research Council.

Weaver, C. N., & Swanson, C. L. (1974). Validity of reported date of birth, salary, and seniority. *Public Opinion Quarterly*, *38*, 69–80.

Webb, E. J., Campbell, D. T., Schwartz, R. D., & Sechrest, L. (1966). *Unobtrusive measures*. Chicago, IL: Rand McNally.

Weick, K. E. (1968). Systematic observational methods. In G. Lindzey & E. Aronson (Eds) *The handbook of social psychology* (Vol. 2, pp. 370–404). Reading, MA: Addison-Wesley.

Zimbardo, P. G., & Meadow, W. (1974). *Sexism springs eternal in the* Reader's Digest. Presented at Western Psychological Association, San Francisco, CA, April.

12.6

ETHICAL ISSUES IN PSYCHOLOGICAL RESEARCH

Anthony Gale

University of Southampton, England

Moral discourse is like the food industry – it is hard to imagine a time when it will be short of business. Moral debate is an essential element in human existence, and ethics has been a central issue in philosophy for centuries. We have a preoccupation with our duties and responsibilities to others, our notions of what is right and wrong, and our positive or negative evaluations of the actions of both ourselves and others. Hardly a day can pass when we do not make a moral judgement about the conduct of others. Philosophers have tried to identify the ethical bases for our relationships with other human beings (for example, why it is wrong to lie, to steal, or to murder), or with society at large (for example, why altruism is better than selfishness, whether we have a moral duty to the poor or to the state). But you will be disappointed if you take a course in ethics in the hope of getting straightforward moral answers about how you should lead your life. As Sartre said, we are condemned to be free.

MORALS, ETHICS, SOCIAL NORMS, AND THE PSYCHOLOGIST

Moral debate is hard work

The outsider to ethical debate finds it hard to appreciate that basic ethical propositions are not reducible to other propositions, such as psychological propositions – for example, that the good is that which makes people happy. Formal ethical debate calls for coherent logical argument among people who typically share basic ethical beliefs but differ as to how such fundamental principles may be applied in a particular case. Moral decisions are almost always a compromise, balancing the imperatives of one principle against the imperatives of another and taking into account the particular circumstances. There are no simple answers. Unfortunately, however, few of us are accustomed to sustained ethical debate. Rollin (1985) suggests that much of the debate about the moral status of research animals in psychology is irrational because

> most people's moral ideas are acquired piecemeal from a variety of sources throughout life, such as parents, teachers, friends, education, reading and films; there is little guarantee that these ideas will form a coherent whole. In fact, most people are not even consciously aware of their moral assumptions. (p. 921)

An informal survey of my academic colleagues shows that few of them remember being taught about ethics during their psychological education. There is little evidence that formal experience of ethical debate is considered an important element in the psychological curriculum (Gale, 1990).

One aspect of ethical conduct in science is taught to students implicitly by a sort of osmosis, and that is the principle that psychology shares with other sciences, for integrity and honesty in the reporting of data. It is not clear how students learn to be honest in their research endeavours, and there are notorious examples of alleged cheating and selectivity in psychological research. For example, Hearnshaw (1979) concluded in his biography of Burt that this distinguished and respected psychologist had for some years been guilty of scientific malpractice, although such conclusions are not shared by others (see Fletcher, 1991; Joynson, 1989).

Ethical debate in psychology is not straightforward

Given that the psychological sciences are concerned with the study of people, the discipline has a special set of moral concerns that do not apply in other sciences. The problem of ethics in psychological research is daunting and *any* psychological research project calls for non-trivial ethical debate. While learned and professional societies such as the American Psychological Association (APA) and the British Psychological Society (BPS) publish ethical guidelines for the conduct of research, such guidelines prove difficult to apply in any hard-and-fast way, in any particular research context, and they remain merely as guidelines. They continue to be criticized on grounds of vagueness (Aitkenhead & Dordoy, 1983) and the majority of scientific journals *assume* that ethical concerns have been considered by the researcher, rather than requiring a formal statement to that effect.

Schlenker and Forsyth (1977) warn psychologists to be aware of the consequences for psychology of different philosophical approaches to ethical principles, which they identify as: *teleological*, where the morality of an action is ultimately judged by its consequences; the *deontological* approach, which rejects consequences as a basis for judgement and appeals to fundamental principles or categorical absolutes derived from natural law; and *skepticism*, which assumes that inviolate moral codes can never be formulated, and includes approaches such as cultural relativism, ethical egoism, and emotivism. They showed experimentally that individuals' moral positions (which of the three approaches they accept) affect their evaluation of the ethicality of particular research studies. Psychological moral discourse is not different from general moral discourse; it will always be hard for participants to agree.

Psychological ethics must keep pace with social change

It is an interesting fact that the APA and BPS codes or guidelines are reviewed periodically; both societies published revised codes in 1990, showing that some aspects at least cannot depend on absolutes or universal truths. One reason for the need to update the codes is the changing context of psychological research and the possibility that new research issues (for example, sexual behaviour in the context of AIDS) might highlight new ethical problems (Melton & Gray, 1988). A more potent reason is the changing views of society at large about the nature of individual rights and the extent to which psychological research is seen to be insensitive to or to invade such rights; thus, for example, the changing approach to adolescent offenders, as people who should be consulted about their treatment rather than as people upon whom decisions should be imposed by experts, has created new restrictions on research into corrective intervention (Mulvey & Phelps, 1988).

Psychology itself might contribute to changing views of the individual. For example, humanistic psychology has had an impact on notions of personal autonomy and freedom of choice and was a reaction to more psychoanalytic-deterministic or behaviourist constructions of the person. More recently, feminist psychology has increased public awareness of institutionalized oppression of women; both the APA and the BPS, in internal documentation and in their scientific journals, prohibit the use of gender-related language, but many further issues remain to be resolved (Denmark, Russo, Frieze, & Sechzer, 1988; see also Condor, 1991, discussed below).

Thus new research, changing views of the person, and the influence of new insights in psychology itself, demonstrate the changing sociocultural background against which ethical codes need to be deployed or are seen to be adequate or salient. New legal rulings might actually restrict psychological research or prove so threatening that research might not be done for fear that the researcher becomes exposed to potential legal action. Appelbaum and Rosenbaum (1989) discuss the implications of the California Supreme Court ruling in the Tarasoff case. Ms Tarasoff was a student; another student informed his therapist at the university counselling centre that he intended to kill her; the therapist informed the police and the second student was detained; but, when the police released him, believing he was not a threat, the counsellors took no further action to warn others or to ensure that he returned to treatment; he then killed Ms Tarasoff. The Supreme Court held the university responsible on the ground that the counsellors were analogous to medical staff who can know the dangers to others of a patient's infectious illness or who negligently allow a violent patient to escape from custody; thus they had a special relationship with the murderer and "a duty to protect" others from his violence. Appelbaum and Rosenbaum (1989) consider analogous research circumstances in which a researcher might be said to have such a duty and conclude that the relationship would need to be analogous to a clinical relationship. Otherwise, they suggest that psychological research on child abuse, violence, substance abuse, and AIDS might be compromised. Similarly, Mulvey and Phelps (1988) appeal for special protection for the privacy of participants in AIDS research, where the researcher might feel pressurized to report to the authorities respondents' confessions to failing to declare their infection when having sexual intercourse.

An interesting feature of current ethical guidelines and psychological research reports is that the term "subjects" has begun, since the early 1980s, be replaced by the term "participants", and this also reflects a changing view of the individual in psychology itself. There has been a historical shift in the perception of the role of the participant in the laboratory from object to person (Silverman, 1977). As Schultz (1969) put it, the I—It relationship has been replaced by the I—You relationship, which in turn has implications for the sorts of procedures that psychological researchers will deploy in the laboratory.

The dilemma: benefits versus costs

Two implicit fundamental ethical beliefs in psychology are first, that the pursuit of psychological knowledge is inherently good, not least because increased understanding could enhance the human condition, and second, that in psychological research participants should be protected from stress, undue invasions of privacy, and other forms of exploitation. These two commitments (to increase knowledge and to protect the individual) can come into direct conflict when the needs of the research seem potentially to undermine the integrity or status of the participant, and that is the central dilemma.

Neff, Iwata, and Page (1986), in a historical review, cite several dramatic examples of medical and psychological/behavioural research which involved the abuse of participants and which caused a public furore: in a stress experiment, participants were led to believe that they were in danger of losing their lives through a simulated plane malfunction; the injection of live cancer cells into chronically ill patients to study the development of antibodies without informing them; the recording of juror behaviour, without their knowledge, with concealed microphones; withholding treatment from 400 subjects in a 40-year study of the long-term effects of syphilis. They might also have included the work of Zimbardo (1973) in which students took the roles of warders and prisoners in a simulated prison, and the researchers had to stop the study early because of the undesirable compliant and punitive behaviours exhibited by participants.

Ask any psychology student about ethics in psychological research and the immediate answer will refer to Milgram's (1963) study of obedience. Milgram believed that context, and in particular obedience to authority, could influence otherwise ordinary and decent folk to act in violent and oppressive ways to others. He thought it was naïve to believe that only certain sorts of people could be guilty of aggression. The abstract of his 1963 paper provides the essential outline of the study:

> This article describes a procedure for the study of destructive obedience in the laboratory. It consists of ordering a naïve S to administer increasingly more severe punishment to a victim in the context of a learning experiment. Punishment is administered by means of a shock generator with 30 gradual switches ranging from Slight Shock to Danger: Severe Shock. The victim is a confederate of the E. The primary dependent variable is the maximum shock the S is willing to administer before he refuses to continue further. 26 Ss obeyed the experimental commands fully, and administered the highest shock on the generator. 14 Ss broke off the experiment at some point after the victim protested and refused to provide further answers. The procedure created extreme levels of nervous tension in some Ss.

Profuse sweating, trembling, and stuttering were typical expressions of this emotional disturbance. One unexpected sign of tension – yet to be explained – was the regular occurrence of nervous laughter, which in some Ss developed into uncontrollable seizures. The variety of interesting behavioral dynamics observed in the experiment, the reality of the situation for the S, and the possibility of parametric variation within the framework of the procedure, point to the fruitfulness of further study. (Milgram, 1963, p. 371)

To the modern critic, the formal technical and matter-of-fact description of the work, the detached clinical description of participants' reactions, and the exhortation to use the technique for further parametric research, add to the sense of horror. Publication of the research brought vilification from other psychologists and from the press; Milgram's study has become a notorious illustration of the alleged wickedness of psychological researchers. Although it occurred many years ago, it is still cited in introductory texts as a key study.

Among the criticisms of Milgram were: making people do things in the laboratory that they would never do in real life, lowering participants' self-esteem by showing them what evil they were capable of, causing long-term harm to their perception of themselves, causing extreme emotional reactions, causing reactions that neither he nor the participants could explain (the laughter), deceiving participants (because no shock was delivered, the apparent recipient of shock was a confederate, and his screams of pain were enacted), instructing people to harm other people, creating experimental conditions under which participants were obliged to follow instructions and found it difficult to withdraw, damaging the reputation of psychology by making it hard for others to conduct research, damaging psychological research by making participants suspicious of being misled, and demonstrating to totalitarian regimes how easy it would be to carry out torture (Baumrind, 1964; Kelman, 1967).

It seems that Milgram was possibly harmed more than were his participants, only 1 per cent of whom said a year later in a follow-up survey that they regretted participating, the majority expressing a positive view of their participation (Milgram, 1977). One participant wrote to Milgram thanking him for making him aware of what he was capable of and the need to resist unacceptable instructions from people in authority. But the harm to psychology itself is hard to calculate.

To illustrate the ethical complexity of the issue and the fact that condemnation of Milgram, while understandable, is not the only possible reaction, let us look further at the positive side of the equation. Did Milgram also instruct us in some important moral lessons, for which some sort of price might be worth paying?

Milgram changed our view of obedience, showing that the majority of us might be capable in appropriate circumstances of committing atrocities, an important if distasteful insight into the human condition. Thus, under appropriate conditions, concentration camps could appear in several cultures or political regimes. Such a revelation could affect not only our explanations for and treatment of those who commit acts of violence but our views of major conflict, undermining xenophobic bigotry, teaching us humility about what could happen in our own society, and enhancing inter alia international understanding, and promoting forgiveness for past wrongs.

It might also serve to explain the fascination people appear to have with human tragedies and disasters as portrayed in the media, and the ready moral condemnation we indulge in when the antisocial actions of others are in the spotlight. In psychoanalytic terms, both contexts enable us to operate ego-defences in socially acceptable ways, revealing to the astute observer both our potential for violence and its social suppression from early childhood. An important lesson for the psychologist is that explanations couched in personal terms (such as "the authoritarian personality") serve to minimize our appreciation of the role that politics, power, and the prevailing ideology may have on individual actions.

The potential for disrepute: can psychology ever win?

The key ethical question raised by Milgram's research is whether the benefits of such revelations justify the steps taken to achieve them. In several areas of psychology it is clear that the results of psychological research could be turned to good or ill; conditioning principles, which have helped so admirably in the rehabilitation of long-term psychiatric patients, might also be deployed in the humiliation and torturing of political prisoners, for which there is a ready audience, as the work of Amnesty International so frequently testifies. Theories and research on attitude change could be used not only in health education (for smoking cessation programmes, say) but also for the promotion of political extremism (such as the acceptance of "ethnic cleansing" in the Balkans). Defendants of research on gender differences and ethnic differences in cognitive processes have had to fight hard to sustain the view that such research is actually potentially beneficial for under-represented minority groups (Scarr, 1988) and need not be merely treated as fuel for right-wing extremists. How easy is it, though, to predict in advance, what use (good or ill?) will be made of your research findings? Einstein is alleged to have said that had he known, he would have become a watchmaker.

Principles governing the scientist–participant relationship

Milgram's studies highlight some of the key issues in psychological research: deception, voluntary consent, subject discomfort, and freedom to withdraw. Other issues that have attracted attention are the role of post-experimental debriefing, and breaches of privacy and of confidentiality. Research does not have to be dramatic nor have the potential notoriety of the original Milgram study to create such concerns. In every research study a calculation needs to be made in advance of the cost–benefit equation.

The social psychology of the psychology experiment reveals an asymmetrical power relationship between experimenter and participant, and the rules and roles of the situation give the experimenter considerable authority. Power is also associated with responsibility. An important issue, even in mundane and apparently non-controversial research, is whether the actions of psychologists in research settings are in any way at variance with what are considered to be the socially or culturally acceptable ways of treating others in everyday social intercourse or in analogous situations of unequal status, such as the classroom or the doctor's surgery (Gale & Chapman, 1984).

Barriers to open debate

Many of the ethical issues surrounding psychological research are too hot to handle. That may be the reason why explicit discussion of ethics is so rarely an essential ingredient of undergraduate curricula. In the past, for example, many undergraduate students were required to participate in research as part of their psychological training, so much so that 80 per cent of the psychological research from 1950 to the mid-1970s could be described as "the psychology of the sophomore" (Silverman, 1977). Clearly, such participation could be beneficial for them, increasing their understanding of psychological science. But such a requirement also creates an opportunity for exploitation, since students might wish to comply with the wishes of their teachers or even fear lower grades as a reprisal if they refuse to participate. Explicit class discussion of the need for voluntary consent might make such students resentful of the requirement to participate. Thus there is an incentive for full discussion of ethical concerns in research to remain on a hidden agenda.

Psychologists are only human

Academic psychologists make a living out of psychological research, and their career, salary, self-esteem, and peer recognition are all based on research achievement. Any prescription that seeks to restrict their freedom also restricts their career prospects. Some commentators have coyly asked why there is relatively little empirical research into the ethics of research (Aitkenhead & Dordoy, 1983), the implication being that failure to address such important issues is a defence mechanism in the form of denial. Psychologists, like everyone else, are subject to value judgements of which they are not necessarily aware and to a tendency to bias judgements to their own benefit; thus persistence in behaviour that is self-serving, without conscious debate on its moral implications, is to be expected.

The danger of public condemnation

As the findings of psychology penetrate public consciousness there is an increasing likelihood that such findings will influence public policy; but public policy is itself influenced by political pressures and beliefs, so that psychological findings in such spheres are always likely to provoke negative public reaction on the part of vested interests. For example, any research into the impact of day-care on young children is likely to offend some interest group: those who defend women's right to work will reject evidence of negative effects, those who defend "traditional family values" will reject evidence of positive effects.

The image of psychological science as value-free has become harder to sustain. Starr (1988), accusing others of moral cowardice, declared that she was prepared to go into exile, in the eventuality of negative public condemnation, if the results of her work on multracial fostering proved to be politically unacceptable. She wanted to know whether ethnic minority children raised in white middle-class homes would show major intellectual gains.

The development of formal guidelines for the conduct of research

Where there is the potential for exploitation and public acrimony it is essential to have formal codes of conduct, both to protect the individual participant and to offer professional protection to the researcher. The history of the evolution of the APA code for research illustrates the effort, dedication, and resources devoted to the development of the code, which had first appeared in 1953. Between 1966 and 1972, when the full ethical code was finally published, the following steps were taken: literature review, pilot questionnaire to 1,000 members, full questionnaire to 9,000 members, soliciting of 2,000 ethical problems from a broad range of researchers, revision of draft principles, further questionnaires to a second sample of 9,000 members and selected groups, soliciting of 3,000 further descriptions of research problems, interviews with 35 experts (journal editors, research directors, experts on ethics, on hypnosis, and so on), discussion of the draft principles at several scientific meetings, consultation with 800 academic institutions requesting full debate and discussion, consultations with members of other disciplines (philosophers, anthropologists, lawyers, and others), publication of the revised version in 1972 including a requirement for five-yearly reviews, which led to revised publication in 1981 and 1990 (American Psychological Association, 1982, 1990). The BPS code also underwent major revisions published in 1978 and 1990 but deploying a much more modest methodology (British Psychological Society, 1991).

Do values differ on the two sides of the Atlantic?

It is clear that both learned societies (which are the largest psychological societies in the world) demonstrated a strong sense of social responsibility and sensitivity in developing their codes, although the element of self-protection is also hard to deny. It is evident, for example, that the APA code is more explicit and more comprehensive than the BPS code (for example, on matters of competence, protection of minority groups, teachers' responsibilities, sensitivity to the influence of personal values, and in the combination of professional practice and research codes and human and animal research within one document).

A brief comment on research with other species

This chapter does not include a detailed debate on the important moral controversy surrounding the use of non-human species in psychological research; the reader may wish to refer to American Psychological Association (1990), Bateson (1986), British Psychological Society (1991), Experimental Psychology Society (1986), Gray (1987), and Miller (1985). Wadeley (1991) lists five key guidelines for animal research in psychology:

1 full knowledge of the law governing animal experimentation
2 thoroughgoing knowledge of the reactions of different species, in the interests of reducing distress
3 humane practices in the breeding, capture, and transport of animals and the use of the smallest samples feasible
4 minimization of pain and distress
5 use of invasive procedures only by competent and fully licensed individuals.

Herzog (1988), in an amusing but challenging article on the moral status of mice, asserts that it rests on the values of humans and the roles humans require mice to play and not in the intrinsic qualities of the mouse. Thus on or within reach of one campus there were four categories of mouse: the *good* mice (used in experiments and protected by legal/ethical codes and veterinary care), the *bad* mice (free-ranging, disease-transmitting pests which suffer painful deaths through traps), *feeder* (morally neutral?) mice used to feed other species, like snakes, required in research, and his son's pet mouse, whose death led to a funeral and tombstone:

> The moral judgements we make about other species are neither logical nor consistent. Rather, they are the result of both cerebral and visceral components of the human mind . . . the roles that animals play in our lives and the labels we attach to them, deeply influence our sense of what is ethical. (Herzog, 1988, p. 474).

Rollin (1985) suggests two principles that should guide decisions to use animals in research: first, the utilitarian principle, by which the potential benefit (to humans or animals) clearly outweighs the pain and suffering to be experienced, and second, the rights principle, whereby the conduct of the research maximizes the animal's potential for living its life according to its nature. Rollin suggests that as a first step we should make the assumption that animals have the same rights as humans, or at least we should use the human case as an analog. That is a most humane principle; unfortunately, our discussion will reveal that consideration of the rights of human participants in psychological research is not straightforward by any means.

ETHICAL GUIDELINES FOR THE CONDUCT OF RESEARCH

An obligation for all psychological researchers

Individuals wishing to conduct psychological research, whether they be fully fledged psychologists, students, or members of another profession, are strongly advised to study both the APA and BPS Principles. The codes reflect careful, humane, and considered attempts to guide the nature of psychological research in the interests of participants. Nevertheless, the codes continue to be criticized for perceived shortcomings (Condor, 1991, see below).

The dangers to the discipline of psychology of failing to enforce such codes are legion. For example, in the United Kingdom, there are upwards of 20,000 18-year-old school students taking the Advanced Level examination in psychology, which typically requires students to conduct five research studies. Many of the teachers are not qualified psychologists; there are thus 100,000 opportunities each year for examples of abuse of participants and for public scandal, easily fed by the prurience of the mass media.

Table 1 provides a schematic version of the key features of a combination of the APA and BPS Principles. The distillation focuses on the aspects of the codes particularly related to research; the APA code refers also to guidelines for professional conduct in the practice of applied psychology, which the BPS deals with in separate documents.

LOOKING CLOSE AT THE PRINCIPLES: CONCEPTUAL ISSUES AND RESEARCH FINDINGS

We shall now examine the central issues of deception and consent and argue that there are dangers of intellectual and practical lip-service to the principles if researchers do not consider the psychological limits to consent and the research that has been conducted about consent itself. In other words, the publication of the Principles and psychologists' acceptance of them should not lead us to a false sense of security, nor indeed to overestimate participants' negative reactions to research procedures. Moreover, the terms used in the Principles are everyday or vernacular terms, lacking legal or technical precision.

Table 1 A distillation of the American Psychological Association and British Psychological Society ethical principles for the conduct of research with human participants

Responsibility
Psychologists are responsible for their research; plan it considering the ethical implications for those involved, conducting a cost−benefit analysis, bearing in mind both the potential gains to psychological science and human welfare, and the risks to participants; appreciate that they might need the advice of others to fully understand its potential impact on particular groups; report it accurately, and are honest about its interpretation, do not suppress disconfirming data, recognizing inter alia that it might be construed to the detriment of others; avoid conflicts of interest which may limit their objectivity; do not lay claim to work that is not their own and acknowledge the contributions of others; prevent distortion of their findings by others; are sensitive to community values; offer a model to students of integrity and objective scholarship; ensure that those conducting research on their behalf share the full sense of ethical responsibility; are aware of political or other pressures that might lead to the misuse of psychological knowledge; treat research participants with respect, avoiding all exploitation, such as sexual harassment; take personal responsibility to correct any harm that occurs to participants as a result of the research; and, where colleagues persist in unprofessional conduct, seek to remonstrate with them and then, if necessary, take formal action against them by reporting them to their professional body.

Competence
To maintain high standards of competence, one has to keep up-to-date with scientific developments in one's field, obtain necessary training where necessary, not claim competence in techniques where one is not qualified, recognize the boundaries of one's expertise, appreciate that one's personal problems might influence professional judgement, and seek the advice of others where appropriate.

Confidentiality
Subject to any overriding legislation, psychologists respect all personal data about participants unless otherwise agreed in advance; resist improper pressures to release such information; conceal the identity of individuals in publishing data or in public lectures; ensure that all stored data are secure; inform participants if the data are to be shared with other researchers; have particular concern for the need to protect the interests of minors or others unable to give voluntary consent; do not reveal personal information to those who might misinterpret it.

Consent
Any feature of a study that might affect participants' willingness to take part should be disclosed in advance; where participants (such as young children or people with intellectual handicaps) might have limited understanding, attempts should be made to obtain real consent, apart from gaining consent from those *in loco parentis* or those with familial or other close links; where persons are detained, limits on true voluntary consent should be recognized; positions of authority over participants should not be used to pressurize them to participate; inducements should not be offered where risk is likely; withdrawal should be allowed at any time and the right to withdraw be made clear from the outset; participants should be free to insist that their data not be used and that records relating to them be destroyed; all promises given when securing consent must be fulfilled; in observational or covert research, where gaining consent

Table 1   (Continued)

is not practicable, due regard should be given to cultural values and people's expectations relating to privacy in public places.

Deception
In many cases, to reveal the full purposes of the study in advance might damage the research; under such circumstances the investigator has a responsibility to assess the scientific benefits, examine fully alternative procedures, consider the possible impact on participants, and ensure they are informed of the true nature of the study at the earliest possible stage; while debriefing after the study is completed is desirable in all cases, it should not be considered as a justification for unethical deception.

Protection of participants
There is a primary responsibility for reducing risk, including identification of factors (such as medical history) that might compound risk; any undesirable consequences should be removed and participants should know that they can contact the investigator if any subsequent discomfort is experienced; care should be taken in discussing children with their parents, because information might be misinterpreted or given undue weight; participants should be informed of any psychological or physical problems that might come to light during the investigation, but bearing in mind the limits to the investigator's own competence.

The psychology of consent

What does consent mean? It must assume three elements: knowledge and understanding of what is involved, competence, and voluntary choice. As Gale and Chapman (1984) point out, the investigator can explain a procedure in detail, but a participant will not have full knowledge of it until she or he has *experienced* it. Indeed, there is no guarantee that the investigators fully appreciate the procedure without undergoing the experience themselves. Given the necessary practice of deception in so much psychological research, it is hard to argue that full prior knowledge is guaranteed. And how much information should be given? Is the participant to receive a mini-lecture on previous research and the statistical robustness of research findings?

Again, the lack of competence of individuals may be the very reason why they are the subject of research (in research with young children, elderly people, infirm or handicapped people, or those in deep emotional distress). In the case of elderly people, some psychologists have too often assumed incompetence (Whitbourne & Hulicka, 1990) and thus sought the permission of others (say, superintendents of rest-homes) too readily.

Without considering the philosophical complexities of the notion of free will, we can appreciate what limits might be operating on voluntary choice: the status of the experimenter, our desire to please others, the desire not to let others down, the desire not to look foolish by insisting on withdrawing when an experiment is already underway. In other words, the social psychology of interpersonal relationships, and the behavioural notion that our actions are controlled by external reinforcement, argue against the truly voluntary action, in its vernacular sense, and apparently assumed in the Principles.

Neef et al. (1986), adopting a behavioural approach, suggest that psychological criteria for operationalizing consent can be devised, including formal tests of the would-be participants' ability to provide accurate descriptions of the experiment and what is involved, if necessary engaging in an iterative procedure until a criterion is reached.

Gale and Vetere (1987), in a critical ethical examination of their own research, confess that in their participant observation studies in family homes they sought the permission of parents (rather than children), did not appreciate the need to inform families of the full implications of publication, found it hard to disguise the identity of families in reports, changed their role inadvertently during the research from scientist to counsellor, and thus, in several ways, breached the full notion of voluntary consent. But the problems they encountered seem insoluble.

Several studies have explored participants' notions of consent, perceptions of deception, and what is acceptable in research, as a research enterprise in itself. For example Gerdes (1979) asked 655 college students of both genders for their reactions to 15 experiments involving various degrees of deception in which they had participated. She received an overwhelmingly positive reaction: respondents did not mind being deceived or having information withheld, and were willing to have a friend participate. In a study involving a factorial design in which stress, degree of deception, considerateness of experimenter, and degree of participation by the participant (active participation versus active role-play) were manipulated, Aitkenhead and Dordoy (1985) again showed that participants' reactions were predominantly positive. Michaels and Oetting (1979) gave participants two check-lists, one relating to personal and social benefits of research, and another specifying a range of stressful manipulations. They showed that their participants did not conduct a cost—benefit analysis; potential benefit did not influence their willingness to participate in a study, rather their primary concern was how much stress they might undergo. Finally, a study of cost—benefit analysis of students by Skinner, Berry, Biro, and Jackson (1991) showed that when the participants' view of the cost—benefit ratio is considered (rather than that of the researcher) subjects do conduct a cost—benefit analysis and are generally more willing to participate than the investigator's cost—benefit analysis predicts.

Studies such as these, stripping aside the possibility of participants' desire to give socially desirable responses (to please the investigator) seem to indicate that student populations are less concerned about the ethicality of some

1169

aspects of psychological research than are psychologists or learned societies. However, consideration of the distinctions drawn by Schlenker and Forsyth (1977) above will lead the reader to appreciate that for the deontological view, students' willingness to participate is irrelevant, since certain studies by virtue of their very nature will be seen to breach morality; for example, Baumrind (1971) in her critique of Milgram states: "Fundamental moral principles of reciprocity and justice are violated, when the research psychologist, using his position of trust, acts to deceive or degrade" (p. 890). Even broader moral issues might need to be considered in evaluating psychological research.

WIDER ISSUES: THE MORAL STATUS OF PSYCHOLOGY WITHIN SOCIETY

Special implications of socially sensitive research

Sieber and Stanley (1988) claim that some researchers have avoided conducting socially sensitive research through fear of the possible personal consequences, and they offer a taxonomy to guide the development of research proposals. They cite the study of Ceci, Peters, and Plotkin (1985), which showed that ethical review committees were twice as likely to reject hypothetical research proposals when they were socially sensitive (discrimination in job appointments) and that the grounds for rejection were largely in terms of potential political impact independent of the presence of ethical problems, such as deception. Sieber and Stanley (1988) list four stages of the research process at which ethical concerns arise: (1) formulation of the research question, (2) conduct of the research, (3) the research setting, and (4) the interpretation and application of findings.

The mere formulation of a research proposal, such as the measurement of ethnic differences in IQ or the genetic origins of violent dispositions can, they claim, raise ethical issues, even though the work is never carried out. Sieber and Stanley (1988) cite the impact of Freud's notion of women's sexual fantasies, anatomical inadequacy, and consequential penis envy (see Brennan, 1992), as still influencing social attitudes and social policy in spite of a 50-year lack of evidence to support the theory. Only public concern about the realities of child abuse has served to undermine the pervasiveness of Freud's views. Again, Sieber and Stanley (1988) point to the misleading ideas of Margaret Mead (1928, 1935, 1949) based on questionable methodology, as the source of the United States' sexual revolution. The failure, in the cultural revolution that her ideas promoted, to set limits on children's behaviour has, they claim, damaged a generation. Mead's notions of children's inherent goodness, combined with American optimism, served to promote and sustain particular views of child-rearing.

During the course of research, participants need to be protected, and the primary concern of ethical codes (as revealed in Table 1) is to focus on issues such as confidentiality, protection from harm, privacy, and deception. But as we saw earlier, information revealed by participants (say, concerning drugs, child abuse, intention to commit crime, or sexual behaviour in the context of AIDS) can create conflict between individual protection and the protection of society at large. In spite of a confidentiality undertaking, should a researcher seek to inform the sexual partner of an AIDS-carrying respondent? One consequence of such breaches of confidentiality could be the withdrawal of consent by particular groups and the undermining of future research, demonstrating yet again how one ethical principle fights against another.

In relation to institutional settings, Sieber and Stanley (1988) make the point that the organizational structure and atmosphere of the context of the research can have an impact on the consequences of publication. For example, publication of reading ages of children in particular schools, or productivity and absenteeism in particular commercial enterprises, could have effects on public reaction and the well-being of participants.

Finally, as a warning against lack of caution in relation to the application of research findings, Sieber and Stanley claim that the combination of new discoveries in genetics and mental testing in the first quarter of the twentieth century contributed to public policy which promoted compulsory sterilization of mentally retarded people, institutionalization, and restrictions on immigration. Several distinguished social scientists contributed, through their research, to such repressive policies.

Does psychology support the status quo?

Prilleltensky (1989), taking up the issue of social responsibility, argues that psychology, rather than promoting human welfare, might actually hinder social progress by protecting the status quo and the selfish interests of those in power in society. Psychologists, like everyone else, are conditioned intellectually by the belief systems of the culture and unconsciously support an implicit political ideology. Psychologists rarely challenge prevailing beliefs but often actively endorse them.

Such issues are crucially important in a century when psychology appears to be taking over many of the functions formerly supported by religion. But rather than criticise the social order, psychology tends to reinforce and ratify it. Prilleltensky (1989) claims that every organized community has a ruling group which seeks to perpetuate its position through various mechanisms including cultural mechanisms that sustain social order. Psychology has played a part in seeking the causes of action *within the individual* rather than within society at large. This dichotomy between individual and society gives an ideological benefit since the individual is seen as asocial and ahistorical, disconnected from wider sociopolitical contexts. Thus, solutions for human problems are seen within the person rather than in major social change. As examples of psychology's role in sustaining this view, Prilleltensky (1989) cites the testing movement, social Darwinism, individualism, male supremacy, political conformity, and the claim that technology (rather than moral reform) has the capacity to solve human problems. Most psychologists, he claims, are socialized to accept the belief systems of the ruling social class, since they themselves are members of it. Various rites of passage, within (say) the educational system, serve to socialize the individual and help to define self and society.

Again, the belief that psychology is scientifically neutral and value-free helps to represent it as depoliticized, which in turn helps to sustain the dominant ideology. Thus through the guise of objectivity, prescription is seen as description. Prilleltensky (1989) examines the assumptions underlying B. F. Skinner's (e.g., 1974) technology of behaviour and the concept of human engineering; the limitations for social change imposed by functionalism, the emphasis on the organism, and genetics; the naïve neglect of socio-economic factors by humanism, and Carl Rogers's (1951, 1970) apparent belief that the world is full of well-meaning therapists; and cognitivism's focus on perceived rather than external reality. He concludes that psychologists should be more active in entering the debate about what is "the good society"; by making people aware that what we take as facts are actually assumptions, we can educate them to think for themselves.

Research on ethnicity and gender and the failure of ethical codes to be sensitive to the reactions and feelings of minority groups offers an example of ways in which psychological research has served to sustain social roles in society.

Race and gender as psychological variables

Scarr (1988) argues that "cowardice about minority and gender differences will lead us nowhere" (p. 56). She claims that psychologists studying sensitive issues such as social class or child-rearing practices rarely highlight race or gender as an issue because of the potential consequences for the researcher, such issues being too controversial. Alternatively, having included different ethnic or gender groups in a research design to ensure representativeness of the sample, researchers might post hoc discover differences as an afterthought. Starr claims that both approaches are reprehensible. Psychologists, by ignoring minority groups, might fail to represent those groups fairly, identify their strengths, or create appropriate understandings. Rather than protect such groups, she claims, they damage them. What is needed is good-quality, value-free research, that tells us what society needs to do to help minority groups succeed.

For example, if research questions, influenced by prevailing values, focus on deficiencies or needs, then research outcomes will be negative. If particular gender styles or family arrangements are seen as healthy, then other gender styles or family arrangements (which might well interact with ethnicity) will be shown to be deficient. There is, she claims, relatively little research on the *strengths* of under-represented groups because of the implicit biases in psychologists' belief systems.

Condor (1991) argues that the BPS Principles, focusing on the relationship between experimenter and participant, neglect the possibility that the research might be offensive to particular groups. She cites published studies that use blatantly sexist material, for example, the use of pornographic films in the study of aggression in men. Male participants might not object to such material, but its very use is an insult to women. Denmark et al. (1988) provide a check-list for avoiding sexism in psychological research. Condor argues that such check-lists have actually had little impact, either on research itself, or on the role of journal editors as ethical gatekeepers.

Researchers on ageing have similarly been accused of sustaining stereotypes of elderly incompetence and aiding the stigmatization of elderly people. Schaie (1988) has identified a number of sources of ageist bias in research, and Whitbourne and Hulicka (1990) analyse the content of 139 textbooks, showing that the negative portrayal of elderly people as incompetent in several respects is common, in spite of much research to the contrary.

Thus issues concerning the role of psychologists in society at large, and claims that psychologists are not objective scientists but even pawns of the ruling classes, offer a much greater challenge to psychological ethics than do the more traditional issues of confidentiality, deception, or privacy, for they have major implications for psychology's influence on social policy and social change.

CONCLUSION

Ethical issues arise in psychology in five major ways: first, in the commitment to the pursuit of truth and the need for integrity in scientific research; second, in the uses (good or ill) to which the results of research might be put; third, in the way psychology projects an image of the person into broader social consciousness; fourth, in selective decisions to conduct research in particular ways and from particular viewpoints, thereby sustaining bias against stigmatized social groups; and finally, in the treatment of participants in the laboratory and other research settings. Learned societies have focused their concerns on the protection of participants, but there is an urgent need to consider the broader issues.

ACKNOWLEDGEMENTS

I wish to thank the following colleagues, who drew my attention to relevant published material for the preparation of this chapter: Mr Richard Hastings, Dr Stephen MacKeith, Dr Don Marcer, Dr Sheila Payne, and Professor Bob Remington.

FURTHER READING

American Psychological Association (1982). *Ethical principles in the conduct of research with human participants*. Washington, DC: APA.

British Psychological Society (1991). *Code of conduct, ethical principles and guidelines*. Leicester: BPS.

Bulmer, M. (Ed.) (1982). *Social research ethics*. London: Macmillan.

Fairbairn, S., & Fairbairn, G. (Eds) (1987). *Psychology, ethics and change*. London: Routledge & Kegan Paul.

Prilleltensky, I. (1989). Psychology and the status quo. *American Psychologist, 44*, 795–802.

REFERENCES

Aitkenhead, M., & Dordoy, J. (1983). Research on the ethics of research. *Bulletin of the British Psychological Society, 36*, 315–318.

Aitkenhead, M., & Dordoy, J. (1985). What the subjects have to say. *British Journal of Social Psychology, 24*, 293–305.

American Psychological Association (1982). *Ethical principles in the conduct of research with human participants*. Washington, DC: APA.

American Psychological Association (1990). Ethical principles of psychologists (amended 2 June 1989). *American Psychologist, 45*, 390–395.

Appelbaum, P. S., & Rosenbaum, A. (1989). *Tarasoff* and the researcher: Does the duty to protect apply in the research setting? *American Psychologist, 44*, 885–894.

Bateson, P. (1986). When to experiment on animals. *New Scientist, 109*, 30–32.

Baumrind, D. (1964). Some thoughts on the ethics of research after reading Milgram's "Behavioral Study of Obedience". *American Psychologist, 19*, 4211–4223.

Baumrind, D. (1971). Principles of ethical conduct in the treatment of subjects: Reaction to the draft report of the committee on ethical standards in psychological research. *American Psychologist, 26*, 887–896.

Brennan, T. (1992). *The interpretation of the flesh: Freud and femininity*. London: Routledge.

British Psychological Society (1990). Ethical principles for conducting research with human participants. *The Psychologist, 3*, 270–272.

British Psychological Society (1991). *Code of conduct, ethical principles and guidelines*. Leicester: BPS.

Ceci, C. J., Peters, D., & Plotkin, J. (1985). Human subjects review, personal values, and the regulation of social science research. *American Psychologist, 40*, 994–1002.

Condor, S. (1991). Sexism in psychological research: A brief note. *Feminism & Psychology, 1*, 430–434.

Denmark, F., Russo, N. F., Frieze, I. H., & Sechzer, J. A. (1988). Guidelines for avoiding sexism in psychological research: A report of the ad hoc committee on nonsexist research. *American Psychologist, 43*, 582–585.

Experimental Psychology Society (1986). *The use of animals for research by psychologists*, London: EPS.

Fletcher, R. (1991). *Science, ideology and the media: The Cyril Burt scandal.* London: Transaction.

Gale, A. (1990). Applying psychology to the psychology degree: Pass with first class honours, or miserable failure? *The Psychologist, 3,* 483–488.

Gale, A., & Chapman, A. J. (1984). The nature of applied psychology. In A. Gale & A. J. Chapman (Eds) *Psychology and social problems: An introduction to applied psychology* (pp. 1–26). Chichester: Wiley.

Gale, A., & Vetere, A. (1987). Ethical issues in the study of family life. In A. Vetere & A. Gale (Eds) *Ecological studies of family life* (pp. 79–86). Chichester: Wiley.

Gerdes, E. P. (1979). College students' reactions to social psychological experiments involving deception. *Journal of Social Psychology, 107,* 99–110.

Gray, J. A. (1987). The ethics and politics of animal experimentation. In H. Beloff & A. M. Colman (Eds) *Psychology survey 6* (pp. 218–233). Leicester: British Psychological Society.

Hearnshaw, L. S. (1979). *Cyril Burt: Psychologist.* London: Hodder & Stoughton.

Herzog, H. A. Jr (1988). The moral status of mice. *American Psychologist, 43,* 473–474.

Joynson, R. B. (1989). *The Burt affair.* London: Routledge.

Kelman, H. C. (1967). Human use of human subjects: The problem of deception in social psychological experiments. *Psychological Bulletin, 67,* 1–11.

Mead, M. (1928). *Coming of age in Samoa: A psychological study of primitive youth for western civilization.* New York: Morrow.

Mead, M. (1935). *Sex and temperament in three primitive societies.* New York: Morrow.

Mead, M. (1949). *Male and female.* New York: Morrow.

Melton, G. B., & Gray, J. N. (1988). Ethical dilemmas in AIDS research: Individual privacy and public health. *American Psychologist, 43,* 60–64.

Michaels, T. F., & Oetting, E. R. (1979). The informed consent dilemma: An empirical approach. *Journal of Social Psychology, 109,* 223–230.

Milgram, S. (1963). Behavioral study of obedience. *Journal of Abnormal and Social Psychology, 67,* 371–378.

Milgram, S. (1977). Ethical issues in the study of obedience. In S. Milgram (Ed.) *The individual in the social world* (pp. 188–199). Reading, MA: Addison-Wesley.

Miller, N. E. (1985). The value of behavioral research on animals. *American Psychologist, 40,* 423–440.

Mulvey, E. P., & Phelps, P. (1988). Ethical balances in juvenile justice research and practice. *American Psychologist, 43,* 669.

Neef, N. A., Iwata, B. A., & Page, T. J. (1986). Ethical standards in behavioral research: A historical analysis and review of publication practices. In A. Poling & R. W. Fuqua (Eds) *Research methods in applied behavior analysis: Issues and advances* (pp. 233–263). New York: Plenum.

Prilleltensky, I. (1989). Psychology and the status quo. *American Psychologist, 44,* 795–802.

Rogers, C. R. (1951). *Client-centred therapy.* Boston, MA: Houghton Mifflin.

Rogers, C. R. (1970). *Carl Rogers on encounter groups.* New York: Harper & Row.

Rollin, B. E. (1985). The moral status of research animals in psychology. *American Psychologist, 40,* 920–926.

Scarr, S. (1988). Race and gender as psychological variables: Social and ethical issues. *American Psychologist, 43,* 56–59.

Schaie, K. W. (1988). Ageism in psychological research. *American Psychologist*, *43*, 179–183.

Schlenker, B. R., & Forsyth, D. R. (1977). On the ethics of psychological research. *Journal of Experimental Social Psychology*, *13*, 369–396.

Schultz, D. P. (1969). The human subject in psychological research. *Psychological Bulletin*, *72*, 214–228.

Sieber, J. E., & Stanley, B. (1988). Ethical and professional dimensions of socially sensitive research. *American Psychologist*, *43*, 49–55.

Silverman, I. (1977). *The human subject in the psychological laboratory*. New York: Pergamon.

Skinner, B. F. (1974). *About behaviorism*. New York: Alfred A. Knopf.

Skinner, L. J., Berry, K. K., Biro, M., & Jackson, T. (1991). Research ethicality: The perceptions of participants and their participation willingness. *Current Psychology: Research & Reviews*, *10*, 79–91.

Wadeley, A. (1991). *Ethics in psychological research and practice*. Leicester: British Psychological Society.

Whitbourne, S. K., & Hulicka, I. M. (1990). Ageism in undergraduate psychology texts. *American Psychologist*, *45*, 1127–1136.

Zimbardo, P. G. (1973). On the ethics on intervention in human psychological research: With special reference to the Stanford prison experiment. *Cognition*, *2*, 243–256.

13
THE PROFESSIONS OF PSYCHOLOGY

INTRODUCTION

Alongside the academic discipline of psychology are a number of associated practices and professions, the most important of which are discussed in this final section. The major professions of psychology are discussed in chapters 13.1, 13.2, 13.3, and 13.4, while chapter 13.5 deals with a practice that is closely associated with psychology but is not one of its recognized professions – psychoanalysis.

In chapter 13.1 Graham E. Powell introduces the professions of clinical and counselling psychology, which (as he points out) are closely related to each other. He outlines the ideas behind more than a dozen of the main approaches to psychotherapy or counselling including behaviour therapy and cognitive behaviour modification (see also chapter 5.2, Donald M. Baer, on applied behaviour analysis), attributional approaches (see also chapter 9.3, David J. Schneider, on attribution and social cognition), and Freudian and post-Freudian theories (see also chapter 13.5 on psychoanalysis). Powell also outlines the main problems that clinical and counselling psychologists deal with, and he concludes by commenting on several professional issues. For more detail about mental disorders see section 10 on abnormal psychology; for more on social skills deficits and training see chapter 5.5 (Michael Argyle).

In chapter 13.2 David Fontana discusses educational and school psychology, which are concerned with the study of psychological factors that affect the learning process and the development and application of psychological methods to improve that process. Fontana outlines the historical development of educational/school psychology and discusses its content under the headings "What is to be learned?" "Who is to learn it?" "How is it to be learned?"

In chapter 13.3 Wendy Hollway introduces industrial (occupational) and organizational psychology. There is some confusion over terminology in these fields, and Hollway prefers to subsume them all under the umbrella of "work psychology". This chapter covers psychological contributions to scientific management and the task idea, human factors, selection psychology, and human relations.

Chapter 13.4, by Clive R. Hollin, is devoted to forensic (criminological) psychology, which includes psychological applications to all aspects of crime and punishment. Hollin's wide-ranging review covers psychological aspects of courtroom evidence, theories of criminal behaviour, crime prevention, and offender rehabilitation. For a slightly different perspective on some of the issues raised by Hollin, see chapter 11.4, in which Robert T. Croyle and Elizabeth F. Loftus examine psychology and the law from a more academic perspective.

Finally, chapter 13.5, by Peter Fonagy, is on psychoanalysis. This is not one of the professions of psychology, and psychoanalysts do not necessarily have degrees in psychology, but it is a practice that is obviously very closely related to psychology. Fonagy, who is trained as both a psychologist and a psychoanalyst, traces the development of psychoanalytic theory and post-Freudian psychoanalysis before describing the actual procedure of full psychoanalysis and psychoanalytic psychotherapy. For a detailed discussion of Freudian theories of personality, see chapter 7.4 (Richard Stevens).

A.M.C.

13.1

CLINICAL AND COUNSELLING PSYCHOLOGY

Graham E. Powell
University of Surrey, England

Models and approaches	Problems and their management
Behaviourism and behaviour therapy	The definition of a problem
Cognitive behaviour modification cognitive therapy	Stress
	Anxiety and panic
	Phobias
	Obsessions and compulsions
Rational-emotive therapy	Depression
Social learning theory	Interpersonal problems
Attributional approaches	Marital and relationship problems
Personal construct theory	
Person- or client-centred therapy	Health problems
	Contribution to different client groups
Gestalt therapy	**Professional issues**
Existential therapy	Range of roles
Systems approaches	Training
Freudian theory	Code of conduct
Post-Freudian developments	**Further reading**
Eclecticism	**References**
Evaluation of models	

Clinical and counselling psychology are the two professional branches of the discipline of psychology which together form a seamless robe comprising the application of psychological knowledge to the maintenance of mental and physical health and the generation of psychological well-being. They overlap to the extent that they both draw on the same sources, namely the empirical knowledge generated by scientific studies and research, and the theoretical knowledge as embodied in a wide range of principles, models, and approaches. They both espouse the scientist-practitioner model of helping people. This means that clinical and counselling psychologists are trained in both scientific method (for example, statistics, research design, evaluation) and in practical skills (for example, treatment and assessment methods and professional skills). It also implies that a broadly scientific approach is taken with clients: making objective observations, collecting the required information, formulating a psychological explanation for the problems at hand, developing an approach to dealing with the problem, and monitoring progress carefully, revising ideas as necessary in the light of progress and new developments (Brammer, Shostrom, & Abrego, 1989). However, the emphases of clinical and counselling psychology are different. Clinical psychology has a longer professional history, and has its roots in the development of psychometric assessment methods and the management of mental illness, while counselling psychology has developed out of the need for people to make decisions about their problems and to make psychological growth in terms of their abilities to help themselves. I shall make no further attempt to distinguish the two, and will concentrate on how psychology as a whole is used to help people with behavioural, cognitive or emotional difficulties.

The plan of this chapter is to divide the field, first, by the models and approaches that are used to guide the helping process – such theories provide a framework for observation, formulation, and treatment, and can be developed to advance fundamental knowledge – and second, by the commonest problems presented by clients. Finally, I shall mention training and professional issues.

MODELS AND APPROACHES

Behaviourism and behaviour therapy

The roots of behaviourism are in operant conditioning, in which behaviour is shaped by the positive and negative rewards or reinforcements that follow it, and classical conditioning, in which psychophysiological responses such as anxiety become associated with stimuli in the environment that happen to be around when this response is experienced (see Bandura, 1969). Treatment begins with an analysis of what stimuli trigger the behaviour that is the problem, and what consequences follow from emitting this behaviour. The treatments themselves often stem directly from the work of Skinner (1974) on how rats learn to press a lever for food, and Pavlov's (1927) on how dogs can come to salivate to the sound of a bell. If the client wishes to strengthen a behaviour, then positive reinforcement can be arranged for it. If new behaviours are to be learned, they can be "shaped up" by expecting and rewarding closer and closer approximations and by arranging for the right environmental cues or triggers to be present. New behaviour can also be learned by having it modelled by others, and all new behaviours can be maintained by ensuring that some intermittent reinforcement continues. Inappropriate behaviour can be eliminated by having the person keep doing it until sated, by removing any positive reinforcement, or by arranging for an incompatible behaviour to be elicited by the triggering stimuli. Emotional "behaviour" can be modified by deconditioning, breaking the association that has been built up between, say, anxiety and the presence of thunder. This is known as desensitization. Conversely, a negative emotion, such as disgust, can be deliberately conditioned to something that is liked too much, perhaps alcohol. This is known as sensitization.

Behaviour therapy rapidly won many advocates because of its clarity of model and scientific approach, and throughout the 1960s empirical studies emerged on treating phobias, inability to relax, inappropriate sexual attractions, sexual problems, obsessions, enuresis, disruptive behaviour, deficits in self-help skills, problems in rehabilitation, and so forth. However, this impressive contribution to the skills of the clinician or counsellor could not disguise its limitations. It tended to be mechanistically applied; there were still many treatment failures, often to do with cognitive aspects such as motivation; it had little success with several important and common problems, especially depression; and models of learning taking over from those of Skinner and Pavlov were explicitly beginning to recognize cognitive factors. For example, the clients' expectations or beliefs about reward contingencies are often just as important as the actual contingencies themselves. Behaviourism, then, has been a tremendous spur but is somewhat limited in application and is not a comprehensive theory of human behaviour. Later cognitive and cognitive-behavioural approaches developed, and some of them will be discussed next.

Cognitive behaviour modification

Meichenbaum (1977) developed and investigated the theme that how you talk to yourself is crucial in determining both behaviour and feelings. Since self-guiding speech directs much of what we do, it becomes an appropriate target for assessment and treatment. The general strategy is to identify dysfunctional self-speech, for example, "I knew I would never do it right anyway", and to teach adaptive strategies, for example, "It's not going well, but I can see what the problem is and I must work out a plan to solve it". Initially, the client practises self-speech aloud and then silently until it is habitual. Self-praising statements are also practised. Applications have included anger control, stress management, coping with anxiety, and social skills.

Cognitive therapy

Beck and his colleagues (Beck, Rush, Shaw, & Emery, 1977) have extensively studied the influence on behaviour and emotions of what people think and say about themselves and the world. They have found that problems are frequently associated with warped or erroneous thinking. Such thoughts must be identified and reformulated, and this changes the way that stimuli in the environment are perceived, interpreted, and ultimately reacted to. In other words, this approach concerns the cognitive interface between stimulus and response that was not acknowledged in classic behaviourism. In treatment, the client learns that the perception of reality is different from reality and that such perceptions are often based on faulty thinking. The client tries to observe his or her own thoughts objectively and identifies distortions in thinking, such as over-reactions, over-generalizations, and a failure to take into account all the relevant information. The client then practises arguing against and countering these distortions, putting it in writing first and practising until it becomes habitual. The technique shows particular promise in relation to depression and anxiety disorder, and is generating a good deal of empirical research.

Rational-emotive therapy

Ellis (Ellis & Whitely, 1979) introduced logic and reason into counselling in quite an extreme way. He pointed out that people hold beliefs that cause problems and that thinking about problems is often muddled. He set out to make people appreciate what assumptions or rules about life they were making and to rationally consider whether other assumptions or rules were more logical and helpful in terms of adjustment. Common irrational ideas or values are that it is essential to be loved by everyone; that a person must be perfectly competent; that it is easier to avoid difficulties than to face them; and that the influence of past events are the determinants of present behaviour and cannot be eradicated. Rational-emotive therapy (RET) is a process of detection and reeducation, with dispute and discussion of how such beliefs are contributing to a problem and whether such beliefs should not be rethought and changed. As with cognitive therapy, with which RET plainly overlaps, this method has been particularly examined in relation to depression and anxiety, but it is also relevant to many quality-of-life issues, such as adjusting to role change during the lifespan and recurrent difficulties in personal relationships.

Social learning theory

Bandura (1986) developed a model of behaviour centred on the finding that people can learn many complex skills through observation alone, that is, by a process of modelling, rather than by overt practice. He therefore stressed the cognitive mediation of learning in which people do not learn by piecemeal trial and error, but acquire whole patterns which, when emitted in their entirety, may then be subject to reinforcement – for example the abused child who may then abuse as an adult. Learning is taken to be specific to situations, and so the role of traits in determining behaviour is seen to be much less than normally believed. However, people can *believe* in cross-situational consistency and this can cause problems. This is especially important in relation to "self-efficacy", which is perceived competence to be able to do something. Clients often over-generalize, and if their confidence or competence in just one area is challenged or undermined, they often feel incompetent across the board and self-evaluations become negative. In therapy, the perception of self-efficacy is defined and discussed and the client tries to develop skills, normally by a series of practice steps, in those areas where self-efficacy is judged lowest. These ideas have for the most part been incorporated into related therapies rather than standing alone as a therapy, and have helped develop the experimental literature.

Attributional approaches

Attribution theory (Jones et al., 1972) stems from the research literature on how people explain their own and others' behaviour. Attributions of the same event may differ between people. If two people receive an invitation to a party, one may see it as a reflection of friendship, and the other may feel invited out of duty or politeness. Some people may believe that they failed an exam because it was very hard, others because they are useless. Misattributions can cause problems and misunderstandings, especially if they cause people to deny their own abilities and qualities, and this is especially true in the case of depression and social anxiety. Therapy consists of identifying the clients' explanations and changing dysfunctional ones, by a consideration of alternative explanations. These ideas have been incorporated into several related therapies, particularly cognitive therapy and rational-emotive therapy.

Personal construct theory

Kelly (1955) developed a highly articulated and coherent theory of personality, called personal construct theory (PCT), which has generated a large and growing body of empirical literature. The central notion is that people make sense of the world by judging or "construing" events on a set of internal, bipolar, cognitive "constructs" or dimensions, such as *this will be stressful for me* versus *I will be able to relax*, or *upsetting* versus *irrelevant to me emotionally*. This helps people anticipate subsequent events and to adjust their behaviour accordingly, or to react accordingly. Every individual has a different set of constructs because each has had different experiences. Individuals will also vary in the number of constructs they have, how they are organised, the degree to which they are shared with other people, and the ease with which they can be modified. Problems in life often stem from a mis-construing of events, so events might seem threatening when they should not be, and there may be distressing misunderstandings of other people, especially partners. Problems also arise when new events come along that cannot easily be construed or when our most basic constructs are called into question. Therapy consists of changing troublesome construct systems. The constructs are elicited and the construing of key events defined. The construct system is thus opened up to discussion and also to validation by careful observation of events from then on. PCT has a wide range of application including couple counselling, specific anxieties, social skills problems, coping with stammering and other stigma, and preparing for role transitions.

Having dealt with the main cognitive-behavioural approaches, we shall turn to three "humanist" approaches which aim primarily to help people get in touch with themselves and to acknowledge their true feelings. We shall then tackle systems approaches, followed by Freudian and related models.

Person- or client-centred therapy

Rogers (1942) began an influential movement in which the self-generated and self-propelled growth of the individual is given paramount importance and respect. The therapist does not judge or condemn the clients' beliefs or plans, does not give specific advice or instruction, and does not give advice on how in general to live. The client, not the therapist, develops the treatment plan, the direction of the dialogue comes from the client, and it is not the therapist who interprets the client's experience. The therapist tries to create an atmosphere of non-possessive warmth, accurate empathy, and genuineness, and these three aspects of the relationship have generated a variety of empirical research into the psychotherapeutic process (Truax & Carkhuff, 1967). Warmth involves acceptance and respect and caring to help build client trust, motivation, and willingness to communicate. Empathy exists when therapists can decentre or see things from the client's perspective, setting aside their own feelings and understanding what the client would be experiencing. These feelings are reflected back to the client who comes to feel understood and to develop self-understanding. Genuineness implies honesty, openness, and a degree of self-disclosure, which can give feedback to clients on what effect their behaviour is having on another person, the therapist. By the end of the therapy, it is hoped that the client will be more open to their experiences and less defensive, be more realistic in perceiving events and in self-perception, have a more positive self-regard, and be more effective at independent problem solving.

Gestalt therapy

Perls (1973) encapsulated a tradition of analysis of the here-and-now and the sharing of that experience in a therapeutic relationship. The goal is to promote growth by increasing awareness and insight, and in this there are obvious similarities to client-centred therapy. Gestalt therapy involves exploration with the therapist providing direct experience. Three principles of therapy have been described. "I and thou" implies an open, shared therapeutic climate, "what and how" refers to exercises to expand the clients' experiences, and "here and now" reinforces the orientation of the therapy to present, actual experience. Gestalt approaches have not been subject to any great amount of empirical research, which is in part a consequence of the ethos of the movement and the lack of precision in specifying models and methods. But some of the techniques are appealing, for example the empty chair technique in which the client switches between two chairs as he or she role-plays both sides of an argument, and the notion of unfinished business (that is, an incomplete Gestalt) is in common parlance.

Existential therapy

This is rooted in the philosophy of existentialism, and is an approach more than a specific therapy, although it is often described as such. The notion of phenomenology, from which existentialism developed, is that all knowledge is subjective and that the client has to clear the path of accurate perception by examining preconceptions and assumptions, to consider things in fresh ways. The work of Laing (1974) in attempting to understand schizophrenia is an example of how the existential perspective can lead to a new way of looking at old problems. However, it is a diffuse and fragmented movement which has not resulted as yet in much empirical research, or even systematic description and discussion of methods.

Systems approaches

There is no one model here but a widely endorsed movement which emphasizes the context of the behaviour as an explanation or cause, whereas many other approaches emphasize individuals themselves as responsible for their own behaviour. The relationship system of the client (for example, family, friends, working colleagues) is examined and the meaning or importance of the problem behaviour for the relevant system drawn out. For example, a child's school refusal may be instrumental in preventing the parents from splitting up. There is an inter-generational approach which suggests that the origin of difficulties lies with the previous generation and that trends are passed on and elaborated until emerging as a real problem. Structural therapies focus on family problems and try to help a family develop an internal structure or organization, involving boundary definition, that allows for both a sense of belonging and individuation. Strategic therapy focuses on the problem as the unit to be treated and how a system comes to be organized about a problem, often reinforcing it in the process. Much of the empirical work in this field has been with the families of children presenting problems, and a range of studies show how useful this approach can be (Minuchin & Fishman, 1981).

Freudian theory

Freud (1943) developed a model of personality which dramatically changed the way that a whole society thought about people, their behaviour, and their problems.

Freud described how the mind or psyche is divided metaphorically into the id (unconscious energy for the mind comprising all the basic drives such as urges for affection, warmth, food and sex, present from birth), the ego (developing later in the first year of life and dealing with reality), and the superego (the personality including morals, standards, and conscience). The interplay between these three is referred to as psychodynamics. For example, the id operates on a pleasure principle, wanting immediate gratification of any unmet need, but the ego realises that this is not the most effective way of dealing with reality and planning life. In developing a personality structure, a person goes through various stages to do with what gratifies the id. These are the oral stage (sucking and feeding), anal stage (elimination and retention), phallic stage (around age 5–6 years, involving stimulation of the genitalia), latency period (reduced interest in sex until about 12 years old), and genital stage (adult heterosexual interest).

Problems can arise in a variety of ways. For example, development can become "stuck" or fixated at a certain stage if the appropriate balance is not achieved between what the id wants and what the environment can provide. Another example of problems occurring is neurotic anxiety, which stems from the blockage of unconscious impulses. The ego can defend against feeling this anxiety by various mechanisms such as repression (pushing impulses into the unconscious), projection (perceiving the emotion as existing in other people rather than oneself), displacement (redirecting the emotion into something acceptable), and rationalization (inventing an acceptable reason for the emotion).

The classic therapy, psychoanalysis, is concerned with how the ego reacts with anxiety when a repressed impulse pushes for expression. It can be seen that such anxiety can be the effect of conflicts from a long time previously that were repressed rather than solved. The patient may be asked to free associate, and the chain of such associations or blocks to saying certain things gives clues to sensitivities and repressed areas. Dreams may be analysed, because during sleep the defence of the ego is relaxed and repressed ma   ial may emerge. The therapist will offer interpretations of associations, dreams, behaviour, and resistance to therapy, in the hope of lifting repression and thereby stimulating insight, understanding, and adjustment. Healthy impulses are to be freed and the superego is to encourage humane and not punitive standards.

Particular interpretation is made of transference, which occurs when attitudes and feelings from an earlier life situation are apparent in the client's behaviour towards the therapist in either a positive or negative direction (for example, either friendliness, love, and affection, or hostility and anger). The client is helped to see that relationships, in this case with the therapist, are being influenced unduly by issues that are not now pertinent. (Sometimes there is counter-transference, when the therapist transfers elements from his or her past on to the analytic relationship with the client, and so therapists are trained to be aware of this and to avoid it.)

Freud's ideas and methods have drawn criticism from both within the movement (overemphasis on the id and lack of recognition of the role of the ego; relative balance of instincts versus sociocultural factors; and an overemphasis of sexuality) and from scientific psychologists (limited range of application of treatments; based on a small and biased sample of people; ill-defined and diffuse methods; outcomes that are very difficult to define or operationalize). But no one denies the brilliance of debate that Freud stimulated.

Post-Freudian developments

Jung (1982) in his "analytical psychology" de-emphasized the sexual nature of the libido and saw it as representing a more general biological force, and introduced the concept of the "collective unconscious" in addition to our own personal unconscious. This is the repository of people's experiences over the centuries.

Adler (1929) developed "individual psychology". In doing so he attributed less of a role to instincts and developed the importance and relevance of striving for superiority, dominance, and mastery, all in a manner that is compatible with the needs of society and the social good.

Erickson (1959) examined closely how the ego developed an identity through the process of psychosocial development. Instead of seeing development as virtually ending early in life, he espoused a "lifespan development psychology", in which people grow psychologically to the moment of death.

An important psychodynamic development since Freud has been object relations therapy. This concerns past interpersonal relationships and how childhood experience can unconsciously determine adult patterns of behaviour. Patterns of living and lifestyle are formed by early relationships and repeated in many variations through life. The task of the therapist is to uncover this process and thereby encourage change in the repeating pattern of living, hopefully to a less problematic one (Eagle, 1984; Klein, 1975).

Eclecticism

Eclecticism is not a theory but a way of working which involves drawing on aspects from different models. It is productive if it encourages awareness of a variety of processes, open-mindedness, a critical appreciation of what therapeutic tools are available, and a desire to fit the treatment to the client, rather than vice versa. It is poor practice if it stems from an unwillingness or inability to make discriminations between the quality, applicability, and efficacy of methods, or from a naïve belief that all approaches are equal, or if different approaches are used without a genuine attempt to integrate them.

Evaluation of models

All models and approaches should be examined and evaluated for strength and weakness in order for them to improve and grow. Good models will have clearly stated principles which can be identified sufficiently well to be challenged; basic concepts should be defined and unambiguous; the range of applicability will be made explicit; methods and techniques will be defined sufficiently well to be understood and acquired by others; a body of empirical research will build up to identify the model as valuable in terms of its ability to predict and explain human behaviour and cognition; a similar body of empirical research will be established as regards efficacy of outcome (Smith, Glass, & Miller 1980). Poor models will have diffuse and ambiguous principles difficult to pin down sufficiently well to challenge; will have difficulty in specifying the essential skills to be taught to potential therapists; methods and techniques will seem ad hoc; explanatory concepts will be unreasonable or weak; there may be internal inconsistencies in the model as a whole; and a body of empirical data will not have been stimulated, especially in relation to outcome or efficacy (Garfield & Bergin, 1986). There is widespread support for the effectiveness of the behaviour therapies and good support for the effectiveness, range of applicability, and general usefulness of some of the cognitive-behavioural methods, especially rational-emotive therapy. There is a burgeoning research interest in cognitive therapy, which has made a special name for itself in regard to depression, and deservedly so. In the systems area, the structural models have been particularly well supported. Psychodynamic (Freudian and post-Freudian) therapies for a long time were removed from traditional scientific evaluation, but this is now changing (Horowitz, 1988) and one senses that important areas of efficacy will emerge. Of the humanistic approaches, client-centred therapy stands out in terms of supporting research.

PROBLEMS AND THEIR MANAGEMENT

The definition of a problem

There is no straightforward dividing line between concepts such as "normal–abnormal", "functional–dysfunctional", or "problematic–problem free". For example, one definition of abnormal is statistical, when the behaviour or capacity in question is rare (for example, those with an uncommonly low IQ); another is to do with suffering, so that something is abnormal if it involves marked personal distress, such as in bereavement; another definition is to do with disability, such as the effect of substance abuse on work performance; a further definition concerns whether the behaviour violates a social norm, such as the sociopath's callousness towards others. In psychiatry, abnormalities and problems are defined in the American Psychiatric Association's *Diagnostic and Statistical Manual of Mental Disorders* (3rd edition, revised), often referred to simply as DSM-III-R (American Psychiatric Association, 1987). It is a useful summary of the most serious problems that people face. There are five dimensions or axes.

Axis I covers clinical syndromes: disruptive behaviour disorders; anxiety disorders of childhood or adolescence; eating disorders; gender identity disorders; tic disorders; elimination disorders; speech disorders not elsewhere classified; other disorders of infancy, childhood, or adolescence; dementia arising in the senium and presenium; psychoactive substance-induced organic mental disorders; organic mental disorders associated with physical disorders; psychoactive substance use disorders; schizophrenia; delusional (paranoid) disorder; psychotic disorders not elsewhere classified; mood disorders; anxiety disorders; somatoform disorders; dissociative disorders; sexual disorders; sleep disorders; factitious disorders; impulse control disorders not classified elsewhere; adjustment disorder; psychological factors affecting physical condition.

Axis II covers developmental and personality disorders: mental retardation; pervasive developmental disorder; specific developmental disorders; other developmental disorders; personality disorders (Cluster A, paranoid, schizoid, schizotypal; Cluster B, antisocial, borderline, histrionic, narcissistic; Cluster C, avoidant, dependent, obsessive compulsive, passive aggressive).

On Axis III are the physical conditions and disorders. Axis IV and V are for research purposes, and are a severity scale and global functioning scale respectively.

There are a number of substantial criticisms of DSM-III-R. For example, words such as "elevated" or "excessive" are not defined and are a judgement on the part of the therapist; there seems to be little empirical evidence for grouping certain symptoms together into a "syndrome"; and the reliability and validity of the categories is generally unknown or uncertain. From a psychological perspective, it has been argued that one should measure symptoms and then see which ones cluster together to form syndromes, and not start with the premise that particular syndromes exist. None the less, DSM-III-R has provided a much-needed common and for the most part neutral language with which to describe problems and to carry out preliminary differential diagnosis. It is then a matter for the psychologist to provide a psychological explanation for the specific problems of the specific patient.

Some of the common ways of treating particular types of problems will now be described.

Stress

When stressed, we prepare our bodies for fight or flight. Powerful stimulants such as adrenalin are released into the bloodstream, along with thyroid hormones to increase metabolism and cholesterol to boost energy. These chemicals, if released on a long-term basis, can cause heart disease and strokes, exhaustion, weight loss, and hardening of the arteries – good reasons to cope with stress effectively. Other reasons are to do with our performance, in that with chronic stress, concentration and attention decrease, memory and speed of thinking become patchy, error rates increase, long-term planning deteriorates, and thinking becomes more confused and irrational (Powell & Enright, 1990). In addition, physical tension increases, personality changes, people feel depressed and helpless, self-esteem falls, interests diminish, sleep is disrupted, drug abuse rises, and people stop trying to solve the fundamental problems. The most stressful sorts of experiences are such things as death of a spouse, divorce or separation, and personal injury or illness. Medium stresses are taking on a major mortgage, changing one's line of work, or having more arguments with one's spouse. Lower level stresses are caused by having a change in sleeping habits, social activities, or vacations. Personality is also important. Particularly vulnerable to self-induced stress are people with Type A behaviours – those who feel an intense sense of time urgency, inappropriate hostility, and aggression, always try to do two things at once, and who try to achieve goals without proper planning.

A variety of methods are helpful. Insight into the situation is mandatory; the individual must recognize the emotional and behavioural patterns as a reaction to stress, and the precise stresses have to be identified, not always an easy matter if the client is "denying" certain sources of stress. A plan has to be made about how to tackle each of the stresses, perhaps by using a client-centred approach to reinforce the clients themselves as the main agents of change. Solutions to some problems may need other kinds of help. For example, if one of the sources of stress is taking on too much work, the client may need assertion training to learn to say "no". If another source of stress is taking on a new financial responsibility, then a cognitive approach could be taken to turn dysfunctional thoughts ("I could be bankrupt tomorrow") into more realistic ones ("This new business loan has been very well planned and there are many things I can do to help the expansion succeed"). A self-instruction approach can be used to cope with the immediate unpleasant emotional feelings ("I have coped with this sort of problem before", "If I can look the problem in the eye it will help", "I know I am feeling on the edge, but I have made sensible plans to improve the situation"). Finally, the client may well have some difficult decision to make about setting clear life goals and priorities.

Anxiety and panic

There are two main kinds of anxiety state (Barlow, Blanchard, Vermilyea, Vermilyea, & Di Nardo, 1986). First, when the main problem is one of panic attacks, there is a sudden overwhelming feeling of apprehension and fear coupled with a wide variety of intense physical distress symptoms such as palpitations, trembling, and dizziness, which often make clients feel that they are dying or going mad. Second, when there is excessive anxiety and worry in general, a variety of chronic feelings such as fatiguability, insomnia, irritability, and restlessness develop. In anxiety the individual systematically overestimates the danger or difficulty of a situation, and there are many negative automatic thoughts and dysfunctional assumptions and rules. For example, with generalized anxiety, people who experience anxiety in social situations may say very little for fear of being ridiculed, but this makes them outsiders, reinforcing their belief that they are likely to be rejected. Dysfunctional rules, such as "Everything must be done perfectly or I will fail" or "Anyone who criticizes me dislikes me", are common. In panic disorders, the main dysfunctional element is the tendency to interpret bodily sensation in a catastrophic fashion. For example, feeling breathless after walking fast to make an appointment on time becomes a palpitation signalling an imminent heart attack, or a racing of thoughts becomes imminent total loss of mental control. The first step in treatment is to develop an objective insight into these processes, often by taking careful notes about what one is thinking or feeling when anxious or when about to panic, or by discussing a recent experience in detail.

The dysfunctional beliefs identified can then be challenged, by gauging the evidence for the thought, asking how another person would feel, asking whether all the facts have been taken into account, asking whether one is thinking in an all-or-none manner, gauging whether the degree of control is being underestimated, considering whether one is overestimating the negative consequences, or asking whether one is underestimating the skills and problem-solving abilities that can be brought to bear. Distraction techniques can also be used, for example concentrating on actual performance rather than the associated negative thoughts, and there can be behavioural experiments, such as hyperventilating to produce dizziness to prove this does not cause a heart attack. More behavioural methods can be used to reduce avoidant behaviour, gradually reintroducing clients into feared situations in a calm way to break up the association with anxiety. This technique is called desensitization.

Phobias

Desensitization is worth describing in some detail as it is one of the most widely applied and effective of behavioural methods (Du Pont, 1982). The main types of phobia are simple (for example, irrational fear of blood, heights), social (for example, irrational fear of negative evaluation, feelings of rejection), or agoraphobia (for example, irrational fear of being trapped or confined, being far from home). The symptoms include marked avoidance of the feared situations, anxiety, or even panic when actually in them, and dysfunctional beliefs about what there is to worry about. The aim in desensitization is to unlearn the association between the situation and anxiety, by a series of graded exposures, to bring the client nearer to the object of fear in a series of small and manageable steps. Each step is repeated until minimal anxiety is felt before moving on to the next step. At each step, once contact is made the person resolves not to withdraw until the anxiety lessens, because withdrawing from a situation while anxiety is at its highest would only make the phobia worse. If one is afraid of heights, the hierarchy could begin with standing on a staircase looking down, moving on to leaning out of a first-floor window, then climbing a ladder, walking across a bridge, then sitting at the top of a cliff face, and finally looking out from the top of a tower block. In fact, it is not always necessary to do these things in real life. Working up a graduated hierarchy in one's imagination, known as "imaginal desensitization", can also be very effective, and at least will reduce some of the anticipatory anxiety prior to doing things in real life – "*in vivo* desensitization". Supplementary techniques will concern managing anxiety until it reduces (for example, relaxation, distraction, and challenging dysfunctional thoughts), and having the therapist model appropriate coping.

Obsessions and compulsions

Obsessions are unwanted thoughts, images, and impulses which intrude into thinking and behaviour. The person usually sees them as senseless, useless, and often repugnant or very distressing, but they cannot be easily dismissed. The obsession may be triggered by a variety of things, such as the presence of dirt or a certain sort of item on the news, perhaps about a murder; this causes a variety of uncomfortable feelings which are neutralized by performing compulsive behaviour or thought (for example, washing, or thoroughly checking where one was at the time of the murder). These compulsions are frequently highly stereotyped, for example washing the hands in a particular way with a certain depth of water at a certain temperature, taking the fingers one at a time in a strict order, then the palms, and finally the backs of the hands. These compulsions bring temporary relief from the anxiety (Turner & Beidel, 1988); anxiety is also reduced by the great deal of avoidance that is built up to prevent coming across the triggers in the first place. The two arms of treatment are therefore first, to expose the person gradually to those things that are being avoided, and second, to encourage ways of coping with the triggers that do not involve the compulsions, a technique often referred to as response prevention. The rationale for treatment is presented in the context of how the pattern of behaviour may have developed (perhaps, for example, the child had similar patterns modelled or encouraged by parents) and how the person reacts to the triggers (for example, dysfunctional thoughts) or what they believe to be the utility of the compulsions (irrational beliefs). Next, the patient is exposed to a gradual hierarchy of triggers. The therapist models appropriate coping, which is copied by the patient, who agrees to delay performing the compulsion until the anxiety has reduced. Feedback is given as to how the anxiety is reduced each time response prevention is practised, and how the thoughts about the triggers and compulsions change.

Depression

The word depression describes a mood (unhappy, fed-up, self-deprecating, listless, apathetic) and a syndrome (depressed mood, loss of interest, anxiety, sleep disturbance, loss of appetite and energy, suicidal thoughts). Depression can also be subdivided, for example into bipolar (swinging from low to high mood), endogenous (no obvious cause), and reactive (attributable to the effects of an identifiable experience). Sometimes these problems are treated by physical methods such as antidepressant medication including tricyclics and lithium, but increasingly the efficacy of psychological methods, especially cognitive therapy, are being acknowledged. Dobson (1989) found that cognitive therapy patients did better than 98 per cent of non-treatment controls, 67 per cent of behaviour therapy clients, 70 per cent of antidepressant clients, and 70 per cent of other psychotherapy clients. It will be recalled from earlier in this chapter that depressed affect is held in cognitive therapy to be the result of negative thoughts and negatively biased perceptions. There is a "negative triad" involving self (seen as inadequate and defective), life (seen as making extreme demands and repeatedly defeating the person), and the future (bound to hold failure). Early in treatment the problem is assessed, the patient is taught about the model, and any pessimism about treatment has to be tackled. Patients are taught how to list their thoughts on a record sheet, noting when they happened, the situation they were in, and the emotions that accompanied them. The intensity of the emotion and degree of belief in the thought can be rated on a scale. The automatic negative thoughts thus identified are then systematically challenged, just as described earlier in relation to anxiety. Once this can be done, more general maladaptive assumptions, such as Ellis's "irrational beliefs" can be similarly approached. Many problems can arise in cognitive therapy for depression including lack of collaboration, over-anticipation of failure, lack of the skills necessary to carry out homework assignments (for example, to tackle a financial problem or deal with a difficult work colleague in a different way), lack of motivation, trying to move too fast, and worries about the consequence of change. Each of these needs to be tackled within therapy, and other techniques or approaches can be used to circumvent the problem (for example, social skills training for the client who would not try behaving with his work colleagues in a different way). New applications of cognitive therapy concern group treatment approaches, therapy for those with long-term mild but chronic depression, identifying negative thought patterns established early in childhood, and specific groups such as adult survivors of child sex abuse.

Interpersonal problems

Quite a wide variety of effective methods for tackling the enhancement of interpersonal competence are now available (Spence, 1993). In overt behavioural social skills training, the micro-skills (for example, eye contact, posture) and macro-skills (for example, giving compliments, making a complaint, and so on), are both taught. Training begins with instruction, coaching, and discussion, and the therapist will model appropriate skills. The session will include behavioural rehearsal or role-playing, about which feedback and reinforcement are given. The client will then have homework assignments to do. Another treatment is training in social-perception skills, to help the person identify the appropriate dynamic cues in others. The client then imagines and carries out various possible responses to these cues and monitors his or her own dynamic cues and how they influence communication. There can also be training in social problem-solving skills when possible solutions to problems are critically examined to evaluate likely outcomes of each so that the most suitable course can be chosen. Of particular importance in forensic work is training in affect control, especially anger. The client is taught to identify the situations that trigger anger and are trained to "stop" rather than react when the trigger occurs, and to use interpersonal problem-solving strategies as just discussed. Finally, the role of maladaptive cognitions again has to be acknowledged and cognitive therapy methods are again relevant.

Marital and relationship problems

Much of the early empirical work on marital and relationship problems was quite behavioural in nature and centred on the notion that partners exchange or reciprocate behaviours or reinforcers (reciprocity). Marital disharmony arises when rates of exchange are low, problem-solving skills poor, rates of conflict produced by the behaviour high, and when the behaviours exchanged are mainly negative (negative reciprocity). Interactions therefore comprise communication training, training in problem-solving skills and the negotiation of a "contract" to exchange behaviours that are constructive and rewarding to the other person (Jacobson & Gurman, 1986). These methods have developed by application of a more cognitive approach. Perceptions of what events occur are compared; attributions about why these events happened are analysed; expectations about the future become important; and the couple's general assumptions or beliefs drawn out. For example, a thoughtlessly hurtful word by a partner can be perceived as a deliberate needle, attributed to a malign intent to cause distress, confirming the expectation that the relationship will be hurtful in the future, and be worsened by an underlying belief that once a relationship goes wrong it cannot be retrieved. Systems theory approaches are also very important. The therapist works with the clients to produce a map of the organisation, roles, boundaries, and rules of the relationship. The concepts of enmeshment and disengagement are especially relevant. An enmeshed style is when there is little separateness or autonomy — the couple will think or act as one. At the opposite end of the spectrum, in a disengaged style, the couple make minimal contact and provide little support in difficult times. Treatment aims to help couples adopt an appropriate style in relation to any particular life task. For example, one needs to be enmeshed to deal with crises, but more disengaged when one partner is striving to confirm his or her identity.

Health problems

Increasingly, psychologists are contributing to the maintenance of physical health. Two examples illustrate this in regard to asthma and diabetes. Asthma is an intermittent difficulty in breathing due to bronchoconstriction, and swelling and mucus secretion in the lungs. It can be precipitated by irritants such as pollen or smoke, physical agitation, and the intake of cold air. A psychological package to help children cope has been developed by Creer (1982). Children as young as 5 years of age can be taught to identify the first stage of an attack and then to adopt a coping routine involving a restriction of physical activity, relaxation to counter any feelings of panic, and drinking a warm liquid. Once settled, the bronchodilator may be used.

Diabetes occurs when the pancreas fails to produce enough insulin to metabolise glucose, leading to heart disease and circulatory problems. Changes in blood glucose are notably related to psychological stress. The role of psychological intervention concerns the situation in which the diabetes is poorly controlled, particularly in children. The child is taught how to monitor his or her own urine levels reliably and regularly, by a process of training and feedback, and how to relate these levels to immediate dietary needs. There can also be training in how to recognize hyper- and hypoglycaemia even without the urine test.

Contribution to different client groups

The work of clinical and counselling psychologists varies considerably depending on the client groups that they work with. For example, in child and adolescent settings there is a greater emphasis on family interventions. In adult work, there is a special problem in dealing with long-term, chronic illness, especially schizophrenia, and how to maintain people with these problems in the community (Lavender & Holloway, 1988). In working with elderly people, one especially has to confront issues to do with the burden on relatives and carers. Those who work with people with learning difficulties have to tackle a whole range of challenging behaviours that stem from poor impulse control and delayed social learning. Psychologists working in health care have developed special interests in the role of health education and illness prevention. Even this brief list should dispel the notion that sitting face-to-face with a client is the only, or even the main, way of working. This important point is taken up again in the next part of the chapter.

PROFESSIONAL ISSUES

Range of roles

As just mentioned, there is a danger that in presenting models of therapy followed by strategies of treating merely a small sample of the great variety of problems posed by clients, groups of clients, or the system, that the impression will be created that face-to-face therapy contact is the primary kind of work. This is absolutely not the case. Psychologists work at a variety of levels. In addition to individual therapy, psychologists have an assessment role, particularly important in neuropsychology, to diagnose brain injury and impaired cognitive function; in childwork to assess cognitive development and specific cognitive defects; and in forensic work to assist in the placement of offenders. There is an immensely important training role, to "give away" intervention skills to parents, teachers, nurses, and so forth, so that the psychologist then acts as an adviser and source of support. Health education, especially to do with smoking, drug taking, AIDS, alcohol abuse, and heart disease, has an increasingly substantial role, involving the psychologist in issues of attitude change, social representation, health belief models, and advertising strategy. Many psychologists work not as individuals but as part of a team – community mental health teams working towards the placement of clients in community settings is just one example. Many psychologists now see no individual clients at all, but work entirely at the system level to improve strategies of health care and to design systems of service delivery. Other psychologists work primarily as researchers, developing fundamental knowledge, applying such knowledge in clinical settings within a research design, undertaking outcome research to determine efficacy and cost-effectiveness, and carrying out consumer research to see if the system is living up to its promises and aspirations.

Training

Training varies considerably between countries, but certainly in the USA and UK there are courses that are formally accredited; every few years they are revalidated by the American Psychological Association or the British Psychological Society, which hold lists of such approved courses. Training lasts usually for three years or more subsequent to a first degree in psychology. Training comprises a balance of supervised clinical work, academic study and research, and it is necessary to pass in all three areas. Training places are in great demand, and so it is often difficult to gain entrance without relevant experience and a very good academic record. Once on a course, the training is demanding because of the stressful nature of working with clients and the sheer breadth of material that has to be learned. However, there is a very wide diversity of employment opportunities available which enables graduates to pursue a career of great personal satisfaction.

Code of conduct

In order to protect clients, accredited psychologists (for example, "chartered" psychologists in the UK) are entered on to a register available to the public and are bound by a code of conduct. Registered, licensed, or chartered psychologists are expected to maintain and develop their professional competence and to work within its limits. They are not allowed to claim competence they do not possess, and are not allowed to make unjustifiable claims for the efficacy of their methods. They must preserve confidentiality in all its modalities, and conduct themselves in a manner not likely to damage their clients or the profession.

FURTHER READING

Barlow, D. H., Hayes, S. C., & Nelson, R. O. (1984). *The scientist practitioner*. New York: Pergamon.

Brewin, C. R. (1988). *Cognitive foundations of clinical psychology*. Hove: Lawrence Erlbaum.

Heppner, P. P., Kivlighan, D. M., Jr, & Wampold, B. E. (1992). *Research design in counseling*. Pacific Grove, CA: Brooks/Cole.

Lindsay, S. J. E., & Powell, G. E. (1987). *A handbook of clinical adult psychology* (3rd edn). Aldershot: Gower.

Patterson, C. H. (1986). *Theories of counseling and psychotherapy.* New York: Harper & Row.

REFERENCES

Adler, A. (1929). *Problems of neurosis.* New York: Harper & Row.

American Psychiatric Association (1987). *Diagnostic and statistical manual of mental disorders* (3rd edn, revised). Washington, DC: APA.

Bandura, A. (1969). *Principles of behavior modification.* New York: Holt, Rinehart & Winston.

Bandura, A. (1986). *Social foundations of thought and action: A social cognitive theory.* Englewood Cliffs, NJ: Prentice-Hall.

Barlow, D. H., Blanchard, E. B., Vermilyea, J. A., Vermilyea, B. B., & Di Nardo, P. A. (1986). Generalized anxiety and generalized anxiety disorder: Description and reconceptualization. *American Journal of Psychiatry, 143*, 40–44.

Beck, A. T., Rush, A. J., Shaw, B. F., & Emery, G. (1977). *Cognitive therapy of depression.* New York: Guilford.

Brammer, L. M., Shostrom, E. L., & Abrego, P. J. (1989). *Therapeutic psychology: Fundamentals of counseling and psychotherapy* (5th edn). Englewood Cliffs, NJ: Prentice-Hall.

Creer, T. L. (1982). Asthma. *Journal of Consulting and Clinical Psychology, 50*, 912–921.

Dobson, K. S. (1989). A meta-analysis of the efficacy of cognitive therapy for depression. *Journal of Consulting and Clinical Psychology, 59*, 414–419.

Du Pont, R. L. (Ed.) (1982). *Phobias: A comprehensive summary of modern treatments.* New York: Brunner/Mazel.

Eagle, M. N. (1984). *Recent developments in psychoanalysis: A critical evaluation.* New York: McGraw-Hill.

Ellis, A., & Whiteley, J. M. (Eds) (1979). *Theoretical and empirical foundation of rational-emotive therapy.* Monterey, CA: Brooks/Cole.

Erikson, E. H. (1959). *Identity and the life cycle: Selected papers.* New York: International Universities Press.

Freud, S. (1943). *A general introduction to psychoanalysis.* New York: Garden City.

Garfield, S. L., & Bergin, A. E. (1986). *Handbook of psychotherapy and behavior change* (3rd edn). New York: Wiley.

Horowitz, M. J. (Ed.) (1988). *Psychodynamics and cognition.* Chicago, IL: University of Chicago Press.

Jacobson, N., & Gurman, A. (1986). *Clinical handbook of marital therapy.* New York: Guilford.

Jones, E. E., Kanouse, D. E., Kelley, H. H., Nisbett, P. E., Valins, S., & Weiner, B. (Eds) (1972). *Attribution: Perceiving the causes of behavior.* Morristown, NJ: General Learning Press.

Jung, C. G. (1982). *Contributions to analytical psychology.* New York: Harcourt Brace Jovanovich.

Kelly, G. A. (1955). *The psychology of personal constructs (vols 1 & 2).* New York: Norton.

Klein, M. (1975). *Envy and gratitude and other works. 1946–1963.* London: Hogarth.

Laing, R. D. (1974). *The divided self.* Harmondsworth: Penguin.

Lavender, A., & Holloway, F. (Eds) (1988). *Community care in practice: Services for the continuing care client.* Chichester: Wiley.

Meichenbaum, D. (1977). *Cognitive behavior modification: An integrative approach.* New York: Plenum.

Minuchin, S., & Fishman, H. C. (1981). *Family therapy techniques.* Cambridge, MA: Harvard University Press.

Pavlov, I. P. (1927). *Conditioned reflexes. An investigation of the physiological activity of the cerebral cortex* (G. V. Anrep, ed. and trans.) Oxford: Oxford University Press (original work published 1923).

Perls, F. S. (1973). *The Gestalt approach.* Palo Alto, CA: Science and Behavior Books.

Powell, T. J., & Enright, S. J. (1990). *Anxiety and stress management.* London: Routledge.

Rogers, C. R. (1942). *Counseling and psychotherapy.* Boston, MA: Houghton Mifflin.

Skinner, B. F. (1974). *About behaviorism.* New York: Alfred A. Knopf.

Smith, M. L., Glass, G. V., & Miller, T. I. (1980). *The benefits of psychotherapy.* Baltimore, MD: Johns Hopkins University Press.

Spence, S. H. (1993). Interpersonal problems: Treatment. In S. Lindsay & G. E. Powell (Eds) *A handbook of clinical adult psychology* (pp. 240–255). London: Routledge.

Truax, C. B., & Carkhoff, R. (1967). *Toward effective counseling and psychotherapy: Training and practice.* Chicago, IL: Aldine.

Turner, S. M., & Beidel, D. C. (1988). *Treating obsessive-compulsive disorder.* New York: Pergamon.

13.2

EDUCATIONAL (SCHOOL) PSYCHOLOGY

David Fontana
University of Wales, Cardiff, Wales

The term *educational psychology* has traditionally covered two related but functionally distinct activities, first, the courses in psychology offered in the initial and continuing education of teachers, and second, the activities of psychologists whose main function is to assess children with learning and behaviour problems and make (or recommend) provision for their special educational needs. This dual terminology has led to some confusion; a partial solution has been to use *the psychology of education* to refer to the former activities, and *school psychology* to refer to the latter. However, there remains a clear need not only for more formalization in the use of these subgroup labels and in the generic term educational psychology, but also to ensure that all those offering services as educational psychologists have similar training and qualifications. Any understanding of the current role played by educational psychology demands that we keep in mind both uses of the term. However, both strands of educational psychology have their origin in a common source, as we shall see in an overview of the historical perspective of the subject.

THE GENESIS OF EDUCATIONAL PSYCHOLOGY

Educational psychology has an interesting and distinguished history (see, e.g., Child, 1985; Sutherland, 1985). Its formative influences can be traced to child psychology (e.g., the developmental norms established by authorities such as Gesell, together with the socio-emotional findings of McDougall, Goldfarb, Bowlby, and others), the study of mental testing (e.g., the work of Binet, Spearman, Thurstone, and Terman), psychodynamic psychology (in particular the writings of Freud and the neo- and post-Freudians), and the experimental investigation of human and animal learning (especially by pioneers like Pavlov, Watson, and Thorndike from behaviourism, and Kohler, Koffka, and Wertheimer from Gestalt psychology). Additional influences came from educational methods developed by non-psychologists such as Froebel and Montessori in continental Europe, Dewey in the USA, and the Macmillans and Susan Isaacs in the UK.

The formalization of these disparate influences into a subject worthy of the name of educational psychology owed much to the work of Sir Cyril Burt, who (in spite of the controversy surrounding his later experimental findings) did much to persuade both teachers and administrators of the crucial role that psychology can play in assessing children's educational needs and in informing classroom interaction. Over a long career stretching from 1912 (the date of his appointment by the London County Council in the first ever official post of educational psychologist) to his death in 1971, Burt remained a major influence on the subject, enjoying the respect of teachers and psychologists, through both his professional work (particularly his tenure of the Chair of Education in the University of London from 1931 to 1951) and his stream of publications.

Perhaps the main criticism that can be levelled at the general direction taken by educational psychology in these early years, however, is that it placed its emphasis primarily upon mental abilities and their assessment. From an initial concern to identify those children suffering from what were seen as mental disabilities, and who were consequently in need of special education and training, this emphasis soon spread to a more general attempt to test and categorize all children in terms predominantly of intelligence and of the verbal and spatial abilities of which intelligence was held to be composed.

Laudable enough in motive, since the expressed intention was to identify children with high potential abilities who were being under-served by the educational system, this emphasis not only tended to typecast children in terms of a somewhat simplistic mentalism, but also distracted attention from the range of other psychological factors that influence child behaviour and educational performance. In particular, it neglected social and affective factors, attitudes, motivation, self-concepts, classroom interaction, and teacher–child relationships. Furthermore, it placed undue stress upon the inheritance of mental abilities, and undue faith in the "scientific" nature of available mental tests. Arguably, the mistakes implicit in this approach, though long since discarded by educational psychology itself, remain as a potent influence on those responsible for educational policy and planning.

DEVELOPMENTS FROM THE 1950s TO THE 1970s

In the 1950s, 1960s, and 1970s, educational psychology became characterized by a much more child-centred approach, with the emphasis more upon the study of children's actual behaviour (both as individuals and as members of groups and subgroups) than upon the application of models of the mind or mental abilities. This change of emphasis was prompted by a number of factors, the most important of which will now be discussed.

First, there was the availability of new sources of psychological data with specific relevance to education, such as those from cognitive psychology (e.g., the work of Piaget, Bruner, and Vygotsky), personality theory (Allport, Erikson, and Maslow), psychometrics (Eysenck and Cattell), counselling and pastoral care (Rogers), and various approaches to learning theory and educational technology (Skinner, Gagné, Bloom, and Kelly).

Second, the increasing sophistication of research methods and techniques of statistical analysis greatly enhanced the database available within educational research.

Third, there were rapidly accumulating findings of sociology (particularly those relating to the family, ethnic groups, sub-cultures, and language), together with the greater awareness shown by society at large of the influence of social factors on child development and on educational opportunity and performance.

Finally, there was a portfolio of findings from across the whole spectrum of psychological research, including those produced by Harlow and Harlow on early attachment, Festinger on cognitive dissonance, Witkin, Kagan, and others on cognitive style, Guildford and others on creativity, McClelland on motivation, Kohlberg on moral development, Bandura on social learning, Rotter on locus of control, and Osgood on semantic space.

DEVELOPMENTS IN THE 1980s AND 1990s

With such a rich and varied field upon which to draw, and with the obvious

1202

relevance of educational psychology to classroom practice, it might be supposed that the 1980s and 1990s would see a major expansion of the influence and use of educational psychology. Unfortunately, within teacher education (the psychology of education), the subject is facing a major struggle both to retain its integrity as an identifiable domain and to be a major influence on classroom practice. Educational psychology has failed to demonstrate how the recommendations generated by psychological theory and research can be operationalized by the busy classteacher.

This failure in the view of many is a consequence of the dichtomy that developed during the 1970s within the teacher education curriculum between educational psychology and teaching method. Given the considerable amounts of specialist knowledge needed, it has proved increasingly difficult for any but a few exceptional individuals to be proficient in both areas, particularly when it comes to the preparation of teachers for work with older children. Tutoring in the two areas has therefore been carried out by specialists with different professional backgrounds, often working separately from each other. Thus the educational psychologist discusses children in isolation from the educational process, while the teaching methods tutor describes the educational process in isolation from the children who are its consumers. Where a team teaching approach has been adopted, the educational psychologist is usually reduced to a resource within the teaching methods curriculum, unable to teach the deep structure of educational psychology essential to a proper understanding of the discipline.

This erosion of educational psychology within teacher education has been exacerbated by the arrival of a number of hybrid subjects, each laying claim to some of its traditional territory. Educational technology and educational management have moved into such areas as learning, social relationships, and classroom control; special education (originally concerned primarily with teaching methods) has taken over work on individual needs; school effectiveness has appropriated work on social organization and assessment; and pastoral care has annexed work on psychological counselling. Extensive use is made of psychological knowledge in these areas, and qualified psychologists sometimes operate within them, but these are fields of study bidding to become disciplines in their own right, reducing educational psychology to what is effectively an auxiliary presence.

However, educational psychology has retained its importance in its second area of activity, the assessment of children with learning and behaviour problems (school psychology), primarily because it alone possesses expertise in the application and interpretation of the battery of diagnostic tests that such assessment demands. However, in face of the emphasis that modern industrial societies – for social and political as well as educational reasons – place upon assessment, educational (school) psychologists may well be manoeuvred into the role of psychological technicians, to the neglect of the other services that they are qualified to offer (discussed in more detail below).

DEFINITION OF EDUCATIONAL PSYCHOLOGY

Definitions are precarious things, often open to endless dispute and debate. However, a useful definition of educational psychology in both its *psychology of education* and *school psychology* roles is that it is, first, the study of those psychological factors that influence the educational process, and second, the development and application of psychological strategies in order to assist and where necessary improve this process. Like any scientific undertaking ("scientific" is used in its loosest sense − the social sciences cannot aspire to the precision of the natural sciences), educational psychology has a descriptive and an active function. It establishes *what is*, and then uses its methods and procedures to help bring about *what can be*. Both aspects are of equal importance; it is imperative that the first function, which involves well-conceived and meticulously executed fieldwork, does not become overshadowed by the second, with its perhaps more fashionable emphasis on the creation and testing of hypotheses.

THE CONTENT OF EDUCATIONAL PSYCHOLOGY

With the exception of the actual content of the school curriculum, educational psychology appears to cover virtually the whole of educational life, because education is about the very things (learning, child development, social relationships and interactions, assessment, motivation, social control, individual differences, and so on) that psychology claims for its own. Education is a psychological process, and much of our understanding of it comes from the findings of psychological research. Educational psychology is best grouped under a number of subheadings, which may suggest that it is a topic-driven subject, but this would be incorrect. One of the hallmarks of a discipline is that it carries a deep structure (referred to above) consisting of an interlaced framework of knowledge and methodology within which individual topics are recognized as points of emphasis rather than as discrete units. Thus each bears a clear relationship to the others and to the whole. Personality, for example, cannot be understood or sensibly taught without reference to learning; motivation without reference to self-concepts; social control without reference to social perceptions and social relationships; child development without reference to cognition; and so on. Thus the subheadings are simply a way of guiding the reader through the field, and should be interpreted only at this level. One useful way in which the various subheadings can themselves be grouped is to look at each of the three main interrelated questions with which the educational process is primarily concerned: What is to be learned? Who is to learn it? How is it to be learned?

WHAT IS TO BE LEARNED?

Decisions on what is to be included in the school curriculum for children of all ages and all abilities are not psychological decisions, but educational psychology has a great deal to say about how curriculum content should be presented to pupils if learning is to be optimized; this involves drawing attention to the importance of educational objectives and the deep structure of what is to be learned.

Educational objectives

In the mid-1950s, Bloom, Engelhart, Furst, Walker, and Krathwohl (1956) identified the general and specific categories that encompass all the learning outcomes that might be expected in the cognitive domain, while Krathwhol, Bloom, and Masie (1964) identified those in the affective domain, and Simpson (1972) those in the psycho-motor domain. The practical value of work of this kind is that it allows teachers to select and specify those aspects of curriculum content that are actually to be presented to pupils, and to monitor subsequently whether or not effective learning has taken place.

Wheldall has shown (e.g., Wheldall & Merrett, 1984, 1989) how the use of appropriate educational objectives not only can enhance the effectiveness with which classroom material is presented to pupils, but also can be readily accepted and used by teachers (see also Pearson & Tweddle, 1984). The precision teaching approach of Raybould (1984) is another example of how classroom material can be structured into a form which assists pupil understanding and learning. It is interesting to note how, outside the classroom, there is little doubt of the major contribution that the objectives approach can make to effective learning and behaviour (see, e.g., management training and practice – Seiwert, 1991).

The importance of structure

Bruner (1966) drew attention to the importance of organizing the material to be learned into a form that allows the pupil to recognize its deep structure, and to relate new information meaningfully to it. This calls for close cooperation between the educational psychologist and the teaching methods tutor so that the structure of classroom subjects can be properly identified and presented to pupils in a psychologically accessible form (i.e., one most suited to the ways in which individuals process incoming information and integrate it into existing cognitive structures).

The use of educational objectives is associated with the behavioural approach to human learning, while the identification and use of structure is related to the cognitive approach. These two approaches are sometimes seen as antipathetic to each other: it is important to point out that from the standpoint of educational psychology there is nothing contradictory about laying equal emphasis upon both. Structure identifies what needs to be learned, while objectives organize it into manageable units and make clear the whole point and purpose of the educational enterprise.

WHO IS TO LEARN IT?

This question brings us to the main focus of educational psychology, the children themselves. Under this heading comes the whole range of variables associated with child development, abilities and attainment, affective and social factors, and self-concepts and self-awareness. Given the long association of educational psychology with mental testing and child development, one might suppose that it has few problems either in identifying what teachers need to know about children, or in instructing teachers on how to make practical use of this knowledge within the classroom. However, this is not the case; the fault lies either with children themselves for being so complex, or with psychologists for being so pluralistic in their approach. Smith (1992) – to take a prime example – shows the conflict of opinion raging among psychologists over the quality and applicability of the research findings of Jean Piaget, previously the unquestioned authority on children's cognitive development. Other examples range from the classroom utility of personality trait theories to the long-term effects of early conditioning. Although the following are the main areas of psychology that have potential relevance to education, there is no consensus on how each of them can best be translated into classroom practice (a point to which I return in due course).

Pupil abilities

There is a whole range of variables within the individual which influence the efficacy of the learning act. Traditionally, psychology has assigned labels such as intelligence, creativity, memory, and motivation; of these, psychology has had most to say about intelligence. Yet even granted their validity, it is unclear how teachers can use psychological models of intelligence in their classroom work. Even a knowledge of children's test scores, however derived, is of doubtful practical value for most teachers, and can even be counter-productive (contributing, for example, to the well-known self-fulfilling prophecy). Unless educational psychology can make clear either how intelligence can be improved (if indeed it can), or how it relates directly to the way in which children learn, the situation (outside the assessment of children with special needs, dealt with below) is unlikely to change markedly.

Similarly with creativity: after the upsurge of interest shown by psychologists in the subject during the 1960s and 1970s, things have gone remarkably quiet, at least within the context of education. Various attempts have been made to demonstrate how teachers can enhance child creativity (e.g., Pickard, 1979), but many of these could equally well have been proposed by good art teachers or teachers of creative writing. Having set the stage, educational psychology failed to indicate the activities that should take place thereon.

Despite everything that psychology has to say about memory (e.g., Baddeley, 1983), for the average teacher a gap still yawns between the findings of psychological research and their application to classroom activities, while motivation, perhaps because it is so readily reduced to a few practical strategies (e.g., teaching through success rather than failure, through relevance and interest rather than through boredom, through intrinsic motivators as well as extrinsic) merely emphasizes what teachers already know. The relative impotence of educational psychology to make statements about individual abilities capable of greatly influencing day-to-day classroom practice may well be a reflection of the impotence of psychology itself. It could be argued that psychology has paid insufficient attention to human abilities in the normal population (particularly the normal population of older children), and to the ways in which these abilities influence behaviour and can be usefully enhanced.

Affective factors

Educational psychology embraces the ways in which affective factors influence both learning and the personal-social development of the child. A number of studies have used the personality measures of Eysenck and/or Catell and identified correlations between personality type and responses to the learning environment (Fontana, 1986); the pioneering work of Bennett (1976) was particularly notable in relation to the interaction between child personality and teaching styles. Within the personal-social development of the child, educational psychology has had to fight a battle against the traditional tendency of formal education to concentrate upon what I have referred to as an education for knowing rather than an education for being (Fontana, 1987). The overt curriculum has paid little more than lip-service to ways of helping children experience their lives and their relationships in a positive way, or for developing those qualities which psychologists equate with maturity of personality. A number of studies (e.g., Eisenberg & Strayer, 1987) make clear explicitly or by implication the scope possessed by the educational process to provide this kind of help, and the relevant skills, which educational psychology could make accessible to the classteacher.

Through its involvement in guidance, counselling, and pastoral care, educational psychology can also provide practical strategies for identifying and helping children with personality and/or social problems (Murphy and Kupshik, 1992; Nelson-Jones, 1986). Although not normally regarded as its direct concern, educational psychology can also assist in careers counselling (Ball, 1984).

The self and self-perceptions

Linked to both cognitive and affective factors, the child's view of him- or herself can be a crucial variable in both formal classroom learning and personal development (Burns, 1982). There is no shortage of psychological material on the self and the growth of self-awareness (Kegan, 1982); Burns (among others) has shown how much of this material can be suitably operationalized within education (Burns, 1982). If there is a resistance to progress here, it comes more from formal education, with its lack of proper concern for an education for personal development, than from any lack of knowledge within educational psychology.

Child development

Child development is a vast, well-researched subject within psychology (Bee, 1989; Kagan, 1984); although marked by pluralism (mention has been made of the debate surrounding Piaget's experimental findings), major areas are relevant to education (see, e.g., Branthwaite & Rogers, 1985). It is perhaps unfortunate that psychology has concentrated more on early childhood than on adolescence – the developmental stage that occasions teachers most heartache – but educational psychology is replete with knowledge of the many, subtle ways in which development influences a child's ability to learn, to relate to others, and to grow in self-awareness. Across a spectrum of topics, including the development of perception, cognition, social identity and relationships, language, moral behaviour, play, personality, psychosexuality, and creative abilities, educational psychologists could make this knowledge available to teachers in a form that has direct impact upon the way in which they understand and relate to children (see, e.g., Desforges, 1989; Fontana, 1984a, 1984b; Hartley, 1985; Stubbs, 1983).

Classroom interaction

The analysis of classroom interaction has been of interest both to educational psychology and to educational sociology (Delamont, 1983), as it identifies the incidents during teacher–child interactions that effect significant changes in children's behaviour (and less obviously in their cognitive and affective processes) in both desirable and undesirable directions. Such changes have important implications for children's learning and for the teacher's ability to maintain classroom control; since the introduction in 1970 of properly constructed instruments for recording and analysing this interaction (Flanders,

1970) student teachers have been able to learn a great deal about the consequences of their own classroom behaviour (see, e.g., Bennett, 1985). The findings from both interaction analysis and cognitive and behavioural psychology have enabled educational psychology to advise more fully on classroom management (Laslett & Smith, 1984) and classroom control and discipline (Fontana, 1985; Wheldall, 1992).

Teacher behaviour

Teacher behaviour is another area where educational psychology links closely with work on teaching method. The aim of both educational psychologists and teaching method tutors is to enhance teacher effectiveness in the presentation of the learning act and in classroom management and control (referred to above). Educational psychology also attempts to help teachers identify those psychological variables within themselves that contribute towards professional success. Longitudinal studies (e.g., Cortis, 1985) have drawn attention to these variables, while work on teacher stress (Cole & Walker, 1990; Greenberg, 1984) has helped furnish educational psychology with a range of stress-reducing strategies available for use in in-service teacher education (Fontana, 1989).

Assessment

The detailed assessment (or screening) of children with special educational needs is central to the function of educational psychologists engaged in school psychology. The assessment tests used (which include structured and unstructured interviews, time-sampling, classroom observation, and verbal and written tests) are so varied, with many having been developed in response to specific needs, that it would be impossible to list them all here. Together they cover the major categories as follows:

1 *learning difficulties* e.g., numeracy, literacy, reasoning, language, and memory tests
2 *sensory impairment* e.g., visual, speech, and auditory tests
3 *physical impairment* e.g., tests for motor handicap, laterality problems, and physical injury
4 *behaviour difficulties* e.g., observation and interviews for hyperactivity, aggression, delinquent acts, school refusal, and truancy
5 *emotional problems* e.g., tests for anxiety, personality difficulties, withdrawal, and fantasizing.

In the application and interpretation of various tests and measures, the educational psychologist will often work with other child and health-care specialists such as doctors, physiotherapists, and social workers. On completion of testing, the educational psychologist presents the results to the educational authorities and (where required) to the parents, and offers recommendations as to the kind of educational provision that the child may need. This could consist of remedial help within the child's own school or (more rarely) transfer to a school specially equipped to cater for his or her special requirements.

The age at which children are first screened for special needs depends on both the child and the policy of the educational psychologists concerned. It is generally felt inappropriate (and often impossible in practice, since they may not have entered formal schooling) to screen children before they are 5 or 6 years old. Screening before this age often proves unreliable, as psychological development in young children tends to be uneven, and the children may refuse to cooperate with the tester. Furthermore, early screening carries the risk that the child will be labelled in the eyes of parents and teachers, and become the victim of a self-fulfilling prophecy. However, if screening is left too late, it simply confirms that the child is having educational difficulties, instead of identifying his or her problems before these difficulties have a chance to arise.

HOW IS IT TO BE LEARNED?

Learning is the prime concern of both psychology and education, and should be the area on which educational psychology speaks with most authority. Although both behavioural and cognitive theories of learning have obvious relevance to our understanding of the way in which children approach and perform the learning act, it is less clear that a knowledge of them is a significant stimulus to good practice. It is unclear whether a teacher who is familiar with these theories is a more successful (or even a markedly different) practitioner from one who is not. This is why many educational psychologists involved in teacher education currently doubt the efficacy of their own subject (see, e.g., Burden, 1992; Tomlinson, 1992; for an examination of some of the issues being raised). However, the problem lies not in the failure of psychological knowledge, but in the absence of consensus on how this knowledge translates into good classroom practice. This lack of consensus is puzzling, given the various authoritative texts addressing the issue (e.g., Bigge, 1982; Fontana, 1984a, 1988; Gronlund, 1978; Howe, 1984; Wheldall & Merritt, 1989), and in view of the evidence that educational psychologists working alongside serving teachers can initiate them into the use of psychological strategies that can materially assist them in their task (Thacker, 1990).

In addition, current work in repertory grids, computer-assisted learning, and self-organized learning (Thomas & Harri-Augstein, 1985), on peer-tutoring (Foot, Morgan, & Schute, 1990) and on how to relate learning to evolving models of mind (Claxton, 1990) provides not only a major stimulus for new thinking in educational psychology, but also an array of practical strategies which most teachers find no difficulty in learning, enjoying, and applying. The debate among educational psychologists on how best to help teachers understand and apply a useful and practical psychology of learning would seem to have more to do with their own uncertainty about their professional role than to any lack of material suitable for the task concerned.

OTHER ASPECTS OF THE EDUCATIONAL PSYCHOLOGIST'S ROLE

Educational psychologists are equipped by their training and experience to undertake a number of functions (in addition to those mentioned above), and can work effectively in any situation involving not only formal and informal education but also the processes of human change and development. They may work in psychological counselling, primarily with children and also on occasions with adults; their duties frequently include child guidance and working alongside teachers in schools to develop counselling and pastoral care networks. With additional training, they may practise psychotherapy with a wide range of disorders, including social and emotional problems, eating problems, anxieties and phobias, and low self-esteem.

In family work, skills range from simple advice to parents on appropriate child-rearing practices to in-depth family therapy work. Educational psychologists may work with groups of children and adolescents to assist the development of social competence and human relationship skills, and with groups of teachers and other professionals to offer guidance on stress management, study skills, classroom control, and child assessment.

Educational psychologists may advise on organizational matters, on the running and management of a school, on appropriate channels of communication, and in the general area of school effectiveness. Many educational psychologists carry out research, often linking up with developmental, clinical, and social psychologists. They may also work in teams with creative arts therapists, such as drama and music therapists, and with allied professionals such as social workers and community care agents.

CONCLUSION: WHAT MORE SHOULD EDUCATIONAL PSYCHOLOGY DO?

The future of educational psychology is intimately bound up with the future both of psychology and of education. Educational psychologists are concerned with the professional training of specific groups of students if they are involved in *the psychology of education*, and with specific duties in connection with schools if they are engaged in *school psychology*. Changes in the content or structure of teacher education will have repercussions on their work, as will changes in school policy consequent upon the actions of national and local politicians.

Educational psychology is not entirely at the mercy of factors beyond its control, however. There is a need for it to assert its own identity more clearly within both psychology and education: the time has come for it to play a role in urging the need for more attention and resources to be devoted to applied educational psychology. Non-psychologists expect psychology to provide insights that relate directly to personal and professional life. Educational psychology is primarily an applied exercise: as such, it has much to teach the parent discipline of psychology. It needs to assert more clearly the psychological content of education, and the fact that education cannot be fully understood and conducted without appropriate psychological knowledge.

Teaching cannot be a fully effective exercise unless the teacher understands and can apply the psychological elements involved in the three interrelated educational questions: *What is to be learned? What is to learn it? How is it to be learned?* The best setting in which to make this plain is the classroom itself, working alongside serving teachers. Within the classroom, teachers can be taught by the educational psychologist to operate as researchers, capable of monitoring their own behaviour, together with that of the children, in order to identify where psychological factors are hindering learning or personal-social development, and where changes in strategy are therefore needed.

This is not to deny the place for a study of educational psychology by student teachers in the lecture room, and by serving teachers on in-service training courses. No profession (e.g., medicine, engineering, law, or dentistry) would pretend that students or serving professionals can do all their learning while on task. Various attempts have been made to set out the major areas to be studied in college-based educational psychology courses, while comprehensive textbooks also exist (see below). But it is within the school setting that educational psychology can most emphatically demonstrate its value. And it is within the school setting that it must in the future seek fully to demonstrate its worth.

FURTHER READING

Bennett, N., & Desforges, C. (1985). *Recent advances in classroom research.* Edinburgh: Scottish Academic Press and British Journal of Educational Psychology.

Fontana, D. (1988). *Psychology for teachers* (2nd edn). London: British Psychological Society and Macmillan.

Francis, H. (Ed.) (1985). *Learning to teach: Psychology in teacher training.* London: Falmer.

Jones, N., & Frederickson, N. (Eds) (1990). *Refocusing educational psychology.* Basingstoke: Falmer.

REFERENCES

Baddeley, A. (1983). *Your memory: A user's guide*. Harmondsworth: Penguin.

Ball, B. (1984). *Careers counselling in practice*. London: Falmer.

Bee, H. (1989). *The developing child* (5th edn). New York: Harper & Row.

Bennett, N. (1976). *Teaching styles and pupil progress*. London: Open Books.

Bennett, N. (1985). Interaction and achievement in classroom groups. In N. Bennett & C. Desforges (Eds) *Recent advances in classroom research* (pp. 105–119). Edinburgh: Scottish Academic Press and British Journal of Educational Psychology.

Bigge, N. (1982). *Learning theories for teachers* (4th edn). New York: Harper & Row.

Bloom, B. S., Engelhart, M. D., Furst, E. J., Walker, M. H., & Krathwohl, D. R. (1956). *Taxonomy of educational objectives*. London: Longmans Green.

Branthwaite, A., & Rogers, D. (Eds) (1985). *Children growing up*. Milton Keynes: Open University Press.

Bruner, J. S. (1966). *Towards a theory of instruction*. New York: Norton.

Burden, R. (1992). Educational psychology: A force that is spent or one that never got going? *The Psychologist, 5*(3), 110–111.

Burns, R. (1982). *Self-concept development and education*. London: Holt, Rinehart & Winston.

Child, D. (1985). Educational psychology, past, present and future. In N. J. Entwistle (Ed.) *New directions in educational psychology: I. Learning and teaching* (pp. 9–24). London: Falmer.

Claxton, G. (1990). *Teaching to learn: A direction for education*. London: Cassell.

Cole, M., & Walker, S. (Eds) (1990). *Teaching and stress*. Milton Keynes: Open University Press.

Cortis, G. A. (1985). Eighteen years on: How far can you go? *Educational Review, 37*(1), 3–12.

Delamont, S. (1983). *Interaction in the classroom* (2nd edn). London: Methuen.

Desforges, C. (Ed.) (1989). *Early childhood education*. Edinburgh: Scottish Academic Press and British Journal of Educational Psychology.

Eisenberg, N., & Strayer, J. (Eds) (1987). *Empathy and its development*. Cambridge: Cambridge University Press.

Flanders, N. A. (1970). *Analyzing teaching behavior*. New York: Addison-Wesley.

Fontana, D. (Ed.) (1984a). *Behaviourism and learning theory in education*. Edinburgh: Scottish Academic Press and British Journal of Educational Psychology.

Fontana, D. (Ed.) (1984b). *The education of the young child* (2nd edn). Oxford: Basil Blackwell.

Fontana, D. (1985). *Classroom control: Understanding and guiding classroom behaviour*. London: Methuen and British Psychological Society.

Fontana, D. (1986). *Teaching and personality* (2nd edn). Oxford: Basil Blackwell.

Fontana, D. (1987). Knowing about being. *Changes, 5*, 344–347.

Fontana, D. (1988). *Psychology for teachers* (2nd edn). London: Macmillan and British Psychological Society.

Fontana, D. (1989). *Managing stress*. London: Routledge and British Psychological Society.

Foot, H., Morgan, M., & Schute, R. (1990). *Children helping children*. Chichester: Wiley.

Greenberg, S. F. (1984). *Stress and the teaching profession*. London: Paul Brooks.

Gronlund, N. E. R. (1978). *Stating objectives for classroom instruction* (2nd edn). London: Collier Macmillan.

Hartley, J. (1985). Developing skills in learning. In A. Branthwaite & D. Rogers (Eds) *Children growing up* (pp. 112–121). Milton Keynes: Open University Press.

Howe, M. J. (1984). *A teacher's guide to the psychology of learning*. Oxford: Basil Blackwell.

Kagan, J. (1984). *The nature of the child*. New York: Harper & Row.

Kegan, R. (1982). *The evolving self: Problems and process in human development*. Cambridge, MA: Massachusetts University Press.

Krathwohl, D. R., Bloom, B. S., & Masie, B. B. (1964). *Taxonomy of educational objectives: Handbook II. The affective domain*. New York: David McKay.

Laslett, R., & Smith, C. (1984). *Effective classroom management*. London: Croom Helm.

Lindsay, G. (Ed.) (1984). *Screening for children with special needs*. London: Croom Helm.

Murphy, P. M., & Kupshik, G. A. (1992). *Loneliness, stress and well-being: A helper's guide*. London: Routledge.

Nelson-Jones, R. (1986). *Human relationship skills: Training and self-help*. London: Cassell.

Pearson, L., & Tweddle, D. (1984). The formulation and use of behavioural objectives. In D. Fontana (Ed.) *Behaviourism and learning theory in education* (pp. 75–92). Edinburgh: Scottish Academic Press and British Journal of Educational Psychology.

Pickard, E. (1979). *Development of creative ability*. Slough: National Foundation for Educational Research.

Raybould, E. C. (1984). Precision teaching and pupils with learning difficulties: Perspectives, principles and practice. In D. Fontana (Ed.) *Behaviourism and learning theory in education* (pp. 43–74). Edinburgh: Scottish Academic Press and British Journal of Educational Psychology.

Seiwert, L. (1991). *Time in money*. London: Kogan Page.

Simpson, E. J. (1972). *The classification of educational objectives in the psychomotor domain*. Washington, DC: Gryphon.

Smith, L. (1992). *Jean Piaget: Critical assessments*, 4 vols. London: Routledge.

Stubbs, M. (1983). *Language, schools and classrooms* (2nd edn). London: Methuen.

Sutherland, M. B. (1985). Psychology and the education of teachers. In H. Francis (Ed) *Learning to teach: Psychology in teacher training* (pp. 6–21). London: Falmer.

Thacker, V. J. (1990). Working through groups in the classroom. In N. Jones & N. Frederickson (Eds) *Refocusing educational psychology* (pp. 8–83). Basingstoke: Falmer.

Thomas, L., & Harris-Augstein, S. (1985). *Self-organised learning*. London: Routledge & Kegan Paul.

Tomlinson, P. (1992). Psychology and education: What went wrong – or did it? *The Psychologist*, 5(3), 105–109.

Wheldall, K. (Ed.) (1992). *Discipline in schools: Psychological perspectives on the Elton Report*. London: Routledge.

Wheldall, K., & Merrett, F. (1984). The behavioural approach to classroom management. In D. Fontana (Ed.) *Behaviourism and learning theory in education* (pp. 15–42). Edinburgh: Scottish Academic Press and British Journal of Educational Psychology.

Wheldall, K., & Merrett, F. (1989). *Positive teaching in the secondary school*. London: Paul Chapman.

13.3

INDUSTRIAL (OCCUPATIONAL) AND ORGANIZATIONAL PSYCHOLOGY

Wendy Hollway
University of Bradford, England

The subject first emerged as *industrial psychology* in the early years of the twentieth century. In Britain, it came to be known as *occupational psychology*. Following broader trends in social science, the title *organizational psychology* has emerged for a sibling subject with less of a focus on the individual. *Work psychology* is a term used in continental Europe, but only just appearing in Britain and unfamiliar in the United States. It is used in this chapter, to avoid the historical and geographical specificity of the terms contained in the title, when it is necessary to refer to the topic in a general way.

Work psychology applies psychology in the workplace. It sounds simple and clear-cut: there is a scientific body of knowledge about the individual called psychology and in this branch it is applied to the study of individuals at work. In this chapter I point out the deficiencies of this definition, emphasizing in contrast the effects of workplace practices in the production of knowledge about people at work.

The present-day *Journal of Occupational Psychology* (subtitled "an

International Journal of Industrial and Organizational Psychology") defines its subject matter as follows:

> The journal's domain is broad, covering industrial, organizational, engineering, vocational and personnel psychology, as well as behavioural aspects of industrial relations, ergonomics, human factors and industrial sociology. Interdisciplinary approaches are welcome. (Guide notes for referees)

Managers, not psychologists, are the largest group who practise, and are trained in, work psychology (Shimmin & Wallis, 1989). Other practitioners who often have some training in work psychology are consultants, trainers, and researchers (few of whom would carry the label "psychologist"). They are employed by organizations to do the following:

1 help select employees
2 devise appraisal systems
3 design systems and methods of work organization
4 instigate change in the organization
5 advise on the introduction of new technology
6 advise on personnel planning and succession plans
7 enhance safety
8 enhance productivity
9 cope with stress and conflict
10 help to problem solve
11 improve decision-making and team-work
12 find out what employees think about their jobs and about the company
13 negotiate pay and conditions
14 counsel people when they lose their jobs
15 advise people on what jobs suit them and how to create a favourable impression on application
16 train managers to manage people and supervisors to supervise them in ways that will promote a climate favourable to the work of the organization.

The list is impressive in its diversity; what the items have in common is that they require knowledge about how people work, for the purpose of improving it.

As is evident from this list, the problems and practices concerning the regulation of people at work are diverse and not shaped by conventional categories of psychology. None the less, they have been influential in defining what work psychology is: in this they have been more influential than the discipline of psychology has been. Indeed, where psychology had little relevant to offer, as in the case of motivation theory (Hollway, 1991, pp. 8–10 and chap. 6), the practical problems of motivating people at work led to an unrelated body of motivation theory which is particular to work psychology (Herzberg, 1968; Herzberg, Mausner, & Snyderman, 1959; McClelland, 1961).

Three questions will protect readers from uncritically accepting the over simplified definition of work psychology with which this chapter began. First, what does being scientific mean in the context of application, and does it provide the guarantees that science implies? Second, to what end, and on whose behalf, do psychologists study individuals at work, and what effects do they have? Is the purpose to enable them to be happier workers, or better workers? Is it primarily on behalf of the employee or the management? Efficiency or welfare, or both? Third, what were the conditions for the emergence of the various strands of work psychology?

I start with a historical approach to the different labels, which gives insight into the changes in the discipline since the early 1920s and reminds us that work psychology is not a consistent, coherent body of knowledge, but a pragmatic amalgam without clear boundaries of potentially useful approaches to a practical problem: the regulation of the individual at work. The other two questions provide themes which run through this chapter and to which I return at the end.

LABELS AND THEIR ORIGINS

When the subject first emerged as industrial psychology after the First World War, it was rather different in character in Britain and the United States. Prior to that war, the practical space into which industrial psychology was to enter was dominated by scientific management (see below). Industrial psychology's focus is on the individual worker, and because scientific management was the first discourse systematically to target the individual worker, industrial psychology claims F. W. Taylor as its forefather and sometimes as its founding father. Although scientific management had profound effects on management practice in Europe (Devinat, 1927) and in Britain ("Some Principles of Industrial Organization . . . "), it was most influential in the United States, its birthplace (Hoxie, 1915).

In Britain, industrial psychology was launched on the reputation of fatigue research (see below), which seemed to promote both industrial welfare and industrial efficiency. The method was experimental and the perspective psychophysiological (Myers, 1926). This approach was also termed *human factors*. In the United States and Germany the initial paradigm was the same, borrowing the dominant experimental method and psychophysiological perspective from the emerging scientific psychology. In 1932 in Britain the *Journal of the National Institute of Industrial Psychology (JNIIP)* changed its name to *Human Factors*. In 1938 it was changed again to *Occupational Psychology* in order that "its coverage should be even wider than that suggested by the adjective 'industrial'" (Rodger, 1972). Charles Myers, the head of the NIIP, wanted the *JNIIP* to be concerned with "psychological problems arising in work of every kind and every level in organizations of every sort and every size" (Rodger, 1972). Out of line with the rest of the western world, "occupational psychology" remains the accepted title in Britain, although there has been a debate about changing the title of the *Journal of Occupational Psychology* (Occupational Psychology Section and Division joint meeting 1990, p. 375).

A consensual definition in British occupational psychology for several decades, until the influx of human relations approaches in the 1970s, was the one given by the first British professor of Occupational Psychology, Alec Rodger. It was concerned with

> practical and theoretical problems arising from "fitting the man to the job" (through vocational guidance, personnel selection and occupational training) and "fitting the job to the man" (through methods development, equipment design and layout, and the arrangement of working conditions and rewards. (Birkbeck College, 1961, describing the new postgraduate department in Occupational Psychology)

Thus it became known as the FMJ–FJM approach (fitting the man to the job – fitting the job to the man).

In the United States, the use of psychometric testing to place over 1 million personnel in the armed services changed the course of industrial psychology almost at the outset to a discipline where psychological measurement provided the method and the psychology of individual differences provided the perspective. This tradition, which has no theoretical or methodological base in common with human factors, was before long the dominant practice of industrial psychology. It has retained the status of the "jewel in the crown" of work psychology and since the early 1980s has renewed its position of dominance as the influence of human relations psychology has declined. The specific field is sometimes referred to as personnel psychology (more commonly in the USA) or vocational psychology. Whereas personnel psychology reflects the point of view of the employer interested in selection, placement, and promotion, vocational psychology has been applied both to this and to the individual, often school-leaver, deciding on the kind of work she or he would like to do.

Starting in the 1920s in the United States, the Hawthorne research (discussed below) was applying new socio-psychological approaches to address problems of worker satisfaction in machine-paced jobs. This was the beginning of the human relations paradigm, which still underpins "organizational behaviour". Organizational behaviour (OB) is an initially American label for a human-relations-based subject allied to work psychology, using neither laboratory experiment nor psychometrics, which attempts an organizational and socio-emotional perspective on its subject (Hollway, 1991, pp. 109ff). In Britain, OB owes more to a "scientific" social-psychological tradition. Organizational psychology is that part of OB, the greater part, which is not sociology.

Work psychology can be placed in relationship to a number of adjoining disciplines. At the social end, industrial sociology overlaps with organizational behaviour. At the physiological end, ergonomics overlaps with industrial psychology, through the psycho-physiological, experimental tradition. According to the British Ergonomics Research Society, ergonomics is the study of the relation between humans and their occupation, equipment, and environment, and particularly the application of anatomical, physiological, and psychological knowledge to problems arising therefrom (Shackel, 1974).

In the United States, industrial psychology and human relations or organizational behaviour have existed relatively independently of each other, the latter being fraternized by a majority of non-psychologists and identified with management ideas. In the expansion of the 1970s, human relations principles infiltrated eventually into British occupational psychology where they cohabited uncomfortably with the scientific tradition. Since much of occupational psychology was practised by non-psychologists and there was no career path and there were few specific jobs for occupational psychologists as such, the demands of the market (for students, consultancy, and research grants) dictated that human relations paradigms be accepted into work psychology. Organization development (OD) became a high-profile and attractive area for work psychologists.

In the recessions of the 1980s the trend reversed back to a dependence on work psychology's core skill of psychometrics. Instead of developing their middle and senior level staff through expensive human relations programmes, organizations were interested in selecting them correctly in the first place. In Britain and the rest of Europe, following the American trend, there was a spectacular growth of small commercial companies whose primary stock-in-trade was psychological measurement (Shimmin & Wallis, 1989). Since many of the central tests used in personnel selection are restricted to qualified users, these companies wanted qualified psychologists. In addition, these psychologists might be expected to perform most of the activities listed at the beginning of this chapter.

Work psychology has thrived by mingling with management training, human resource development, and personnel management. In the current climate, where psychological practice is subject to professional regulation, this poses a dilemma: who is allowed to practise what? It is impossible and undesirable for psychologists to control most of the practices concerning the regulation of the individual at work. Psychometric testing, however, is restricted, and this has confirmed its place as the core of work psychology.

I shall now trace the development of the different discourses within work psychology, starting with the conditions for the emergence of industrial psychology in the first decades of the twentieth century.

SCIENTIFIC MANAGEMENT AND THE TASK IDEA

Scientific management in its widest sense refers to the attempts made to

1219

devise efficient systems of industrial production and organization. In its narrower sense, it refers to the specific principles advocated by the US engineer F. W. Taylor before the First World War. Taylor's aim was increased productivity and the elimination of waste through management control of the labour process: "As to the importance of obtaining the maximum output of each man and each machine, it is only through the adoption of modern scientific management that this great problem can be finally solved" (Taylor, 1967, p. 27).

Three areas of scientific management became the province of industrial psychology: training workers in new methods devised by management; design of tools; and selection. The task idea, "the most prominent single element in modern scientific management" (Taylor, 1967, p. 64), meant that "the task of every workman is fully planned out, and each man usually receives written instructions describing in the minutest detail the work which he is to accomplish, as well as the means to be used in doing it" (Cadbury, 1914, p. 101). The task idea is significant for the emergence of management and for industrial psychology in two ways: its object was the individual worker, and it systematized the removal of autonomy from the workforce and transferred knowledge and further control into the hands of management.

Industrialization established the ground for management to emerge: increasingly the machinery developed for production necessitated the containment of labour in factories, rather than the old system of "putting out". Partly governed by the new machinery and partly by the desire to limit workers' control over their work, jobs became narrow, specialized, and stripped of the craft skill previously associated with them.

The deskilling of labour produced a new management class to deal with a problem of control which has been fundamental to the history of western capitalism and of industrial psychology. In the mid-nineteenth century in the United States, there were no middle managers. Fifty years later, management was well established with its own training institutions and journals: "Rarely in the history of the world has an institution grown to be so important and so pervasive in so short a period of time" (Chandler, 1977, p. 4).

Scientific management claimed that, through the task idea, industry would become more productive and trouble-free as it "gathers up, systematizes and systematically transmits to the workers all the traditional craft knowledge and skill which is being lost and destroyed under current industrial methods" (Taylor, quoted in Hoxie, 1915, p. 10). In effect this was a transfer of control from workers to management and was a significant part of the creation of management. To set the task, and to control it, management had to transfer all the specific knowledge and skill required to do particular jobs into its own hands.

The task idea is significant for a second major reason: it provided an industrial relations strategy which changed the focus from workers en masse (the response to which was unionization) to workers as individuals. This shift of focus to regulation of the individual worker was an essential condition of the emergence of industrial psychology, as well as being a political tool to counter increasing organization of labour into trade unions.

Scientific management also prepared the ground for industrial psychology by offering the means for workplace discipline to shift from the reign of arbitrary personal authority to the rule of law, procedure, and science. In Taylor's discourse (consistent with the wider status of natural science at the time), science functions as the neutral arbiter, outside the interests both of management and labour. The appeal to science denies power relations, since it produces "natural" laws which management too must observe: "It substitutes joint obedience of employers and workers to fact and law for obedience to personal authority" (Taylor, quoted in Hoxie, 1915, p. 9). Although science is supposedly the neutral arbiter, in practice "every protest of every workman must be handled by those on management side" (ibid). This "science" was produced on behalf of management.

Scientific management did not achieve the desired social regulation. With the destruction of the craft tradition and the introduction of machine-paced jobs, the control of the workforce became an issue of the utmost importance to employers. Absenteeism, restriction of output, and sabotage were rampant, even though supervision reached marathon proportions (Goldman & van Houten, 1979).

Scientific management targeted the individual as the problem of control, but since it stripped workers of any vestige of responsibility for their own work and yet failed to curb the foreman's arbitrary personal authority (for example Mayo, quoted in Hollway, 1991, p. 82), it exacerbated the problem. It required the counselling and interpersonal skills training programmes at the Hawthorne works to tackle the arbitrary authority of the foreman (Hollway, 1991, chap. 5). In this sense, scientific management ushered in human relations, which grew and became influential on the basis of its claim to get workers to regulate themselves. The concepts of motivation, job satisfaction, interpersonal skills for managers, and the long-running attempt at democratic leadership style, all testify to the shift from coercion of bodies to the attempted production of self-regulated individuals in managerial knowledge and practice. The primary problem still being addressed by contemporary work psychology is how to place responsibility for the work back in the hands of the worker. Whereas quantity could be partly regulated by the production line, quality has continued to evade supervision.

The greater strength of trade unions in Britain was an important factor in the take-up of scientific management, in regard both to its extent and emphasis. In the eyes of progressive British employers, the sorts of exploitation that were attributed to scientific management in the United States would court industrial unrest and possibly revolution in Britain:

The reduction of the workman to a living tool, with differential bonus schemes to induce him to expend his last ounce of energy, while initiative and judgement and freedom of movement are eliminated, in the long run must either demoralise the workman, or more likely in England, produce great resentment and result in serious differences between masters and men. (Cadbury, 1914, p. 105)

Industrial psychology in Britain emerged in close cooperation with the industrial welfare movement, that is, with progressive employers who had learned that it was necessary not to antagonize organized workers (Hollway, 1993).

HUMAN FACTORS

The problem of fatigue became prominent in the British munitions industry during the First World War, where the productivity of workers was improved at the same time as reducing hours of work and introducing improvements in working conditions.

During the nineteenth century, industrial workers organized to combat excruciatingly long hours; however, no attention was paid to the relation of hours to productivity. Workers were regarded as "hands", and from this perspective, employers assumed that the more hours they were put to work, the more they would produce. It took the conditions of war, and the reputation of science, to produce a wider acceptance of the principle that longer hours did not necessarily mean greater output.

Trade union organization, industrial unrest, and government response in the form of legislation on hours and working conditions, had succeeded in reducing working hours dramatically by the First World War. Then hours were increased to 70–90 a week, over 90 hours being not infrequent (Hearnshaw & Winterbourn, 1945). Studies showed the advantage in reduced hours: "In one investigation concerned with the heavy work of sizing fuse bodies, reducing the hours worked from 58.2 per week to 51.2 resulted in an increased total output of 22 percent. The hourly output increased from 100 to 139" (Hearnshaw & Winterbourn, 1945, p. 22). The findings of the wartime fatigue studies can be summarized as follows:

An extension of the usual hours of work does not – except for short periods during an emergency – give a proportional increase of output; on the contrary it causes the rate of output to fall off with increasing rapidity. . . . After a continuous period of overtime, improvement in output rate does not take place for some time after the re-introduction of shorter hours. . . . An unbroken spell of four and a half to five hours is generally too long. Man must rest even at work. (Industrial Health Research Board, 1940, quoted in Hearnshaw & Winterbourn, 1945, pp. 22–24)

The question of fatigue united concerns that were already of political importance: national efficiency, the health of the labouring classes and, because of trade union demands, working conditions in factories.

Psychologists were able to take much of the credit for this noteworthy achievement of advancing the goals of efficiency and welfare simultaneously (Mansion House meeting, 1922, p. 60) and it was on the basis of this reputation that psychology claimed a useful place in British industry and, in 1921, established the National Institute of Industrial Psychology (NIIP), an independent, self-financing organization, supported by politicians and progressive employers.

At one of its early fund-raising events in London, the aims of the NIIP were summarized in a speech as

> to assist employers in finding the best way to do each piece of work by the aid of scientific knowledge and scientific methods; and in addition to finding the best way to do each piece of work, we also want to help the employer to find the best job for each worker. (Mansion House meeting, 1922, p. 60)

None the less, industrial psychology was associated by many with scientific management, efficiency engineering, and "speeding up":

> It was obvious that the workers were straightway prejudiced against it by such terms as "efficiency" and "scientific management". By improvement in efficiency they feared speeding-up and the dismissal of their less competent comrades. The mention of scientific management made them suspect that all their craft knowledge would pass from them into the hands of their employers and that they would be degraded to the position of servile mechanisms. (Myers, 1926, p. 26)

Myers distinguished industrial psychology from efficiency engineering in the following way:

> It was sought not to press the worker from behind, but to ease the difficulties which may confront him. It has aimed at removing the obstacles which prevent the worker from giving his best to the work and it has almost invariably succeeded in increasing output by this method. (ibid., p. 28)

A report by consultants from an NIIP team who worked on contract for Rowntree's Cocoa Works before it established a Psychological Department provides an example of this approach:

> Under the new method here described, output increased by over 35% and the workers were unanimous in their appreciation of a considerable saving of fatigue at the end of the day, spontaneously expressing to the investigators their gratitude. (Farmer & Eyre, 1922, p. 12)

Psychologists in the human factors tradition are reputed for their meticulous scientific study of working conditions (Shimmin, 1986). However, the NIIP became increasingly dependent on work based on psychometric testing which employers wanted in order to improve selection. There was a retreat from working conditions research, partly because legislation and the factories inspectorate covered these areas, but also because of the move towards the individual as the object of strategies of regulation.

SELECTION

Since the First World War, the use of psychometric tests in an attempt to fit the worker to the job has dominated industrial psychology (Hollway, 1992). While training workers in the use of new methods was a significant early part of industrial psychology's work, selecting applicants for the various types of machine-paced work became increasingly prominent. Selection was based on the use of psychological tests for the measurement of various job-related skills such as visual acuity and finger dexterity. In 1933 Rowntree's labour manager published an article which claimed that the new methods "proved to be right in approximately 95% of instances" and that "the misfits have been practically halved" (Northcott, 1933, p. 168). Selection appeared to take over from fatigue as the practice which could be claimed as uniting the interests of efficiency and welfare: by "fitting the man to the job", he or she would not only be more efficient but more contented and "reduce to an almost negligible number the cases in which work is felt to be monotonous" (J. S. Rowntree, 1923, p. 245). It was claimed that even the most monotonous of jobs were suitable to some individuals, namely "the lowest grade of worker" (ibid). Women's "nature" provided a justification for situating them in dead-end and monotonous jobs (B. S. Rowntree, 1979, p. 139).

The *New York Times* of 17 February 1922, announcing the new Psychological Corporation whose aim was described as "the application of psychology to business", claimed: "Some of the backers of the Psychological Corporation believe that it would be possible to increase by $70,000,000,000 the national wealth each year by properly fitting every man, women and child to the kind of work each could best perform" (New Psychological Corporation in the USA, 1922, p. 76). Psychometrics, with its unique cocktail of "scientific" measurement, mass regulation, and the claim of enhanced productivity for business and the nation, put industrial psychology on the map.

Where psychometrics provided the method, the psychology of individual differences supplied the theory, which derived from social Darwinism and eugenics (Burt, 1953; Rose, 1985). The psychology of individual differences was recognized as quite distinct from laboratory psychology, as can be seen from Münsterberg's claim that "a complete change can be traced in our science" (1913, p. 10) and Burt's assertion of a "new, advanced and separate branch" which he called "individual differences in mind" (1924, p. 67). Viteles, whose textbook on industrial psychology succeeded Münsterberg's as the classic American text in the 1930s, explained the new psychology as follows:

> Industrial psychology is interested in the individual – in his reactions to a specific situation. The growth of industrial psychology has been associated with the development of psychology interested not in general tendencies, but in problems of a single individual and in the nature and extent of the variation of his response from the reactions of other individuals. (Viteles, 1933, p. 29)

This new emphasis brought engineering psychology and personnel psychology into "active conflict":

> The program of applied experimental psychology is to modify treatments so as to obtain the highest average performance when all persons are treated alike – a search, that is, for "the one best way". The program of applied correlational psychology is to raise average performance by treating persons differently – different job assignments, different therapies, different disciplinary methods. The correlationist is utterly antagonistic to a doctrine of "the one best way".... The ideal of the engineering psychologist, I am told, is to simplify jobs so that every individual in the working population will be able to perform them satisfactorily, i.e. so that differentiation of treatment will be unnecessary. (Cronbach, 1957, p. 678)

In the 1950s, however, the engineering tradition of job design, beseiged by its connections with scientific management, linked up with the new motivation theorists to produce ideas and practices concerning job enlargement and job satisfaction (Hollway, 1991, chap. 6) and thus started a not-too-successful move away from deskilling of jobs (Davis, Canter & Hoffman 1955; Walker, 1950).

HUMAN RELATIONS

Between the 1930s and the 1960s human relations became the dominant paradigm within which the management of people in organizations was understood and its practices modified. In its most popular and well-established sense, human relations "is simply a catch-all term for describing the way in which the people who comprise an organization think about and deal with each other' (Gellerman, 1966, p. 1). More precisely, it refers to a social-psychological paradigm for understanding the individual at work and to recommendations for management practice which stem from this approach. It is no more the exclusive property of psychology than of sociology or management theory. The practice of planned change outside the financial and technical spheres has taken place predominantly according to human relations emphases, notably motivation, leadership, and interpersonal skills.

A series of famous studies were conducted at "Hawthorne", a site of the Western Electric Company in a Chicago suburb, in the second half of the 1920s. Describing the reasons for the transition from the early illumination studies, Mayo (1949) comments:

> The conditions of scientific experiment had apparently been fulfilled – experimental room, control room; changes introduced one at a time; all other conditions held steady. And the results were perplexing. (p. 61)

Experimenters measured the effect on the productivity of women workers of a great variety of changes in working conditions, including illumination and rest pauses. Productivity increased under all conditions, a result that was attributed to the improved social relations. The extent to which this experiment became synonymous with the Hawthorne studies is evident in the way that this phenomenon is called the "Hawthorne effect". In 1928, Mayo (from the Harvard Business School) visited the plant. Also in 1928, an internal Industrial Research Division was set up to develop a massive interviewing programme to find out what was on employees' minds (Hollway, 1991, pp. 79ff; Roethlisberger & Dickson, 1970). According to Roethlisberger, one of the Harvard research team, in 1928 a new era of personnel relations began: "It was the first real attempt to get human data and to forge human tools to get them. In that year a novel idea was born; dimly the experimenters perceived a new method of human control" (Roethlisberger, 1949, p. 16)

The counselling programme which developed from this research at the Hawthorne works continued until 1956. In 1931, observation began in the Bank Wiring Room (all men employees), where restriction of output was first formally documented and investigated. The formal involvement of the Harvard team ended in 1932. The counselling programme led to training programmes in interpersonal skills (Roethlisberger, 1954) for supervisors, thus initiating a practice that was to become the bread and butter of human relations psychology.

The Hawthorne studies combined two radical departures from previous industrial psychology. The first involved a shift from the psychophysiological approach to the worker to a socio-emotional one. The second was a change in method from an experimental one whose object was the body (or the inter-face between the body and the job), to one whose object was attitudes as the intervening variable between situation (working conditions) and response (output). As Roethlisberger describes the conclusions of one set of studies (in the Relay Assembly Test Room): "What all their experiments had dramatically and conclusively demonstrated was the importance of employee attitudes and sentiments" (1949, p. 15). According to Roethlisberger (1949) the important characteristic of sentiments was that "they cannot be modified by logic alone" (p. 31). He described the early experimenters at Hawthorne as

> Carrying around in their heads the notion of "economic man", a man primarily motivated by economic interest, whose logical capacities were being used in the service of this self-interest. Gradually and painfully the experimenters had been forced to abandon this conception of the worker and his behavior . . . they found that the behavior of workers could not be understood apart from their feelings or sentiments. (p. 19)

Human relations not only made possible the production of different kinds of information for the first time in the workplace, but also had a powerful effect on the workers themselves. The Hawthorne interview programme discovered that a sympathetic interview technique not only could elicit new information that was valuable to management, but also could itself be instrumental in effecting a change in employees' attitudes. Human relations training was later to be based on this insight (Hollway, 1991, chaps 5 & 6).

Attitudes and sentiments became the central human relations problematic because they gave conceptual leverage to a problem of resistance to control by workers in large organizations. Commentators as far apart politically as Braverman (famed for his Marxist analysis of deskilling and the labour process) and Drucker (the popular management writer) are of the opinion that scientific management was not superseded but was built into the technology of the production line. Drucker (quoted by Braverman, 1974, p. 87) states that Taylorism "is no longer the property of a faction, since its fundamental teachings have become the bedrock of all work design". Braverman develops this by examining the role of management and related behavioural sciences once the technology is in place:

> Work itself is organized according to Taylorian principles, while personnel departments and academics have busied themselves with the selection, training, manipulation, pacification, and adjustment of "manpower" to suit the work processes so organized. Taylorism dominates the world of production; the practitioners of "human relations" and "industrial psychology" are the maintenance crew for the human machinery. (p. 87)

During the 1960s, full employment, strong trade unions, and an anti-authoritarian culture combined to maintain the centrality of motivation as management's way of viewing the problem of employee regulation (Hollway, 1991, chap. 7). In the 1980s and 1990s unemployment and the curtailment of trade union power meant that the problematic shifted away from motivation towards efficiency. Encouragement to self-regulation is still a central issue, but in practice is increasingly targeted towards a core – professional, managerial, and technical – workforce (Hollway, 1991, chap. 9). In the future, the difference between core and peripheral workers will probably be the basis for differences in regulatory practices: the use of psychometric testing to determine who gets a job and who does not and developmental methods including the use of selection tests, but also counselling and human relations-type training for a core workforce which would be expensive to replace and on whose commitment the organization depends. The way that work is structured in future will affect the relative dominance of problems concerning the individual at work. If "the days of the large employment organization are over" (Handy, 1984, p. 86), the problematic of motivation, based on the imperative to produce employee self-regulation, is likely to be modified or transformed.

CONCLUSION

Each regulation strategy associated with work psychology has used a different lens through which to view the individual: scientific management, human factors, selection, interpersonal skills training, work design, and leadership. They vary in their success and in the advantages that accrue to employees from their use. Among these there is little theoretical coherence, and even within each broad strategy there are differences. This is because they are not primarily the products of theorizing, but of changing regulative problems in a variety of workplaces. They do share one common feature, however, and this testifies to the power of work psychology: they all target the individual.

Work psychology's legitimacy hinges on its claim to be scientific and therefore neutral. The historical evidence demonstrates, however, that this very claim was part of a wider set of power relations which meant that work psychology has predominantly been produced from a vantage point of management's concerns with the regulation of individual employees. The extent to which this functions on behalf of employees is a question that can be answered only by looking at specific practices in specific locations. None the less, work psychology's utility to management hinges on its claim to be in the interests of both efficiency and welfare simultaneously.

FURTHER READING

Baritz, L. (1965). *Servants of power.* Middletown, CT: Wesleyan University Press.
Hollway, W. (1991). *Work psychology and organizational behaviour: Managing the individual at work.* London: Sage.
Münsterberg, H. (1913). *Psychology and industrial efficiency.* Boston, MA: Houghton Mifflin.
Roethlisberger, F. J., & Dickson, W. J. (1970). *Management and the worker.* Cambridge, MA: Harvard University Press (original work published in 1939).
Rose, M. (1975). *Industrial behaviour: Theoretical development since Taylor.* Harmondsworth: Penguin.

REFERENCES

Baritz, L. (1965). *Servants of power.* Middletown, CT: Wesleyan University Press.
Birkbeck College (1961). *Birkbeck College Calendar.* London: Birkbeck College.
Braverman, H. (1974). *Labour and monopoly capital: The degradation of work in the twentieth century.* New York: Monthly Review Press.
Burt, C. (1924). The mental differences between individuals. *Journal of the National Institute of Industrial Psychology 11*(2), 67–74.
Burt, C. (1953). *Contribution of psychology to social problems.* London: Oxford University Press (originally L. T. Hobhouse memorial lecture no. 22).
Cadbury, E. (1914). Some principles of industrial organization: The case for and against scientific management. *Sociological Review, 7*(2), 99–117.
Chandler, A. D. (1977). *The visible hand: the managerial revolution in American business.* Cambridge, MA: Harvard University Press.
Cronbach, L. (1957). The two disciplines of scientific psychology. *American Psychologist, 12*, 671–684.
Davis, L., Canter, R., & Hoffman, J. (1955). Current job design criteria. *Journal of Industrial Engineering, 6*(2), 21–33.
Devinat, P. (1927). *Scientific management in Europe.* Geneva: International Labour Organization.

Farmer, E., & Eyre, A. B. (1922). An investigation into the packing of chocolates (1). *Journal of the National Institute of Industrial Psychology*, *1*(2), 14–16.

Gellerman, S. W. (1966). *The management of human relations*. Chicago, IL: Holt, Rinehart & Winston.

Goldman, P., & Van Houten, D. R. (1979). Bureaucracy and domination: Managerial strategy in turn-of-the-century American industry. In D. Dunkerley & G. Salaman (Eds) *International yearbook of organisation studies* (pp. 108–141). London: Routledge & Kegan Paul.

Handy, C. (1984). *The future of work*. Oxford: Basil Blackwell.

Hearnshaw, L., & Winterbourn, R. (1945). *Human welfare and industrial efficiency*. Wellington, NZ: Reed.

Herzberg, F. (1968). One more time: How do you motivate employees? *Harvard Business Review*, *46*, 53–62.

Herzberg, F., Mausner, B., & Snyderman, B. (1959). *The motivation to work*. New York: Wiley.

Hollway, W. (1991). *Work psychology and organizational behaviour: Managing the individual at work*. London: Sage.

Hollway, W. (1992). Occupational psychology and the regulation of work: The case of vocational selection. *Occupational Psychologist*, *16*, 2–9.

Hollway, W. (1993). Efficiency and welfare: Industrial psychology at Rowntree's cocoa works. *Theory and Psychology*, *3*.

Hoxie, R. F. (1915). *Scientific management and labor*. New York: Appleton.

McClelland, D. (1961). *The achieving society*. New York: Van Nostrand.

Mansion House meeting (1922). *Journal of the National Institute of Industrial Psychology*, *1*(2), 59–61.

Mayo, E. (1949). *The social problems of an industrial civilization*. London: Routledge & Kegan Paul.

Münsterberg, H. (1913). *Psychology and industrial efficiency*. Boston, MA: Houghton Mifflin.

Myers, C. S. (1926). *Industrial psychology in Great Britain*. London: Cape.

New Psychological Corporation in the USA (1922). *Journal of the National Institute of Industrial Psychology*, *1*, 76–78.

Northcott, C. H. (1933) Industrial psychology at Rowntree's cocoa works. (2) Statistical note upon the results of vocational selection, 1923–1931. *The Human Factor*, 166–168.

Occupational Psychology Section and Division joint meeting (1990). *The Psychologist*, *3*(8), 375.

Rodger, A. (1972). *Training and development* (unpublished course notes of Birkbeck College, Department of Occupational Psychology).

Roethlisberger, F. J. (1949). *Management and morale*. Cambridge, MA: Harvard University Press.

Roethlisberger, F. J. (1954). *Training for human relations*. Cambridge, MA: Harvard University Press.

Roethlisberger, F. J., & Dickson, W. J. (1970). *Management and the worker*. Cambridge, MA: Harvard University Press (original work published in 1939).

Rose, N. (1985) *The psychological complex: Psychology, politics and society in England, 1869–1939*. London: Routledge & Kegan Paul.

Rowntree, B. S. (1979). *The human factor in business*. New York: Arno Press (original work published 1921).

Rowntree, J. S. (1923). The scope of vocational selection in industry. *Journal of the National Institute of Industrial Psychology*, *1*(6), 240–245.

Shackel, B. (Ed.) (1974). *Applied ergonomics*. Guildford: IPC Science and Technology Press.

Shimmin, S. (1986). *History and natural history in occupational psychology* (keynote address to the BPS Occupational Psychology conference, University of Nottingham).

Shimmin, S., & Wallis, D. (1989). *Change and survival in occupational psychology*. Paper presented at the 4th West European Congress on The Psychology of Work and Organisation, Cambridge, 10–12 April.

"Some principles of industrial organization: The case for and against scientific management" (1914). *Sociological Review*, 7(2), 99–117.

Taylor, F. W. (1967). *The principles of scientific management*. New York: Norton (original work published 1911).

Viteles, M. S. (1933). *Industrial psychology*. London: Cape.

Walker, C. R. (1950). The problem of the repetitive job. *Harvard Business Review*, 58(3), 54–58.

13.4

FORENSIC (CRIMINOLOGICAL) PSYCHOLOGY

Clive R. Hollin
University of Birmingham, England

Psychology in the courtroom
Eyewitness evidence
  The law–psychology debate
Confession evidence
The jury
  Jury selection and
    composition
  Extra-evidential influences
Strengths and weaknesses
Theories of criminal behaviour
Social learning theory
Cognition and crime:
  cognitive style
Empathy
Locus of control
Moral reasoning
Self-control

Cognition and crime: social
  information processing
Disposition or rational
  choice?
Crime prevention
Situational crime prevention
  Reducing opportunity
  Increasing the risk of
    detection
  Displacement
  Civil liberties
Offender rehabilitation
  A brief summary of the
    meta-analytic studies
Conclusion
Further reading
References

The application of psychology to the fields of law and criminal behaviour has become one of the growth areas of applied psychology since the early 1980s. Research has flourished, for example, in such diverse areas as crime detection, exemplified by offender profiling; police selection and training; courtroom dynamics, including the impact of expert psychological evidence and legal decision-making (in both civil and criminal courts); rules of law in mental health and juvenile and family legislation; the study of offenders, as with sex offenders and juvenile delinquents; and the design and impact of crime prevention programmes. While there is a fine line to be drawn in much of this research between criminology, sociology, psychiatry, and psychology, there are several texts that offer an overview of psychology, law, and criminal behaviour from a psychological perspective (Hollin, 1989, 1992; Kagehiro & Laufer, 1992; Lloyd-Bostock, 1988; Quay, 1987; Raskin, 1989).

While driven by theory and empirical research, forensic psychology is very much an applied field. Forensic psychologists work in many different settings, including prisons, courts, hospitals and other treatment facilities, probation services, police services, and government departments. They tackle a vast array of work, spanning consultancy, training, research, management, treatment, and giving expert evidence in court. Clearly it is not possible to cover all these topics in one chapter. Therefore I shall concentrate here on three areas that exemplify the range and scope of both theory and practice in contemporary forensic psychology – psychology in the courtroom, advances in theories of criminal behaviour, and impact of these theories on crime prevention strategies.

PSYCHOLOGY IN THE COURTROOM

The idea that psychology might have something to offer in the courtroom is not a new one. As long ago as 1908 Hugo Münsterberg suggested that psychology could usefully be applied to the study of eyewitness evidence and to the dynamics of the jury, while the psychologist would have much to offer in the role of an expert witness. Münsterberg's choice of topics for psychological research has stood the test of time, although as Diamond (1992) remarks, "Vigorous and sustained research in the field is a recent phenomenon. It is only 15 years since the first review of psychology and law appeared in the *Annual Review of Psychology*" (p. v).

Many forensic psychology practitioners will appear in the courtroom. The discussion below on the topic of evidence illustrates the theoretical, professional, and applied issues that face psychologists engaged in this type of work.

Eyewitness evidence

With a relatively long history, the psychological study of eyewitness memory provides an excellent illustration of the methods and controversies in legal psychology. It is not difficult to see why psychologists turned to the study of eyewitness memory, involving as it does the psychological processes of perception and memory, together with the opportunity to address a major concern of all those working in the justice system – the possibility of a wrongful conviction. Indeed, Huff and Rattner (1988) have suggested that "the single most important factor contributing to wrongful conviction is eyewitness misidentification" (p. 135).

The study of eyewitness evidence has generated a vast body of research collected in a number of books (e.g., Lloyd-Bostock & Clifford, 1983; Wells & Loftus, 1984), and discussed in several review articles (e.g., Goodman & Hahn, 1987; Williams, Loftus, & Deffenbacher, 1992). The force of this research has been to show how a range of variables can influence eyewitness memory and hence eyewitness evidence. These variables are generally referred to in the context of the three stages of *acquisition, retention* (or *storage*), and *retrieval* traditionally delineated in memory research. Through laboratory research it has become clear that memory for real-life events can be significantly affected at all three stages. Thus, variables operative at the stage of acquisition, such as the length of time spent in observation and the level of violence, can influence the accuracy of eyewitness recall and recognition. Storage variables, such as the length of time between viewing and recollection and talking with other witnesses can similarly influence eyewitness testimony. Finally, the same is true for retrieval factors as exemplified by the style of questioning used to elicit testimony and the impact of misleading information. In addition, individual differences such as the age of the witness may play a role across all three stages.

While much of the early research pointed to the somewhat fragile nature of eyewitness evidence, this knowledge base proved to be the foundation for a further research effort with the practical goal of enhancing eyewitness evidence. A body of psychological research has developed around, for example, the design and use of face recall systems such as the photofit and identikit procedures (Davies, 1983); the fairness of the identity parade or line-up (Cutler & Penrod, 1988); artist sketches (Davies, 1986); and improved interview techniques such as the cognitive interview (Fisher, Geiselman, & Amador, 1989).

The law–psychology debate

The psychological study of eyewitness evidence has generated debate in three areas. The first hinges on the theoretical interpretation of the findings from the research into leading questions. Specifically, there is a view that misleading information actually changes memory, so that recall of the original event is impossible (Loftus & Ketcham, 1983). Alternatively, other theorists hold that the misleading information coexists with the original memory and can be accessed given the right retrieval cues (Zaragoza, McCloskey, & Jarvis, 1987). These different positions and the experimental studies they generate clearly add to the richness of theoretical discussion within cognitive psychology.

The second area of debate centres on the generalizability of the experimental evidence, that is, the degree to which findings from mainly laboratory-based studies can be applied to "real-world" issues. Two studies have found high levels of similarity between eyewitness performance in laboratory and real-world settings (Brigham, Maass, Snyder, & Spaulding, 1982; Sanders & Warnick, 1981). Yuille and Cutshall (1986) found, however, that eyewitnesses to a real-life incident did not perform in a manner consistent with the research literature. This is an area in which further empirical studies are needed, gathering data from an amalgam of methodologies including laboratory studies, case-studies, field-studies, and study of archival sources.

The third area of debate, flowing from the second, concerns the presentation in court by forensic psychologists of the research findings, neatly including Münsterberg's role for the psychologist as an expert witness. The argued lack of generalizability of the findings is said by critics to restrict their usefulness generally, and may act to increase juror scepticism resulting in wrong verdicts being reached. In addition, the suggestion has also been advanced that jurors have an intuitive, commonsense appreciation of human behaviour that will allow them to judge when an eyewitness is likely to be inaccurate. The nature of the results from psychological research has also been a cause for debate. The experimental studies on which the forensic psychologist draws typically produce findings based on probabilities rather than statements of what is certainly true or false or right and wrong. Thus psychological research cannot predict whether a given eyewitness is correct or incorrect in, say, his or her identification of a suspect. Williams, Loftus, & Deffenbacher (1992) discuss these objections and conclude that confidence can be held in the reliability of the research findings; that expert testimony is needed to inform lay understanding of eyewitness testimony but that this does not adversely affect juror scepticism; and that probabilistic statements do not necessarily conflict with the role of the expert witness. In the final analysis the issue facing the forensic psychologist is one of individual ethical and moral judgement: potential expert witnesses must consider their belief in the strength of the evidence then, as Wells (1986) notes, "consider the potential effects of not giving expert testimony" (p. 83).

Confession evidence

Whatever the finer points of debate concerning the research evidence, it is undeniable that psychologists have brought the complexity of the issue of eyewitness evidence squarely into the public domain. The same is also true of another form of evidence – confessional evidence. As was once the case with eyewitness evidence, confessional evidence is accorded a great deal of weight in reaching decisions of guilt and innocence. If a person confesses to a crime, then this counts significantly towards a guilty verdict. However, a number of cases in England in the early 1990s, including the Guildford Four and the Birmingham Six, have shaken the public's faith in a criminal justice system that places such high value on uncorroborated confessional evidence. As with eyewitness evidence, forensic psychologists have been in a position to offer the courts both empirical evidence and a coherent explanation for the phenomenon of false confessions (Gudjonsson, 1992).

Kassin and Wrightsman (1985) outlined three types of false confession: first, the *voluntary confession* offered in the absence of any external pressure; second, the *coerced-compliant confession* made during police interrogation and which the confessor knows to be false; and third, the *coerced-internalized confession* in which during interrogation confessors come wrongly to believe, either temporarily or permanently, that they committed the crime of which they are accused. While voluntary confessions may be a sign of psychological distress, it is the latter two types of confessions that have attracted most attention from researchers.

The research into confessions has focused on the conditions under which the interrogation takes place, the tactics of police interrogation, and the psychological characteristics of the individual likely to make a false confession. In terms of conditions, it is plain that the experience of police custody can be stressful, placing the suspect in a vulnerable position. With regard to interrogational tactics, the police have developed sophisticated questioning techniques designed to exert maximum pressure on the suspect to confess (e.g., Inbau, Reid, & Buckley, 1986). Gudjonsson and Clark (1986) suggested that in seeking to cope with the demands of stress and interrogation, some individuals will be coerced into making false confessions. The *compliant* suspect, who knowingly gives a false confession, is characterized by generally low intelligence, high acquiescence (i.e., a tendency to answer questions in the affirmative), and a high need for social approval. *Suggestible* suspects, however, internalize the interrogator's messages and come to believe that they committed the crime, leading to false confessions. A summary of the experimental findings, reviewed by Gudjonsson (1992), describing the characteristics of the suggestible individual is shown in Table 1.

Psychological research has contributed significantly to the legal debate on the standing of uncorroborated confessions. It will doubtless be the case that the same issues detailed above in the law–psychology debate regarding eyewitness evidence will again be rehearsed for confessions. None the less, to be debating the issues from a psychological perspective is rapid progress, given the recent nature of much of the empirical work.

The jury

As Hans (1992) notes, while jury trials are decreasing in frequency, the jury continues to attract a great deal of research. Alongside the intricacy of the psychological processes involved, the jury continues to interest researchers, Hans suggests, because jury trials are often of social and political significance, including a critical role in death penalty cases in most US states.

Table 1 Psychological correlates of suggestibility

Psychological factor	Relationship with suggestibility
Acquiescence	Positive
Anxiety	Positive
Assertiveness	Negative
Facilitative coping style	Negative
Fear of negative evaluation	Positive
High expectation of accuracy	Positive
Intelligence	Negative
Memory ability	Negative
Self-esteem	Negative
Social desirability	Positive

Note: A positive relationship predicts that, say, as anxiety increases so suggestibility also increases; a negative relationship predicts, say, that as assertiveness increases suggestibility decreases.

The concerns of psychologists have been mainly in the four areas of jury selection and composition, extra-evidential influences, the impact of evidence, and decision-making.

Jury selection and composition

There are criteria, such as age and eligibility to vote, that inform the selection of individuals to sit on juries. However, the issue runs rather deeper than these formal criteria, in that an ideal juror would have sufficient intelligence to comprehend the evidence; would have the verbal and social skills to contribute to jury discussion prior to reaching a verdict; and would be unbiased and non-prejudicial at all times. In the real world, unfortunately, the ideal juror is a rare commodity: a number of studies have shown that juror verdicts can be heavily influenced by the age, sex, and psychological attributes of the jurors. For example, some people place undue faith in the state and the prosecution, believing that mistakes in the criminal justice system are infrequent. Clearly, it would not be in the best interests of justice to have a jury stacked with such individuals, and therefore some means of selection for jury service is needed. In the USA particularly psychologists have made their voice heard in the debate over the utility of "scientific jury selection". This approach to selection utilizes techniques such as polling public opinion to gauge normative attitudes and hence to profile ideal jurors; analysis of mock juror debates to inform selection and presentation of evidence; and assessment of jurors before the trial begins to identify "unsuitable" candidates. This procedure has generated considerable controversy, both in terms of the ethics of selection and the validity of the techniques themselves.

Extra-evidential influences

While one might hope that juror decision-making would be entirely based on the evidence presented in court, there are fears that extra-evidential factors may influence jurors. There are three likely sources of extra-evidential influence: pre-trial publicity, witness confidence, and the juror's perceptions and attitudes towards others in the courtroom.

Looking first at pretrial publicity, the typical experimental strategy is to give groups of mock jurors newspaper cuttings about a defendant in which details of previous criminal history, retracted confession, and so on are varied. In their overview of this research, Linz and Penrod (1992) drew the conclusion that "information about prior convictions and confessions may indeed be detrimental to criminal defendants. Emotional, sensational, or gruesome descriptions of the crime may also have an impact on juror decision making" (p. 11). Of course, judges can instruct jurors to disregard pre-trial publicity, but do such instructions translate into action? From the limited experimental evidence, the answer is in the negative. Judges' instructions appear to do little to eliminate the biasing influence of pre-trial publicity.

With regard to the impact of witness confidence, the weight of evidence from mock juror studies strongly suggests that jurors are more likely to return a guilty verdict after hearing evidence from a confident witness. Similarly, less credibility is accorded to the evidence from a hesitant, uncertain witness (Penrod & Cutler, 1987). Now, if confidence is a reliable index of accuracy, then this is not a matter for undue concern. On the other hand, if there is a grain of truth in Ambrose Bierce's observation that to be positive is to be wrong at the top of one's voice, then clearly this introduces a source of extra-evidential influence. The findings from studies of the relationship between confidence and accuracy bear witness to the truth of Bierce's witticism: at best confidence is arguably but a weak predictor of witness accuracy.

Finally, can jurors' perceptions, attitudes, and judgements be swayed by interpersonal factors rather than the evidence? In their overview of the research, Hans and Vidmar (1986) identified a range of such potential influences: for example, the physical attractiveness of the defendant can lead to a favourable outcome for the defendant (although more attractive defendants who offered little justification for their actions were seen as deserving a *more* severe sentence); defendants with high socio-economic status were seen as less blameworthy for their crime; and women are less likely than men to be found guilty for reasons of insanity. Other subtle influences on jurors include "powerful speech" (speaking clearly and without hesitation) by witnesses and defendants; the age of the witness; and the defendant's demeanour in court.

Strengths and weaknesses

Any field of applied psychology is bound to meet its critics who dismiss its theories, its methods, its appreciation of real world issues, and the generalizability of the evidence it produces. It would be naïve in the extreme to deny that there are strengths and weaknesses in studies in forensic psychology. Mock jury studies, for example, are easy meat for critics: they are removed from the drama of the courtroom, they do not always use trial procedures, they concentrate unduly on one variable, they rely heavily on undergraduate participants, and so on. However, rather than dismissing the research findings as worthless, as do some critics, it is more constructive to acknowledge the limitations of the studies and to seek to improve and broaden research methods. In that way weak findings can be identified and robust findings presented with greater certainty. Indeed, cases in which findings from social psychology were used to set legal precedence (Colman, 1991) should motivate researchers to seek ways to strengthen their procedures so that their findings can have an even greater impact on legal proceedings.

THEORIES OF CRIMINAL BEHAVIOUR

The search for an explanation for criminal behaviour has a long history, with distinguished contributions from many disciplines including psychology. As mainstream psychological theories rise to favour, so they have been applied to the phenomenon of criminal behaviour: for example, there have been psychoanalytic and psychodynamic theories, personality theories, constitutional theories, and learning theories (Hollin, 1989). While these theories all have their modern-day advocates, the current trends in psychological theorizing lie in the application of social learning theory and cognitive theory to formulate explanations of criminal behaviour. As will be seen, after a discussion of the theory, these theoretical advances have had a significant practical impact on crime prevention.

Social learning theory

The emergence of a social learning approach to the explanation of criminal behaviour can be traced to a line of theorizing, beginning with Sutherland's (1939) *differential association theory*, that emphasized the importance of learning in understanding criminal behaviour. Briefly, Sutherland took the view that crime itself is defined by those people within society with the power to make laws. Once defined, there are some people who abide by the rules and others who transgress. Why this difference in law-abiding behaviour? The answer, Sutherland proposed, is to be found in learning – learning that is no different in nature from any other human learning. Through association with individuals disposed to break the law, some people acquire not only the specific skills to commit offences but also the attitudes and motivations that favour breaking the law. In total, differential association theory incorporates three fundamental psychological assumptions: first, the crucial learning takes place within close social groups; second, the learning has both a cognitive and a performance component; and third, criminal behaviour is acquired behaviour and not a sign of deep-seated psychopathology. While all three assumptions would meet with sympathy from contemporary psychologists, at the time Sutherland was writing the basic theoretical structures to explain learning were not well advanced.

In seeking to offer an account of the process of learning, Jeffery (1965) suggested that operant theory could be used to refine differential association theory, giving *differential reinforcement theory*. In essence, Jeffery proposed that criminal behaviour is an operant behaviour: in other words, criminal behaviour is acquired and maintained by the reinforcing and punishing consequences it produces for the individual concerned. For example, in most cases of acquisitive criminal behaviour, such as theft and burglary, the consequences are financial gain. In turn, these gains make it more likely that the behaviour will be repeated when the occasion for a successful crime arises.

The advent of social learning theory (Bandura, 1977), in part an extension of operant principles, heralded the next theoretical step. Social learning theory departs from operant theory in the way it explains the acquisition of behaviour and the forces that maintain behaviour. In operant theory the acquisition of behaviour is through direct environmental reinforcement, in social learning theory the process of acquisition is extended to include modelling and imitation. The specific models for criminal behaviour are to be found in the social environment: in the actions of family and peers, in the prevalent sub-culture, and in cultural symbols as found on television and in magazines. The maintenance of criminal behaviour is, as in operant theory, not only via external reinforcement such as financial and social gain, but also through *internal* rewards such as increased self-esteem and self-reinforcing thoughts and through the nature of the appraisals of one's actions. These self-appraisals or *definitions* may be positive, in that the criminal behaviour is seen as desirable: for example, football hooligans may define their actions as exciting. Alternatively, the definitions may be neutralizing, serving to justify the criminal behaviour: for example, people who falsify their tax returns may say that the sums are so small that they do not matter, or that as there is no real victim so no harm is done as with "real" crimes. These definitions, clearly demanding complex cognitive processes, serve to set the meaning of their behaviour for the individuals concerned. As Akers (1990) suggests, social learning theory offers perhaps the most psychologically complete theory of criminal behaviour. One of the impacts of social learning theory, and of the cognitive revolution generally in mainstream psychology, has been to turn researchers' attention to the nature and role of cognition.

In the study of criminal behaviour, this trend has been manifest in studies of social cognition both in terms of cognitive style and cognitive processing.

Cognition and crime: cognitive style

In their review of cognition and crime, Ross and Fabiano (1985) make the distinction between *im*personal cognition and *inter*personal (i.e., social) cognition. The former is concerned with our knowledge of our physical world, the latter with our attitudes and beliefs about our social world. Various styles of social cognition have been associated with criminal behaviour, particularly juvenile delinquency, as outlined below. It should be noted, however, that these are trends in the literature: it is not the case that every study reaches the same conclusion, findings can vary for reasons such as sampling and design. Further, it should not be assumed that every offender will display these cognitive styles: these are general trends in offender populations *not* the defining characteristics of all offenders.

Empathy

The ability to see the world, including one's own behaviour, from another person's point of view is to display empathy. A number of studies have suggested that offender populations do not score highly on measures of empathy.

Locus of control

The concept of locus of control refers to the degree to which individuals perceive their behaviour to be under their own *internal* control, as opposed to being under the control of *external* forces such as luck or authority. The general empirical trend is that offenders see themselves as externally controlled. However, this may vary with the type of offence: violent young offenders, for example, show greater external control than non-violent young offenders (Hollin & Wheeler, 1982).

Moral reasoning

The broad conclusion across studies is that delinquency is associated with a delay in the development of moral reasoning (Nelson, Smith, & Dodd, 1990). However, as with locus of control, this may be tempered by type of offence. Thornton and Reid (1982) found that young offenders who had committed offences without financial gain, such as assault, murder, and sex offences, displayed more mature moral judgement than offenders convicted for crimes of acquisition such as burglary and theft.

Self-control

A lack of self-control is often associated with impulsive behaviour: a failure to stop and think between impulse and action. It is a finding of long standing in psychological research that offender populations are characterized by low levels of self-control (and hence high levels of impulsivity).

Knowledge of these styles of social cognition offers a general impression of the way that some offenders may view their social world. However, to achieve a more rounded picture, these "fixed" styles should be set in the more dynamic context of social information processing.

Cognition and crime: social information processing

The impact of theories of social information processing have been most keenly felt in the study of aggressive and violent behaviour. Dodge (1986) defined a sequence of steps in the effective cognitive processing of social information leading up to a given action: (1) the encoding of social cues; (2) the cognitive representation and interpretation of these social cues; (3) searching for the appropriate ways to respond in a given situation; (4) deciding on the optimum response.

The first part of this cognitive sequence involves the individual in perceiving and interpreting situational cues, especially the words and actions of other people. There is a body of research evidence that strongly suggests that aggressive and violent people, perhaps particularly aggressive and violent children and adolescents, search for and perceive *fewer* social cues than non-violent people. Yet further, it is likely that violent individuals will interpret the behaviour of others in a hostile manner (Slaby & Guerra, 1988). Indeed, this hostile aggressive interpretation of the actions of other people may well be a fundamental component of violent behaviour.

The next part of the sequence, following one's understanding of the situation, involves the generation of suitable responses for that situation. This particular cognitive ability is referred to as *social problem solving*. A number of studies with both male and female young offenders have shown that, compared to non-delinquents, offenders used a more limited range of alternatives to solve interpersonal problems, and in selecting a response rely more on verbal and physical aggression (Freedman, Rosenthal, Donahue, Schlundt, & McFall, 1978). It also appears that in many instances the violent response is seen as legitimate and acceptable. Yet further, it is now generally accepted that emotional arousal can have a complex interaction with angry cognition, intensifying the person's aggression and increasing the likelihood of a violent outburst (Novaco & Welsh, 1989).

There are two competing explanations for the finding of limited social problem solving in offenders. The first is in terms of a "cognitive skills deficit", in that for whatever reason some offenders have not mastered the skills necessary to generate a range of alternative solutions to cope with social problems. The second explanation focuses on the offender *defining* a given interaction as aggressive or hostile. Once this meaning is ascribed to a situation, albeit on the basis of limited utilization of social information, then it may well be the case that violent situations simply offer less alternatives for action. Following this line of thought, the decision to act in a violent manner becomes more reasonable: if you perceive that you are being threatened, then to decide to retaliate in kind is a defensible, even rational and legitimate, response.

These two interpretations of the research highlight a debate that has been running for centuries and has once again come to the forefront in contemporary exchanges (Roshier, 1989). With a "deficit" approach the antisocial behaviour is explained in terms of a failure to acquire cognitive skills and hence control over one's actions. Thus the individual's disposition to act in a criminal manner is seen as being determined by interactions between psychological, biological, social, and cultural forces. Alternatively, one might follow the rational "free choice" position, in which it is held that the person could equally as well have decided not to behave in a criminal manner as to elect to commit an offence.

Disposition or rational choice?

While dispositional theories of criminal behaviour were popular among many human scientists in the first decades of the twentieth century, during the 1970s there was a growing disenchantment with this approach to understanding criminal behaviour. Around this time a new approach began to emerge that saw human actions not as the product of social or psychological dispositions, but as the product of rational decisions motivated simply by self-interest and the expected gain to be had from the criminal behaviour. According to this latter view, there are two necessary events that must coincide for a crime to take place. First, there must be the opportunity for the crime; second, the individual must freely decide that the potential gains to be had from seizing the opportunity outweigh the potential losses if apprehended. A body of research evidence has, indeed, shown that many forms of criminal behaviour are related to increased opportunity and that offenders do make rational choices when faced with the opportunity to commit a crime (Cornish & Clarke, 1986). Now, while the conflict between dispositional and rational choice approaches raises several obvious philosophical and theoretical points, it also has an applied element in terms of crime prevention.

CRIME PREVENTION

There is nothing so useful as a good theory, and there are two crime prevention strategies in which the theoretical advances noted above have played a prominent role. The first strategy attempts to change the environment in which crime takes place; the second strategy seeks to change the person who commits the crime. The former approach has become known as *situational crime prevention*, the latter as *offender rehabilitation*.

Situational crime prevention

If we take the view that criminal behaviour stems from the opportunity to commit a crime in the knowledge that the potential gains outweigh the penalties, then it follows that in order to prevent crime we must reduce opportunity and/or increase the risk of detection. Such an approach holds, therefore, that crime prevention should focus on changing the situations in which crime takes place, rather than attempting to change the person after the crime has been committed. This approach to crime prevention has attracted the attention not only of researchers (e.g., Heal & Laycock, 1986), but also of politicians. As will be seen, many of the initiatives that have sprung from this political (and financial) investment have become part of our everyday lives.

Reducing opportunity

One way to reduce the opportunity for crime is known as *target hardening*: in practice this means physically strengthening the target or using security devices. The British Telecommunications company, for example, adopted this strategy by replacing aluminium coin boxes with steel boxes in seeking, with some degree of success, to reduce theft from telephone kiosks. Similarly, car damage and theft can be discouraged by the use of stronger and more sophisticated door locks, lockable wheel nuts, security coded sound systems, and car alarms. *Target removal* is another strategy aimed at reducing opportunity: payment of wages by direct bank credit, for example, removes the target of large amounts of cash being transported in public.

Increasing the risk of detection

One of the most obvious ways to increase the risk of detection is to increase levels of *formal surveillance*, particularly in situations where there is an increased likelihood of crime. While a police officer on every street corner would probably cut down crime significantly, this would have costs in terms of money and civil liberties. However, it does make sense for the police force to be present in increased numbers at sporting events such as football matches, and to patrol video and amusement arcades where truants from school (a high crime group) may congregate during school hours.

Alongside a human presence, such as a police officer, shop assistant, or car park attendant, technological advances have increased the potential for formal surveillance. Since closed-circuit television (CCTV) was used to cut down crime on the London Underground (Burrows, 1980), it has become widely used in banks, shops, and at sporting events. CCTV can, in theory, both deter and help to apprehend offenders. One of the most recent technological advances lies in the procedure known as *electronic monitoring* or *tagging*. Tagging involves convicted offenders wearing a small transmitter on their bodies, usually on the arm, ankle, or wrist. In one system the offenders are required to log in to a central computer via a telephone link in their homes: failure to log in would alert monitoring officers who are sent to investigate. Another system allows for constant monitoring via a device attached to the telephone system that picks up the transmitter's signals and relays them to a computer. If the offender moves out of a predetermined range from the telephone, say 30 metres, the monitoring officers are alerted. As noted by both British (e.g., Nellis, 1991) and US sources (e.g., Maxfield & Baumer, 1990), tagging has increased greatly in use since the mid-1980s.

Given the high cost of formal surveillance, strategies designed to increase *informal surveillance* have also been developed during the 1980s. Of the various strategies, there can be little doubt that Neighbourhood Watch (sometimes called Block Watch) has proved the most pervasive. Watch schemes have proliferated in North America (Brantingham & Brantingham, 1990), while Mayhew, Elliott, and Dowds (1989) estimate that in excess of 2.5 million households in England and Wales are Watch members. The principle underlying Watch schemes is simple: with the support of the police, people living close to one another take responsibility for the surveillance of each others' property, look out for suspicious characters, and report any signs of suspicious activity to the police. Indeed, the co-operation between police and public is a corner-stone of the scheme, encapsulated in the much-vaunted slogan "Crime: Together We'll Crack It".

Do Watch schemes work? In truth, the evidence is mixed, depending greatly on the operational definition of "work". Brantingham and Brantingham (1990) offer a concise statement: "The weight of evidence accumulated through evaluation studies conducted in North America and Britain now suggest that Watch programs may substantially improve participants' general attitudes about their neighbourhoods and may reduce participants' fear levels, but may not have much impact on crime" (p. 24).

There are other strategies, such as the design of streets and buildings, and the development of personal skills and strategies to avoid crime-prone settings, employed in situational crime prevention. However, there are complications to situational approaches to crime prevention that revolve around displacement and civil liberty.

Displacement

Do situational crime prevention strategies stop crime, or do they simply move it to another setting, time, or victim? It is clear that displacement can occur:

the evaluation of the introduction of CCTV on the London Underground hinted that crime had been displaced to those stations without CCTV close by those with the increased surveillance. Unfortunately, one of the major problems when attempting to establish whether an initiative has caused displacement on a large scale lies in untangling the crime statistics. Changes in the number of recorded crimes can be caused by many factors, making the influence of displacement effects, if any, extremely difficult to estimate. However, all things considered, it is unlikely that the human element can be discounted. It is plausible that some "occasional offenders" will be deterred by situational measures, while "professional offenders" will displace their criminal activity.

Civil liberties

Given that they change our environment, situational crime prevention measures raise questions about the society in which we live. A one level there are personal issues such as being recorded on videotape in banks and stores, carrying a personal identification card, and so on. At another level there are the implications of initiatives such as tagging: do we want a criminal justice system that uses electronic monitoring of fellow citizens? As discussed by Nellis (1991), technological advances may well make it feasible to implant transmitters under the skin so that in conjunction with CCTV the system could be used to monitor and hence control an individual's movements with hitherto undreamed-of precision. It is clear that society has some hard decisions to make regarding the balance between tolerance of crime and preservation of existing freedoms.

Offender rehabilitation

In 1974 Robert Martinson published a paper entitled "What works? Questions and answers about prison reform". The message that this paper delivered was that when it comes to the rehabilitation of offenders, "nothing works". This doctrine of "nothing works" has, in the time since Martinson's paper, become an article of faith, accepted by both academics and policymakers alike. It is interesting to speculate as to why the "nothing works" doctrine found such ready acceptance.

If we follow the reasoning of researchers such as Andrews (e.g., Andrews, 1990; Andrews et al., 1990), then we see that the idea of rehabilitation must have a large psychological component. To design and conduct effective rehabilitation programmes, some sophistication in the skills needed to work with individual offenders is a necessity. This focus on the individual is clearly an area in which psychologists might claim some expertise. Yet, the concept of rehabilitation implicitly contains the assumption, with all the associated theoretical connotations, that criminal behaviour can be changed by working with the offender. As Andrews suggests, this focus on the individual offender – in both a practical and theoretical sense – runs counter to the sociological and political dominance evident in some mainstream criminology. The concept of rehabilitation, with its emphasis on understanding and working with the individual offender, stands in stark contrast to theories of crime that emphasize, for example, the role of a capitalist economy in creating crime. It follows that such theories see not rehabilitation but political change as the means by which to reduce crime. Thus the "nothing works" position is entirely suited to those theorists who espoused theories of crime that paid little attention to the offender and were hence opposed to the need for any psychologically oriented account of criminal behaviour. However, as West (1980) points out, the goals of social reform and individual change do not have to be exclusive.

At a political level the view that nothing works in offender rehabilitation received a favourable reception in the political climate of the 1970s and 1980s. The marked political swings to the right in the USA, the UK, and parts of continental Europe brought about changes in the criminal justice system based not on the soft liberal ideal of rehabilitation, but on policies steeped in the hard conservative neo-classical assertions of the need for deterrence and justice through punishment. Thus, as Cullen and Gendreau (1989) note, the "nothing works" doctrine perfectly suited the mood of the times, and was elevated from the status of theoretical argument to socially constructed reality. Against this academic and political backdrop the policies generated by a belief in the futility of rehabilitation were easy to implement – where, after all, was the opposition? Who was there to produce the evidence to state the case for effective rehabilitation? (Assuming, of course, that policies are based on reasoned empirical debate – which might be a very large assumption to make.)

In fairness there was always a voice of opposition with some writers – most notably Paul Gendreau and Robert Ross (e.g., Gendreau & Ross, 1979, 1987) – holding the line that effective rehabilitation was not an impossible goal and pointing to examples of success. However, a problem faced by these champions of rehabilitation lay in making a coherent case from a myriad of research findings. In the field of offender rehabilitation, reviewers are faced with many different types of interventions, conducted in different settings, with different measures of "success". As there are hundreds of outcome studies, it is very difficult, if not impossible, to draw meaningful conclusions about what works, for whom, and under what conditions, simply by pooling the results of several hundred studies and "vote counting". Indeed, as Gendreau and Andrews (1990) note, such an approach can lead to the neglect of key information, the formulation of imprecise conclusions, and even author bias. However, the development of the statistical technique of *meta-analysis* has gone some way towards providing a means by which to produce a standardized overview of many empirical studies.

A brief summary of the meta-analytic studies

As Izzo and Ross (1990) explain, meta-analysis is

a technique that enables a reviewer to objectively and statistically analyze the findings of each study as data points.... The procedure of meta-analysis involves collecting relevant studies, using the summary statistics from each study as a unit of analysis, and then analysing the aggregated data in a quantitative manner using statistical tests. (p. 135)

For example, in a typical meta-analytic study, Garrett (1985) included in her analysis 111 studies reported between 1960 and 1983, involving data gathered from a total of 13,055 young offenders. From this type of large-scale analysis, informed conclusions can be made about whether treatment works, and estimates made of what type of intervention works best in what setting.

When considering the findings of the meta-analytic studies, it is important to make a clear distinction between *clinical/personal and criminogenic* outcome variables. The former can be thought of as some dimension of personal functioning, such as psychological adjustment, cognition, anger control, skill level, and academic ability; while the latter refers specifically to variables concerned with crime, recidivism, type of offence, and so on. As a generalization, rehabilitation programmes with specific *clinical* aims tend to produce beneficial *clinical* outcomes regarding personal change. Thus, for example, programmes designed to improve social skills in offender populations do generally lead to positive changes in social competence (Hollin, 1990a). However, it is possible for programmes to produce significant outcomes in terms of positive personal change, but for that personal change to have no impact on *criminogenic* variables (Hollin, 1990b; Hollin & Henderson, 1984). One contribution of the meta-analytic studies is that they allow us to begin to untangle the confusion in the literature between these two types of outcome measure.

In the field of offender rehabilitation there have been several meta-analytic studies since Garret's 1985 publication; as with most research, later studies are able to build upon and avoid the criticisms levelled at earlier efforts. The discussion below is guided by the findings of two important meta-analytic studies (Andrews et al., 1990; Lipsey, 1992). In particular, the Lipsey study is a major piece of work, involving an analysis of 443 outcome studies in field of juvenile delinquency.

The first point to emerge from the meta-analyses is that there is a substantial variability of criminogenic outcome in the literature. As Lipsey notes, some studies show high effects of intervention on recidivism, in keeping perhaps with the position of writers such as Paul Gendreau and Robert Ross; while other studies show either no treatment effect or even a negative effect, in line with the views of the advocates of "nothing works". Given this variability it is understandable that different reviewers, depending on their sampling of the literature and their definitions of "success", have arrived at different conclusions.

What elements of a rehabilitation programme are associated with changes in offending? The meta-analysis studies allow an identification of the factors that characterize intervention programmes that show a high effect in *reducing criminal behaviour*.

First, indiscriminate targeting of treatment programmes is counterproductive in reducing recidivism: important predictors of success are that medium to high-risk offenders should be selected, and that programmes should focus on criminogenic areas. Second, the type of treatment programme is important: the structured and focused treatments, typically behavioural, skill-oriented, and multimodal programmes are more effective than less structured approaches such as counselling. Third, the most successful studies, while behavioural in nature, include a cognitive component to focus on the attitudes, values, and beliefs that offenders use to support and justify their antisocial behaviour. Fourth, regarding the type and style of service, Andrews et al. (1990) in particular suggest that some therapeutic approaches are not suitable for general use with offenders. Specifically, they argue that 'traditional psychodynamic and nondirective client-centered therapies are to be avoided within general samples of offenders' (p. 376). Fifth, treatment programmes conducted in the community have a stronger effect on delinquency than residential programmes. While residential programmes can be effective, they should be linked structurally with community-based interventions. Finally, the most effective programmes have high "treatment integrity" in that they are carried out by trained staff and the treatment initiators are involved in all the operational phases of the treatment programmes. In other words, there is effective management of a sound rehabilitation programme based on social learning and cognitive principles (Hollin, 1990b). Added to this list is the further conclusion made by Roberts and Camasso (1991), following their meta-analysis, that interventions specifically targeted at the family are also successful in reducing delinquency.

In total, given the above conditions, the meta-analysis studies suggest that the high-effect outcome studies can produce decreases in recidivism of the order of 20–40 per cent over and above the baseline levels from mainstream criminal sanctioning of offenders. On this basis it is fair to conclude that it is not the case that "nothing works" in attempts to rehabilitate offenders. Indeed, this point is reinforced by Thornton's (1987) searching re-examination of the studies cited by Martinson (1974); although Martinson (1979) had himself begun to withdraw from the "nothing works" position. It can be stated with confidence that rehabilitation programmes, particularly those based on the principles detailed above, can be effective in significantly reducing recidivism. Of course this conclusion has obvious benefits at every level: it offers the potential to reduce victimization; it takes the offender out of the criminal justice system, to the potential benefit of both individual offenders and their families; and it reduces the financial burden on taxpayers.

CONCLUSION

While this chapter has illustrated some of the topics in forensic psychology, the field is rich and psychological theory and research continue to be applied across the criminological and legal fields. One of the challenges for those who work in this area is the range of material with which they must be familiar before advancing into the real world. I find myself reading almost as much criminology and law as I do psychology books and journals. There are, I think, a number of advantages in reading seriously across disciplines. For example, one reads criticism of psychological research from outside mainstream psychology. This outside view, so to speak, sharpens one's own critical faculties in both the theoretical and applied domains. However, there is a sense that currently the application of research is outstripping the development of theory. The next fundamental step to be taken is to attempt a meta-theoretical explanation of criminal behaviour, incorporating what is known from criminological, legal, and psychological research. The impact of such a meta-theory on forensic practice *would* be interesting to behold.

FURTHER READING

Gudjonsson, G. (1992). *The psychology of interrogations, confessions and testimony.* Chichester: Wiley.

Hollin, C. R. (1989). *Psychology and crime: An introduction to criminological psychology.* London: Routledge.

Kagehiro, D. K., & Laufer, W. S. (Eds) (1992). *Handbook of psychology and law.* New York: Springer-Verlag.

Quay, H. C. (Ed.) (1987). *Handbook of juvenile delinquency.* New York: Wiley.

Weiner, I. B., & Hess, A. K. (Eds) (1987). *Handbook of forensic psychology.* New York: Wiley.

REFERENCES

Akers, R. L. (1990). Rational choice, deterrence, and social learning theory in criminology: The path not taken. *Journal of Criminal Law and Criminology, 81,* 653–676.

Andrews, D. A. (1990). Some criminological sources of anti-rehabilitation bias in the Report of the Canadian Sentencing Commission. *Canadian Journal of Criminology, 2,* 511–524.

Andrews, D. A., Zinger, I., Hoge, R. D., Bonta, J., Gendreau, P., & Cullen, F. T. (1990). Does correctional treatment work? A clinically relevant and informed meta-analysis. *Criminology, 28,* 369–404.

Bandura, A. (1977). *Social learning theory.* Englewood Cliffs, NJ: Prentice-Hall.

Brantingham, P. L., & Brantingham, P. J. (1990). Situational crime prevention in practice. *Canadian Journal of Criminology, 32,* 17–40.

Brigham, J. C., Maass, A., Snyder, L. D., & Spaulding, K. (1982). Accuracy of eyewitness identification in a field setting. *Journal of Personality and Social Psychology, 42*, 673–681.

Burrows, J. (1980). Closed circuit television and crime on the London Underground. In R. V. G. Clarke & P. Mayhew (Eds) *Designing out crime* (pp. 75–83). London: Her Majesty's Stationery Office.

Colman, A. M. (1991). Crowd psychology in South African murder trials. *American Psychologist, 46*, 1071–1079.

Cornish, D. B., & Clarke, R. V. G. (Eds) (1986). *The reasoning criminal: Rational choice perspectives on crime.* New York: Springer-Verlag.

Cullen, F. T., & Gendreau, P. (1989). The effectiveness of correctional rehabilitation: Reconsidering the "nothing works" debate. In L. Goodstein & D. L. MacKenzie (Eds) *The American prison: Issues in research and policy* (pp. 23–44). New York: Plenum.

Cutler, B. L., & Penrod, S. D. (1988). Improving the reliability of eyewitness identification: Lineup construction and presentation. *Journal of Applied Psychology, 73*, 281–290.

Davies, G. M. (1983). Forensic face recall: The role of visual and verbal information. In S. M. A. Lloyd-Bostock & B. R. Clifford (Eds) *Evaluating witness evidence: Recent psychological research and new perspectives* (pp. 103–123). Chichester: Wiley.

Davies, G. M. (1986). Capturing likeness in eyewitness composites: The police artist and his rivals. *Medicine, Science and the Law, 26*, 283–290.

Diamond, S. S. (1992). Foreword. In D. K. Kagehiro & W. S. Laufer (Eds) *Handbook of psychology and law* (pp. v–ix). New York: Springer-Verlag.

Dodge, K. A. (1986). A social-information processing model of social competence in children. In M. Permutter (Ed.) *Minnesota symposium on child psychology* (vol. 18, pp. 77–125). Hillsdale, NJ: Lawrence Erlbaum.

Fisher, R. P., Geiselman, R. E., & Amador, M. (1989). Field test of the cognitive interview: Enhancing the recollection of actual victims and witnesses of crime. *Journal of Applied Psychology, 74*, 722–727.

Freedman, B. J., Rosenthal, L., Donahue, C. P., Schlundt, D. G., & McFall, R. M. (1978). A social-behavioral analysis of skills deficits in delinquent and non-delinquent adolescent boys. *Journal of Consulting and Clinical Psychology, 46*, 1448–1462.

Garrett, C. J. (1985). Effects of residential treatment of adjudicated delinquents: A meta-analysis. *Journal of Research in Crime and Delinquency, 22*, 287–308.

Gendreau, P., & Andrews, D. A. (1990). Tertiary prevention: What the meta-analyses of the offender treatment literature tell us about "what works". *Canadian Journal of Criminology, 32*, 173–184.

Gendreau, P., & Ross, R. R. (1979). Effective correctional treatment: Bibliotherapy for cynics. *Crime and Delinquency, 25*, 463–489.

Gendreau, P., & Ross, R. R. (1987). Revivification of rehabilitation: Evidence from the 1980s. *Justice Quarterly, 4*, 349–407.

Goodman, G. S., & Hahn, A. (1987). Evaluating eyewitness testimony. In I. B. Weiner & A. K. Hess (Eds) *Handbook of forensic psychology* (pp. 258–292). New York: Wiley.

Gudjonsson, G. (1992). *The psychology of interrogations, confessions and testimony.* Chichester: Wiley.

Gudjonsson, G., & Clark, N. K. (1986). Suggestibility in police interrogation: A social psychological model. *Social Behaviour, 1*, 83–104.

Hans, V. P. (1992). Jury decision making. In D. K. Kagehiro & W. S. Laufer (Eds) *Handbook of psychology and law* (pp. 56–76). New York: Springer-Verlag.

Hans, V. P., & Vidmar, N. (1986). *Judging the jury.* New York: Plenum.

Heal, K., & Laycock, G. (Eds) (1986). *Situational crime prevention: From theory into practice.* London: Her Majesty's Stationery Office.

Hollin, C. R. (1989). *Psychology and crime: An introduction to criminological psychology.* London: Routledge.

Hollin, C. R. (1990a). Social skills training with delinquents: A look at the evidence and some recommendations for practice. *British Journal of Social Work, 20,* 483–493.

Hollin, C. R. (1990b). *Cognitive-behavioral interventions with young offenders.* Elmsford, NY: Pergamon.

Hollin, C. R. (1992). *Criminal behaviour: A psychological approach to explanation and prevention.* London: Falmer.

Hollin, C. R., & Henderson, M. (1984). Social skills training with young offenders: False expectations and the "failure of treatment". *Behavioural Psychotherapy, 12,* 331–341.

Hollin, C. R., & Wheeler, H. M. (1982). The violent young offender: A small group study of a Borstal population. *Journal of Adolescence, 5,* 247–257.

Huff, C. R., & Rattner, A. (1988). Convicted but innocent: False positives and the criminal justice process. In E. Scott & T. Hirschi (Eds) *Controversial issues in crime and justice* (pp. 130–144). Beverly Hills, CA: Sage.

Inbau, F. E., Reid, J. E., & Buckley, J. P. (1986). *Criminal interrogation and confessions* (3rd edn). Baltimore, MD: Williams & Wilkins.

Izzo, R. L., & Ross, R. R. (1990). Meta-analysis of rehabilitation programs for juvenile delinquents: A brief report. *Criminal Justice and Behavior, 17,* 134–142.

Jeffery, C. R. (1965). Criminal behavior and learning theory. *Journal of Criminal Law, Criminology and Police Science, 56,* 294–300.

Kagehiro, D. K., & Laufer, W. S. (Eds) (1992). *Handbook of psychology and law.* New York: Springer-Verlag.

Kassin, S. M., & Wrightsman, L. S. (1985). Confession evidence. In S. M. Kassin & L. S. Wrightsman (Eds) *The psychology of evidence and trial procedure* (pp. 67–94). Beverly Hills, CA: Sage.

Linz, D., & Penrod, S. (1992). Exploring the First and Sixth Amendments: Pretrial publicity and jury decision making. In D. K. Kagehiro & W. S. Laufer (Eds) *Handbook of psychology and law* (pp. 3–36). New York: Springer-Verlag.

Lipsey, M. W. (1992). Juvenile delinquency treatment: A meta-analytic inquiry into the variability of effects. In T. D. Cook, H. Cooper, D. S. Cordray, H. Hartmann, L. V. Hedges, R. J. Light, T. A. Louis, & F. Mosteller (Eds) *Meta-analysis for explanation: A casebook* (pp. 83–127). New York: Russell Sage Foundation.

Lloyd-Bostock, S. M. A. (1988). *Law in practice.* London: British Psychological Society and Routledge.

Lloyd-Bostock, S. M. A., & Clifford, B. R. (Eds) (1983). *Evaluating witness evidence: Recent psychological research and new perspectives.* Chichester: Wiley.

Loftus, E. F., & Ketcham, K. E. (1983). The malleability of eyewitness accounts. In S. M. A. Lloyd-Bostock & B. R. Clifford (Eds) *Evaluating eyewitness evidence: Recent psychological research and new perspectives* (pp. 159–171). Chichester: Wiley.

Martinson, R. (1974). What works? Questions and answers about prison reform. *Public Interest, 35,* 22–54.

Martinson, R. (1979). New findings, new views: A note of caution regarding sentencing reform. *Hofsta Law Review, 7,* 242–258.

Maxfield, M. G., & Baumer, T. L. (1990). Home detention with electronic monitoring: Comparing pretrial and postconviction programs. *Crime and Delinquency*, *36*, 521–536.

Mayhew, P., Elliott, D., & Dowds, L. (1989). *The 1988 British Crime Survey*. London: Her Majesty's Stationery Office.

Münsterberg, H. (1908). *On the witness stand: Essays on psychology and crime*. New York: Clark, Boardman.

Nellis, M. (1991). The electronic monitoring of offenders in England and Wales. *British Journal of Criminology*, *31*, 165–185.

Nelson, J. R., Smith, D. J., & Dodd, J. (1990). The moral reasoning of juvenile delinquents: A meta-analysis. *Journal of Abnormal Child Psychology*, *18*, 231–239.

Novaco, R. W., & Welsh, W. N. (1989). Anger disturbances: Cognitive mediation and clinical prescriptions. In K. Howells & C. R. Hollin (Eds) *Clinical approaches to violence* (pp. 39–60). Chichester: Wiley.

Penrod, S. D., & Cutler, B. L. (1987). Assessing the competence of juries. In I. B. Weiner & A. K. Hess (Eds) *Handbook of forensic psychology* (pp. 293–318). New York: Wiley.

Quay, H. C. (Ed.) (1987). *Handbook of juvenile delinquency*. New York: Wiley.

Raskin, D. C. (Ed.) (1989). *Psychological methods in criminal investigation and evidence*. New York: Springer.

Roberts, A. R., & Camasso, M. J. (1991). The effect of juvenile offender treatment programs on recidivism: A meta-analysis of 46 studies. *Notre Dame Journal of Law, Ethics and Public Policy*, *5*, 421–441.

Roshier, B. (1989). *Controlling crime: The classical perspective in criminology*. Milton Keynes: Open University Press.

Ross, R. R., & Fabiano, E. A. (1985). *Time to think: A cognitive model of delinquency prevention and offender rehabilitation*. Johnson City, TN: Institute of Social Sciences and Arts.

Sanders, G. S., & Warnick, D. H. (1981). Truth and consequences: The effect of responsibility on eyewitness behavior. *Basic and Applied Social Psychology*, *2*, 67–79.

Slaby, R. G., & Guerra, N. G. (1988). Cognitive mediators of aggression in adolescent offenders: 1. Assessment. *Developmental Psychology*, *24*, 580–588.

Sutherland, E. H. (1939). *Principles of criminology*. Philadelphia, PA: Lippincott.

Thornton, D. M. (1987). Treatment effects on recidivism: A reappraisal of the "nothing works" doctrine. In B. J. McGurk, D. M. Thornton, & M. Williams (Eds) *Applying psychology to imprisonment: Theory and practice* (pp. 181–189). London: Her Majesty's Stationery Office.

Thornton, D. M., & Reid, R. L. (1982). Moral reasoning and type of criminal offence. *British Journal of Social Psychology*, *21*, 231–238.

Wells, G. L. (1986). Expert psychological testimony: Empirical and conceptual analyses of effects. *Law and Human Behavior*, *10*, 83–95.

Wells, G. L., & Loftus, E. F. (Eds) (1984). *Eyewitness testimony: Psychological perspectives*. Cambridge: Cambridge University Press.

West, D. J. (1980). The clinical approach to criminology. *Psychological Medicine*, *10*, 619–631.

Williams, K. D., Loftus, E. F., & Deffenbacher, K. A. (1992). Eyewitness evidence and testimony. In D. K. Kagehiro & W. S. Laufer (Eds) *Handbook of psychology and law* (pp. 141–166). New York: Springer-Verlag.

Yarmey, A. D. (1979). *The psychology of eyewitness testimony*. New York: Free Press.

Yuille, J. C., & Cutshall, J. L. (1986). A case study of eyewitness memory to a crime. *Journal of Applied Psychology*, *71*, 291–301.

Zaragoza, M. S., McCluskey, M., & Jarvis, M. (1987). Misleading post-event information and recall of the original event: Further evidence against the memory impairment hypothesis. *Journal of Experimental Psychology: Learning, Memory and Cognition*, *13*, 36–44.

13.5

PSYCHOANALYSIS

Peter Fonagy
University College London, England

Psychoanalysis is at least four things. First and foremost, it is a method of psychotherapeutic treatment originated by two Viennese physicians, Joseph Breuer and Sigmund Freud, who first described "the talking cure" in their visionary book *Studies on Hysteria* published in 1895. It was elaborated and extended in the corpus of Freud's work as well as that of psychoanalysts who followed him.

The psychoanalytic method is deceptively simple. Two people meet daily for a set period of time, usually 50 minutes, in surroundings designed to minimize extraneous stimuli. Traditionally the room has a couch on which the analysand (the patient) can lie comfortably and a chair for the analyst, who normally sits out of range of the patient's vision. The analysand speaks spontaneously of whatever is passing through his or her mind. Analysts normally restrict themselves to listening, and they try to make sense of what they hear and observe and communicate their conclusions to the patient from time to time.

Among the techniques described by Freud as part of psychoanalysis are *free association* (encouraging patients to tell their therapist all their thoughts without attempt at censorship) and *interpretation* (the attempt on the part of the therapist to identify feelings, links, and ideas in the patient's verbalization of which the patient was unaware). Other phenomena that serve the psychoanalytic process are *transference* (the tendency of patients to re-experience, in the context of the therapeutic relationship, their feelings and conflicts associated with early caregiving figures) and *insight* (the curative effect of arriving at a conscious understanding of the unconscious and mostly childlike reasons that underlie maladaptive behaviour). Psychoanalysis is a form of therapy that is at the same time a source of psychological data. Psychoanalysts use their clinical experience with patients as a basis for generalizations about psychopathology, personality, and human psychology.

Second, psychoanalysis is a theory of mental illness, particularly of neurosis. It holds that many maladaptive behaviours, such as anxiety or depression, for which individuals seek psychological help, are symptoms of a dysfunctional mental system. More specifically, symptoms serve to help the individual to resolve conflicts between conscious and non-conscious feelings, ideas, and fantasies. For example, the neurotic symptom of depression may represent a way of avoiding conscious confrontation with a much-loved figure towards whom the individual unconsciously experiences feelings of violent rage. If anger in connection with that individual is felt to be intoler-able – perhaps the object of the anger is perceived as fragile or as potentially dangerous – the person may resolve the conflict by turning the anger against him- or herself. The result will be the experience of pervasive self-criticism, a sense of total inadequacy, and a painful sense of worthlessness.

Third, psychoanalysis is a theory of individual differences and personality. It is constructed to account for differences in character that we all observe in people we know: family, friends, and colleagues. Why is one person more self-assured, confident, and apparently unconcerned about criticism than another? The psychoanalytic account of such differences would reach into the nature of early relationships that individuals had with their primary caregivers. People who are diffident and constantly in need of reassurance and praise might have had parental figures who were less attentive or simply less perceptive of their early childhood achievements. They have had no opportunity to internalize the ability to judge the value of actions, and conse-quently they remain uncertain of the worth of their achievements despite con-siderable evidence to the contrary (that is, their past history of significant personal accomplishments). They thus find themselves constantly turning to the outside world for an affirmation of the appropriateness of their actions. Psychoanalysts have made considerable efforts to draw up a typology of human character and to provide explanations, in terms of common patterns of childhood experience and reactions to these, for individual differences in personality.

Fourth, psychoanalysis is a psychology; it is a collection of theories or generalizations made about the functioning of human minds based on psychoanalytic clinical experience. Freud and his followers constructed a model of the mind, consistent with their clinical experience, which has been very influential in general psychology. Freud drew attention to the limited access that the conscious mind has to all the mental processes one needs to postulate to provide an adequate account of human behaviour. He likened the mind to an iceberg, and awareness to its very tip, the only part of the structure above the waterline. He also conceived of the need for mechanisms of psychological defence, mental operations, with the function of reducing anxiety. Thus he noted that we often choose to forget aspects of our life that carry painful connotations, and he hypothesised that this phenomenon was underpinned by the defensive manoeuvre of repression.

Finally, psychoanalysis also encompasses Freud's most ambitious project. He intended it to be a general theory of human civilization with the potential to enrich the description of social phenomena and cultural products and codes, in addition to being a psychology of the unconscious and a theory of individual differences and psychopathology. For example, he contemplated the nature of humour, in particular jokes. He noted that rarely, if ever, are jokes genuinely innocent, free of sexual or aggressive innuendo. He proposed that jokes permit a temporary suspension of culturally imposed constraints on human thoughts, fantasies, and emotions and thus bypass the forces of repression. Perhaps this is why it is notoriously difficult to remember jokes. We hear literally thousands of jokes and humorous remarks over the course of our lives, yet most of us find it well-nigh impossible to recall successfully more than a handful of genuinely funny stories.

Freud also commented on art. He was convinced that psychoanalysts, through their understanding of the individual psyche, achieved unique insights into aesthetic experience. Through art the contents of the unconscious mind can be communicated rapidly and in all its complexity, and aesthetic experience is the appreciation of the artist's ability to perform this remarkable feat.

THE DEVELOPMENT OF PSYCHOANALYTIC THEORY

Not surprisingly, psychoanalysis has undergone several major transformations between its inception in the late nineteenth century and its current form nearly 100 years later. What makes this development somewhat difficult to follow is that these changes to psychoanalytic ideas tend not to be transformations or substitutions of one theoretical framework for another. Rather, new ideas were added to old ones, enriching existing theoretical frameworks and developing alternative formulations, but stopping short of discarding previous proposals. The end result is a body of knowledge containing very many inherent contradictions and inconsistencies.

This is one of the greatest weaknesses of psychoanalytic epistemology;

psychoanalysis seems unable to discard plausible ideas once proposed and accepted, even if alternative formulations would provide a better account of the same phenomenon. Psychoanalysts have become accustomed to this state of affairs, and psychoanalysis is taught in most institutes in a historical manner, starting with Freud's earliest ideas and building up to more recent formulations. I shall follow this tradition.

The affect trauma model

Freud's first major psychoanalytic proposal concerned the nature of hysteria. This is a condition in which the patient experiences physical symptoms, for example blindness or paralysis, without obvious organic cause. Breuer and Freud (1895) discovered that such symptoms were not due to the degeneration of the nervous system (as previously thought), but rather were frequently responses to a major emotional trauma of which the patient appeared to have no conscious knowledge. The experiences were of such emotional force that the patient's mind failed in its attempt to exclude the experience from consciousness, and the affect associated with the trauma broke through and manifested as the symptom which had hidden connections to the original experience. For example, a 45-year-old man suffered temporary unexplained blindness after witnessing his wife having sex with his best friend.

Freud's idea was less than popular; this was primarily because he dared to suggest that, most commonly, hysterical symptoms are the consequence of the psychic trauma associated with the physical or sexual abuse of children. More recently, it has become generally accepted that, in the majority of cases of severe personality disorder of the kind discussed by Freud at this time, childhood maltreatment *is* an important causal factor.

One of several reasons for the failure of Freud's early formulation was the inadequacy of the treatment. Freud's therapy involved the release of pent-up emotion (catharsis) associated with early trauma by helping patients to bring the experience fully into consciousness (abreaction). Freud attempted to use hypnosis to achieve this effect, but it was a method in which he was not particularly proficient. Abreaction and catharsis, abandoned for many years by psychotherapists, are once again key components in many current treatments of post-traumatic stress disorder.

The topographical model

By 1900, Freud had discarded his childhood-seduction theory, constructed a new general model of mental function, revised his theory of neurotic disturbance, and laid down the principles of psychoanalytic treatment as described above. The corner-stone of Freud's (1900) new theory was the assumption that much human thought inevitably takes place outside consciousness. He distinguished the conscious, preconscious, and unconscious systems of the mind. Psychological difficulties could be explained by a conflict between unconsciously held, childlike wishes and the largely socially acceptable ideas which constitute the contents of consciousness.

He postulated that sexual and aggressive mental contents are repudiated by consciousness. These arise out of instinct-driven motives and dominate the *System Unconscious*. The *System Preconscious* is the middle layer within this topographical model and plays a primary role in the distortion and censorship of forbidden instinctual wishes; it permits thoughts from the *System Unconscious* to access consciousness only if they are already so distorted that their unconscious origins can no longer be detected.

Freud's (1905) dual instinct theory postulated a sexual and, later, an aggressive drive. The individual was seen by Freud as "defending" against aggressive and sexual wishes by *repressing* them into the non-conscious part of the mind. Repression was assumed not to function under certain conditions and these permitted insight into the functioning of the unconscious.

During sleep, the part of the mind responsible for protecting consciousness from unacceptable impulses (which Freud called the censor) weakens in its function; thus the mental content of sleep (the dream) contains more or less direct reflections of unconscious mental contents. Repressed wishes find expression through dreams, albeit in an indirect form. Thus the dream of a small child about losing a favourite pet might be interpreted as an expression of an unconscious wish to "lose", or at any rate to be rid of, a younger sibling.

Freud realized that the conscious contemplation of instinct-driven wishes would create anxiety; hence the need for repression and censorship even in dreams. The expression of forbidden impulses in dreams may explain why most of our dreams are associated with the experience of anxiety and are distorted to circumvent understanding by the censor. The mode of thinking in the System Unconscious was seen by Freud as fundamentally different from conscious thought. The unconscious was assumed to be dominated by primary process thinking: impulsive, disorganized, and bizarre visual images, untroubled by considerations of time, order, or logical consistency. Freud claimed that the bizarre, irrational nature of dreams reflected the functioning of primary thought processes and could be understood if the mechanisms of distortion were carefully unravelled. Freud (1900) reported a dream he had had of seeing his sleeping mother being carried into a room by some bird-headed people. Freud interpreted the dream as a disguised expression of his sexual feelings for his mother. The word for bird (*Vogel*) is similar to the German slang word for having sex (*vögeln*).

Unconscious wishes are also directly expressed in jokes. It is hard to think of genuinely humorous stories that do not involve a certain degree of aggressive content which, outside the permissive atmosphere created by humour, would be totally unacceptable. Slips of the tongue − also called "Freudian slips' − may occasionally directly express unconscious concerns.

For example, a US woman senator spoke in highly indignant terms about ideological repression in the United States "of feminists, homosexuals, and other perversions – I mean persuasions".

Freud (1905) constructed a view of human life determined by primitive human urges that we need to master, over the first years of life, in order to conform to the demands of society. These drives were assumed to be rooted in the body; their mental representation occurs in terms of the wish for gratification directed towards external figures (objects). The biological evolution of the instinct over the course of life provided the principal framework for the psychoanalytic theory of development. The sexual instinct was thought to develop through a predictable sequence of stages marked by specific bodily concerns.

The early stages of psychosexual development were assumed by Freud to be organized around oral pleasures and anal concerns. In the fourth and fifth years of life the child is thought to enter into a particularly formative phase. Children develop close ties with the caregiver which they wish to maintain as an exclusive bond. Their increased cognitive awareness leads them to consider other individuals, particularly siblings and the other parent, as threatening the exclusivity of the relationship to the primary caretaker.

Freud's notion of the *Oedipus complex* concerns the child's feelings about the other parent, this "third" potentially rivalrous figure. Classically, the little boy's exclusive relationship with his mother is threatened by the father's presence, which leads the little boy to harbour powerful unconscious feelings of hostility towards his rival. His fear of retaliation leads him to identify with his father instead of opposing him. A similar process is thought to take place for girls, although the fear of retribution in girls is less intense than in boys, with the result that Oedipal attitudes tend to be less strongly repressed in women, and the father remains a sexually attractive figure.

Pre-eminent in Freud's view of neurosis at this time was the individual's need to maintain unconscious wishes and drives outside consciousness. He made an important distinction between neurotic symptoms and character traits. While the latter owe their existence to a successful defence against instinctual impulses, neurotic symptoms come into being as a result of the failure of repression. When sexual drives find expression they create anxiety or guilt.

The First World War led Freud to broaden his theory of drives to include primary aggression as well as sexuality. He concluded that much of human behaviour, including the destructiveness of war, and crimes of people against one another, could not be explained unless some basic aggressive destructive drive were postulated. Indeed, subsequent events have shown all too clearly the precariousness of human civilization when confronted with basic human motives of territoriality, vengefulness, bigotry, and self-interest. Throughout the evolution of psychoanalytic theory, the concept of anxiety-producing wishes, experiences, and desires that are pushed from conscious awareness but re-emerge in neurotic symptoms has remained constant.

The structural model

Freud gradually realized that there was more to mental functioning than could be encompassed in a simple distinction between unconscious, preconscious, and conscious mental processes. In 1923 he spelt out the structural viewpoint of psychoanalysis in *The Ego and the Id*. This work for the first time integrated Freud's concepts of drives, defences, and affects, and indicated his aspiration to provide a fully-fledged general psychology rather than a theory of maladjustment. He described three sets of mental processes or structures.

The first, entirely unconscious structure, the id, is the reservoir of sexual and aggressive drives.

The second structure, the superego, was seen as the organized psychic representation of childhood parental authority figures. The child's picture of his or her parents is naturally not realistic. The internalized authority figure is far stricter and harsher in most cases than the parents would actually have been. The superego contains both the goals and the aspirations derived from parents and society (the ego ideal) and the self-corrective functions mediated by guilt. Guilt is an unpleasant sensation, or affect, and individuals do much, including resisting the instinctual aggressive and sexual pressures of the id, in order to avoid being overwhelmed by it.

The third component of the model is the ego. The ego encapsulates mental processes such as thinking, memory, and perception, which collectively enable the individual to cope with the demands and restrictions of external reality. The ego mediates initially between the drives and reality, and later on, as moral sense develops, between the drives and the superego.

This new model represented an extension of Freud's thinking in a number of ways. First, social acceptability was no longer synonymous with consciousness. In this view, most sophisticated psychological processes could function without the benefit of consciousness. Second, anxiety which was previously seen by Freud as undischarged sexual energy was here seen as a signal of danger arising within the ego whenever external demands or internal impulses represented a major threat. This might occur under the danger of loss of love or of enormous guilt as well as danger of physical injury.

The identification of defence mechanisms was one of Freud's early achievements, but it was not until the advent of the structural model that their function and organization could be elaborated adequately. Defences were seen by Freud and his daughter Anna Freud as unconscious mental processes mediated within the ego to prevent the development of painful affect, particularly anxiety or guilt.

Defence mechanisms involve distortions of the way an individual perceives and experiences aspects of his world. *Reaction formation* is a mechanism that serves to maintain repression by intensifying its antithesis. For instance, people disturbed by cruel impulses towards animals might find it helpful to offer their services to the Royal Society for the Prevention of Cruelty to Animals. This would protect them from expressing aggressive impulses by channelling all their energies into preserving rather than destroying life.

Other defence mechanisms include *denial* (refusal to acknowledge that an event has occurred or is likely to occur, for example that one has a terminal illness); *displacement* (transfer of affect from one person or situation to another); *isolation* (splitting feelings off from thought, for example immediately following severe trauma); *suppression* (the conscious decision to avoid attending to anxiety- or guilt-provoking circumstances); *sublimation* (the gratifying of an instinctual impulse by giving it a socially acceptable aim, for example sublimated aggression in violent sports); *regression* (reversion to a childlike manner of behaving that was safe, acceptable, and gratifying); *acting out* (allowing direct expression of an unconscious impulse, for example by slips of the tongue); and *intellectualization* (separating a threatening impulse from its emotional context and placing it in a sometimes inappropriate, rational framework).

Psychopathology is substantially more complex in the structural model than it was within the topographical view. In the structural model the neurotic symptom is seen as representing a combination of unacceptable impulses which threaten to overwhelm the ego and the defences utilized by the individual against them. Anxiety, the hallmark of most neurotic reaction types, was seen by Freud as the reaction of the ego, signalling its imminent danger of being overwhelmed and mobilizing its defensive capabilities. An often-quoted analogy compares anxiety to a fire alarm, set off at the first sign of smoke, aimed at summoning the assistance of the fire brigade. The neurotic reaction types are distinguished by the manner in which the ego defends itself against the anxiety and guilt engendered by childhood instinctual impulses. Thus, in phobias Freud saw the operation of the mechanisms of projection and displacement. A little boy projects his own envious and jealous anger on to his father because it is inconsistent with the love and fear he also feels. The projection of these feelings distorts the boy's perception of his father and he begins to see him as a murderously angry man. This experience may also be too painful and frightening to bear, particularly if he is a lovable and valued object to the child. The fear is then displaced on to objects with whom he has less intimate ties: thus he may become terrified of burglars whom he fears may come to kill him during the night. A paranoid person was thought to use reaction-formation as a defence against conflictual homosexual impulses. "I love him" turns into "I hate him", which by projection becomes "He hates me". These early psychoanalytic theories of homosexuality have been the subject of substantial revision.

In obsessive-compulsive neurosis, Freud thought that individuals defend against aggressive impulses by reaction-formation. Thus they might turn the feared wish to murder brutally, for example, into endless worry over the safety of the person concerned. Sometimes the aggression is fended off by isolation, so that individuals continue to experience the violent images consciously but feel that they are bizarre, do not belong, and are being thrust upon them from outside.

POST-FREUDIAN PSYCHOANALYSIS

Following Freud's death, psychoanalytic thought developed in two fundamentally different ways. In the United States, and to a lesser extent in Britain, certain psychoanalysts grew dissatisfied with the limitations of Freud's approach. These analysts tried to elaborate further the functioning of the ego, focusing on those parts not actively involved in the struggles with the id or the superego. Meanwhile, mainly in Britain, another group of analysts worked on the effects of early relationships, especially those between the infant and his mother. Many other important theorists developed new ideas from Freud's work, those of Jung, Horney, Sullivan, and Adler being examples. Later, however, the most prolific theorists were in the areas of *ego psychology* and various *object-relations theories*.

Ego psychology

Heinz Hartmann (1958) originated a new psychoanalytic approach based on the study of the ego which he felt was a notion neglected by Freud. The central theme of Hartmann's conception was that the ego is not solely involved in conflicts with warring internal structures but is also able to function independently of drives or of involvement in conflicts. The ego was seen as capable, given an adequate environment, of perceiving, learning, remembering, thinking, moving, acting, organizing, synthesizing, and achieving a balance. These capabilities were referred to as the autonomous functions of the ego.

From this background, Erikson (1959) proposed a psychosocial model of ego development. He emphasized the notion of developmental crises. These were held to occur at each of eight stages of development (corresponding in part to Freud's psychosexual stages but taking into account also the problems of transition to early, middle, and late adulthood) and arose from the individual's need to adapt to changed circumstances and social expectations brought about through the process of maturation.

Each crisis is characterized by its own pair of opposing (desirable and undesirable) personality traits (for example, the stage of basic trustfulness versus mistrustfulness from birth to 18 months). With the resolution of each crisis, the individual acquires a relatively permanent balance between the desirable and undesirable traits designating that stage. Among all of

Erikson's stages, the stage of adolescent crisis (the opposition of identity and role confusion) has made most impact.

A major innovation introduced by Hartmann concerns the gratification available to the organism from the sheer exercise of its functions (for example the pleasure a child gains from learning to walk or draw). Additionally, ego psychologists (notably Rapaport, 1967) emphasized that the seeking of stimuli, described as a search for novelty (or curiosity), is necessary for normal development. This enabled some psychoanalysts to move away from Freud's severely criticized motivational system (cf. G. S. Klein, 1976), which had tension-reduction as its sole aim. In the current psychoanalytic view, the ego is a balance-inducing system striving to find an optimal level of tension, using induction as well as reduction.

Ego psychology has undoubtedly been the most influential psychoanalytic model in the United States. Furthermore, of all the major psychoanalytic approaches it has come the closest to achieving a unification with general psychology; yet since the 1970s it has met with a substantial amount of criticism as being confused and conceptually inadequate. Holt (1976) called instinct theory, which remained a corner-stone of ego psychology, the "shame of psychoanalysis", so riddled was it with philosophical and factual errors and fallacies that nothing short of discarding the concept would do. George Klein (1976) recommended the abandonment of all of psychoanalytic theory not directly concerned with the understanding of clinical problems presented by psychoanalytic clients. It was felt by some that psychoanalytic theory should abandon any claim to identify general psychological structures and mechanisms such as the ego and instincts and apply itself to clinical problems only. Perhaps in response to these inadequacies of the ego psychological approach, US analysts are increasingly turning to the British tradition of psychoanalytic thought.

Melanie Klein and her followers

Developments in Britain and most recent developments in the United States represent a movement away from the formal mechanistic framework of structures, forces, and energies that characterized Freud's structural model and Hartmann's ego psychology. The move is towards a more clinically oriented theory, primarily concerned with the development of infants, their sense of self, their relationships with their caregivers (their objects), and the implications of the internal representations of such relationships on future development. Thus psychoanalytic attention has shifted to the examination of self-other relationships using a language much closer to that of day-to-day experience. Melanie Klein's (1932, 1948) approach is chiefly distinguished by being the first to emphasize the importance of infants' earliest relationships. In developing Freud's ideas, she discovered that children's play could be interpreted in a way similar to that used to interpret the verbal associations of adults.

Perhaps the most far-reaching of her theoretical contributions has been her insistence that neurosis has its origins in the first year of life. The main source of difficulty at this stage is the infant's innate ambivalence about his or her most important object relationship: the nourishing but sometimes frustrating breast. A basic assumption of Klein's theory was that from their earliest times infants' mental lives are dominated by unbearable conflicts between love (the manifestation of the libido) and hate (the aggressive instinct). This conflict is reduced, and a feeling of safety promoted, by putting or projecting the aggressive impulses into the breast. However, in this way the breast could also at times become a frightening and dangerous object for them. At other times, the breast was felt as good, was cherished and loved.

Klein called the normal working-through by infants of their fear and suspicion of the breast the "paranoid-schizoid position". During the second half of the first year the painful discovery is made that the loved and the hated breasts are one and the same object. Klein maintained that until the infant could become confident of being loved in spite of his/her rage, every occasion when the breast was removed would be interpreted by the infant as a loss due to the infant's own destructive fantasies. This would be accompanied by feelings of sadness, guilt, and regret. Klein believed that all infants go through this repeated experience of sorrow for the loved object, fear of losing it, and then longing to regain it. The infant can get beyond this "depressive position" only when assured of having maternal love. The infant needs to accept responsibility for the destructive fantasies and follow this by mental acts of reparation (sorrow and sadness); only then would the depressive position be overcome. Klein explained later psychological disturbance less in terms of actual experiences than the internal experience of infancy, in which unconscious fantasies and wishes predominate. If the depressive position was not adequately negotiated in infancy, the individual would never succeed in establishing a stable internal image of a good and loving object. There would be a predisposition to return to the depressive position with consequent feelings of loss, sorrow, guilt, anxiety, and low self-esteem: in other words, such individuals would be likely to feel insufficiently loved and would be particularly prone to depression and other psychological problems.

Kleinian theory has been very influential in British psychoanalysis (Spillius, 1988) and is receiving increasing attention in the United States. Kleinian writers since the early 1950s have worked to understand the mental processes underlying psychotic disturbance, where the patient loses the capacity reliably to distinguish reality from fantasy, and severe character pathology such as borderline states characterized by poor interpersonal relationships, violent changes of mood, impulsivity, and self-destructiveness.

Kernberg's (1975, 1984) highly influential psychostructural model emphasizes the inevitability of psychic conflict and its by-products of anxiety, guilt, and shame in the course of early human development. The root cause of severe personality disturbance, such as borderline states, in Kernberg's model is the intensity of destructive and aggressive impulses and the relative weakness of ego structures available to handle them. Kernberg sees such individuals as using developmentally early defences in an attempt to separate contradictory images of self and others, in order to protect positive images from being overwhelmed by negative and hostile ones. The infant's attempts to protect the object from destruction with the only rudimentary psychic mechanisms at his or her disposal, leads to the defensive fragmentation of self and object representations. Later manifestations of the borderline condition therefore represent a developmentally unresolved infantile conflict state. These conflicts may reasonably be expected to continue within the context of treatment and their interpretation is assumed to have therapeutic effects.

Kernberg's approach has much in common with followers of Melanie Klein (Bion, 1957; Klein, 1957; Segal, 1964) who also stress the inevitability of pathological sequelae arising out of innate destructiveness. The crucial difference lies in later Kleinian thinking (see Spillius, 1988) concerning the common defensive organization that appears to exist in much borderline pathology. The term "organization" – for example narcissistic organization (Rosenfeld, 1987; Sohn, 1985), defensive organization (O'Shaughnessy, 1981), pathological organization (Steiner, 1987) – refers to a relatively firm construction of impulses, anxieties, and defences, creating stability, but at the expense of more advanced modes of psychic functioning which would lead to intolerable depressive anxiety. The psychic defences work together in an extremely rigid system making therapeutic progress difficult and rarely entirely successful. It is as if the psychic structure itself becomes the embodiment of the destructive impulses which called it into existence in the first place. Bion (1962) provides one explanation. He sees the ego's identification with an object, felt to be full of envy and hate, as resulting in an early disabling of certain psychic processes having to do with the capacity to understand cognitive and affective aspects of interpersonal relationships.

Kernberg (1967, 1975, 1976, 1984) conceived of borderline personality disorder as a level of psychic functioning referred to as borderline personality organization. In this respect he continued Melanie Klein's emphasis on defensive personality organization. The borderline personality organization, according to Kernberg, rests on four critical features of the patient's personality-structure: first, non-specific manifestations of ego weakness, including difficulty in tolerating anxiety, controlling impulses, or developing socially productive ways of channelling energy (sublimation); second, a propensity to shift towards irrational, dream-like thinking patterns in the context of generally intact reality-testing; third, predominance of early psychological defences such as splitting, projection, and projective identification; fourth, diffusion of identity, and the related pathology of internal object relations, such that mental representations of important others are fragmented and strongly charged as either good or bad. Thus Kernberg's concept of borderline personality includes a range of disorders such as infantile personalities, narcissistic personalities, antisocial personalities, as-if personalities, and schizoid personalities. In fact, any patient manifesting significant disturbance of identity in Kernberg's system is either psychotic or, if in possession of intact reality-testing, borderline.

In their emphasis on instincts, the theories of both Klein and Kernberg are more uncompromising than those of Freud. The main impact on psychoanalysis has been its stress on infants' ambivalent relationship with their mothers and the consequences of inadequate resolution. It should be noted, however, that Klein attaches little importance to the infant's actual experience of mothering. Thus, as her statements about the inner world of children are not linked to anything in the external world, her views are more or less impossible to verify empirically. Her numerous unwarranted assumptions concerning infants' fantasy lives must make us regard her theory with a certain scepticism. It is perhaps more important to stress the theoretical developments that Klein's ideas have stimulated than the ideas per se.

Fairbairn and Winnicott

Fairbairn (1952, 1963) and Winnicott (1953) were British psychoanalysts who were greatly affected by Melanie Klein's views on early development, although both found it hard to accept her emphasis on the classical theory of instincts (notably of innate aggression and destructiveness). Fairbairn considered the main source of motivation to be the establishment of a human relationship through which needs could safely be gratified. Thus Fairbairn reformulated Freud's theory of the libido. No longer was it seen as a system directing the person towards physical pleasure; rather, what impressed Fairbairn was its tendency to send individuals in search of particular patterns of relationships, in search of objects.

The essence of Fairbairn's approach lay in his emphasis on the strivings of the ego in its endeavour to reach an object (a person-relationship) from whom it might find support. For Fairbairn, the ego was not a mechanism of control over other psychic systems but was conceptualized as the self. He believed that the self was made up of internal images of past persons of importance to the individual. These internalized early relationships and the feelings that accompanied them, so he claimed, made up our current experience of ourselves.

One of Fairbairn's major contributions was the description of the schizoid personality. Such a person is not psychotic and may appear outwardly quite successful, but is in fact a solitary figure who, even when in a relationship, gives little or nothing to the other person. Fairbairn viewed this personality type as arising from a weak, underdeveloped self produced by the mother's failure to love the child for his/her own sake, to give the child spontaneous and genuine expressions of affection which the child could internalize and use as the basis of a sound ego structure. This left the child unsure of the reality of his/her own ego (self) and therefore constantly playing a role, indulging in exhibitionism, and afraid that "giving" in a relationship might result in permanent loss or self-emptying.

Winnicott (1953) was also concerned with the earliest phase of the mother–child relationship and the importance of what he described as "good-enough" mothering for the child's personality development. The child's potential for development from absolute dependence to relative independence was, he believed, strongly influenced by the quality of maternal care. The earliest stage in the infant's experience is one of undifferentiated fusion with and attachment to his/her primary object, most likely the mother. The "good-enough" mother reflects this, and at the child's birth loves the baby as an extension of herself, thus enabling her to become emphatically tuned to the child's inner needs. As the child develops and becomes aware of his/her own needs and of the separate existence of the mother, the optimal mother–child relationship changes to allow a careful balance between gratification and frustration. The separation from the mother permits the infant to express his/her needs and initiative (the basis of the emerging sense of self). A mother who intrudes too much would short-circuit the infant's initiatives and restrict the development of the self. A too distant mother creates anxiety accompanied by the fading of the infant's internal representation of her. Either of these failures at "good-enough" mothering could result in the development of a "false self" based on the necessity for compliance with the demands of the external environment. As adults, such individuals would relate to the world through a compliant shell: they would not be entirely real to themselves or to others.

The transition from absolute dependence (undifferentiated fusion with mother) to relative dependence (awareness of mother's separateness) is accomplished, according to Winnicott, by the development of "transitional phenomena" of which the most obvious are transitional objects. These are often actual objects, such as a blanket, pillow, or favourite teddy bear, to which the child becomes intensely attached and separation from which stirs up extreme anxiety. Attachment to the object as an immediate displacement from attachment to the mother, enables the child gradually to separate from her. Children know that the blanket or teddy bear is not mother, and yet they react emotionally to these objects as if they were her. Such external objects, which offer comfort and security at times of anxiety and danger, permit children to explore the world around them more freely (Eagle, 1983).

Object-relations theory as outlined by Fairbairn, Winnicott, and other British psychoanalysts is currently perhaps the most widely accepted psychoanalytic approach in the United Kingdom. Its fundamental postulate, concerning the formative relationship between mother and infant during the first year of life, has become generally accepted in the psychoanalytic world.

However, whereas ego psychology attempted to improve psychoanalysis by refining its conceptual framework, object-relations theory introduced new concepts which, though not in direct conflict with empirical evidence, are none the less open to criticism. Many assumptions are made concerning the inner world of the infant which are difficult, if not impossible, to substantiate and are justified only if no simpler model can be advanced to account for the same data. Sandler and Sandler (1978) suggested that much of Fairbairn's and Winnicott's clinical material could be explained by a far less complex model. They put forward the idea that the fulfilment of wishes (seen by Freud as the gratification of instincts) could indeed be looked at in simpler terms, namely as the wish to repeat interactions that in the past had given pleasure or comfort. They proposed the theory that each partner in every relationship at any given time had a role for the other and explicitly (in real relationships) or implicitly (in fantasy) negotiated with that person in order to get them to respond in such a way as to restore the wished-for feeling of well-being and safety; for example, a young man might develop a relationship with a shy and diffident girl in order to restore the comfort he experienced in the early feeling of being totally in control of his mother. Many psychological problems could be looked at as being attempts to repeat comforting or gratifying early relationships. Thus an agoraphobic woman, whose fear so restricted her life that she stayed in bed most of the day, might actually be fulfilling a wish to have her husband "mother" her.

Kohut's theory

Kohut (1971), following similar lines to Winnicott, saw infants as perceiving the mother (the object) as part of themselves. Through her soothing and mirroring of infants' needs, she supplies them with the necessary functions of self-cohesion which infants cannot yet perform for themselves. Kohut suggested that when the child's self-love (narcissism) is undermined by the mother's inevitable occasional failure to provide care, the child defensively develops a protective, somewhat megalomaniac self-image (which Kohut termed the 'grandiose self'). The grandiose self is expected to moderate during maturation and in response to changes in the parents' responses: for example, a 2 year old who is able to ride a tricycle would receive attention and praise in contrast to an older sibling. It was suggested that narcissistic personality patterns are the result of the arrest of this normal developmental sequence. This childish grandiosity might remain unaltered if, for example, the mother's confirming responses were never forthcoming or where, alternatively, they were unpredictable or entirely unrealistic.

For Kohut and his North American followers the excessively unempathic responses of the self-objects result in the frustration of normal developmental needs and fixate the child's self at a fragile, archaic level. The narcissistic individual thus finds it necessary to make use of highly primitive self-object relationships (grandiosity, rage or excitement, or sedation through drugs or other addictions) to support self-cohesion as well as self-esteem. Such extremely sensitive individuals are said to be suffering from "narcissistic personality disorder". Kohut also evocatively described the subjective experience of emptiness that is secondary to an inadequately developed self. Such individuals tend to exploit others in social relationships and to treat their love objects as nothing more than extensions of themselves (Akhtar, Thomson, & Anderson, 1982). Lasch (1978) suggests that this personality type may be characteristic of contemporary western civilization.

This theory is essentially a deficiency theory: deficiency of necessary facilitating experiences leading to a psychic deficit (that is, an inadequately developed sense of self). The characteristic manifestations of the borderline states may be understood as indications of the individual's tragic attempts to cope with the profound limitations of his/her intra-psychic world. The clear therapeutic implication is that meaningful intervention must focus on the nature of the individual's deficit and, through a therapeutic environment that may be expected to lead to personal growth, make good the early deprivation: in Kohutian terms to provide a soothing and mirroring function leading to the restoration of the self.

PSYCHOANALYSIS

Although psychoanalytic theory has changed substantially since Freud's time, the treatment he pioneered remains relatively unchanged. The client (analysand) lies on a couch with the analyst sitting behind, out of the client's field of vision. The client is asked to talk honestly about whatever comes to mind and to follow the thoughts through, however embarrassing or trivial they might seem. In the United Kingdom, full psychoanalysis requires attendance for fifty-minute sessions five days per week over several years, although in some countries three or four sessions per week are regarded as sufficient.

The aim of psychoanalysis is the undoing of repression and other defences, the recovery of lost memories, and the achievement of insight or a fresh understanding of previously puzzling behaviour. The analysis may also provide a corrective emotional experience, in that the relationship with the analyst may help to undo the effects of previous deprivation (Alexander & French, 1946). As the analysis proceeds, the analytic situation encourages the development in the analysand of strong feelings for the analyst. The analyst gives little away about him- or herself, so that the influence of significant aspects of the clients' early relationships may be seen in their thoughts and fantasies about the analyst. This process, in which emotions rightly belonging to childhood relationships are transferred on to the analyst, is called *transference*.

The analyst's task is to clarify clients' emotional conflicts. This should start with the interpretation of their defences (for example the tendency to deal with anger by turning it on oneself). This can then be linked with past events to provide an account of the clients' forbidden impulses (for example anger aimed at an apparently uncaring mother). In doing this, the analyst works in the transference, allowing the analysand to feel these conflicts; thus anger towards the analyst for lateness or insufficient attentiveness may well feel frightening and be fended off initially, just as anger with mother was strongly defended against during childhood. In this way clients can work in the "here-and-now" with thoughts and feelings that belong in some way to the past. With a successful analysis, clients gain a better understanding of their behaviour in current relationships, in early relationships, and in the relationship with the analyst.

Thus psychoanalysis is aimed not at removing particular problem behaviours or symptoms but at a far-reaching and radical restructuring of the personality. How far it is successful in achieving this goal is a point of considerable contention. From a review of all studies of the effectiveness of psychoanalysis up to about 1990, Bachrach, Galatzer-Levy, Skolnikoff, and Waldron (1991) have shown that the rate of improvement, with symptom removal as the criterion, is about 64.5 per cent, which is roughly comparable to the effectiveness of other therapeutic approaches. There is little evidence concerning claims of more fundamental personality changes following full psychoanalysis. Such changes are in any case very difficult, if not impossible, to assess reliably. A tentative indication that full, five-times-weekly classical psychoanalysis may give the client something that alternative therapies do not, comes from studies of the client population of psychoanalysts. From a number of investigations it appears that more than half the patients of most psychoanalysts, at least in the United States, are mental health professionals, themselves involved in the administration of forms of therapy that have been advanced as alternatives to psychoanalysis (Kadushin, 1969).

PSYCHOANALYTIC PSYCHOTHERAPY

Psychoanalytic psychotherapy is practised much more widely than psychoanalysis, from which it has evolved. The analyst and client both sit in armchairs in full view of one another and meet only once or twice a week. The therapy tends to focus on specific psychological problems, to emphasize interpersonal events in the client's current life, and to consider the possible displacement of emotions from earlier relationships to current ones (generally excluding that with the analyst). Malan (1976), on the basis of some empirical evidence, strongly advocates the use of interpretations that emphasize the similarity between clients' responses to the analyst and to their parents. Some therapists go so far as to induce anxiety deliberately in their clients by provocative transference interpretations – for example, "You want to murder me just like you wanted to murder your father!" (Sifneos, 1972).

Many of these approaches aim at substantially shorter treatments than psychoanalysis and focus on a single conflict (for example, an inability to be assertive with father and hence with other male authority figures). Therapist and patient often make a "contract" for a particular number of sessions rather than entering an open-ended arrangement.

Such dynamically oriented psychotherapies rely on a distillation of fundamental psychoanalytic concerns: defences, drives, and the transference. In a number of studies (e.g., Sloane, Staples, Cristol, Yorkston, & Whipple, 1975) where the effectiveness of therapies based on psychoanalytic insights were contrasted clinically with that of other therapeutic approaches for neurotic problems, little difference in effectiveness was found. These are important findings since, while classical psychoanalysis compares very unfavourably with more modern therapeutic approaches in terms of time and cost, psychoanalytic psychotherapy is very much less intensive and in most cases takes no longer than do alternative modes of intervention.

Although in principle the practice of psychoanalysis requires lengthy specialist training, including the psychoanalysis of the trainee analyst, many clinical psychologists, as well as psychiatrists and social workers, practise psychotherapy guided by psychoanalytic principles without receiving a full psychoanalytic training.

EVALUATION

Finally, it must be asked, what is the value of the psychoanalytic approach? For psychology, its value is synonymous with its scientific status. Efforts have been made to demonstrate the scientific validity of psychoanalysis by replicating in the laboratory clinical phenomena such as projection, repression, and dream symbolism. These attempts constitute a substantial body of evidence, some consistent with and some failing to support psychoanalytic contentions (see reviews by Fisher & Greenberg, 1977; Fonagy, 1981; Kline, 1981). Although of great interest in their own right, such investigations have no real relevance to psychoanalysis. Attempting to replicate such complex processes as projection, for example, is impossible when so many of the factors normally responsible for their occurrence in real life and in the consulting room are absent in the laboratory.

This does not mean, however, that experimental investigations have no relevance to psychoanalysis. Experimentalists can examine the psychological processes that may underlie phenomena described in the clinical situation without attempting to recreate these phenomena in the laboratory. I have argued (Fonagy, 1982) that experimental studies cannot ever hope to validate psychoanalytic ideas in the sense of demonstrating their existence to observers not participating in the psychoanalytic encounter. Nevertheless, it is quite possible for laboratory studies to demonstrate the existence of psychological processes that underlie the phenomena described by psychoanalysts.

Taking this approach, we can be a little more optimistic about the potential scientific status of psychoanalysis. The rapid expansion of psychological knowledge has already provided much evidence consistent with psychoanalytic assumptions. Both psychoanalysis and psychology will continue to develop and grow for a long while yet. Eventually, adequate common ground may emerge so that psychoanalysis may become acceptable as a branch of psychological science. Until such a time, however, psychologists are correct in treating the unique but clinically based psychological models of psychoanalysts with interested and perhaps sympathetic scepticism.

FURTHER READING

Etchegoyen, R. (1991). *The foundations of psychoanalytic technique*. London: Karnac.

Greenberg, J. R., & Mitchell, S. A. (1983). *Object relations in psychoanalytic theory*. Cambridge, MA: Harvard University Press.

Sandler, J., Dare, C., & Holder, A. (1973). *The patient and the analyst: The basis of the psychoanalytic process*. London: Allen & Unwin.

Tyson, P., & Tyson, R. L. (1990). Psychoanalytic theories of development. New Haven, CT: Yale University Press.

REFERENCES

Akhtar, S., Thomson, J., & Anderson, T. (1982). Overview: Narcissistic personality disorder. *American Journal of Psychiatary*, *139*, 12–19.

Alexander, F., & French, T. M. (1946). *Psychoanalytic therapy*. New York: Ronald.

Bachrach, H. M., Galatzer-Levy, R., Skolnikoff, A., & Waldron, S., Jr (1991). On the efficacy of psychoanalysis. *Journal of the American Psychoanalytic Association*, *39*, 871–916.

Bion, W. R. (1957). Differentiation of the psychotic from the non-psychotic personalities. *International Journal of Psycho-Analysis*, *38*, 266–275.

Bion, W. R. (1962). Learning from experience. In W. R. Bion, *Seven servants: Four works by Wilfred R. Bion* (pp. 1–111). New York: Aronson, 1977.

Breuer, J., & Freud, S. (1895). *Studies on hysteria*. In J. Strachey (Ed. and trans.) *Standard edition of the complete psychological works of Sigmund Freud* (vol. 2). London: Hogarth.

Eagle, M. (1983). Interests as object relations. In J. Masling (Ed.) *Empirical studies of psychoanalytic theory* (pp. 159–187). Hillsdale, NJ: Analytic Press.

Erickson, E. H. (1959). Identity and the life cycle: Selected papers. *Psychological Issues*, Monograph vol. 1, whole no 41.

Fairbairn, R. (1952). *Object relations theory of the personality*. New York: Basic Books.

Fairbairn, R. (1963). Synopsis of an object-relations theory of the personality. *International Journal of Psychoanalysis*, *44*, 224–225.

Fisher, S., & Greenberg, R. (1977). *The scientific credibility of Freud's theories and therapy*. Brighton: Harvester.

Fonagy, P. (1981). Research on psychoanalytic concepts. In F. Fransella (Ed.) *Personality: Theory, measurement and research* (pp. 56–72). London: Methuen.

Fonagy, P. (1982). The integration of psychoanalysis and experimental science: A review. *International Review of Psychoanalysis*, 9, 125–145.

Freud, S. (1900). *The interpretation of dreams*. In J. Strachey (Ed. and trans.) *Standard edition of the complete psychological works of Sigmund Freud* (vols 4–5). London: Hogarth.

Freud, S. (1905). *Three essays on sexuality*. In J. Strachey (Ed. and trans.) *Standard edition of the complete psychological works of Sigmund Freud* (vol. 7). London: Hogarth.

Freud, S. (1923). *The ego and the id*. In J. Strachey (Ed. and trans.) *Standard edition of the complete psychological works of Sigmund Freud* (vol. 19). London: Hogarth.

Hartmann, H. (1958). *Ego psychology and the problem of adaptation*. New York: International Universities Press (original work published 1939).

Holt, R. R. (1976). Drive or wish: A reconsideration of the psychoanalytic theory of motivation. *Psychological Issues*, Monograph 36, 158–197.

Kadushin, C. (1969). *Why people go to psychiatrists*. New York: Atherton.

Kernberg, O. (1967). Borderline personality organization. *Journal of the American Psychoanalytic Association*, 15, 641–685.

Kernberg, O. (1975). *Borderline conditions and pathological narcissism*. New York: Aronson.

Kernberg, O. (1976). Technical considerations in the treatment of borderline personality organization. *Journal of the American Psychoanalytic Association*, 24, 795–829.

Kernberg, O. (1984). *Severe personality disorders: Psychotherapeutic strategies*. New Haven, CT: Yale University Press.

Klein, G. S. (1976). Freud's two theories of sexuality. *Psychological Issues*, Monograph 36, 14–70.

Klein, M. (1932). *The psycho-analysis of children*. London: Hogarth.

Klein, M. (1948). *Contributions to psycho-analysis. 1921–1945*. London: Hogarth.

Klein, M. (1957). Envy and gratitude. In M. Klein, *The writings of Melanie Klein* (vol. 3, pp. 176–235). London: Hogarth.

Kline, P. (1981). *Fact and fantasy in Freudian theory* (2nd edn). London: Methuen.

Kohut, H. (1971). *The analysis of the self*. New York: International Universities Press.

Lasch, C. (1978). *The culture of narcissism: American life in an age of diminishing expectations*. New York: Norton.

Malan, D. (1976). *Toward the validation of dynamic psychotherapy*. New York: Plenum.

O'Shaughnessy, E. (1981). A clinical study of a defensive organization. *International Journal of Psycho-Analysis*, 62, 359–369.

Rapaport, D. (1967). *The collected papers of David Rapaport*. New York: Basic Books.

Rosenfeld, H. (1987). *Impasse and interpretation*. London: Tavistock.

Sandler, J., & Sandler, A.-M. (1978). On the development of object relationships and affects. *International Journal of Psycho-Analysis*, 59, 285–296.

Segal, H. (1964). *Introduction to the work of Melanie Klein*. New York: Basic Books.

Sifneos, P. E. (1972). *Short-term psychotherapy and emotional crisis*. Cambridge, MA: Harvard University Press.

Sloane, R. B., Staples, F. R., Cristol, A. H., Yorkston, N. J., & Whipple, K. (1975). Short-term analytically oriented psychotherapy versus behavioral therapy. *American Journal of Psychiatry, 132*, 373–377.

Sohn, L. (1985). Narcissistic organization, projective identification and the formation of the identificate. *International Journal of Psycho-Analysis, 66*, 201–213.

Spillius, E. B. (1988). General introduction. In E. B. Spillius (Ed.) *Melanie Klein today: Developments in theory and practice* (vol. 1, pp. 1–7). London: Routledge.

Steiner, J. (1987). The interplay between pathological organizations and the paranoid-schizoid and depressive positions. *International Journal of Psycho-Analysis, 68*, 69–80.

Winnicott, D. W. (1953). Transitional objects and transitional phenomena. *International Journal of Psychoanalysis, 34*, 1–9.

GLOSSARY

This glossary is confined to a selection of frequently used psychological terms that merit explanation or comment. Its informal definitions are intended as practical guides to meanings and usages. The entries are arranged alphabetically, word by word ("natural selection" comes before "naturalistic observation" because "natural" comes before "naturalistic"), and numerals are positioned as though they were spelled out ("5-hydroxytryptamine" is under f for "five").

abnormal psychology a branch of psychology, sometimes called psychopathology, concerned with the classification, aetiology (causation), diagnosis, treatment, and prevention of mental disorders and disabilities. *Cf.* clinical psychology.

absolute threshold in psychophysics (q.v.), the minimum physical energy of a sensory stimulus that allows it to be detected by an observer.

acetylcholine one of the neurotransmitter (q.v.) substances that play a part in relaying information between neurons.

accommodation 1. In Piaget's theory of cognitive development, the type of adaptation in which old cognitive schemata (q.v.) are modified or new ones formed in order to absorb information that can neither be ignored nor adapted through assimilation (q.v.) into the existing network of knowledge, beliefs, and expectations. 2. In vision, modification of the shape of the eye's lens to focus on objects at different distances. 3. In social psychology, the modification of behaviour in response to social pressure or group norms, as for example in conformity (q.v.).

ACh a common abbreviation for acetylcholine (q.v.).

achievement motivtion *see* need for achievement (achievement motivation).

ACTH *see* adrenocorticotropic hormone (ACTH).

action potential the momentary change in electrical potential that occurs when an impulse is propagated along a neuron.

adolescence from the Latin *adolescere*, to grow up, the period of development between puberty and adulthood.

adrenal glands from the Latin *ad*, to, *renes*, kidneys, a pair of endocrine glands (q.v.), situated just above the kidneys, which secrete adrenalin (epinephrine), noradrenalin (norepinephrine) (qq.v.), and other hormones into the bloodstream. *See also* adrenocorticotropic hormone (ACTH).

adrenalin(e), noradrenalin(e) hormones secreted by the adrenal glands (q.v.), causing an increase in blood pressure, release of sugar by the liver, and several other physiological reactions to perceived threat or danger. *See also* antidepressant drugs, endocrine glands.

adrenocorticotropic hormone (ACTH) a hormone secreted by the pituitary gland that stimulates the adrenal gland to secrete corticosteroid hormones such as cortisol (hydrocortisone) into the bloodstream, especially in response to stress or injury.

affect any subjectively experienced feeling state or emotion (q.v.), such as euphoria, anger, or sadness.

affective disorders an alternative term for mood disorders (q.v.).

afferent neurons from the Latin *ad*, to, *ferre*, to carry, neurons that transmit impulses from the sense organs to the central nervous system (CNS). *Cf.* efferent neurons.

agoraphobia from the Greek *agora*, market-place, *phobia*, fear, an irrational and debilitating fear of open places, often associated with panic attacks; one of the most common phobias (q.v.) encountered in clinical practice.

Agreeableness one of the Big Five personality factors (q.v.), sometimes called Pleasantness, characterized by traits such as kindness and trust, and the relative absence of hostility, selfishness, and distrust.

alarm reaction the first stage in the general adaptation syndrome (q.v.) according to Hans Selye's three-stage interpretation of an organism's physiological reaction to stress. It is characterized by an initial fall in body temperature and blood pressure, and a subsequent counter shock phase during which hormones (q.v.) are secreted into the bloodstream and a biological defensive reaction begins.

allele from the Greek *allel*, one another, one of two or more genes (q.v.) responsible for alternative characteristics of a phenotype (q.v.), for example different eye colours.

alpha waves high-amplitude brain waves with frequencies of 8–12 Hz, recorded in an electroencephalogram (q.v.), characteristic of relaxed wakefulness in subjects whose eyes are closed. *Cf.* delta waves.

altered state of consciousness (ASC) a state of consciousness induced by drugs, hypnosis, meditation, or other deliberate means that differs from ordinary wakefulness or sleep.

alternative hypothesis in statistical tests, a hypothesis that, in contrast to the null hypothesis (q.v.), typically asserts that the independent variable has an effect on the dependent variable that cannot be explained by chance alone. It is also called an experimental or research hypothesis. *See also* significance (statistical).

altruism in social psychology and sociobiology, behaviour that benefits another individual or individuals in terms of safety, monetary or other advantages, or chances of survival and reproduction, at some cost to the benefactor. *See also* reciprocal altruism.

Alzheimer's disease named after the German physician who first identified it, a degenerative form of presenile dementia (q.v.), usually becoming manifest between the ages of 40 and 60, characterized by loss of memory and impairments of thought and speech. *See also* senile dementia.

amnesia partial or complete loss of memory. Anterograde amnesia is loss of memory for events following the amnesia-causing trauma, or loss of the ability to form long-term memories for new facts and events; retrograde amnesia is loss of memory for events occurring shortly before the trauma.

amphetamine any of a class of commonly abused drugs including Benzedrine, Dexedrine, and Methedrine that act as central nervous system stimulants, suppress appetite, increase heart-rate and blood pressure, and induce euphoria.

anal stage in psychoanalysis (q.v.), the second stage of psychosexual development, in approximately the second and third years of life, following the oral stage and preceding the phallic stage, characterized by preoccupation with the anus and derivation of pleasure from anal stimulation and defecation. *Cf.* genital stage, latency period, oral stage, phallic stage.

analytic psychology a school of psychoanalysis founded by the Swiss psychiatrist Carl Gustav Jung following a rift with Sigmund Freud.

androgens from the Greek *andros*, man, *genes*, born, any of a number of male sex hormones, notably testosterone, secreted by the testes and the adrenal glands in males and in small amounts by the ovaries and the adrenal glands in females, responsible for the development of masculine secondary sexual characteristics.

androgynous from the Greek *andros*, man, *gyne*, woman, having both masculine and feminine qualities.

anorexia nervosa from the Greek *an*, lacking, *orexis*, appetite, an eating disorder, mostly of women, characterized by self-induced weight loss, a morbid fear of fatness which does not diminish as weight decreases, and a disturbance of body image (feeling fat even when emaciated). *Cf.* bulimia nervosa.

anosmia loss of the sense of smell as a result of damage to the olfactory nerve or some other cause.

anterograde amnesia *see* amnesia.

anti-anxiety drugs an umbrella term for a number of drugs, including the benzodiazepine drugs (q.v.) and the muscle relaxant meprobamate, that are used for reducing anxiety, also sometimes called minor tranquillizers.

antidepressant drugs drugs that influence neurotransmitters (q.v.) in the brain, used in the treatment of mood disorders (q.v.), especially depression. The monoamine oxidase inhibitor (MAOI) drugs block the absorption of amines such as dopamine, adrenalin, and noradrenalin (qq.v.), allowing these stimulants to accumulate at the synapses in the brain, and the tricyclic antidepressants such as imipramine act by blocking the re-uptake of noradrenalin in particular, thereby similarly increasing its availability.

antipsychotic drugs a general term for all drugs used to alleviate the symptoms of psychotic disorders (q.v.). Major tranquillizers, including especially the phenothiazine derivatives such as chlorpromazine (Largactil) and thioridazine, are used primarily in the treatment of schizophrenia and other disorders involving psychotic symptoms; lithium compounds are used primarily in the treatment of bipolar (manic-depressive) disorder. *See also* tardive dyskinesia.

antisocial personality disorder a condition characterized by antisocial behaviour (such as lying, stealing, sometimes violence), lack of social emotions (guilt and shame), and impulsivity.

anxiety disorders a group of mental disorders in which anxiety is an important symptom. *See also* obsessive-compulsive disorder, panic disorder, phobia, posttraumatic stress disorder (PTSD).

anxiolytic drugs another name for anti-anxiety drugs (q.v.).

aphasia loss of language abilities, whether partial or complete, invariably due to an organic brain lesion. There are many forms of aphasia, depending largely on the site of the lesion.

applied behaviour analysis the application of learning theory to behavioural problems in everyday settings, including hospitals, clinics, schools, and factories. Research and practice in this field is described by its practitioners as applied, behavioural, analytic, technological, conceptually systematic, effective, and capable of generalized effects. *See also* behaviour modification.

applied psychology the application of psychological theories and research findings to practical problems of everyday life. The major fields of applied psychology are the professions of clinical psychology, counselling psychology, educational (school) psychology, industrial (occupational) psychology, organizational psychology, and forensic (criminological) psychology (qq.v.).

aptitude tests tests designed to measure people's potential abilities or capacities for acquiring various types of skills or knowledge.

archetypes according to the Swiss psychiatrist Carl Gustav Jung and his followers, universal, symbolic images that appear in myths, art, dreams, and other expressions of the collective unconscious.

arithmetic mean *see* mean.

arousal a general term for an organism's state of physiological activation, mediated by the autonomic nervous system. *See also* Yerkes-Dodson law.

articulatory loop a system in working memory or short-term memory (q.v.) that holds and uses inner speech. *Cf.* central executive, visuo-spatial sketchpad.

artificial intelligence (AI) the science of designing machines or computer programs to do things normally done by minds, such as playing chess, thinking logically, writing poetry, composing music, or analysing chemical substances. Largely unconscious functions of intelligence, such as those involved in vision and language, present especially difficult challenges to AI.

assimilation thy process of absorbing new information into existing cognitive structures and modifying it as necessary to fit with existing structures. In Piaget's theory of cognitive development, the type of adaptation in which existing cognitive schemata (q.v.) select for incorporation only those items of information that fit or can be forced into the existing network of knowledge, beliefs, and expectations. *Cf.* accommodation.

association areas parts of the cerebral cortex (q.v.) not primarily devoted to sensory or motor functions.

attachment in developmental psychology, an emotional bond between babies and their primary caretakers. In later life, any strong emotional tie or binding affection between people.

attitude a fairly stable evaluative response towards a person, object, activity, or abstract concept, comprising a cognitive component (positive or negative perceptions and beliefs), an emotional component (positive or negative feelings), and a behavioural component (positive or negative response tendencies).

attribution in social psychology, the ascription of motives, attitudes, traits, or other characteristics to oneself or another person, especially in order to explain or understand that person's behaviour. *See also* fundamental attribution error.

audience effect *see* social facilitation.

audition the sense of hearing.

auditory nerve the nerve connecting the auditory (hearing) receptors to the brain.

authoritarian personality a personality (q.v.) type strongly disposed to racial and other forms of prejudice (q.v.), first identified in 1950, characterized by rigid adherence to conventional middle-class values, submissive, uncritical attitudes towards authority figures, aggressive, punitive attitudes towards people who violate conventional norms, avoidance of anything subjective or tender-minded, an inclination to superstition, preoccupation with strong-weak dichotomies, cynical distrust of humanity in general, a tendency towards projection (q.v.) of unconscious emotions and impulses, and preoccupation with the sexual activities of other people.

autokinetic movement from the Greek *autos*, self, *kinesis*, movement, a visual illusion involving the apparent movement of a stationary point of light viewed in a completely dark environment.

autonomic nervous system a subdivision of the nervous system that regulates (autonomously) the internal organs and glands. It is divided into the sympathetic nervous system and the parasympathetic nervous system (qq.v.).

availability heuristic a heuristic (q.v.) in which the frequency or probability of an event is judged by the number of instances of it that can readily be brought to mind and that are thus cognitively available. It can generate biased or incorrect conclusions, as when people are asked whether the English language contains more words beginning with the letter *r* or more with *r* as the third letter. Most people find it easier to think of instances of the former than the latter and so conclude wrongly that there are more words beginning with *r*.

avoidance conditioning a form of operant conditioning (q.v.) in which, in order to avoid an aversive stimulus, the animal or person being conditioned must learn to make some evasive response.

axon from the Greek word meaning axis, a process or extending fibre of a neuron (q.v.) which conducts impulses away from the cell body and transmits them to other neurons.

barbiturates chemical compounds derived from barbituric acid, including barbitone and phenobarbitone, used as hypnotic or sedative drugs, liable to cause strong dependence when abused.

basilar membrane the membrane in the inner ear in which the auditory receptor cells are embedded.

behaviour genetics an interdisciplinary field of study concerned with the genetic or hereditary bases of animal and human behaviour.

behaviour modification the application of techniques of operant conditioning (q.v.) to reduce or eliminate maladaptive or problematic behaviour patterns or to develop new ones. *See also* applied behaviour analysis, cognitive behaviour modification, flooding.

behaviour therapy a therapeutic technique based on the principles of conditioning and behaviour modification (qq.v.).

behavioural ecology a branch of psychology devoted to understanding behaviour in terms of natural selection (q.v.) and adaptation.

behavioural medicine an interdisciplinary field of study devoted to behavioural aspects of health and illness.

behaviourism a school of psychology founded by John B. Watson in 1913 which considers objectively observed behaviour rather than inner mental experiences to be the proper subject for study. Behaviourists tend to stress the importance of the environment as a determinant of human and animal behaviour.

benzodiazepine drugs any of a group of chemical compounds that are used as anti-anxiety drugs (q.v.) and hypnotics (sleeping drugs), including diazepam (Valium) and chlordiazepoxide (Librium).

Big Five personality factors the following factors, derived from factor analysis (q.v.) and widely accepted since the 1980s as the fundamental dimensions of human personality (q.v.): Extraversion, Agreeableness, Conscientiousness Neuroticism, and Openness to Experience or Intellect (qq.v.) .

binocular disparity the slight difference between the two retinal images, due to the slightly different vantage points of the two eyes, which serves as the basis of stereoscopic depth perception.

biological clock *see under* biological rhythm.

biological rhythm any periodic, more-or-less regular fluctuation in a biological system controlled by a biological clock, for example a circadian rhythm (q.v.). Biological rhythms should not be confused with the pseudo-scientific doctrine of biorhythms according to which the interaction of three perfectly periodic rhythms, fixed at the time of birth, determine "good" and "bad" days throughout life.

bipolar cell　a neuron (q.v.), usually a sensory nerve cell, with two processes, axon and dendrite, extending in opposite directions from the cell body.

bipolar disorder　a mood disorder (q.v.) in which depression alternates with mania, also known as manic-depressive psychosis.

blood-brain barrier　a complex physiological mechanism whose function is to allow blood to flow freely to the brain but to prevent some chemicals present in the blood from reaching the brain.

borderline personality disorder　a mental disorder in which a person hovers on the borderline between normal and disordered functioning, typically with disturbed social relations, dramatic mood swings, and often outbursts of anger and impulsive episodes of antisocial behaviour.

bottom-up processing　in cognitive psychology, information processing that proceeds from "raw" sensory stimuli and then works up to more abstract cognitive operations, as for example in a computational theory (q.v.) of vision. *Cf.* top-down processing.

bulimia nervosa　from the Greek *bous*, ox, *limos*, hunger, an eating disorder, confined almost exclusively to women, characterized by recurrent episodes of binge eating, usually followed by self-induced vomiting and/or laxative abuse, and a morbid fear of fatness. *Cf.* anorexia nervosa.

case-study　a research method involving a detailed investigation of a single individual or a single organized group, used extensively in clinical psychology and less often in other branches of psychology.

CAT (computerized axial tomography)　*see* JCT (computerized tomography).

catecholamine　any member of the group of hormones (q.v.) that are catechol derivatives, especially adrenalin, nor adrenalin, and dopamine, (qq.v.), all of which are involved in the functioning of the nervous system.

cell body　sometimes called the *soma*, the central part of a neuron (q.v.), containing the nucleus and other structures that keep the cell alive.

central executive　the attentional coordinating system of working memory or short-term memory (q.v.). *Cf.* articulatory loop, visuo-spatial sketchpad.

central limit theorem　in statistics, a theorem showing (roughly) that the sum of any large number of unrelated variables tends to be distributed according to the normal distribution (q.v.). It explains why psychological and biological variables that are due to the additive effects of numerous independently acting causes are distributed approximately normally.

central nervous system (CNS)　the part of the nervous system (q.v.) that controls behaviour and bodily functioning. In human beings and other vertebrates it consists of the brain and spinal cord.

centration　Piaget's term for the tendency of children in the pre-operational period (q.v.) to focus on only one aspect of a problem at a time, one consequence of which is their failure to solve problems involving conservation (q.v.) of number, substance, mass, and volume.

cerebellum　from the Latin diminutive form of *cerebrum*, brain, one of the main divisions of the brain, situated beneath the back of the main part of the brain, involved in the regulation of movement and balance.

cerebral cortex　from the Latin *cerebrum*, brain, *cortex*, bark, the thin layer of cells covering the cerebrum (q.v.), largely responsible for higher mental functions.

cerebral hemispheres　the two halves of the cerebrum (q.v.), which have slightly different functions in human beings.

cerebrum from the Latin word meaning brain, the largest brain structure, comprising the front and upper part of the brain, of which the cortex (outer layer) controls most sensory, motor, and cognitive processes in human beings.

chemical senses the senses of olfaction (smell) and gustation (taste) (qq.v.).

chlordiazepoxide one of the benzodiazepine drugs (q.v.), commonly called Librium.

choice reaction time *see* reaction time.

chromosomes from the Greek *chroma*, colour, *soma*, body, so called because they stain deeply with basic dyes, the microscopic rod-shaped structures in the nucleus of every cell containing deoxyribonucleic acid (DNA) (q.v.) which carries the genes (q.v.) that determine hereditary characteristics. There are 46 chromosomes in every human body cell, apart from the sex cells which carry 23 each.

chronological age *see* intelligence quotient (IQ).

circadian rhythm from the Latin *circa*, about, *diem*, day, any biological rhythm with a period (from peak to peak or trough to trough) of about 24 hours, including the sleep-wake cycle and other metabolic and physiological processes in human beings.

clairvoyance *see* extrasensory perception (ESP).

classical (Pavlovian) conditioning the process, first described by the Nobel Prize-winning Russian physiologist Ivan Petrovich Pavlov, sometimes called respondent conditioning, by which an initially neutral stimulus acquires the capacity to elicit a response through association with a stimulus that naturally elicits that response. *See also* conditional (conditioned) response (CR). *Cf.* operant conditioning.

client-centred therapy a method of psychotherapy or counselling pioneered by the American psychologist Carl Rogers in which the therapist refrains from advising, suggesting, or persuading, but tries instead to establish empathy with the client by clarifying and reflecting back the client's expressed feelings; the therapist tries to convey an attitude of "unconditional positive regard" in the context of a permissive, non-threatening relationship; hence this method of psychotherapy is also called non-directive therapy or non-directive counselling.

clinical psychology one of the major professions of psychology, concerned with the prevention, diagnosis, treatment, and study of mental disorders and disabilities, to be distinguished from abnormal psychology (q.v.), which is the academic study of these matters.

CNS *see* central nervous system (CNS).

co-action effect *see* social facilitation.

cochlea from the Greek *kochlias*, snail, a fluid-filled spiral tube in the inner ear, shaped like the shell of a snail, containing the basilar membrane and the receptors for hearing that convert sound waves into nerve impulses.

cognition from the Latin *cognoscere*, to know, attention, thinking, problem-solving, remembering, and all other mental processes that fall under the general heading of information processing.

cognitive behaviour modification a technique of psychotherapy based on methods of behaviour modification (q.v.) with an emphasis on the learning of cognitive responses involving imagery, fantasy, thoughts, and above all beliefs.

cognitive dissonance a motivating state of tension first identified by the American psychologist Leon Festinger that occurs when a person simultaneously holds two cognitions – items of knowledge, attitudes, or beliefs – that are psychologically inconsistent. A person in a state of cognitive dissonance is motivated to eliminate or reduce the dissonance, and this often involves changes in attitudes or beliefs.

1281

cognitive psychology the branch of psychology devoted to the study of attention, memory, imagery, perception, language, thinking and problem solving, artificial intelligence (AI), and generally all mental operations that involve information processing.

cognitive schema (pl. schemata or schemas) an integrated network of knowledge, beliefs, and expectations relating to a particular subject; in Piaget's theory of cognitive development, the basic element of mental life.

cognitive science an umbrella term for an interdisciplinary enterprise, involving cognitive psychology, the brain sciences, computer science, artificial intelligence, linguistics, and philosophy, to construct theoretical models of cognition.

cohort from the Latin *cohors*, company of soldiers, a group of people who share some experience or demographic trait in common, especially being of similar age (an age cohort).

compulsions repetitive, ritualised, stereotyped actions, such as hand-washing, that a person feels unable to stop performing in spite of realizing that the behaviour is inappropriate or excessive, often associated with obsessions (q.v.).

computational theory a formal approach to the study of vision, pioneered by David Marr in the late 1970s, which is intended to show how the pattern of light falling on the retinas of the eyes is transformed into a symbolic representation of the shapes, colours, and movements of what is observed. The first stage is the construction of the primal sketch based on individual intensity changes within a map based on the retina, with edge fragments grouped into meaningful clusters relating to surfaces; then depth cues are used to form the viewer-centred $2\frac{1}{2}$D sketch, which is insufficient for object recognition because it is not invariant with respect to the observer's viewpoint; and the final stage is the construction of the object-centred 3D model description.

concordance rate in the study of behaviour genetics (q.v.), the proportion of identical twins (or other relatives of known degrees of genetic relatedness) who display the same characteristic or phenotype (q.v.).

concrete operations in Piaget's theory of cognitive development, a class of cognitive operations that are logical but tied to the physical (concrete) world and not abstract, and are characteristic of children between the ages of approximately 7 and 11 years, after the pre-operational period but before the stage of formal operations (q.v.) involving abstract thinking. *Cf.* formal operations, pre-operational period, sensori-motor period.

conditional (conditioned) reinforcer a reinforcer (q.v.) whose reinforcing properties are due to association with another reinforcer rather than being intrinsic.

conditional (conditioned) response (CR) the term used in classical (Pavlovian) conditioning (q.v.) for a response that is elicited by an initially neutral conditional stimulus (CS) after it has been associated with an unconditional stimulus (UCS). In Pavlov's original experiments with dogs, for example, an initially neutral stimulus (the sound of a bell) was repeatedly paired with a stimulus (food) that produced a response (salivation) unconditionally and was therefore called an unconditional stimulus (UCS). Eventually the bell came to elicit the salivation response, which in that context is called a conditional response (CR) because its appearance is conditional on the learning process having taken place.

conditional (conditioned) stimulus (CS) *see* conditional (conditioned) response (CR).

conditioning *see* classical (Pavlovian) conditioning, conditional (conditioned) response (CR), operant conditioning.

cone any of the conical cells in the retina of the eye, sensitive to bright light and colour. *Cf.* rod.

conformity the modification of attitudes, opinions, or behaviour in response to social pressure from group members or prevailing social norms.

confounding in experimental design, the problem that arises when two or more causal variables are not properly controlled so that their independent effects cannot be disentangled.

connectionism an approach to artificial intelligence (q.v.) involving the design of intelligent systems composed of groups of interconnected processing units, in which items of knowledge are represented not at single locations but as patterns over collections of units, and these patterns are adaptive inasmuch as they are capable of learning from experience. It is also called parallel distributed processing.

consanguinity study in behaviour genetics (q.v.), a comparison of the correlations between pairs of relatives of different known degrees of genetic relatedness on a measurable trait in order to estimate the heritability (q.v.) of the trait. It is also called a family study or a kinship study.

Conscientiousness one of the Big Five personality factors (q.v.), sometimes called Dependability, characterized by traits such as organization, thoroughness, and reliability, and the relative absence of carelessness, negligence, and unreliability.

conservation Piaget's term for the developing child's understanding of the way in which number, substance, mass, and volume are unaffected by certain transformations. For example, most 5-year-old children do not understand that pouring liquid from a flat bowl into a tall thin bottle does not increase its quantity, which shows that during this pre-operational period (q.v) they have not yet mastered the conservation of volume. *See also* centration.

construct validity in psychometrics (q.v.), the validity (q.v.) of a test established by investigating whether it yields the results predicted by the theory underlying the trait that the test purports to measure.

content validity in psychometrics (q.v.), the validity (q.v.) of a test estimated via a systematic examination of the items of which it is composed.

continuous reinforcement in learning theory, a schedule of reinforcement (q.v.) in which every response is reinforced. *Cf*. intermittent (partial) reinforcement.

control group in experimental design, a comparison group of subjects who, when the independent variable (q.v.) is manipulated, are not exposed to the treatment that subjects in the experimental group (q.v.) are exposed to, but who in other respects are treated identically to the control group, to provide a baseline against which to evaluate the effects of the treatment.

convergent thinking thinking characterized by synthesis of information, especially in the course of arriving at a unique solution to a problem; analytical, usually deductive thinking in which formal rules are followed, as in arithmetic. *Cf*. divergent thinking.

corpus callosum from the Latin *corpus*, body, *callosum*, callous, the band of white fibres that connects the left and right cerebral hemispheres of the brain.

correlation in statistics, the relationship between two variables such that high scores on one tend to go with high scores on the other or (in the case of negative correlation) such that high scores on one tend to go with low scores on the other. The usual index of correlation, called the product-moment correlation coefficient and symbolized by r, ranges from 1.00 for perfect positive correlation, through zero for uncorrelated variables, to -1.00 for perfect negative correlation.

correlation coefficient *see* correlation.

correlational study a non-experimental type of research design in which patterns of correlations (q.v.) are analysed.

cortex *see* cerebral cortex.

cortisol *see* adrenocorticotropic hormone (ACTH).

counselling psychology a branch of applied psychology, related to clinical psychology (q.v.), devoted to helping people to solve problems of everyday living.

counterconditioning a learning process in which a new response is associated through classical conditioning (q.v.) with an established conditional (conditioned) stimulus (CS) (q.v.).

counter-transference in psychoanalysis, the displacement by an analyst on to a client of emotions, often sexually charged, from earlier relationships. *Cf.* transference.

criminological psychology *see* forensic (criminological) psychology.

criterion validity in psychometrics (q.v.), the validity (q.v.) of a test determined by applying it to groups of people who are known to differ on the trait that the test purports to measure.

critical period a biologically determined stage of development at which a person or animal is optimally ready to acquire some pattern of behaviour. *See also* imprinting.

cross-sectional study a research design for investigating questions of developmental psychology in which samples of subjects of different ages are studied simultaneously and their behaviour compared. In contrast to a longitudinal study (q.v.), this design does not control for cohort (q.v.) effects.

CT (computerized tomography) a non-invasive method of scanning the brain or other body organ by means of an X-ray beam passed through it repeatedly from different angles, enabling a computer to build up a visual picture, formerly called a CAT (computerized axial tomography) scan. Tomography, from the Greek *tome*, a cutting, is any of a number of techniques used to obtain images of selected plane sections of the human body or other solid objects. *Cf.* magnetic resonance imaging (MRI), PET (positron emission tomography).

culture-fair tests psychometric tests, especially intelligence tests, that are designed to minimize the biasing influence of cultural knowledge associated with particular ethnic groups, social classes, and other cultural and sub-cultural groups. Culture-free tests (q.v.) are those, if any such exist, entirely free of cultural bias.

culture-free tests *see* culture-fair tests.

DA a common abbreviation for dopamine (q.v.).

dark adaptation the process by which the eyes adjust from bright light to low levels of illumination. The cones (q.v.) in the retina adapt within about seven minutes, and the rods (q.v.) within about four hours.

decibel (dB) a unit commonly used for measuring the physical intensity of sound, equal to ten times the logarithm to the base 10 of the ratio of the intensity of the sound to the intensity of a reference sound, usually the faintest sound audible under ideal listening conditions (conventionally 0.0002 dynes/cm^2).

defence mechanisms a term used originally in psychoanalysis (q.v.) and later more widely in psychology and psychiatry to refer to patterns of feeling, thought, or behaviour that arise in response to perceptions of psychic danger and enable a person to avoid conscious awareness of conflicts or anxiety-arousing stressors; among the most important are denial, displacement, intellectualization, projection, rationalization, reaction formation, regression, and repression (qq.v.).

de-individuation the loss of one's sense of individuality, personal accountability, and self-monitoring that as occurs in some crowd situations when individual behaviour gives way to mob action. *See also* diffusion of responsibility.

déjà vu from the French for already seen, an illusion of having previously seen or experienced something that, in reality, one is seeing or experiencing for the first time. Analogous illusions are sometimes referred to as *déjà entendu* (already heard), *déjà pensé* (already thought), and so on.

delta waves   low frequency (1–3 Hz), high amplitude (approximately 150 microvolts) brain waves, recorded on an electroencephalogram (q.v.), characteristic of deep, dreamless sleep. *Cf.* alpha waves.

delusion   a false personal belief, maintained in the face of overwhelming contradictory evidence, excluding religious beliefs that are widely accepted by members of the person's culture or sub-culture, characteristic especially of delusional (paranoid) disorder (q.v.). *Cf.* hallucination.

delusional (paranoid) disorder   formerly called paranoia, a mental disorder characterized by delusions (q.v.), especially of jealousy, grandeur, or persecution, but with otherwise unimpaired intellectual functioning.

demand characteristics   features of an experimental situation that encourage certain types of behaviour from the subjects and can contaminate the results, especially when this behaviour arises from subjects' expectations or preconceptions or their interpretations of the experimenter's expectations. *Cf.* experimenter effects.

dementia   from the Latin *de* away from, *mens*, mind, any mental disorder characterized by a failure or loss of mental powers, especially memory, intelligence, and orientation. *See also* Alzheimer's disease, dementia praecox, presenile dementia, senile dementia.

dementia praecox   from the Latin for dementia of youth (as opposed to senile dementia), an obsolete term for schizophrenia.

dendrite   from the Greek *dendron*, tree, the collection of branched, threadlike extensions of a neuron (q.v.) that receives impulses from other neurons or from a receptor and conducts them towards the cell body.

denial   a defence mechanism (q.v.) involving a failure to acknowledge some aspect of reality that would be apparent to other people.

deoxyribonucleic acid (DNA)   a self-replicating molecule, the major constituent of chromosomes (q.v.), containing the hereditary information transmitted from parents to offspring in all organisms apart from some viruses (including the AIDS virus), and consisting of two strands coiled into a double helix linked by hydrogen bonds between the complementary chemical bases that encode the genetic information – between adenine and thymine and between cytosine and guanine. *See also* gene.

dependent variable   in experimental design (q.v.), a variable that is potentially liable to be influenced by an independent variable (q.v.). The purpose of an experiment is typically to determine whether one or more independent variables influence one or more dependent variables in a predicted manner.

depersonalization   a form of dissociation (q.v.) involving a feeling of loss of the sense of self, sometimes accompanied by an out-of-body experience (OBE) – a sense of perceiving oneself from a distance, usually from above – associated with sleep deprivation, some forms of drug intoxication, and various mental disorders including some forms of schizophrenia and dissociative disorder (qq.v.).

depression   a sustained negative mood state characterized by sadness, pessimism, a general feeling of despondency, passivity, indecisiveness, suicidal thoughts, sleep disturbances, and other mental and physical symptoms, associated with some mood disorders (q.v.).

descriptive statistics   methods of summarizing numerical data in ways that make them more easily interpretable, including calculations of means (averages), variabilities, and correlations (qq.v.). *Cf.* inferential statistics.

developmental psychology   a branch of psychology concerned with the development over the lifespan from birth to old age of all aspects of behaviour and mental experience.

diazepam   one of the benzodiazepine drugs (q.v.), commonly called Valium.

difference threshold in psychophysics (q.v.), the smallest difference in physical intensity between two stimuli that can be perceived.

diffusion of responsibility the reduced sense of personal responsibility and individual accountability experienced in some circumstances by members of a group, often leading to behaviour untypical of any of the group members when alone. *See also* de-individuation, social loafing.

disparity, binocular *see* binocular disparity.

disparity, retinal *see* binocular disparity.

displacement a defence mechanism (q.v.) involving redirection of feelings about a person or object on to another, usually less threatening target.

dissociation a process involving a group of psychological functions having a degree of unity among themselves which become detached from the rest of personality and function more or less independently, as in multiple personality disorder (q.v.).

dissociative disorder an umbrella terms for psychological disorders, such as multiple personality disorder and the non-organic amnesias, involving dissociation (q.v.) and general disintegration of the functions of consciousness, self-concept, or perceptual-motor coordination.

divergent thinking imaginative thinking characterized by the generation of multiple possible solutions to a problem, often associated with creativity. *Cf.* convergent thinking.

dizygotic (fraternal) twins from the Greek *dis*, double, + zygote, a fertilized egg cell, from the Greek *zygon*, yoke, non-identical twins arising from the fertilization of two separate eggs by two separate sperms at about the same time, who like ordinary siblings share half their genes in common. *Cf.* monozygotic (identical) twins.

DNA *see* deoxyribonucleic acid (DNA).

dominant gene a gene (q.v.) inherited from one parent that produces the same phenotype (q.v.) in the organism whether the corresponding allele (q.v.) inherited from the other parent is the same or different. *Cf.* recessive gene. *See also* epistasis.

dopamine a catecholamine (q.v.); one of the neurotransmitter (q.v.) substances significantly involved in central nervous system functioning. *See also* antidepressant drugs.

double-blind study a research design in which, in order to control for experimenter effects and the effects of demand characteristics (qq.v.), neither the experimenter nor the subjects know, until after the data have been collected, which experimental treatment has been applied to which subjects. This type of design is used, for example, in drug trials, with the help of placebos (q.v.), to avoid contamination of the results from biases and preconceptions on the part of the experimenter or the subjects.

DSM-IV the common name of the fourth edition of the *Diagnostic and Statistical Manual of Mental Disorders* of the American Psychiatric Association, published in 1994, replacing DSM R, the revised version of the third edition published in 1987, containing the most authoritative classification and definitions of mental disorders.

echoic store the sensory memory (q.v.) register or store for auditory information. *Cf.* iconic store.

ECT *see* electroconvulsive therapy (ECT).

educational (school) psychology one of the major professions of psychology, devoted to psychological factors affecting learning, adjustment, and behaviour in children, and the application of psychological methods to provide practical help to children with learning or behaviour problems and to their teachers and parents.

efferent neurons   from the Latin *e*, from, *ferre*, to carry, neurons that transmit impulses away from the central nervous system (CNS) towards the muscles, glands, etc. *Cf*. afferent neurons.

ego   from the Latin word for I, in English language versions of psychoanalysis one of the three major divisions of the psyche, and the one that is conscious and governed by the reality principle (q.v.); Freud originally used the more familiar and informal German word *Ich*, which also means I. *Cf*. id, superego.

ego ideal   *see* superego.

eidetic image   from the Greek *eidos*, shape, an exceptionally vivid, virtually "photographic" visual memory image, much more common among children than adults. The term is occasionally applied by analogy to auditory memories.

electroconvulsive therapy (ECT)   a psychiatric method of treating certain symptoms of mental disorder by passing a weak electric current (20–30 milliamps) through the brain to induce *grand mal* epileptic-type convulsions in patients who are usually first given sedative and muscle relaxant drugs. Sometimes called shock therapy or electroshock therapy (EST).

electrodermal response (EDR)   *see* galvanic skin response (GSR).

electroencephalogram (EEG)   from the Greek *electron*, amber (in which electricity was first observed), *en*, in, *kephale*, head, *gramme*, line, a visual record of the electrical activity of the brain, recorded via electrodes attached to the scalp. The recording apparatus is called an electroencephalograph. *See also* alpha waves, delta waves.

electroshock therapy (EST)   *see* electroconvulsive therapy (ECT).

emotion   from the Latin *e*, away, *movere*, to move, any evaluative, affective, intentional, short-term psychological state. *See also* expressive behaviour, James-Lange theory, opponent-process theory of motivation, primary emotions.

empirical   from the Greek *en*, in, *peira*, trial, derived from observation or experiment rather than speculation or theory.

endocrine gland   any ductless gland, such as the adrenal gland or pituitary gland (qq.v.), that secretes hormones directly into the bloodstream. The endocrine system functions as an elaborate signalling system within the body, alongside the nervous system.

endorphins   from the Greek *endon*, within, and morphine, from *Morpheus*, the Greek god of sleep and dreams, any of a class of morphine-like substances occurring naturally in the brain that bind to pain receptors and thus block pain sensations.

engineering psychology   *see* ergonomics.

epinephrine, norepinephrine   from the Greek *epi*, upon, *nephros*, kidney, alternative words for adrenalin and noradrenalin (qq.v.), especially in United States usage. *See also* endocrine gland.

episodic memory   a type of memory for specific experiences or episodes, generally stored together with information about where and how the information was acquired. *Cf*. semantic memory.

epistasis   from the Greek word meaning stoppage, in genetics, the suppression by a gene of the effect of another gene that is not its allele. *Cf*. dominant gene.

equivalent-form reliability   a measure of the reliability (q.v.) of a psychological test based on the correlation (q.v.) between scores obtained on two equivalent versions of the test; if the test measures reliably, and if the equivalent forms really are equivalent, the correlation should be high. *Cf*. split-half reliability, test-retest reliability.

ergonomics from the Greek *ergon*, work, *nomia*, law, a branch of industrial (occupational) and organizational psychology (q.v.) concerned with designing jobs, equipment, and workplaces to maximize performance and well-being and to minimize accidents, fatigue, boredom, and energy expenditure, also called engineering psychology, especially in the United States.

ESS *see* evolutionarily stable strategy (ESS).

ethology from the Greek *ethos*, character, *logos*, study, the study of the behaviour of animals in their natural habitats.

evoked potential a characteristic pattern in an electroencephalogram (EEG) in response to a specific stimulus.

evolutionarily stable strategy (ESS) in behaviour genetics and behavioural ecology, any genetically determined pattern of behaviour that is stable in the sense that it would be favoured by natural selection (q.v.) in competition with alternative behaviour patterns. The word "strategy" in this context comes from game theory (q.v.).

experiment a research method whose defining features are manipulation of an independent variable (q.v.) or variables and control of other (extraneous) variables that might influence the dependent variable (q.v.). Experimental methods are uniquely powerful in allowing rigorous examination of causal effects without the uncertainties of other research methods. *See also* control group, experimental group, quasi-experiment.

experimental group in experimental design, a group of subjects exposed to an independent variable (q.v.) in order to examine the causal effect of that variable on a dependent variable (q.v.). *Cf.* control group.

experimental hypothesis *see* alternative hypothesis.

experimenter bias *see* experimenter effects.

experimenter efects biasing effects on the results of an experiment caused by expectations or preconceptions on the part of the experimenter; also called experimenter bias. *Cf.* demand characteristics.

expressive behaviour behaviour, especially facial expressions and other forms of non-verbal behaviour, that expresses emotional states or attitudes. *See also* emotion, primary emotions, non-verbal communication.

extinction in classical conditioning (q.v.), the repeated presentation of a conditional stimulus without its associated unconditional stimulus, which leads in certain circumstances to the gradual elimination of the conditional (conditioned) response (qq.v.); in operant conditioning (q.v.), a process whereby the relative frequency of a learned response decreases when reinforcement is withdrawn.

extrasensory perception (ESP) in parapsychology (q.v.), perception supposedly occurring without the use of sense organs. Extrasensory perception of other people's thoughts is sometimes called telepathy, extrasensory perception of objects or events at a distance is called clairvoyance, and extrasensory perception of other people's future thoughts or of future events is called precognitive telepathy or clairvoyance, or simply precognition. The reality of all of these phenomena is highly controversial.

Extraversion one of the Big Five personality factors (q.v.). sometimes labelled Surgency, ranging from extreme extraversion. characterized by traits such as sociability, talkativeness, and assertiveness, to extreme introversion, characterized by reserve, passivity, and silence.

factor analysis a statistical technique for analysing the correlations between a large number of variables in order to reduce them to a smaller number of underlying dimensions, called factors, in a manner analogous to the way in which all spectral colours can be reduced to combinations of just three primary colours.

family study *see* consanguinity study.

feature detectors sensory neurons that are particularly responsive to specific features of stimuli, for example a line detector, a corner detector, or a voice-onset detector.

Fechner's law in psychophysics (q.v.), the law discovered by the German philosopher and mystic Gustav Theodor Fechner in 1850, which states that sensations increase by equal steps as stimulus intensity increases by equal proportions; this is usually expressed mathematically by stating that magnitude of sensation is a logarithmic function of stimulus intensity: $\psi = k \log \phi$, where ψ is the magnitude of the sensation, ϕ is the physical intensity of the stimulus, and k is a constant. *Cf.* Weber's law

field experiment an experiment (q.v.) carried out in a natural setting rather than in the artificial environment of a laboratory.

field study a research investigation, not necessarily a field experiment (possibly a non-experimental study) carried out in a natural setting rather in the artificial environment of a laboratory.

5-hydroxytryptamine (5-HT) another name for serotonin (q.v.).

fixed interval (FI) schedule *see* schedules of reinforcement.

fixed ratio (FR) schedule *see* schedules of reinforcement.

flashbulb memory a vivid, detailed, long-term memory (LTM) (q.v.) for the surrounding circumstances in which one experienced or learned about some historical or significant event.

flooding a technique of behaviour therapy (q.v.) for treating phobias (q.v.) in which the client is exposed to the phobic stimulus for extended periods of time without the opportunity of escape.

forensic (criminological) psychology a branch of applied psychology concerned with all aspects of criminal behaviour and the application of psychology to practical problems of crime and punishment.

formal operations in Piaget's theory of cognitive development, the stage from about 11 years old, following the period of concrete operations, characterized by operations involving deductive reasoning. *Cf.* concrete operations, pre-operational period, sensori-motor period.

fraternal twins *see* dizygotic (fraternal) twins.

free association a therapeutic technique, used in psychoanalysis (q.v.) for recovering unconscious material, in which clients are encouraged to verbalize their stream of consciousness without hesitation or censorship.

fundamental attribution error a pervasive tendency to overestimate the importance of internal, dispositional factors, and to underestimate external, situational factors, when explaining the causes of other people's behaviour. *See also* attribution.

g factor the factor of general intelligence, first identified by the British psychologist Charles Spearman through factor analysis (q.v.).

galvanic skin response (GSR) a fall in the resistance of the skin to the passage of a weak electric current, indicative of emotion or arousal, also called psycho galvanic response (PGR) and electrodermal response (EDR).

game theory a branch of mathematics, with applications in social psychology, behavioural ecology, and sociobiology, devoted to the analysis of interdependent decision-making in any situation in which two or more decision makers, called players, each choose between two or more options, called strategies, and the outcome depends on the choices of all players. *See also* evolutionarily stable strategy (ESS).

ganglion cells neurons in the retina of the eye that receive impulses from receptor cells and whose axons constitute the optic nerve.

gene   from the Greek *genes*, born, the unit of hereditary transmission encoded in deoxyribonucleic acid (DNA) (q.v.), occupying a fixed locus on a chromosome (q.v.), and either specifying the formation of a protein or part of a protein (structural gene) or regulating or repressing the operation of other genes (operator or repressor gene). The complete human genome contains between 50,000 and 100,000 genes. *See also* allele, dominant gene, epistasis, recessive gene.

general adaptation syndrome (GAS)   the three-stage biological response of an organism to severe stress according to Hans Selye, comprising the alarm reaction (q.v.), resistance stage, and exhaustion stage.

genital stage   in psychoanalysis (q.v.), the final stage of psychosexual development. beginning in early adolescence following the latency period (q.v.), characterized by affectionate sexual relationships with members of the opposite sex. *Cf.* anal stage, latency period, oral stage, phallic stage.

genotype   the complete genetic constitution of an organism. *See also* gene.

gerontology   from the Greek *geron*, old man, *logos*, study, the study of aging and the problems associated with old age.

Gestalt psychology   from the German *Gestalt*, configuration or form, a school of psychology that flourished in Germany from 1912 until the rise of the Nazis and emphasized the importance of studying patterns, configurations, and wholes, which are sometimes more than the sum of their parts, rather than isolated elements.

Gestalt therapy   a method of psychotherapy devized by Fritz Perls in the United States in the 1960s in which clients are encouraged to concentrate on the immediate present and to express their true feelings openly.

glial cells   cells forming the connecting tissue that surrounds and supports neurons (q.v.) in the nervous system.

group polarization   a tendency for group decisions to be more extreme, in the direction of the predominant group opinion, than the individual opinions of the group members. In the special case of decisions involving risk if the predominant group opinion favours a risky decision, the phenomenonis called the risky shift.

GSR   *see* galvanic skin response (GSR).

gustation   from the Latin *gustare*, to taste, the sense of taste.

hallucination   from the Latin *alucinari*, to wander in the mind, a false perception, most commonly visual or auditory, subjectively similar or identical to an ordinary perception but occurring in the absence of relevant sensory stimuli, characteristic in particular of some forms of schizophrenia. False perceptions occurring during sleep, while falling asleep (hypnagogic image), or while awakening (hypnopompic image) are not normally considered to be hallucinations. *Cf.* delusion.

hallucinogenic drugs   drugs such as lysergic acid diethylamide (LSD) or mescaline that induce hallucinations.

health psychology   a branch of psychology concerned with psychological factors relevant to the promotion and maintenance of health, the prevention of illness, and the identification of psychological causes and correlates of health and illness.

heritability   the proportion of variance (q.v.) in a phenotypic trait that is attributable to genetic variance in a specified population.

heuristic   from the Greek *heuriskein*, to discover, any of a number of methods of solving complex problems by means of rough-and-ready rules of thumb. *See also* availability heuristic.

hippocampus   from the Greek *hippos*, horse, *kampos*, sea monster, a structure in the brain, whose cross section has the shape of a sea horse, involved in emotion, motivation, learning, and the establishment of long-term memory.

homeostasis from the Greek *homos*, same, *stasis*, stoppage, the maintenance of equilibrium in any physiological or psychological process by automatic compensation for disrupting changes.

hormone from the Greek *horman*, to stir up or urge on, a chemical substance secreted into the bloodstream by an endocrine gland (q.v.) and transported to another part of the body where it exerts a specific effect.

hypnagogic image *see* hallucination.

hypnopompic image *see* hallucination.

hypnosis from the Greek *hypnos*, sleep, an altered state of consciousness or a pattern of behaviour resembling such an altered state, characterized by apparently sleep like passivity, heightened responsiveness to suggestions from the hypnotist, narrowed attention, and various exotic phenomena.

hypnotics barbiturates and benzodiazepine drugs (qq.v.) used as sleeping drugs to treat insomnia (q.v.) and known informally as sleeping drugs.

hypothalamus a pea-sized structure situated (as its name indicates) below the thalamus at the base of the brain, crucially involved in the regulation of the autonomic nervous system (q.v.) and the control of temperature, heart-rate, blood pressure, hunger, thirst, and sexual arousal.

hypothesis a tentative explanation for a phenomenon, subject to refutation by empirical (q.v.) evidence. *See also*, alternative hypothesis, null hypothesis.

iconic store from the Latin *icon*, image, the sensory memory register or store for visual information. *Cf.* echoic store. *See also* sensory memory.

id from the Latin word meaning it, in English language versions of psychoanalysis (q.v.) one of the three major divisions of the psyche, governed by the pleasure principle (q.v.), from which come blind, instinctual impulses towards the immediate gratification of primitive urges. Freud originally used the more informal and familiar German word *Es*, which also means it. *Cf.* ego, superego.

imipramine *see* under antidepressant drugs.

imprinting in ethology (q.v.), a form of rapid learning that takes place during a critical period (q.v.) of development and is extremely resistant to extinction (q.v.). The most familiar example is the behaviour of newly hatched ducklings, which will become imprinted on, and subsequently follow around, virtually any moving object that is presented during this critical period.

independent variable in experimental design (q.v.), a variable that is varied by the experimenter independently of other variables in order to examine its effects on the dependent variable (q.v.).

individual differences psychological differences between people, notably those that form the subject matter of the study of personality (q.v.).

industrial (occupational) and organizational psychology one of the major fields of applied psychology (q.v.), sometimes called work psychology, concerned with the application of psychological knowledge to problems of people in work and unemployment and with the structures and functions of organizations and the activities of people within them. *See also* ergonomics.

inferential statistics techniques for inferring conclusions about populations on the basis of data from samples. The major objective is usually to decide whether the results of research are statistically significant. *See* significance (statistical).

insomnia difficulty in falling or remaining asleep. Initial insomnia is difficulty in falling asleep; middle insomnia is waking up and going back to sleep only with difficulty; and terminal insomnia (which is less lethal than other terminal disorders) is waking up at least two hours before one's normal waking time and being unable to fall asleep again. *See also* hypnotics drugs.

1291

instrumental conditioning *see* operant conditioning.

Intellect (personality factor), *see* Openness to Experience or Intellect.

intellectualization a defence mechanism (q.v.) involving excessive abstract thinking designed to block out disturbing emotions.

intelligence from the Latin *intelligere*, to understand, the ability to think, in itself not directly observable, but manifested in such examples of intelligent behaviour as reasoning and problem solving, and measurable by intelligence quotient (IQ) (q.v.) tests.

intelligence quotient (IQ) a term introduced by the German psychologist William Stern in 1912 to denote a person's mental age divided by his or her chronological (actual) age. It became customary to multiply this quotient by 100 in order to express mental age as a percentage of chronological age, but in contemporary psychometric practice IQ scores are defined statistically without reference to the ratio of mental to chronological age: a person's IQ is defined by reference to a hypothetical population of IQ scores in a normal distribution (q.v.) with a mean (q.v.) of 100 and a standard deviation (q.v.) of 15.

interference *see* proactive interference (PI), retroactive interference (RI).

intermittent (partial) reinforcement in learning theory, any schedule of reinforcement (q.v.) in which not all responses are reinforced. *Cf.* continuous reinforcement.

introspection from the Latin *intro*, towards the inside, *specere*, to look, the act of examining one's own mental experiences.

introversion *see* extraversion.

inventories ordered lists of items or more specifically questionnaires consisting of ordered lists of items designed to measure attitudes, personality traits, or other psychological attributes.

IQ *see* intelligence quotient.

James-Lange theory a theory proposed independently by William James in the United States and Carl Lange in Denmark asserting that bodily changes precede subjective emotional experiences and that it is the perception of these bodily changes that are (or cause) the subjective emotional experiences. *See also* emotion.

just noticeable difference (jnd) in psychophysics (q.v.), the difference between two sensory stimuli that is only just detectable under ideal experimental conditions.

kinesthesis from the Greek *kinein*, to move, *aisthesis*, feeling, the sensory modality, also called muscle sense, through which bodily position, weight, muscle tension, and movement are perceived.

kinship study *see* consanguinity study.

Largactil the trademark of a preparation of one of the anti psychotic drugs (q.v.), chlorpromazine.

latency period in psychoanalysis (q.v.), the period following the phallic stage but preceding the genital stage, from about the age of 5 until early adolescence, during which the sexual drive is thought to be sublimated. *Cf.* anal stage, genital stage, oral stage, phallic stage.

law of effect a law first propounded by the American psychologist Edward Thorndike in 1904 stating that any behaviour followed by reward is more likely to occur in the future.

LD-50 the dosage of any drug that is lethal to 50 per cent of subjects. *Cf.* minimum effective dose (MED-50). *See also* therapeutic index.

learning the relatively permanent change in behaviour that occurs as a result of experience. *See also* classical (Pavlovian) conditioning, conditional (conditioned) response (CR), operant conditioning.

libido from the Latin word for desire, in psychoanalysis (q.v.), psychic energy emanating from the id (q.v.).

Librium the trademark of a preparation of the drug chlordiazepoxide (q.v.). *See also* benzodiazepine drugs.

lie detector *see* polygraph.

limbic system a ring of structures surrounding the brain stem concerned with emotion, hunger, and sex.

linkage in genetics, the occurrence of two genes close together on the same chromosome (q.v.) so that they are unlikely to become separated and tend to be inherited together.

lithium *see* anti psychotic drugs.

locus of control in personality theory and social psychology, the perceived source of control over one's behaviour, on a scale from internal to external.

longitudinal study a research design in which the same sample of subjects is examined repeatedly over an extended span of time, typically to investigate problems of developmental psychology. *Cf.* cross-sectional study.

long-term memory (LTM) relatively long-lasting memory for information that has been deeply processed. *Cf.* sensory memory, short-term memory (STM).

Machiavellianism a personality trait (named after the sixteenth-century Italian political philosopher) associated with devious manipulativeness and opportunism, often shortened to Mach.

magnetic resonance imaging (MRI) a non-invasive method of examining the brain or other body organs by recording the responses of atoms, molecules, or nuclei in a magnetic field to radio waves or other forms of energy. *Cf.* CT (computerized tomography), PET (positron emission tomography).

major tranquillizers *see* antipsychotic drugs.

mania a mood disorder characterized by extreme elation, expansiveness, irritability, talkativeness, inflated self-esteem, and flight of ideas.

manic-depressive psychosis *see* bipolar disorder.

MAO inhibitor *see* antidepressant drugs.

mean short for arithmetic mean, the technical word in descriptive statistics (q.v.) for the most common measure of central tendency, popularly known as the average. The mean of a finite set of scores is normally calculated by adding the scores together and then dividing the total by the number of scores. *Cf.* median, mode.

median a measure of central tendency in descriptive statistics (q.v.), the middle score in a series of scores arranged in order of magnitude, or the average of the two middle scores if there is an even number of scores. *Cf.* mean, mode.

medulla short for medulla oblongata, the lower stalk like part of the brain stem, attached to the spinal cord, involved in vegetative processes such as heartbeat and breathing.

memory the mental processes of encoding, storage, and retrieval of information. *See also* amnesia, episodic memory, flashbulb memory, long-term memory, semantic memory, sensory memory, short-term memory (STM), state-dependent memory.

mental age (MA) *see under* intelligence quotient (IQ).

mental disorder   according to DSM-IV (q.v.), a psychological or behavioural syndrome or pattern associated with distress (a painful symptom), disability (impairment in one or more areas of functioning), and a significantly increased risk of death, pain, disability, or an important loss of freedom, occurring not merely as an expectable response to a disturbing life-event.

meta-analysis   a technique for combining the results of a number of research studies and analysing them statistically as a single data set.

minimum effective dose (MED-50)   the lowest dosage of a drug required to produce the desired effect in 50 per cent of subjects. *Cf.* LD-50. *See also* therapeutic index.

minor tranquillizers   another name for anti-anxiety drugs (q.v.).

mode   a measure of central tendency in descriptive statistics (q.v.), the most frequently occurring score among a collection of scores. *Cf.* mean, median.

monoamine oxidase inhibitor (MAOI)   *see* antidepressant drugs.

monozygotic (identical) twins   from the Greek *monos*, single, + zygote, a fertilized egg cell, from the Greek *zygon*, yoke, twins who are formed when a single egg is fertilized by a single sperm and then splits into two. Unlike the more common dizygotic (fraternal) twins, monozyotic (identical) twins share identical genes.

mood disorders   a group of mental disorders characterized by disturbances of affect or mood, including especially depression, bipolar disorder and mania (qq.v.).

motivation   the motive forces responsible for the initiation, persistence, direction, and vigour of goal-directed behaviour.

multiple personality disorder   a rare dissociative disorder (q.v.) in which two or more markedly different personalities coexist within the same individual, popularly confused with schizophrenia (q.v.).

muscle sense   *see* kinesthesis.

NA   a common abbreviation for noradrenalin (q.v.).

natural selection   the evolutionary process whereby those individuals from a population that are best adapted to the environment survive and produce more offspring than others, thus altering the composition of the population and eventually the characteristics of the species as a whole.

naturalistic observation   a research method involving the passive observation of behaviour in naturally occurring situations.

NE   a common abbreviation for norepinephrine. *See* noradrenalin.

need for achievement (achievement motivation)   a social form of motivation (q.v.) involving a competitive drive to meet standards of excellence, traditionally measured with a projective test such as the Thematic Apperception Test (TAT) (q.v.). *Cf.* need for affiliation.

need for affiliation   a social form of motivation (q.v.) involving a drive to associate and interact with other people. *Cf.* need for achievement (achievement motivation).

negative reinforcement   reinforcement (q.v.) that results from the removal rather than the presentation of the reinforcer (which, by implication, is an aversive or punishing negative reinforcer). *Cf.* positive reinforcement.

nervous system   *see* autonomic nervous system, central nervous system (CNS), parasympathetic nervous system, sympathetic nervous system.

neural network   in cognitive science and artificial intelligence, a type of abstract model of knowledge representation, characteristic of connectionism (q.v.).

neuron   from the Greek word for nerve, a nerve cell, which is the basic structural and functional unit of the nervous system, consisting of a cell body, axon, and dendrites (qq.v.). *See also* afferent neuron, efferent neuron.

neurophysiology   the study of the functions of the nervous system (q.v.).

neuropsychology the study of the psychological effects of damage to the central nervous system.

neuroscience an interdisciplinary field of study concerned with the anatomy, physiology, development, and biochemistry of the nervous system.

neurosis an obsolescent umbrella term for a group of mental disorders that are distressing but do not involve gross impairment of psychological functioning or any loss of self-insight or contact with reality. *See* anxiety disorders, obsessive-compulsive disorder, panic disorder, phobia, post-traumatic stress disorder (PTSD).

Neuroticism one of the Big Five personality factors (q.v.) ranging from one extreme of neuroticism, characterized by such traits as nervousness, moodiness, and temperamentality, to the opposite extreme of emotional stability.

neurotransmitter a chemical substance such as acetylcholine, dopamine, serotonin, or noradrenalin (qq.v.) by which a neuron (q.v.) communicates with another neuron or with a muscle or gland.

nocioceptor a receptor (q.v.), generally in the skin, sensitive to pain, sometimes called a nocioreceptor.

nondirective therapy (counselling) *see* client-centred therapy.

nonsense syllables consonant-vowel-consonant trigrams, such as VUD or KEJ, presumed to be relatively meaningless, used in the study of memory.

non-verbal communication the collective name for all forms of communication apart from language, including vocal quality, facial expression, postures, and gestures.

noradrenalin one of the catecholamine (q.v.) hormones and an important neurotransmitter (q.v.) in the nervous system, also called norepinephrine, especially in United States usage.

norepinephrine *see* noradrenalin.

normal distribution a symmetrical, bell-shaped probability distribution, with the most probable scores concentrated around the mean (average) and progressively less probable scores occurring further from the mean: 68.26 per cent of scores fall within one standard deviation (q.v.) on either side of the mean, 95.44 per cent fall within two standard deviations, and 99.75 fall within three standard deviations. Because of the central limit theorem (q.v.), the normal distribution approximates the observed frequency distributions of many psychological and biological variables and is widely used in inferential statistics (q.v.).

null hypothesis in statistical hypothesis testing, the provisional hypothesis that there is no difference or no relationship and that the observed experimental results can be attributed to chance alone. If the statistical test rejects the null hypothesis, then the alternative hypothesis (q.v.) may be entertained and the effect that has been observed may be considered statistically significant. *See also* significance (statistical).

observational learning *see* vicarious learning.

obsessions recurrent, persistent, irrational ideas, thoughts, images, or impulses that are experienced not as voluntary but as unwanted invasions of consciousness, characteristic especially of obsessive-compulsive disorder (q.v.).

obsessive-compulsive disorder one of the more common anxiety disorders characterized, as the name suggests, by obsessions and compulsions (qq.v.).

Oedipus complex in psychoanalysis (q.v.), a normally unconscious desire in a child, especially a boy, to possess sexually the parent of the opposite sex and to exclude the parent of the same sex. It is named after a character in Greek mythology who killed his father, being unaware of his kinship, and unwittingly married his mother.

oestradiol the most potent of the oestrogen (q.v.) hormones.

oestrogen any of a number of female sex hormones.

olfaction the sense of smell.

Openness to Experience or Intellect one of the Big Five personality factors (q.v.), characterized at the one extreme by such traits as imagination, curiosity, and creativity, and at the other by shallowness and imperceptiveness.

operant conditioning a type of learning, sometimes called instrumental conditioning, which focuses on the process by which behaviour changes as a result of its consequences, in particular the way in which an individual's behavioural responses become more or less frequent as a consequence of reinforcement (q.v.). *Cf.* classical conditioning.

opponent-process cells cells in the visual system that respond to light of a specific range of wavelengths and are actively inhibited from responding by other wavelengths.

opponent-process theory of motivation any of several theories that state that, because of homeostasis (q.v.), any emotion is likely to be followed by its opposite, which in turn will become stronger over time.

optic chiasma the area in the brain behind the eyes where the optic nerves cross.

oral stage in psychoanalysis (q.v.), the earliest, infantile, stage of psychosexual development during which libido (q.v.) focuses on the mouth and has not been differentiated, so the ingestion of food has a sexual quality and pleasure is derived from sucking, chewing, licking, and biting. *Cf.* anal stage, genital stage, latency period, phallic stage.

organ of Corti named after the nineteenth-century Italian anatomist Alfonso Corti, the array of tiny hair cells attached to the basilar membrane (q.v.) that form part of the auditory receptor in the inner ear and whose movements in response to sound waves trigger nerve impulses to the brain.

organism in biology, any life form. In psychology, any human or animal life form whose behaviour might be the subject of research.

organizational psychology *see* industrial (occupational) and organizational psychology.

out-of-body experience (OBE) *see* depersonalization.

panic disorder an anxiety disorder characterized by panic attacks, overwhelming apprehension, dread or terror, fear of going insane or dying, and fight or flight behaviour.

parallel distributed processing *see* connectionism.

paranoia *see* delusional (paranoid) disorder.

parapraxis (pl. parapraxes), in psychoanalysis (q.v.) an everyday absent-minded error, such as a slip of the tongue, assumed to be caused by repressed impulses.

parapsychology from the Greek *para*, beyond + psychology, the study of psychological phenomena that appear to be paranormal (beyond the normal), notably extrasensory perception and psychokinesis (qq.v.).

parasympathetic nervous system one of the two major division of the autonomic nervous system; its general function is to inhibit arousal and maintain calmness. *Cf.* sympathetic nervous system.

partial reinforcement *see* intermittent (partial) reinforcement.

Pavlovian conditioning *see* under classical (Pavlovian) conditioning.

PDP parallel distributed processing. *See* connectionism.

peptides chemical substances such as endorphins (q.v.) that regulate various bodily functions and play an important part in the experience of pain.

perception the processing of sensory information from the receptors (q.v.). *Cf.* sensation.

perceptual constancy the tendency for a perceived object, or a perceptual quality such as colour, to appear the same even when the pattern of sensory stimulation changes because of a change in orientation, distance, illumination, or some other influencing factor.

personality from the Latin *persona*, mask, the sum total of all the behavioural and mental characteristics that distinguish an individual from others. *See also* Big Five personality factors.

personality disorder any of a group of mental disorders characterized by deeply ingrained, enduring, maladaptive patterns of behaviour that cause suffering to the person with the disorder or to others.

PET (positron emission tomography) a non-invasive technique for scanning the brain and studying its function by recording the emission of positrons when radioactive glucose, introduced into the brain, is metabolized by neurons (q.v.) as they are activated. Tomography, from the Greek *tome*, a cutting, is any of a number of techniques used to obtain images of selected plane sections of the human body or other solid objects. *Cf.* CT (computerized tomography), magnetic resonance imaging (MRI).

phallic stage in psychoanalysis (q.v.), a stage of psychosexual development following the anal stage but before the latency period, between the ages of about 2 and 5, characterized by preoccupation with the penis or clitoris. *Cf.* anal stage, genital stage, latency period, oral stage.

phenotype the physical and psychological characteristics of an organism, determined jointly by its genetic constitution and its environment.

pheromone from the Greek *pherein*, to bear, *horman*, to stimulate, any chemical substance with a communicative function, secreted externally by an organism and affecting the behaviour or physiology of other members of the same species.

phobia from the Greek *phobos*, fear, an irrational, debilitating, persistent, and intense fear of a specific type of object, activity, or situation, which, if certain diagnostic criteria are fulfilled, may be considered a mental disorder. *See also* agoraphobia.

phoneme from the Greek *phonema*, a sound, any class of speech sounds regarded in a given language as merely variant pronunciations of the same speech sound.

physiological psychology the branch of psychology concerned with the relationships between physiological and psychological processes.

pinna the external part of the ear, sometimes called the auricle.

pituitary gland the master endocrine gland (q.v.), attached by a stalk to the base of the brain, which secretes into the bloodstream hormones affecting bodily growth and the functioning of other endocrine glands. *See also* adrenocorticotropic hormone (ACTH).

placebo from the Latin word meaning I shall please (the opening words of the Roman Catholic office or service for the dead are *Placebo Domino*, I shall please the Lord), an inactive substance or dummy treatment administered to a control group (q.v.) to compare its effects with those of a real drug or treatment. *See also* double-blind study, placebo effect.

placebo effect a positive or therapeutic benefit resulting from the administration of a placebo (q.v.) to someone who believes that the treatment is real.

pleasure principle in psychoanalysis (q.v.), the doctrine that psychological processes and behaviour are governed by the gratification of needs. It is seen as the governing process of the id (q.v.), in contrast to the reality principle (q.v.) which is the governing process of the ego (q.v.).

1297

polygraph from the Greek *polus*, many, *graphein*, to write, an instrument for the simultaneous recording of several largely involuntary physiological responses, notably galvanic skin response (GSR) (q.v.), heart-rate, and respiration, sometimes used as a lie detector.

pons from the Latin word meaning bridge, short for pons Varolii (bridge of Varoli, after the Italian anatomist Costanzo Varoli), a rounded structure connecting the two halves of the brain at the level of the brain stem.

population in statistics, the entire aggregate of individuals from which samples are drawn and to which the results of research investigations may be generalized. *Cf.* sample.

positive reinforcement a process of reinforcement (q.v.) in which the relative frequency of the response is increased by the presentation of a reinforcer with rewarding properties. *Cf.* negative reinforcement.

positron emission tomography *see* PET (positron emission tomography).

post-traumatic stress disorder (PTSD) an anxiety disorder resulting from experience of a major traumatic event, characterized by obsessive reliving of the trauma in fantasies and dreams, a feeling of emotional numbness and lack of engagement in the world, sleep disturbances, an exaggerated startled response, general symptoms of anxiety, and in some cases (e.g. survivors of concentration camps) guilt about having survived.

precognition *see* extrasensory perception (ESP).

prejudice literally prejudgment, that is, a preconception or a premature opinion based on insufficient evidence; more specifically, a negative attitude (q.v.) towards a whole category of people, especially a minority group within society. *See also* authoritarian personality.

pre-operational period in Piaget's theory of cognitive development, the period from about 18 months to 7 years, following the sensori-motor period but before the stage of formal operations, during which object permanence is mastered and thinking is perceptually driven and intuitive rather than logical, but without mastery of conservation (q.v.). *Cf.* concrete operations, formal operations, sensori-motor period.

presenile dementia a form of dementia (q.v.) of unknown cause starting before old age. *See also* Alzheimer's disease.

primal sketch *see* computational theory.

primary emotions the six emotions of happiness, sadness, disgust, fear, anger, and surprise, so-called because their associated facial expressions are evidently innate: they appear soon after birth, even in infants born blind and deaf, and have been found to be similar in all cultures that have been studied. *See also* emotion, expressive behaviour, non-verbal communication.

proactive interference (PI) the inhibitory effect of information learned in the past on the learning of new information, especially noticeable when the two sets of material are very similar. *Cf.* retroactive interference (RI).

process in anatomy, an axon or a dendrite extending from a neuron.

product-moment correlation coefficient *see* correlation.

progesterone a female sex hormone that prepares the uterus for the fertilized ovum and maintains pregnancy.

projection a defence mechanism (q.v.) in which unacknowledged feelings, impulses, or thoughts are falsely attributed to other people.

projective tests psychological tests designed to tap deep-lying psychological processes, usually consisting of weakly structured or ambiguous stimulus materials on to which the perceiver is assumed to project ideas, which may be unconscious. *See also* Rorschach test, Thematic Apperception Test (TAT).

prosocial behaviour any form of socially cooperative behaviour, including especially altruism (q.v.) and helping behaviour.

psychoactive drug any drug such as lysergic acid diethylamide (LSD), opium, or a barbiturate, that is capable of affecting mental activity. *See also* amphetamine, anti-anxiety drugs, antidepressant drugs, antipsychotic drugs, barbiturates, benzodiazepine drugs, hallucinogenic drugs, psychopharmacology.

psychoanalysis a theory of mental structure and function and a method of psychotherapy based on the writings of Sigmund Freud and his followers, focusing primarily on unconscious mental processes and the various defence mechanisms that people use to repress them. *See also* anal stage, defence mechanisms, ego, free association, genital stage, id, latency period, libido, Oedipus complex, oral stage, phallic stage, pleasure principle, reality principle, sunmation, superego, transference, unconscious.

psychodynamic relating to psychological systems and theories that place heavy emphasis on motivation (q.v.), especially psychoanalysis (q.v.) and its offshoots.

psychogalvanic response (PGR) *see* galvanic skin response (GSR).

psychokinesis from the Greek *psyche*, mind, *kinesis*, movement, in parapsychology (q.v.), the movement or change of physical objects by purely mental processes, without the application of physical forces.

psycholinguistics the psychology of language, including language acquisition in children, the mechanisms underlying adult production and comprehension of language, and language disorders.

psychology from the Greek *psyche*, mind, *logos*, study, the study of the nature, functions, and phenomena of behaviour and mental experience.

psychometrics from the Greek *psyche*, mind, *metron*, measure, mental testing, including IQ, ability, and aptitude testing and the use of psychological tests for measuring interests, attitudes, and personality traits and for diagnosing mental disorders.

psychoneuroimmunology the study of the interrelationships between psychology, the nervous system, and the immune system.

psychopathology *see* abnormal psychology.

psychopharmacology the study of drugs that have psychological effects. *See also* amphetamine, anti-anxiety drugs, antidepressant drugs, antipsychotic drugs, barbiturates, benzodiazepine drugs, hallucinogenic drugs, LD-50, minimum effective dose (MED-50), psychoactive drugs, therapeutic index.

psychophysics the study of the functional relationships between physical properties of stimuli and psychological responses to them. *See also* absolute threshold, difference threshold, Fechner's law, just noticeable difference, signal detection theory, Weber's law.

psychosis gross impairment of psychological functioning, including loss of self-insight and of contact with reality, such as is found in mental disorders involving hallucinations and delusions (qq.v.). *Cf.* neurosis.

psychosomatic from the Greek *psyche*, mind *soma*, body, of or relating to disorders thought to be caused or aggravated by psychological factors such as stress.

psychotherapy the treatment of mental disorders by psychological methods. *See also* behaviour modification, behaviour therapy, client-centred therapy, cognitive behaviour modification, flooding, Gestalt therapy, psychoanalysis, rational-emotive therapy, systematic desensitization, token economy.

psychotic disorders *see* psychosis.

puberty from the Latin *purer*, adult, the period of development that marks the onset of adolescence when secondary sexual characteristics emerge.

quasi-experiment   any research method that is not strictly experimental but that has some of the features of an experiment (q.v.).

quota sampling   a non-random method of drawing a sample from a population so that its composition in terms of sex, age, social class, or other demographic characteristics matches the known proportions in the population. *Cf.* random sampling.

random sampling   any method of drawing a sample from a population in such a way that every member of the population is equally likely to be selected. *Cf.* quota sampling.

rapid eye movement (REM)   rapid movement of the eyeballs behind closed eyelids during sleep, when the sleeper is in REM sleep, a state that occurs approximately every 90 minutes when sleeping and is characterized by vivid dreaming. *See also* REM rebound effect.

rational-emotive therapy   a method of psychotherapy originated by the American psychologist Albert Ellis in which the therapist actively challenges the irrational beliefs of the client.

rationalization   a defence mechanism (q.v.) in which false but reassuring or self-serving explanations are contrived to explain one's own or others' behaviour.

reaction formation   a defence mechanism (q.v.) in which a person replaces unacceptable thoughts, feelings, or behaviour with ones that are diametrically opposite.

reaction time   the minimum time between the presentation of a stimulus and a subject's response. In experiments involving choice reaction time, the subject is presented at unpredictable times with one of two or more stimuli, each of which requires a different response.

reality principle   in psychoanalysis (q.v.), the governing principle of the ego (q.v.), which exerts control over behaviour to meet the demands and constraints imposed by the external world. *Cf.* pleasure principle.

receptor   a sense organ or structure that is sensitive to a specific form of physical energy and that transmits neural information to other parts of the nervous system.

recessive gene   a gene (q.v.) inherited from one parent that produces its characteristic phenotype (q.v.) in an organism only when the corresponding gene inherited from the other parent is the same. *Cf.* dominant gene.

reciprocal altruism   altruism (q.v.) or helping behaviour whose performance or continuation is conditional on the recipient behaving altruistically or helpfully in return.

recombinant DNA techniques   techniques involving the joining together by chemical means of DNA molecules extracted from different sources, for example when DNA from a human gene is recombined with DNA from a bacterium in order to create a new genetic form.

regression   a defence mechanism (q.v.) in which an adult or an adolescent behaves in a manner more appropriate to a child in order to avoid or reduce anxiety.

reinforcement   in learning theory, the strengthening of the bond between a stimulus and a response (qq.v.) or anything that increases the relative frequency of a response. *See also* conditional (conditioned) reinforcer, continuous reinforcement, intermittent (partial) reinforcement, negative reinforcement, positive reinforcement, reinforcer, schedules of reinforcement, secondary reinforcement.

reinforcer   any stimulus or event that increases the relative frequency of a response during the process of reinforcement (q.v.).

reliability   in psychometrics (q.v.), the consistency and stability with which a measuring instrument performs its function. *See also* equivalent-form reliability, split-half reliability, test-retest reliability. *Cf.* validity.

REM rebound effect   the tendency for people who are deprived of REM sleep to show increased proportions of REM sleep on subsequent nights.

REM sleep *see* rapid eye movement (REM).

repression a defence mechanism (q.v.) involving an inability to recall disturbing desires, feelings, thoughts, or experiences.

research hypothesis *see* alternative hypothesis.

respondent conditioning *see* classical conditioning.

response any behavioural or glandular activity of a person or an animal, especially as a reaction to a stimulus (q.v.).

responsibility diffusion *see* diffusion of responsibility.

reticular activating system (RAS) a large bundle of neurons in the brain stem responsible, as its name suggests, for controlling the level of arousal or activation of the cerebral cortex (q.v.), and generally involved in consciousness, sleep, and muscular tone.

reticular formation *see* reticular activating system.

retinal disparity *see* binocular disparity.

retroactive interference (RI) the inhibiting effect that the learning of new information has on the recall of material learned previously, especially when the two sets of material are very similar. *Cf.* proactive interference (PI).

retrograde amnesia *See* amnesia.

risky shift *See* group polarisation.

rod any of the elongated cylindrical cells in the retina of the eye, containing rhodopsin (visual purple) and sensitive to dim light but not to colour. *Cf.* cone.

Rorschach test a projective test (q.v.) named after the Swiss psychiatrist Hermann Rorschach consisting of 10 cards on which are printed bilaterally symmetrical inkblots to which the testes responds by describing what the inkblots look like or what they bring to mind.

saccade from the French word meaning a jerk on the reins of a horse, a sudden movement of the eyes from one fixation point to another, such as occurs when reading.

sample a number of individuals selected from a population (q.v.) to test hypotheses about the population or to derive estimates of its characteristics.

schedules of reinforcement in operant conditioning (q.v.), a rule describing the functional relationship between reinforcement (q.v.) and an organism's responses. In a fixed ratio (FR) schedule, reinforcement occurs regularly after a fixed number of responses; in a fixed interval (FI) schedule, reinforcement occurs after fixed intervals irrespective of the organism's responses; variable ratio (VR) and variable interval (VI) schedules are defined *mutatis mutandis.*

schema *see* cognitive schema.

schizophrenia from the Greek *schizein*, to split, *phren*, mind, a group of mental disorders characterized by incoherent thought and speech, hallucinations (q.v.), delusions (q.v.), flattened or inappropriate affect, deterioration of social functioning, and lack of self-care. In spite of its derivation, the word does not refer to multiple personality disorder (q.v.).

school psychology *see* educational (school) psychology.

secondary reinforcer *see* conditional (conditioned) reinforcer.

semantic memory memory for information encoded verbally according to its meaning. *Cf.* episodic memory.

semicircular canals the three looped, fluid-filled tubes, set at right angles to one another, that form the labyrinth of the inner ear and play a crucial role in the sense of orientation, balance, and movement.

senile dementia from the Latin *senilis*, old, + dementia, dementia (q.v.) of unknown cause in old people, often associated with Alzheimer's disease (q.v.).

sensation acquisition by the body's internal and external sense organs or receptors (q.v.) of "raw" information. *Cf.* perception.

sense organ *see* receptor.

sensori-motor period in Piaget's theory of cognitive development, the first period, before the pre-operational period, from birth until about 18 months, during which an infant functions without fully developed internal representations of objects or mental images but merely with sensori-motor schemata (q.v). *Cf.* concrete operations, formal operations, pre-operational period.

sensory adaptation the diminution or disappearance of responsiveness that occurs when an unchanging stimulus is repeated or continued.

sensory deprivation an experimental situation in which sensory input to all receptors (q.v.) is severely reduced.

sensory memory a form of memory, necessary for normal vision and hearing, which allows images to be stored for about half a second and sounds for up to two seconds. Sensory memory enables television, which presents 30 still images per second, to convey the illusion of a single moving image. It also makes speech intelligible, because without it, by the end of each spoken word the hearer would have forgotten its beginning. *See also* sensory registers. *Cf.* long-term memory, short-term memory.

sensory registers subsystems of sensory memory (q.v.), such as the iconic store and the echoic store (qq.v.), generally assumed to exist separately for each sensory modality.

serial position effect a tendency for items that are positioned towards the beginning and end of a list to be remembered better than those in the middle positions.

serotonin one of the neurotransmitter (q.v.) substances in the nervous system, also known as 5-hydroxytryptamine or 5-HT.

shadowing a technique for studying attentional processes in which the subject listens to two messages simultaneously and attempts to repeat, or shadow, one of them.

shaping a method of training animals and people to exhibit novel forms of behaviour by using a suitable schedule of reinforcement to reward successive approximations to the target behaviour, beginning with existing elements of the subject's behavioural repertoire.

shock therapy *see* electroconvulsive therapy (ECT).

short-term memory (STM) a memory store, also called working memory, consisting of a central executive, visuo-spatial sketchpad, and articulatory loop (qq.v.) that is used for storing small amounts of information for periods of time ranging from a few seconds to a few minutes. It has a severely limited capacity of about seven or eight items of information, such as digits of a telephone number, and the information is rapidly forgotten unless it is refreshed by rehearsal, following which it may eventually be transferred to long-term memory (LTM) (q.v.) . *See also* sensory memory.

signal detection theory a mathematical theory derived from psychophysics (q.v.) to explain the detection of a sensory signal, taking into account the intensity of the signal, the amount of background noise, the level of motivation of the subject, and the criterion for responding.

significance (statistical) a property of the results of an empirical investigation suggesting that they are unlikely to be due to chance factors alone. The 5 per cent level of significance has become conventional in psychology; this means that results are normally considered to be statistically significant if statistical tests show that the probability of obtaining results at least as extreme by chance alone is less than 5 per cent, usually written $p < .05$. *See also* alternative hypothesis, inferential statistics, null hypothesis.

size-weight illusion a compelling illusion whereby, if two objects are of equal weight but markedly different sizes, the smaller object feels much heavier than the larger. Sometimes called Charpentier's illusion.

Skinner box named after the American psychologist B. F. Skinner, a device for studying learning in animals, especially rats and pigeons, consisting of a box in which the animal can move a lever or peck a target to obtain reinforcement (q.v.), usually in the form of food.

sleeping drugs also called hypnotics. *See* barbiturates, benzodiazepine drugs.

slow-wave sleep deep, dreamless sleep, characterized by high-amplitude (150 micro volts), low-frequency (1–3 Hz) electroencephalogram (EEG) waves called delta waves (q.v.).

social cognition from the Latin *socius*, a companion, + cognition, the study of how people perceive and understand all aspects of their social environments, especially the behaviour of other people and themselves. *See also* attribution.

social facilitation the enhancing effect on behaviour of the mere presence of others, either as passive spectators (audience effect) or as co-actors (co-action effect). It is a misnomer, because the effect is often inhibiting rather than enhancing or facilitative.

social learning learning that occurs through observation of the behaviour of others, called models, together with imitation, and vicarious learning (q.v.).

social loafing the tendency for individual effort to diminish in group task situations, partly as a consequence of diffusion of responsibility (q.v.).

social motivation any form of motivation (q.v.) associated with social behaviour, manifested in such phenomena as need for achievement (achievement motivation). need for affiliation, social facilitation, and social loafing (qq.v.).

social psychology from the Latin *socius*, a companion, + psychology, a branch of psychology concerned with the study of social behaviour and the mental experience of individuals in social contexts.

socialization in developmental psychology, the modification from infancy of a person's behaviour to conform with the demands of society.

sociobiology the study of the biological bases of social behaviour.

sociogram a pictorial representation derived from sociometry (q.v.) of the social relationships in a group.

sociometry from the Latin *socius*, a companion and the Greek *metron*, measure, the measurement of social relationships, especially friendship patterns, within groups. *See also* sociogram.

soma *see* cell body.

somatoform disorders a class of mental disorders characterized by deterioration of physical functioning without any discernable physiological cause, specifically when there is evidence that the physical symptoms have psychological causes and there is lack of voluntary control over the physical symptoms and indifference to the deterioration of physical functioning.

split-half reliability a measure of the reliability (q.v.), more specifically the consistency, of a psychological test determined by calculating the correlation (q.v.) between scores obtained on half the test items, arbitrarily chosen, with scores obtained on the other half; if the test measures consistently, the correlation should be high. *Cf.* equivalent-form reliability, test-retest reliability.

spontaneous recovery in conditioning (q.v.), the reappearance of a response after its extinction (q.v.), following a period of rest.

standard deviation in descriptive statistics (q.v.), a measure of dispersion or variability expressed in the same units as the scores themselves, equal to the square root of the variance (q.v.).

standard score the score on any measuring instrument expressed in units of standard deviations (q.v.) of the distribution of scores in the population, also called a z-score.

state-dependent memory memory for information learned in a particular state of consciousness – for example, in a particular emotional state or under the influence of alcohol or drugs – that can be recalled only when in a similar state. Thus material learned in an intoxicated state is sometimes remembered only in a later intoxicated state, and a person in a depressed state is sometimes more likely to remember unhappy experiences from the past, which exacerbates the depression and creates a vicious circle.

statistical significance *see* significance, statistical.

statistics, descriptive *see* descriptive statistics

statistics, inferential *see* inferential statistics

stereopsis the visual perception of objects in three dimensions, or stereoscopic vision.

stereotype from the Greek *stereos*, solid, *typos*, type, an over-simplified, biased, and above all inflexible conception of a social group. The word was originally used in the printing trade for a solid metallic plate which was difficult to alter once cast.

stimulants hormones such as adrenalin, noradrenalin, and dopamine (qq.v.), and drugs such as amphetamines (q.v.), that increase physiological arousal in general and central nervous system activity in particular.

stimulus (pl. stimuli) any objectively discernable event capable of evoking a response (q.v.) in an organism.

stimulus generalization in classical (Pavlovian) conditioning (q.v.), the tendency to respond, after conditioning, to stimuli that resemble the conditioned stimulus; in operant conditioning (q.v.), the tendency to respond, after conditioning, to stimuli that were present during reinforcement.

stressor any stimulus, event or state of affairs that causes stress.

subjects from the Latin *sub*, under, *jacere*, to throw, people or other organisms whose behaviour or mental experience is investigated in psychological research.

sublimation in psychoanalysis (q.v.), the redirection of libido or psychic energy originating in sexual impulses into non-sexual, especially artistic or creative activity.

subliminal from the Latin *sub*, beneath, *limen*, threshold, below the threshold of consciousness; used in perception for a stimulus of very small intensity of duration that can be shown to have been perceived without conscious awareness.

superego in English language versions of psychoanalysis (q.v.), one of the three major divisions of the psyche, which develops out of a conflict between the id and the ego (qq.v.) and incorporates the moral standards of society. It consists of two parts: the ego ideal (a narcissistic image of one's own perfection and omnipotence) and the conscience (one's moral scruples, the part of the superego said to be most readily soluble in alcohol).

survey methods research methods for investigating the distribution of attitudes, opinions, and other psychological attributes in specific sections of a population or in whole populations.

sympathetic nervous system one of the two major divisions of the autonomic nervous system; it is concerned with general activation, and it mobilises the body's reaction to stress or perceived danger. *Cf.* parasympathetic nervous system.

synapse the junction between two neurons (q.v.), where nerve impulses are relayed from the axon (q.v.) of one neuron to the dendrites (q.v.) of another.

systematic desensitization   a technique of behaviour therapy (q.v.) pioneered by the South African psychiatrist Joseph Wolpe for treating phobias and specific anxieties, in which the client enters a state of deep muscle relaxation and is then exposed to a hierarchy of progressively more anxiety-arousing situations, real or imagined.

tardive dyskinesia   from the Latin *tardus*, sluggish, and the Greek *dys*, bad, *kinesis*, movement, an irreversible neurological side-effect of over-use of antipsychotic drugs (q.v.), the symptoms of which include repetitive sucking, lip-smacking, and characteristic tongue movements.

telepathy   *see* extrasensory perception (ESP).

testosterone   one of the most important of the androgens (q.v.).

test-retest reliability   a measure of the reliability (q.v.) of a psychological test, more specifically its stability, determined by calculating the correlation (q.v.) between scores obtained by a group of subjects on the test on two separate occasions; if the test measures stably, and if the psychological characteristic being measured is stable over time, the correlation should be high. *Cf.* equivalent-form reliability, split-half reliability.

thalamus   from the Greek *thalamos*, an inner room or bedroom, a major interior brain structure that serves as a relay centre to the cerebral cortex for all sensory impulses except those arising from olfaction.

Thematic Apperception Test (TAT)   a projective test (q.v.) based on a series of somewhat ambiguous pictures about which the testee is asked to tell imaginative stories.

therapeutic index   the ratio obtained by dividing the LD-50 of a drug by its minimum effective dose (MED-50): mathematically, the therapeutic index $TI = (LD-50)/(MED-50)$. If the ratio is equal to 10 or more, it indicates that a lethal dose is at least ten times the minimum effective dose. *See also* LD-50, minimum effective dose (MED-50).

3D model description   *see* computational theory.

timbre   from the Old French word meaning bell, the sound quality that distinguishes one spoken vowel from another, one voice from another, or one musical instrument from another when pitch and loudness are held constant.

tip-of-the-tongue (TOT) phenomenon   the frustrating feeling of certainty that a particular name, word, or other item of information is available in long-term memory even though one cannot recall (the whole of) it.

token economy   a method of behaviour modification (q.v.) in which people living in an institution or other controllable environment are assigned target behaviour patterns and are rewarded for achieving them with tokens that they can exchange for privileges.

top-down processing   in cognitive psychology, information processing that proceeds from general assumptions or presuppositions about the material being processed. *Cf.* bottom-up processing.

trait   from the Latin *trahere*, to draw, any enduring physical or psychological characteristic that distinguishes one person from another. *See also* personality.

tranquillizers   *see* anti-anxiety drugs, antipsychotic drugs.

transference   in psychoanalysis, the displacement by a client on to an analyst of emotions, often sexually charged, that have been carried over (transferred) from earlier relationships, especially with parents. *Cf.* counter-transference.

trichromatic theory   a theory of colour vision based on three primary colour receptors. *See also* Young-Helmholtz theory.

tricyclic antidepressants   *see* antidepressant drugs.

$2\frac{1}{2}$D sketch   *see* computational theory.

two-point threshold   the minimum distance apart at which two pinpricks on a specified area of the body are perceived as two separate pricks.

Type A behaviour pattern   a personality type, possibly associated with an increased risk of coronary heart disease, characterized by an exaggerated sense of urgency, competitiveness, ambition, and hostile aggressiveness when thwarted.

unconditional (unconditioned) response (UR)   in classical (Pavlovian) conditioning (q.v.), a response evoked by a stimulus before any conditioning has taken place.

unconditional (unconditioned) stimulus (UCS)   *see under* conditional (conditioned) response (CR).

unconscious   occurring without awareness or intention; in psychoanalysis (q.v.), the name for the part of the mind containing instincts, impulses, images, and ideas of which one is not normally aware.

validity   from the Latin *validus*, strong, in psychometrics (q.v.), the degree to which a measuring instrument measures what it purports to measure. *See also* construct validity, content validity, criterion validity. *Cf.* reliability.

Valium   a trademark of a preparation of the drug diazepam (q.v.). *See also* benzodiazepine drugs.

variability   in statistics, the degree to which a set of scores is scattered. Thus two sets of scores with identical means (averages) may have widely different variabilities. The usual measures of variability are the variance and the standard deviation (qq.v.).

variable   anything that is subject to variation; in psychological research, any stimulus, response, or extraneous factor that is not necessarily fixed and may influence the results of the research. *See also* dependent variable, independent variable.

variable interval (VI) schedule   *see* schedule of reinforcement.

variable ratio (VR) schedule *see* schedule of reinforcement.

variance   in descriptive statistics (q.v.), a measure of the dispersion or variability (q.v.) of a set of scores; it is equal to the mean (average) of the squared deviations of the scores from their mean. *See also* standard deviation.

vicarious learning   from the Latin *vicarius*, substituted, learning that occurs through the observation of others' behaviour and its consequences, also called observational learning. *See also* social learning.

visuo-spatial sketchpad   a system in working memory or short-term memory (q.v.) that is used for setting up and manipulating visual images. *Cf.* articulatory loop, central executive.

WAIS-R   the revised version of the Wechsler Adult Intelligence Scale.

Weber fraction   *see under* Weber's law.

Weber's law   in psychophysics (q.v.), the law of sensation discovered by the German physiologist Ernst Heinrich Weber in 1846, which states that the just noticeable difference between two stimuli is a constant fraction of the lesser stimulus; for example, the just noticeable difference between two weights is 1/53 of the lighter weight. Thus the Weber fraction for weight discrimination is 1/53; for visual brightness discrimination it is 1/62, for auditory pitch discrimination it is 1/333, for loudness discrimination it is 1/11, and so on. The usual mathematical expression of Weber's law is $\Delta I/I = k$. where ΔI is a small increment in the physical intensity of the stimulus, I is the initial stimulus intensity, and k is a constant equal to the Weber fraction. *Cf.* Fechner's law.

Wechsler tests   *see* WAIS-R, WISC-R, WPPSI.

WISC-R   the revised version of the Wechsler Intelligence Scale for Children.
working memory   *see* short-term memory (STM).
WPPSI   the Wechsler Preschool and Primary Scale of Intelligence.

Yerkes-Dodson law   a psychological law named after its proposers stating that optimal performance on a variety of tasks occurs at intermediate levels of arousal (q.v.).
Young-Helmholtz theory   a theory of colour vision, named after its originators, which turned out to be essentially correct, based on the assumption that all colours are reducible to combinations of three basic colour components, each of which stimulates a specific receptor (q.v.) in the retina of the eye.

z-score   another name for a standard score (q.v.).
zygote   from the Greek *zygon*, yoke, a fertilized ovum or egg.

INDEX

Bold entries denote figures.